VIRGINIA WOOLF: TURNING THE CENTURIES

Selected Papers from the Ninth
Annual Conference on Virginia Woolf

VIRGINIA WOOLF: TURNING THE CENTURIES

Selected Papers From the Ninth
Annual Conference on Virginia Woolf

University of Delaware
June 10-13, 1999

Edited by Ann Ardis & Bonnie Kime Scott

New York
Pace University Press
2000

Copyright © 2000 by
Pace University Press
One Pace Plaza
New York NY 10038

All rights reserved
Printed in the United States of America

Library of Congress Cataloging-in-Publication Data

Conference on Virginia Woolf (9th : 1999 : University of Delaware)
Virginia Woolf : turning the centuries : selected papers from the ninth annual Conference on Virginia Woolf : University of Delaware, June 10-13, 1999 / edited by Ann Ardis & Bonnie Kime Scott.
 p. cm.
Includes bibliographical references and index.
ISBN 0-944473-51-2 (pbk.: alk.paper)
1. Woolf, Virginia, 1882-1941--Criticism and interpretation--Congresses.
2. Women and literature--England--History--20th century--Congresses. I. Ardis, Ann L., II. Scott, Bonnie Kime III. Title.

PR6045.O72 Z5787 1999
823'.912--dc21   00-025621

"Repression of War Experience," from COLLECTED POEMS OF SIEGFRIED SASSOON by Siegfried Sassoon, copyright 1918, 1920 by E. P. Dutton. Copyright 1936, 1946, 1947, 1948 by Siegfried Sassoon. Used by permission of Viking Penguin, a division of Penguin Putnam, Inc.

Contents

Abbreviations ix

Introduction
Ann Ardis and Bonnie Kime Scott 1
    Virginia Woolf: Turning the Centuries

Scanning the Centuries

Stephen J. Ramsay 6
    "On Not Knowing Greek": Virginia Woolf
    and the New Ancient Greece
Sally Greene 11
    Virginia Woolf, Renaissance Woman
Gabrielle Dane 16
    Thinking Back through Her Fathers: Virginia
    Woolf and Edward Gibbon
Alison Booth 24
    Those Well-Lit Corridors of History
Pamela L. Caughie 34
    Virginia Woolf in the Age of Mechanical Reproduction
Charles Boebel 40
    From *Orlando Ever After: A Dramatic Speculation*

Remote Inscriptions

Gyllian Phillips 56
    "She Was No Scholar": Placing Mrs. Browning
Tracey Sherard 62
    "Parcival in the Forest of Gender": Wagner,
    Homosexuality, and *The Waves*
Lisa Golmitz Weihman 69
    The Problem of National Culture: Virginia Woolf's
    Between the Acts and Elizabeth Bowen's *The Last September*
Catherine Sandbach-Dahlström 78
    Feminist Conversation: Virginia Woolf, Simone de Beauvoir,
    and the Dialogics of Criticism
Mónica Ayuso 86
    Remote Inscriptions: *To the Lighthouse* and *The Waves*
    in Julieta Campos' Caribbean

New Applications of Queer Theory

Judith Roof — 93
    Hocus Crocus
Troy Gordon — 102
    The Place of Cross-Sex Friendship in Woolf Studies
Eileen Barrett — 111
    Response
Patricia Cramer — 116
    Response

Trauma and Wellness

Diane Gillespie — 127
    Metaphors of Illness and Wellness: John Donne, Virginia Woolf, and Susan Sontag
David Eberly — 134
    Semicolons and Safety Pins
Judith Greenberg — 140
    Woolf's Ancient Song: Traces of the Dead Echoing into the Future
Suzette Henke — 147
    Virginia Woolf and Post-Traumatic Subjectivity
Jane Lilienfeld — 153
    Accident, Incident, and Meaning: Traces of Trauma in Virginia Woolf's Narrativity
Marilyn Schwinn Smith — 158
    Narration, Memory, and Identity: *Mrs. Dalloway* at the End of the Century

Life and Death Writing

Julia Briggs — 166
    In Search of New Virginias
June Elizabeth Dunn — 176
    "Beauty Shines on Two Dogs Doing What Two Women Must Not Do": Puppy Love, Same-Sex Desire and Homosexual Coding in *Mrs. Dalloway*
Val Gough — 183
    "A Responsible Person Like Her": Woolf's Suicide Culture

Textual Re-takes

Kathryn N. Benzel — 192
    Woolf's Early Experimentation with Consciousness:
    "Kew Gardens," Typescript to Publication, 1917-1919
Peter Naccarato — 199
    Re-Defining Feminist Fiction in *The Years*
Jane de Gay — 207
    An Unfinished Story: The Freshwater Drafts of "The
    Searchlight"
Wayne K. Chapman — 215
    Leonard Woolf, Cambridge, and the Art of the English Essay

Pressing the Public Sphere

Patrick Collier — 223
    Woolf, Privacy, and the Press
Melba Cuddy-Keane — 230
    "A Standard of One's Own": Virginia Woolf and the Question
    of Literary Value
John Young — 236
    Canonicity and Commercialization in Woolf's Uniform Edition

Moving Images

Suzanne Bellamy — 244
    "Painting the Words": A Version of Lily Briscoe's Paintings
    from *To the Lighthouse*
Isota Tucker Epes — 252
    The Liberation of Lily Briscoe
Anna Snaith — 256
    "At Gordon Sq. and nowhere else": The Spatial and Social
    Politics of Bloomsbury
Leslie Kathleen Hankins — 266
    Tracking Shots Through Film History: Virginia Woolf,
    Film Archives and Future Technologies
Lesley Higgins and Marie-Christine Leps — 276
    From Contingency to Essence: Fictions of Identity in
    Novels and Films
Michelle N. Mimlitsch — 283
    Envisioning/Revisioning Woolf in Film at the End
    of the Twentieth Century

Disciplinary Traversals

Shiela Pardee   291
    Assuming Psyche's Task: Virginia Woolf Responds to
    James Frazer
Elyse Myers   298
    Virginia Woolf and the "Voyage Out" from Victorian Science
Michael Whitworth   304
    "The Lighted Strip of History": Virginia Woolf
    and Einsteinian Simultaneity
Edward Barnaby   311
    Visualizing the Spectacle: Woolf's Metahistory Lesson
    in *Between the Acts*
Ann Murphy and Jeanne McNett   317
    Women's Learning, Women's Work
Laurie Quinn   325
    A Woolf with Political Teeth: Classing Virginia Woolf
    Now and in the Twenty-First Century

Notes on Contributors   331

Conference Program   336

Index   348

Abbreviations

AHH	*A Haunted House*
AROO	*A Room of One's Own*
BP	*Books and Portraits*
BTA	*Between the Acts*
CDB	*The Captain's Death Bed and Other Essays*
CE	*Collected Essays* (4 vols.)
CR 1	*The Common Reader*
CR 2	*The Common Reader, Second Series*
CSF	*The Complete Shorter Fiction*
D	*The Diary of Virginia Woolf* (5 vols.)
DM	*The Death of the Moth and Other Essays*
E	*The Essays of Virginia Woolf* (6 vols.)
F	*Flush*
FR	*Freshwater*
GR	*Granite & Rainbow: Essays*
JR	*Jacob's Room*
L	*The Letters of Virginia Woolf* (6 vols.)
M	*The Moment and Other Essays*
MEL	*Melymbrosia*
MOB	*Moments of Being*
MT	*Monday or Tuesday*
MD	*Mrs. Dalloway*
ND	*Night and Day*
O	*Orlando*
PA	*A Passionate Apprentice*
RF	*Roger Fry: A Biography*
TG	*Three Guineas*
TTL	*To the Lighthouse*
TW	*The Waves*
TY	*The Years*
VO	*The Voyage Out*

Introduction

Ann Ardis and Bonnie Kime Scott
Virginia Woolf: Turning the Centuries

The Georgian architecture of the University of Delaware's main mall provided an appropriate setting for the Ninth Annual Virginia Woolf Conference, which took Woolf studies toward the new millenium by inviting participants both to focus on Woolf's work as a feminist historian, and to think ahead to the concerns of the twenty-first century. We solicited papers, performances, exhibitions, and original one-act plays related to the following: transitional moments and markers in Woolf's career or her mappings of (feminist) literary history; the problems with and possibilities of period designations; her treatment of the Greeks, the Elizabethans, the eighteenth century, the nineteenth century, the Victorian fin-de-siècle, and of issues of modernization unique to her own age; and extensions of Woolf's experimental spirit. Furthermore, we encouraged such topics as: lesbian and gay readings of her work; new perspectives on issues of race, sexuality, subjectivity, and ecology in her writings; presentations dealing with the ways Woolf's work has "traveled" into other disciplines or responds to new developments in disciplines outside the field of literary studies; reassessments of feminist literary recuperation; Woolf's role in current attempts to articulate the future of literary studies; and the impact of electronic archivalization on Woolf studies.

Not surprisingly, given the conference's over-arching theme, the spirit of *Orlando* reigned over all of the conference's events and performances. Evoked first by Melba Cuddy-Keane's performance of Pamela Caughie's paper on "Woolf in the Age of Mechanical Reproduction" at the first plenary session, then extended on Friday evening in Charles Boebel's original one-act play, "*Orlando* Ever After," it erupted quite gloriously in the "*Orlando* Costume Ball and Banquet" on Saturday evening, which gave everyone an opportunity to join in the pageant of Woolf's historical imagination. Orlando in doublet and hose and Mrs. Manresa were clear favorites, as characters to assume at the ball, but we welcomed also Maisie Johnson, Lily Briscoe, Sasha, Peter Walsh (unbeknownst to himself), at least one pirate, a suffragette, a spirited group rendition of the great frost, and several Virginias. For us as conference organizers, though, the spirit of Orlando hovered perhaps most closely over our meetings throughout the preceding year with our graduate student planning committee. Not unlike Orlando's private interactions with Nell and the prostitutes in Woolf's eighteenth century London, these meetings were punctuated by raucous laughter, community-mindedness, and good cheer that carried over into the conference itself.

Those "thin threads that connect us to each other, our past, and our future" (Davis 10) emerged first in the first plenary session, "Virginia Woolf: Scanning the Centuries," which reunited, quite unexpectedly, Sally Greene, Alison Booth, and Melba Cuddy-Keane, who had opened the seventh annual Virginia Woolf Conference, "Influence, Intertext, Context." However nice it might have been to hear Pamela Caughie read her own paper, Cuddy-Keane's rendition of it—in the same dress that Sally Greene happened to choose for the occasion—was one of the events that this volume of conference proceedings can allude to but never recapture. Truly, we were blessed at this conference with a multiplicity of splendid performances: Cuddy-Keane's evocation of Caughie; Suzanne Bellamy and Isota Tucker Epes' exchange about their mutual challenge to recreate Lily Briscoe's paintings from *To The Lighthouse*; the dramatization, mainly by the Delaware graduate students, of Boebel's "*Orlando* Ever After"; an exciting set of demonstrations on hypertexts and electronic archives; and to finish things off, Ntozake Shange's dramatic reading, "Many Trails of a Poet," which included reflections on her experiences reading and teaching Virginia Woolf, and her sense of "history without an omniscient narrator" (Davis 10). Shange attracted additional audience members from campus and community, at a time when conference numbers might have been expected to dwindle.

Papers for the volume were chosen on the basis of the recommendations made by those who attended the conference, support of our "Turning the Centuries" theme, balance in representing the full range of the conference, and our commitment to featuring some new voices in Woolf studies. We are pleased to be able to represent several non-hierarchical, group sessions that broke out of conventional conference formats, including here the example of Anne Murphy and Jeanne McNett's "Women's Learning, Women's Work: A Dialog." We are sorry that the "Electronic Archives" panel cannot be contained in these pages, as it provides a fine introduction of things to come: the networked history of women's writing in English of "The Orlando Project," as presented by Patricia Clements, Susan Brown, and Kathryn Harvey, the hypertext of *Ulysses* conceived by Michael Groden, now under construction by a community of Joyce scholars, and Clifford Wulfman's *Waves* "breaking on an electronic shore." Mark Hussey's cautionary message has since been published in Pamela Caughie's new collection, *Virginia Woolf in the Age of Mechanical Reproduction*.

It is possible to chart the places where "the accent falls a little differently" (*CR*1 156) in Woolf studies at the end of the twentieth century by noting topics that generated multiple sessions in this conference, and ones that

Introduction

reverberate as well from the Seventh and Eighth Annual Conferences and look toward the Tenth. The volume sustains interest in gay and lesbian studies of Woolf. This occurs both with individual papers distributed throughout the volume, such as Tracy Sherard's "Percival in the Forest of Gender" and June Dunn's "Beauty Shines on Two Dogs Doing What Two Women Must Not Do," and in the only conference session we have chosen to reproduce in its original form here, "New Applications of Queer Theory." This featured panel offered an exchange among Judith Roof, Troy Gordon, and their respondents, the editors of *Virginia Woolf: Lesbian Readings*, Eileen Barrett and Patricia Cramer. This exchange usefully frames and "teaches the conflicts" within Woolf scholarship regarding the value of postmodern approaches to subjectivity and textuality. An important connection with the Eighth Conference comes from the sessions on Woolf and trauma, an emerging focus of biographical as well as literary study that has developed since the publication of Louise DeSalvo's *Virginia Woolf: The Impact Of Childhood Sexual Abuse On Her Life and Work*. Connections to trauma as studied in the wake of experiences of war, as an issue in holocaust studies, or as theorized as post-traumatic stress disorder add new complexity to these recent studies. Finally, the multiple panels on "Remote Inscriptions" and "Disciplinary Traversals," represented in individual sections of this volume, look forward to the Tenth Annual Virginia Woolf Conference, which will be hosted by Jessica Berman at the University of Maryland, Baltimore County in 2000. There the topic of "Virginia Woolf Out of Bounds" will encourage participants to cross "regional, temporal, and disciplinary boundaries" of all kinds and invite reflection on "the future of Woolf study, especially as an opportunity for new intellectual exchanges and mixtures." Our boundaries here extend to Ireland, France, and the Caribbean, and take time from the era of Classical Greece to the temporal possibilities of the theory of Relativity, considering Woolf's imaginative powers at every turn. These essays also acknowledge her most difficult traversals of property, class, and the public sphere.

Except for the panel on "Queer Theory," conference sessions have undergone a sea change in the arrangement of this volume. Although we have retained many of the titles of featured sessions, re-clustering the papers enables some exciting new juxtapositions. "Scanning the Centuries" now includes a richer complement of historical samplings, with Woolf both framing and framed by history. Borrowing its title from one of its papers, "Remote Inscriptions" now looks backward as well as forward from Woolf, featuring her readings of earlier writers' work as well as contemporaneous and later, geographically far-flung writers' dialogic relationships with her. "Trauma and Wellness" melds papers from two conference sessions on these issues. "Life and Death Writing" brings Julia Briggs' keynote, "In Search of New Virginias," into conversation with papers presenting the cultural codes of lesbian desire and the cultural context of Victorian suicide, all of these allowing

3

for new definition of Woolf's creative life. Indeed, both biography and subjectivity are concerns for numerous sections of the collection.

Orlando aside, *The Voyage Out*, and *Mrs. Dalloway* commanded the most attention among Woolf's texts. It is also significant that many less well-known materials—published and unpublished—received attention, including Leonard Woolf's youthful essays, drafts of "The Searchlight," Hogarth Press ads, and Woolf's introduction to Margaret Llewelyn Davies' *Life as We Have Known It*. This in part manifests the recent turn in modernist studies toward cultural studies and the material history of literary production, most visible in two sections of the volume, "Textual Re-Takes" and "Pressing the Pubic Sphere," both of them pulling from multiple panels at the conference. "Moving Images" foregrounds continuing interest in the films inspired by Woolf, with Michelle Mimlitsch encouraging us to re-examine the criterion of "fidelity" when judging films, and Leslie Hankins searching out the archive of films that might have influenced Woolf. In this section, film is also enriched by urban photography and original paintings, joining new directions toward popular culture and the visual in modernist studies. "Disciplinary Traversals" points us all in the direction of next year's conference by inviting us, not only to consider Woolf's reactions to new developments in disciplines such as anthropology, physics, female anatomy, and classics at the turn of the twentieth century, but also to reflect on how we can use her writings to deal with issues and concerns unique to *our* turn of the century, including shifting concerns of pacifism and feminism, and challenges for Woolf studies now that they have securely entered the academy.

We want to thank the University of Delaware Library, and particularly Shiela Pardee, for mounting a display that demonstrates the extent of Woolf's influence and the diversity of materials that have been published in response to the lively and continuing interest in her life and work. Selections ranged from Vanessa Bell's sketches to Woolfian offerings on the web. Examples from the extensive collection of the Hogarth Press imprints in the Library's Special Collections department were well represented. In addition to the Library, the conference had a number of other generous University sponsors: the English Department, the Office of the Dean of Arts and Science, International Programs and Special Sessions, the Office of Women's Affairs, Black American Studies, the University Honors Program, and the Women's Studies Program. Additionally, we had seed money from the International Virginia Woolf Society and the 8th Annual Virginia Woolf Conference. Invaluable support and effort were provided by: members of the University of Delaware student planning committee, which included Patrick Collier (bookstore liaison and paper selection), Lil Crisler (program), Karen Gaffney (publicity), Jennifer Guarino (paper selection), Kathryn Miles (play), Shiela Pardee (library exhibit and silent auction liaison), Sara Triller (library exhibit), Sara Whitehead (play), Anne Thalheimer (banquet), Greg Weight (web site), Lejla Kucakalic (database and play), Laurie Frankel (administration); the Woolf

Introduction

Conference steering committee, composed of previous organizers Mark Hussey, 1991; Vara Neverow, 1992; Jane Lilienfeld, 1993; Beth Rigel Daugherty, 1995; Wayne Chapman and Elisa Sparks, 1996; Jeanne Dubino, 1997. Special thanks go to the constantly helpful Georgia Johnson, 1998. We appreciate that University of Delaware President, David Roselle, permitted us to have the *Orlando* Ball and Banquet in the appropriate setting of Gore Hall, and that colleagues from throughout the university chaired panels and otherwise took interest in the Conference. Our paper selection committee was composed of Judith Allen, Ann Ardis, Patrick Collier, Beth Rigel Daugherty, Jen Guarino, Patricia Moran, Vara Neverow, Bonnie Scott, and Pierre-Eric Villeneuve. We had invaluable advice and help from: Margaret Anderson (Interim Dean of Arts and Science), Deborah Lyall (secretarial), Linda Russell (budget administration), George Miller (Chair, Dept. of English), Ruth Hurst, Mary Luciano, and Jan Ziesing (Conference Services), Jewel Walker (Theatre), Richard Davison, Barbara Gates, Lois Potter, J.J. Wilson, Phil Mink, and Tom Scott.

Works Cited

Davis, Laura. "International Virginia Woolf Society Column." *Virginia Woolf Miscellany* 54 (Fall 1999): 10.

Woolf, Virginia. "Modern Fiction." *The Common Reader*. New York: Harcourt, Brace & World, 1953. 150-58.

Scanning the Centuries

Stephen J. Ramsay

"On Not Knowing Greek:" Virginia Woolf and the New Ancient Greece.

Virginia Woolf's famous encomium on Greek literature contains some of that subtle posturing commonly directed, in nineteenth-century introductions and apologia, at those who do not know Greek by those who do. The essay confidently assumes the "common reader's" acquaintance with ancient Greek literature, and repeatedly offers up, by way of example, some of the most impenetrable lines in the Greek corpus without benefit of English translation. Yet this essay effectively argues that the opacity of this ancient language—the mysterious and relentless difficulties for which it is (not unjustifiably) famous—extends not only to those who do not know Greek, but to those who do. These include, presumably, the author herself:

> For it is vain and foolish to talk of knowing Greek, since in our ignorance we should be at the bottom of any class of schoolboys, since we do not know how the words sounded, or where precisely we ought to laugh, or how the actors acted, and between this foreign people and ourselves there is not only difference of race and tongue but a tremendous breach of tradition. (*CR*1 23)[1]

In Woolf's day, as in our own, information concerning "how the actors acted" and "how the words sounded" is infuriatingly scant. Yet the implicit cultural continuity between the civilization which had emerged on the heels of the Athenian victory at Salamis in the fifth century and the civilization which had emerged after the Anglo-Saxon defeat in the eleventh, had been repeatedly affirmed and celebrated since the time of Dryden. The translators Woolf does quote were full of the old language of effusion, admiration, and deference. The English translation of *The Greek Anthology*, according to its translator, J. W. MacKail, is "an epitome, sketched in a facile hand, of the book of Greek life" (iv); Jebb's *Antigone*, the best example of "ideal beauty attained by truth to human nature" (vi). To place such scholars at the bottom of "a class of schoolboys" was criticism indeed. Many a schoolboy, with varying degrees of faith in the Greek Ideal, had labored through Aeschylus' curious manipulations of the optative mood in the hopes of gaining that promise of culture which Woolf here declares insuperable. On the surface, Woolf's essay urges what it represents: "a tremendous breach of tradition."

Yet for all the apparent boldness of this declaration, much of the effusive longing found in the hellenophilic writings of Winckelmann, Schlegel, Arnold, Pater, and Symonds, remains curiously, though perhaps somewhat anxiously, intact. Greek literature is still, in Woolf's estimation, the "literature of masterpieces"—and moreover, the literature of the very first masterpieces (*CR*1 37). English literature may have its heroes and its marriage plots, but Greek drama offers us "heroism itself," "fidelity itself" in all their metaphysical splendor (*CR*1 27). In Aeschylus and Sophocles we witness the primal theatrical emotions given to us "before [they] have been worn into uniformity" (*CR*1 28); the nightingale "whose song echoes through English literature singing in her own Greek tongue" (*CR*1 28). Chaucer may lay significant claim to our emotions, but Antigone, Ajax, and Electra are "the originals, Chaucer's the varieties of the human species" (*CR*1 27).

> But again (the question comes back and back), Are we reading Greek as it was written when we say this? When we read these few words cut on a tombstone, a stanza in a chorus, the end or the opening of a dialogue of Plato's, a fragment of Sappho, when we bruise our minds upon some tremendous metaphor in the *Agamemnon* instead of stripping the branch of its flowers instantly as we do in reading *Lear*—are we not reading wrongly? losing our sharp sight in the haze of associations? reading into Greek poetry not what they have but what we lack? . . . Back and back we are drawn to steep ourselves in what, perhaps, is only an image of the reality, not the reality itself, a summer's day imagined in the heart of a northern winter. (*CR*1 35)

Woolf appears to struggle here with what amounts to a deep, and eminently modern, epistemological problem. Ancient Greece—the traditional psychic homeland of the West for close to four centuries—stands as an unknowable entity. We are severed forever from that pristine, idyllic culture by too much ignorance. Like cultural analysands, we are destined to speak always of ourselves whenever we would intend to speak of another. Yet her response to this metaphysical crisis consists not in the abandonment of our illusory association with the Acheans, but with a nascent recognition of the fact that any hermeneutic circle purporting to bind one completely may likewise be re-envisioned as a peculiar form of freedom. A truly unknowable Greece would necessitate our silence. Woolf seems to acknowledge the fact that the impulse to create a psychic homeland out of the vague palimpsest of our ignorance makes such silence impossible. Are we imagining a summer's day in the heart of a northern winter? Yes. And why not? Dispense with the need for verisimilitude and linguistic empiricism, and one is left free to imagine more perfectly a Greece permeated with what we lack. Woolf's response to the question that comes "back and back" is, put simply, to ignore it.

7

Ramsay

The old ancient Greece—the ancient Greece of Arnold and Symonds—had sought to relate the Greek experience to the experience of contemporary England.[2] The new ancient Greece celebrates the foreignness, the strangeness of ancient Greece. Words like *peripeteia, páthos,* and *hamartía* do not appear in Woolf's essay. Nor do the various Hellenic imports which have formed the mainstay of introductions to tragic literature since Castelvetro: tragic flaw, relentless Necessity, ruinous temptation, the immutable forms. Such things deceive us with their pretensions toward anthropological certainty. For Woolf, the demonstrable "otherness" of Greek literature and experience is the most attractive element of all—the otherness of the culture, but moreover, the otherness of its language. Nothing, writes Woolf, can come "between us and the naked cry

ὀτοτοτοῖ πόποι δᾶ. ὦ 'πολλον, ὦ 'πολλον   (*CR*1 31)

Nothing, including English translation. Translate Aristotle's famous dictum—ὁ ἄνθρωπος φύσει πολιτικόν ζῷον(1253a 2-3)—and you end up with a line that Locke or Hume might have written ("man is by his nature an animal who lives in a polis"). Translate Cassandra's naked cry, and you end up with an elegiac farewell to the presumed continuity between what the Greeks said about their world and what the English can say about their own: ὀτοτοτοῖ πόποι δᾶ. ὦ 'πολλον,—"Oh, woe, woe, woe! Alas! Apollo! Apollo!" (Fraenkel 155).[3]

I do not believe we are witnessing a simplistic preference for the Dionysian over the Apollonian in this essay. Woolf has no interest in embracing what Nietzsche exuberantly referred to as "the original titanic hierarchy of terror" (Nietzsche 30). For Woolf, the chief advantage of our insistent desire to imagine Greek literature, is that to do so requires that one "annihilate the smoke and the damp and the thick wet mists" of the English Midlands (*CR*1 24). Where previous critics had sought to correct our fantasies by appealing to reality, Woolf endeavors to dispense with the need for a fantasy which requires a reality. Nineteenth-century positivistic scholarship had managed to make Sophocles look more and more like a broad-churchman. Woolf's Sophocles looks more and more like a modernist. Sophocles knew that his genre required, "something emphatic, familiar, brief, that would carry, instantly and directly, to an audience of seventeen thousand people perhaps, with ears and eyes eager and attentive, with bodies whose muscles would grow stiff if they sat too long without diversion" (*CR*1 25). Such lines come rather close to Brecht's epic theater, and closer still to Artaud's theater of cruelty—perhaps closest of all to Woolf's own vision of literary art. Where classical scholarship had stood firm in believing the chorus to be the collective voice of the audience, Woolf sees a proto-modern taste for the self-referential: a chorus which represents (like the characters in *The Waves*) "the undifferentiated voices who sing like birds in the pauses of the wind; who can comment, or sum up, or allow the poet to speak himself or supply, by contrast, another side to his conception" (*CR*1 29). The legendary difficulties of Greek choric odes are (or should be) part of the experience of literature—a place we turn for relief from "the atmosphere of doubt, of suggestion, of questioning," but which, like the notes to *The Wasteland*, leave us "baffled rather than instructed" (*CR*1 29). And if all of this amounts to little more than a fantasy borne of our own longings, Woolf seems to say, then so be it. These are fantasies worth having.

Even Plato himself, the metaphysician *sans pareille*, becomes an advocate for the pleasures of the text: "Are pleasure and good the same? Can virtue be taught? Is virtue knowledge?" (*CR*1 32). Kant might strive to emulate the mind-numbing progress of Socrates and Protagoras on these matters; for Woolf, "what matters is not so much the end we reach as our manner of reaching it" (*CR*1 32). Heretical from a Platonic standpoint, perhaps, but perfectly in accord with what Woolf would go on to say of realism, the omniscient narrator, and the linear narrative: "[T]ruth is various; truth comes to us in different guises; it is not with the intellect alone that we perceive it" (*CR*1 32). Language is the thing that comes "back and back" in Woolf's essay. For in Woolf's formulation, one need not understand Greek so much as poetry. She demonstrates a marked impatience with the "servile and snobbish passion" evident in those who would endeavor to alleviate our misunderstandings by striking upon the exact place where one should laugh when reading *The Odyssey* (*CR*1 37). Woolf leaves lines untranslated in the firm belief that the only truly adequate paraphrase of a line of Greek verse is the line itself.

One of the resounding ironies of Woolf's essay, of course, is that it provides incontrovertible proof that the author, a Georgian woman writing occasional essays for the *Times*, not only knows Greek, but knows it rather shatteringly well. One is reminded of the American linguist Benjamin Whorf whose understanding of Hopi was so deep as to allow him to declare it utterly untranslatable—a principle he was able to demonstrate using hundreds of well-translated examples. But Woolf's conception of the Greek language provides a foil not to our conceptual scheme with regard to time or causality, but to a well-established social order. Greek may be the language of *eidola*—of phantasmal images and truths only half-gleaned by the modern reader. It is likewise the language of *hoi eugenes anthropoi*: well-born British men. Woolf's essay is in this sense as much a declaration of the New Greece as of the New Woman.[4] Women are beginning to learn the old cabalistic language of privilege and status. They are, of course, at the bottom of a class of schoolboys. But then, so are all the other schoolboys—and the master besides.

There is, to be sure, a note of nostalgia—even naiveté—in Woolf's creation of this new psychic homeland. She writes, after all, on the heels of an age in which Thomas Arnold had looked to Thucydides for a response to agitation over reform bills while Gladstone sought answers to the Irish Question in the pages of *The Odyssey*. Whatever change Woolf's essay marks in the development of British philhellenism, it is one that cannot entirely forsake the desire to see Ancient Greece as a practical metaphor for modern England. Yet ultimately, there can be no comparison between Victorian Hellenism and

Woolf's recalibration of it. For Arnold, for Symonds, and for countless other philhellenes, something essential in the modern landscape could remain intact after Hellenism has taken its rightful place as the infallible guide to cultural reform. Previous critics, eager to make Greek polytheism consonant with Christian virtue or Athenian radical democracy indistinct from the modern parliamentary state, were quick to say what was right about modern life and what was savage about the sons of Peleus. Woolf asks us to turn to the Greeks "when we are sick of the vagueness, of the confusion, of the Christianity and its consolations, of our own age" (*CR*1 38). In so doing, she is willing to own the very savagery which her forebears had rejected. Or rather, to own savagery as the Greeks understood it. As *bárbaros*—our word for barbarian, the Greek word for those who said "bar bar"—the inarticulate grumblings of those who do not know Greek.

Notes

[1] The shifting rhetorical terrain of Woolf's essays—and this essay in particular—have been well charted by Melba Cuddy-Keane and Edward L. Bishop. For Cuddy-Keane, the "constant shifts in focalization" which mark these essays as conversational likewise place them into a long-standing tradition of feminist writing in which conversation is "conscientious political action" (143, 137). See Bishop and Cuddy-Keane, op. cit.

[2] As Linda Dowling has recently demonstrated, even Oscar Wilde's provocative statements on Hellenic Love at the end of the century may be seen as a continuation of this basic impulse in nineteenth-century thought; yet another attempt to guide social and intellectual reform by appealing to the authoritative model of ancient Greece, and one largely well received by the audience at the first trial. See Dowling, op. cit.

[3] A legendarily difficult line which well illustrates Woolf's point. Fraenkel's translation, as with most Victorian and early twentieth-century translations, appeals to the language of Shakespeare and the King James Bible. In Greek, the phrase opens with what amounts to a stuttering scream, followed by an exclamation generally connoting pain, shame, and distress, and then two apostrophic invocations of Apollo.

[4] For a general introduction to the issue of women and the classics in Victorian and early twentieth-century England, see Fowler, op. cit.

Works Cited

Aristotle. *Politics*. Loeb Classical Library 264. Trans. H. Rackham. 1944. Cambridge: Harvard UP, 1990.

Bishop, Edward L. "Metaphor and the Subversive Process of Virginia Woolf's Essays." *Style* 21 (1987): 573-88.

Cuddy-Keane, Melba. "The Rhetoric of Feminist Conversation: Virginia Woolf and the Trope of the Twist." *Ambiguous Discourses*. Ed. Kathy Mezei. Chapel Hill: U of North Carolina P, 1996. 137-61.

Dowling, Linda. *Hellenism and Homosexuality*. Ithaca: Cornell, 1994.

Fowler, R. "'On Not Knowing Greek': The Classics and the Woman of Letters." *Classical Journal* 78 (1983): 337-349.

Fraenkel, Eduard, ed. and trans. *Aeschylus: Agamemnon*. Vol. 1 Oxford: Clarendon, 1950.

Jebb, R. C., ed. *The Antigone*. 2nd edition. Vol. 3. Cambridge, 1891.

MacKail, J. W., trans. *Select Epigrams from the Greek Anthology*. London: Longman's, 1923.

Nietzsche, Friedrich. *The Birth of Tragedy and The Genealogy of Morals.* New York: Anchor-Doubleday, 1956.
Woolf, Virginia. *The Common Reader: First Series.* Ed. Andrew McNeillie. 1925. San Diego: Harcourt, 1984.

Sally Greene
Virginia Woolf, Renaissance Woman

Here I'd like to continue a conversation we began in New Hampshire two years ago in a similar forum, where the topic was Woolf in intellectual history. I wondered out loud then why it is that Woolf's Renaissance still fascinates us—some of us, at least—whereas our more historically driven Renaissance colleagues have all but dismissed early twentieth-century interpretations of the Renaissance.[1]

Early twentieth-century readings, these critics would say, are fundamentally flawed, because they buy into totalizing, limiting notions about the past that never were the whole story in the first place. The noted Swiss historian Jacob Burckhardt, whose book *Civilization of the Renaissance in Italy* gives us the concept of "Renaissance man" in all his imperious and male glory, is a favorite whipping-boy.[2] Woolf's Renaissance, however, seemed to me to have very little to do with Burckhardt's.

Newly energized by that conference, I decided that as I finished editing my collection of new essays on Woolf and the Renaissance (*Virginia Woolf: Reading the Renaissance*) it would be fruitful to dig more deeply into what the Renaissance looked like in the nineteenth and early twentieth centuries, to try to place Woolf's reception in a broader context.[3] What I found is what many of you here tonight, in your own projects, have already discovered about Virginia Woolf: that when you start to grapple with her work in its own context, you find her tapping into movements and ideas that over time have become lost or written out of existence. Your own work becomes what Woolf's often was: a process of recovery, of rediscovery.

In my project, I learned that Burckhardt was neither the first nor the last word after all. His famous book, though first published in 1860, was not translated from the German into English until 1878, by which time a well-defined debate over what the Renaissance meant was in progress.

To understand this debate in England in the nineteenth and early twentieth centuries, we need first to look to France, where, by around 1860, the issues were already joined. To the Jesuits, the conservative defenders of a state-authorized Catholicism, the Renaissance was seen as a threat: it was an "aggressively secular movement and the embodiment of religious infidelity" (Bullen 11) that followed the more agreeable Middle Ages. But to the secular intellectual classes, the Renaissance symbolized humanity's successful struggle against repressive dogmatism.

An important spokesman for the secular intellectuals was Jules Michelet, an extraordinary historian who made his name at the Collège de France, which itself was founded by François I, France's Renaissance king, in a burst of humanistic fresh air that was emphatically opposed to the theological dogmatism of the Sorbonne and the University of Paris.[4] In time, Virginia Woolf would become fascinated with Michelet's dynamically revisionist historical practice (as would, later still, Roland Barthes, who also taught at the Collège de France); but before turning to that discussion it will be helpful to consider a bit more fully the contrasting example of Burckhardt.

To be fair, it may be that he has been taken for saying more than he said. He does not proclaim a Catholic party line. To use Hayden White's taxonomy of narrative modes, Burckhardt writes history as ironic satire—it is not intrinsically good or bad (though certainly capable of being manipulated for the bad). Burckhardt linked the inception of "individualism" with the decline of feudal despotism. His theory, which can be challenged from any number of directions, was that when you're a feudal serf, individualism is essentially forced upon you: you're driven to discover "all the inward resources of [your] own nature." And that, he said, was "neither good nor bad, but necessary" (455). The result may be Michelangelo or Machiavelli.

There is nothing progressive about history for Burckhardt. It leads neither to hope nor necessarily even to action. Strictly speaking, Burckhardt cannot be aligned with the conservatives. Yet it's fairly easy to see how his message would have been ripe for appropriation by those who viewed the Renaissance as the end, rather than the beginning, of civilization.

As the debate over the significance of the Renaissance is taken up in England, we find Ruskin on the one hand and Pater on the other. Ruskin's myth of the Renaissance, like the Jesuits', is dire. The period is a "foul torrent" that "swept away" the Middle Ages, spoiling "all unity and principle." Or even colder: "the Renaissance frosts came, and all perished."[5] You will probably pause here to think, as I do, of *Orlando* (speaking of satire). And let's not forget that a little later, E. M. W. Tillyard (*The Elizabethan World Picture*) picks up this theme. Renaissance scholars have scorned him for decades, for his glorification of the great chain of being and all that, but I find it at least worth smiling about that the first move Tillyard makes in that book, which came out in 1943, was to dismiss *Orlando* out of hand.[6]

Pater, who was much influenced by Michelet, is an entirely different story. We have some understanding of Pater's influence on Woolf, from Perry Meisel's book and other work, but what I concluded when I looked particularly at Pater's *Renaissance* is that we may have been selling him short. We know Pater's precious aesthetics, we remember how he said "[n]ot the fruit of experience, but experience itself, is the end" (188). But listen to what else he said about the Renaissance: he calls it "that movement in which, in various ways, the human mind wins for itself a new kingdom of feeling and sensation and thought, not opposed to but only beyond and independent of the spiritual system then actually realised" (5). "[W]ithin the enchanted region of the Renaissance," he writes, "one needs not be for ever on one's guard," for "there are no fixed parties, no exclusions" (20).

Here, we are approaching something like Woolf's Renaissance, not just aesthetically but politically: no fixed parties, no exclusions. Equally Woolfian (as we shall see), it's hard to tell what Pater's Renaissance looks like.

Now let's turn to Michelet's Renaissance, which Pater takes and aestheticizes but Woolf takes straight up. It's a fascinating, if imaginary, place. He wrote it out of disappointment with the failed promise of the French Revolution. The Revolution was born in 1789; he was born in 1798, of revolutionary parents. He grew up to watch the dream rise and die, not once but several times. And so his Renaissance is just that: the story of repeated attempts of the human spirit to wrest itself from oppressive medieval systems. He's especially hard on the tedious, head-of-a-pin-spinning scholastics. It's wickedly ironic, often hilarious, but the dominant "mode of emplotment," to return to Hayden White's terms, is romantic. Like the poets of Romanticism who are more familiar to us, he is calling out to a better world that is not yet, but is yet to be—one that we can reach only by way of a kind of subjective and spiritual quest.

Michelet calls the whole sixteenth century a "hero," but his particular heroes include da Vinci, Galileo, Brunelleschi—men who married art and reason, the beautiful and the true. Reason is what he saw missing from the Middle Ages. He celebrates Brunelleschi's dome in Florence, for example, for being a feat of physics as well as art. In Michelet's Renaissance there is much uncertainty, no guarantee that the hoped-for ends will come about; but as in Pater and in Woolf it's a kind of productive uncertainty.

Perhaps one of the most interesting characteristics of Michelet's Renaissance, from a Woolfian perspective, is that it is precisely not a Carlylean pageant of "great men": rather it is a call, issuing out of the past to the present, for the living spirit of *la Renaissance* to rise up collectively. Throughout his text he notes that the achievements of these great men (and it is men: his views on women were complicated and time-bound, as Bonnie Scott has noted in another context) seem to be singular, isolated, rising up randomly out of the unenlightened masses. But that's only because "the people" or populace was not yet born that could support them, and that's what he really longs for. He wants the spirit of the Renaissance—figured female in his narrative as a lucky accident of French grammar—to rise up *as a body*. Do not give up, he says to her: "No, go, march, have confidence, enter [the future] without fear. Let one sole word reassure you: *A world of humanity is beginning, of universal sympathy*" (211, trans. mine, emphasis in original).

For Michelet, history itself was prophetic, was redemptive even. His tombstone at the Père-Lachaise cemetery in Paris is a bas-relief sculpture representing his reclining mortal body, out of which a female body is rising. The inscription is from his own pen: "*L'histoire est une résurrection.*"[7]

". . . and the dead poet who was Shakespeare's sister will put on the body which she has so often laid down" (*AROO* 114).

Woolf's Renaissance is out of this prophetic line. The important message is not so much that fact alone, but that Woolf is carrying on a tradition, one we have to call an alternative tradition now, when we think not just of Burckhardt's triumph but also of T. S. Eliot's, for example, of his success in redefining the Renaissance along lines more consistent with Ruskin. To understand the larger debate I've been talking about is to discover a context for discussing Woolf's Renaissance *versus* Eliot's, among other things.

Now I'll leave you near the beginning of Woolf's Renaissance, with Katharine and Ralph in *Night and Day*, two romantic modern souls, who both dream of voyages to the New World, setting out to nowhere yet known, just an image of "[s]hips vanishing on the horizon" (334). As they talk their conversation becomes broken; they can't quite think how to say what they mean. Finally Ralph writes her a note in defense of the idea of communication, communication being at least a window upon other worlds, even "a world such as he had had a glimpse of the other evening when together they seemed to be sharing something, creating something, an ideal—a vision flung out in advance of actual circumstances" (487).

Scanning the Centuries

This could be Pater, or Michelet: a yearning toward something other and better than what we are or have, but as yet inexpressible. In the end, Ralph resorts to "little figures in the blank spaces, heads meant to resemble her head, blots fringed with flames meant to represent—perhaps the entire universe" (487). Katherine says, "'Yes, the world looks something like that to me too'" (493).[8]

Or as David McWhirter writes in the last chapter of my collection, which considers Woolf's and Eliot's very different Renaissances in the context of *Between the Acts* ("Woolf, Eliot, and the Elizabethans: The Politics of Modernist Nostalgia," Greene 245-66), Woolf resists nostalgia, resists any conception of history other than as a process, ever capable of new directions. By thinking differently, she reaches out—and encourages us in our own work to reach out—toward a future of ever-expanding horizons.

Notes

[1] The forum was the plenary panel "Influence, Intertext, Context," at the Seventh Annual Conference on Virginia Woolf. My remarks, together with those of the other panelists, are abstracted in Davis and McVicker, 55-62.

[2] See, e.g., the introduction to Ferguson et al. Among feminist Renaissance scholars, Woolf herself is criticized for failing to recognize that there were, after all, women writers in Shakespeare's time. For a recent example, see Cerasano and Wynne-Davis, whose introduction begins, "Recalling the dismal fate of Virginia Woolf's fictional playwright, Judith Shakespeare, we might be prompted to ask why Early Modern women such as Mary Sidney, Elizabeth Cary, Mary Wroth and the Cavendish sisters dared to write a play at all?"

[3] The full results of my research are incorporated in the collection's introduction and in my Ch. 1, "Michelet, Woolf, and the Idea of the Renaissance." Readers will find there a more extensive version of the remarks made here. Special thanks are due to Pierre-Eric Villeneuve for his comments at the seventh Woolf Conference and elsewhere.

[4] For a brief but fascinating political history of the universities of the Left Bank from the Middle Ages through *les événements de mai* 1968, see Vallois 155-63.

[5] Ruskin, in *The Seven Lamps of Architecture* (1846), in *Works*, 8:97-98; and *The Stones of Venice* (1853), in *Works*, 9:278.

[6] Woolf is upbraided because the opening pages of *Orlando* "do not tell us that Queen Elizabeth translated Boethius, that Raleigh was a theologian as well as a discoverer, and that sermons were as much a part of an ordinary Elizabethan's life as bear-baiting" (Tillyard 3).

[7] Barthes writes that Michelet's tomb at Père-Lachaise is an "official and elaborate mausoleum" that his widow chose, in violation of what Michelet would have wished (87). Citing an apocryphal story that he "wanted his own body, upon his death, to be exposed to the sun until dissolution" (85), Barthes regrets that by virtue of this monumental monument Michelet "entered into that motionless enchantment of which he had always been afraid" (87). And yet, as Barthes recognizes, history cannot really be frozen: "[T]he goal of history is to rediscover in each piece of the past's flesh the corruptible element par excellence, not the skeleton but the tissue" (87).

[8] Other strategic "doodles" in Woolf's work will come to mind at this point. See further Anne E. Fernald, "The Memory Palace of Virginia Woolf," in Greene 89-114.

Works Cited

Barthes, Roland. *Michelet.* Trans. Richard Howard. London: Blackwell, 1987.
Bullen, J. B. *The Myth of the Renaissance in Nineteenth-Century Writing.* Oxford: Clarendon P, 1994.
Burckhardt, Jacob. *The Civilization of the Renaissance in Italy.* 1878. 2d ed. Rev. and trans. S.G.C. Middlemore. New York: Oxford UP, 1945.
Cerasano, S. P., and Marion Wynne-Davis, eds. *Readings in Renaissance Women's Drama: Criticism, History, and Performance 1594-1998.* New York: Routledge, 1998.
Davis, Laura, and Jeanette McVicker, eds. *Virginia Woolf and Her Influences: Selected Papers from the Seventh Annual Conference on Virginia Woolf.* New York: Pace UP, 1998.
Ferguson, Margaret, Maureen Quilligan, and Nancy J. Vickers, eds. *Rewriting the Renaissance: The Discourses of Sexual Difference in Early Modern Europe.* Chicago: U of Chicago P, 1986.
Greene, Sally, ed. *Virginia Woolf: Reading the Renaissance.* Athens: Ohio UP, 1999.
Meisel, Perry. *The Absent Father: Virginia Woolf and Walter Pater.* New Haven: Yale UP, 1980.
Michelet, Jules. *Renaissance et Réforme. Histoire de France au XVIe siècle.* Pref. Claude Mettra. Paris: Robert Laffont, 1982.
Pater, Walter. *The Renaissance: Studies in Art and Poetry.* Ed. Donald L. Hill. Berkeley: U of Calif. P, 1980.
Ruskin, John. *The Works of John Ruskin.* 39 vols. New York: Longmans, Green, 1903-12.
Scott, Bonnie Kime. "Joyce and Michelet: Why Watch Molly Menstruate?" *Joyce in Context.* Ed. Vincent J. Cheng and Timothy Martin. Cambridge: Cambridge UP, 1992. 122-37.
Tillyard, E. M.W. *The Elizabethan World Picture.* 1943. Rpt. New York: Vintage, n.d.
Vallois, Thirza. *Around and About Paris.* Vol. 1. London: Iliad Books, 1995.
White, Hayden. *Metahistory: The Historical Imagination in Nineteenth-Century Europe.* Baltimore: Johns Hopkins UP, 1973.
Woolf, Virginia. *Night and Day.* 1919. New York: Harcourt Brace Jovanovich, 1973.
———. *A Room of One's Own.* 1929. New York: Harcourt Brace Jovanovich, 1989.

Gabrielle Dane
Thinking Back Through Her Fathers: Virginia Woolf and Edward Gibbon

"History will be a good thing for her to take up as I can give her some hints" (qtd. in Lee 57), the historical biographer Leslie Stephen wrote in 1893 to his wife Julia, voicing his expectations of their daughter Virginia's future career. A child of the Stephen lineage, Virginia was bred to feel the influence of numerous British historiographers such as Edward Gibbon. I'd like to investigate Woolf's conflicted relationship with this prototypical British historian, analyzing how his influence shapes Woolf's thinking about writing and history.

Marveling at the clarity, economy, and euphony of "one of Gibbon's pictures," Woolf compares his ability to conjure past scenes to that of "the historical novelist—to Scott or to Flaubert" (*DM* 57, 58). In this perceived blurring of the boundaries between history and fiction, Woolf suggests that Gibbon conflates genre categories, becoming a composer of novelistic history. Of course, his intense commitment to truth, which causes him to remain ultimately faithful to fact rather than imagination, curtails his imaginative flights. Woolf finds fault with Gibbon's devotion to fact, a presumed objectivity unfettered by one's own subject position. Still, his unique ability to blend imagination and fact, to cloud the distinction between history and fiction, causes Woolf to describe him as a literary historian, "a master of the pageant and the story" (*DM* 58).

Of course, Gibbon's project was not mainly aesthetic. Gibbon speaks of the historian as architect crafting the lasting edifices through which future generations might step into the past (*Essays* 538). In fact, Gibbon raises the historian to noble heights since he (or she) wields the pen that saves great nations from obscurity: "For the losses of history are indeed irretrievable... [N]ew poets may invent, and new philosophers may reason; but if the inscription of a single fact be once obliterated, it can never be restored by the united efforts of Genius and industry" (*Essays* 535). But despite his ardent belief in the preservation of historical fact, Gibbon wanted not merely to conserve the past, but to submit that past to the rigorous scrutiny of present (eighteenth-century) reason. According to Peter Gay, Gibbon attempted a discourse free "from constricting prejudgements and from unquestioning acceptance of authority" (30). Vindicating himself from attacks on the *Decline and Fall*, Gibbon reveals his resolve to undermine the irrational superstition of religious zealots such as these "Watchmen of the Holy City," the "adversaries, whom it is impossible for [him] to consider as objects either of terror or of esteem," who have spilt ink assaulting his history (*Essays* 311). As Gibbon lambastes the idiocy of his critics' cant, he exposes his own politico-philosophical bent—an urge to dispel the "phantoms" of the dogma that cloud enlightened thought.

Woolf cherishes Gibbon not only for his mastery as a storyteller; she also lauds him as "the critic and the historian of the mind" (*DM* 58). As he erases the clear distinction between history and fiction, Gibbon acknowledges the fictionality of his project, gravely mocking the ostensible infallibility of historians. Exposing the faulty vision of past historians, Gibbon implies that our version of the past is no more than a reflection of the biased perspectives of those who compile it. Yet historians are not the only sacred cows open to Gibbon's contempt. "Few virgins or matrons, nuns or monks leave his pages with their honour entirely unscathed," Woolf claims, delighted. "But his most insidious raillery, his most relentless reason, are directed, of course, against the Christian religion" (*DM* 59). The agnostic Leslie Stephen's daughter applauds Gibbon's assault on "the terrible grip" of Christianity, as she believes that "the fear of God" remains more than a hundred years after Gibbon's enlightened study as "the chief enemy" to intellectual freedom (*D*1 165). In Woolf's eyes, Gibbon's political philosophy was predicated on his contempt for all things fanatical and superstitious. Wherever he encountered these evils he attacked them with his most powerful tool: irony.

However, despite appreciating the power of Gibbon's irony, Woolf also understands its potential pitfalls, declaring that

> the pressure of public opinion forced [Gibbon] to be covert, not open. And irony is a dangerous weapon; it easily becomes sidelong and furtive; the ironist seems to be darting a poisoned tongue from a place of concealment. However grave and temperate Gibbon's irony at its best, however searching his logic and robust his contempt for the cruelty and intolerance of superstition, we sometimes feel, as he pursues his victim with incessant scorn, that he is a little limited, a little superficial [. . .] (*DM* 59-60)

For Woolf, Gibbon's example underlines the fact that irony, often her own weapon of choice, is a dangerously tenuous one. Certainly public opinion, including sometimes even the opinions of those closest to her, forced Woolf to be covert, to mask her anger beneath a sidelong and furtive irony. Reading Gibbon, Woolf sees that the sarcasm erupting out of untempered irony disables the speaker, rendering her limited, shallow. Throughout her life, Woolf struggled to find the tone of restraint in her own works that she found wanting in writers such as Gibbon, believing that a writer's most potent abilities involve "the strength to leave things unsaid; the strength required not to preach; not to extemporise" (*D*4 26).

Despite her marked admiration of Gibbon's ability as a storyteller, Woolf reads his work with a critical eye. After remarking on Gibbon's pompous diction, stereotypical syntax, and crudely hewn characters, Woolf goes on to underline the weakness of his characters. In the interest of order and drama, Gibbon erases the features that would describe individualized faces:

> Here are none of those violent gestures and unmistakable voices that fill the pages of Carlyle and Macaulay with living human beings who are related to ourselves. . . . Time has cut off those quick reactions that make us love and hate. The innumerable figures are suffused in the equal blue of the far distance. They rise and fall and pass away without exciting our pity or our anger. (*DM* 57)

For Woolf, the story of a people is a story of individuals whose actions motivate what will come to be called their history. Since he fails to infuse his pages with the violent gestures and unmistakable voices of living human beings, memorable characters able to excite the reader's pity and anger, Gibbon's history making elicits Woolf's critique.

Indeed, although Gibbon appears in Woolf's essays and novels as well as in her diaries and letters, he often stands as a rather chilly figure, an encyclopedic reference evoked by the particular Cambridge-educated character under Woolf's narrative scrutiny. At such times, the (home-schooled) female figure tends to look on, mute, in the face of this quintessential voice—decid-

Scanning the Centuries

edly conventional and male—of British history. Woolf offers this fraught interchange around the great Gibbon most explicitly in her first novel, *The Voyage Out*. Here, St. John Hirst employs Gibbon in order to sound the worth of a woman as well as to flaunt his "masculine acquirements" in order to veil his sexual unease in her presence (*VO* 154). Stunned to learn that Rachel Vinrace, who like Woolf lacked a university education, had reached the advanced age of twenty-four years without having read Gibbon, St. John demands that she begin her intellectual odyssey the following day. Still, despite his eagerness to ameliorate her supposed deficiency, St. John poses a lingering question: "D'you think you'll be able to appreciate [Gibbon]? He's the test, of course. It's awfully difficult to tell about women [. . .] how much, I mean, is due to lack of training, and how much is native incapacity" (*VO* 154). The man and woman stand on opposite edges of a chasm, between them the crucial experience of Cambridge. In order to craft a female able to engage in stimulating discourse, Hirst must feed her intellect with the appropriate fodder—if, that is, she can prove her ignorance is inexperience and not incapacity. Like Henry Higgins sounding out initial vowel sounds for Eliza Doolittle, St. John extends Gibbon to Rachel—a cornerstone for the educated mind (after having served its preliminary function as I.Q. test).

Yet St. John's attempt to play Pygmalion to Rachel's Galatea crumbles when the pianist Rachel ultimately fails to find the music in Gibbon's prose (*VO* 201). Initially, Rachel's reading of Gibbon had fired her imagination when she felt that "never had any words been so vivid and so beautiful." Indeed, the historian's words

> seemed to drive roads back to the very beginning of the world, on either side of which the populations of all times and countries stood in avenues, and by passing down them all knowledge would be hers, and the book of the world turned back to the very first page. Such was her excitement at the possibilities of knowledge now opening before her that she ceased to read, and a breeze turning the page, the covers of Gibbon gently ruffled and closed together. (*VO* 175)

For Rachel, Gibbon stands as an entrée into the world of the mind. Casting Woolf in the role of her protagonist, one might add that Gibbon represents not only the actual visceral pleasure of intellectual activity, but the deeply exciting terrain of history, of the book of the world turned back to the very first page. But here Gibbon serves as liaison; after opening the vista onto unfamiliar roads and inciting her to explore unknown populations and countries, his text is shut, lacking the music that will move her imagination.

The music to which Gibbon marches is, at heart, a tune strident to Woolf's ear. In an essay written after the *Decline and Fall*, Gibbon calls for a national history of England equivalent to certain continental efforts, hoping "to enrich [Britain's] common treasure of national glory" through historical narrative (*Essays* 534). "Without indulging the fond prejudices of patriotic vanity," Gibbon insists, "we may assume a conspicuous place among the inhabitants of

19

the Earth. The English will be ranked among the few nations, who have cultivated with equal success the arts of War, of learning and of commerce" (*Essays* 534-35). Juxtaposing this proposal for a history of their own alongside Gibbon's completed masterwork, certain similarities appear. Studying the contents of the *Decline and Fall*, one finds a saga of education, of economics—but especially of war. As Roy Porter states, "Through perusing his book, Gibbon tells his readers, 'the most voracious appetite for war will be abundantly satisfied'" (94). Indeed perusing the six volumes, a reader finds that 68 of the 71 chapters contain war-related entries, where "war-related" covers both internal and external issues, including armies, assassination and usurpation, religious persecution, repression and rebellion, and imperialist conquest. Although Gibbon's tome focuses much attention on the subject of religion, the story that he tells of Christianity vs. paganism is one of violent conflict, an ongoing war that is waged throughout the six volumes. When Gibbon mentions the subject of non-military education, he speaks primarily of the intellectual and moral development (or lack thereof) of civic and religious leaders, or the philosophical evolution of government and its policies. And when he covers economic issues, he focuses mainly on the commerce of empire, the funding of a government which tends to acquire or require war-related monies. For Gibbon, the story of the bloody decline of Rome was in a sense a cautionary tale of the fall of an unparalleled civilization. Thus, in the *Decline and Fall*, Gibbon mourns the demise of a superior power which cultivated with equal success the nationalistic arts of war, learning, and commerce.

But for Woolf, these categories suggest the "great movements" of traditional historiography that inherently exclude women's experience (*AROO* 46). In *Three Guineas*, she translates this triumvirate—the economic, university, and war machine—into an interdependent mechanism. The university breeds and the government funds the patriotic fervor that results in war. The nationalist urge that leads to wars of conquest and to the domination of a "feminized" other is but one end of a continuum at the other end of which is the related nationalist urge to keep women enslaved for the purposes of racial purity. Woolf figures this imperialist impulse as a larger than life (if less than adult) force, a sort of isolated Tweedledum lacking his rattle: "a monstrous male, loud of voice, hard of fist, childishly intent upon scoring the floor of the earth with chalk marks, within whose mystic boundaries human beings are penned, rigidly, separately, artificially" (*TG* 105). Ultimately, Gibbon's history, the story of the decline and fall of a great imperialist power, is the lavish tale of a people whose chalk marks might have faded into obscurity, except that they've been made indelible via the pens of historians such as Gibbon. Yet for Woolf, Gibbon's history remains the superficial account of an imperfect past which the historian views with equanimity, the saga of an empire whose established order he admires. "Gibbon," claims Porter, "like so many of his fellow Englishmen, saw reflected in the politics of the Roman Republic the qualities ideally displayed in Georgian England" (96). Conversely, Woolf's rendering of Britain's interdependent nationalistic mechanism—the economic, university, and war machine—represents her attempt not only to penetrate to the underlying determining conditions that drive English history, but to launch an attack on the politics that led to the construction of the machine.

Woolf also figures Gibbon as a vanguard of aesthetic convention, perpetrator of what she terms the "man's sentence." Remarking on a brief passage taken from Samuel Johnson, Woolf states, "The sentence that was current at the beginning of the nineteenth century [. . .] is a man's sentence; behind it one can see Johnson, Gibbon and the rest. It was a sentence that was unsuited for a woman's use" (*AROO* 79-80). Johnson's, and by extension Gibbon's, sentence has a regular, linear structure intended to provide a well-reasoned, clearly-constructed summary remark. A composite of such remarks erects a discourse of facts building toward a solid rational conclusion. Coupled with Gibbon's presumed freedom from cant (also a Johnsonian urge), this discourse assumes the detached status of an objectivity divorced from personal bias. Now, in contradistinction to the notion of the "man's sentence," one might attempt to construe what Woolf might call a "woman's sentence." Yet although Woolf seems to be raising the call for such a construct, the reader of her essay searching to clarify this notion will emerge dissatisfied since Woolf herself intentionally refrains from coining such a phrase. And this crucial omission cuts to the heart of Woolf's project and implicitly underlines her criticism of Gibbon's.

Throughout her life, Woolf struggled with the notion of an experimental aesthetics based in her experience of how human consciousness works. The proper stuff of human experience, Woolf insists, is the life of the mind. And this "truth" has no predetermined plot since consciousness lacks a neat conventional structure. In the *Decline and Fall*, Lionel Gossman claims, "division and multiplicity are always seen . . . as error, weakness, decline, decay" (26). But Woolf figures division and multiplicity as the stuff of life, of possibility, the very essence of human experience. What Woolf calls for then, in opposition to the Gibbonian "man's sentence," is an open-ended, always experimental discourse, willing to discard decisive (and static) conclusion in favor of the free play of innovation, of indecision, of the narrative uncertainty bespeaking the truly skeptical, non-traditional mind. Thus Woolf refuses to raise the phantom of a gender-based "woman's sentence" designed simply to replace one stultifying convention for another. A discourse in opposition to the "man's sentence," then, is an ideal notion, one which is not the province of biological womanhood. Instead Woolf imagines the possibility of a discourse that defies gender restrictions, erupting from an androgynous mind that outlines an all-human experience. For Woolf, the androgynous mind translates as an unhindered intellect able to reside outside of (or at least to remain in contention with) conventional categories, such as aesthetic and historiographical ones. The androgynous mind is both and neither; like Orlando, it wants—and needs—to have it both ways. In order for an act of creation to be accomplished it must be fertilized, "some marriage of opposites has to be consummated. The whole of the mind must lie wide open if we are to get the sense that the writer is communicating his experience with perfect fullness" (*AROO* 108). The androgynous mind is a mind of experiment, of play, a mind that refuses to choose an absolute truth that would force it to acquiesce to a limited methodology.

Attempting to imagine a more fluid form of historiography, Woolf employs the figure of the prototypical historian himself in order to probe the notion of writing the lives of great men. In her essay, "Reflections at Sheffield Place" (1937), Woolf uses Gibbon as a figure around whom to puzzle over a number of rhetorical questions: What is (a) history? How can we know an historical figure (or any human being)? What are the contours of a "life"? How does context impinge upon the historical artifact? Perhaps inspired by her subject to make "pictures," Woolf examines moments, snapshots of the man and his surroundings. Instead of focusing her gaze on the ostensible subject of her narrative, Woolf glances all around him, providing an almost accidental sketch of the historian painted against a domestic backdrop. The snatches of information revealed about Gibbon are filtered through the eyes and the experiences of the women who surround (and care for) him. If Gibbon disregarded character, Woolf seems determined to exploit it, offering images of the historian as they flit through the consciousness of Gibbon's surrogate daughter, Maria. Through her ruminations we meet Gibbon's disapproving, pious Aunt Hester, and his doting, tolerant caretaker, Aunt Kitty. Also using Maria as conduit, we anticipate her future granddaughter, Kate.

Woolf tells the history of Gibbon both by thinking back through his female caretakers (whose daughters in turn think back through their mothers), and by exploring the domestic conditions that helped to shape both the historian's intellect and his nature. Gibbon's "life" begins as a twentieth-century narrator attempts to imagine his formidable bulk reflected against the fantastic flowered grounds of the contemporary tourist site, Sheffield Place. But the narrator's train of thought is interrupted by the consciousness of the eighteenth-century mistress of the estate who corrects these anachronistic speculations as she gazes out onto the swans currently in residence where rhododendrons will later wave. This young woman's mixed reflections of her adoptive uncle, who "looked different [when viewed through Maria's eyes] from Gibbon seen by himself," are filtered through her concerns about running a large household, including the problems of managing her restless father who was only restrained by the good sense of his dear friend, "le grand Gibbon" (*DM* 64).

In apparent extension of Maria's thoughts, we enter the perspectives of the historian's two aunts, Hester and Kitty, the former whose ferocious piety helped ignite Gibbon's religious skepticism and the latter whose freethinking indulgence inspired his "love of pagan literature" (*DM* 67). This "life" makes clear that should Kitty not have taken charge of young Gibbon, inspiring his curiosity by granting him free access to the books he fancied, repressive parenting might well have robbed the world of a great historian. Nonetheless, these two incompatible adult models combined to produce his conflicted nature. Asked to imagine the "strange mixture" of Gibbon's aloof, caustic intellect juxtaposed alongside his capacity for familial devotion, the apparent dichotomy between his scathing ridicule of the eccentric Hester versus his patient tenderness toward the "rather tedious" Kitty, we return to the frame of Maria's silent musings:

> Very strange, Maria may have thought as she sat there listening to his talk while she stitched: selfish yet tender; ridiculous but sublime. Perhaps human nature was like that—by no means all of a piece; different at different moments; changing, as the furniture changed in the firelight, as the waters of the lake changed when the night wind swept over them. (*DM* 68)

History can never be a static enterprise, since its human subjects are never still; a "life" can never be an absolute account, since it must always be informed by the shifting subjectivity of the speaking voice. Thus Woolf offers a series of diverse perceptions intended to suggest the outline of an historical figure. And while her impressionistic portrait of Gibbon ends with his death, she extends Maria's life past the confines of her pages, concluding her history of the uncle by tracing the familial line of the niece.

Crafting her history of the great Gibbon, Woolf underlines the subjectivity of her interested position, tacitly acknowledging her biases as she tells Gibbon's story through the eyes of his female intimates. Offering a version of Gibbon's life which is patently a product of the imagination, Woolf implies that history is more fabricated than found, more fictional than factual. Rather than providing a seamless narrative in which we are offered an integral picture of the great man, Woolf's disjointed account provides merely glimpses, biographical snippets. Through Gibbon's sporadic and nebulous presence, Woolf acknowledges the lacunae which must exist in our knowledge of either another human being or a past event. Moreover, she explodes the pretense both of a disembodied narrator able to avoid the distortions of perspective and of a history able to escape the circumstance of its production. Alongside Woolf's fleeting series of impressions of her subject, she also includes a number of ostensibly peripheral portraits—of both person and place—suggesting that what we can know about any subject depends upon an understanding of an entire complex of interpersonal relationships and situated contexts. In sum, while the immortal Gibbon both inspires and intimidates Woolf, she ultimately rejects the substance and the structure of his project, choosing to reconfigure his lessons into a form that she can fruitfully apply to her own method of imagining history.

Works Cited

Gay, Peter. *Style in History: Gibbon, Ranke, Macaulay, Burckhardt*. New York: Norton, 1988.

Gibbon, Edward. *The English Essays of Edward Gibbon*. Ed. Patricia B. Craddock. Oxford: Clarendon, 1972.

———. *The History of the Decline and Fall of the Roman Empire.* Ed. David Womersley. 6 vols. New York: Penguin, 1994.
Gossman, Lionel. *The Empire Unpossess'd: An Essay on Gibbon's Decline and Fall.* New York: Cambridge UP, 1981.
Lee, Hermione. *Virginia Woolf.* New York: Knopf, 1997.
Porter, Roy. *Gibbon: Making History.* New York: St. Martin, 1988.
Woolf, Virginia. *The Diary of Virginia Woolf.* Ed. Anne Olivier Bell and Andrew McNeillie. 5 vols. New York: Harcourt: 1977-84.
———. "The Historian and 'The Gibbon.'" *The Death of the Moth and Other Essays.* London: Hogarth, 1943. 55-63.
———. "Reflections at Sheffield Place." *The Death of the Moth and Other Essays.* London: Hogarth, 1943. 63-68.
———. *A Room of One's Own.* New York: Harcourt, 1957.
———. *Three Guineas.* New York: Harcourt, 1966.
———. *The Voyage Out.* New York: Harcourt, 1948.

Alison Booth
Those Well-Lit Corridors of History

At the 1997 Virginia Woolf Conference in New Hampshire I picked a fight with Woolf that happily has done no harm whatsoever to her reputation. I was hardly the first to challenge the partial cultural history inscribed in *A Room of One's Own*, *Three Guineas*, and the essays, but I took my turn to point out what was missing—not only a host of seventeenth- or eighteenth-century women writers, working class women or women of color, essayists or poets (Ezell, Sandbach-Dahlström), but also a substantial archive of bio-historical records of women published since the eighteenth century. How could she say that women are "all but absent from history" and biography, given a long-standing tradition of a history of women in the form of collective biographies (*AROO* 43-44)? On this occasion, I propose to substantiate my claim, broached in 1997, that her vocabulary of historical women was developed in the collections of female biography readily available since the 1830s.

Although Woolf participated in a modernist craze for sets of short biographical studies, she hardly made a habit of reading role model anthologies addressed to the female common reader. Woolf's well-known fascination with biography appears traceable to full-length solo lives, though apart from *Roger Fry*, *Orlando*, and *Flush*, her own biographical writings mostly appear in collections. Fortunately, I have no need to prove that Woolf was directly influenced by or indebted to particular collections of female biographies.[1] In the field of biography, questions of authorship, originality, influence, or sources are more than usually unprofitable, as the genre circulates sets of subjects and their narratives rather than monumental classics. As William H. Epstein suggests, "the biographical subject" dominates the genre, ensuring "the virtual disappearance of the biographer" (80), and I would add, of the particular textual version of the subject. The genre's diffusion of authority is further propelled by the tropism of women's lives toward collections, and of collections themselves toward anonymity and typology. Woolf almost entirely ignored the hundreds of biographical collections that cobbled together a history of educated European women for her day. I would not suggest that Woolf was willfully blind to the archives that surrounded her; rather she followed a set of conventions, too overdetermined and complex to examine in full here. Among the various incentives that may have led Woolf to claim the absence of women from history and biography, the most pertinent is the convention of performative mourning for "the lives of the obscure" which effectively deepens that obscurity. Woolf's blindness to the light in history's corridors proves to be characteristic of recuperative collective biographies themselves, which ritually identify the supposedly unidentified, and grieve for the loss of many foremothers.

Collections of women's biographies have been a favored mode of argument in centuries of feminist and anti-feminist debate; a few feminist scholars, such as Margaret Ezell, Natalie Zemon Davis, Martha Vicinus, and Sybil Oldfield have begun to examine this neglected body of work. My bibliography of nearly 800 all-female collections of three or more *narrated* lives (I exclude most reference works) published in English between 1830-1940 includes works well within Woolf's purview, some of which I indicate here. Victorians on both sides of the Atlantic already possessed something of the "supplement to history" that Woolf tentatively solicits from the college women of the future in *A Room of One's Own* (*AROO* 45). Suffice it to say, here, that most of the women featured in Woolf's own multivolume records of women's lives were kept in contemporary currency in collections of biographies published between 1880 and 1930 alone: there were the perennial favorites Austen, the Brontës, George Eliot, Florence Nightingale, Madame de Sévigné, Elizabeth Barrett Browning, as well as the less popular Duchess of Newcastle, Fanny Burney, Hester Thrale, Dorothy Wordsworth, Jane Carlyle, Mary Russell Mitford, Maria Edgeworth, Laetitia Pilkington, Ellen Terry, Mary Kingsley, Lady Hester Stanhope, Joanna Baillie, Sappho, George Sand.[2] But rather than consume this essay with roll-calling or bibliography, I propose to highlight the form itself, collective biography, in Woolf's career and context. Above all, I want to examine the convention of the missing pantheon. Generations of tributes to historical women lament that women are all but absent from history.[3]

Woolf stands as the model of the feminist scholar perennially "looking about the shelves for books that were not there" (*AROO* 45). The record may actually be on the shelves in a spectral form whose disappearance the scholar reenacts. Further, the reclamation of the obscure promotes a myth of hegemonic recognition. Thus, Woolf and others assail History as the Biographies of Great Men as though it were omnipresent and universal, whereas any pantheon is built on the graves of the unknown (Garber 42-43). "There were the biographies: Johnson and Goethe and Carlyle and Sterne and Cowper and Shelley and Voltaire and Browning and many others" (*AROO* 90). Undoubtedly, this masculine canon has overshadowed the majority of lives, but it is a list that already ends elliptically in "many others." A sense of metonymic contingency pervades some of the most notorious promotions of hero-worship. When for example Emerson praises great men, he suggests that they are interchangeable types of "the genius of humanity" (23); we should outgrow "idolatry" of individuals as, collectively, we are "multiplied by our proxies" (9). Such cracks in the facade of hero-worship led the later Victorians and modernists to abandon monumental biography in favor of fragmented memorial impressions (already anticipated by Hazlitt, Carlyle, and Pater). Yet brief collected lives had been favored since the first secularizations of hagiography, and records of women had largely taken that form. Only in the later nineteenth century were middle-class Englishwomen thought to merit a full-length biography of one's own, and such monographs still monopolized the reviewer's attention during Woolf's career in spite of the fashion for elite collections such as Lytton Strachey's *Eminent Victorians* or Harold Nicolson's *Some People.*

Indeed, it is remarkable the extent to which Woolf and her contemporaries and friends were immersed in female collective biography. Let me recall a few instances, besides the famous collections by Leslie Stephen, Strachey, and Nicolson.[4] A sort of tradition of thinking back through mothers had also thrived. Woolf's aunt (sister of her father's first wife), Anne Thackeray Ritchie, published *A Book of Sibyls* in 1883, a reprint of essays published in *The Cornhill Magazine* during Leslie Stephen's editorship; the *Cornhill* later helped to launch Virginia Stephen as a reviewer in 1908. Ritchie's engaging studies, dedicated to Margaret Oliphant, portray strong female predecessors in the literary field, "Mrs. Barbauld, Mrs. Opie, Miss Edgeworth, and Miss Austen." The Duckworth house, which published Woolf's first two novels, published collections of women, including *Historic Nuns* (1899) by the mid-Victorian feminist Bessie Rayner Parkes, now Mme. Belloc (mother of Hilaire).[5] The Hogarth Press in 1937 began a series of short volumes known as World-Makers and World-Shakers, in an attempt, in Leonard's words, to "explain history" to "young people" "through the lives of great men and women." The second of four books actually published was *Joan of Arc* by Vita Sackville-West (Hoberman 3; L. Woolf, *Journey* 98-99)—the one female subject in this series being the most popular subject in all collective female biographies in English, according to my records.[6] J. H. Willis links this and other Hogarth series to a widespread publishing practice, then as now often structured upon groups of biographies, "such as Constable's Makers of the Nineteenth Century (8 titles in 1936), Duckworth's Great Lives (57 titles in 1936)" (109-10). Professional writers were often recruited into the multibiography industry; besides the volume on Joan of Arc, Sackville-West also contributed an Orlando-esque portrait of Aphra Behn to a collection produced by Woolf's friend Francis Birrell, *Six Brilliant English Women* (1930). As common publishing ventures, collective biographies also might serve differing political or institutional agendas, from the revolutionary—as in Margaret Goldsmith's *Seven Women Against the World* (London, 1935), including Flora Tristan and Emma Goldman— to the pious—as in the Rev. Joseph B. Code's tribute to pioneer Catholic women, *Great American Foundresses* (New York, 1929). The organizing principle of such collections corresponds with their rhetorical aims, their designs upon particular audiences. During Woolf's lifetime, we can trace two new, intertwined impulses in compilations of eminent women, bids for the status of high art and campaigns for the political status entailed in suffrage. In 1889, the suffrage leader Millicent Garrett Fawcett published *Some Eminent Women of Our Time*, addressed "chiefly to working women and young people," representing eleven famous women writers out of twenty-six subjects.[7] In 1909, Edith Craig produced Cicely Hamilton's *A Pageant of Great Women*, an honor roll in which eminent Edwardian women reincarnated Learned Women (from Hypatia to Mme. Curie), Artists (including Sappho and Rosa Bonheur), Saintly Women (including the perennial favorites, Elizabeth Fry and Catherine of Siena), Heroic Women (including Charlotte Corday), Rulers (including Victoria of course), and Warriors from Joan of Arc to Florence Nightingale (see Green 75-78).[8] Yet canons of great women also formed without espousing feminist activism of any kind; most often they modeled a liberal ideal of education and opportunity for middle-class women, as in William Henry Davenport Adams's 1884 *Celebrated Englishwomen of the Victorian Era*, from Eliot and Mitford to Sara Coleridge and Jane Carlyle, designed to "illustrate the remarkable intellectual activity of woman in this nineteenth century" (iii-iv).[9] If it seems unlikely that Woolf *needed* to read popularizing collections, she could expect her audience to be familiar with such figures as Eliza Carter, "the valiant old woman who tied a bell to her bedstead in order that she might wake early to learn Greek" (*AROO* 65-66), through worthy sources such as Ethel Rolt Wheeler's *Famous Blue-Stockings* (London, 1910: 264).[10]

I have suggested that there were overlapping barriers to an open acknowledgment of the records of women's lives widely available. Woolf's own near-silence on the subject of these collections only seems the more peculiar because she appears to deplore the lack of just such a supply. Although *Three Guineas*, for instance, compiles the life-narrative of a "collective 'us,'" as Georgia Johnston has observed (322), its documented sources are numerous separate biographies of women, apart from four collections: Ray Strachey's *The Cause* (a biographical history of the British women's movement), Margaret Llewelyn Davies' collection of working women's testimonies, *Life as We Have Known It* (published, with Woolf's introduction, by Hogarth in 1931), George Ballard's 1752 *Memoirs of Several Ladies of Great Britain*, the great-grandaddy of Victorian collective biographies of women, and of course *The Dictionary of National Biography*. Remember that *Three Guineas* takes the form of letters addressed to a middle-aged lawyer-narratee: "your prosperity .

. . has been deserved. . . . You are writing letters, . . . presiding over this and that" (*TG* 3-4). The implied reader may relish her distance from this narratee's gentlemanly privileges, yet Woolf seems aware that his sort enforce contemporary literary standards: in spite of celebrations of the Common Reader, she sought recognition of readers in the Oxbridge-Westminster-Bloomsbury realm. If she were to participate, instead, in the exchange of popular biographical history in a Society of Outsiders, she would risk joining the "mass" of "the lives of the obscure behind . . . lives that were . . . actually written." Although "biography is many-sided," the narrator of *Three Guineas* continues, and although it records such "civilized" subjects as "Florence Nightingale, Anne Clough, Emily Brontë, Christina Rossetti, Mary Kingsley," obscurity lurks behind that series, among women undeserving of a solo volume. To have commended one of the tools of Victorian women's "unpaid-for education," reading material for the suburban parlor (*TG* 78-79), might have risked her reputation as a critic and writer.

Woolf equivocates, moreover, on the question of the presences and absences of male and female, elite and common biographies within tradition. She famously lures us into "those almost unlit corridors of history," where the "generations of women" are only "dimly" recorded ("Women and Fiction" 76). Yet in *Three Guineas* she invites a thorough reading of biography, "that witness which anyone who can read English can consult on the shelves of any public library"; a record, she suggests, that does include "the lives of the poor, of the obscure, of the uneducated" (*TG* 24-25). In context, she refers here to unprivileged men who covet a university education. But why imagine that men's biography and history are intact and transparent, women's a jumble of shards? Any library would include traces of lives of women, poor and uneducated if not obscure. Woolf perhaps prefers to continue the search for something more precious. Evocatively, *A Room of One's Own* sketches what is desired: "For one often catches a glimpse of [women] in the lives of the great, whisking away into the background, concealing, I sometimes think, a wink, a laugh, perhaps a tear. And, after all, we have lives enough of Jane Austen. . . ." (*AROO* 45). That is an awkward break, I thought!—as Woolf writes of *Jane Eyre* (*AROO* 69). Apparently, we have more than enough biography of all sorts of men, and a redundancy of some kinds of female biography (Woolf would be happy never to hear of Mary Russell Mitford again). What is the female biography that we have in spades? Woolf concedes, "Occasionally an individual woman is mentioned, an Elizabeth, or a Mary; a queen or a great lady. But by no possible means could middle-class women with nothing but brains and character at their command have taken part in any one of the great movements" of history (*AROO* 44-45). On the contrary, since the time of Dr. Johnson and Mary Astell (*TG* 153, n.21), Englishwomen of middling as well as high ranks had been repeatedly honored—honored we might say in droves—for their part in historical movements such as the Civil War or penal, educational, or religious reform. It is always useful to recall that Woolf writes (especially in *A Room of*

One's Own) not as a historian but as a literary critic, at a time when "literature" has been restricted to poetry, fiction, and drama; hence her distorting focus on a few great women novelists, a poet or two. Although the archives that recognized Englishwomen had long privileged women of letters, they also encompassed writers in many genres. Victorian collections of biography accommodate eminent women in many fields of work, and only begin to favor novelists and poets, as Woolf does, at the turn of the century. Altogether, Woolf's reviews, essays, and manifestos acknowledge a remarkable range of women of the past, but she scarcely challenges the conception, shared by the common reader of the *TLS*, of women's historical nullity. Perhaps having reviewed too many solitary biographies of women writers; or perhaps feeling some ambivalence about Judith Shakespeares who were not anonymously buried at the crossroads; or guided, as I have suggested, by her sense of the arbiters of literary value in her audience, Woolf neglects the middle-to-lowbrow anthologies that made available a diverse and substantial history of women of middle-class brains and character.

To Woolf, it seems, the lost biography is much more desirable than the accessible. This is not at all extraordinary; elegies for lost canons seem self-perpetuating. Champions of different groups are compelled to call up again and again the lists always under erasure. There is, at least, an uncanny anticipation of *A Room of One's Own* in a collection published in London and New York in 1880, *Six Life Studies of Famous Women* by Matilda Betham-Edwards.[11] The neglected exemplars—Fernan Caballero (Spanish novelist), Alexandrine Tinné (African explorer), Caroline Herschel (astronomer), Marie Pape-Carpantier (education reformer), Elizabeth Carter (scholar), Matilda Betham (the compiler's aunt, a writer and artist)—arouse a "keen regret" for the missing, the "glorious women of all ages and countries" to whom "history has been indeed unjust"—thus Betham-Edwards sounding highly Woolfian. "Here and there [sic] imperious queen or saintly devotee has won recognition. We know something about Louise of Savoy, Anne of Brittany, Margaret of Parma; from earliest childhood we have been taught to admire Joan of Arc, Elizabeth of Hungary, and Saint Theresa. But there are heroic women of another type of whom we would fain know something also; fireside heroines whose lives are more in sympathy with our own." Betham-Edwards continues with a list of famous names, from Aspasia to Elizabeth I to Joan of Arc, that "do not fairly represent" ordinary heroism, followed by a few snapshots of "intermediate notabilities . . . worthy of a biographer," such as Sarah Fielding (v-xiv). In effect, Betham-Edwards, like Woolf and many others, reiterates a ghostly catalogue of women from the books that elude recognition on the shelves. An imaginary plenitude of one sort of archive, great men or great women, heightens the desire for the perfect encyclopedia of nonentities, those anonymous complements to one's own bid for humanity. The facade of this hall of fame is always under scaffolding, while some Mrs. Martin, Mrs. Bast, Mrs. Brown scrubs the floors.

Recognition seems to flaunt its contradictions: How can we call up lists of the truly anonymous? Why are we always having to repeat the summons? Yet such ironies do not bring me to deplore the effort, in which I participate. Woolf restimulated the historical recuperation of women, and she revitalized legends of unsung heroism that have been productive for generations of feminists. I invite us, however, to observe the conventions of "looking about the shelves for the books that were not there." I am tempted to conclude with a catalogue of Woolfian perceptions of absences: the discourse of collective biographies of women or people of color often features an autobiographical scene recalling by name the forebears once unknown. One example of the orphaned but now affiliated will have to do: Paule Marshall recalling Harlem in the 1930s:

> No . . . teacher of mine had ever mentioned [Paul Laurence] Dunbar or James Weldon Johnson or Langston Hughes. I didn't know that Zora Neale Hurston existed... Nor . . . Frederick Douglass and Harriet Tubman . . . or . . . Sojourner Truth. What I needed was an equivalent of the Jewish shul, someplace where we could . . . . read works by those like ourselves and learn about our history." [12]

Marshall can name *now* whom she should have venerated *then*; she imagines that Jewish children knew their models all along. Structurally, this is much the same as Woolf's supposition that men's biographical history suffices, women's evanesces and eludes. A projection of wholeness seems to invite a complementary display of lack—a lack nevertheless filled in surprising detail. (Collective biographies of African Americans, beyond anthologized slave narratives, had been published across the decades since the Civil War, and handfuls of all-female multibiographies appeared after 1893, until an eruption of recognition in the 1970s. It would have been possible, however difficult, for the young Marshall to consult, among numerous sources, *Who's Who in Colored America* [Boris, 1927], or *The Negro in Literature and Art* [Brawley, 1930], or a few women's anthologies [Brown, 1926; Daniel, 1931; Davis, 1934].)[13] How do we name the truly missing? More disturbingly, where do these waves of recognition get us, beyond cycles of erosion?

Notes

[1] It would be nice, but not necessary, to know whether the nursery at Hyde Park Gate held copies of Charlotte M. Yonge's *Biographies of Good Women* (1865, third edition 1893) or Matilda Betham-Edwards' *Six Life Studies of Famous Women* (1880), honoring middle-class women such as Dorothy Wordsworth and Elizabeth Carter as models for the young.

[2] Omissions are always telling in lists of significant people. Woolf includes later Victorian campaigners who had not made it into collections (besides *The Cause* and a few others) by the 1920s and 1930s—Josephine Butler, Anne Clough, Emily Davies—but she neglects many favorites of standard Victorian, Edwardian, and Georgian collections, including the more nonliterary or the pious: Harriet Martineau, Hannah More, Joan of Arc. Woolf has no time for most missionaries to the poor, Mary Carpenter, Elizabeth Fry, Sister Dora, etc., though she favored Octavia Hill with

notice. A few other names prominent in Woolf's essays and manifestos that rarely appear in collections of 1830-1940: Lady Winchelsea, Margaret Oliphant, Mary Wollstonecraft. Sophia Jex-Blake is not a figure in the anthologies, and curiously, neither Christina Rossetti nor Aphra Behn (favored by Woolf) crops up frequently (Vita Sackville-West's portrait of Behn was published in a collection in 1930 [see Birrell]). Behn and Wollstonecraft could equally be banned from most collections for their sexual transgressions.

3 Rosemary Hennessy cautions that feminist revisionist history founders when it relies on "dynamics of new-ness" that have repeatedly constructed "'Woman's' contradictory position under capitalism and patriarchy" (102, 104). Historical narratives may remain intact, as a New Woman—and I would add, versions of the Old Woman, embodiment of origin, national tradition, memory—is reincarnated by generations of feminist discourse.

4 Leslie Stephen himself published collections of largely biographical essays, such as *Men, Books, and Mountains.*

5 Duckworth also published Mabel Richmond Brailsford's *Quaker Women* in 1915.

6 I am currently compiling charts of subjects in non-specialized collections, 1850-1870, 1880-1900, 1910-1930, which indicate that Joan of Arc is the most frequent subject or among the two or three most frequent, across the decades.

7 Collections might attach themselves to signs of prestige, as in Esther Singleton's *Famous Women As Described by Famous Writers* (New York, 1907), including Mary Queen of Scots by Algernon Charles Swinburne, Marie de Mancini by Alexandre Dumas, and la Duchesse du Maine by Charles Augustin Sainte-Beuve. In contrast, Fawcett's pieces originally appeared in *The Mother's Companion*; apart from Queen Victoria and Queen Louisa of Prussia, all examples, from Caroline Herschel and Mary Somerville to Jane Austen and Hannah More, are middle-class women of brains and character, with a preponderance of achievement in *belles lettres*. Fawcett was president of the National Union of Women's Suffrage Societies and one-time opponent of Woolf's uncle Fitzjames Stephen (Lee 62). In 1931, Woolf and Ethel Smyth appeared at a meeting of the London and National Society for Women's Service in a hall named in honor of Millicent Fawcett; among the invited guests were Vita, Vanessa, and Cicely Hamilton (Lee 590). Woolf later donated books, "especially biographies," to the Millicent Fawcett Library (Lee 593).

8 I have not confirmed that Woolf attended, or read the pageant when published in 1910, though she was active in the adult suffrage movement for a brief time in that year. She was certainly acquainted with the actress Edy Craig, at whose theater Vita Sackville-West held a reading of her poem *The Land* in 1932 (Lee 623).

9 His models seem Woolfian enough: Queen Victoria, Harriet Martineau, Charlotte Brontë, Mary Russell Mitford, Mary Somerville, Sara Coleridge, Mary Carpenter, Adelaide Anne Procter, George Eliot, and Jane Welsh Carlyle.

10 Margaret E. Tabor published in London in 1929 a collection entitled *Four Margarets*, biographies of Renaissance and Restoration women of the English court suggestive of Woolf's four Marys in *A Room* (only Margaret Roper, the daughter of Thomas More, is well-known). Tabor and Woolf draw on a folk tradition of groups of women who share a holy name, as well as the custom of numbering them, as in the anonymous contemporary collection, *The Six Maries: Devotional Readings* (London, 1930), or many titles similar to those of Birrell or Betham-Edwards.

11 The preface affirms, "ordinary readers, and especially young readers ... read short biographies, or none at all" ; it includes Matilda Betham, "the friend of the Southeys, Coleridge, and Charles and Mary Lamb, and herself the first biographer in our language of celebrated women" (vii-viii). Back in 1804, Mary Matilda Betham compiled *A Biographical Dictionary of the Celebrated Women of Every Age and Country.* As early as 1804, Betham was at least fifty years belated (though ahead of a Victorian

wave), but never mind some family pride; no one had thought to trace a canon of such works.

[12] See Marshall, quoted in Jay, 18-19. Other examples of the autobiographical trope of the missing canon include Kulkin (xv) and Heilbrun (26-27). Alice Walker's famous search for Zora Neale Hurston (93-116) and other models for the black woman writer consciously repeated Virginia Woolf's search in *A Room of One's Own* for signs of Englishwomen's lives (235-40), though Woolf largely elided the question of race. Jo Whitehorse Cochran suggests the receding circles of exclusion: "when the lesbian feminist movement was . . . breaking into the ranks of the feminist movement, there were NO faces, NO words, NO dreams, NO visions I could share in. . . . That place of no voice, no reflection" was shared by "Asian, African, and Chicana/Latina lesbians. . . But it seemed to Native lesbians that we were even further out on the periphery" (64-65).

[13] Jean Fagan Yellin's and Cynthia D. Bond's bibliography, *The Pen Is Ours*, a later addition to the Schomburg Library of Nineteenth-Century Black Women Writers, catches the early multibiographies as sources for a female literary tradition, though early anthologies, such as *The Work of the Afro-American Woman* (Mossell, 1894), canvassed various vocations besides the literary. See Brown, Scruggs, Majors.

Works Cited

Adams, William Henry Davenport. *Celebrated Englishwomen of the Victorian Era*. 2 vols. London: F. V. White, 1881. Rpt. 1884, 1900.

Ballard, George. *Memoirs of Several Ladies of Great Britain*. Ed. Ruth Perry. Detroit: Wayne State UP, 1985.

Betham-Edwards, Matilda. *Six Life Studies of Famous Women*. London: Griffth & Farran, 1880.

Birrell, Francis. *Six Brilliant English Women*. London: Gerald Howe, 1930.

Boris, Joseph J., ed. *Who's Who in Colored America*. New York: Who's Who in Colored America Corp, 1927.

Brailsford, Mabel Richmond. *Quaker Women*. London: Duckworth, 1915.

Brawley, Benjamin G. *The Negro in Literature and Art in the United States*. New York: Duffield, 1918; Dodd, Mead, 1930.

Brown, Hallie Q., ed. *Homespun Heroines and Other Women of Distinction*. Xenia, Ohio: Aldine, 1926. Rpt. New York: Oxford UP, 1988.

Cochran, Jo Whitehorse. "From a Long Line of Contrary Folks." In Bonnie Zimmerman and Toni A. H. McNaron, eds. *The New Lesbian Studies*. New York: Feminist Press, 1996. 61-66.

Code, Joseph Bernard. *Great American Foundresses*. New York: Macmillan, 1929.

Daniel, Sadie Iola. *Woman Builders*. Washington, D.C.: Associated Press, 1931.

Davies, Margaret Llewelyn. *Life as We Have Known It*. Intro. Virginia Woolf. London: Hogarth, 1931.

Davis, Elizabeth. *Lifting as They Climb*. Chicago: National Association of Colored Women, 1933.

Davis, Natalie Zemon. "Gender and Genre: Women as Historical Writers, 1400-1820." In Patricia H. Labalme, ed. *Beyond Their Sex: Learned Women of the European Past*. New York: New York U P, 1980: 153-82.

Emerson, Ralph Waldo. "Uses of Great Men." *Representative Men*. 1850. Rpt. Ed. Pamela Shirmeister. New York: Marsilio, 1995.

Epstein, William H. *Recognizing Biography*. Philadelphia: U of Pennsylvania P, 1987.

Ezell, Margaret J. M. *Writing Women's Literary History*. Baltimore: Johns Hopkins U P, 1993.

Fawcett, Millicent Garrett. *Some Eminent Women of Our Time*. London: Macmillan, 1889.
Garber, Marjorie. *Symptoms of Culture*. New York: Routledge, 1998.
Goldsmith, Margaret L. *Seven Women Against the World*. London: Methuen, 1935.
Green, Barbara. *Spectacular Confessions: Autobiography, Performative Activism, and the Sites of Suffrage, 1905-1938*. New York: St. Martin's, 1997.
Hamilton, Cicely Mary. *A Pageant of Great Women*. [London]: The Suffrage Shop, 1910.
Hennessy, Rosemary. *Materialist Feminism and the Politics of Discourse*. New York: Routledge, 1993.
Heilbrun, Carolyn G. *Writing a Woman's Life*. New York: Ballantine, 1988.
Hoberman, Ruth. *Modernizing Lives: Experiments in English Biography, 1918-1939*. Carbondale: Southern Illinois UP, 1987.
Jay, Gregory S. *American Literature and the Culture Wars*. Ithaca: Cornell U P, 1997.
Johnston, Georgia. "Women's Voice: *Three Guineas* as Autobiography." *Virginia Woolf: Themes and Variations*. Ed. Vara Neverow-Turk and Mark Hussey. NY: Pace UP, 1993. 321-28.
Kulkin, Mary-Ellen. *Her Way: Biographies of Women for Young People*. Chicago: American Library Assoc., 1976.
Lee, Hermione. *Virginia Woolf: A Biography*. New York: Knopf, 1997.
Majors, Monroe Adolphus. *Noted Negro Women, Their Triumphs and Activities*. Chicago: Donohue and Henneberry, 1893.
Marshall, Paule. "The Making of a Writer: From the Poets in the Kitchen." In *Reena and Other Stories*. Old Westbury, N.Y.: Feminist Press, 1983. 1-13.
Mossell, Mrs. N. F. [Gertrude Bustill]. *The Work of Afro-American Woman*. Philadelphia: G. S. Ferguson, 1894. Rpt. New York: Oxford U P, 1988.
Nicolson, Harold. *Some People*. 1927. New York: Atheneum, 1982.
Oldfield, Sybil. *Collective Biography of Women in Britain, 1550-1900: A Select Annotated Bibliography*. London: Mansell, 1999.
Parkes, Bessie Rayner. [Bessie R. Belloc]. *Historic Nuns*. London: Duckworth, 1899.
Ritchie, Anne Thackeray. *A Book of Sibyls*. 1874. London: Smith Elder, 1883.
Sackville-West, Vita. *Joan of Arc*. World-Makers and World- Shakers Series. London: Hogarth, 1937.
Sandbach-Dahlström, Catherine. "'Que scais-je?': Virginia Woolf and the Essay as Feminist Critique." In *Virginia Woolf and the Essay*, ed. Beth Carole Rosenberg and Jeanne Dubino. New York: St. Martin's, 1997. 275-93.
Scruggs, Lawson A. *Women of Distinction: Remarkable Works and Invincible Character*. Raleigh, N.C.: L. A. Scruggs, 1893.
Singleton, Esther, Ed. and Trans. *Famous Women Described by Famous Writers*. New York: Dodd, Mead, 1904.
Six Maries, The : Devotional Readings. London: Skeffington, 1930. 1951.
Stephen, Leslie. *Men, Books, and Mountains*. Intro. S. O. A. Ullmann. Minneapolis: U Minnesota P, 1956.
Stephen, Leslie, and Sidney Lee, eds. *The Dictionary of National Biography*. 66 vols. London: Smith Elder, 1885-1901. Rpt. Oxford: Oxford U P, 1917, 1938.
Strachey, Lytton. *Eminent Victorians*. 1918. Harmondsworth: Penguin, 1986.
Strachey, Ray. *The Cause: A Short History of the Women's Movement in Great Britain*. 1928. Rpt. London: Virago, 1978.
Tabor, Margaret E. *Four Margarets*. London: Sheldon, 1929.
Vicinus, Martha. "Models for Public Life: Biographies of 'Noble Women' for Girls." In *The Girl's Own: Cultural Histories of the Anglo-American Girl, 1830-1915*. Ed. Claudia Nelson and Lynne Valone. Athens: U Georgia P, 1994. 52-70.
Walker, Alice. *In Search of Our Mothers' Gardens*. New York: Harcourt Brace, 1983.

Wheeler, Ethel Rolt. *Famous Blue-Stockings.* London: Methuen; New York: John Lane, 1910.
Woolf, Leonard. *The Journey Not the Arrival Matters.* New York: Harcourt, Brace & World, 1969.
Woolf, Virginia. *A Room of One's Own.* 1929. Foreword by Mary Gordon. New York: Harcourt/Harvest, 1981.
——. *Three Guineas.* New York: Harcourt Brace & World, 1966.
——. "Women and Fiction." 1929. Rpt. in *Granite and Rainbow.* New York: Harcourt/Harvest, 1958. 76-84.
Yonge, Charlotte M. *Biographies of Good Women.* Second series. London: Mozley, 1865.

Pamela L. Caughie
Virginia Woolf in the Age of Mechanical Reproduction[1]

No one need wonder that I start, press my hand to my heart, and turn pale. For what more terrifying revelation can there be than that it is the present moment? (*O* 299). We have arrived at the twentieth century, and my arduous responsibility on this panel is to represent our present era. *That I survive the shock at all is only possible because the past shelters me on one side* [Alison Booth and Sally Green], *the future on the other* [the audience].

Using *Orlando* to segue from the 18th and 19th centuries to the 20th is only too obvious, but I begin by invoking this passage from the novel for a reason other than Orlando's longevity: Orlando enters the twentieth century with the magic of modern technology. The descriptions that follow the passage cited above record a hodge-podge of images, objects, and sounds—a "raging torrent" of sensations—that Orlando experiences while motoring to Marshall & Snelgrove's, where she is "shot smoothly upwards" in the lift: "The very fabric of life now, she thought as she rose, is magic" (*O* 300).

To represent Woolf studies in the twentieth century, I will use the collection of essays I recently edited. *Virginia Woolf in the Age of Mechanical Reproduction* (Garland 2000) explores the ways in which new technologies in the early part of this century produced new sensual experiences (such as those Orlando undergoes while motoring), which in turn led to new concepts of national and personal identity, new understandings of the world around us, new forms of art, and new audiences with new tastes. As Walter Benjamin argues in "The Work of Art in the Age of Mechanical Reproduction," the advent of new technologies like photography, "the first truly revolutionary means of production" (224), means not simply that art can be reproduced more quickly or that new forms of art are at hand; rather, Benjamin argues, mechanical reproduction transforms the very nature and function of art (227), as today's CD-ROMs are changing the very nature of reading, a phenomenon Mark Hussey explores in his closing essay. Human perception, including auscultation (Melba Cuddy-

Scanning the Centuries

Keane's useful coinage for analyzing the reception of sound), is organized differently by new media so that how we see and hear, even what we see and hear, changes. Sensual experience is now understood as historical ("The Work of Art" 222). "Motoring," writes Makiko Minow-Pinkney in this collection, "together with other experiences distinctive to the modern age of technology, affects the human sensory organization itself . . . necessitat[ing] new modes of thought and aesthetic representation adjusted to it" (163).

Any effort to understand Woolf in the context of the twentieth century cannot ignore the relation between modernist representation and new technologies, nor the socio-political consequences of new media. For the 1920s generation was, Bernard Bergonzi remarks, "the first literary generation in England to have to face mass civilization directly" (*Reading the Thirties*; qtd. in Frith 24). From the ashes of the aura destroyed, Benjamin says, by reproductive technologies, mass society emerges like the phoenix. Photography gives rise to picture magazines and postcards; radio and records to mass markets as opposed to particular audiences; letters to the editor allow the newspaper reader to become an author; newsreels and documentaries turn pedestrians into actors. A new relation between artist and audience pertains to the age of mechanical reproduction. "The distinction between [artist] and public," writes Benjamin, becomes merely functional" ("The Work of Art" 232). Art is no longer an object of contemplation absorbing the viewer. Now the pleasures of viewing are connected with the distractions of everyday life. Iris Barry, film critic of the 1920s, compares watching a movie with the "agitation of a day, which includes catching buses, trams, or tubes, manipulating typewriters or telephones or lathes" (31-32). Insofar as technology creates new ways of seeing and hearing, registering "something very profound" (*MD* 18) in the agitations of modern life, it becomes more than a means of mass communication; technology is itself a signifier of modernity.

The rise of mass communication in the late 19th and early 20th centuries at once made possible the formation of a national culture (a possibility both Hitler and the BBC exploited) and undermined the notion of a national identity. "Britain's island insularity offers no protection in the air age," writes Michelle Pridmore-Brown (415), that is, the age of airplanes and air waves. The experience of "voice divorced from sight" that Gillian Beer says was made possible by radio and phonograph (166), the "unconscious optics" (Benjamin's term) introduced by the camera, the new sensory organization produced by motoring, all reveal, in Benjamin's words, "entirely new structural formations of the subject" ("The Work of Art" 236). As Michael Taussig puts it in his fascinating study, *Mimesis and Alterity*, new technologies induced "a tremor in cultural identity . . . in the security of Being itself" (226). Radio, records, and movies were more than a form of national entertainment; mechanical reproduction and the new sensory experiences enabled by it formed the "technological substance of civilized identity-formation" (Taussig 207-208).

Caughie

In "The Work of Art," Benjamin uses Freudian theory to explain by analogy the revolutionary effect the camera has had on our notions of the subject.

> Evidently a different nature opens itself to the camera than opens to the naked eye—if only because an unconsciously penetrated space is substituted for a space consciously explored by man.... Here the camera intervenes with the resources of its lowerings and liftings, its interruptions and isolations, its extensions and accelerations, its enlargements and reductions. The camera introduces us to unconscious optics as does psychoanalysis to unconscious impulses. (236-237)

Even an early novel like *Jacob's Room* (1922), often said to be Woolf's first experimental novel, presents on the narrative level itself the changes in perception and in notions of the subject that the camera came to signify for Benjamin. When we read, "Mrs. Pascoe stood at the gate looking after them; stood at the gate till the trap was round the corner; stood at the gate, looking now to the right, now to the left; then went back to her cottage" (*JR* 55), we might well ask, "What is the optical precedent for this perception?", a question filmmaker Sergei Eisenstein asked of the decidedly low-tech frescoes of Diego Rivera (*Immoral Memories*; qtd. in Karetnikova 162). Such a passage intrudes on the narrative with no obvious function, it seems, other than to slow down the narrative flow. An oddity in a written narrative, the scene would make sense in film where the camera often fades out while lingering on the character perceiving the action. That passage presents the kind of observation Benjamin says is made possible by film. It is not that Woolf was necessarily imitating camera technology; as Cuddy-Keane argues in the Garland collection, it is more a matter of modernist techniques and new technologies mutually shaping one another than of direct influence. New imaginative possibilities identified with new forms of mechanical reproduction were prepared for by new modes of representation in literature and the arts, not just reflected in them.

For example, Woolf not only experiments with new modes of perception in *Jacob's Room*, she calls attention to them, thereby helping to prepare her readers for new media. Describing the "multitudes" of people around St. Paul's, where Jacob is playing tourist, Woolf writes: "They have no houses. The streets belong to them; the shops; the churches; theirs the innumerable desks; the stretched office lights; the vans are theirs, and the railway slung high above the street. If you look closer you will see that three elderly men at a little distance from each other run spiders along the pavement as if the street were their parlour" (66). "If you look closer," she writes, as if the camera were moving in, as if Woolf were explicitly inviting us to look with the "new eye" created by cinematic technology. The narrative perspective—whether distanced or close-up, distracted or attentive—is foregrounded in *Jacob's Room*. And nothing, it seems, escapes the camera's eye. Modernist writers employed mass cultural forms. "The serious artist," writes Simon Frith, "became, by necessity, an observer, a recorder, a camera" (25).

Scanning the Centuries

"In short, the observer is choked with observations" (*JR* 68). In *Jacob's Room*, as in her other novels of the 1920s, Woolf explores the effects of urban mass culture—the omnibus, the movies, motor cars, advertising, the Kodak—on the structure of experience and on new formations of the subject. One passage in particular invokes Georg Simmel's observations on urban life: Woolf writes, "The proximity of the omnibuses gave the outside passengers an opportunity to stare into each other's faces. Yet few took advantage of it" (*JR* 64). In his essay "On Some Motifs in Baudelaire," Benjamin quotes Simmel on the "technological substance" of this perception: "Here is something . . . characteristic of the big city. . . . Before buses, railroads, and streetcars became fully established during the nineteenth century, people were never put in a position of having to stare at one another for minutes or even hours on end without exchanging a word" (191). If *Jacob's Room* was so disconcerting for readers of the time—for example, Arnold Bennett, whose review of the novel was entitled "Is the Novel Decaying?"—it was not, I would suggest, simply because Woolf was experimenting with character and narrative structure in the modernist mode; it was because those narrative experiments captured and reproduced the new sensual experiences of modern urban life, creating a "tremor in cultural identity."

Taussig's important contribution to modernist studies is his argument that recording machines, like the camera and the phonograph, "whose job it is to reproduce likeness" (206), reveal "the intimate relationship between primitivism and the new theories of the senses circulating with the new means of reproduction" (201). Discussing the specifically imperialistic meanings of new technologies, Taussig recounts the exploration of anthropologist George Marsh in 1924 when he traveled into the jungles of Central America looking for "white Indians." Among the many supplies Marsh took on this journey were two Victrolas that proved useful in turning angry natives into curious companions. The "talking machines" provided amusement to those on the expedition, certainly, but that amusement took a specific form: namely, watching the Other's fascination with Western technological prowess, which in turn gave new meaning to the "technological substance" of Western identity. Taussig writes:

> What seems crucial about the fascination with the Other's fascination with the talking machine is the magic of mechanical reproduction itself. . . . To take the talking machine into the jungle is to emphasize and embellish the genuine mystery and accomplishment of mechanical reproduction in an age when technology itself, after the flurry of excitement at a new breakthrough, is seen not as mystique or poetry but as routine. . . . it is to reinstall the mimetic faculty as mystery in the art of mechanical reproduction . . . . (207-208)

Taussig's discussion of Marsh's expedition brings to mind Cedric Gibbons' 1934 film *Tarzan and His Mate* (Woolf was supposedly a fan of Tarzan films) where the men who come to the jungle to reclaim Jane bring with them a Victrola. The machine functions as an instrument by which to lure Jane back to civilization, a signifier of modern life along with perfume and silk stockings; but it also serves as a source of amusement as the men and the audience together watch Tarzan's curious response to this magic. The very enchantment attributed to exotic places and peoples in tourist brochures and road maps of the 1920s is attributed as well to "the mystery of sound reproduction" (Taussig 208).

Taussig's analysis of mechanical reproduction sheds light on passages in Woolf's writing that I have long found troubling if not perverse, from the descriptions of Jacob as "savage" and "barbaric" to the primitivism of *The Waves* and the "hairy man" passage in the last chapter of that novel. It helps to explain in particular that odd opening to Woolf's essay "The Cinema" (1926), written when she was first conceiving *The Waves*: "People say that the savage no longer exists in us, that we are at the fag-end of civilization, that everything has been said already, ... But these philosophers have presumably forgotten the movies. They have never seen the savages of the twentieth-century watching the pictures. . . ." (*CDB* 180). Whether modern savages at the cinema or Marsh's savages in the jungle, technology induces a sense of magic and reveals what Taussig identifies as "Benjamin's enduring theme, the surfacing of 'the primitive' within modernity as a direct result of modernity," especially its "mimetic machinery" (20). The shock and the magic of modern technology is nowhere better captured than in Orlando's entry into the twentieth century with which I began.

Such passages in Woolf, read through Taussig's work, give a new layer of meaning to the term "border crossing," the theme of Garland's series in which *Virginia Woolf in the Age of Mechanical Reproduction* appears. Border crossing refers not just to the crossing of Westerners into other territories, inspired by and transporting new recording devices; not just to the crossing of generic boundaries among the arts by modernists or the crossing of disciplinary boundaries by contemporary cultural critics. Border crossing refers as well to the kind of crossing over signified by what I have termed elsewhere "passing," refiguring that common trope as a modern phenomenon. "The gift of seeing resemblances," Benjamin writes in his essay "On the Mimetic Faculty," "is nothing other than a rudiment of the powerful compulsion in former times to become and behave like something else" (*Reflections*; qtd. in Taussig 33). This compulsion takes many forms in Woolf's day, from tourists dressing in native attire, to hair products promising the Valentino or Josephine Baker look, to D. H. Lawrence searching exotic places for the cosmic harmony that eluded his own techno-culture. Technology has been both an incentive to and a medium for border crossing in this special sense. In her essay on the gramophone in the Garland volume, Bonnie Kime Scott alludes to this aspect of border crossing when she writes, "Victrolas crossed the color line" (98). More than simply acknowledging the democratizing force of this new technology, Scott's wording explicitly invokes the social practice of passing and raises the question of how mechanical reproduction fostered passing in the figurative sense, that desire "to become . . . something else."

The Americanization of popular culture throughout the world (the phenomenon the BBC fought against) "owes an enormous amount to music reproduced by the phonograph," Taussig notes (198), and that musical export was predominantly jazz, "the first British musical culture dependent on recordings" (Frith 58). In his 1925 essay "Jazz at Home," published in Alain Locke's *The New Negro*, J. A. Rogers remarks that jazz "ranks with the movie and the dollar as the foremost exponent of modern Americanism" (216). Scott has noted that T. S. Eliot carried jazz recordings into Woolf's parlor. In her research on British *Vogue* for her essay in the Garland collection, Jane Garrity turned up articles on the New Negro craze, fueled by the primitivism of jazz and propelled across the Atlantic by the "talking machine," the wireless, and later the cinema. Jazz, Rogers says, "bears all the marks of a nerve-strung, strident, *mechanized* civilization" (218; my italics), signifying modernity in the "technological substance" of its identity but also in the way it excited and facilitated the crossing of the color line. "Primitive," "barbaric," "atavistically African," jazz may be "a thing of the jungles," Rogers remarks, but it is "modern man-made jungles." Modern identity, I would argue, was not just mechanized, it was *racialized* by new technologies. It was in part the cultural shifts introduced by mechanical reproduction that necessitated thinking about race as a component of identity formation.

When I was invited to present on this panel, I thought of various schemes for representing Woolf studies in the twentieth century. I might present a linear narrative, from the new critical formalism of the 1940s, 50s, and 60s; to the liberal feminism of the 70s and early 80s; to the poststructuralist criticism of the late 80s and 90s. Or I might represent the twentieth century as Woolf represented her childhood home, as the cohabitation of two clashing generations: in Woolf's case, the late Victorianism of her parents and stepbrothers, and the Georgian sensibilities of herself and her siblings; in ours, the modernists and the postmodernists. If I chose to represent the century by means of this volume of essays—by, if not the clash then the imbrication of technology and modernism—it is because the kind of cultural criticism it models is where I see the exciting potential for the future of Woolf criticism after Y2K.

Notes

[1] A longer version of this essay appears as the introduction to *Virginia Woolf in the Age of Mechanical Reproduction*, edited by Pamela L. Caughie (New York & London: Garland Publishing, Inc., 2000). This conference version is republished here by permission.

[2] Sunny Stalter made this point in her paper at the 1998 Woolf conference, "The Ways of Seeing: The Cinematic Novel in the Age of Mechanical Reproduction." My thanks to the author for permission to cite her paper.

Works Cited

Barry, Iris. *Let's Go to the Movies.* 1926. New York: Arno Press and the New York Times, 1972.
Beer, Gillian. "'Wireless': Popular Physics, Radio and Modernism." *Cultural Babbage: Technology, Time and Invention.* Ed. Francis Spufford and Jenny Uglow. London: Faber and Faber, 1996. 149-166.
Benjamin, Walter. "On Some Motifs in Baudelaire." *Illuminations.* Trans. Harry Zohn. New York: Schocken Books, 1969. 155-200.
———. "The Work of Art in the Age of Mechanical Reproduction." *Illuminations.* 217-251.
Caughie, Pamela L. *Passing and Pedagogy: The Dynamics of Responsibility.* Urbana: University of Illinois Press, 1999.
———, ed. *Virginia Woolf in the Age of Mechanical Reproduction.* New York & London: Garland Publishing, Inc., 2000.
Cuddy-Keane, Melba. "Virginia Woolf, Sound Technologies, and the New Aurality." In Caughie, ed. : 69-96.
Frith, Simon. *Music For Pleasure: Essays in the Sociology of Pop.* New York: Routledge, 1988.
Hussey, Mark. "How Should One Read a Screen?" In Caughie, ed. : 249-265.
Karetnikova, Inga. *Mexico According to Eisenstein.* Albuquerque: U of New Mexico P, 1991.
Minow-Pinkney, Makiko. "Virginia Woolf and the Age of Motor Cars." In Caughie, ed. : 159-182.
Pridmore-Brown, Michele. "1939-40: Of Virginia Woolf, Gramophones, and Fascism." *PMLA* 113.3 (May 1998): 408-421.
Rogers, J. A. "Jazz at Home." 1925. *The New Negro.* Ed. Alain Locke. New York: Antheneum, 1992. 216-224.
Scott, Bonnie Kime. "The Subversive Mechanics of Woolf's Gramophone in *Between the Acts.*" In Caughie, ed. : 97-113.
Taussig, Michael. *Mimesis and Alterity: A Particular History of the Senses.* New York: Routledge, 1993.
Woolf, Virginia. "The Cinema." *The Captain's Death Bed and Other Essays.* New York: HBJ, 1978. 180-186.
———. *Jacob's Room.* 1922. New York: HBJ, 1950.
———. *Mrs. Dalloway.* 1925. New York: HBJ, 1953.
———. *Orlando.* 1928. New York: HBJ, 1956.

Charles Boebel

A Synopsis of *Orlando Ever After: A Dramatic Speculation*

When Virginia Woolf's *Orlando* comes to an end on October 11, 1928, what happens to Orlando? Possibly she dies. She suffers the disintegrating onslaught of the striking clock, which shatters her psyche into thousands of selves; envisions her own burial; visits the ancient oak tree, where she plans to bury the manuscript of her poem; witnesses the ghostly return of the dead queen to the house she no longer owns. Certainly some limit has been reached. But at the end of the novel, Orlando's husband, Marmaduke Bonthrop

Shelmerdine, returns like a god from the sea, and it appears that some passionate reunion is about to take place. Perhaps in some way they are about to become the yolk and white of a single shell; perhaps they are about to be reborn. *Orlando Ever After* assumes rebirth rather than death, and imagines the life of Orlando and to some extent, the life of Shelmerdine, during the last three quarters of the 20th century.

Orlando and Shelmerdine enter the strange airship depicted at the end of the novel and emerge, after an indefinite time, naked on the hills of Cumbria. A transformation has occurred. Orlando has become a man, as he was in the 16th and 17th centuries; and Shel has become a woman. Miraculously, many human beings, petrified in the Great Frost of the early 17th century, now come to life, and dancing, lead Orlando and Shel to the rail station, from which they depart for London. Unfortunately they soon become separated; the play follows the adventures of Orlando, although we learn that Shel, sadly, has had to earn her living as a chanteuse on a trans-Atlantic ocean liner.

It is now the 1930s, and London is no longer the bright, distracted city of Woolf's novel. All is dark and politicized. Orlando returns to his old haunts and briefly discovers a Soho pub where W. H. Auden is holding forth, but he is soon on his way in pursuit of his former love, Sasha, the Russian princess. Having learned that Sasha has joined the retinue of the American poet H. D., Orlando goes in drag to a luncheon at H. D.'s home. There he listens to the poet read from "The Dancer," and observes Sasha perform a modern dance. Unfortunately, he is discovered to be male, when his wig falls into the punch bowl, and he must retire in disgrace—or in his own imagination, hotly pursued by Maenads.

Still in drag, Orlando next finds himself in the midst of the Blitz, and walking down Earls Court Road, he encounters an air raid warden who happens to be T. S. Eliot. After hearing Eliot chant parts of *Four Quartets* and "The Wasteland," and after making appropriate responses based upon his own life experience, Orlando discovers, to his horror, that Eliot is also the Archduke Harry, a would-be lover who has pursued Orlando through the centuries. Again Orlando flees—this time to America.

In the United States, Orlando has no trouble landing an academic job. He has given up poetry, and he has written a book about time and the British novel, but he is completely disgusted at the sexism of his department, and he rushes away from the university club in a frenzy of anger. By this time it is the 1960s, and Orlando comes upon a feminist meeting in which a group of women are discussing *The Feminine Mystique*. He finds that the discussion leader is none other than Shel, who for 30 years has been living as a woman. Together —carried along by Janis Joplin's music—Orlando and Shel escape into the counterculture, and they begin to think seriously about gender. With the help of Hélène Cixous and French feminism, Orlando realizes more strongly than ever that gender is more a state of mind and a social condition than a biological fact. He now learns to identify himself with women—and thus perhaps he again becomes a woman—as characters, including the stiff and pedantic biographer, participate in the ecstasy of a Rave Party. However, Sasha appears once more, and as the play ends, Orlando leaves the party to follow her. His adventures are likely to continue into the 21st century.

    The play is enlivened throughout by music and dance—from renaissance dance music to Wagner to Stockhausen to Hendrix to the Beatles to Joplin to Rave. The play will be greatly strengthened by casting an accomplished dancer as Sasha. The Voice at the Console may be performed by one actor or several. This actor—at the console—may also control the music and lights. Mirrors may be used to show relationships and to enhance the effect of Rave.

CHARACTERS IN ORDER OF APPEARANCE

The Biographer
Orlando
Voice(s)
Dancer(s)

Excerpt from Scene 3

THE BIOGRAPHER

. . . A wail of sirens sprang up on every side as though the earth exhaled pure terror. Ahead sticks of light swept the horizon, crossed each other, like dueling swords, lingered together like dancers, wavered like inquisitive antennae. From far away came the whirring drone of massed aircraft. And in the distance—pom! pom! pom!—like drums beating in solemn ritual, the sound of cannon firing into the sky.

ORLANDO

Rumble of an approaching storm; near at hand, silence, solitude, fear.

THE BIOGRAPHER

He became aware of a tall man walking beside him, step for step, some kind of official, wearing a tin hat and a white arm band.

VOICE AT THE CONSOLE

Eructation of unhealthy souls
Into the faded air, the torpid
Driven on the wind that sweeps the gloomy hills of London . . .
Good evening. My name is Tom.

ORLANDO

Wonderful. Another American, another American poet.
I can think of nothing to say.

VOICE AT THE CONSOLE
Too strange to each other for misunderstanding,
In concord at this intersection time
Of meeting nowhere, no before and after,
We trod the pavement in a dead patrol.

THE BIOGRAPHER
The whir of locust grew louder; beside the square, drums began to beat, muzzle flashes among the trees; a stream of light shot across the sky like a falling star, but angry, red; a faltering rattle amidst the fierce buzz of voracious insects. Three great blasts flung Orlando against the wall—two in Earls Court Square, one, later, and to the west.

ORLANDO
Someone has died.
I think of rising water, brown, swirling, and cold; love, imagination, the light of consciousness are lost; rolled out to sea; tumbled beneath the waves—"a current under the sea picks their bones in whispers."

VOICE AT THE CONSOLE
Time before and time after
In a dim light; neither daylight
Investing form with lucid stillness . . .

ORLANDO
I have lived for hundreds of years; I have learned nothing.

VOICE AT THE CONSOLE
Near the ending of interminable night
At the recurrent end of the unending
After the dark dove with the flickering tongue . . .

ORLANDO
All time is meaningless; all time gathers in the darkness of a single moment.

VOICE AT THE CONSOLE
If all time is eternally present
All time is unredeemable . . .

ORLANDO
And we now—we two—here together amidst death and chaos, in this unredeemable present . . .

VOICE AT THE CONSOLE
At the still point of the turning world, neither flesh nor fleshless;
Neither from nor towards; at the still point there the dance is . . .

ORLANDO
We cannot help being dancers; we dance in place even as we flee across bare hills; even as we ride the spinning ice, the ruined huts, down the strong brown river.

VOICE AT THE CONSOLE
. . .neither arrest nor movement and do not call it fixity . . .

THE BIOGRAPHER
Tom the poet was an American, but not American. He was some kind of prophet—in touch with the underworld.

VOICE AT THE CONSOLE
I, Tieresias, old man with wrinkled dugs
Perceived the scene and foretold the rest.

THE BIOGRAPHER
But not Tieresias.

VOICE AT THE CONSOLE
I caught the look of some dead master
Whom I had known, forgotten, half recalled,
Both one and many . . .

ORLANDO
The eyes of a familiar compound ghost,
Both intimate and unidentifiable.
So I assumed a double part and cried . . .
What! are *you* here?

VOICE AT THE CONSOLE
Orlando! My love! It is you! It is I—

THE BIOGRAPHER
By the flashing light of an ambulance (the Nazi raiders all flown by), Orlando saw Tom's face for the first time—the long mouth turned down in sorrow, tears streaking the dust of each broad cheek.

VOICE AT THE CONSOLE
I am the Archduke Harry. Oh, Orlando, how I have suffered!

ORLANDO

Someone has died.

THE BIOGRAPHER

Orlando ran straight toward the tube station and the conflagration in Earls Court Square. Flames shot above trees and roof lines. He slipped on broken glass, tripped over fire hoses, tangled like nests of serpents. Here was the incandescent terror; here was the demonic pentecost; here was the funeral pyre of innocence.

No one remembers Orlando entering the tube station and descending to the lower level. Years later he wrote in his journal that he had taken the train to Heathrow and flown to New York.

Orlando's chronology must have been faulty, but there can be no doubt that he became an American.

(Fade up and out Jimi Hendrix's "Star Spangled Banner." Blackout during which Orlando changes wigs.)

Scene 4

VOICE AT THE CONSOLE

Some say the world will end in fire,
Some say in ice.
From what I've tasted of desire
I hold with those who favor fire. . . .

THE BIOGRAPHER

Orlando intoned poetry and walked by the window. He had recited the poem a thousand times; the scene before him included neither fire nor ice. He paid scant attention to his students, some of whom nodded and dozed, some of whom seemed to be writing assiduously in their notebooks.

Outside the window, outside a double-thick pane of glass, outside the hermetic seal of an air-conditioned room, Orlando watched palm trees toss in the desert wind like the heads of ecstatic dancers; he watched a lawn sprinkler turn back and forth, making small rainbows of spray against the rich green grass; on the horizon he saw desert hills like the hills of Greece or Turkey, but the foreground of big, brightly colored automobiles sliding smoothly along the palm-lined boulevard had nothing to do with gypsies.

ORLANDO

Time flies from me. I have grown analytical. I observe its passage and note it down. I have attended Oxbridge—as a man, of course. I have walked unimpeded upon the grass; I have studied unescorted in the spacious reading room of a famous library; I have dined with fellows and scholars in the great hall of my college. I have graduated master of arts; I can no longer write poetry.

Instead, I have produced a book on time and the British novel; I have been engaged by an American university.

For a few hundred dollars the university has purchased a holograph copy of "The Oak Tree," written, they believe, by one anonymous. Every day on the way to class I pass the glass case in which it is kept; every day it becomes more remote and more alien.

VOICE AT THE CONSOLE

But if I had to perish twice,
I think I know enough of hate
To say that for destruction ice
Is also great
And would suffice.

THE BIOGRAPHER

Life was good for members of the University Club. And Orlando (his colleagues called him Orlie) was a member in good standing. There's nothing like a British academic to give tone to an English department.

ORLANDO

Three o'clock began with dry martinis, gin and tonic, or scotch on the rocks, depending on your taste. It begins with a discussion of Professor Wank's *Philological Quarterly* article on the authorship of "Epistle to Arabella . . ."

VOICE AT THE CONSOLE

PQ, Wank?
Good job, Wank

ORLANDO

which now, thanks to Wank, can with assurance be attributed to Pope; about the new edition of Swift, which old Cummerbund is proposing; about Cleanth Brooks and Claude Levi-Strauss and Northrop Frye (who will be giving a guest lecture next week); and about T. S. Eliot, who has befriended young Mr Fredericks.

THE BIOGRAPHER.

Poor moist mystical Tom.

ORLANDO

And as the afternoon wears on and ice cubes rattle and ties and tongues are loosened, the conversation devolves upon secretaries and female students.

THE BIOGRAPHER

Orlando writhed; Orlando seethed; Orlando drank his gin and took it.

Scanning the Centuries

VOICE AT THE CONSOLE
Hey, Wank, who's the new chick in your office?
Foxy.
Nice ass.
What do *you* call them, Orlie? Birds?

ORLANDO
My gorge rises; visions riot in my brain. I see once more the hate-filled leers, the condescending sneers of Pope and Swift; the doomed gaiety of Nell; the sad, separate fates of all the world's Sukeys.

THE BIOGRAPHER
Through the double-pane of sealed glass, Orlando watched men and women stagger along the sidewalk, braced against the wind. He feared that he would lose his martinis; olives would become half-masticated, half-digested, vengeful projectiles.

VOICE AT THE CONSOLE
Say, you're not married yet, are you, Orlie?
Nothing like being properly cared for.
Getting *everything* you need right at home.

THE BIOGRAPHER
Orlando lurched to his feet. He hardly knew what he was doing, and as he had always been a trifle clumsy, his martini upset, casting a yellow stain across the white table cloth.

ORLANDO
Drunken sods!

THE BIOGRAPHER
Orlando strode from the refrigerated room and into the superheated air of a desert afternoon. The wind struck him. He breathed deeply until his lungs were seared, revitalized.

VOICE AT THE CONSOLE
Godamit!
What's his problem?
I guess our friend Orlie is a confirmed bachelor.
(The set goes to black. Fade up The Beatles' "She's Got a Ticket to Ride.")

Boebel

Scene 5
THE BIOGRAPHER
That evening Orlando drove toward the city. He kept the air conditioning off, the windows down, and the radio up.

His anger had not cooled; he took personally his colleagues' boorish contempt. We are more than we know—so much more that he despaired of planting even a seed of awareness in their impervious brains. He thought of Sylvia Plath and her poem "Mirror." How superficial his "Oak Tree" seemed in comparison.

VOICE AT THE CONSOLE
Now I am a lake. A woman bends over me,
Searching my reaches for what she really is.

ORLANDO
Not the rearview mirror in which, by craning my neck, I can see a fragment of my face. The real mirror is the windscreen opening upon a lake that reflects the world in pieces.

It seems for a moment to be the Old Kent Road, but no, it is the freeway. Three lanes of tail lights make shifting arcs of fire; headlights leap at me like shoals of phosphorescent fish. The skyline stands unmoved above its wavering reflections, like illuminated icebergs. Pieces of history, of my mind, are on the move. I am struggling with my heart.

THE BIOGRAPHER
With a part of himself, he longed to find comfort on the Boulevard—the Strip—where he would cruise slowly as he had cruised the wharfs in the days of the dead queen and Soho in the 18th century. He would search for Sukey or Nell or young Giles, leaning casually against a lamp post, smoking a cigarette. He was no better than his ignorant colleagues. No, he was much worse. After almost four hundred years, he had not conquered desire. He longed for Shel though he despaired of finding her. He could not stop thinking of Sasha, but after the fiasco in Lowdnes Square, how could he face her. It would be better if hell opened beneath him and extinguished his miserable life forever.

VOICE AT THE CONSOLE
Beauty is a simple passion,
but, oh my friends, in the end
you will dance the fire dance in iron shoes.

THE BIOGRAPHER
He would stop for a drink in the lounge of the Desert Inn. Any bar would do for maintaining the habit of numbed forgetfulness he had long cultivated in America.

Scanning the Centuries

On the way to the bar, Orlando passed a poster–some kind of event: "Understanding the Feminine Mystique." A local women's organization was holding a meeting, which, according to his watch, was already in progress.
As he had done so often in the past, Orlando sought comfort in the company of women.

ORLANDO
One of those boring, beige sterile meeting rooms. Absolutely full. Rows of women, with a sprinkling of men, standing at the back and along the outer aisles. I immediately join the standers. Nothing ceremonial here. No music. No poetry. Rapt attention.
(From this point until the end of the play, the figure at the console (or if there is more than one figure, the Voice representing Shel) is more illuminated; and Orlando is more directed toward her than toward The Biographer.)

THE BIOGRAPHER
A handsome woman stood at the front of the room reading from a book. Orlando could not see her well, but even from a distance, he recognized strength of character. Long fair hair, hanging straight down, half glasses perched on the end of an aquiline nose.

VOICE AT THE CONSOLE
"Could there be a part of themselves they have buried as deeply as Victorian women buried sex? If there is, a woman might not know what it was, any more than the Victorian woman might know she had sexual needs."

ORLANDO
Victorian women had buried sex? It's news to me.

THE BIOGRAPHER
Nevertheless, Orlando felt an interchange of positive energy—call it good vibrations—between himself and this crowd. He stayed and he listened.

THE VOICE AT THE CONSOLE
"The image of woman that emerges is young and frivolous, almost childlike; fluffy and feminine; passive; gaily content in a world of bedroom and kitchen, sex, babies, and home. The only passion, the only pursuit, the only goal a woman is permitted is the pursuit of a man."

ORLANDO
The very image of my loathsome colleagues.
As if our souls did not float freely in the river of time. As we had no knowledge of the eternal sea rising through the white arch of a thousand deaths; of wild geese flashing through the bright empyrean of a thousand dawns.

THE BIOGRAPHER

The presentation slid into discussion—passionate, animated, disjointed—but unified, in all instances, by recognition. Women were on their feet, telling their stories with sarcasm and pathos, affirming, elaborating, sometimes arguing, more often applauding.

Orlando listened and said nothing. But as the crowd drifted from the room, he remained behind, drawn to the speaker by an intuition of sympathy and shared experience. Four or five women stood in a circle, chatting.

VOICE AT THE CONSOLE

I was married once, long ago and under strange circumstances. I have played many parts—more than I can remember.

THE BIOGRAPHER

She recited a list of jobs, slowly at first, then faster, building momentum. Like an echo, Orlando repeated her words.

ORLANDO

Waitress, secretary, receptionist, clerk.

VOICE AT THE CONSOLE

Teacher, technician, hygienist, nurse.

ORLANDO

Telephone operator.

VOICE AT THE CONSOLE

Riveter.

ORLANDO

Personal assistant, lady's companion, chambermaid, governess.

VOICE AT THE CONSOLE

Ballerina, actress.

ORLANDO

Skater (Oh, Sasha!).

VOICE AT THE CONSOLE

Exotic dancer, gentleman's escort, Playboy Bunny, chanteuse.

ORLANDO

Sea captain, horseman—My god, Shel! It's you!

Scanning the Centuries

VOICE AT THE CONSOLE
Orlando?

ORLANDO
My love!

VOICE AT THE CONSOLE
Dear heart!

THE BIOGRAPHER
Shel's fans were not happy to see her disappear so quickly on the arm of a man. They could understand a little, however, for they noticed that his hair clustered darkly around his marble forehead; his pleading eyes were large and brimming and the color of drenched violets; his lips were short and full; his teeth were of an exquisite and almond whiteness.

Nevertheless, the women said to each other, this was, in spite of appearances, a man. And furthermore, an older woman said to a younger, ideology cannot comprehend love.

(The set goes to black. Fade up Janis Joplin's "Me and Bobby McGee." The music continues for a minute or two, then fades before the next speech. This cultural transition becomes a loosening up exercise for the actors, who may dance and may invite the audience to dance.)

Scene 6
THE BIOGRAPHER
At this point the biographer's art becomes immensely difficult. Anything significant that happened to Shel and Orlando seemed to have happened inside. And even their physical presence —we may as well call them apparitions— becomes difficult to locate.

No matter how one tries, it is almost impossible to follow another vehicle through six lanes of bumper-to-bumper traffic.

A few hours—or possibly years—later, they turned up on a different freeway, over a thousand miles away, headed in a different direction. They were driving a yellow 1959 Volkswagen micro-bus, traveling east.

ORLANDO
I never felt a shred of guilt for abandoning the university. Within a month they had hired another Brit from Oxbridge, a fellow named Nicholas Greene, who had written a book on the psycho-sexual Marxist Christianity of W. H. Auden. I will never again wear a striped neck tie, a button-down collar, a three-piece suit. I may never again cut my hair. Fortunately I don't really have to shave.

VOICE AT THE CONSOLE
I did feel a little guilty for giving up the speakers circuit. But what the hell, I felt guilty for joining the circuit in the first place.

Boebel

Ideology, ideology, ideology—working inside like some invisible knitting machine. A curse upon it!

ORLANDO

A joint administered at the proper time, can lay that curse. Gently.

VOICE AT THE CONSOLE

But a joint cannot answer the great questions of life.

ORLANDO

Admittedly.

THE BIOGRAPHER

Evidence shows that Orlando and Shel shared many a joint, that they lived in a commune, that they rented a shack on the outskirts of Milwaukee.

VOICE AT THE CONSOLE

We also lived for three months in our van under a bridge in Cleveland.

THE BIOGRAPHER

I didn't know that!

ORLANDO

We did, most assuredly.
I enjoyed that commune. Such unstriving souls. Meditation without limit, without schedules, classes, committees.

VOICE AT THE CONSOLE

You meditated because they took you for a man. We women traipsed about in our tie-dyed dresses and did the cooking.
Which reminds me. In 1934, why did you abandon me to the trans-Atlantic skin trade?

THE BIOGRAPHER

Their marriage was not always smooth, but it was based upon mutual understanding and unique experience.

VOICE AT THE CONSOLE

None of our friends is as old as I—one hundred fifty years if a day, I reckon.
(Orlando speaks confidentially, to the audience.)

ORLANDO

Four hundred years exactly. Even Shel doesn't know. Didn't want him to think he'd been picked off by an older woman.

(Orlando removes the male wig and puts on the female. He turns to Shel. They examine each other as if looking in a mirror. They embrace.)

THE BIOGRAPHER

Now I am confused. Who is the woman? Who is the man? I am a biographer. I try to present a straight story. I take some pride in being a normal human being, regularly employed.

ORLANDO

My dear Biographer, have I ever said a word to you until now? Did you know I knew you were there?
I have always known; I look over your shoulder as you write.
Listen to me.

VOICE AT THE CONSOLE

Listen to us.

ORLANDO

You must listen to us. Where we are going you cannot follow.

VOICE AT THE CONSOLE

You must wait for our report.

ORLANDO

Do not think, my friend, that we exist in sequence, we first and then you, making your record, at some later date.

VOICE AT THE CONSOLE

At the still point of the turning world, there the dance is.
(Admonishing the Biographer.)
And do not call it fixity.

ORLANDO

Even if we are dancing in ecstasy, like willows whose yellow hair tosses free in the troubled air; like palms wildly tossing their savage head dresses; like the rooted oak tree, which drinks deeply of the dancing place, stamping its earth firmly, formally bowing its saraband.

THE BIOGRAPHER

You mean like "the great-rooted blossomer."

ORLANDO

Even so.

Boebel

The dancing place is on the move, like an ice flow whirling in strong brown current.
(Fade up music for a Rave Party, which continues as background until the end. The lights of a Rave Party illuminate the stage; a dancer or dancers appear, carrying lights.)

VOICE AT THE CONSOLE
The room is turning. The pounding bass, the flashing strobes, the black-lighted walls, the long floating hair of the dancers—psychedelic apparitions—turning, turning in the turning light. Ecstasy, Ecstasy.

THE BIOGRAPHER
All of the dancers seem to be women.

ORLANDO
All of the dancers are women. All of us are women.
We dance our lost selves, our mutilated lives, into existence once more. We dance out of the dark, despised continent of ourselves. We dance the dark river of Lilith, Hecate, and Medusa.
Our river is not lost at sea. Our river is a circling sea, like circling blood, circling a central fire, the rhododendron, the burning rose—
(The Biographer breaks in pedantically.)

THE BIOGRAPHER
But there is a frozen lake at the center of hell. According to Dante.
(The Biographer is ignored.)

VOICE AT THE CONSOLE
O strong
ember
burns in ice,
snow folds over ember;
fire flashes through clear ice.

ORLANDO
And from the marriage of fire and ice, from the dark womb at the center of the world, the body is born.

VOICE AT THE CONSOLE
From the marriage of fire and ice, from the dark womb at the center of the world, the soul is born.

ORLANDO

Whether we dance upon ice floes being swept out to sea; whether we dance the dance of death—

VOICE AT THE CONSOLE

Whether we dance upon the dark, circling river of birth, dancing as midwives and mothers—
(The Biographer also begins to understand and is swept away.)

THE BIOGRAPHER

O body swayed to music, O brightening glance—
Oh–Oh–Ecstasy!

ORLANDO

We have reached the point of balance; we have reached the point of reconciliation, where time pauses, where all lives, all sexes, gather in semblance of eternity.

THE BIOGRAPHER

How can we tell the dancer from the dance?

VOICE AT THE CONSOLE

All have become women out of need and in the fullness of desire. Vacancy will be found and comprehended. The voiceless will speak—yes, will sing to heaven and earth—not only in the dark—and will be understood.

ORLANDO

Now, now . . . always for now . . .
*(The Biographer struggles to regain control;
other actors are dancing; other dancers may also appear;
the audience is also invited to dance. Sasha appears, also dancing.)*

THE BIOGRAPHER

Looking away from Shel and the infinitely receding reflections of myriad dancers, for only an instant, Orlando saw by the door and the mystically lighted wall, the most beautiful, the most exquisite—and now she flashed those eyes, as if drawn from the bottom of the sea—

ORLANDO

Oh, Sasha!

THE BIOGRAPHER

And Orlando strode swiftly from the room.
(Before blackout, the music continues for a time, while actors and audience continue to dance. The Biographer also joins the dance.)

Remote Inscriptions

Gyllian Phillips
"She was no scholar": Placing Mrs. Browning

In her essay "Aurora Leigh," Virginia Woolf describes the limitations placed on Elizabeth Barrett Browning as a Victorian woman and writer by suggesting that the poet had little choice but to live much of her narrow life through books. Woolf insists however, that Browning was by inclination a woman of action and of the world. She was not a scholar, and her rather forced scholarship proved detrimental to her poetry. Both Woolf's mock biography *Flush* and her essay examine Browning's ambivalent relationship with forms of literary expression and literary history. The difficulties of Browning's historical circumstances lead, in Woolf's estimation, to substantial flaws in her poetry. Woolf's essay, and especially *Flush*, pick up on some of these flaws, like the tendency to magnify insignificant events, and use them implicitly to question the value of traditional scholarship as seen in the biography and in the essay. Of particular interest to me is the intersection between the serious essay and the mock biography and the way in which Woolf uses scholarly forms to re-read Browning's work and life and uses Browning's life to rework scholarly forms.[1] Ultimately, the supposedly unitary subject of biography and of literary history undergoes substantial revision in Woolf's whimsical portrait.

In her essay "Aurora Leigh," Woolf makes the distinction between reading as a second best alternative to real life and real life as a potentially dangerous intrusion on writing. Woolf reads Browning in her historical context. She attempts to identify and evaluate the ambivalent relationship between books and life and more broadly between traditional literary forms and contemporary projects. In the essay, Woolf argues that Browning was a woman who focused her energy and attention on immediate experience; she preferred the study of her world and the people who inhabited it, to the study of texts: "she was no scholar" says Woolf (*CR*2 187). Woolf's reading of Aurora Leigh's education in the poem seems implicitly to support this idea about Browning. Woolf quotes Aurora Leigh's account in Browning's poem of her "real" education in the attic of her aunt's house: "'I had found the secret of the garret room/ Piled high with cases in my father's name,/ Piled high, packed large, where creeping in and out . . . like some small nimble mouse between the ribs of a mastodon' she read and read." (*CR*2 185). Woolf's selection of this passage is significant for its focus on the substitution of reading for living, but also for the way in which it marks books, or traditional scholarship, through imagery. On the one hand, the secret books in the attic open the world of literature to Aurora Leigh, one that her aunt attempts to close off; on the other hand, Aurora's exploration of books can be seen as a furtive and diminishing encounter with the bones of an extinct tradition. She creeps in and out of the remnants of the name of the Father. In a sense, her education is an education in a forbidden patriarchal tradition. The books marked with the name of the father are signs of the secondhand masculine literary tradition to which (Woolf seems to suggest) Browning was also relegated. She was in fact a woman who needed the stimulations of life and people to produce ideas and Woolf notes how Browning laments being cloistered with texts.

Woolf applauds Browning's theory, as outlined in Book V of *Aurora Leigh*, that contemporary literature should deal directly with contemporary life. Browning argues that the epic can be used in this contemporary context and that it should not be concerned with ancient history or myth. And of course the poem is itself an example of this combination of epic form and contemporary conditions. Woolf praises Browning for creating a vivid embodiment of the general sense of the times: "The aunt, the antimacassars, and the country house from which Aurora escapes are real enough to fetch high prices in the Tottenham Court Road at this moment" (*CR*2 191). It seems that the poem captures, in a general way, something of the real life that Browning inhabits. But Woolf also condemns the poem for its choice of an ancient mold to contain this modern world. The scholarly container is inadequate, Woolf seems to imply, to the contemporary context. The blank verse makes the smallest event appear ridiculously elevated and makes impossible the range of shading and character available to prose fiction. Woolf says "Romney . . . rants and reels like any of those Elizabethan heroes whom Browning had warned so imperiously out of her modern living room" (*CR*2 190). The form is in an uncomfortable logical juxtaposition with the content of the poem. The bookishness of blank verse and epic isolate and magnify (to a tedious degree) the life that the poem is attempting to shape and represent.

The imbalance and magnification of life that Browning's choice of traditional formal structures seems to introduce are echoed, Woolf implies, in Browning's personal history. Her confinement and isolation cause her to magnify apparently insignificant elements of her life. However, this flaw in her life and writing pointed out in the straight-up literary essay crosses over with the mock biography to form the creative centre of the latter. In so doing, I argue, Woolf suggests an uncomfortable inadequacy of the traditional forms of canonical reevaluation (like the essay or the conventional Victorian biography) to the subject of a literary life. In describing Browning's problematic relationship to life, Woolf says, "it cannot be doubted that the long years of seclusion had done her irreparable damage as an artist. She had lived shut off, guessing at what was outside, and inevitably magnifying what was within. The loss of Flush, the spaniel, affected her as the loss of a child might have affected another woman" (*CR2* 187). Browning's isolation and the resulting attachment of symbolic importance to the minor characters and incidents of life, serious problems for the poet, provide Woolf with an unconventional focus on Flush the dog for her own playful reevaluation of the literary biography. That is, Browning's response to the constrictions of Victorian culture gives Woolf a starting place to shift the emphasis of traditional literary scholarship. By trying to get more people to read Browning, Woolf has already started down this road, and by pushing the subject of literary biography further to centre not on the obscure woman poet but on that poet's dog, Woolf exaggerates the limitations of traditional forms. Woolf flouts the scholarly conventions by replacing a central, "important" unified subject with a marginal (and as we shall see) multiple subject. To complicate matters further, the biography mimics Browning's own distorted sense of importance—both Woolf and Browning place the dog at the centre of Browning's life narrative.

This displacement of the traditional subject and order of literary biography opens the debate also to the formal structures of biography. I hope to suggest a parallel between Woolf's narrative strategy and her play with the textual conventions of scholarship, particularly endnotes. In conventional biographical narrative, Flush the dog would be a footnote in Browning's life, a favorite pet but hardly comparable to family, publishing record, and the other usual concerns for the biographer. But in Woolf's reading of literary history, there seems to be an analogy between Flush's place and Browning's own place in that narrative. Woolf suggests that Browning was herself only a footnote to literary history: "the only place in the mansion of literature that is assigned her is downstairs in the servants' quarters, where, in company with Mrs. Hemans, Eliza Cook, Jean Igelow, Alexander Smith, Edwin Arnold, and Robert Montgomery she bangs the crockery about and eats vast handfuls of peas on the point of her knife" (*CR2* 183). In my view, this metaphor resembles the idea of the footnote as tangential—related but unimportant to the main part of the text. But the metaphor from the essay is explored in the actual structure of the biography *Flush*. That is, the life of the servant (Wilson), marginal to the literary biography, is both expanded and elided by its position in the endnotes of the book. Her marginal status is identified and represented by her relegation to the notes, but at the same time her status is critiqued by the inclusion of a biography in the margins of a biography (of an already doubly marginal subject). The sketch of Wilson's life points explicitly to a gap in conventional biography, the elitism contained in the fact that "the life of Lily Wilson is extremely obscure" (*Flush* 155). And, as Debra Cumberland points out in "'A Voice Answering a Voice,'" this provocative note opens the possibility for a dialogue with later texts. In effect textual marginalia, like endnotes (and in *Orlando*, index), serve a double function: they establish the generic credentials of the text as embodying a scholarly form, but with the element of "mock" factored in, they also disrupt the assumptions of unified, verifiable certainty that supposedly attach themselves to scholarly genres.

The textual apparatus of notes and index conventionally represent the 'scaffolding' that supports and authorizes the building of personality. In *A Room of One's Own*, the subject headings (which read rather like indexes) quoted in Woolf's narrative of her exploration of women's history (*AROO* 29, 44) are figures for the patriarchal values supporting traditional scholarship. Textual apparatus represents the artificial and limiting nature of scholarship, on the one hand, and its assumption of transparent authority on the other. I think that the notes in *Flush* are, to some extent, an antidote to those subject headings in *A Room*. *Orlando* must be mentioned here as well. Its index also serves a dual purpose: it identifies and defines the novel as "literary biography" and it undermines its own authority by playing with the conventions of indexes. References to people ("Louise [the house maid], 188), places ("Abbey, Westminster, 34"), and events ("Orlando: his loves, 17") all frustrate the conventional research tool of the index (*O* 206-207).

I hope it is clear by now that the relationship of margin to centre in the subject(s) of biography is rather in flux between Woolf's essay and *Flush*. That flux or excessive play is represented by the textual apparatus that marks the biography as scholarship and yet also criticizes its function there. The notes to the text themselves emphasize the construction of history and subject. Mock biography telescopes literary history by taking a marginal poet and then displacing her with a dog and by setting the servant's biography hovering in the wings. This strategy also points to the instability of truth and authority by centering on amusing, apparently random, and trivial bits of information. The narrative proper is interrupted not by documents and asides augmenting the main events and important people of the text but instead fuller explanations of the suicide attempt of Carlyle's dog and the pervasive nature of the flea in nineteenth-century Italy.

The end of the narrative comes with the death of its subject, but even that is interrupted and undermined by the note. In reference to "he was now dead," the note declares that only the event of Flush's death is known "but the date and manner of his death are unknown" (*Flush* 162). Yet in the body of the text, the death is described specifically, as a room, once full, now empty: "He had been alive; he was now dead. That was all. The drawing-room table, strangely enough, stood perfectly still" (150). The note belies the rather poetic representation of the death of Flush, by pointing to an absence of verifiable "fact." Yet it also helps to augment the evocation of absence in the death of the subject. But is not the subject of biography necessarily characterized, in part, by absence?

In both *Flush* and *Orlando* the construction of the biographical subject, along with text, is multiple and shifting. Both Sheila Kineke and Pamela Caughie (in "The Woman Artist in Virginia Woolf's Writings") have pointed out that Orlando is a divided, multiple, and performative subject, and so too, I argue, is Flush. While Orlando's multiplicity comes from that novel's play with gender and the nature of the writer, Flush's comes from his place in the narrative as a centralized footnote to Elizabeth Barrett Browning's life. Clearly the parallels between Browning and her dog are more than their historical coincidence or even than their lives in the margins of history. They are doubles of one another figuratively as well. The biographer describes each as a mirror image of the other as they meet face to face for the first time: "Broken asunder, yet made in the same mould, could it be that each had completed what was dormant in the other? She might have been—all that; and he—But no. Between them lay the widest gulf that can separate one being from another. She spoke. He was dumb" (*Flush* 27). The subject of this biography is twofold; Browning and her dog are both central characters in the narrative. But the subject is also double; she and Flush complete each other. Significantly, the element of character that keeps them apart, language, is also absent from the crux of their completion. Whatever might bring them together is replaced with inarticulate dashes in the text. That silence may in fact be a more profound connection than separation, as Browning muses after drawing a picture of Flush made to look like herself. Again their merged and distinct subject status is defined in opposition to language: "the fact was that they could not communicate with words.... Yet did it not lead also to a peculiar intimacy?... After all, she may have thought, do words say everything? Can words say anything? Do not words destroy the symbol that lies beyond the reach of words?" (*Flush* 38). Language, silence and symbol appear to be at the root of subjectivity as another curiously Lacanian moment of doubling demonstrates: "she would make him stand with her in front of the looking-glass and ask him why he barked and trembled. Was not the little brown dog opposite himself? But what is 'oneself'? Is it the thing people see? Or is it the thing one is?" (46). This doubling and questioning of the status of the subject suggests that the intersection between life and art or experience and representation is always marked by a silence somewhere. As well, this division and combination of opposing or at any rate differing subjectivities further unpacks the aims of the traditional biographer or literary historian. The portrait of a self is dependent solely on the conventions of language and image, the conventions of the symbolic. The search for an essence of self is doomed, because such a self is silent, as the intersection between Flush and Browning shows.

Biography is ostensibly the representation of a life in language, but both "Aurora Leigh" and *Flush* self-consciously demonstrate that the molds for representation, for identities, are made from without and help to determine their subjects. In order to undermine the unconscious reification of social structures and notions of unified identity, Woolf engages in a play and a disruption of the certainties of conventional biography—and through that she seems to propose a shifting and contingent model of identity.

Notes

[1] I am indebted to the growing body of critical work on *Flush* for the foundation of my ideas. Pamela Caughie's article *"Flush* and the Literary Canon: oh where oh where has that little dog gone?" has continued to be a valuable resource for me. As well, I have gained inspiration and insight from a number of other contributions to Woolf scholarship to be found in past proceedings from this conference: Ruth Vanita "'Love Unspeakable:' The Uses of Allusion in Flush" and David Eberly "Housebroken: The Domesticated Relations of *Flush.*" Also useful is Thomas Lewis's article "Combining 'the advantages of fact and fiction:' Virginia Woolf's Biographies of Vita Sackville-West, Flush and Roger Fry."

Works Cited

Caughie, Pamela. "'I must not settle into a figure': The Woman Artist in Virginia Woolf's Writings." *Writing the Woman Artist: Essays on Poetics, Politics, and Portraiture.* Ed. Suzanne Jones. Philadelphia: U of Pennsylvania P, 1991.

———. *"Flush* and the Literary Canon: oh where oh where has that little dog gone?" *Tulsa Studies in Women's Literature* 10.1 (1991): 47-66.

Cumberland, Debra. "'A Voice Answering a Voice': Elizabeth Barrett Browning, Virginia Woolf, and Margaret Forster's Literary Friendship." *Virginia Woolf: Text and Contexts: Selected Papers from the Fifth Annual Conference on Virginia Woolf.* Ed. Beth Rigel Daugherty and Eileen Barrett. New York: Pace UP, 1996.

David Eberly "Housebroken: The Domesticated Relations of *Flush.*" *Virginia Woolf: Text and Contexts: Selected Papers from the Fifth Annual Conference on Virginia Woolf.* Ed. Beth Rigel Daugherty and Eileen Barrett. New York: Pace UP, 1996.

Kineke, Sheila. "Subject to Change: The Problematics of Authority in Feminist Modernist Biography." *Rereading Modernism: New Directions in Feminist Criticism.* Ed. Lisa Rado. New York: Garland, 1994. 253-271.

Lewis, Thomas. "Combining 'the advantages of fact and fiction:' Virginia Woolf's Biographies of Vita Sackville-West, Flush and Roger Fry." *Virginia Woolf: Centennial Essays.* Eds. Elaine Ginseberg, Laura Moss Gottlieb and Joanne Trautman. Troy, N.Y.: Whitston, 1983. 295-324.

Vanita, Ruth. "'Love Unspeakable:' The Uses of Allusion in Flush." *Virginia Woolf: Themes and Variations: Selected Papers from the Second Annual Conference on Virginia Woolf.* Eds. Vara Neverow-Turk and Mark Hussey. New York: Pace UP, 1993.

Woolf, Virginia. "Aurora Leigh." *The Second Common Reader.* New York: Harcourt, Brace and Co., 1932.

———. *A Room of One's Own.* 1929. New York: Harcourt, 1989.

———. *Flush: A Biography.* 1933. London: Hogarth Press, 1963.

———. *Orlando: A Biography.* 1928. New York: Harcourt, 1956.

Tracey Sherard
"Parcival in the forest of gender"[1]: Wagner, Homosexuality, and *The Waves*

In *The Waves,* Woolf's characterization of Percival draws on the discourses of Christianity, nation, and gender consolidated by the nineteenth century revival of Arthurian lore. A "flat" character whose function is his absence, or psychological opacity, his alignment with the traditional male quest, Christianity, and imperialism centers him as the simulacrum of cultural myths the others feel responsible to fulfill,[2] each through their own gendered script, or narrative. The signification of male homosexuality, in particular, is made possible by the correspondences between Neville's descriptions of the specificity of his desire and the character of Amfortas, and his wound, in Wagner's *Parsifal.* Woolf was familiar with the opera, and through her use of the leitmotif she signifies the "heteroideology"[3] to which each character is subject.

The "despotism" (Peter 63) Leonard Woolf sensed in Wagner's art (*Beginning Again* 50) seems to have resulted in a tendency to discount *Parsifal* "as the *source* for the thematic and even structural devices" (Jacobs 236) in the novel. Nevertheless, while she was no doubt influenced by Leonard's "strong opinion" (Jacobs 235), and was not impressed after reading the libretto of the opera, after seeing it a second time, Woolf admits to pondering how it achieved its effects (Jacobs 234)—which perhaps suggests her interest in the opera's "overwhelming unity" was technical.[4]

In *The Waves*, Woolf draws not only thematically, but structurally on Wagner's *Parsifal*. John DiGaetani points out convincing thematic parallels between Parsifal's and Percival's "resurrections," and their continued influence on other characters (123).[5] However, his positive treatment overlooks the "despotic" effect many, including Woolf herself, perceived in Wagner's art.[6] For the similarities between the opera and the novel are structural as well, and complicate any straightforward relation. Woolf utilizes the leitmotif in order to signify the characters' ongoing struggle with the oppressive discourses of gender by which they are interpellated—discourses for which the character of Percival serves as a sort of "spool."

Though Peter Jacobs does not see Woolf's use of leitmotivs as having any "conscious Wagnerian origin," (236), there is a strong affinity between the way the two use the device. Wagner used various leitmotifs not only to carry the thematic material of the opera, but also to indicate character and "relations between people, events and things" (Peter 63). Harvena Richter asserts that in *The Waves* verbal refrains build up "a fund of emotion around the remembered event," noting that they "recur with fairly constant phrasing whenever the memory of a particular character's emotion is to be recalled." She contrasts these phrase refrains with "symbolic images," either a "phrase or a single noun or verb," which "undergo . . . a series of constant transformations, shifting either in the mind of the character or moving from the mind of one character to another with a change in meaning" (166). Richter terms this dynamic a *"matrix of memory,* an extremely complicated nesting of schema which, lifted to consciousness, can revive forgotten complexities of feeling" (167). The ultimate result is that "we become . . . the repository of collective memory, looking back over the past with its lived connections" (Richter 169). In *The Waves,* the collective memory of the discourses and symbols of Christianity and nationhood that constitute Percival plays a large role in the characters' reactions to him, as well as in the verbal phrases and imagery that make up their various leitmotifs.

For example, Louis's desire for the authority Percival embodies manifests itself in his attraction towards Christianity; he admires the "orderly, processional, into chapel"; "I become a figure in the procession, a spoke in the huge wheel that turning, at last erects me, here and now" (34). Wagner's stage directions for the first Grail ceremony display similar language and reification of the rituals of authority: "Through the opposite door *Amfortas* is brought in on his litter by *Esquires* and serving brethren; before him march boys who bear a shrine draped in purple-red cloth. This procession wends to the centre of the background" (Wagner 17).

Despite the love of order he shares with Louis, however, Neville instinctively recoils from a religion which deems his desire a perversion. While Louis rejoices in Dr. Crane's "authority" (34), Neville thinks: "The brute menaces my liberty . . . his words fall cold on my head like paving-stones, while the gilt cross heaves on his waistcoat" (35). Neville's protest is characteristic of his position throughout the novel. When he learns Latin, the language of the church, he notes that tenses of words "mean differently. There is an order in this world; there are distinctions, there are differences . . . upon whose verge I step" (21). This difference, no doubt, refers to gender, which Neville recognizes as inherent in language—as does Louis when he says: "I know my cases and my genders; I could know everything in the world if I wished" (21). Because such mastery "presupposes a causal relation among sex, gender, and desire" (Butler 22), an epistemological relation from which same sex desire is excluded, Neville feels uneasy about its entrenchment in language and narratives inextricable from Christian discourses of heterosexuality: "One pellet was a man, one was a woman. We are all pellets. We are all phrases" in Bernard's story" (70).

The reign of this "heteroideology" permeates the novel through its many allusions to the Garden of Eden. Louise Poresky astutely points out that "[t]he Eden story connects Elvedon to Neville's early and recurring vision of 'death among the apple trees'" (24); but the relationship between Neville's vision and his homosexuality has so far gone unnoticed.[7] Poresky's interpretation of the apple tree as the tree of knowledge, however, provides an opportunity to contextualize Neville's struggle with linguistic and cultural narratives of gender that serve to exclude him, narratives which intersect distinctly with imagery in Wagner's *Parsifal.*[8]

Neville condenses his account of hearing about a man having his throat slashed with a knife into the symbolic image, "death among the apple trees," a phrase which appears with minor variation throughout the novel. This initial account [9] appears just prior to Susan's narration of a kiss between Florrie and Ernest, mirrored both by Jinny kissing Louis in the garden *and* by Kundry's kissing of Parsifal in Wagner's opera. John Peter explains that "Kundry's kiss is Parsifal's first erotic experience, and its effect on him . . . is convulsive" (Peter 88). Peter's description of the intensity of such an impact certainly fits Louis's reaction to Jinny's kiss, which becomes one of his defining leitmotifs in the novel: "All is shattered" (13).

References to events early in the novel in the garden at Elvedon, which sounds similar to both "Eden" and "Eve," evoke narratives of gender resulting from Genesis's account of the Fall, which in Western culture informs humans' perception of nature. The garden, as "root" of the characters' leitmotifs, stands in not merely for nature, but culture as well, and more specifically the relationship between them. The recurrence of these leitmotifs in fact defines character much in the way Wagner's leitmotifs do in *Parsifal*. In Neville's case, however, the man with the bleeding gash in his throat, perhaps analogous to Amfortas's unhealing wound, becomes hidden, or closeted, in his abbreviated symbolic phrase for the event, "the immitigable tree" (24), or the tree of knowledge in Eden.

What becomes Neville's leitmotif in the novel, the "immitigable apple tree which we cannot pass" (25) is precisely Christianity's myth of Adam and Eve, the masternarrative of heterosexuality in our culture. *The Waves* leaves no doubt as to the tyranny of this narrative. Louis, who has the first extended soliloquy in the novel, imagines his eyes as "green leaves, unseeing," perhaps a reference to prelapsarian innocence. Immediately, however, he describes himself as a boy "with a belt fastened by a brass snake," which brings to mind the serpent in the Genesis account of the Fall.

Woman's role in the Fall is emphasized in Jinny's Eve-like desire for knowledge, emotions that lead to her kiss with Louis: "What moved the leaves? What moves my heart, my legs?" (13). Susan's reaction to the kiss is reminiscent of the language in Genesis of humankind's punishment for Eve's transgression: "I shall eat nuts and peer for eggs through the brambles and my hair will be matted and I shall sleep under hedges and drink water from ditches and die there" (13-14). Throughout the novel it is precisely this set of narratives, and their condensation into various leitmotifs, that serve to define each character's struggle.

Neville, for example, seeks to transform such narratives into his own private symbolic system in a way that at least attempts to avoid the negation of his desire.[10] To counter the novel's perpetual references to twos, pairs, and difference, Neville initially recasts desire in terms of singularity and sameness. Although feeling the need to hide his "wound," Neville begins to create an alternative to the mythical, heterosexual site of Eden when he thinks "I shall be free to enter the garden where Fenwick raises his mallet . . . bound, surely, to discover my desire in the end . . . I will shade my eyes . . . to hide one tear . . . to peep at one face" (60). In the second dinner scene Neville incorporates this alternative imaging of the garden in the articulation and defense of his desire to Susan, whose alignment with nature[11] embodies one aspect of the traditional feminine that has rendered him, like Forster's Maurice, an "unspeakable of the Oscar Wilde sort" (*Maurice* 159).

At the first dinner, however, Neville clearly "lacks" the discursive agility to do so. Just as in *Parsifal* Amfortas receives his spear-wound in succumbing to the sexual desire aroused in him by Kundry in Klingsor's garden, Neville's "wound" is an imagination still governed by Western, Edenic configurations of desire. Amfortas's wound marks sexual transgression as feminine, an effect similar to that of the story of Genesis. Neville's desire for men is coded as feminine through his association with the "gash," or "wound" which can only be healed, presumably, by the phallic spear of Percival, whom he desires for most of the novel. But like Amfortas's wound in Wagner's opera, Neville's wound is not healed by Percival's presence at the first "communion"; he is unable to conceptualize his desire in terms other than lack. Ironically, it is Percival's absence from the second dinner at Hampton Court which allows Neville to forget his "wound," caused by what Jonathan Dollimore and Jamake Highwater[12] describe as the Christian discourse of desire as perversion.

The association of Neville with Amfortas's "feminine" wound marks the intersection of exegetical conflations of evil and perversion (Dollimore 124) with that of what Foucault has described as the nineteenth century's "psychiatrization" of perverse pleasure, and the creation of the homosexual (43). Neville's "wound" signifies the lack of the "normal" proportion of masculinity, "enabled by the [theological] view of perversion as an inimical threatening absence" (Dollimore 204). While Neville *begins* to subvert the Edenic narrative of heterosexuality, at the farewell dinner for Percival—analogous to the first, failed Grail ceremony in *Parsifal*—he still figures his desire in terms of lack, both in the general sense of femininity as lack, and in the more specific sense of the semiotics of homosexuality specified by Foucault and Dollimore.

Neville describes the pleasure he derives from waiting for Percival in terms of lack: "There is a morbid pleasure in saying, 'No; it is not Percival'" (118). As he waits, Neville's suspense "sharpens," a verb which evokes the weapon that cut the throat of the man, or the spear that inflicted Amfortas's wound. Until Percival arrives, Neville believes, "things have lost their *normal* uses—this knife blade is only a flash of light, not a thing to cut with. The *normal* is abolished" (119; emphasis added). "Normality" is precisely what Neville as a homosexual male, lacks.

Rhoda observes that the "swing-door," associated with Neville's "wound," "goes on opening" (122), just as Amfortas's wound continues to "burst out afresh" (Wagner 19). The whole farewell dinner scene, in fact, incorporates images and motifs in this way. Like Rhoda, Bernard notes the swing-door "opening perpetually": "its glass cage solicits us with myriad temptations and offers insults and wounds to our confidence" (123). This juxtaposition of the swing-door with "temptations" and "wounds," signifies the theological apparatus that marks Neville as feminine and perverse, an apparatus in which Wagner's opera participates.

Neville initially seems to think that Percival's presence will "heal" his wound, which he masks with the image of the tree of knowledge, and he wishes to be unburdened from the secrecy, or "relations of the closet" (Sedgwick 3) that action seems to have entailed for him.[13] While it is true that some sense of community is achieved at the initial farewell dinner, which all of the characters attribute in some fashion to Percival, Neville's "wound" is not healed by the spear, or masculine heterosexual myth of unified subjectivity Percival representationally wields: "But I shall never have what I want, for I lack bodily grace and the courage that comes with it" (129). His "wound," and all its significations of lack, cannot be healed by the heritage of discourses which Percival carries into the restaurant and into the social text, a heritage of mythology and culture that includes the biblical, exegetical tradition of the Fall, the various versions of the Grail myth, most specifically Wagner's, and the nineteenth-century's "psychiatrization" of perverse pleasure (Foucault 43). The model of wound and spear, the story of Eden, is precisely the model of compulsory heterosexuality that has "wounded" Neville in the first place.

In the second dinner scene, Neville feels "sorrow" because he knows for sure that Percival, the object of his desire will not appear: "The door will not open; he will not come" (211). Here he does not express pleasure through lack, but rather resignation. He fumbles in his "private" ("closeted"?) pocket for his "credentials," which he carries to "prove" his "superiority" (211). While they seem to be literal, physical pieces of paper (possibly poems that he has written), I would like to suggest that these "credentials" also represent Neville's success at subverting the discourses of gender that have figured his desire as lack. He tries to communicate to Susan that he has "passed" (211), an ambiguous yet loaded term in discussions not only of race but also of sexuality. It could signify that Neville has succeeded in passing for heterosexual and thus in avoiding social persecution. But it more probably refers to what he has not been able to pass for most of the novel, "the immitigable tree" (25), which has played an integral role in negating the specificity of his desire. Significantly, his certainty wavers because of Susan and the physically-based ideology of femininity in which she is implicated: "Now it has died down altogether, under Susan's stare . . . I hear only the wind sweeping over the ploughed land and some bird singing—perhaps some intoxicated lark" (212).

Neville's confidence also seems shaken by couples in the restaurant, "looking at the trees which are not yet dark enough to shelter their prostrate bodies" (212). Although there are trees here, and bodies beneath them that recall the man with the bleeding throat, Neville seems to be more aware of that image's investment in heterosexuality. What he wishes to convince Susan he has "passed" is that very tree, the line which distinguishes male presence from female absence, and which configures his desire as feminine, perverse lack.

Neville attempts to create a reverse discourse of the one that aligns the feminine with the predictable cycles of nature and the body by employing some of its elements to privilege artifice and discontinuity. Fruit embroidered on his curtain "swells so that parrots can peck it" and milk is "opal, blue, rose" (212). Embroidery, gems, and vibrant colors mark his relationships as he imagines winters in a "red cave" and the chaotic breaking of pipes: "We stand in a yellow tin bath in the middle of the room. We rush helter-skelter for basins . . . We shout with laughter at the sight of ruin. Let solidity be destroyed" (213). Susan's marriage, on the other hand, he depicts as monotonous, and his awareness of the discourse of feminine lack that impacts his gender identity is evident: "You say nothing. You see nothing. Custom blinds your eyes. At that hour your relationship is mute, null, dun-coloured. Mine at that hour is warm and various. There is no repetition for me. Each day is dangerous" (213).

Neville disrupts the different/same binary informing the hetero/homosexual one by representing his relationships with other men in terms of difference, and the marriage of Susan, who has "stuck like a limpet to the same rock" (213), in terms of the same, doing so in a way that foregrounds the semiotic nature of discourses of gender: "The snow, the burst pipe, the tin bath, the Chinese goose—these are *signs*, swung high aloft upon which, looking back, I *read* the character of each love; how each was different" (213; emphasis added). Neville sees himself not as occupying either side of a binary divided by a line, or tree, but as "a net whose fibers pass imperceptibly beneath the world" (214).

Neville concludes the carefully wrought and highly symbolic defense of his desire to Susan by expressing nostalgia for the solidity Percival and the various symbolic systems that comprise him offered: "But there was another glory once, when we watched for the door to open, and Percival came" (214). In Susan's "reply" to Neville, she acknowledges that the idea of femininity in which she is implicated legitimates itself by negating his desire: "Yet look, Neville, whom I discredit in order to be myself" (215). She attempts to render the artificiality Neville strategically deploys lifeless: "Seen through your pale and yielding flesh, even apples and bunches of fruit must have a filmed look as if they stood under glass" (215). And yet, given the reference to fruit and apples, which evoke both sexuality and knowledge, Susan might be recognizing the unnatural quality the Edenic narrative must have for Neville. Neville's "wound" is healed at Hampton Court because he is speaking his desire, rather than letting his culture's myths render it unspeakable; he heals his wound by forgetting Percival's spear.

Notes

[1] I borrow "Parcival in the forest of gender" from Rachel Blau DuPlessis's "Pater-Daughter: Male Modernists and Female Readers" in her book, *The Pink Guitar*.

[2] Though its implications are similar, my argument differs from M. K. Booker's in that I see Percival's character not as defined by others, but as definitive of others.

[3] Roof's discussion of "heteroideology" (42) informs this analysis of *The Waves*.

[4] Woolf wrote a review for the London *Times* in 1909, in which she praised the Bayreuth festival of that year and Wagner's *Parsifal* in particular for its "overwhelming unity" (qtd. in DiGaetani 112).

[5] DiGaetani points out that only in Wagner's opera is the figure of Percival central, rather than peripheral, as in other accounts such as Malory's and Weston's *From Ritual to Romance* ; "Moreover, these other versions do not portray Parsifal as a sacrificial victim, as Wagner does" (123).

[6] See James Knapp for a discussion of the history of nationalist uses of the Percival myth (including Wagner's opera) as "old words to validate new social power" (157).

[7] Poresky, however, makes an interesting, if unintentional, sexual connection between Susan and Bernard's flight from the garden and Neville's sexuality when she says "Eden becomes Sodom, and humankind is driven by fear into an alien and mortal world" (65).

[8] Percival seems to appear out of nowhere at the British *public* school the *male* characters attend, which suggests his connection with the various linguistic and symbolic systems the upper class male British subject internalizes through education—systems of meaning which the figure of Percival, in its various manifestations, has a history of being used to uphold.

[9] For the full text of Neville's account, see pages 24-25 in *The Waves*.

[10] Foucault remarks that the discourse on homosexuality "made possible a strong advance of social controls into this area of 'perversity'; but it also made possible the formation of a 'reverse' discourse: homosexuality began to speak in its own behalf, to demand that its legitimacy or 'naturality' be acknowledged, often in the same vocabulary, using the same categories by which it was medically disqualified" (101).

[11] Throughout the novel Susan is described by the other characters and by herself with language evocative of nature, animals, and materiality. See J. W. Graham and M. K. Booker.

[12] For discussions of the Christian discourse of desire as perversion and its effects on the signification of homosexuality, see Eve Kosofsky Sedgwick, Jonathan Dollimore, and Jamake Highwater.

[13] For a discussion of the exegetical "exfoliation" of the Eden story "by which 'knowledge' and 'sex' become conceptually inseparable from one another," see Sedgwick (73).

Works Cited

Booker, M. K. "Tradition, Authority, and Subjectivity: Narrative Constitution of the Self in *The Waves*." *LIT* 3.1 (1991): 33-55.

Butler, Judith. *Gender Trouble: Feminism and the Subversion of Identity*. Thinking Gender. Ed. Linda J. Nicholson. New York and London: Routledge, 1990.

DiGaetani, John Louis. *Richard Wagner and the Modern British Novel*. Rutherford: Fairleigh Dickinson UP, 1978.

Dollimore, Jonathan. *Sexual Dissidence: Augustine to Wilde, Freud to Foucault*. Oxford: Clarendon Press, 1991.

DuPlessis, Rachel Blau. *The Pink Guitar: Writing as a Feminist Practice*. New York: Routledge, 1990.

Forster, E. M. *Maurice: A Novel.* 1971. New York and London: W. W. Norton & Co., 1993.
Foucault, Michel. *The History of Sexuality.* Vol. 1. Trans. Robert Hurley. New York: Pantheon Books, 1978.
Graham, J. W. "Manuscript Revision and the Heroic Theme of *The Waves.*" *Twentieth Century Literature* 29.3 (1983 Fall): 312-332.
Highwater, Jamake. *The Mythology of Transgression: Homosexuality as Metaphor.* New York and Oxford: Oxford UP, 1997.
Jacobs, Peter. "'The Second Violin Tuning in the Ante-room': Virginia Woolf and Music." *The Multiple Muses of Virginia Woolf.* Ed. Diane F. Gillespie. Columbia and London: U of Missouri P, 1993. 27-260.
Knapp, James F. "Discontinuous Form in Modern Poetry: Myth and Counter Myth." *Boundary 2: A Journal of Postmodern Literature and Culture* 12.1 (1983 Fall): 149-166.
Peter, John. *Vladimir's Carrot: Modern Drama and the Modern Imagination.* London: Andre Deutsch, 1987.
Poresky, Louise. "Eternal Renewal: Life and Death in Virginia Woolf's *The Waves.*" *Virginia Woolf Miscellanies. Proceedings of the First Annual Conference on Virginia Woolf.* New York: Pace UP, 1992. 148-154.
Richter, Harvena. *Virginia Woolf: The Inward Voyage.* Princeton: Princeton UP, 1970.
Roof, Judith. *Come As You Are: Sexuality and Narrative.* New York: Columbia UP, 1996.
Sedgwick, Eve Kosofsky. *Epistemology of the Closet.* Berkeley: U of California P, 1990.
Wagner, Richard. *Parsifal: A Festival Drama.* Trans. H.L. and F. Corder. New York: Fred Rullman, Inc., n.d.
Woolf, Leonard. *Beginning Again: An Autobiography of the Years 1911-1918.* London: The Hogarth Press, 1964.
Woolf, Virginia. *The Waves.* 1931. San Diego: Harcourt Brace & Co., 1978.

Lisa Golmitz Weihman
The Problem of National Culture: Virginia Woolf's *Between the Acts* and Elizabeth Bowen's *The Last September*

Virginia Woolf began writing *Between the Acts* in early 1938, and finished the final draft just weeks before her own suicide in 1941. These years saw the bombing of her London home by the Germans, which forced the Woolfs to live full-time in Rodmell, on the Sussex downs, where the threat of invasion was imminent. What was salvageable from the Mecklenburgh Square ruins was sent to rented rooms in Sussex. Most of the books and papers landed at Monk's House, where the disordered past lay in mildewed piles on Woolf's chairs and kitchen table: her journals were rescued, as were most of her father's library and a few pieces of Omega workshop pottery (Lee 730-31). The comforting chronology of storage violated, it was as though a volcano had pushed to the surface random, decontextualized fragments of her past. *Between the Acts*, the product of these disordered years, shares much in common with the Monk's House cottage: the novel, like the home, is a warehouse of memory, a collection of literary and historical fragments of English culture. Woolf juxtaposes these fragments—literary artifacts—with contemporary political analysis in order to interrogate the ideological power of art and the value of collective memory. The novel asks if a shared national culture is possible, if such a culture is beneficial to the artist, and how art functions in relation to the community.

The interrelationship between nationalism and the forces that authorize political violence is a theme Woolf explores in much of her writing in the 1930s, and in *Between the Acts* Woolf centers the action around a symbol, the Big House, that catches within it the forces she critiques: class division, sexual violence, and patriarchal tyranny within the home. Pointz Hall is the symbolic fortress guarding an increasingly untenable national inheritance, and at the end of the novel, Woolf metaphorically burns the house to the ground with an array of smoldering images. The first occurs as Miss La Trobe's audience leaves the scene of the pageant, and Pointz Hall comes into view: "*Dispersed are we*, the gramophone repeated. And the audience turning saw the flaming windows, each daubed with golden sun" (196). The gramophone is silenced, bringing to a close the illusion of community that moments before had brought audience and actors together in the familiar chorus of *God Save the King*.[1] The sentimentality of national bonding is parodied in the image of the flaming sunset, which dismisses the community and leaves behind a vision of Pointz Hall in flames. The setting sun metaphor resonates with the disintegration of the British Empire, with the threat of the coming war, and with the potential destruction of domestic life symbolized by Pointz Hall. Pointz Hall is a place holder for the nation in this novel, the symbolic point where the private world of the home becomes the mirror image of the national crisis.

The Oliver family returns to Pointz Hall following the pageant to find the solidity of the home threatened by Miss La Trobe's literary deconstruction and by their failure to communicate with one another, a dangerous state of affairs Woolf critiques through her use of incendiary imagery within the home. The class tensions brought out by the afternoon's drama are reinforced when the narrator reports that the house is now a "shell" where the servants feed the flames: "The usual sounds reverberated through the shell; Sands making up the fire; Candish stoking the boiler" (215). Isa, whose "hand burnt in the sun on the window sill," (215) pays the household bills, which are said to "crackle" in her hand. Miss La Trobe, sitting alone in the local pub, is the designated arsonist: "The cheap clock ticked; smoke obscured the pictures. Smoke became tart on the roof of her mouth. Smoke obscured the earth-coloured jackets" (212). As she sits amid the smoke and ashes, the first lines of her next play rise up in her mind. The novel ends with an image, perhaps Miss La Trobe's, of England as a primordial swamp. Windows take the place of solid wall to reveal the "enmity. . . also love" of husband and wife to the reader and the world outside: "The window was all sky without colour. *The house had lost its shelter*" (my emphasis, 219). Pointz Hall is dismantled by Miss La Trobe's art, offering two interpretive possibilities for the novel's closure: the nation will be destroyed by the coming apocalypse, signified by the disappearance of the house. But perhaps the community may survive even the death of nation, if the community can discover new modes of communication.

Virginia Woolf's diaries and letters attest to her fascination with her own nationalist impulses during the war, impulses she ultimately rejects but continually explores in her writing. Most of Woolf's literary contemporaries responded to the Nazi threat with more ambivalence toward national culture, and one writer, the Irish novelist Elizabeth Bowen, spoke with Woolf about her divided loyalties and the need to do something productive to help the war effort. Bowen was a good friend to Woolf during the 1930s, and by 1941 was a regular visitor and correspondent. The two women had much in common. Both Woolf and Bowen lost their mothers at an early age. Both shared a circle of influential friends, and were introduced at a party thrown by Ottoline Morrell. Eddy Sackville-West was a close friend of Bowen's, and Bowen was born, like Eddy and his cousin Vita, into a fading aristocratic family. Like Vita Sackville-West and like Woolf herself, Bowen was also a happily married woman who loved other women. While Bowen became a good friend to Woolf in her final years, and was in fact one of the last guests at Monk's House before Woolf's death, the friendship was complicated by the seventeen year age gap between Woolf and the younger Bowen, by Woolf's sense of Bowen as a literary rival, and by Bowen's increasingly conservative political leanings. In July, 1940, Bowen writes to Woolf about her decision to spy for the war effort in Ireland, where her contacts in Anglo-Irish society could make her a valuable source of information to the English government should Germany invade. She writes,

> I think I told you I had asked the Ministry of Information if I could do any work, which I felt was wanted, in Ireland. On Saturday morning I had a letter from them saying yes, they did want me to go. Now it has come to the point I fear, rather a feeling of dismay and of not wanting to leave this country. I am to see Harold Nicolson on Thursday and go to Ireland on Friday night next. I don't expect it will be for very long. . . . I hope I shall be some good: I do feel it's important. . . . If there's to be an invasion of Ireland, I hope it may be while I'm there—which I don't mean frivolously—but if anything happens to England while I'm in Ireland I shall wish I'd never left, even for this short time. (Berg Collection, NYPL).

Bowen writes of her divided loyalties, caught between the Anglo and the Irish of her heritage. There is no record of Woolf's reply to Bowen's crisis of national identity. As for Bowen's confessional mode with Woolf, one has to wonder what sort of spy she could have been, and Bowen was not an astute reader of *Three Guineas* if she thought Woolf would be sympathetic to her English patriotism. While the private writing gives no direct support for this assumption, there are clues within *Between the Acts* which suggest that Woolf's examination of nationalism within her final novel stems in part from a close reading of her friend's views on the value of national culture. Among the dozens of literary echoes resonating throughout *Between the Acts* are repeated allusions to Bowen's 1928 novel *The Last September*, in which Bowen connects the development of women's subjectivity and artistic growth with the ability to "conceive of one's country emotionally" (*LS* 101).

The Last September and *Between the Acts* share a number of striking similarities. Both novels investigate the connection between the cult of female domesticity and the production of national identification. Both link patriarchal forces within the home with external political violence, and critique the social and political insularity of the upper classes. Woolf and Bowen share a suspicion that the heterosexual marriage plot is outmoded, and both novels feature women artist figures grappling with an inadequate or inaccessible literary and cultural history. Both are also "Big House" novels, comedies of manners revolving around a large country home, which serves to parody class snobbery and the work of Empire. The connections between the two novels are so pervasive that it is impossible to conclude that Woolf was unaware of the use she was making of her friend's earlier novel, which Bowen sent to her in May, 1934, after the Woolfs visited her in Ireland (*L5* 304). That critics of both novels have failed to note the intertextual resonances of *The Last September* within *Between the Acts* is certainly the result of Elizabeth Bowen's lowly place within the canon of Modernism, and the misidentification of her work as elitist, apolitical, and lacking in feminist virtue—accusations which must sound familiar to us as Woolf critics. Elizabeth Bowen's literary reputation is minor today; the feminist and political analysis brought to bear on Woolf's writing in the past two decades has only just begun to touch Bowen's work. Woolf, as usual, is a better reader of her contemporaries than we are.

The Last September is set, like *Between the Acts*, in the months preceding the outbreak of war. Bowen's terrain is Ireland in 1920, when tensions are mounting between rebel nationalists and the forces of the British Empire. Danielstown, the estate of Lady and Lord Naylor, is a symbol of the Protestant Ascendancy class that is rapidly losing political and economic power. Danielstown is also a symbol of ambivalent nationalism: the rebel nationalists see the estate as the spoils of Empire, while the home's occupants see the Big House as the fruition of Irish identity—the best model of Irish domestic and political life. The coming war will dislocate these beliefs, and will call into question the nature of Irish national identity. Violence encroaches on the landscape, but the Naylors continue to host tennis parties and to wonder at their friends who have fled to the safety of England. Lois Farquar, Sir Richard's orphaned niece, arrives at Danielstown after graduating from a boarding school in London. Two possible futures are prepared for Lois: she may marry Gerald

Lesworth, a British soldier, or she may be sent to the Slade School of Art in London. Neither option will be realized.

Lois is the age of the century, about to turn 21. She is revealed to be an amateur artist, though her drawings are scorned as derivative and "Pre-Raphaelite": too Victorian for modern tastes. The front cover of her sketchbook states "Lois Honoria Farquar: Her Book." But the epigraph to the title page reveals just how little of Lois is to be found within:

> I am a painter who cannot paint;
> In my life, a devil rather than a saint;
> In my brain, as poor a creature too:
> No end to all that I cannot do!
> But do one thing at least I can—
> Love a man or hate a man
> Supremely— (*LS* 97).

Lois defines herself with Robert Browning's words from *Pippa Passes* as someone with "no end to all that I cannot do," as a failed artist, a painter who cannot paint, and she ironically uses another artist's words to communicate the gap where her self should be. In her incapacity and self-effacement Lois bears a compelling resemblance to Woolf's Isa Oliver, who hides scraps of derivative poetry from her husband in a false account book. Isa, like Lois, is weighed down by tradition and cliché. Both Lois and Isa are caught between roles, and both novels suggest that the self is nothing but a theatrical conceit, a choice of mask placed over a void.

Woolf's Isa Oliver picks up Lois's quotation of Browning in *Between the Acts:* "But do one thing at least I can— /Love a man or hate a man/Supremely." Love and hate for her husband Giles burn through Isa throughout the novel: "Isabella felt prisoned. Through the bars of the prison, through the sleep haze that deflected them, blunt arrows bruised her of love, then of hate" (66). Lois is 20 in 1920, Isa is 39 in 1939, making both characters the same age as Elizabeth Bowen herself. Like Lois and Bowen, Isa is Anglo-Irish with a mixed colonial inheritance: we are told that her mother died in India (159) and that she is the "niece of the two old ladies at Wimbledon who were so proud, being O'Neils, of their descent from the Kings of Ireland" (16). Lois Farquar is Sir Richard Naylor's niece; Isa Oliver, in *Between the Acts*, "looked like what she was: Sir Richard's daughter" (16). Woolf's portrait of Isa serves to remind Bowen of her own more complicated if also ambivalent portrayal of the problem of national culture in *The Last September*. By 1940, Bowen has moved from questioning the value of nationalism to debating which country, England or Ireland, she would prefer to die in should the Germans invade.

Reading Isa as a continuation of Bowen's ingénue also clarifies Woolf's physical description of her: "'Abortive,' was the word that expressed her. . . . Thick of waist, large of limb, and, save for her hair, fashionable in the tight modern way, she never looked like Sappho, or one of the beautiful young men whose photographs adorned the weekly papers" (16). This unflattering portrait of Isa is illuminated by comparison with Bowen's description of Marda Norton, the disruptive visitor to Danielstown who is Lois Farquar's only true romantic attachment in *The Last September*. Bowen's description of Marda invests her with the qualities Isa lacks:

> [Marda] was tall; her back, as she stood looking over the fields, *was like a young man's* in its vigorous slightness. She escaped the feminine pear-shape, her shoulders were square, legs long from the knee down. Her light brown dress slipped and fitted with careless accuracy, defining spareness negatively under its slack folds. (My emphasis, 79)

Entranced by Marda's sophistication, Lois slips on her fur coat: "Her arms slipped silkily through; her hands appeared, almost tiny, out of the huge cuffs. 'Oh the escape!' she thought. . . . 'Oh, the *escape* in other people's clothes!'" (76). Lois's game of dress-up and the illusion of her possible "escape" from the feminine self prescribed by Anglo-Irish custom is undermined by Marda Norton's capitulation to marriage with an Englishman ironically named Leslie Lawe. Marda, as her name suggests, is the sacrificed martyr at the altar of heterosexual convention.

Isa Oliver is a still bleaker portrait of Lois Farquar's future. Isa's failure to write poetry or to finish her unexpressed thoughts is contrasted in *Between the Acts* with the ambitious pageant written and directed by Miss La Trobe, who does resemble Sappho in being both an artist and a lesbian. Bowen's Lois Farquar is also caught in this struggle to love women and art, and Lois's deep attraction to Marda is her true sexual awakening. When the two women encounter an abandoned mill, "Marda put an arm round her waist, and in an ecstasy at this compulsion Lois entered the mill. Fear heightened her gratification; she welcomed its inrush" (124). This moment of ecstasy is contrasted with the emptiness Lois feels when Gerald kisses her. "So that was being kissed: just an impact, with inside blankness. She was lonely and saw there was no future" (88-89). Isa, in her unhappy middle age, represents what Lois most fears she will become if she cannot escape the restrictive domesticity of Anglo-Irish womanhood.

Woolf's evocation of *The Last September* in *Between the Acts* extends her critique of English imperial policy. Artifacts of colonial expansion molder throughout both Danielstown and Pointz Hall:

> Lois often tripped with her toe in the jaws of the tiger; a false step at any time sent some great claw skidding over the polish. Pale regimental groups, reunions a generation ago of the family or the neighbourhood gave out from the walls a vague depression. There were two locked bookcases of which the keys had been lost, and a troop of ebony elephants brought back from India by someone she did not remember paraded along the tops of the bookcases. (*LS* 10)

Pointz Hall is similarly troubled by inherited imperial treasure in *Between the Acts*. The house overflows with colonial and military artifacts ("a watch that had stopped a bullet on the field of Waterloo"; Sohrab, the "crusader's" dog), paintings of ancestors both actual and adopted, and half-remembered books. In the passage above, Bowen's narrator comments that the bookcases at Danielstown are locked, their keys forgotten. In *Between the Acts*, Isa considers the books in her father-in-law's library, and finds them wanting; for this generation, "the newspaper was a book," a commodity fought over "like fish rising to a crumb of biscuit" (216). The books Isa notes on her father-in-law's shelves reflect a gentleman's canonical education, equated with the shilling shockers abandoned at the home by visitors. With the exception of Lucy Swithin's natural history text, books at Pointz Hall reflect only the anti-intellectual acquisition of a "gentleman's education" or the boredom of a long train ride. Allusions to the English literary canon are juxtaposed with the bleak political realities intruding on the home, and throughout *Between the Acts* Woolf implicates the privileging of English literary culture with increasing political and social violence—books become talismans of English cultural life rather than opportunities for intellectual engagement.

Gerald Lesworth in *The Last September* is similarly addicted to the newspaper, repeating the information in the *Morning Post* as though it contained insider information from the garrison, to which he is not privy. Gerald looks for a narrative to support his involvement in Ireland and finds it in the anti-Irish *Post*, but the irony lies in the psychological release the newspaper gives him from the history he is in fact helping to create. The newspaper distances him from the violence, contains it, and its reductive summaries of the political tension in Ireland give Gerald a false sense of security and mastery of the Irish situation. The impression of immediacy and accuracy, the dependable recurrence each day of the newspaper substitutes for more direct engagements with reality. The communities in both novels allow the newspapers to speak their values for them, to define their political views not with the intention of bringing the news closer for more analysis but with the assurance that further analysis is not necessary. Bart and Giles Oliver can gobble their paper like fish because it takes no more time than that for the newspaper to do its cultural work. Gerald Lesworth becomes a zombie in the presence of the paper, and is described as "half-hypnotized, consciously barren," when he repeats to the Naylors the news of the day (94). Lady Naylor remarks, "it was extraordinary how no amount of experience shook these young Englishmen up. Their minds remained cutting books"—repositories of decontextualized bits of received information rather than engines of original thought (94).

One of the most compelling connections between the two novels is this sustained critique of the mass media, and both texts share a suspicion of reproduced sound. The importation of modern conveniences from the dominant, imperial culture, such as automobiles, refrigerators, and gramophones, seduces and pacifies individuals in both novels, rendering them more open to mass messages broadcast via radio and newspaper. Woolf invokes Bowen when Miss La Trobe brings a gramophone out of doors, where it is hidden behind hurdles—barricades—and camouflaged with leaves like a weapon of war. A gramophone is also brought out of doors in *The Last September*, held by a British subaltern so that Lois might dance with Gerald in the lanes. Bowen repeatedly conflates the music of the gramophone with imperial power, something Lois will theoretically gain through a marriage with Gerald. The sinister gramophone makes a second appearance at a dance Lois attends at the army barracks. A brutal, shell-shocked soldier named Daventry suggests that if only the rebels would declare themselves and fight, then the troops could wage an all-out war. "The Miss Raltes. . . looked down their noses. There was a moment of slight discomfort, of national consciousness. 'Wouldn't it be a rag,' said Moira, relieving the tension tactfully, 'if they tried to fire in at the window while we were dancing?'" (143). The "tactful" suggestion of violence is repeated in the dancing: "Cicely glanced at the gramophone, hummed a fox-trot and tapped her heel on the floor, looking most unconscious. But the subalterns continued to slide violently, rebounding against each other. . . . The gramophone spurted hoarse music" (143). The anthropomorphic gramophone, here as in *Between the Acts*, responds to the tenor of the conversation, heightening the emotional intensity with the threat of sexual violence. Lois arrives, and is caught up in the momentum of the music. In the course of her conversation with Gerald she inadvertently agrees to marry him: "'What have I done?' she thought" (158). She then encounters the drunken, demonic Daventry, who has just molested one of the Irish girls:

> If they were not careful, *they would knock over the gramophone. Mr Daventry thought it was time they did. It was time something happened.* He danced the D. I.'s niece down the passage and kissed her with her head pressed back in the coats. She struggled, futile, slippery as a weasel. As he kissed her again, her face went stiff and she shut her eyes. When these opened, they were as shrewd as ever: still he did not know what she thought. . . .
> 'Do you get kissed a lot?'
> 'Englishmen never could keep their mouths to themselves.'
> 'You won't know yourselves when we're gone!'
> 'You should get back home while you can, the lot of you.' (My emphasis, 156-57)

Sexual predation is linked to national violence, and the dance between colonized women and the colonizing military officers is described as a battle.

Daventry is reportedly shell-shocked from his experiences in World War I; his job in Ireland is to ransack the bedrooms of suspected rebel families, where "nearly all beds contained old women or women with very new babies" (*LS* 144). Woolf borrows Daventry's mix of instability, cruelty, and misogyny for *Between the Acts*. Isa is haunted by a newspaper article recounting the rape of a young girl by soldiers in an army barracks, who lure her in with the promise of showing her "a horse with a green tail" (20). Both Woolf and Bowen reveal the misogyny that military culture enforces, and depict rape as a weapon of political domination. Isa, like Lois, is haunted by the soldier's actions, and fragments of the story recur to her throughout the day of the pageant. Miss La Trobe's pageant offers a context for the soldier's behavior, demonstrating that the values of English society support the political, sexual and economic domination of women and of the colonies.

The symbolic burning of Pointz Hall at the end of *Between the Acts* recalls the actual burning of Danielstown at the end of *The Last September*. The political violence that destroys Danielstown liberates its occupants from the past, from the insular conventions of Anglo-Irish society. Nationalist rebels set the fire, but the text suggests the true arsonists to be the home's occupants, whose social and political isolation have become intolerable. The narrative draws to a matter-of-fact close, not a tragic one:

> At Danielstown, half-way up the avenue under the beeches, the thin iron gate twanged (missed its latch, remained swinging aghast) as the last unlit car slid out with the executioners bland from accomplished duty. The sound of the last car widened, gave itself to the open and empty country and was demolished. Then the first wave of silence that was to be ultimate flowed back, confident, to the steps. Above the steps, the door stood open hospitably upon a furnace.
> Sir Richard and Lady Naylor, not saying anything, did not look at each other, for in the light from the sky they saw too distinctly. (206)

The "bland" executioners set fire to the house, which stands with its doors open to the inferno, "hospitably" welcoming its own destruction. Lady and Lord Naylor are not within the house when it burns, and remain silent; their emotional detachment from the home and from each other ends the novel. The "burning" of Pointz Hall at the end of *Between the Acts* similarly implicates the occupants of the home with the nation's destruction, connecting the restrictive roles for women within the home with the reproduction of self-aggrandizing national narratives. The "Big House" in both novels functions as a symbol of female domestic entrapment, fading patriarchal authority, and lost class privilege. Woolf's "fire" is only the setting sun, but it removes the walls of the house as surely as Miss La Trobe's pageant exposes the lies and frauds of British imperial culture.

Notes

[1] Beth Rigel Daugherty acknowledges Woolf's critique of patriotism: "Art fails to lift people out of their individual concerns. . . . Outside circumstances fragment them so that they *desire* unity, but they infrequently feel it; when they do, it is usually during patriotic numbers that both the pageant and the novel critique" (78).

[2] On July 5, 1940, Woolf writes of a long walk with Bowen: "We walked from 37 through Temple, along river, up Thames Street, to the Tower, talking talking about what? her going to Ireland on a Govt mission; leaving Clarence Terrace; writing, it was my 'greatness' as we circled the town. No, I don't think it was only flattery I wanted. Something warmer" (*D5* 301).

[3] Patricia Laurence argues, "These emergent media [newspaper, radio, photography and cinema] and the 'authority' that 'facts' and 'truth' and certain worldviews were acquiring in relation to art led Woolf through a period of intense questioning of the

distinctions between fact and fiction, history and literature, and 'high' and 'low' art" (229).

[4] Judith Johnston writes, "Throughout the pageant, Miss La Trobe's use of the gramophone to dominate her audience, to impose into their consciousness certain repeated phrases. . . . recalls the propagandistic use of recorded speeches and patriotic songs broadcast to radio audiences before and during the Second World War. The 'tick tick tick' of the needle scratching on the record calls attention to the mechanical reproduction of speech and suggests how repetition of selected ideas and feelings blots out individual differences" (266).

Works Cited

Bowen, Elizabeth. *The Last September*. London: Penguin Books, 1987.

———. Unpublished letter to Virginia Woolf, July 1940. Courtesy of the Henry W. and Albert A. Berg Collection, New York Public Library, Astor, Lenox, and Tilden Foundations.

Daugherty, Beth Rigel. "Face to Face with 'Ourselves' in Virginia Woolf's *Between the Acts*." *Virginia Woolf: Themes and Variations*. Ed. Vara Neverow-Turk and Mark Hussey. New York: Pace UP, 1992.

Johnston, Judith L. "The Remediable Flaw: Revisioning Cultural History in *Between the Acts*." *Virginia Woolf and Bloomsbury: A Centennial Celebration*. Ed. Jane Marcus. Bloomington: Indiana UP, 1987.

Laurence, Patricia. "The Facts and Fugue of War: From *Three Guineas* to *Between the Acts*." In Mark Hussey, ed. *Virginia Woolf and War: Fiction, Reality, and Myth*. Syracuse:Syracuse U P, 1991. 225-45.

Lee, Hermione. *Virginia Woolf*. New York: Alfred A. Knopf, 1996.

Woolf, Virginia. *Between the Acts*. New York: HBJ 1941.

———. *The Diary of Virginia Woolf*, Vol. 5. Ed. Anne Olivier Bell. New York: HBJ 1984.

———. *Three Guineas*. New York: Harcourt, Brace, 1938.

Catherine Sandbach-Dahlström
Feminist Conversation: Virginia Woolf, Simone de Beauvoir and the Dialogics of Criticism

Even if Virginia Woolf's feminist writings, *A Room of One's Own* and *Three Guineas*, and Simone de Beauvoir's *The Second Sex,* were written at very different historical moments and in very different circumstances, the apparently prophetic and revolutionary character of these texts has elevated their authors to singular icons of feminist struggle. As icons they have become a locus of feminist conversation, or a site where some feminism's understanding of itself is played out. A recent student handbook for gender studies may be seen as emblematic of this tendency. Placing pictures of Woolf and de Beauvoir side by side on one of the first pages, the accompanying text simplifies history by asserting that "Early 'European' feminist theoretical writings began with the work of Simone de Beauvoir, while 'Anglo American' writing is often associated with Virginia Woolf" (Goodman, xi). It is easy enough to fault this handbook for omitting mention of other prominent feminist thinkers and writers in Europe, Britain, and the United States, or for re-creating erroneous distinctions between feminisms, but it serves nonetheless to highlight the problems of selection and organization that we encounter in the writing of feminist history.

Woolf and de Beauvoir are central to this project since in their lives and works, as well as in their posthumous reputations, they demonstrate the tensions and ambiguities that would seem to be inherent in the figuration of the exceptional (intellectual) woman and/or feminist pioneer. Outspoken as they were in the cause of women's liberation, they were also visibly dependent upon men both for emotional confirmation and intellectual stimulus.[1] Embedded in groups dominated by men, Bloomsbury or the Left Bank, both Woolf and de Beauvoir present a challenging and at times an uncomfortable reminder of our own vulnerability as academics in a world still much determined by androcentric values. As Toril Moi writes in her introduction to *The Making of an Intellectual Woman*, it is this very dilemma that makes de Beauvoir so important as a feminist emblem. Since "even in the 1990s women who set out to become intellectuals have to face personal, social and ideological obstacles not generally placed in the way of aspiring male intellectuals," they "cannot afford not to take [Simone de Beauvoir] seriously as a thinker, particularly in an educational context"(3).

While acknowledging the validity of Moi's point, I believe that we should be self-conscious about the way that we appropriate both Woolf and de Beauvoir for our own ends. Therefore, I intend to discuss "Woolf" and "de Beauvoir" (I use the citation marks this once to indicate that these are posthumous constructions rather than reincarnations of living beings) here as focal points for feminism's discourse of resistance. My aim is not to determine the degree, or quality, of de Beauvoir's intellectual debt to Sartre (or other important influences such as Hegel, Marx, and Merleau-Ponty) or the exact nature of Woolf's emotional need of Leonard Woolf or her indebtedness to her father, to Roger Fry, or George Moore. I wish rather to point to the constraints of criticism that would have us determine the issue one way or another. In an often-quoted passage, Nancy Miller insists that "...the signature of the woman writer who is also a feminist writer is the mark of resistance to dominant ideologies; for the feminist critic, the signature is the site of a possible disruption" (17). If the feminist project is by definition one of resistance and rewriting, then we are driven to look for this factor or to note its absence. We are, in other words, complicit in a pre-established binary.

There are various ways of theorizing the dilemma facing the feminist historian. One would be to refer to Hayden White's essay "The Historical Text as Literary Artifact." According to White, "The historical narrative . . . mediates between the events reported in it on the one side and pre-generic plot structures conventionally used in our culture to endow unfamiliar events and situations with meanings, on the other" (88). In other words, the unfamiliar nature of the life of the intellectual woman in the earlier years of our century leaves us dependent on earlier plots of heroic resistance, romantic love and/or female victimization.[2] We can also approach the issue via Bakhtin's concept of the dialogic relation of utterances:

> Very frequently the expression of our utterance is determined not only—and sometimes not so much by the referentially semantic content of this utterance, but also by others' utterances on the same topic to which we are responding or with which we are polemicizing.... The expression of an utterance always responds to a greater or lesser degree, that is, it expresses the speaker's attitude towards others' utterances and not just his attitude toward the object of his utterance. (91-92)

This is to say, the scholar cannot speak of any topic without also entering into a dialogue with previous utterances on the same topic. Critical discourse is thus in itself in a dialogic relation to previous utterances, aesthetic and philosophical, as well as social and psychological. Whenever we write of the exceptional woman, we willy-nilly express an attitude to other utterances derived not only from the general ideological framework of feminism but also from the more general figurations of our culture. To recognize this is to experience, though perhaps without much hope of change, what Rosi Braidotti has called "the radical consciousness of one's own complicity with the very power one is trying to deconstruct" (qtd. in Miller 115).

I would like to approach the issue of complicity from two angles first by looking at some instances of—for feminism—troubling elements in Woolf and de Beauvoir and then by turning to examples of the plots or attitudes that affect our critical response.

Woolf in her private writing and in her polemics—from her picture of Joyce in her diary as self-conscious adolescent to the image of the "infantile fixation" of the fathers in *Three Guineas*—is outspoken in her critique of masculine egotism. Yet, as Alison Booth has suggested, like George Eliot before her, she cast herself in the mold of "The Grand Old Woman of English Letters" (1). And even if, as Booth argues further, Woolf's fiction puts forward "female self sacrifice" as an "antidote to male egotism" she was also "intent on [her] own success within a masculinist tradition" (3). The maintenance of the position of "Grand Old Woman" paradoxically both requires the valorization of female qualities and the suppression of the modifier woman (sometimes by dint of a pseudonym) since within the masculinist tradition the epithet works pejoratively. This may explain why both Woolf and de Beauvoir fail to do full justice to the extent of female accomplishment in the past and in their own time.

Woolf, for instance, downplays the extent of female journalism in the nineteenth century and women's contribution to science and scholarship.[3] In "A Scribbling Dame," Woolf responds to contemporary moves to rediscover lost women writers by vehemently rejecting the suggestion that Elizabeth Heywood could have paved the way for Jane Austen (*E2* 22-26). We might think that at this early date Woolf was required to speak "in the voice required and often demanded by the editorial policy of the relevant journal" (Brosnan 61). But essays written much later create related problems. In 1931 Woolf expresses admiration for Elizabeth Barrett's high ambitions, but condemns *Aurora Leigh*'s artistic imperfection, its lack of consistency, lack of impersonality (*CR2* 208). And despite her recorded admiration elsewhere for Jane Austen and George Eliot, despite the evocation of literary mothers, in both "Women and Fiction" and "The Leaning Tower" Woolf presents the full flowering women's writing as Utopia, as belonging to the future.

It would seem as if Woolf's theory of female disadvantage, the tale of Shakespeare's sister, forces her to disregard or qualify contemporary achievement and look to a future where women's writing will flower. It can be argued that de Beauvoir's description of contemporary women is also determined by the need to fit the cartography to the theory. It would be impossible to deny that *The Second Sex* is a tremendous indictment of patriarchal society and what it has done to women—in this it resembles both Mary Wollstonecraft's *A Vindication of the Rights of Woman* and *Three Guineas*. But the latter differs from *The Second Sex* in so far as Woolf suggest that women's position under patriarchy has promoted specific female values, the civilized qualities that a woman's college would preserve, for instance. For de Beauvoir, conventional womanhood, because it denies women their condition as free transcendent subjects, because it condemns them to immanence, is without redeeming features. Consequently her representation even of independent women is contemptuous: women doctors lack authority, independent women lack the adventurous spirit, and actresses indulge in narcissistic self-worship. Indeed the professional woman exists, for de Beauvoir, in a kind of limbo. "In so far as a woman wishes to be a woman," she notes, "her independent status gives rise to an inferiority complex: on the other hand her femininity makes her doubtful of her professional future" (708).

Given the dilemma of the independent, or intellectual, woman mapped out in *The Second Sex* then, de Beauvoir's denigration of female achievement is comprehensible. *The Second Sex*, in fact, condemns almost all female authorship out of hand. Noting the domestic or romantic thematics of much women's writing in Britain, France, America, Canada, and Scandinavia, de Beauvoir criticizes them for their bourgeois values, remarking that they "exalt the middle-class ideal of well-being and disguise the interests of their class in poetic colors; they orchestrate the grand mystification intended to persuade women to 'stay womanly'" (718). Even the few prominent women novelists remain trapped in their womanhood: "Jane Austen, the Brontë sisters, George Eliot have had to expend so much energy negatively in order to free themselves from outward restraints that they arrive somewhat out of breath at the stage from which masculine writers of great scope take their departure" (718).

Interestingly, Woolf's views, more specifically her essays on Austen, Brontë, and Eliot, as well as *A Room of One's Own,* provide the authority for this particular statement. De Beauvoir, however, expands the argument beyond the attack on the aesthetic limitations of anger, arguing more radically that since women have scarcely attained "the human situation," their works "for the most part lack metaphysical resonances" (*Second Sex* 720). Women's incapacity, their inability to know that "truth is ambiguity, abyss, mystery," derives logically from their present condition as inessential human subjects, conceived only as the Other (718).

Of course, there is an autobiographical dimension both to Woolfs' polemics and to *The Second Sex.* Woolf's address to "the daughters of educated men," for instance, and de Beauvoir's agonized account of the abject intellectual woman expose the constraints placed upon such women in our time (*Second Sex* 689–724). Faced with this problem in the lives of their subjects, biographers make heroines of them. Troubled as she is by the final "unprecedented failure" of Virginia Woolf's "imaginary voyage," Lyndall Gordon, nonetheless, decides to interpret her suicide as an act of daring comparable to Septimus Smith's jump onto the railings below in *Mrs Dalloway* (281). "Virginia Woolf," writes Hermione Lee of Woolf's mental disease, "was a person of exceptional courage, intelligence and stoicism, who made the best use she could, and came to the deepest understanding possible of her condition" (175). If Lee merely implies the heroic quest here, Mary Evans is specific in placing her subject in this mode: "Reading de Beauvoir in the late twentieth century," she remarks, "it is difficult to avoid reading her as a woman writer in the heroic tradition—a person who wished to conquer the world and was able to do so because she found in a male companion the sustaining symbolic presence which made the hero's quest for immortality possible" (85).[4] Toril Moi's version is more tempered, insofar as she recognizes the emotional sacrifices involved in de Beauvoir's existential choices. Yet, while pointing to a masochistic dimension to de Beauvoir's lifelong alliance with Sartre, she nonetheless praises, as exemplary, "her courage, patience and fortitude. Her absolute insistence, in the face of patriarchal prejudice, on her self-evident right to emotional and sexual happiness . . . " (256).[5]

Apart from a tendency to make heroines of the exceptional woman, the belief that resistance or revision is the hallmark of feminist writing is another of our most common "attitudes," and a good deal of Woolf scholarship has been devoted to the search for resistance and disruption. "I want to suggest," wrote Jane Marcus, setting the tone in 1984, "that Virginia Woolf deliberately fashioned for herself a role in which reading, writing and speaking were feminist and radical acts, a role in which she, as novelist and as feminist critic, became her sister's voice, as Procne read the text of Philomel's woven story in the tapestry and spoke for her against the patriarchy" (139). More moderately, Sue Roe argues that "to the extent that Woolf's writing is feminist, it is so because she attempts to re-formulate meaning within fictitious forms" (171).

Recently, Maggie Humm, writing of Strachey and Woolf and of Woolf's productive dialogue with her father's essays, demonstrates a number of subtle shifts away from Stephen's positioning.[6] Even the deconstructive story tells a similar tale of an alternative viewpoint when Rachel Bowlby aims "to show that it is precisely in her insistence on the sexual inflection of all questions of historical understanding and literary representation that Woolf is a feminist writer" (15).

Much writing on de Beauvoir's thought also seeks to place her within a discourse of re-writing or reformulation. An extreme version is to be found in Kate and Edward Fulbrook's *Simone de Beauvoir and Jean Paul Sartre: The Remaking of a Twentieth Century Legend*, where they argue for Beauvoir as an independent philosopher who inspired Sartre rather than the other way around. Michèle Le Doeuff argues in *Hipparchia's Choice* that Beauvoir converts existentialism "into operative philosophy and makes it think above and beyond its means" (115). Eva Lundgren-Gothlin more modestly writes that an analysis of *The Second Sex* "reveals implicit criticism and a transformation of Sartre's ontology and anthropology which makes the conceptual similarity confusing and misleading" (2).

However, even in rewriting, de Beauvoir inevitably remains partially dependent on the models that are her starting point. The consequence can be the repetition of misogynist tendencies. Since, as Lundren-Gothlin observes,

> Both Hegel and Marx saw motherhood, and the activities related to it, as closer to the animal than were the activities of men, and since unfortunately Beauvoir (sic) does not criticize this androcentric view, she is apt to reproduce it. There is a tendency to regard woman as more animal, closer to nature per se, than man, and thus inevitably subordinate in the historical process (81).

It is evident, in fact, that de Beauvoir and her commentators—because of the very nature of the discourse—reproduce an image of men and women as other to one another. Debra Bergoffen, in a recent extended account of de Beauvoir's philosophy, stresses her resistance to the "Hegelian model of recognition" and her debt to Merleau-Ponty in creating her "ethic of the erotic"; but she also puts this ethic in direct contrast to the implicitly male ethic of the earlier thinkers.

The most significant aspect of Bergoffen's account is the prism she uses to argue her case, namely the essentially metaphorical concept of dominant and muted voices where de Beauvoir's rewriting of Hegel and Sartre is presented as the muted voice.[7] It would seem fairly obvious that what is being suggested here is a dialogic quality within the text itself—the dynamic interrelation of the voice of the transcendent human subject with its Other. What is significant is the implicit reintroduction of a gendered dichotomy. Despite the denial of any opposition between the two voices, the very terms dominant and muted immediately remind us of the Ardners' theory of masculine domination in all societies. Consequently, de Beauvoir's dominant voice must inevitably carry all the weight of masculinist or patriarchal thought and thereby her muted feminine voice is disadvantaged, or at least sufficiently veiled to require postfeminist exegesis to bring it out. Even if the ethic of the erotic is not specifically feminine, its elements of generosity, vulnerability and bonding bear feminine connotations. Bergoffen implicitly reproduces what Le Doeuff has described as the conviction in "the social doxa" that there are masculine and feminine "intelligences" which are "radically heterogeneous," and that since feminine difference has "been repressed by modern society," it is "necessary to bring specifically feminine values to light once more" (96).

While, as Le Doeuff suggests, there is a danger that such beliefs may constitute normative models of sexual difference, the feminist project makes little sense if it does not embrace the history of women, and give some credence to the notion of the feminine. In other words Bergoffen's comment— and our reading of it—is a telling example of the dialogics of feminist argument, of the "expression of the utterance being determined by similar utterances on the same topic."

To sum up: if we consider how our own utterances are constrained by the often unspoken assumptions of our discourse, it becomes easier to recognize the intradiegetic nature of our writing. Put more specifically, we are bound to find both a discourse of resistance and one of accommodation at one and the same time in our objects of study; and since both are necessary to the internal as well as to the external debate, they are present in our own writings as well. Ironically enough, then, rather than simply demonstrating the mode of resistance and rewriting that their own polemics would seem to demand, Woolf and de Beauvoir apparently provide us with exemplary cases of the reproduction within discourse of the very patterns that we also critique.

Notes

[1] The actual nature of the private relations of Sartre and de Beauvoir, or de Beauvoir and Algren in contrast to Virginia Woolf's relationship with Leonard is too complex for discussion here. Suffice it to say that the Woolfs' relationship appears to have been an inversion of Sartre and de Beauvoir's with Leonard taking on the kind of practical supportive role played by de Beauvoir.

[2] One of the reasons why the Woolfs' marriage has proved so controversial is presumably that it both endorses and undermines the ideal of heterosexual union. Extreme versions of the use of the plot of victimization are Roger Poole's *The Unknown Virginia Woolf* and Louise DeSalvo's *Virginia Woolf: The Impact of Childhood Sexual Abuse on Her Life and Work*.

[3] There are a number of references to Jane Harrison and although Woolf does indirectly acknowledge her scientific achievement, the humorous account of the distinguished entomologist Miss Ormerod in *The Common Reader*, while it ironically highlights her modesty, is also a reproduction, if playful, of the contempt in which the exceptional woman is held.

[4] Similarly, Carolyn Heilbrun has chosen to see the mode of Woolf's private life as a positive alternative life.

[5] Deirdre Bair also stresses de Beauvoir's indomitable nature and her courageous ability to live her life on her own terms (617-618).

6 Naturally concerned mostly with Woolf's refashioning of a critical stance suited to feminist purposes, Humm does not approach the thorny issue of Woolf's dedication to the contemporary ideal of impersonality, and she attempts to play down what she calls "errors, not so much of judgment but of conservatism" (132). Another critic to investigate the issue of debt and resistance is Perry Meisel in *The Absent Father*.

7 "Discerning the sounds of Beauvoir's (sic) muted voice—the voice that develops the erotic and radical implications of Beauvoir's theses of ambiguity and generosity—I hear the difference between Beauvoir's thought and the thought of Hegel and Sartre, and am struck by the affinity between Beauvoir and Merleau-Ponty. Further, understanding that Beauvoir's muted voice, like her dominant voice, is grounded in the idea of ambiguity, I find that its challenge to the project ethic of transcendence is not an oppositional challenge, but a dynamic one. It is not intended to negate the ethic of the project but to remind us of its limits and dangers" (186).

Works cited

Ardner, Edwin and Shirley. *Perceiving Women*. London: Malaby, 1975.
Bair, Deirdre. *Simone de Beauvoir: A Biography*. London: Cape, 1990.
Bakhtin, Michael. "The Problem of Speech Genres" in *Speech Genres and Other Late Essays*. Trans. Vern W. McGee. Ed. Caryl Emerson and Michael Holquist. Austin: U of Texas P, 1986. 60-102.
Beauvoir, Simone de. *The Second Sex*. 1949. Trans. H. M. Parshley. 1953. Picador Classics. London: Pan Books, 1988.
Bergoffen, Debra. *The Philosophy of Simone De Beauvoir: Gendered Phenomenologies, Erotic Generosities*. New York: State U of New York P, 1997.
Booth, Alison. *Greatness Engendered: George Eliot and Virginia Woolf*. Ithaca and London: Cornell UP, 1992.
Bowlby, Rachel. *Virginia Woolf. Feminist Destinations*. Oxford: Oxford UP, 1988.
Brosnan, Leila. *Reading Virginia Woolf's Essays and Journalism*. Edinburgh: Edinburgh UP, 1997.
DeSalvo, Louise. *Virginia Woolf: The Impact of Childhood Sexual Abuse on Her Life and Work*. Boston: Beacon Press, 1989.
Evans, Mary. *Simone de Beauvoir*. London: Sage Publications, 1996.
Fulbrook, Kate and Edward. *Simone de Beauvoir and Jean Paul Sartre: The Remaking of a Twentieth Century Legend*. New York: Harvester Wheatsheaf, 1993.
Goodman, Liz Beth, ed. *Literature and Gender*. London: The Open UP, 1996.
Heilbrun, Carolyn G. *Writing a Woman's Life*. New York: Ballantine Books, 1988.
Humm, Maggie. *Feminist Criticism: Women as Contemporary Critics*. Brighton: The Harvester Press, 1986.
Le Doeuff, Michèle. *Hipparchia's Choice: An Essay Concerning Women, Philosophy, etc.* trans. Trista Selous. Oxford: Blackwell, 1989. 1990.
Lee, Hermione. *Virginia Woolf*. London. Chatto & Windus, 1996.
Lundgren-Gothlin, Eva. *Sex and Existence: Simone de Beauvoir's 'The Second Sex'*. Hanover & London: U P of New England, 1996.
Marcus, Jane. "Taking the Bull by the Udders: Sexual Difference in Woolf—a Conspiracy Theory." *Virginia Woolf and the Languages of Patriarchy*. Bloomington & Indianapolis: Indiana UP, 1987. 136-162.
Meisel, Perry. *The Absent Father: Virginia Woolf and Walter Pater*. New Haven: Yale UP 1980.
Miller, Nancy K. *Subject to Change: Reading Feminist Writing*. New York: Columbia UP, 1988.

Moi, Toril. *Simone de Beauvoir, The Making of An Intellectual Woman*. Oxford: Basil Blackwell, 1994.
Poole, Roger. *The Unknown Virginia Woolf*. Cambridge: Cambridge UP, 1978.
Roe, Sue. *Writing and Gender: Virginia Woolf's Writing Practice*. Hemel Hempstead: Harvester Wheatsheaf, 1990.
White, Hayden. "The Historical Text as Literary Artifact." *Tropics of Discourse: Essays in Cultural Criticism*. Baltimore & London: Johns Hopkins UP, 1978. 81-100.
Woolf, Virginia. "Lives of the Obscure." *The Common Reader: First Series*. Ed. Andrew McNeillie. New York: Harcourt Brace Jovanovich, 1984.
——. *The Essays of Virginia Woolf*. Vol. 2. Ed. Andrew McNeillie. London: Hogarth Press, 1987.

Mónica Ayuso
Remote Inscriptions: *To the Lighthouse* and *The Waves* in Julieta Campos' Caribbean

Over the decades, the work of Virginia Woolf has been scrutinized by women writers throughout the world. A diverse Spanish-American community of women who wrote in relative isolation until very recently—"with less writerly contact and less of an eventual audience than their male counterparts" (Miller 23)—responded intimately to Woolf's influential voice because she was interpreted as "the woman writer *par excellence*" (Bowlby 12) and "a textual model for women's writing in general and Spanish America in particular" (Chevigny 155). This study concentrates on the record of one such writer, Cuban-born Julieta Campos, as a means of interpreting the impact that Woolf had on one of those who read her work from the periphery, as most Spanish Americans did. Campos did from Mexico, the country where she has resided since 1955. The purpose of this essay is to extend the limits of previous studies—those intuiting, but seldom detailing—the possibility of considering Woolf as a textual model for women who may have read her in English but who wrote in Spanish. In this paper I argue that Campos inscribes Woolf's *The Waves* and *To the Lighthouse* in a literary context peopled by male models of textual authority.

Julieta Campos (b. 1932) has a Ph.D. from the University of Havana and did graduate work in France, where she met her husband, political scientist Enrique González Pedrero. She has had a distinguished career as a prolific writer of fiction, a literary critic, and a translator. Profoundly influenced by the noveau roman, she wrote a number of ambitious novels. With *Tiene los cabellos rojizos y se llama Sabina* (1974)—translated into English as *She Has Reddish Hair and Her Name is Sabina* (1993)—she won the prestigious Xavier Villaurrutia Prize.

Sabina is a novel that defies classification. Most critics agree on little more than its reflexive, fragmentary, and obsessively repetitive nature. The few efforts made to approach this text have been mostly channeled through the French tradition. Hugo Verani recognizes its links with Mauriac's *L'Aggrandisement* and calls it a novel devoid of the specificity given by the anecdotal (145) ; Bruce-Novoa likens its absence of character development and dialogue to Robbe-Grillet. Martha Paley Francescato has rightly pointed out both the inadequacy of critical discourse in tackling it and the defiance the novel evinces against the modernist dictum elaborated by Ortega y Gasset in which novels necessarily belong to one genre like animals to a particular species (161). Debra Castillo has called this novel a "hyper-confused text" (155) while Klarén, Molloy, and Sarlo have described it as "the inner adventure of a search for glimpses of meaning and awareness of the self in memory" (68). Not only are most readings indicative of critical puzzlement at the absence of conventional anecdotal content but also none is able to account for the format of the novel as a whole because any one reading approach seems unable to encompass the whole of *Sabina*.

Clearly, *Sabina* anticipated narrative tactics of the mid-70's later fleshed out by post-structuralist theory. Among these are the disruption of the rules of conventional fictional decorum and crystallization of diverse conceptual shifts in our understanding of representation. Another approach congruous with *Sabina* is found in Bakhtin's theory of language. Campos' propensity for finding musical metaphors to describe the writing endeavor makes her texts a congenial ground for the application of Bakhtin's concept of language as polyphonic. In her metaphorical terms, any novel is a musical composition with variations (*Imagen* 85). She calls the writer "an empty sounding board" on which the magnified echoes of other magnified voices converge (*Sabina* 67); and a "herald" (spokesperson) through whose mouth other voices may be heard. The Spanish term she uses in this last case is "portavoz," literally "he or she who transports the voice." She is likewise aware of the "dialogue"—her choice as it is Bakhtin's (*Imagen* 83)—unavoidably triggered (quite apart from authorial intention) by other utterances articulated within the same genre. Most important, *Sabina* dramatizes ambivalence, especially feminist hyper-anxiety, toward textual authority. In the introduction to the belated English translation, Lelland Chambers hailed this novel as "a feminist work that attempts to dislodge the prevailing masculine logocentrism of our culture" (xv). But it was years ago when Bruce Novoa attempted a description of *Sabina* as "a feminist deconstruction of male logocentrism" that clearly linked Campos with Virginia Woolf (88). As authors and women, both were in marginal positions. Undertaking to write, to speak, and to read against the silencing voice of male writers made their fiction a site where they both faced the omissions and exclusions of the past.

Like so many other Spanish-American women writers in search of models, Campos turned to Woolf and recorded personal, intensely passionate encounters with her writings as a means of relating to realities of oppression which were culturally quite different. In an essay entitled "El universo artístico de Virginia Woolf" (1958), she discussed Woolf's essential themes, those that Campos would incorporate in her own work later on. In another essay entitled "La función de la novela" (1973), she argued for the novel as an integrative form with the function of counteracting the dispersion of the female self—more dangerously acute than that of the male self (140-41). She, like Woolf, queried the understanding of a discrete and autonomous subjectivity and preferred the potentiality of fluctuation over fixity:

> [The] true self [is] neither this nor that, neither here nor there, but something so varied and wandering that it is only when we give the rein to its wishes and let it take its way unimpeded that we are indeed ourselves. Circumstances compel unity; for convenience sake a man must be a whole. The good citizen when he opens his door in the evening must be banker, golfer, husband, father; not a nomad wandering the desert. (*CE*4 161)

In *Sabina*, Campos carries Woolf's modernist ideas to incommensurable extremes and violates all the rules of conventional fictional decorum. She discards "comedy, tragedy, love interest, and. . .air of probability" ("Modern Fiction"*CR*1 153); and abides by Woolf's injunction that absolutely everything is "the proper stuff of fiction, every feeling, every thought; every quality of the brain and spirit. . . . no perception comes amiss" (158). If Woolf's *Mrs. Dalloway* and Joyce's *Ulysses* depict the longest days in English fiction, Campos' *Sabina* comprises the longest minute in Spanish. Campos textualizes Woolf's legendary disruption of the spaces registered by clock time, suspending it during one hyper-extended minute. The reference to markers of chronological time so frequent in Woolf's fiction—the palpability of minutes ticking, of bells chiming, and of the hour striking—is foregone in *Sabina* for an equally reiterative reference to the time of day: four o'clock in the summer afternoon on May 8, 1971. Both writers accomplish the expansion of the moment, otherwise muted and invisible. Woolf fills it with the flood of consciousness and Campos with the flow of a subjectivity made up of texts.

Campos rejects the fixity of plot such as Woolf described it in *A Writer's Diary* so completely that in this novel there is no plot to discuss. Simply stated, the recessive "plot" of this non-narrative narrative consists of the ramblings of a polyphonic, dialogic, disembodied voice, engaged in the recreation of some undefined, but clearly transcendent, vision during which, for a brief moment, everything made sense. Its flow is the more conspicuous by contrast to Sabina's static female body. She stares vacantly towards the ocean off Acapulco on a summer afternoon at the end of a seven-day stay at the beach and the holiday season. In symmetry with her voice/body stands the sea/promontory. Occasionally, the two-hundred-page-long paragraph that quite literally arrests the moment in an effort to capture it makes graphic the extended monologue and provides laconic clues to whatever minimal action there is. One such clue is that Sabina holds a camera in her hand. Its appearance limns solutions to important issues inherent to Sabina. Because its referent is frozen in time, photography instantly places viewers in a reflective mood, requiring them to make a connection between the flow of experience and the image produced by the camera. Also, the camera reproduces mechanically as it fixes reality permanently. Human memory, on the other hand, is selective, and it changes through time. Sabina is ready to use the camera as an expedient means of capturing her vision at first glimpse. But later, she discards this idea, like so many others that she contemplates briefly.

So Woolf's multiple-character flood of consciousness changes into the manifestations of Campos' single-character gendered subjectivity. This subjectivity reveals awareness of the paucity of female systems of representation, the terms of representation themselves being male. An avid reader in at least three languages, Sabina is a labile narrator (who proliferates into numerous narrators) and inserts herself (like Campos) into pre-existing narratives. The novel is a mosaic of canonized male writers. It is as if its voices were evidence of a subjectivity generated not so much by a thinking subject as by prior discourse. This voice swings between a doomed referential function ("every attempt at literary formulation of the adventures of the conscious mind is by its very nature an artifice, as is the fact that any expression of reality through words is a fiction") (79) and an intertextual interference that it cannot escape, and which leads to rambling: "Would you dare describe the Caribbean after Carpentier?" (68).

Would indeed anyone dare, dare to inscribe one's voice in a context so dominated by male models? Campos is aware of the historicity of language, of the fact that it has been inherited from generations of other users. In her essay on de Beauvoir, Campos asserts the existence of a "collective memory," handed down through writing from generation to generation (*Imagen* 123). No matter how hard she researches, topics bear the imprint of previous users. The malleability of language comes down to her severely limited. Granted her case is no different from that of the numerous authors she names in the novel, this text is special in its explicit awareness of this characteristic, made the sharper by the international scope of the text, which spans at least four traditions and languages (French, British, Anglo-American and Spanish-American). In a scene of reading, one of Campos' narrators consults a reference and finds the entry "sea" already rendered in multiple stock metaphors. Among others, the sea as metaphor is:

> a mirror of free man (Baudelaire). . . .an accomplice of human uneasiness (Joseph Conrad). . . .our powerful mother figure (Joyce-Buck Mulligan); sad (Victor Hugo). . . .heartless (Henry Miller); inconsolable (César Vallejo). . . .desolate night sea (Xavier Villaurrutia). . . .a source of temptation. (168-9)

Conspicuously, those quoted are male. The omission of Woolf, in whose fiction the sea is ubiquitous, is quite significant for any avid reader of the British writer. So this proliferation of narrators writes Woolf into the tradition by inscribing her novels in *Sabina*.

Sabina recalls themes from Woolf's *The Waves* and *To the Lighthouse*. The obvious ones are the seascape, the holiday, and the descriptions thereof; the de-emphasis of plot, outward occurrence and character; and the fragmented, obsessively repetitive nature of the narrative. Integral to the plot of all three, the sea is in dynamic relation with the mainland. The two are poles across which oscillate two alternative currents, whipping back and forth: fluidity and constraint. Also, the sea harbors in itself another bipolar set of values: life and death (*Sabina* 71). In counterpoint to the rhythmic rolling of the water, representing a life-affirming movement, is a darker movement, the undertow, that makes the sea a harbinger of death. In *The Waves*, the corrosion of life is inscribed in the images of decay: "rotten apples" (236); "gusts of dead smells;" (74); "matter oozing" (75); in *Sabina*, in the references to destruction and insidious malaise: cancer, cholera, pneumonia and madness. Finally, in neither work is time a fixed entity. What Campos says of Woolf's use of time as flux is also true of her own. The flow that the two try to capture paradoxically contains both the essence of life and the seed of death ("El universo artístico de Virginia Woolf" 21).

In *Sabina*, Campos pits, among many others, Woolf against Borges as models of textual authority (44). The unexpected assertion that Borges does not like Woolf—somewhat hard to explain especially in view of his anglophilic taste and the successful undertaking of the translations into Spanish of *A Room of One's Own* and *Orlando* for *Sur* in the mid-thirties—is not delivered by this text. The reader needs to intervene actively to make sense of it; (s)he needs to be sufficiently informed to speculate on this vexing assertion. Its cryptic, puzzling nature is in keeping with the mode of a text in which "meaning" appears briefly only to slip and fail.

At the intertextual level, the assertion is justified since Borges lambastes novelists who uphold the tenets of the "psychological" novel, Woolf's specialty. Such a form, he states in the prologue to *The Invention of Morel*, "Would have us forget that it is verbal artifice." At the opposite end of the spectrum is detective fiction. This genre appealed to him because it afforded "the classic virtues of a beginning, a middle, and an end—of something planned and executed" (5-6).

The assertion that Borges does not like Woolf can also be explained by the fact that Borges' postmodern denial of individual agency opposes the relational, socially-developed self exemplified in the work of the British writer, which is closer to that of *Sabina*. In other words, both adhere to a model of feminine subjectivity that is open, dispersed; its ego boundaries are so relaxed that they expand to merge with what is outside. Mrs. Ramsay is a good example of the process of becoming one with the world. When, after a hectic day, she retires to be alone—with some knitting or sewing still to do—she watches the three strokes until she and the light become one:

> The long steady stroke, for watching them in this mood always at this hour one could not help attaching oneself to one thing especially of the things one saw; and this thing, the long steady stroke, was her stroke. . . .she became the thing she looked at—that light for example. (73)

In *Sabina*, the narrator is as absorbed with the marine surroundings as Mrs. Ramsay is: "A few minutes more and I will cease to see that light which dazes me in order to become that light, to turn incandescent" (34). Later the narrator is invaded by an urge to incorporate herself with other beloved surroundings. The interesting play of reflexives in the Spanish original emphasizes the shifting nature of subject and object identities. Personal identity surrenders to a fusion with nature that poses no threat:

> The sea undulates and murmurs. . . .She imagines freedom, openness, and flight. One imagines oneself an object obsessively caressed by its gaze, looked at by the sea. . . . One imagines oneself the sea. I, myself, the sea.

And earlier, "The balcony, the promontory, and I are a single entity" (26). In both writers, the oceanic flux seems to be an especially suitable landscape to mirror the expansion of the self. The most conspicuous are the narrator's shifts between the self and the characters she is creating. There is also a dispersion mirrored in the flow of words, never reaching a climactic end, toward which it might seem to be moving.

The here and the now are essential to Sabina because, as Campos maintains in *La imagen en el espejo*, the present is all that matters (*Imagen* 79). Meaning in this novel seems in the process of being formed, and textual authority is caught in the act of "composing" its own image; subjectivity is never reified and fixed. I believe Sabina's affirmation is to propose a plumb to the depths of the literary past, not to preserve it the way it was but to break clear from it. This means that the past can be both preserved and cancelled at the same time. In descriptive language, this Cuban/Mexican writer bears the burden of a context, the Caribbean, preempted by the lingering echoes of male precursors. Like Bathsheba in *Far from the Madding Crowd*, Sabina says, again and again, "I have the feelings of a woman but I have only the language of men" (quoted in "Men and Women" 67). This statement expresses what could potentially be a real impasse. But the narrators do not become tongue-tied nor give up the Caribbean. They plunder female archives and inscribe one of the omitted—Woolf—in whom marine renditions are so prevalent. So these responses add themselves to the existing layers of interpretation. They establish a dialogue with the literary past; they subvert objectionable conventions installed in the past; otherwise, they let them stand. To the troubling question, "Do you dare describe the Caribbean after Carpentier?" they are now equipped to respond: "I would not dare. I would not dare even try. I would have to describe it, unfortunately, as one describes a state of mind" (68). And that is precisely what Campos does.

Works Cited

Borges, Jorge L. Prologue. *The Invention of Morel and Other Stories*. By Adolfo B. Casares. Trans. Ruth L. S. Simms. Austin: UT, 1986. 5-7.

Bowlby, Rachel. *Virginia Woolf*. Harlow: Longman Group Ltd., 1992.

Bruce-Novoa, Juan. "La Sabina de Julieta Campos en el laberinto de la intertextualidad." *La sartén por el mango*. Ed. Patricia González y Eliana Ortega. Río Piedras: Ediciones Huracán, 1982.

Campos, Julieta. "El universo artístico de Virginia Woolf." *La imagen en el espejo*. Ciudad de Mexico: Universidad Autónoma de Mexico, 1965. 11-22.

———. *Función de la novela*. Cuidad de Mexico: Joaquin Mortiz, 1973. 11-157.

———. *Tiene los cabellos rojizos y se llama Sabina*. Joaquin Mortiz: Nueva Narrativa Hispánica, 1974.

Castillo, Debra A. *Talking Back: Toward a Latin American Feminist Literary Criticism*. Ithaca: Cornell UP: 1992.

Castro-Klarén, Sara, Sylvia Molloy and Beatriz Sarlo, eds. *Women's Writing in Latin America: An Anthology*. Boulder: Westview Press, 1991.

Chambers, Lelland. "Introduction." *She Has Reddish Hair and Her Name is Sabina*. By Julieta Campos. Athens: U of Georgia P, 1993.

Chevigny, Bell Gale. *Reinventing the Americas: Comparative Studies of Literature of the United States and Spanish America*. Ed. Gale Chevigny and Gari Laguardia. Cambridge: Cambridge UP, 1986.

Francescato, Martha Paley. "Un desafío a la crítica literaria: *Tiene los cabellos rojizos y se llama Sabina* de Julieta Campos." *Revista de Crítica Latinoamericana*, 7.13 (1981): 121-125.

Miller, Beth. *Mujeres en la literatura*. Mexico: Fleischer Editora, S. A., 1978.

Ortega y Gasset, José. *The Dehumanization of Art, Culture and Literature*. Trans. Helene Weyl. Princeton: Princeton UP, 1968.

Verani, Hugo. "Julieta Campos y la novela del lenguaje." *Teatro Crítico* 2.5 (1975): 132-149.

Woolf, Virginia. "Men and Women." *Women and Writing*. Ed. Michèle Barrett. New York: Harcourt Brace Jovanovich, 1979. 64-67.

———."Modern Fiction." *The Common Reader. First Series*, 1925. New York: HBJ, 1953. 150-158.

———. *Mrs. Dalloway*. 1925. New York: HBJ, 1990.

———. *The Waves*. 1931. Harcourt Brace & Co., 1931.

———. *To the Lighthouse*. 1927. Harcourt Brace & Co., 1927.

New Applications of Queer Theory

Judith Roof
Hocus Crocus

"Then, for a moment, she had seen an illumination; a match burning in a crocus; an inner meaning almost expressed" (32). Mrs. Dalloway's "illumination" has hovered for years in and around the insights of Woolf scholars trying to locate and decode the lesbian sexuality—one of the "inner meanings"—Woolf's texts express. Since Jeannette Foster's pioneering exhumation of the passage as an unmistakable moment of lesbian consciousness, attempts to illuminate the lesbian and the problem of "almost" expressing her have become the two most prominent strains of critical work around issues of sexuality in Woolf's oeuvre. I want to come back to the match and the crocus, not to rehash the many figural and (c)literal interpretations that have produced the astounding body of scholarship locating lesbian sexuality in Woolf's texts, but rather to see what critical assumptions Woolf scholars have adopted to investigate sexuality, and what other ways we might think about the relations between sexuality and textuality in Woolf's writing.

Looking for the lesbian in Woolf's work has for the most part been just that: looking for the lesbian and employing the fact of her presence as one key to interpreting Woolf's fiction. Excavating repressed and masked sexualities has a strategic urgency in an 80s and 90s politics where visibility is paramount; discerning the lesbian is undeniably a crucial first step in attempts to understand the functions of sexuality in Woolf's work. Woolf's critics disinter the lesbian by means of three inter-related and often combined modes of interpretation: 1) psycho-biography which draws evidence from Woolf's life, letters, and diaries to discern and elucidate lesbian moments in her texts; 2) historical materialism which posits contemporaneous social conditions as both the referents and the rationale for the ways Woolf represents sexuality; and 3) encodement theories which, assuming the historical repression of lesbian sexuality, work to decode what they perceive as masked lesbian representations.[1]

These three approaches rely upon the same set of critical assumptions about the relations between author and text, and between sexuality and representation. This critical uniformity may exist because the essayists all draw from one or more of the same few critical ur-texts: Blanche Wiesen Cook's "Women Alone Stir my Imagination," published in *Signs* in 1979, several of Bonnie Zimmerman's essays from the 1980s, Jane Marcus's examinations of Woolf's understandings of patriarchy and her formulation of "saphhistry," Marilyn Farwell's conception of lesbian narrative, and Catherine Stimpson's theory of encodement in "Zero Degree Deviancy."[2] The work of these five critics is complex, sophisticated, and central to studies of women and modernism, but all depend upon the same several assumptions about the character of lesbian sexuality and the relations between sexuality and textuality. The most basic assumption is that there is such a creature as a lesbian and we know what that is, an assumption that exists in contradistinction to contemporaneous lesbian theory which struggled continually with understandings of what lesbian sexuality might be and how it relates to larger systems of gender, power, and representation.[3] Jeannette Foster certainly assumed there were clearly-definable lesbians in 1956, and that presumption still weaves through the majority of the essays on lesbians in Woolf, but most notably through work theorizing encodement. Decoding what is perceived as encoded depends upon a belief in the hidden presence of a pre-existent lesbian content that must be unmasked; the ability to decode depends on knowing what we are looking for.[4] The issues of what might constitute a lesbian and the differences that exist among lesbians rarely arise, even if such differences might in fact operate in Woolf's texts.

Often accompanying this lesbian certitude is the idea that lesbian constitutes an identity rather than a desire or a structural position co-existing with other, even contradictory desires and positions. A noun rather than an adjective, the term "lesbian" is plagued with immanence; it is distinguished by lesbians' desire for sameness rather than difference, at least according to Marilyn Farwell, whose essay, "Heterosexual Plots and Lesbian Subtexts," governs most considerations of narrative in Woolf's treatments of lesbian sexuality.[5] Understanding the lesbian as engaged in a dynamic of sameness does link the lesbian figure to the gender homogeny perceived to constitute the larger community of women; the lesbian becomes a synecdoche of this continuum in a perverse reversal of Adrienne Rich's "lesbian continuum" (648). (Rich's continuum makes all women lesbian in an attempt to dismantle lesbophobia; it does not suggest that lesbians represent all women. Rich's strategy does not work in reverse). The slippage present in some Woolf criticism—most notably in Jane Marcus's sapphistries—between lesbian and female desire is a symptom of the lesbian's function as representative of the continuum, of what Marcus calls "the double difference within difference," and of a tendency to erase lesbian desire (whatever that may be) just when one thinks one is talking about it ("Saphhistory" 174).

Another assumption of this critical tradition is that identity (and sexuality) must be expressed in art; creative production is in thrall to—and according to some, is determined by—the author's biography and psychology. If the author is a lesbian, then her literary works must express lesbianism in some way. Related to this is the assumption that artistic endeavors of necessity reflect the social, historical, and literary contexts in which they are created and that understanding these contexts provides valuable insight into the workings of texts. Even when the author plays with history, as Woolf does in *Orlando*, the assumption is that this playing is made necessary by an oppressive culture that restricts Woolf's free expression of her biographical truth—her love for Vita Sackville-West. Assumptions about the relation between author and text, thus, are that the text exists in a one-to-one relation to the author whose life to a large degree defines her work, and those things her life can't resolve Bloomsbury, World War I, sexology, and intertextuality can. In other words, art is perceived as a transformation of material fact.

In this historical, biographical, material framework, the lesbian as excavated in Woolf's texts tends to fulfill two functions: 1) it emblemizes fruitful relations among women as an alternative to patriarchy; and 2) it represents the rupture or subversion of patriarchy. As Jane Marcus demonstrates in *Virginia Woolf and the Languages of Patriarchy* (1987), Woolf's texts are often a sharp critique of the ubiquitous oppressive power of patriarchy. As Woolf herself eloquently argues, the gender disparities of patriarchy silence women and relegate them to the position of second class citizens whose role is to mirror man. Focused on men and on women's presumed need for men, patriarchy thus excludes the lesbian whose independence and strength put the lie both to assumptions about gender inequality and the necessity of heterosexuality. A seeming anomaly, the lesbian turns what appears to be oppression into victory, making relations with women a positive virtue and a viable alternative. Shari Benstock, Marcus, Jessica Tvordi, Donna Risolo, Toni McNaron, Jane Lilienfeld, Janet Winston, Corinne Blackmer, Tuzyline Allan, and others link the lesbian figure to the larger community of women. This community enables women's connections with one another through the provision of saphhified opportunities for identification: through the seductions of reading (comprised of the seductions of identification), the shared codes of counter-patriarchy (identification through experience), or the projects of recovering women's lives (identification through history). The direction of this criticism is almost uniformly gyre-like, not opening out but narrowing in to the specifics, the details, the facts, the identity increasingly isolated from the play of signifiers around them. Some critics laudably have gestured towards a historical understanding of the inter-relatedness of various gendered and sexual positions within the texts: Marcus, Pamela Olano, Eileen Barrett, and David Eberly introduce the problem of how to understand the relations among lesbian sexuality and the male homosexuality that infused Bloomsbury and provide possible readings of the connections between lesbian and gay male characters in *Mrs. Dalloway* and

The Waves. I want to return to this inclusive gesture in a moment as a way to reread the match in the crocus.

A significant number of the essays characterize the lesbian figure as subversive, resistant, a rupture, and even, in an extreme moment, as the structure of the unconscious. Shari Benstock sees Woolf's "sapphic" texts as interruptions within Woolf's own oeuvre (191), while Olano, Tvordi, Farwell, Patricia Juliana Smith, and Ruth Vanita see the lesbian as subversive. Following Bonnie Zimmerman, Diana Swanson situates this subversive lesbian within an intriguing binary map of what she calls "the current critical debate over the definition of 'lesbian': on the one hand, the lesbian theorized as outlaw and transgressor, and on the other hand, the lesbian theorized as inevitably a part of, or situated within, patriarchal discourse and the institution of heterosexuality"(39). Swanson ends this long-overdue acknowledgment of the "current" discussion (in 1994 when Swanson gave her paper this discussion had been going on since the early 1980s [6]) with Bonnie Zimmerman's formulation of "both/and" which situates insideness and outsideness as inter-related virtues, the former enabling lesbian critique of patriarchy, the latter grounding her separate identity. In a gesture that makes quite visible another critical map, Swanson adds in a footnote that Zimmerman aligns Elizabeth Meese, Farwell, Judith Fetterley, and Monique Wittig among the outsiders, and Meese (again) and Diana Fuss among the insiders.

The critical split mapped by Swanson, which seems to occur somewhere down the middle of Meese, is in fact the very essence of a way of thinking about criticism as a them/us endeavor. This has possibly impoverished lesbian studies of Woolf as those studies fairly consistently align themselves with the "outsiders," not so much because they are outside, but because those same critics (with the exception of Wittig, whose analysis of the outside position of the lesbian rests on very different reasoning than Farwell and Fetterley) also belong to a tradition of essentialized understandings of lesbian identity, the transparency of texts, and the certainties of history. In other words, the split is one between literary historical scholarship that imagines that reality precedes discourse and that accepts without critical examination cultural configurations of lesbian sexuality (i.e., sameness, subversive, outside) and structuralist/post-structuralist critics who think that discourse shapes reality and who are more interested in the problems of representation and the status of the text. The split here masks a battle in which the "insiders" (what is in the tradition of some feminist thought identified as male or "theoretical") bring into question the assumptions of the "outsiders" (the women in their struggle against patriarchy). In stalwartly remaining insular outsiders, Woolf scholars tend to eschew the insights of post-structuralism.

The symptom of this critical bifurcation is the surprising absence of most deconstructive, psychoanalytic, or post-structuralist lesbian theory which probably represents more the mainstream of lesbian studies from the late-1980s through the 90s.[7] The formulations of Meese, Judith Butler, Teresa de Lauretis,

New Applications of Queer Theory

Fuss, Renée Hoogland, Terry Castle (who would hate to be called a theorist), and even me are pretty much absent from the bibliographies of the 30+ essays I read that were published after the advent of *Gender Trouble* (1991) and *(Sem)Erotics* (1992). While one might normally assume that if someone is going to look at representations of lesbian sexuality they might want to be conversant with the major ideas and theories about lesbianism, part of this absence could be simply a question of discipline. In an overwhelming plethora of publications, scholars tend to read the materials that seem most directly related to their work, in this case a tradition of feminist literary critics of modernism who seem focused on individual authors. But it might also represent a particular ideological bent that prefers for both political and aesthetic reasons to understand lesbian sexuality as a concrete and provable presence. Part of this may be linked to the exigencies of a liberationist politics that depends to a large extent on visibility. Part may also relate to the aesthetics of a 1970s womanist feminism that wants to believe in the positive power of women emancipated from patriarchy. In any case, one telling symptom of the critical direction of lesbian studies in Woolf is the total absence of any mention of Michel Foucault, whose understandings of the relations among sexualities and discursive formations would seem to be useful in conceiving the functions of sexuality in modernism.

For the remainder of this paper, I'm going to take the "inside" tack even though I'm an outsider (while Woolf critics who are insiders take the outside tack), and assume that the lesbian is an intrinsic and necessary part of the sexual system we call heterosexuality and the gender/power system we call patriarchy.[8] Apart from heterosexuality and a system of binary gender, lesbianism has no meaning as such. The question here is not how heterosexuality oppresses lesbians, but rather how lesbian sexuality inflects the heterosexual, what functions it has in the complex problems of representation, power, cultural anxiety, and aesthetics.

Upon returning from her excursion to buy flowers, Mrs. Dalloway mounts the stairs ruminating about that "something central" she seems to lack (31). Thinking of her room and its association with her various failures, Clarissa comes, via a list of elements which are *not* what she lacks, to the acknowledgment that while she cannot conceive of heterosexual passion, she can "dimly perceive" women together (31). She is attracted, she insists, to "a woman," and not "a girl," "confessing" (32). The distinction between woman and girl is important, not as an assurance of sameness but as a reflection of the power disparity upon which Clarissa builds an erotic wherein she "yields" to "the charm" of a woman who first subordinates herself to Clarissa by confessing "some scrape, some folly" (32). Clarissa's dynamic of seduction involves first being placed in a position of power by an equal, then yielding to the weaker party. In this drama Clarissa "did undoubtedly then feel what men felt," not only because of an understanding of lesbian desire as simple inversion, but also because of the power dynamic already established where Clarissa assumes the position of the one with power (32). Her heady second of dominance "was enough" she says for a "sudden revelation," insight mingled with arousal which takes over, "gushing and pouring" over the "cracks and sores" (32). The passage's climax, this "illumination; a match burning in a crocus; an inner meaning almost expressed" is more than thinly-veiled clitoral imagery or an acknowledgment of lesbian desire. It already engages the complex relations among power, gender, and knowledge that constitute one version of same-sex desire.

Her love for Sally Seton whose wrapped diamond kiss was "the most exquisite moment of her whole life" is another version that appears later in the same passage, linked to the match in the crocus by the bridge of what Clarissa calls "this question of love" (35, 32). Where in the first case Clarissa responds erotically to women who put her in a position of power, she admires Sally to whom she subordinates herself and whom she strives to emulate. The "infinitely precious" quickly interrupted moment with the charismatic Sally provides almost a "religious feeling" as it radiates, a "disinterested" generosity "not like one's feeling for a man," characterized by the sustained but fleeting joy that Sally "is beneath this roof"(35, 36, 34). Billowing outward in their energy, Clarissa's feelings for Sally are very different from the staid, almost cloistered scene of confession. Both versions of lesbian desire are, however, different from and in contrast to Clarissa's other connections in the novel (those with her husband, her daughter, her maids, Miss Kilman, Peter, Dr. Bradshaw, the stranger Septimus, and the woman across the way into whose window she gazes), and the novel's many versions of desire (Dalloway, Hugh Whitbread who dances attendance on the invalid Evelyn, the Bradshaws, Septimus and Rezia, mid-life crisis Peter and Daisy, the inter-species love of Elizabeth and Clarissa for dogs, Miss Kilman's religious sublimations, Peter's narcissism, and Septimus's tragic, arguably homosexual attachment to Evans).[9]

Within this range of gendered, species, and sexual relations, the differences between Clarissa's two versions of lesbian desire are significant. That they occur in the same extended passage is not simply a matter of their thematic affinity; rather, it signals a difference made through a deliberate contrast that illuminates not only different lesbian desires as they co-exist in one person, but also the different contexts within which these desires arise. While in the earlier passage Clarissa's solitary ruminations butt up against those signifiers of celibacy and lack that began her contemplations—her narrow bed and half-burnt candle—Sally's kiss, that exemplum of love, occurs in the context of a garden stroll with Peter and old Joseph Breitkopf and is interrupted by Peter's jealous hostility, "like running one's face against a granite wall in the darkness!"(36). The contrast between Clarissa's rapturous insight and the narrow bed in the first passage situates her desire for the confessing woman as involuntary, something "she could not resist," that though in opposition to her empty bed and half-burnt candle also bespeaks the virginal quality of those who do not act on desire, or whose yielding is a species of acquiescence (31-32). Her receptiveness to Sally in the blooming garden on the other hand is entirely voluntary and sought. The former desires arise in the company of women; the latter in a familial context. The former are more cerebral; the latter more the effects of sustained courtship. The former are present; the latter "meant absolutely nothing to her now" (34).

The difference here is not just that one is a predilection, the other true love, or differences in age, experience, and social position, but rather is linked (textually and emotionally) to Clarissa's perceptions of her life's course, her feeling of diminishment and narrowing. In this sense Clarissa's complex sexuality signifies not a quintessential sexual identity, but serves as one of the several motifs that measure her vitality and insight. The link between sexual desire and life is reiterated in the similarities between Clarissa's metaphor of "running one's face against a granite wall" when Peter interrupts and her empathetic imaging of Septimus's death: "up had flashed the ground; through him, blundering, bruising, went the rusty spikes" (184). And in her comparison of Septimus's experience with her own in the paragraph that immediately follows, Clarissa contrasts Septimus who "had flung it away" with "They (all day she had been thinking of Bourton, of Peter, of Sally), they would grow old" (184). As she thinks about Septimus and watches the old lady go to bed alone while Peter and Sally are downstairs awaiting her, Clarissa is conscious of the clash of these different modes of existing and dying and her place within them, fearing no more the heat of the sun. Clarissa's lucid moments of desire just evade being lucid moments of insight; only death completes the circuit and makes insight available.

The connections among sexual desire, life, and death as well as among various configurations of gender/power/desire manifested throughout *Mrs. Dalloway* provide an outline of the discursive formation underwriting modernism. While this is a very textual example, it is an exercise of Foucault's idea of a discursive formation that reads multiple regimes as they cooperate and collide. It is informed as well by a more flexible notion of sexualities which focuses on the way sexualities arise from and in turn inform other categories of activity and signification.[10] In *Mrs. Dalloway* multiple and variable sexualities exist in figurative relations to life, death, and failures to signify even as those failures—those "inner moments almost expressed"—perform the very relations and desires they say they cannot express. The "inner meaning almost expressed" is in fact expressed. The paradox of this performance of communicating both the desires and the failure through a statement of failure is an essence of a modernism that seduces through the indirection that is produced, again paradoxically, by subjective mimesis. For modernism says what it wants to say at the very moment it fails to say it, produces desire through the metaphors that supplant it, enacts consciousness unconsciously (and vice versa), and is most experimental when it doesn't try. While it is a huge jump to leap from *Mrs. Dalloway*'s complex system of sex/life/death to modernism's discursive paradoxes, I want to suggest that they belong to the same impetus, embody the same contradictions, and have as their stake the same questions of vitality and meaning inextricably linked to a very complex landscape of sexual desires that are no longer contained within their categories. In this failure of boundary—or success at interconnection—modernists perform what only post-structuralists can perceive; in this modernism is ahead of its time. And Woolf's match burning in a crocus is not only an emblem of genital fire and lesbian desire, a canny rendering of the seductive indirection, holding back, and flirtation that characterize desire, but is also an Olympian flame of modernism itself.

Notes

1. I speak of general trends which represent the majority of essays on Woolf and lesbian sexuality. Given the constraints of time, I am not able to map also the unique contribution each of the essays makes.
2. These five authors function as the founding "mothers" of this criticism. All except Zimmerman are more firmly grounded in modernism or women's writing than they are in lesbian theory. My sense of their centrality is based both on the number of times they are cited and the propositions for which they are cited.
3. From the mid-80s until the mid-90s, such critics and theorists as Judith Butler, Teresa de Lauretis, Elizabeth Meese, Diana Fuss, Biddy Martin, Elizabeth Grosz, Sue-Ellen Case, Terry Castle, Renée Hoogland, Annamarie Jagose, Sally Munt and others worked on showing the political and social stakes of the sexual system, the instability of both heterosexual and patriarchal formations, and the ways in which the lesbian functions as a figure. In some ways this work would seem to be questioning some of the premises of more traditional author-centered feminist literary criticism.
4. For a more developed critique of encodement theory, see my *A Lure of Knowledge*.
5. Farwell's surprising acquiescence to the cultural stereotype of the lesbian as having no difference surpasses even Freud who was loathe to make an easy equation between lesbian sexuality and sameness and/or narcissism.
6. In her often reprinted early 80s essay "What Has Never Been: An Overview of Lesbian Feminist Criticism," Bonnie Zimmerman raises the problem of definition as one that leads to some of the same problematic critical assumptions that I have identified in this essay and that arise in articles written after Zimmerman's landmark piece. If some of the readers of Woolf's lesbian representations employ this essay, they must be ignoring some of it. This suggests that there is something else at stake—identity, self-affirmation—in some literary criticism.
7. By mainstream I am referring to work read by academics generally interested in ideas about lesbian sexuality.
8. For this proposition I'll cite briefly Butler's *Gender Trouble*, de Lauretis's *The Practice of Love*, Foucault's *History of Sexuality*, and my own *A Lure of Knowledge*.
9. In "Unmasking Lesbian Passion: The Inverted World of *Mrs. Dalloway*," Eileen Barrett shows the variety of lesbian relations as well as the ways Septimus and Clarissa are connected and their relations to the novel's various versions of heterosexuality.
10. Some work centered around gay male sexuality has recently taken a more poststructuralist perspective, but gay male and lesbian sexualities represent very different cultural configurations and critical histories. See for example, Joseph Boone's *Libidinal Currents: Sexuality and the Shaping of Modernism*

Works Cited

Allan, Tuzyline. "The Death of Sex and the Soul in *Mrs. Dalloway* and Nella Larsen's *Passing*." *Virginia Woolf: Lesbian Readings*. 95-113.

Barrett, Eileen. "Unmasking Lesbian Passion: The Inverted World of *Mrs. Dalloway*." *Virginia Woolf: Lesbian Readings*. 146-164.

Barrett, Eileen and Patricia Cramer, eds. *Virginia Woolf: Lesbian Readings*. NY: NY UP, 1997.

——. *Re: Reading, Re: Writing, Re: Teaching Virginia Woolf: Selected Papers from the Fourth Annual Conference on Virginia Woolf*. NY: Pace UP, 1995.

Benstock, Shari. "Expatriate Sapphic Modernism: Entering Literary History." *Lesbian Texts and Contexts*. 183-203.

Blackmer, Corinne. "Lesbian Modernism in the Shorter Fiction of Virginia Woolf and Gertrude Stein." *Virginia Woolf: Lesbian Readings*. 78-94.

Boone, Joseph. *Libidinal Currents: Sexuality and the Shaping of Modernism*. Chicago: U of Chicago P, 1998.

Butler, Judith. *Gender Trouble*. New York: Routledge, 1990.

Cook, Blanche Wiesen. "'Women Alone Stir My Imagination': Lesbianism and the Cultural Tradition." *Signs* 4 (1979): 718-739.

Cramer, Patricia. "Notes From Underground: Lesbian Ritual in the Writings of Virginia Woolf." *Virginia Woolf Miscellanies*. 177-188.

Eberly, David. "Talking It All Out: Homosexual Disclosure in Woolf." *Virginia Woolf: Themes and Variations*. 128-134.

Farwell, Marilyn. "Heterosexual Plots and Lesbian Subtexts: Toward a Theory of Lesbian Narrative Space." *Lesbian Texts and Contexts*. Ed. Karla Jay and Joanne Glasgow. NY: NY UP, 1990. 91-103.

Foster, Jeannette. *Sex Variant Women in Literature*. Tallahassee: The Naiad Press, 1985.

Hussey, Mark and Vara Neverow-Turk, eds. *Virginia Woolf Miscellanies*. NY: Pace UP, 1992.

de Lauretis, Teresa. *The Practice of Love: Lesbian Sexuality and Perverse Desire*. Bloomington: Indiana UP, 1994.

Lilienfeld, Jane. "'The Gift of a China Inkpot': Violet Dickinson, Virginia Woolf, Elizabeth Gaskell, Charlotte Brontë, and the Love of Women in Writing." *Virginia Woolf: Lesbian Readings*. 37-56.

Marcus, Jane. *Virginia Woolf and the Languages of Patriarchy*. Bloomington: Indiana UP, 1987.

——. "Sapphistory: The Woolf and The Well." *Lesbian Texts and Contexts*. 164-179.

McNaron, Toni. "'The Albanians, or was it the Armenians?': Virginia Woolf's Lesbianism as Gloss on her Modernism." *Virginia Woolf: Themes and Variations*. 134-141.

Meese, Elizabeth. *(Sem)Erotics: Theorizing Lesbian Writing*. NY: NY UP, 1992.

Neverow-Turk, Vara and Mark Hussey, eds. *Virginia Woolf: Themes and Variations*. NY: Pace UP, 1993.

Olano, Pamela. "'Women alone stir my imagination': Reading Virginia Woolf as a Lesbian." *Virginia Woolf: Themes and Variations*. 158-171.

Rich, Adrienne, "Compulsory Heterosexuality and Lesbian Existence." *Signs* 5 (1980): 631-660.

Risolo, Donna. "Outing Mrs. Ramsay: Reading the Lesbian Subtext in Virginia Woolf's *To the Lighthouse*." *Virginia Woolf: Themes and Variations*. 238-248.

Roof, Judith. *A Lure of Knowledge: Lesbian Sexuality and Theory*. NY: Columbia UP, 1991.

Smith, Patricia Juliana. "'The Things People Don't Say': Lesbian Panic in *The Voyage Out*." *Virginia Woolf: Lesbian Readings*. 128-145.

Stimpson, Catherine. "Zero Degree Deviancy: The Lesbian Novel in English."

Feminisms: An Anthology of Literary Theory and Criticism. Ed. Robyn Warhol and Diane Price Herndl. New Brunswick: Rutgers UP, 1991. 301-15.

Swanson, Diana. "The Lesbian Feminism of Woolf's *To the Lighthouse.*" *Re: Reading, Re: Writing, Re: Teaching Virginia Woolf.* 38-44.

Tvordi, Jessica. "*The Voyage Out*: Virginia Woolf's First Lesbian Novel." *Virginia Woolf: Themes and Variations.* 226-237.

Vanita, Ruth. "'Love Unspeakable': The Uses of Allusion in *Flush.*" *Virginia Woolf: Themes and Variations.* 248-257.

——. "'Throwing Caution to the Winds': Homoerotic Patterns in *The Waves.*" *Re: Reading, Re: Writing, Re: Teaching Virginia Woolf.* 299-304.

Winston, Janet. "Reading Influences: Homoeroticism and Mentoring in Katherine Mansfield's 'Carnation' and Virginia Woolf's *Moments of Being*: "Slater's Pins Have No Points"'. *Virginia Woolf: Lesbian Readings.* 57-77.

Woolf, Virginia. *Mrs. Dalloway.* New York: Harcourt Brace Jovanovich, 1981.

——. *Orlando.* New York: Harcourt Brace Jovanovich, 1928.

Zimmerman, Bonnie. "What Has Never Been: An Overview of Lesbian Feminist Literary Criticism." *The New Feminist Criticism: Essays on Women, Literature, Theory.* Ed. Elaine Showalter. New York: Pantheon, 1985. 200-224.

——. "Lesbians Like This and That: Some Notes on Lesbian Criticism for the Nineties." *New Lesbian Criticism.* Ed. Sally Munt. NY: Columbia UP, 1992. 1-16.

Troy Gordon
The Place of Cross-Sex Friendship in Woolf Studies

"The friendship between a man and woman," Carolyn Heilbrun observed in 1973 in her literary study of androgyny, "is one of the most unexplored of all human experiences" (100). More recently Terry Castle argued in her book on Radclyffe Hall and Noël Coward that "cross-sex friendship may indeed be one of the most productive models we have for thinking about a nonpatriarchal world of social relations" (109). Heady claims: "one of the most unexplored ... experiences" and "one of the most productive models." Such a rhetoric of superlatives asserts that the critical examination of cross-sex friendship is not only possible, but also imperative.

Yet the topic also seems resistant to exploration, as indicated by the relative paucity of work, not to mention the quarter-century gap between Heilbrun's and Castle's isolated comments, 1973 to 1996.[1] Perhaps that's because common wisdom, even through three decades of feminist, lesbian and gay movements, continues to claim that men and women can *never* be *just* friends. In popular culture lately, gay men are finally coming out as a straight woman's best friend—that is, if he is cute, compassionate yet funny, generally asexual yet full of advice about romance, like some strange 1990s incarnation of a black mammy figure.[2] We are only now beginning to talk about nonsexual friendships across sex, even though such relationships are common in many people's social lives, common also in twentieth-century fiction. Heterosexual romance has been rife with 'answers' to the following question: what does it mean to desire or to like someone whose sex differs from one's own? But what if one takes away the element of sexual attraction and asks the question again: what does it mean to desire or to like someone whose sex differs from one's own? It stops one short to realize how much there is still to say about those ways of desiring and liking.

Building on feminist work, lesbian and gay studies has made addressing this question more possible, in large part by making nonheterosexual subjectivities and desires more visible. So far, however, we have no single theoretical apparatus within which we can place the study of cross-sex friendship. The most promising seems to be the area of queer theory, where friendships between men (mostly gay) and women (mostly straight) are beginning to get some attention. Queer theory may be well suited because of its denaturalizing of identity based on the trope of 'crossing'—crossing gender, crossing race, crossing sexuality (Prosser 21-60)—and because of its ability to straddle feminist, lesbian, and gay male studies. Certainly if this topic needs anything, it needs to do a bit of crossing and straddling.

But as various critics such as Biddy Martin, Jacqueline Zita, Judith Butler and Rosemary Hennessy all began pointing out around 1993, queer criticism often has blind spots and imbalances, not least in recognizing when and why certain differences like gender still sometimes matter. Queer theorist Stephen Barber, for instance, looks at gay man/straight woman friendships in Virginia Woolf's *The Years* and *Between the Acts*. He reads nonromantic cross-sex intimacies as evidence of "Woolf's queer aesthetic" (402), 'queer' here being definitionally dependent on the trope of secrecy and the presence of gay male subjectivity. Most tellingly, 'queer' for Barber serves as a conceptual means of overcoming gender difference in favor of sameness, a move that makes me highly skeptical. As a theoretical rubric for the study of cross-sex affiliations, queer theory, in Barber's formulations of it, needs a subtler apparatus for reading gender differences.

I want to develop a slightly different framework for talking about nonsexual social attachments across sex by reorienting 'queer' in a feminist context. The theoretical category I propose to develop is that of 'the heterosocial.' It is a term that has yet to be theorized in detail, and to help me sketch out some initial parameters I want to turn, like Stephen Barber, to the work of Virginia Woolf.

Woolf stocks her fiction with numerous cross-sex combinations that defy the normative model of the heterosexual couple and its social and narrative counterpart, the patriarchal family. To list a few: Helen Ambrose and St. John Hirst in *The Voyage Out*, Clarissa Dalloway and Septimus Smith in *Mrs. Dalloway*, Lily Briscoe and William Bankes in *To the Lighthouse*, Rhoda and Louis in *The Waves*, and the dual focus of Barber's essay, Eleanor and Nicholas in *The Years* and Isa Oliver and William Dodge from *Between the Acts*.[3] I want to illuminate a different portrait of one particular pairing from Woolf's work, a portrait of two people framed in the window of a country house—and it is not Mrs. Ramsay and James.

In *Between the Acts*, lunch is finished and the villagers are beginning to arrive for the pageant. Lucy Swithin, an elderly widow, has been showing William Dodge, a young, married gay man, the strangely aestheticized house in which she grew up, empty of people at the moment. Their perambulating tour reaches its apogee in an upstairs window, where the two assume a tableau as aloof observers. Woolf writes, "The audience was assembling. But they, looking down from the window, were truants, detached. Together they leant half out of the window" (*BTA* 72).

I am especially struck by that seemingly contradictory pairing of words, "detached. Together. . . ." They indicate Mrs. Swithin and William's privileged status as outsiders from the group. They also contain the philosophical paradox, so sought-after in Woolf's writing, of the single self that yet stands in relation to another, discrete but not alone, different but not ranked hierarchically: "detached" yet "[t]ogether." Even more, detachment is at once an affective and an aesthetic mode. Together, Mrs. Swithin and William can be emotionally indifferent to the heterosexual drama of masculine/feminine that holds other couples in its thrall, and disinterested enough to perceive something beautiful or interesting apart from their own egos. In short, as a combination of two characters, Mrs. Swithin and William exemplify nearly everything Virginia Woolf prizes most in human relations. I want to translate this portrait of a woman and a man "detached. Together" into the theoretical concept of 'the heterosocial,' to offer some general guidelines for reading nonsexual cross-sex relations, and finally to consider the place of heterosocial affiliations in Woolf Studies. The following observations serve as preliminary notes theorizing the heterosocial as a distinct category of social relations.[4]

I. The heterosocial is not the same as the heterosexual.

Adrienne Rich and Eve Sedgwick have both theorized a same-sex continuum joining the homosocial to the homosexual, Rich in the idea of a lesbian continuum of the 'woman-identified woman' that seeks to bridge differences among feminists, Sedgwick in the idea of a male homosocial continuum that seeks to link forms of male social bonding to sexual desire, which homophobic pressure attempts to deny and regulate. In both cases, the sexual and the social within a gender group (homo) needed to be brought together for analytical and political purposes. But as Victor Luftig has pointed out, the task with the heterosocial is quite the opposite: one must pry it loose from the heterosexual presumption that mandates *any* two differently sexed people automatically be inscribed in a sexual narrative. I use 'hetero' as in 'heterosocial' to refer to two differently sexed people in some social relation with one another. That is, hetero as the mark of sexual difference, rather than that of sexual desire.

New Applications of Queer Theory

Yet to define it this way is only a start. It is a doomed strategy to assume that removing the element of sexual desire is, by itself, ever enough to guarantee that a woman and a man will like each other or find something interesting to say or do together. For Virginia Woolf of course, gender is always a complex social formation that characters must constantly negotiate. Reading the heterosocial thus entails initially moving beyond the mere absence of erotic desire: it requires that one carefully trace a specific social landscape showing separately how each person's subject position materializes in the text. Neither Mrs. Swithin nor William sexually desires the other, but not simply because she is an old woman who presumably does not think about sex and he is a gay man who supposedly does not desire women. If this were enough, then all elderly women and gay men would spontaneously bond, which is certainly not the case. One must get specific: what kind of 'old woman'? and what kind of 'gay man'? How is her old age or his homosexuality gendered in the novel? Again, I am shifting 'hetero' away from a discourse of sexual desire to a question about social and textual constructions of gender for two differently sexed people.

On these questions queer criticism has some limitations. Unlike most old women consigned to post-romance roles such as matchmaker, widow or grandmother, Mrs. Swithin reads poetry and history, even though her Victorian upbringing denied her a public education; her brother got the family copy of Byron and he no longer even reads poetry. She is not a typical old woman, and given her generation one might easily call her relationship to gender 'queer,' unconventional. Moreover, William is one of Woolf's most overtly gay characters, but his homosexual desire performs a lesser function in defining his gendered subjectivity than does his oppression as a clerk who works in an office but would rather be doing something artistic; his constant appreciation of paintings and antique teacups makes this clear. The problem with queer criticism, evident for example in Barber's analysis, is that it tends to overlook the historical conditions that create Mrs. Swithin's queer, nonnormative relationship to femininity and the socio-economic system of capitalist labor that entraps the artistically inclined William as male wage earner, uncomfortably forcing him into a normative, bourgeois, masculine role. In other words, to figure out why this particular cross-sex friendship works for Woolf, the first task is to broaden the scope of queer criticism beyond the presence of a gay character and epistemological issues of secrecy to include a more complex vision of the historical, social, and economic configurations of gender that produce various subject positions.

II. The heterosocial looks at a dynamic cross-sex interaction.

It is one thing to ask specifically, who is she? and who is he? But one must then ask, what do they become together? Queer theory so far has worked best in theorizing the subjectivity of one person, not two in relation, and above all not a woman and a man. To generalize, the quintessential queer subject is often one person interacting with some cultural form, like a book, an advertisement, or a movie. A second task for queer studies, then, is to expand the notion of 'cross-gender identification,' the cornerstone of queer theory's concept of gender performativity (see Prosser), to the more relational concept of 'cross-sex friendship.' This means moving queerness from a one-person to a two-person theoretical category. Most of all, such a move requires close attention to the *interactive* articulations of gender and power, how two people together mutually affect and change one another.[5]

One of Virginia Woolf's principal literary preoccupations is to explore how two people of different sex can relate without falling into the masculine/feminine roles of a patriarchal script that devalues and oppresses the one in the feminine position. Achieving a workable heterosocial association for Woolf means eliminating differences of gender and power by rewriting both the male and female characters in a nonhierarchical relation.

Let me offer just one example of how Woolf effects this transformation. An astonishing exchange between Mrs. Swithin and Dodge occurs in the room where Mrs. Swithin was born. While Dodge stands in one corner, his tour guide sits on the bed. "[H]e saw her eyes reflected in the glass," Woolf writes. "Cut off from their bodies, their eyes smiled, their bodiless eyes, at their eyes in the glass" (*BTA* 71). For one fleeting moment, they have neither a gender nor its most fundamental signifier, a sexed body. Even more, the woman does not occupy the position of the 'feminine,' objectified as mirror reflecting the masculine subject back to itself—and at twice his natural size, Woolf memorably writes in *A Room of One's Own* (35)—but she is instead a subject in relation to another subject. This is true even at a grammatical level. The plural "their eyes," his and hers possessively joined, reflexively occupies both subject and object positions in the sentence: "their eyes smiled, their bodiless eyes, at their eyes in the glass." To gauge the significance of this radically egalitarian cross-sex visual connection in the mirror I would point to the final sequence of the more public pageant. Miss La Trobe's enormous mirror, "the inquisitive, insulting eye" (*BTA* 186), reflects the gathered audience back to itself in "orts, scraps and fragments" (*BTA* 188); except for Mrs. Manresa, a paragon of heterosexual femininity, no one can even bear to look. The private heterosocial pairing of two achieves what the collective public group cannot: a nonhierarchical connection beyond power-inflected differences of feminine and masculine, audience and stage.

III. The heterosocial forms a narrative.

Another way of asking, what do two people become in each other's presence, is to ask, what do they *do* together? What activity triangulates their interaction? Queer criticism in general has had a very difficult time asking these sorts of narrative questions. But for the heterosocial to be differentiated from the heterosexual one must consider questions of plot and narrative. A standard reading of *Between the Acts* cites Isa's final lament, "Surely it was time someone invented a new plot" (215), as evidence that no new plot has been created. For the younger Isa, trapped in the related romance narratives of marriage and infidelity, it has not. But Woolf has created a new plot with the elderly Mrs. Swithin and William, the heterosocial plot of "detached. Together" that is propelled by a mutual, disinterested responsiveness to culture rather than a romantic engagement with each other.[6]

Like Lily Briscoe and William Bankes in several passages of *To the Lighthouse*, William Dodge and Mrs. Swithin do something together that takes them out of the gendered roles of the romance narrative. Content to consume the beauty and meaning of a landscape view, a portrait of a woman, an empty room or the pages of a book, all while moving through the rooms of the family home, this tour guide and her guest meet on the common ground of aesthetic and intellectual perception. This kind of disinterested activity, where sexual difference is no longer a question of hierarchy and oppression, is for Woolf the principal alternative to the narratives of patriarchal family and heterosexual romance that are leading the world to war. It is obviously a vision of aesthetic sensibility the access to which is distinctly privatized and classed; after all, it takes place inside a country house. This indicates how narrow is the strip of narrative turf within which Woolf maneuvers, but she does in fact stake out that territory. She even gives this heterosocial narrative between Mrs. Swithin and William a proper, gentle closure that is neither the dull repetition nor the sudden death she associates with romance endings. Dodge seeks out Mrs. Swithin to say goodbye and to thank her. "He took her hand and pressed it," Woolf writes. "Putting one thing with another, it was unlikely that they would ever meet again" (*BTA* 207).

IV. The heterosocial can be a lesbian category.

Writing publicly about the heterosocial certainly does not pose the same literary challenge for Woolf as writing publicly about Chloe liking Olivia. For one thing, women alone together evoke some of Woolf's most erotic passages, whereas when she imagines women with men in legitimate heterosocial interaction (in her published fiction, that is), the erotic has no place. Yet to the extent that Woolf envisions a viable cross-sex combination principally by critiquing the heterosexual couple, the patriarchal family, and the heterosexual plot, her angle of vision on the heterosocial emerges from what Julie Abraham has cogently defined as the place of lesbian writing in the twentieth century (*Are Girls Necessary?* 1-37). A critique of the conventions of the heterosexual plot enables Woolf to imagine, on the one hand, women together socially and erotically, and on the other, women with men in friendship. In other words, Woolf's particular representations of cross-sex associations to my mind make her *more* of a lesbian writer, not less of one, and make lesbian writing itself an expansive category.

I do not mean to suggest that the heterosocial is only a lesbian category, or mostly a lesbian category, more than, for example, a category amenable to gay male studies. But for Woolf it is. As a conceptual framework the heterosocial has the capacity to sustain and make visible important differences, rather than cover them up or pretend to resolve them in liberal-humanist concepts of gender reconciliation, like androgyny (Heilbrun) or queer (Barber). My own research at the moment looks at cross-sex friendships by pairing Woolf with Lytton Strachey, modernist lesbian writing with modernist gay male writing; the heterosocial applies to both, but in distinctly different ways. For instance, Woolf seeks to eliminate inflections of power in a cross-sex association, but Strachey seeks to reverse inflections of power by giving the woman more social and cultural clout, which is why he is so interested in Queen Elizabeth, Queen Victoria, and the less powerful men with whom they interact. Woolf strives to make a heterosocial relation nongendered, whereas Strachey strives to make it cross-gendered. Both writers use unconventional friendships to challenge the social arrangements and literary representations of gender, but they have quite different goals. They even choose to work predominantly in different genres, the novel for Woolf and biography for Strachey. The heterosocial as a two-person theoretical category can accommodate these differences and form a valuable dialogue between lesbian studies and gay male studies without occluding one or the other.

V. The heterosocial belongs in a feminist theoretical framework.

That is to say, the place of cross-sex friendship in Woolf Studies must ultimately be rooted within feminist discourses. After all, Mrs. Swithin and William meet inside the family house, the locus of middle-class women's oppression as 'feminine.' Woolf's female artists generally work outdoors: Lily Briscoe paints canvases on the lawn, Orlando writes poetry from the hill above Knole, Miss La Trobe stages dramas on the grassy terrace. But with Mrs. Swithin, Woolf daringly places a woman, with a man no less, inside the domestic interior of a country house, and astonishingly she becomes something other than its angel.

At the same time, cross-sex friendship in Woolf's work provides one way for feminist criticism to revisit the vital question of how and why women and men form attachments with one another. On this score, the work of many African-American and Latina feminist scholars, such as bell hooks and Cherríe Moraga, gives a crucial and guiding perspective. Bonds across sex often become primary and imperative alliances for women who advocate feminism within non-white ethnic groups, particularly in American culture. The binary view that feminists must either resist or collude with men and male dominance not only reduces both feminism and masculinity to monolithic entities, but also presumes that no other axis of difference matters besides sexual difference. The stultifying assumption that women and men cannot be friends may not only be heterosexual, but also implicitly middle-class and white, dependent on privileged categories of class and ethnicity as well as sexuality.

New Applications of Queer Theory

What I am suggesting, of course, is nothing new for the generation of feminist writers that continues to work with inclusive understandings of difference and conflict. My purpose in reiterating some of those claims here is to situate the under-examined topic of cross-sex friendship solidly within this feminist intellectual genealogy. I do this for two main reasons. In large part I want to warn against invoking a potentially liberal discourse like that of 'friendship' as a magical leap beyond power relations. The most useful work on cross-sex friendship will critique not only the ideology underpinning the assumption that 'men and women can never be friends,' but will equally expose the ideological limitations of 'can't we all just get along' (see DeMott). And there is another reason as well. In writing about Virginia Woolf, I have returned again and again to feminist criticism from the 1980s, with 1990s queer theory tucked under my arm. Work by such Woolf critics as Jane Marcus, Rachel Blau DuPlessis, Rachel Bowlby and Anne Herrmann offers a rich critical foundation for launching a feminist and queer inquiry of cross-sex bonds in Woolf Studies. As a younger male academic in the late 1990s, I am in the historically unique position of being able to look to an older, established generation of feminist scholars, from hooks to Bowlby to Moraga to Herrmann, with whom I feel an easy and complicated affinity—an affinity within the late-twentieth-century academy akin perhaps to the one between the younger Mr. Dodge and the older Mrs. Swithin within Woolf's modernist country house. At the turn of this century I am intrigued to see how these unconventional cross-sex friendships alter our visions of modernist writing, our experiences in the postmodern academy.

In the dining room of Pointz Hall hang two separate portrait paintings, visual emblems of the heterosexual couple within a patriarchal social structure, which Woolf challenges throughout her career. One portrait represents a named male ancestor, inherited; the other renders an unknown woman, purchased because she was beautiful to a male buyer. But with Mrs. Swithin and William in the upstairs window, Woolf paints a different picture of cross-sex association. The country house literally frames them, but in a more important way they are conceptually framing the house by redefining it as the aestheticized, cultured domain of the heterosocial—the nonhierarchical relation of a woman and a man, "detached. Together," leaning out from a room of their own.

Notes

[1] For examples of work on the topic representing a range of literary criticism, social scientific approaches and autobiographical narratives, see Barber, Boone, Luftig, Nestle and Preston, Vanita, and Werking, in addition to Castle and Heilbrun.

[2] I am indebted to Antonio Brown for this observation about black mammies. For a journalistic appraisal of gay man/straight woman friendships in contemporary popular culture, see McCauley.

[3] Pairing Isa and Dodge, heterosexual woman with gay man, happens frequently in Woolf criticism. Missing is often a comparison between this younger cross-sex couple, still inscribed in a romance narrative, and the factor of age, which Woolf uses in representing the bond between Mrs. Swithin and William. See Bonnie Kime Scott for discussions of both couples (57, 65-66).

4 I have benefited greatly from Victor Luftig's work on idioms of heterosexual friendship, particularly his distinction between heterosexual romance and friendship, his emphasis on looking at shared activities, and his focus on moments more than narratives. My approach differs from Luftig's by moving out of an explicitly heterosexual framework and drawing on work in lesbian, gay, queer, and feminist theory. Thinking only about cross-sex friendships between ostensible heterosexuals, as Luftig does, may limit one's vision of the myriad ways women and men interact, indeed may limit differences between men, differences between women.

5 In this respect queer theory benefits immensely from closer dialogue with colonial/postcolonial theories, the best work of which has always analyzed a colonial encounter from multiple positions, including both colonizing and colonized subjects; see for instance McClintock.

6 To use Stephen Barber's essay again as an example, I am critical of the fact that he privileges Isa Oliver and William Dodge as his exemplary cross-sex friendship, because such a reading overlooks the multiple ways Virginia Woolf inscribes this couple indelibly within the script of the heterosexual plot, if primarily as its inversion. Their meeting in the cathedral-like greenhouse, their parodic inversions of Miss La Trobe's romantic vignettes, their sense that they are 'conspirators,' all attest to their entrapment in a narrative of marriage and romance. To invert that narrative is not to escape it. The only cross-sex pairing in *Between the Acts* not inscribed in some fundamental way in a narrative of romance is that between William and Mrs. Swithin. For another example of this critical tendency to overlook narrative issues, see also Ruth Vanita's chapter on William Bankes and Lily Briscoe in *To the Lighthouse*, in her book *Sappho and the Virgin Mary* (165-86). She argues that the two are friends because they are both "homoerotically inclined" (175), but she never discusses what they actually do together, or what they even talk about. Addressing narrative and discursive concerns such as these is necessary if one is to specify what exactly 'cross-sex friendship' might mean, what conditions make it possible, and how it might be used to think about bridging lesbian, gay male, and feminist studies. For excellent discussions of narrative questions in reading relations between women in modernist writing, see the work of Julie Abraham and Suzanne Raitt.

Works Cited

Abraham, Julie. *Are Girls Necessary? Lesbian Writing and Modern Histories*. New York: Routledge, 1996.

Barber, Stephen. "Lip Reading: Woolf's Secret Encounters." *Novel Gazing: Queer Readings in Fiction*. Ed. Eve Kosofsky Sedgwick. Durham: Duke UP, 1997. 401-443.

Boone, Joseph. *Libidinal Currents: Sexuality and the Shaping of Modernism*. Chicago: U Chicago P, 1998.

Bowlby, Rachel. *Virginia Woolf: Feminist Destinations*. Oxford: Basil Blackwell, 1988.

Butler, Judith. "Against Proper Objects." *differences* 6.2-3 (1994): 1-26.

Castle, Terry. *Kindred Spirits: Radclyffe Hall and Noël Coward*. New York: Columbia UP, 1996.

DeMott, Benjamin. *The Trouble With Friendship: Why Americans Can't Think Straight About Race*. New York: Atlantic Monthly Press, 1995.

DuPlessis, Rachel Blau. *Writing Beyond the Ending: Narrative Strategies of Twentieth-Century Women Writers*. Bloomington: Indiana UP, 1985.

Heilbrun, Carolyn. *Toward a Recognition of Androgyny*. London: W.W. Norton, 1973.

Hennessy, Rosemary. "Queer Theory: Review of the *differences* Special Issue and Wittig's *The Straight Mind*." *Signs* 18.4 (Summer 1993): 964-72.

Herrmann, Anne. *The Dialogic and Difference: "An/Other Woman" in Virginia Woolf and Christa Wolf*. New York: Columbia UP, 1989.

hooks, bell. "Feminism: A Movement to End Sexist Oppression." *Feminist Theory: From Margin to Center.* Boston: South End Press, 1984. 17-31.
Luftig, Victor. *Seeing Together: Friendship Between the Sexes in English Writing from Mill to Woolf.* Stanford: Stanford UP, 1993.
Marcus, Jane. *Virginia Woolf and the Languages of Patriarchy.* Bloomington: Indiana UP, 1987.
Martin, Biddy. "Sexualities Without Genders and Other Queer Utopias." *diacritics* 24.2-3 (Summer-Fall 1994): 104-21.
McCauley, Stephen. "He's Gay, She's Straight, They're a Trend." *New York Times,* 20 September 1998, sec. 2:31+.
McClintock, Anne. *Imperial Leather: Race, Gender and Sexuality in the Colonial Contest.* New York: Routledge, 1995.
Moraga, Cherríe. "From a Long Line of Vendidas: Chicanas and Feminism." *Loving in the War Years.* Boston: South End Press, 1986. 90-144.
Nestle, Joan and John Preston, eds. *Sister and Brother: Lesbians and Gay Men Write About Their Lives Together.* London: Cassell, 1994.
Prosser, Jay. *Second Skins: The Body Narratives of Transsexuality.* New York: Columbia UP, 1998.
Rich, Adrienne. "Compulsory Heterosexuality and Lesbian Existence." *The Lesbian and Gay Studies Reader.* Ed. Henry Abelove, Michèle Aina Barale, and David Halperin. New York: Routledge, 1993. 227-254.
Scott, Bonnie Kime. *Refiguring Modernism: Postmodern Feminist Readings of Woolf, West, and Barnes.* Vol. 2. Bloomington: Indiana UP, 1995.
Sedgwick, Eve Kosofsky. *Between Men: English Literature and Male Homosocial Desire.* New York: Columbia UP, 1985.
Vanita, Ruth. *Sappho and the Virgin Mary: Same-Sex Love and the English Literary Imagination.* New York: Columbia UP, 1996.
Werking, Kathy. *We're Just Good Friends: Women and Men in Nonromantic Relationships.* New York: Guildford Press, 1997.
Woolf, Virginia. *Between the Acts.* New York: Harcourt Brace & Co., 1970.
——— . *A Room of One's Own.* New York: Harcourt Brace Jovanovich, 1989.
Zita, Jacqueline N. "Gay and Lesbian Studies: Yet Another Unhappy Marriage?" *Tilting the Tower: Lesbians Teaching Queer Subjects.* Ed. Linda Garber. New York: Routledge, 1994. 258-76.

Eileen Barrett
Response to Papers by Judith Roof and Troy Gordon

With "Hocus Crocus," Judith Roof revisits the moment of Clarissa Dalloway's illumination that is the focus of critical attention in her 1989 essay, "'The Match in the Crocus': Representation of Lesbian Sexuality." Paula Bennett's response in "Critical Clitoridectomy" and Teresa De Lauretis's reading of the Roof and Bennett essays in *The Practice of Love: Lesbian Sexuality and Perverse Desire* are part of the scholarship that sheds light not only upon this luminous Woolfian moment but also upon the ongoing discussions between queer theory and lesbian feminism. Today Roof traces Clarissa's solitary ruminations, her imagined scenes with younger women, and her remarkable memory of Sally's kiss to reveal Clarissa's layers of desire. At the same time the hocus with which Roof modifies Woolf's crocus warns how tricky is the art of reading texuality/sexuality, how wily the search for the literal in Woolf's clitoral moments.

This play with language also signals an omission that Roof discerns in recent lesbian readings of Woolf. Except for Diana Swanson's 1993 essay, Roof detects an absence of attention to the post-structuralist theory that informs queer studies. Roof's explanations for this absence are to a large degree correct. Schooled in radical feminist practice and theory of the late 70s, Woolf scholars find affinity with such lesbian feminist critics as Bonnie Zimmerman, Catherine Stimpson, Jean Kennard, Toni McNaron, Blanche Wiesen Cook, and Marilyn Farwell, among others, whose work suggests the many ways in which feminism and lesbianism inform modernism. More recently, however, these critics explore intersections between lesbian feminism and post-structuralist theories in such collections as *Cross Purposes: Lesbians, Feminists, and the Limits of Alliance, Professions of Desire,* and *New Lesbian Studies: Into the Twenty-first Century,* to mention three which should provide multiple points of departure for future lesbian readings of Woolf. At the same time, the past twenty years reveal lesbian feminist theory alive with attention to difference as well as sameness, and lesbian identity neither essentialized nor fixed but envisioned as one among many critical vantage points. Since the practical and political need for lesbian visibility continues unabated, lesbian critics will continue to attend to the material and historical conditions of lesbian existence both in literature and in life.

I also agree with Roof that much lesbian criticism of Woolf attempts to make visible in her life what previous biographers have elided and obscured, the centrality of her emotional and erotic attraction to women. Yet I would stress the importance of this project. "Now then will you believe that I am devoted to every hair, and every ridge and every hollow, and every spot upon your body?" Virginia Stephen asked of Violet Dickinson (*L1* 245). Jane Lilienfeld is the most recent critic to show how the passion between these two women that this exemplary quote suggests inspired Woolf's early and lifelong efforts to write love between women in all its permutations. Nonetheless the current spate of highly visible biographies of Woolf that minimize or ignore such erotically charged addresses to women illustrates how easily lesbianism can be erased. "When it comes to lesbians," as Terry Castle reminds us, "many people have trouble seeing what's in front of them" (2).

In her autobiographical writings Woolf revels in the power of her narratives to seduce a lesbian reader, writing proudly to Vita Sackville-West, for example, after receiving letters from readers of *Orlando,* "The percentage of Lesbians is rising in the States, all because of you" (*L4* 14). Lesbian reader-response theory offers another opportunity for figuring lesbian desire in Woolf's texts as work by Elizabeth Meese, Toni McNaron, and Suzanne Bellamy demonstrates. As a teacher at a comprehensive state university, I, like

Woolf, am interested in the common reader and her pleasure in the text, a pleasure that such personal narratives can movingly recreate and that abstruse theories often obscure.

Roof, rightly I think, argues that lesbian feminist critics envision the lesbian narrative as the story that resists compulsory heterosexuality and subverts patriarchy through the creation of an alternative community of women. Much like archaeologists, to borrow Roof's metaphors, we excavate, disinter, and exhume the lesbian and her sexuality from Woolf's texts. In other words, we reveal the ghostly presence that Terry Castle names the apparitional lesbian and describes as "always somewhere else: in the shadows, in the margins, hidden from history, out of sight, out of mind, a wanderer in the dusk, a lost soul, a tragic mistake, a pale denizen of the night" (2).

Much like the apparitional lesbian that Terry Castle argues haunts the narratives of western culture, Doris Kilman haunts Clarissa's private sexual desire and suggests yet another troubling lesbian difference within. Doris functions in Woolf's narrative as Clarissa's uncanny other, an outsider to her insider, the visible expression of her almost expressed. Whereas Clarissa enters her cloistered attic room to experience the privacy of her soul and her lesbian desire, Doris enters the "double darkness" of the public Abbey, where she is seen as "a soul haunting the same territory; a soul cut out of immaterial substance; not a woman, a soul" (134). Clarissa's orgasmic revelations leave her swollen with rapture then alleviated. Doris's unrequited desire for Elizabeth leaves her agonized and "split asunder." Clarissa treasures Sally's kiss long after her departure, while Elizabeth's departure eviscerates Doris, who feels Elizabeth draw out "the very entrails in her body, stretching them as she crossed the room." "She had gone," Doris thinks. "Mrs. Dalloway had triumphed. Elizabeth had gone. Beauty had gone, youth had gone" (133).

At the same time, images of Doris with "her Elizabeth" trouble Clarissa's sleep until Doris becomes "one of those spectres with which one battled in the night; one of those spectres who stand astride us and suck up half our life-blood" (12). This narrative struggle with the spectre of the vampiric lesbian frames Clarissa's day. Later that evening, she detects "a hollowness" about her party (174) that brings back thoughts of Doris: "Kilman her enemy. That was satisfying; that was real. Ah, how she hated her—hot, hypocritical, corrupt; with all that power; Elizabeth's seducer; the woman who had crept in to steal and defile . . . She hated her: she loved her" (175).

On the one hand, to apply Castle's argument, the spectral figure allows Clarissa a vehicle for recognizing her lesbianism through negation, what Castle refers to as the psychological and rhetorical means for objectifying—and ultimately embracing—that which otherwise could not be acknowledged" (60). On the other hand, the narrative reveals how Clarissa's negation traumatizes Doris. Roof argues that Woolf's match burning in a crocus is an emblem of lesbian desire and a flame of modernism. What I'd suggest today is that the complex dynamic between Clarissa and Doris, the lesbian narrative that frames this emblematic moment, evokes another lesbian feminist desire that is, to paraphrase Michelle Cliff, to claim an identity they taught me to despise.

Troy Gordon turns us in another direction. Calling our attention to the relatively unexplored area of same-sex friendship, he outlines a theoretical apparatus with which to place such varieties of friendship in literature. Whereas Roof wants to push feminist theory in post-structuralist directions, Gordon uses Woolf to push queer theory in feminist directions, a project which I welcome, although with skepticism. As Leslie Hankins writes elsewhere, "a queer theory into which feminism disappears without a trace cannot contain Woolf's texts" (182). Gordon, then, proposes to theorize the heterosocial through an examination of some of Woolf's depictions of cross-sex friendship.

Woolf's novels are a wonderful site for such a discussion, as Gordon suggests with his heterosocial pairing of Helen Ambrose and St. John Hirst, Septimus and Clarissa, Lily Briscoe and William Bankes. Taking a similar approach in an essay titled "Bringing Buried Things to Light: Homoerotic Erotic Alliances in *To the Lighthouse*," Ruth Vanita proposes how such cross gender friendships can illuminate Woolf's gay and lesbian narratives. Vanita juxtaposes the heterosexual (Rachel and Terence) and heterosocial (St. John and Helen) narratives in *The Voyage Out* and shows how in *To the Lighthouse* the friendship between Lily Briscoe and William Bankes calls forth their respective homoerotic desires, hers for Mrs. Ramsay and his for Mr. Ramsay. As Vanita writes of the friendship between Lily and William, "In a heterosexually defined world, the homosexually inclined man and woman share their buried secrets and develop a lifelong alliance. In the closing section of the book, Lily reflects: 'Indeed, his friendship had been one of the pleasures of her life. She loved William Bankes'" (Vanita 176). It seems to me that Gordon's construct of the "detached. Together" plot would help us to discover further how the story of Lily and William functions both literally and figuratively outside heterosexual narrative space.

Whereas critics such as Stephen Barber and Vanita have begun the textual analysis, Gordon offers us a model for analyzing narratives that might also move us beyond the confines of the hetero-patriarchal text. Gordon theorizes the heterosocial with attention to the "social landscape" that reveals the material being of characters within the text, thus allowing for what he calls "a more complex vision of the historical, social and economic arrangements of gender." Gordon raises a central question about Woolf when he asks "how can two people of different sex relate without falling into the masculine/feminine roles of heterosexual romance that devalue and oppress the one in the feminine position?" As Gordon shows with the moment between William Dodge and Lucy Swithin in the mirror, we move from the mirror of women magnifying men to the mirror as vehicle for cross gender equality. When the lesbian artist La Trobe shatters our memory of that magnifying mirror and invites her audience to a similar re-envisioning of themselves in its fragments, the cross-sex friendship becomes part of a lesbian category and a feminist theoretical framework.

Here, as Patricia Cramer has already proposed, I suggest that we consider *Three Guineas* as another invitation to cross-sex friendship. During the past several weeks as pictures of mass destruction in Eastern Europe were covering our daily newspapers, I was reminded once again of the relevance of Woolf's pacifist, feminist essay. Gordon's thesis encourages me to see as well the optimistic gesture that this female narrator's letter to her male correspondent inscribes: "But with your letter before us we have reason to hope. For by asking our help you recognize that connection; and by reading your words we are reminded of other connections that lie far deeper than the facts on the surface" (143). Although the sounds of guns and pictures of dead bodies and ruined houses focus Woolf's narrator upon practical strategies for peace, this outsider longs to discuss with this insider the capacity of the human spirit to overflow boundaries and make unity out of multiplicity" (143). Woolf's political solution—"We can best help you to prevent war not by joining your society but by remaining outside your society but in co-operation with its aims" (143)—echoes in a very different context the heterosocial plot of "detached. Together" that Gordon thoughtfully theorizes.

Works Cited

Barrett, Eileen and Patricia Cramer, eds. *Virginia Woolf: Lesbian Readings.* NY: New York UP, 1997.

Bellamy, Suzanne. "The Pattern behind the Words." Barrett and Cramer, *Virginia Woolf: Lesbian Readings.* 21-36.

.Bennett, Paula. "Critical Clitoridectomy: Female Sexual Imagery and Feminist Psychoanalytic Theory." *Signs: Journal of Women in Culture and Society* 18 (1993) : 235-59.

Castle, Terry. *The Apparitional Lesbian: Female Homosexuality and Modern Culture.* NY : Columbia UP, 1993.

Cliff, Michelle. *Claiming an Identity They Taught Me to Despise.* Watertown, MA: Persephone, 1980.

Cramer, Patricia. "'Plain as a Pike's Staff'" A Response to Recent Biographers." Woolf and Traumatic Narrative: Fictional Strategies and Cultural Responses. Woolf Conference. U of Delaware. 12 June 1999.

De Lauretis, Teresa. *The Practice of Love: Lesbian Sexuality and Perverse Desire.* Bloomington: Indiana UP, 1993.

Haggerty, George and Bonnie Zimmerman, eds. *Professions of Desire: Lesbian and Gay Studies in Literature.* NY: MLA, 1995.

Hankins, Leslie. "*Orlando*: 'A Precipice Marked V': Between 'A Miracle of Discretion' and 'Lovemaking Unbelievable: Indiscretions Incredible.'" Barrett and Cramer, *Virginia Woolf: Lesbian Readings.* 180-202.

Heller, Dana, ed. *Cross-purposes : Lesbians, Feminists, and the Limits of Alliance.* Bloomington : Indiana UP, 1997.

McNaron, Toni. "A Lesbian Reading Virginia Woolf." Barrett and Cramer, *Virginia Woolf: Lesbian Readings.* 10-20.

McNaron, Toni and Bonnie Zimmerman, eds. *The New Lesbian Studies: Into the Twenty-first Century.* NY : Feminist Press, 1996.

Meese, Elizabeth. "When Virginia Looked at Vita, What Did She See; Or, Lesbian:

Feminist: Woman - What's the Differ(e/a)nce?" *Feminist Studies* 18 (1992): 99-117.
Roof, Judith. "The Match in the Crocus: Representations of Lesbian Sexuality." *Discontented Discourses: Feminism/Textual Intervention/Psychoanalysis.* Eds. Marleen Barr and Richard Feldstein. Urbana: Illinois UP, 1989. 100-16.
Vanita, Ruth. "Bringing Buried Things to Light: Homerotic Alliances in *To the Lighthouse.*" Barrett and Cramer, *Virginia Woolf: Lesbian Readings.* 165-79.
Woolf, Virginia. *The Letters of Virginia Woolf.* Eds. Nigel Nicolson and Joanne Trautmann. 6 vols. NY: HBJ, 1975-80.
———. *Mrs. Dalloway.* 1925. NY: HBJ, 1981.
———. *Three Guineas.* 1938. NY: HBJ, 1966.

Patricia Cramer
Response

> The problem, the personal problem, was not what our enemies might be doing, but what our friends were doing.
> Hannah Arendt (qtd. in Young-Bruehl 108)

My response to papers by Judith Roof and Troy Gordon is shaped by my standpoint, political allegiances, and experiences as a radical feminist and lesbian with strong separatist loyalties.[1] I am very aware that just my unapologetic use of words like "standpoint," "experience," and even "I" places me gladly and irrevocably outside the theoretical tradition to which Troy and Judith refer. And just as I do not recognize myself in Judith's renditions of lesbian-feminism, Troy and Judith also may not recognize themselves in my summaries of their comments and the issues they raise. This lack of a "common language"[2]—of even the fundamentals for mutual understanding—is symptomatic of a "gulf so deeply cut between us" that, like Virginia Woolf as she began her response to the man from a peace society in *Three Guineas*, I sit on my side of it wondering "whether it is any use to try to speak across it" (4).

The topic of greatest concern for both our speakers is the relevance of structuralist/post-structuralist and queer theories to readings of Virginia Woolf. Both Troy Gordon and Judith Roof have defined a rift between theorists who employ deconstructive, psychoanalytic, structuralist/post-structuralist theories (Judith Roof's classification), and queer theorists (Troy Gordon's classification) in opposition to feminist and lesbian-feminist approaches. Both in different ways urge a rapprochement between these, as I believe they've represented it, competing communities of inquiry. Although Troy is drawn to queer studies for its openness to diverse peoples and theorists—its ability to, in his words, "cross" various disciplines and identities,[3] he feels queer theory lacks some of the strengths of feminist studies. Troy suggests feminism can broaden queer scholarship by adding feminist perspectives on the social and historical conditions of gender and extend critical attention from the solitary queer of queer theory to a community of two: this male/female couple could be modeled on Woolf's frequent pairing of women with gay men in her novels. In particular, Troy focuses on the relationship between Lucy Swithin and Dodge in *Between the Acts* as a model for a nonhierarchical, nonsexual coalition between feminism and queer studies.

While Troy finds feminist perspectives expansive in their theoretical possibilities, Judith Roof criticizes lesbian-feminist readings of Woolf for our "critical uniformity." We have, Judith suggests, possibly "impoverished lesbian studies" by our adherence to essentialist notions—for example, our search for "the lesbian" in Woolf's texts; our belief that lesbianism is an identity rather than a desire or structural position; our expectation that lesbian decoding will uncover a hidden preexistent lesbian content and our assumption that a lesbian author must necessarily express lesbianism in her creative work.

Like Troy, Judith claims that lesbian studies should seek coalitions with gay male studies; toward this end, Judith also urges Woolf scholars to study connections between lesbian and gay male characters in Woolf's work. Judith suggests that we begin to use the theorists she recommends (Elizabeth Meese, Judith Butler, Teresa de Lauretis, Diana Fuss, herself and, inevitably, Foucault). These theorists, she says, progress beyond the simplistic issues which preoccupy lesbian-feminist studies—like how lesbians are oppressed— "to more complex questions of how lesbians function within representation, power, cultural anxiety, and aesthetics." These theorists and the tradition of lesbian theory they represent, Judith claims, encompass "the mainstream of [contemporary] lesbian studies," "the major ideas and theories about lesbianism."[4] Have lesbian readings of Woolf tended to ignore these theorists "because of a particular ideological bent" or "simply a matter of discipline?" Judith asks.

While I agree with Audre Lorde that we do not have to become each other in order to work together—we do, as Bernice Reagon notes, need to have a few beliefs in common in order for coalitions to have any meaning at all (366). This lack of common ground is why some of us have found structuralist/post-structuralist and queer theories irrelevant to lesbian readings of Woolf. Whether we adopt Judith's or Troy's rubric for the theoretical tradition they refer to, this tradition—most often referred to as queer—differs from lesbian-feminist traditions in origins, membership, methodology, and aim. "[T]he result is that though we look at the same things, we see them differently"; and perhaps "we cannot understand each other because of these differences" (*TG* 9, 6). For example, structuralist/post-structuralist and queer theories derive primarily from male theorists (Foucault, Derrida, et al.), with queer theorists adding to this the influence of gay male and lesbian activism around AIDS. In contrast, lesbian-feminist theories derive from lesbian life experiences and the interactions between lesbian and feminist movements which Bonnie Zimmerman has aptly described as "coterminous if not identical social phenomena" (165). Poets, playwrights, and musicians (Gloria Anzaldua, Alix Dobkin, Carolyn Gage, Paula Gunn Allen, Judy Grahn, Pat Parker, Audre

Lorde, Cherríe Moraga, Adrienne Rich, and Irena Klepfisz, to name but a few) and lesbian gatherings outside academia have influenced lesbian-feminist theory and activism rather than the male-derived theories Judith recommends.

Queer constituencies are not gender- nor even gay- or lesbian-based, but are broadly defined by their sexual practices and ideologies. Jagose explains "queer may be used to describe an open-ended constituency, whose shared characteristic is not identity itself but an anti-normative positioning with regard to sexuality" (98). In contrast, lesbian-feminism is defined by lesbians who generally seek closer ties with non-lesbian-identified women than with gay or otherwise-defined men.

In methodology, structuralist and post-structuralist theorists prefer analysis of, for example, as Judith mentions, "the way sexualities arise from and in turn inform other categories of activity and signification" over politically motivated questions of lesbian visibility and oppression. Gregory W. Bredbeck explains that queer "enacts a programme of *pure* critique, a process deeply inflected by poststructuralist literary theory and postmodern social theory"; in this system of thought, he adds, "intervention in the system is labelled useless" (479; 491; italics in original). Judith Butler claims political status for theory in and of itself: "[i]f the political task is to show that theory is never merely *theoria*, in the sense of disengaged contemplation, and to insist that it is fully political (*phronesis* or even *praxis*), then why not simply call this operation politics, or some necessary permutation of it?" ("Imitation" 14-15; italics in original).

Lesbian-feminism, however, has always been unapologetically activist and idealistic in its origins and aims—claiming lesbianism as a base from which to analyze and overthrow male supremacy and, to borrow Woolf's words, work for "justice and equality and liberty for all men and women" (*TG* 106). From the radical lesbian claim in the 1970s that lesbians represent "the rage of all women condensed to the point of explosion" through the 1980s, when Cheryl Clark proclaimed lesbian "passion will ultimately reverse the heterosexual imperialism of male culture" (1981)—this conjunction of lesbian desire with feminist idealism has been sustained (qtd. in Russo 277-78). Despite the wishful thinking of some post-structuralist and queer theorists who are fond of announcing the death of lesbian-feminism as we have known it (e.g., Lamos 94; Morton 121), lesbian-feminists continue our varied work "[e]ven," as Bonnie Zimmerman notes, "if that political program was, is, and ever will be utopian" (160). Thus in the 1990s, lesbian-feminists continue to argue that lesbians can change themselves and the world; for example, Irene Reti writes that even "in an era where earnestness is caricatured more and more as old-fashioned, and silly, uncool, uptight, I still believe in the potential of lesbian-feminism to change the world" (2, 3). Similarly, Sheila Jeffreys explains that lesbian-feminism was and is "an alternative universe" for "construct[ing] a new sexuality, a new ethics, a new culture in opposition to malestream culture" (ix). Analysis is key to lesbian-feminism, but transformation and social action are its goals.

Many have been and will probably continue to be attracted to queer precisely because of its refusal to clearly articulate its political agenda. Annamarie Jagose, for example, claims that "indeterminacy [is] one of its widely promoted charms" (1, 3). But, like Troy, feminist and lesbian critics are uneasy with queer's dissociation from feminism and like Judith, we are reluctant to adopt a theory and terminology that reflects gay male interests more prominently than lesbian. Suzanna Danuta Walters expresses a common complaint when she argues that "[d]estabilizing gender (or rendering its artifice apparent) is not the same as overthrowing it" (866). Furthermore, as Lillian Faderman notes, "perhaps the most substantive parting of the ways between lesbian-feminism and queer is queer theory's rejection, in the guise of challenging the binary gender system, of almost any focus on the politics of female sex and sexuality" (226).

I would now like to turn to a necessarily abbreviated discussion of Woolf's attitudes toward the politics of sexuality in order to suggest how closely Woolf's ideas about lesbian sexual desire coincide with radical lesbian-feminist sexual idealism, and to illustrate why some of us have found lesbian-feminist theories more useful than queer theory and post-structuralism for understanding Woolf's lesbian politics and aesthetics.

As Troy notes, Woolf proudly declared herself an outsider to her culture. In *Moments of Being* she describes herself and Vanessa as born "explorers, revolutionists, reformers" in "that world of many men" (123); in 1933, while fascism spread through Europe, she describes herself and Stephen Spender as "think[ing] how to improve the world" (*D4* 303). Although writing was her chosen form of activism—"[t]hinking is my fighting," she wrote in response to Hitler's war successes—thinking for her was not divorced from political aims: "[t]his pitter patter of ideas is my whiff of shot in the cause of freedom" (*D5* 285, 235). Woolf was loathe to convert, but her fiction interweaves harsh "criticis[m] of the social system & . . . [how] it work[s]" (*D2* 248) with dreamlike portraits aimed at seducing us to seek freer ways of being, loving, and living.

She was profoundly opposed to war and domination of any kind. As early as March 19, 1918, she writes "[a]nd more & more I come to loathe any dominion of one over another; any leadership, any imposition of the will" (*D1* 256). In this sense, I entirely agree with Troy that nonhierarchical partnerships and coalitions are crucial to Woolf's aims. Like lesbian-feminists of today, Woolf considered gender and sexuality central to her feminist approach to the question of how to end war: in 1940, when sharing her views with Lady Shena Simon on how to end war, Woolf thinks in gender terms: "[c]an one change sex characteristics?" she asks, can "the sexes . . . adapt themselves?" (*D6* 379). She disparaged heterosexuality as eroticized domination over women. For example, in *Between the Acts* she explores the interconnections between sexual love patterns and world wars. When Mrs. Manresa is turned on by Giles' bloody boots, Woolf links female sexual masochism with the adoration of dictators; Woolf attaches images of blood and death to Isa's memories of her first sexual feelings for her dominating husband, Giles, by comparing this "falling in love" to being caught like a salmon. Woolf portrays Isa as trapped, not liberated, by her sexual enthrallment to violence. Significantly, it is Isa and the lesbian LaTrobe who most actively seek the "new plots" that would transform sexual and social relations.

Woolf's attitude toward dominant-submissive sexuality is similar to that of lesbian-feminists who have opposed sadomasochistic practices that eroticize dominance, submission, and violence. Postmodern lesbians and queers have separated sexuality from gender as the primary site of oppression (Butler, "Against Proper Objects" 1). As Donald Morton notes, "[q]ueer [t]heory in all its variants works to displace gender as a category in an analytical, concept-based materialism . . . with sexuality as libidinalism so pleasure-saturated that it can disrupt and indeed dispense with conceptuality and analytics . . . " (141). Among structuralist/post-structuralists and queer theorists opposition to the political analyses of sexuality by Andrea Dworkin and Catherine MacKinnon is assumed (Butler 11, Tucker); support for sadomasochistic sexual practices is pervasive (see Lynda Hart, Lamos et al.); and they typically disparage any opposition to sadomasochistic sexual practices as moralistic and oppressive. Judith Halberstam's opposition to political programs that would "impose moralistic codes of behavior on sex by assuming that there should be some continuity between what people believe in politically and what they do sexually" is typical (see also Grosz 77). Queer theorists also tend to favor sexual practices in which fantasies of violation are repeated rather than, as lesbian-feminists prefer, transformed. For example, Lynda Hart explains why queer theatrics in which, for example, a "psychologically precarious female patient . . . is catheterized by a 'slightly disturbed male doctor,'" can provide feminists with "a way out of the endlessly repetitive oedipal drama" in the following way: "[t]he struggle is not to avoid repetition, but to repeat [our illusions] with differences that are transformative" (55; 63). Similarly, Ann Cvetkovich praises sadomasochistic scenes in which women playing "dyke daddies" reenact scenes of abuse with their partners as "healing rituals" offering "[t]he subversive possibilities of repetition with a difference" (355).[5]

Woolf's use of the erotic is closer to what Audre Lorde has defined as the power of the erotic to transform rather than repeat inherited sexual and social patterns: "[R]ecognizing the power of the erotic within our lives can give us the energy to pursue genuine change within our world, rather than merely settling for a shift of characters in the same weary drama" ("The Uses of the Erotic" 59). Repetitions of oedipal and other patterns of patriarchally constructed behaviors seem to have bored, not titillated Woolf: think of the mindless repetitions of phrases, behavior, and thought patterns which entrap rather than liberate the characters in *The Years*; or her comparison in *Three Guineas* of "human nature" to a "gramophone whose needle has stuck . . . now grinding out with such disastrous unanimity" (59). Woolf did not exempt sexual desire from her political judgments about which types of repetitive behaviors she sought to transform. For example, bored by the courting rituals of her friends Dora Carrington and Ralph Partridge, she writes "[i]t was the stupidity of virility that impressed me—& how, having made those convenient railway lines of convention, the lusts speed along them, unquestioning" (*D2* 177-78). In 1935, after her nephew Julian tells her men need war for the "danger emotion" she writes, "Lust & danger. Cant cut them out at once. Must divert them on to some harmless object. . . . Some fantasy must be provided. I say many people have found life exciting without war and bull fighting" (*D4* 307).

As Kathy Miriam notes, for many lesbian-feminists, "transformation of desire *is* a critical part of the liberating process" (38; emphasis in original), at least for those of us who have chosen, as Karman Kregloe and Jane Caputi suggest, "to explore, both privately and in public discussion, our sexual practices as they are infused with our feminist desire" (151). I believe we can reclaim Virginia Woolf as a radical sex pioneer in this lesbian-feminist adventure of exploring the possible interconnections between lesbian desire and feminist ideals in our private as well as public lives—even at the level of sexual fantasy and practices.

Most of us are by now familiar with the extent to which Woolf's metaphors for lesbian desire deliberately reverse Freudian, Christian, and sexological equations of lesbians with unnatural acts by linking lesbian emotions with images of natural fertility: spring coming, grapes, nuts, apricots, streams flowing free, beach trees, waterfalls, bumble bees and suet pudding are typical. Less obvious perhaps is the extent to which Woolf attaches lesbian desire to feminist insight, rebellion, and coalition-building. For example, Clarissa Dalloway's lesbian desire for Sally motivates her to temporarily suspend her class isolation to identify with the point of view of the working class homosexual Septimus; but Clarissa and Septimus are bonded not only by their sexual "difference" but by shared values—their shared opposition to war and the warlike values embodied in Bradshaw and Holmes. In *The Waves*, the lesbian Rhoda is driven by memories of her girlfriend, Alice, and beckoned by a mysterious goddess figure, out of the world which holds the militaristic Percival as ideal; in so doing, Rhoda's lesbian desire causes her to turn away not only from the compulsory heterosexuality of this social system, but also the imperialism and class arrogance Percival embodies. In *The Years*, feeling the glow on her cheek from Miss Fripp's kiss, Kitty stands at the open window dreaming of escape to America and then decides "she didn't want to be a don's wife and live in Oxford forever. No, No, No!"(61-62). In a chapter excluded from *The Years*, Eleanor finds herself unexpectedly aroused by Kitty's kiss. The "tingling, the tension" Eleanor feels from Kitty's kiss lead to her feminist rage at heterosexual norms and male sexual violence against women. She disaprovingly connects her parents' "brass bed" with her father's affair with Mira and the heterosexual arrogance which could put her homosexual friend, Nicholas, in prison. Then, Eleanor suddenly "gets" why she cannot walk alone at night (Galley F 19-30; see Radin).

In these and other passages linking lesbian desire with feminist rebellion, Woolf solicits the power of sexual love to inspire heroic ambitions, what Carl Goldberg has identified as the potential of "passionate yearnings . . . to vitalize our personality and influence our willingness to pursue the conditions of self-worth in social and political missions" (14). We can also recognize here what lesbian-feminist Nett Hart has defined as the power of lesbian desire "to lead us out of confinement to duty," "to envision and enact a new reality" (298).

Although Woolf's fiction favors ideal versions of lesbian love, of course Woolf's feelings about Vita Sackville-West could not always be truthfully compared to "sunny patch[es] on a hot bank" and "[b]ees[ ] mingling in the asparagus beds"(L3 440, 275). For example, Woolf's jealousy over Vita's other love affairs could give rise to fantasies of violence avoided in the fiction—as when Woolf warns Vita to be "careful . . . in [her] gamboling, or [she'll] find Virginia's soft crevices lined with hooks"(L3 395); Woolf's 1940 nightmare in which Vita appears with a blackened nose blown up like a pig (L6 396) exposes feelings of revenge and violence toward her beloved. In the fiction Woolf exhibits a range of lesbian types who exhibit varied relationships to Woolf's lesbian-feminist ideals. The lesbian Rose in *The Years* is a feminist activist who supports the war; the closeted Kitty (whose butch tendencies are discernible despite her feminine attire) opposes war; and the lesbian LaTrobe while writing on the side of peace curses her audience and carries a whip.[6]

Nevertheless, Woolf tends toward a one-sidedness in her idealized representations of lesbian desire because she is a visionary as well as an historian of romantic love: an explorer and creator, not simply repeater of her own and her culture's sexual fantasies. She intervenes into that "twilight zone between fantasy and reality" (Moller 162) where long-standing cultural patterns are eroticized and acted out, and she constructs romantic ideals and metaphoric alliances consistent with her feminist political aims. Woolf commingles lesbian sexual desire with fantasies of feminist freedom and action to create a sexual ideology as "exhilarating" (Julia Penelope's words) and "transformative" (Adrienne Rich's) as the aims of lesbian-feminism in our own time.

Like feminist and other political movements, I expect lesbians and gay men will soon move beyond arguing about the allegedly bifurcated traditions of queer and lesbian-feminism that Troy and Judith identify: how much more interesting it is when we argue in ways that make visible the multiply-sited distinctions among us, rather than absorbing us all into the amorphous universality and "either/or" thinking queer claims. The fact that during our discussion Troy expressed discontent with queer theory and Judith won't even adopt the term suggests that these separations will occur from within as well as from outsiders to this tradition, like me. Perhaps by standing our ground lesbian-feminists can serve as a model for the kind of separatism that I believe is the basis for coalitions that work. This is a time, therefore, when sorting out our real differences—not the made-up ones like "essentialist feminist" vs "complex avant-garde structuralist/post-structuralist queer"—is more important than making mergers through which our differences, and unique gifts, will disappear.

As for lesbian-feminism, I wholeheartedly agree with Bonnie Zimmerman that our challenge now "is to individuate [lesbian-feminism] from gay and queer studies, not feminist studies" (166). And to structuralist/post-structuralists and queers, I say, since our "causes it seems are [not] connected" (*TG* 84), let us each live out the consequences of those differences and, like Lucy and Dodge at the end of the novel, go our separate ways.

Notes

[1] On separatism and coalition-building, see Hill Collins (on standpoint theory). Frye; Lugones; Penelope, *For Lesbians Only;* Reagon (especially on the concept of "space within coalition" and "allowing people to name themselves. And dealing with them from that perspective") (363; 367). On Woolf and separatism, see Bellamy. This political strategy has been caricatured by structuralist/post-structuralist and queer theorists as essentialism and identity politics despite the fact that, as Faderman notes, lesbian-feminism has always been social constructivist in emphasis (223). For lesbian-feminist perspectives on the lesbian "self" as fluid, definable/indefinable, see Brossard, Lugones, Penelope, *Call Me Lesbian*; Nett Hart. I am aware that in this essay I may seem to narrow lesbian-feminism to just lesbians who have opposed pornography and sadomasochism but this is not my intention. I have kept a focus on this sector within lesbian-feminism partly because I am comfortable there and partly because these are the women and lesbians most demonized by structuralist/post-structuralists and queers. The common ground among lesbian-feminists, as I understand it, is that we do not separate our lesbian analyses from the oppression of women. On debates among lesbian-feminists see *Sinister Wisdom*, passim.

[2] For a tradition which has taken such strong stands against moral imperatives, queer theorists are surprisingly fond of telling others what is "no longer thinkable" (Fuss 1); "no longer theoretically feasible" (Lamos 99); "no longer to be seen" (de Lauretis iii). The "things we can no longer say, do or dream about" are usually the categories of analysis that have been most successfully explored by feminists and lesbian-feminists: gender categories—especially "woman" and "lesbian" (e.g. Morton 141, Butler, "Imitation" 13); standpoint theories (Bredbeck 488); ethical idealism (e.g. Grosz 77; Tucker); first person narratives of disclosure, especially coming out (McRuer 33) and incest autobiographies (Cvetkovich 359); experience-based theories (Morton 142); and lucid, accessible prose (see Fuss' dismissal of "the dream of a common language" 7; see also, Butler, "Imitation"). For excellent critiques of queer theory and post-modernist theories, see Daly, Dobkin, Faderman, Jeffreys, Kregloe and Caputi, Modleski, Walters, Reti, Turcotte, Zimmerman; see also *Deconstruct This: Radical Feminism Fights Back Against Postmodernism.*

[3] That the much touted inclusivity of queer gatherings does not, in practice, welcome lesbian-feminists was recently illustrated at the "First Annual Philadelphia Dyke March" in June, 1999 which attempted to exclude Alix Dobkin, a founder and leading theorist/activist in lesbian-feminist circles, due to her reputation for defending womyn-only spaces. The march Planning Committee informed Dobkin that she had

been disinvited because she "might make some transsexuals uncomfortable." See Dobkin for a full account of this incident.
4 Structuralist/post-structuralist and queer theorists are fond of declaring themselves the "mainstream" of lesbian and gay studies as Judith does here, and "the lesbian and gay avante garde" (Hennessey 964). Bredbeck is more accurate when he states that gay activism (but I would add lesbian-feminism) and queer activism are concurrent social and literary phenomena originating in the United States in the 1970s. (See also Jeffreys, who dates these debates as beginning in the late nineteenth century.) As Gunn Allen notes, what is "new" is not always better: queer theory's colonialist model of linear progress does not serve the interests of despised groups who are regularly asked to "repudiate their origins" (Allen 224) and accept what is, in fact, backlash, as progress.
5 Here, Woolf might ask, "And most persistent and difficult of all the questions that our silence covers, what possible satisfaction can dominance give to the dominator?" (*TG* 129)
6 Here, I have just the space to agree with Judith that Woolf's versions of lesbian desire are more varied than, say, Clarissa's retreat to a narrow bed and attachment to flowers. Woolf eroticizes personal power in women mingled with other more conventionally recognized "feminine qualities" but she imagines forms of power divorced from the impulse to hurt or control others. Because lesbian-feminists dream this same dream, Woolf's lesbian eroticism may be more easily accessible to us at this early stage in the scholarship than to readers saturated in structuralist/post-structuralist and queer theories.

Works Cited

Allen, Paula Gunn. "Who Is Your Mother?: Red Roots of White Feminism." *Sinister Wisdom: The Fifteenth Anniversary Retrospective.* 43/44 (1991): 224-36.

Bellamy, Suzanne. "The Pattern behind the Words." *Virginia Woolf: Lesbian Readings.* Ed. Eileen Barrett and Pat Cramer. NY: New York UP, 1997. 21-36.

Bredbeck, Gregory W. "The New Queer Narrative: Intervention and Critique." *Textual Practice* 9 (1995): 477-502.

Brossard, Nicole. Trans. Marlene Wildeman. *The Aerial Letter.* Toronto: The Women's Press, 1988.

Butler, Judith. "Against Proper Objects." *differences* 6.2-3 (1994): 1-26.

——. "Imitation and Gender Insubordination." *inside/out: Lesbian Theories, Gay Theories.* 13-31.

Cvetkovich, Ann. "Sexual Trauma/Queer Memory: Incest, Lesbianism, and Therapeutic Culture." GLQ 2 (1995): 351-77.

Daly, Mary. *Quintessence . . . Realizing the Archaic Future: A Radical Elemental Feminist Manifesto.* Boston: Beacon Press, 1998.

Deconstruct This: Radical Feminism Fights Back Against Postmodernism (We Won't Be Fooled Again). Spec. issue. *Off Our Backs.* xxix.8 (August-September 1999).

De Lauretis, Teresa. "Queer Theory: Lesbian and Gay Sexualities." *differences* 3 (1991): iii-xviii.

Dobkin, Alix. "The Philadelphia Story" (part 1); "Banned and Unbanned in Philadelphia"(part 2); "The (Post March) Meeting" (part 3); "The Philadelphia Story" (part 4); "Big Al from Philly" (part 5). *Chicago Outlines.* 8 July 1998; 22 July 1998; 12 August 1998; 26 August 1998; 19 September 1998.

Faderman, Lillian. "Afterword." *Cross-Purposes: Lesbians, Feminists, and the Limits of Alliance.* Ed. Dana Heller. Bloomington: Indiana UP, 1997. 221-29.

Frye, Marilyn. *The Politics of Reality*. Freedom, CA: The Crossing Press, 1983.
Fuss, Diana, Ed. *inside/out: Lesbian Theories, Gay Theories*. NY: Routledge, 1991.
Goldberg, Carl. "The Role of Passion in the Transformation of Anti-Heroes." *Journal of Evolutionary Psychology* 9.1-2 (1989): 2-16.
Grosz, Elizabeth. "Refiguring Lesbian Desire." *The Lesbian Postmodern*. Ed. Laura Doan. NY: Columbia UP, 1994. 67-84.
Hart, Lynda. "Blood, Piss, and Tears: The Queer Real." *Textual Practice* 9.1 (1995): 55-66.
Hart, Nett. "Lesbian Desire as Social Action." *Lesbian Philosophies and Cultures*. Ed. Jeffner Allen. NY: New York UP, 1990. 295-304.
Halberstam, Judith. "Who's Afraid of Queer Theory?" *Class Issues: Pedagogy, Cultural Studies and the Public Sphere*. Ed. Amitava Kumar. NY: New York UP, 1997. 256-75.
Hennessy, Rosemary. "Queer Theory: A Review of the *differences* Special Issue and Wittig's *The Straight Mind*." *Signs: Journal of Women in Culture and Society* 18 (1993): 964.
Hill Collins, Patricia. *Black Feminist Thought*. Boston: Unwin Hyman, 1990.
Jagose, Annamarie. *Queer Theory: An Introduction*. NY: New York UP, 1996.
Jeffreys, Sheila. *The Lesbian Heresy*. North Melbourne, Australia: Spinifex Press, 1993.
Kregloe, Karman and Jane Caputi. "Supermodels of Lesbian Chic: Camille Paglia Revamps Lesbian/Feminism (while Susie Bright Retools)." *Cross-Purposes: Lesbians, Feminists, and the Limits of Alliance*. Ed. Dana Heller. Bloomington: Indiana UP, 1997. 136-56.
Lamos, Colleen. "The Postmodern Position: On Our Backs." *The Lesbian Postmodern*. Ed. Laura Doan. NY: Columbia UP, 1994. 84-155.
Lugones, Maria. "Playfulness, 'World' Traveling, and Loving Perception." *Lesbian Philosophies and Cultures*. Ed. Jeffner Allen. NY: New York UP, 1990. 159-80.
Lorde, Audre. *Sister Outsider*. Freedom, California: The Crossing Press, 1984.
McRuer, Robert. *The Queer Renaissance*. NY: New York UP, 1997.
Miriam, Kathy. "From Rage to All the Rage: Lesbian-Feminism, Sadomasochism and the Politics of Memory." *Unleashing Feminism: Critiquing Lesbian Sadomasochism in the Gay Nineties*. Ed. Irene Reti. Santa Cruz: HerBooks, 1993. 7-70.
Modleski, Tania. "The White Negress and the Heavy-Duty Dyke." *Cross-Purposes: Lesbians, Feminists, and the Limits of Alliance*. Ed. Dana Heller. Bloomington: Indiana UP, 1997. 64-84.
Moller, Herbert. "The Social Causation of the Courtly Love Complex." *Comparative Studies in Society and History*. 1 (1958-59): 137-63.
Morton, Donald. "The Politics of Queer Theory in the (Post)Modern Moment." *Genders* 17 (1993): 121-50.,
Penelope, Julia. *Call Me Lesbian. Lesbian Lives, Lesbian Theory*. Freedom, CA: Crossing Press, 1992.
Radin, Grace. "Two enormous chunks': Episodes Excluded During the Final Revisions of *The Years*." *Bulletin of the New York Public Library* 80.2 (1977): 221-51.
Reagon, Bernice Johnson. "Coalition Politics: Turning the Century." *Home Girls: A Black Feminist Anthology*. Ed. Barbara Smith. NY: Kitchen Table: Women of Color Press, 1983. 356-68.
Reti, Irena. Introduction. *Unleashing Feminism: Critiquing Lesbian Sadomasochism in the Gay Nineties*. Ed. Irene Reti. Santa Cruz: HerBooks, 1993. 1-3.
Russo, Ann. et al. *A Feminist Dictionary*. Boston: Pandora Press, 1985. *Sinister Wisdom: The Fifteenth Anniversary Retrospective*. 43/44 (Summer 1991).
Tucker, Scott. *The Queer Question: Essays on Desire and Democracy*. Boston: South

End Press, 1997.
Turcotte, Louise. "Queer Theory: Transgression and/or Regression." *Canadian Woman Studies* 16.2 (1996): 118-21.
Walters, Suzanna Danuta. "From Here to Queer: Radical Feminism, Postmodernism, and the Lesbian Menace (Or, Why Can't a Woman Be More Like a Fag?)." *Signs: Journal of Women in Culture and Society* 21 (1996): 830-69.
Woolf, Virginia. *Between the Acts*. NY: HBJ, 1941.
——. *The Diary of Virginia Woolf*. 6 vols. Ed. Andrew McNeillie. NY: HBJ, 1987.
——. *The Letters of Virginia Woolf*. Ed. Nigel Nicolson and Joanne Trautmann. 6 vols. NY: HBJ, 1975-80.
——. *Moments of Being*. NY: HBJ, 1976.
——. *The Years*. NY: HBJ, 1937.
——. *The Waves*. NY: HBJ, 1931.
——. *Three Guineas*. NY: HBJ, 1938.
Young-Bruehl, Elisabeth. *Hannah Arendt: For Love of the World*. New Haven: Yale UP, 1982.
Zimmerman, Bonnie. "Confessions of a Lesbian-Feminist." *Cross-Purposes: Lesbians, Feminists, and the Limits of Alliance*. Ed. Dana Heller. Bloomington: Indiana UP, 1997. 157-68

Trauma and Wellness

Diane F. Gillespie
Metaphors of Illness and Wellness:
John Donne, Virginia Woolf, and Susan Sontag

Woolf looked backwards in time when she wrote "On Being Ill," most immediately to Henry Dwight Sedgwick's 1916 essay of the same title. In her review of his book, Woolf wryly defines such abstract topics as antiquated, or more characteristic of the eighteenth than of the twentieth century (*E2* 80). Her title, therefore, must be ironic. Familiar with much of John Donne's work, she probably knew his *Devotions upon Emergent Occasions*,[1] a metaphor-filled response to "a dangerous illness in 1623 [that] brought him to the brink of the grave" (in Leslie Stephen's words, 68). Whether or not Woolf had Donne's work in mind, though, is less important than the search of two writers, living with different religious orientations at different cultural moments, for language to describe the experience and the significance of illness.[2] Among its many figures of speech, Donne's *Devotions* incorporates certain metaphors that Susan Sontag challenges in *Illness as Metaphor and AIDS and Its Metaphors* (1989). Sontag, who admits that metaphors are both inevitable and seductive, still thinks there are "some...we might well abstain from or try to retire" (93). Among them are military metaphors—like Donne's—whereby illness, as Sontag says, becomes "an enemy that invades, that lays siege to the body-fortress" (96). In today's discourse, micro-organisms overcome the body's immunological defenses, and "medicine is 'aggressive'" in response (97). Sontag objects to such metaphors because they shape our attitudes and excuse our behavior in potentially dangerous ways. For one thing, "the move from the demonization of the illness to the attribution of fault to the patient is an inevitable one" (99). "We are not being invaded," she insists. "The body is not a battlefield. The ill are neither unavoidable casualties nor the enemy. We—medicine, society—are not authorized to fight back by any means whatever" (183).

Woolf, like Sontag, considers metaphors both seductive and "necessary directly you deal with thought" (Silver 109). In *Orlando* (1928), to cite one example, she not only indulges in them but also mocks them and puts their

127

extravagances and limitations into a historical context (e.g. 27, 47).[3] Of disease and military metaphors Woolf is especially self-conscious. As Daniel Fogel observes, Woolf on occasion "described [literary] influence as a disease, and associated it with influenza" which, "after the . . . pandemic of 1918-19," "no one could take . . . lightly" (70-71). Similarly, as Karen Levenback recently writes, "to Virginia Woolf, . . . after 1914 war was not a figure of speech" (1). If Woolf still uses military imagery after 1914, when war became a horrifying reality, and if she links it with disease—epidemic in her world as it was in Donne's—then one should observe carefully what she does. In "On Being Ill" Woolf connects war not just with the suffering body in the sickroom, as Donne does, but also with the so-called "civilized" and healthy world outside. Anticipating Sontag, Woolf suggests that writers can defuse or ironically recast pernicious metaphors in ways that indict a society overly fond of them. To be physically ill and isolated from a culture that defines health as participation in a battle for power and status, and that defines reading as an organized military exercise led by critics, is also, in an important sense, to be well.

There is some disagreement about the nature of the illness Donne writes about. Similarly, although "On Being Ill" refers to a number of diseases and symptoms, some of them as life-threatening as what Donne must have suffered, Woolf leaves the matter vague.[4] Yet Woolf, like Donne, initially images the body both as a battlefield and as a little world, a landscape buffeted by natural forces. Both writers also express astonishment at the body's sudden transformation by illness and at human mortality. Perhaps these similarities exist not just because suffering has certain commonalities, but because, as Woolf says, of "the poverty of the language." If English literature "has no words for the shiver and the headache" (*E4* 318), then one begins, ironically if necessary, with what one has.

It is the "miserable condition of Man," Donne writes, using the military metaphors Sontag dislikes, that "in a minute a Cannon batters all, overthrowes all, demolishes all." Then he shifts to microcosmic metaphors: "Is this the honour which Man hath by being a *little world*," he asks, "That he hath these *earthquakes* in him selfe, sudden shakings; these *lightnings*, sodaine flashes; these *thunders*, sodaine noises; these *Eclypses*, sodaine offuscations, & darknings of his senses; these *blazing stars*, sodaine fiery exhalations; these *rivers of blood*, sodaine red waters?" (Meditation 1, 7-8). Indeed, he insists gloomily, "A sicke bed, is a grave; and all that the patient saies there is but a varying of his owne *Epitaph*" (Meditation 3, 15).

Woolf, in "On Being Ill," does refer to an "*attack* of influenza" and to the neglect in literature of the "great *wars*" which the body wages by itself. . . in the solitude of the bedroom against the *assault* of fever or the oncome of melancholia" (*E4* 317-18; italics mine). She also exclaims, with the parallel grammatical structures, elaborate microcosmic metaphors, and intimations of mortality reminiscent of Donne,

> how tremendous the spiritual change it [illness] brings, how astonishing, when the lights of health go down, the undiscovered countries that are then disclosed, what wastes and deserts of the soul a slight attack of influenza brings to light, what precipices and lawns sprinkled with bright flowers a little rise of temperature reveals, what ancient and obdurate oaks are uprooted in us in the act of sickness, . . . (*E4* 317).

What in Donne's meditation are frightening and violent bodily symptoms, however—imaged as earthquakes, lightnings, thunders, and eclipses—are, in Woolf's more complex microcosm, darkenings, precipices, and uprootings, yes—but also fascinating and pleasant disclosures, illuminations, and revelations. Woolf goes further. She shifts the military metaphors from the experience of illness to the everyday routine of ostensibly healthy people, to their efforts "to communicate, to civilise, to share, to cultivate the desert, educate the native, to work by day together and by night to sport." The tone forecasts the irony of the passage in *A Room of One's Own*: without women serving as magnifying looking-glasses for men, "probably the earth would still be swamp and jungle. The glories of all our wars would be unknown" (35-6). Yet in illness, "On Being Ill" states, all "this make-believe ceases. . . .we cease to be *soldiers* in the *army* of the upright; we become *deserters*. They *march to battle*. We float with the sticks on the stream. . ." (*E4* 321; italics mine). The respectable, so-called civilized life of the body politic is the scene of warfare, both literal and figurative, and the ailing body in the sickroom is not so much an escape from it as a challenge to its values.

The sickroom in "On Being Ill" is a commentary on related battlefields, those of the practical world where prose defeats poetry and of the academic world where Donne's "Cannons" become literary canons. Indeed, Woolf writes, "illness makes us disinclined for the long *campaigns* that prose exacts. We cannot *command* all our faculties and keep our reason and our judgement and our memory *at attention* while chapter swings on top of chapter, and, as one settles into place, we must be on the watch for the coming of the next, until the whole structure—arches, towers, battlements—stands firm on its foundations" (*E4* 323-4; italics mine). In Woolf's sickroom, poetry is the preferred reading, and "all this buzz of criticism" about it is swept aside. "Shakespeare with his overweening power" speaks directly to outlaw readers with their "overweening arrogance." Such readers even have the temerity to say, "But enough of Shakespeare" and to pick up Augustus Hare's three-volume chronicle of Charlotte, Countess Canning, and Louisa, Marchioness of Waterford, sisters caught in the "web" or "net" of Victorian family life (*E4* 326). The sickroom, in other words, becomes a room of one's own where the hierarchies and reading habits of the so-called healthy, patriarchal world, defined by its endemic military imagery, are set aside.

Woolf also departs from her predecessor Donne, and thus from the pattern Sontag describes, when she deals with the isolation of, and "the attribution of fault to the patient" (Sontag 99). "As Sicknesse is the greatest misery, so the greatest misery of sicknes is *solitude*," Donne observes. "*Solitude* is a torment, which is not threatned in *hell* it selfe." Friends tire of visiting, or they fear infection. Even the "*Phisician* dares scarse come" (Meditation 5, 24-5).[5] Indeed, "an infectious bed" to Donne is "equall, nay worse than a *grave*, that thogh in both I be equally alone, in my bed I *know* it, and *feele* it, and shall not in my *grave*" (26).

It is possible that the speaker of "On Being Ill," like that of Donne's *Devotions*, is an "autobiographical *fiction*" (Rollin 52). Still there is a self-pitying, self-lacerating, and moralizing tone in Donne's meditations not present in Woolf's lighter, more humorous, often ironic presentation. In the expostulation that follows the meditation on solitude, for instance, Donne cites the agonies of scriptural predecessors who have been left, or feared to be left alone (Elias, Martha, Jeremiah, the leper). "Shall this come to such a *Leprosie* in my *body*, that I must die alone? Alone without them that should assist, that shold comfort me?" He reproaches, however, not just the community he fears will cast him out but also himself: "comes not this *Expostulation* too neere a *murmuring*" against an ever-present God and his purposes? (Expostulation 5, 27-28; cf Expos. 23, 123).

Woolf, like Donne, notes the patient's isolation, but her sickbed is no grave. She is neither a metaphorical leper blaming others for casting her out, nor does she blame herself for her reactions. Unlike Donne, she dismisses any identification with family, friends, doctors, or nurses as something "we cannot have" and, moreover, probably do not want. In an age of people "weighted . . . already . . . with sorrow" and focused, of necessity, on the demanding and distracting business of living, those who still sympathize and cater to the whims of the sick are "the laggards and failures," mostly women "who, having dropped out of the race, have time to spend upon fantastic and unprofitable excursions" (*E4* 319-20). There is the usual ironic ambiguity here when Woolf suggests that the current competitive goals of civilization leave no time for "such follies" as procuring the oddities a sick person fancies (*E4* 320). At the same time, she says, were the truth told, "we go alone, and like it better so. Always to have sympathy, always to be accompanied, always to be understood would be intolerable" (*E4* 320-1).

Woolf's essay thus seems to question Donne's famous geographical metaphor in Meditation 17, "No Man is an *Iland*, intire of it selfe; every man is a peece of the *Continent*, a part of the *maine*; . . ." (Meditation 17, 87).[6] On the contrary, she says,

> that illusion of a world so shaped that it echoes every groan, of human beings so tied together by common needs and fears that a twitch at one wrist jerks another, where however strange your experience other people have had it too, where however far you travel in your own mind someone has been there before you—is all an illusion. We do not know our own souls, let alone the souls of others. (*E4* 320)

Woolf had just written in *Mrs. Dalloway* (1925) about the dangers of assuming such knowledge, and of the resulting attempts to force people's souls into predetermined molds, to impose one's "sense of proportion" upon them (*MD* 96). Born into a publicly agnostic family, Woolf presents Conversion, the sister goddess of Proportion, in a similarly negative light (*MD* 100). Donne, however, born Roman Catholic in an era of persecution, took Anglican orders and became dean of St. Paul's in 1621. He is thus preoccupied throughout his meditations with the relationship between the physical and the spiritual, sickness and sin, and life and death, all presided over by the Christian God. Each of Donne's twenty-three meditations is followed by an expostulation based on scripture, and by a prayer. Indeed, the most meaningful written text to Donne's sick person is the Bible,[7] the third of God's books (after the book of life and the book of nature) (Expostulation 9, 49). Mankind is also a metaphorical book, authored by God, in which men are chapters translated by old age and death, sickness and war (Meditation 17, 86). Translated by sickness, Donne uses his rational mind, in turn, to translate into words his struggle against both physical illness and his negative emotions. His *Devotions*, with its linear structure, follows the stages of these efforts and, as he indicates in his dedication, concludes with a "preternaturall Birth, *in returning* to Life, *from this* Sicknes." The patient rises, reborn, to give birth, in turn, to the book (*Devotions* 3).

Woolf, although she wryly describes the experience of coming out of a dentist's anaesthesia as a time of confusion between the doctor and "the Deity" (*E4* 317), dismisses the feeble imaginings of "Heaven, Immortality" characteristic of clergymen and their parishioners, and of most prose writers (*E4* 322-23). The idea of reincarnation into multiple lives provides an agreeable alternative to the "tyrannical 'I'" traditionally dominating both this world and the next. Again, Woolf confronts the inadequacy of words. "The imagination of a poet," she concludes, is what is needed for "Heaven making" (*E4* 323) because, she says, "In illness words seem to possess a mystic quality." Instead of their "surface meaning[s]," we pick up sounds, colors, and rhythms which poets use "to evoke, when collected, a state of mind which neither words can express nor the reason explain" (*E4* 324).

In the experience Woolf describes, the senses dominate. The Bible is not what the sick person reads, or needs. Nor is there any interest in expostulation with its connotations of reason and authority. If Shakespeare is a kind of secular scripture to a writer like Woolf, then in illness, she notes, we want no intermediaries; nor do we presume to teach others how and what to read. Woolf defends her enjoyment of a writer like Hare who, while no Boswell, yet slowly makes the reader "almost one of the family" (*E4* 326). One may be isolated during illness from those engaged in the battles society demands, she implies, but one remains fascinated with human emotions rendered in words. Whereas the final word in Donne's *Devotions*, with its linear structure, is "*pardoned*" (*Devotions* 127), Woolf's associational meditations on illness conclude, not with physical and spiritual recovery, but with the word "agony," the response of Lady Waterford, in Hare's account, to her husband's accidental death.[8] Woolf, with her focus on the circumstances of an "often very lonely," artistically talented woman, circles back to the unpredictable changes in human existence, the fragility of human health and human life, with which she began (*E4* 327). She offers no links between suffering, sin, and conventional spirituality. She produces no moral lesson for her readers' edification.

To be physically ill may contribute, ironically, to new perspectives, signs of intellectual health. For this to happen, the military metaphors associated with physical illness and self-reproach must be placed where they originate, in a competitive and hierarchical society that defines life as war and in academic institutions where critics classify literary texts and march readers through them. Perhaps this is one reason why the scholarly T. S. Eliot, himself soon to be an Anglican convert, showed little enthusiasm for "On Being Ill," an article he had requested from her for the recently founded *New Criterion*. Both Virginia and Leonard Woolf, however, considered the essay among her "best" (*D3* 49).[9]

Notes

[1] I have established in "Through Woolf's 'I's': Donne and *The Waves*" Woolf's long-evolving knowledge of Donne's life and work. Although editions of Donne's *Devotions* appeared in 1839, 1840, 1841, 1923, and 1925 (Donne, *Devotions*, xlv), the one remaining in the Woolf library at Washington State University is dated the same year as the initial January publication of "On Being Ill" (1926). Leslie Stephen described the *Devotions* already in 1899 in his reponse to Edmund Gosse's biography (68-9).

[2] Scholars usually consider passages from "On Being Ill" when they discuss Woolf's creative process or her treatment of illness and perceptions of the body in her fiction. Dusinberre mentions both Donne's *Devotions* and Woolf's "On Being Ill" in the same chapter but does not examine them together. Dubino offers a useful reading of Woolf's essay in the context of Bakhtin's "carnival."

[3] Nick Greene, who in the seventeenth century dismisses Donne as "a mountebank who wrapped up his lack of meaning in hard words," praises him in the twentieth (*O* 88, 284-5).

[4] The two possibilities are "typhus and the seven-day or relapsing fever," both of which have been associated with an epidemic in London in late 1623, early 1624. Raspa admits the possibility that Donne ultimately took liberties with his symptoms "for purposes of devotional speculation" (Donne, *Devotions* xvi-xvii). McNeillie does not identify Woolf's illness (*E4* xviii); Bell speaks of "a long bout . . . , with headaches and exhaustion, partial recoveries and new relapses" (2 114). Lee refers to a fainting spell in August followed by months during which "she was very unwell" (491).

[5] As Rollin observes, however, the physician, his consultants, and even the king's doctor are very much present in Donne's descriptions, and "more important than the physical presence of other human beings . . . is the speaker's growing empathy with them" and with their sufferings (56-7).

[6] In *The Waves* (1931), Woolf's characters reflect both disagreement and agreement, as Schlack points out (111).

[7] The *Devotions* are also filled with allusions to classical writers, to the Book of Common Prayer, and to Renaissance theology, medicine, and astronomy (as Raspa's annotations indicate).

[8] The essay does not conclude with the words Dubino quotes when she calls the ending "highly romanticized" and suggestive of "the end of the patriarchal family and the rise of the woman artist" (43). These socially progressive results are implied, but they come at considerable cost.

[9] "On Being Ill" appeared in January 1926. The following April, in a shorter revised version entitled "Illness—An Unexploited Mine," it appeared in *Forum*. A slightly revised original version became a Hogarth Press pamphlet in 1930 (*E4* 327-8).

Works Cited

Bell, Quentin. *Virginia Woolf: A Biography*. 2 vols. London: Hogarth, 1973.

Donne, John. *Devotions Upon Emergent Occasions*. Ed. Anthony Raspa. Montreal: McGill-Queen's UP, 1975.

Dubino, Jeanne. "On Illness as Carnival: The Body as Discovery in Virginia Woolf's 'On Being Ill' and Mikhail Bakhtin's Rabelais and His World." In *Virginia Woolf: Emerging Perspectives*. Ed. Mark Hussey and Vara Neverow. New York: Pace UP, 1994. 38-43.

Dusinberre, Juliet. *Virginia Woolf's Renaissance: Woman Reader or Common Reader?* Iowa City: U of Iowa P, 1997.

Fogel, Daniel Mark. *Covert Relations: James Joyce, Virginia Woolf, and Henry James*. Charlottesville: UP of Virginia, 1990.

Gillespie, Diane F. "Through Woolf's 'I's': Donne and The Waves." In *Virginia Woolf Reading the Renaissance*. Ed. Sally Greene. Athens: Ohio UP, 1999. 211-44.

Lee, Hermione. *Virginia Woolf*. New York: Knopf, 1997.

Levenback, Karen L. *Virginia Woolf and the Great War*. Syracuse: Syracuse UP, 1999.

Rollin, Roger B. "John Donne's Holy Sonnets—The Sequel: Devotions upon Emergent Occasions." *John Donne Annual* 13.1&2 (1994). 51-59.

Schlack, Beverly Ann. *Continuing Presences: Virginia Woolf's Use of Literary Allusion*. University Park, Pennsylvania: Pennsylvania State UP, 1979.

Silver, Brenda. *Virginia Woolf's Reading Notebooks*. Princeton, N.J.: Princeton UP, 1983.

Sontag, Susan. *Illness as Metaphor and AIDS and Its Metaphors*. New York: Doubleday, 1989.

Stephen, Leslie. "John Donne" (1899). *Studies of a Biographer*. Vol. 3. New York: G. P. Putnam's Sons; London: Duckworth, 1902. 36-82.

Woolf, Virginia. *The Diary of Virginia Woolf*. Vol. 3. Ed. Anne Olivier Bell. New York: Harcourt Brace Jovanovich, 1980.

——. *The Essays of Virginia Woolf*. Ed. Andrew McNeillie. Vol. 2. San Diego: Harcourt Brace Jovanovich, 1987; Vol. 4. London: Hogarth, 1994.

——. *The Letters of Virginia Woolf*. Vol. 3. Ed. Nigel Nicolson and Joanne Trautmann. New York: Harcourt Brace Jovanovich, 1977.

——. *Mrs. Dalloway*. San Diego: Harcourt Brace Jovanovich, 1981.

——. *Orlando: A Biography*. New York: Harcourt Brace Jovanovich, 1956.

——. *A Room of One's Own*. New York: Harcourt Brace Jovanovich, 1957.

David Eberly
Safety Pins and Semicolons

From the start Virginia Woolf's work has been marked by both her supporters and detractors as "feminine," and her strengths and weaknesses (which are often interchangeable) have been characterized as those of a woman writer. Her supposed inability to formulate linear plot and to create robust characters has been juxtaposed with her sensitivity, and her style has been described in terms associated with intercourse. "Lover's talk, yes," Jeanette Winterson writes of *The Waves*, to give one example. "The language of rapture . . . [t]he words in rhythmic motion in and out" (93-94). Winterson's florid assessment was foreshadowed by an earlier and far harsher appraisal, which, perhaps unconsciously, juxtaposed the specifics of Woolf's style to female sexual response. "I cannot escape the feeling," Walter Allen wrote in 1954, "that from time to time the exercise of sensibility has become an end in itself. Nor do the moments of revelation and illumination always seems illuminative in any very real sense, but *rather a succession of short, sharp female gasps of ecstasy* [italics mine]; an impression intensified by Mrs. Woolf's use of the semicolon where the comma is ordinarily enough" (423). It is this relationship between Virginia Woolf's overdetermined use of the semicolon, and her sexuality—troubled by the effects of trauma and abuse—that I wish to explore here and to apply to her texts.

As Bennison Gray writes in *The Grammatical Foundations of Rhetoric*, "The usual punctuation convention for distinguishing between compound sentences whose assertions are linked by conjunctions and those without conjunctions is to strengthen the stopping force of the punctuation mark when there is no conjunction and to mitigate the stopping force when there is a conjunction"(96). As Gray implies, the semicolon, which itself is comprised of two contradictory signs of punctuation—the *stop* of the period and the *go* of the comma—functions in a larger grammatical system which propels or impedes the meaning of a sentence, and paradoxically signals simultaneous interruption and continuation.

Moreover, the semicolon is a punctuation mark of relationship. Required when the second clause is preceded by an adverb, it may in compound sentences also function to mark the omission of "subordinate" conjunctions. As Strunk and White state in *The Elements of Style*, the "simple method" of employing the semicolon to "indicate relationship between statements is one of the most useful devices of composition. The relationship . . . is commonly one of cause and consequence" (6). The semicolon, then, denies or suppresses the causality or agency implied in the relationship of the clauses it joins. In addition the semicolon acts within the sentence to unite, sometimes arbitrarily, disparate clauses to form a sentence and to secure its meaning, much like a grammatical safety pin.

Gray concludes his discussion of punctuation and sentence structure by noting that "[W]ords, assertions, sentences, paragraphs, whole compositions, are meaningful in the final analysis because of the way we interpret them in the largest context we need to envision in order to make complete sense of them" (96). This "largest context" necessarily includes an awareness of Virginia Woolf's sexual abuse and an acceptance of its impact on her writing, and calls for the development of what I suggest be described as a rhetoric of incest.

The effects of sexual abuse have been studied and described in increasing detail for over two decades now. As Howard Levine notes in his study of the aftermath of childhood sexual abuse, "The broad range of possible variables involved in childhood sexual trauma means that adults who were sexually abused as children are members of a heterogeneous group that defies simple characterization" (145). Among the "wide variety of adult symptomatic consequences of childhood sexual trauma" that Levine lists is included "promiscuity, seductive behaviors, sexual inhibitions and dysfunctions." In *Betrayal Trauma*, Jennifer J. Freyd also states that "[s]exual abuse survivors also commonly suffer damage to their ability to enjoy their sexuality. Their sexual behavior may be either excessively restricted or excessively promiscuous; either extreme can restrict both intimacy and pleasure" (173). In her study of brother-sister incest Karin Meiselman reports that of those studied, "85 percent of the sisters had serious problems with orgasmic response as adults, either failing to achieve orgasm at all or achieving it only in very unusual circumstances" (281).

Clearly, the possibility of orgasm raises issues about sexual control in incest survivors. "Impulsivity and concerns about control or loss of control . . . must stem, in part, from the victim's repeated experiences of loss of self-control accompanying environmentally triggered altered states of consciousness, such as . . . abreactions, panic attacks, and regressive states" (Putnam, 124). The *stop/start* signal of the semicolon within the structure of a sentence can be said to simulate the contradictory sexual response of the incest survivor, who may simultaneously seek and avoid the orgasm she wants and dreads. Similarly, the semicolon, which has been shown as a punctuation mark of relationship, may act to disguise or repress causality, imitating the denial mechanism reported to be so prevalent among survivors. In her discussion of repression, Freyd examines at length the relationship between trauma and denial, arguing that the mechanism of repression is motivated not only by the avoidance of pain or by the inhibition of impulse but also by "the need to preserve the love of others, and suggests that the betrayal of trust and not the extremity of abuse may be the cause of memory loss" (23-24, 60-71.) Let me suggest that the subjugation experienced and denied by the victim in her relationship to the perpetrator may be seen as mirrored within a sentence structure that masks the overt relationship between its clauses by employing the semicolon.

Because the denizens of Bloomsbury wrote and preserved an extraordinary amount of gossip, we may know more about the sexual response of Virginia Woolf than almost any other author (Edith Wharton's experience comes to mind, and offers an interesting contrast) and so may discuss it with confidence that our assessment is not conjecture. "Certainly," Woolf reported to Ka Cox, "I find the climax immensely exaggerated. Except for a sustained good humor . . . I might be still Miss S" (*L2* 6). A few months later Vanessa Bell confirmed her sister's self-reported frigidity. Writing to her husband Clive, she observed that both Leonard and Virginia are "a little exercised in their minds on the subject of the Goat's coldness . . . . Apparently she still gets no pleasure at all from the act" (132). Vanessa linked her sister's lack of response to her indifference to men. But we should remember that Vita Sackville-West also mentioned Woolf's sexual dysfunction in her own love affair with Virginia, admitting to her husband that "I am scared to death of arousing physical feelings in her, because of the madness. I don't know what effect it would have, you see; and that is a fire with which I have no wish to play" (159). We should remember that Vita writes this *after* she has twice slept with Virginia. What we find in these documents is a profile of the impact of trauma on Woolf's sexuality that is recognizably similar to that of incest survivors, a profile which includes dysfunction, frigidity, and the threat of being overwhelmed by the experience of orgasm.

This pattern of *stop/start* response to pleasure which characterizes Woolf's sexuality can also be found in her texts, whose narrative flow is so markedly distinguished by the dynamics of impulse and restraint. In an earlier paper I briefly noted the overdetermined use of the semicolon in *Flush* (Eberly 22) and related it to the incest narrative that I found there. Now I would like to examine its use more closely.

"Slater's Pins Have No Points" has been examined for the narrative strategies that conceal its function as a site of homoeroticism. But while the specifically lesbian nature of the relationship the story describes and the coded sexual climax it implies have been revealed, the underlying dysfunction of the sexual impulse depicted in the text has not been fully explored. "Slater's Pins" moves covertly to the recognition of the attraction and implied sexual union of its two characters, Julia Craye and Fanny Wilmot, and culminates in what Janet Winston describes as "lesbian ecstatic bewilderment" in her study of this story (68). But Julia Craye—whose name is a close homonym with *"crave"*—is characterized as a woman hemmed in by obsessive-compulsive behaviors. "She took," Fanny Wilmot notes, "astonishing precautions against chills, fatigue, rich food, the wrong food, draughts, heated rooms, [and] journeys in the Tube." If Craye strings an afternoon upon her "necklace of days," it is as compartmentalized from her other experiences as "this view;" [semicolon] or "that city;" [semicolon]. "[B]eauty; [semicolon]," Julia thinks, "and I can't get at it; [semicolon] I can't have it— [dash]" (*CSF* 213). The dash, I might add, can serve as a substitute for the semicolon, as Gray remarks.

Trauma and Wellness

Although Winston argues that the eroticized descriptions of the women's handling of the carnation evokes what she describes as "forms of lesbian lovemaking," Craye seems an unlikely character for such abandonment. The passage in which Julia retrieves the carnation while Fanny searches for the pin indeed suggests manual stimulation of the clitoris and orgasm: "The pressure of her fingers seemed to increase all that was most brilliant in the flower; to set it off; to make it more frilled, fresh, immaculate." Winston chooses to conclude the quotation here, but Woolf herself continues. "What was odd in her . . . was that this crush and grasp of the fingers was combined with a perpetual frustration. So it was now with the carnation. She had her hands on it; she pressed it; but she did not possess it, enjoy it, not altogether" (*CSF* 211). Woolf darkens the sexual moment; the pleasure sought is not enjoyed. Indeed the last sentence quoted imitates the halting movement toward orgasm—its flow is impeded by two semicolons and two commas and is a masterly depiction of the sexual hesitancy it encodes. When in the penultimate paragraph all seems "transparent for a moment to the gaze of Fanny Wilmot," the prose explodes in what can only be described as a frenzy of semicolons—twelve, to be exact, before she "sees" Julia, who kisses her. Each semicolon joins, distinguishes, secures, and separates.

"Slater's pins have no points," the story concludes. But more than a carnation is lost when a pin provides no security or safety. One cannot read this statement without recalling that Woolf, who suffered agonies over her dress, famously lost her drawers while shopping. It is difficult not to associate this symptom of Woolf's sexual abuse with the story being discussed, and to allow an element of unease to trouble the erotic interchange between the women.

That the representation, however coded, of digital manipulation and penetration of the vagina provokes such defenses in Woolf's writing should not surprise the reader familiar with the account that she gave of her earliest sexual abuse. Indeed, she left a strikingly graphic and public account:

> Once when I was very small Gerald Duckworth lifted me onto this [slab], and as I sat there he began to explore my body. I can remember the feel of his hand going under my clothes; going firmly and steadily lower and lower. I remember how I hoped that he would stop; how I stiffened and wriggled as his hand approached my private parts. But it did not stop. His hand explored my private parts, too. I remember resenting, disliking it—what is the word for so dumb and mixed a feeling? It must have been strong, since I still recall it. (69)

The overwhelming nature of this trauma is indicated by the speechlessness to which it reduces Woolf, who cannot find the words to describe it, and may account for the ambivalence in her work when she describes the mutual masturbation that would be a pleasurable experience for most women. As a result of her abuse, her descriptions of lesbian intimacy, while unmarked by the understanding of the political and social power structures of male dominance which inform her writing on heterosexual relations, are themselves troubled and troubling.

If, as Julie Abraham writes, *"Mrs. Dalloway* has to be central to any reading of Woolf as a lesbian writer because of the ways in which narrative, history, and representations of lesbianism are brought together in this novel" (145), the novel firmly resists any effort to transform it into a meta-narrative of lesbian experience, in part because of Woolf's vicious description of its one identifiable lesbian, Doris Kilman. Eileen Barrett, for one, has sought to ameliorate Woolf's portrait of Kilman by arguing that "the reality of Doris's lesbian existence enables Clarissa to release the lesbian trapped within her soul" (162). But embedded in Woolf's description of Kilman is not only an ambivalence to the lesbian experience, but the trace of sexual trauma as well.

Woolf, for example, describes the interaction between Elizabeth and Kilman in terms remarkably similar to the description of Julia and Fanny in "Slater's Pins." As in the short story, the scene demonstrates a hyper-attentive and I would say phobic description of Doris Kilman's hands. During their tea, Kilman is described as "fingering the last two inches of a chocolate éclair." Her "large hand opened and shut on the table." "If she could grasp her, if she could clasp her, if she could make her hers absolutely and forever and then die; that was all she wanted," Woolf writes. "The thick fingers curled inward." Elizabeth remembers that, offered a bouquet, "Miss Kilman squashed the flowers all in a bunch," in a gesture similar to Julia Craye's (*MD* 131-2). The aversion to Kilman shown in Woolf's narrative rests on a horror deeper than that of homophobia. In fact Miss Kilman's hand most resembles that of Colonel Abel Pargiter. In another passage notable for its semicolons, Woolf describes Pargiter's lovemaking: "He drew her toward him; he kissed her on the nape of the neck; and then the hand that had lost two fingers began to fumble rather lower down where the neck joins the shoulders" (*TY* 9).

Mrs. Dalloway is a novel of interruptions and intrusions. Characterized by a fluidity of movement and moment, it paradoxically reveals a dynamic of hesitancies, halts, and checks. "'I love walking in London,' said Mrs. Dalloway. 'Really it's better than walking in the country.'" But unlike a country stroll, her city walk is a series of stops and starts as she halts for traffic, greets friends, and window shops. It seems, too, that her each step is accompanied in the text by a semicolon, creating in its microcosm a "choreography" that "inevitably develops from the rhythm of broken sequence," as Lucio Ruotolo has described Woolf's fiction as a whole (Ruotolo 2). These interruptions may be as small as a thought or a word or as large as the Great War, which so tragically interrupts the lives of Septimus and Rezia. Peter Walsh, of course, interrupts the kiss between Sally and Clarissa. Walsh, who is associated with a half-opened pocket knife that—if one thinks about it—might recall a safety pin, functions as yet another phallic-finger symbol which intrudes in the novels of Woolf much like Colonel Pargiter. But we should note that the kiss itself in the text is an interrupted event. "Sally stopped; [semicolon] picked a flower; [semicolon] kissed her on the lips" (MD 35).

"There is a jouissance of the body that is," Lacan has written, "'beyond the phallus.... There is a jouissance that is hers (à elle), that belongs to that 'she' (elle) that doesn't exist and doesn't signify anything. There is a jouissance that is hers about which she perhaps knows nothing if not that she experiences it" (74). It is this jouissance, absent the phallus—the pin with no point, or Peter Walsh, if you prefer—that Julia Craye and Fanny Wilmot, and Clarissa Dalloway and Sally Seton seek to discover in their relationships with one another. But the phallus is never not absent; instead it is present in the trauma memory of the penetrating finger that interrupts the very structure of the sentences that Woolf uses to describe the pleasure she seeks to create. An "imaginary signifier," it nevertheless leaves real traces of its presence in the semicolons of Virginia Woolf's texts.

Works Cited

Allen, Walter. *The English Novel: A Short Critical History.* New York: E. P. Dutton & Co., Inc., 1954.

Barrett, Eileen. "Unmasking Lesbian Passion: The Inverted World of *Mrs. Dalloway.*" *Virginia Woolf: Lesbian Readings.* Ed. Eileen Barrett and Patricia Cramer. New York: New York UP, 1997. 146-164.

Bell, Vanessa. *Selected Letters of Vanessa Bell.* Ed. Regina Marler. New York: Pantheon Books, 1993.

Eberly, David. "Housebroken: The Domesticated Relations of *Flush.*" *Virginia Woolf: Texts and Contexts. Selected Papers from the Fifth Annual Conference on Virginia Woolf.* Ed. Beth Rigel Daugherty and Eileen Barrett. New York: Pace UP, 1996.

Freyd, Jennifer. *Betrayal Trauma; The Logic of Forgetting Childhood Abuse.* Cambridge, Massachusetts: Harvard UP, 1996.

Gray, Bennison. *The Grammatical Foundations of Rhetoric: Discourse Analysis.* The Hague: Mouton Publishers, 1977.

Lacan, Jacques. *On Feminine Sexuality: The Limits of Love and Knowledge. The Seminars of Jacques Lacan. Book XX Encore 1972-1973.* Translated with notes by Bruce Fink. New York: W. W. Norton & Company, 1998.

Levine, Howard B., M.D. "Repetition, Reenactment, and Trauma: Clinical Issues in the Analytic Therapy of Adults Who Were Sexually Abused as Children." *Victims of Abuse: The Emotional Impact of Child and Adult Trauma.* Ed. Alan Sugarman, M.D. Madison: International Universities Press, Inc., 1994, 141-164.

Meiselman, Karin C. *Incest: A Psychological Study of Causes and Effects with Treatment Recommendations.* San Francisco: Jossey-Bass Publishers, 1978.

Putnam, Frank W., M.D. "Disturbances of 'Self' in Victims of Childhood Sexual Abuse." *Incest-Related Syndromes of Adult Psychopathology.* Ed. Richard P. Kluft. M.D. Washington D.C.: American Psychiatric Press, Inc., 1990. 113-131.

Sackville-West, Vita and Harold Nicolson. *Vita and Harold: The Letters of Vita Sackville-West and Harold Nicolson.* Ed. Nigel Nicolson. New York: G. P. Putnam's Sons, 1992.

Strunk, William Jr. and E. B. White. *The Elements of Style.* Third Edition. New York: Macmillan Publishing Co., Inc., 1977.

Winston, Janet. "Reading Influences: Homoeroticism and Mentoring in Katherine Mansfield's 'Carnation' and Virginia Woolf's 'Moments of Being: Slater's Pins Have No Points.'" Barrett, ed. *Virginia Woolf: Lesbian Readings*. 57-77.

Winterson, Jeanette. *Art Objects: Essays on Ecstasy and Effrontery.* New York: Vintage, 1995.

Woolf, Virginia. *The Complete Shorter Fiction of Virginia Woolf.* Ed. Susan Dick. New York: HBJ, 1985

——. *The Letters of Virginia Woolf.* Volume 2. Ed. Nigel Nicolson and Joanne Trautman. New York: HBJ, 1976.

——. *Moments of Being.* San Diego: Harvest, 1985.

——. *Mrs. Dalloway.* San Diego: Harvest, 1981.

——. *The Years.* New York: HBJ, 1965.

Judith Greenberg
Woolf's Ancient Song: Traces of the Dead Echoing into the Future

> Not all of me is dust. Within my song,
> safe from the worm, my spirit will survive.
> —Pushkin

I. Writing Survival

Trauma poses a crisis of survival. In Cathy Caruth's terms, it creates "an oscillation between a crisis of death and a crisis of life: between the story of the unbearable nature of the event and the unbearable nature of its survival" (9). I want to show that on many levels—from the characters to all of London in 1923 to the narrative voice and the role of literature itself—*Mrs. Dalloway* is a novel about traumatic survival.

In *Beyond the Pleasure Principle,* Freud evokes the story of Tancred and Clorinda from Tasso's *Gerusalemme Liberata* to illustrate what happens to a survivor of trauma:

> Its hero, Tancred, unwittingly kills his beloved Clorinda in a duel while she is disguised in the armour of an enemy knight. After her burial he makes his way into a strange magic forest which strikes the Crusaders' army with terror. He slashes with his sword at a tall tree; but blood streams from the cut and the voice of Clorinda, whose soul is imprisoned in the tree, is heard complaining that he has wounded his beloved once again. (24)

Tancred's reenactment of the original violence, according to Freud, depicts how survivors unknowingly *repeat* a traumatic event. Moreover, Caruth emphasizes that Tasso's story also portrays the survivor's encounter with the *unassimilable* dimension of trauma. The traumatic event returns because it posed such a shock that it was recognized *one moment too late*; it is a missed experience that has yet to be fully known. Surviving trauma involves a "repeated confrontation with the necessity and impossibility of grasping the threat to one's own life" (Caruth 62). By focusing on the otherness of the *voice* heard in the repetition, Caruth emphasizes the witnessing that occurs only belatedly for the survivor. Tancred hears in the voice that cries out from the tree a truth that he could not know fully at the time of the original event.

Mrs. Dalloway analyzes what it means to celebrate life in the aftermath of both war and personal trauma. Many of the novel's characters— Clarissa Dalloway and Septimus Warren Smith in particular—question the solidity of the boundary between life and death. What kind of survival is possible after the death encounter of trauma? How do the living walk with the dead? Do the dead haunt certain places? Like Tasso's story, this novel about survival also frames encounters with strange voices of otherness.

During her morning walk on Bond Street, Clarissa considers what it means to survive. She turns from thoughts of her own mortality to wonder if:

> somehow in the streets of London, on the ebb and flow of things, here, there, she survived, Peter survived, lived in each other, she being part, she was positive, of the trees at home; of the house there, ugly, rambling all to bits as it was; part of people she had never met; being laid out like a mist between the people she knew best, who lifted her on their branches as she had seen the trees lift the mist, but it spread ever so far, her life, herself. (9)

Clarissa blurs the boundary between the living and the dead by imagining existence as some sort of magical forest in which people survive by metamorphosing into others and trees. She refuses to part with the dead. Instead, like the Tasso story, she imagines that people are like trees with branches that extend the survival of the self. But if the trees in Tasso's story reintroduce past trauma (the cry acts as an echo of the original wound), then does Clarissa's tree-filled fantasy also confront some violence and death that can not be assimilated?

Clarissa continues to focus on the possibility of the return of the dead towards the end of the day:

> with her horror of death, allowed her to believe (for all her scepticism), that since our apparitions, the part of us which appears, are so momentary compared with the other, the unseen part of us, which spreads wide, the unseen might survive, be recovered somehow attached to this person or that, or even haunting certain places after death...perhaps—perhaps. (153)

Why does Clarissa turn to a sense of haunting, a belief that the dead remain alive in the world of the living? Although the event never appears directly in her thoughts, Clarissa witnessed the death of her sister, Sylvia, who was hit by a falling tree. Peter Walsh remembers: "that horrible affair. To see your own sister killed by a falling tree (all Justin Parry's fault—all his carelessness) before your very eyes, a girl too on the verge of life, the most gifted of them, Clarissa always said, was enough to turn one bitter" (78). Thus, along with Clarissa's recent confrontation with her own survival after her illness, witnessing the death of her sister may have been an event both seen and unseen. The continual references to trees may allude to the trauma of her having witnessed and survived Sylvia's death.

Of course, the most extreme survivor in the novel is Septimus. Much has been written on Septimus's status as Clarissa's "double" in the novel, as Woolf's own notes state ("Preface" vi).[1] Both characters repeat the refrain from Shakespeare's *Cymbeline*, revealing a shared death wish. But if both focus on the parting—or failure of parting—between the living and the dead, Septimus experiences a more acute confusion in regard to that division. He hears the sparrows sing "from trees in the meadow of life beyond a river where the dead walk, how there is no death" (25). He sees his dead war comrade Evans appear from out of the bushes. He is haunted by his own survival: "The War had taught him. It was sublime. He had gone through the whole show, friendship, European War, death, had won promotion, was still under thirty and was bound to survive. He was right there. The last shells missed him. He watched them explode with indifference" (86). This emotional numbness and the other symptoms Septimus experiences would have been labeled "shell-shock" in the 1922 Report to the War Office Committee (Knox-Shaw 103) and can today be called post-traumatic-stress-disorder (PTSD).[2] In PTSD, the inability for the mind to confront the possibility of its death directly makes the survival an "endless testimony to the impossibility of living" (Caruth 61). Survival for Septimus is a crisis full of repeated and painful confrontations with the dead. And, like many survivors, he makes the ultimate declaration of the *impossibility* of living by his act of suicide.

II. Survival as Echo

The question of survival, according to J. Hillis Miller, exists for *all* of the characters in the novel. "Each man or woman," Miller argues, "possesses a kind of immortality, despite the finality of death" (181). For Miller, such immortality extends to the narrative voice of the novel as well, a narrative voice that lives after the events of the story have taken place, and that, in repeating the past, not only remembers but resurrects the dead.[3] Miller's characterization of the novel as ghostly suggests an oscillation between life and death. I propose that this return is not so much a ghostly resurrection but more of an echoing after trauma. In the place of a supernatural phenomenon, the trope of an echo presents a naturally occurring phenomenon that also produces a ghostly sense of survival. As a disembodied voice, an echo creates a kind of presence in absence. It involves the emergence of a sound after the occurrence of an original and thus resembles the structure of original absence and then belated return in trauma. Both an echo and trauma literally replay the past, carrying a trace of the original after it has disappeared. I thus reread the novel's ghostly structure as an echoing that reintroduces the lack of witnessing of the threat of death. The dead come back to life not because they are resurrected in a supernatural way but because life for the traumatized survivor—or for the narrative voice—replays the unknown event after a gap in time.

This is to argue that echoes are central to the crises of survival at stake in the novel. Not only do "affinities, echoes and chains of imagery throughout the text link Clarissa and Septimus" (Briggs 47) but the entire novel abounds in echoes—verbal refrains and various acoustical "rings" that reverberate throughout the day. To understand the role of echoes as voices of survival in the novel, voices that bear witness, we should turn to the first representation of an echoing voice that blurs the boundaries between the living and the dead. The story of Echo from Ovid's *Metamorphoses* that appears in Book Three (intertwined with the story of Narcissus) can allegorize many of the conditions faced by survivors of trauma. From the outset of her story, Echo's speech is constrained by Juno—she cannot originate her own words but is condemned to mimic what others have said. Like a survivor of trauma, Echo has no access to an original and is compelled to repeat. Her repetitive fragments—her stammer—can be interpreted as the literal reemergence of the traumatic event.[4]

As the story develops, Echo becomes enamored with the beautiful Narcissus who eventually rejects her. Out of grief, she withers away until her bones disintegrate and she becomes pure voice. Ovid does not leave Echo to die, however. He transforms her into eternal reverberation: although physically wasted away, her voice "can be heard [everywhere]; the power of sound still lives in her" (93). Metamorphosed, Echo resembles the state of survivors who have been "through" death. She has experienced death—her body dies—and yet her voice lives. This existence in a ghostly or disembodied state can also depict the place of the survivor's voice—somehow removed or disembodied[5] and yet echoing nevertheless. Finally, at the end of these stories, when Narcissus dies by the side of the pool, a group of dryads weep for the loss of the beautiful boy and Echo joins their "choir of grief" (97) by miming their sounds. In her final condition, Echo sings a song of mourning and eternal repetition. Thus the figure of Echo can allegorize the constraints of traumatic narration, the survivor's sense of disembodiment, and the reverberations of the mourning or traumatized voice.

But this final role—the voice or cry that survives—also becomes a strength. A reference to Echo reappears in Ovid's final lines in the *Metamorphoses*. Ovid reintroduces the echo to symbolize the immortal voice of poetry: "my lines will be on people's lips; and through all time—if poet's prophecies are ever right—my name and fame are sure: I shall have life" (549). Ovid's evocation of the echo of the Other in the form of the audience connotes presence in the form of a listening or reading body, a crossing or exchange between reader and poet, the living and the dead. Thus Echo's final transformation into an acoustical echo provides the poet the acknowledgment that she herself never received from Narcissus. The voice that returns has been transformed from one of constrained speech into the survival of the written word.

This intertext of Ovid's Echo can help us to rethink issues of trauma and survival. Echoing voices and allusions to Echo in the novel ask: "Do repetitive fragments articulate conditions of surviving trauma?" "How does a voice of repeated fragments, a stammer, bear witness?" One echoing passage in *Mrs. Dalloway,* the song of the ravaged beggar woman outside the Regent's Park Tube Station, is particularly emblematic of how such sounds address crises of survival for the novel as a whole. Much as Narcissus encounters Echo as a sound that interrupts him, as Peter Walsh approaches a "crossing":

> A sound interrupted him; a frail quivering sound, a voice bubbling up without direction, vigour, beginning or end, running weakly and shrilly and with an absence of all human meaning into
>
> > *ee um fah um so*
> > *foo swee too eem oo—*
>
> the voice of no age or sex, the voice of an ancient spring spouting from the earth; which issued, just opposite Regent's Park Tube station from a tall quivering shape, like a funnel, like a rusty pump, like a wind-beaten tree for ever barren of leaves which lets the wind run up and down its branches singing
>
> > *ee um fah um so*
> > *foo swee too eem oo*
>
> and rocks and creaks and moans in the eternal breeze. (80-81)

Although this song is repeated three times, the origin or meaning of the sounds are lost. All that return are indecipherable fragments, a kind of pre- or post-linguistic babble that attest to the incommunicable nature of this woman's message. Gilbert and Gubar interpret her babble as symbolic of both women's alienation from language and the ability to imagine a "fantastic new language" (249-50).[6] While I do find something hopeful in the later claim, I consider her sounds to be not only fantastic but the stammer of the survival of trauma.[7] If this woman sings of the dead, then the indecipherability of her lyrics testifies to the impossibility of knowing that death.

Both the beggar woman and Echo personify survival, transcending or blurring the division between life and death. Echo's voice remains, and this woman's sound "rocks and creaks and moans in the eternal breeze." Her voice has survived all ages, it is an "ancient song" that existed "when the pavement was grass, when it was swamp, through the age of tusk and mammoth, through the age of silent sunrise" (81). And as Echo calls and sings for her beloved and unattainable Narcissus, this figure sings of "love which prevails, and millions of years ago, her lover, who had been dead these centuries, had walked, she crooned, with her in May" (81). The beggar-woman now alone remains, the living and the dead have parted. But her song restructures time and history: the dead live with her in an eternal present. Miller reads this passage as Woolf "burying within her novel a clue to the way the day of the action is to be seen as a resurrection of ghosts from the past" (189) and argues that it presents a version of Strauss's *Aller Seelen,* a song about the day of collective resurrection when the beloved return from their graves. (190) Again, I suggest reading the hovering of this woman and her ancient song as traumatic replay. Her sounds that interrupt Peter symbolize how a strange or wounded voice acts as a trace of the past that forces the survivor to bear witness to that which could not be known.[8]

III. Survival of Writing

While this Echo-like figure may seem tangential to the threads of *Mrs. Dalloway*, she embodies a kind of survival central to the novel and that returns in Woolf's writing. In the essay she was working on in 1941, "Anon," Woolf introduces an androgynous and immortal singer—who bears striking resemblance to this beggar woman and to Echo—to represent the history of the song-making instinct. Woolf writes of Anon: "if he cannot speak, he must sing" (Scott 680). Much as Anon's song exists between the "sayable and the unsayable," the space of the "ancient song" of trauma exists between the fragments that return and what cannot be known or communicated. The crisis of survival transforms into the text that survives. Even if the beggar-woman's song is enigmatic, it does leave its mark. Her ancient song "bubbles up" and soaks "through the knotted roots of infinite ages," like a wound from the past, leaving a "damp stain" that bears resemblance to the blood that issues forth from the tree in Tasso's story. (81) A trace of the event writes itself upon the earth. The song becomes an inscription.

In this sense, the beggar woman's song "writes" trauma—in as much as trauma can be written—for the future. Indeed, it will survive the planet. As Ovid transforms Echo's limited language into the future of his lines, the beggar woman's song can signify the potential for echoing fragments to affect listeners. Indeed, some of her words soothe Rezia, who repeats them, suggesting that this echo offers a kind of recognition for another isolated woman. This voice of a haunting echo creates a bond with future listeners.

I close by mentioning that this association of echo with survival exists not only in Woolf's fiction but in her diaries as well. In June, 1940 Woolf uses the word "echo" to signify the continued resonance of her own lines. In her diary entry of June 9, fearing the approach of the Germans, Woolf thinks: " It struck me that one curious feeling is, that the writing "I" has vanished. No audience. No echo. That's part of one's death...But it is a fact—this disparition of an echo" (*D5* 293). "No echo" here indicates a lack of listeners, the death of her writing. She frames the question of survival—this time of the life of writing in a world at war rather than the life of a character—through an echo. Woolf returns to the image of an echo a couple of weeks later: "Further, the war—our waiting while knives sharpen for the operation—has taken away the outer wall of security. No echo comes back. I have no surroundings" (June 22). The absence of an echo indicates a lack of a witness to the ongoing and approaching traumas. The word "echo" reappears yet again a month later: "All the walls, the protecting and reflecting walls, wear so terribly thin in this war. There's no standard to write for: no public to echo back" (July 24). Woolf expresses her isolation—as Septimus put it, the "doom" of being "alone forever" (*MD* 145)—in terms of a loss of an echo. Without this echo, no one will bear witness to the traumatic past. The song comes to an end. If the crisis of survival involves acknowledging the otherness of the echoing voice, then survival itself depends upon the preservation of this ancient song. It becomes our task as readers to listen to Woolf's echoes.

Notes

[1] As J. Hillis Miller reads it, Clarissa is resurrected through Septimus's death back into the world of living and words. Woolf's notes about Clarissa's originally planned death appear in the preface to Modern Library edition. This is noted in Mark Hussey's *Virginia Woolf A to Z,* 172. Elaine Showalter also discusses their parallels, 192.

[2] See Hussey, 174.

[3] "In *Mrs. Dalloway* narration is repetition as the raising of the dead" (Miller 178).

[4] At the same time, Echo's words can symbolize not only the replay of trauma but the cathartic possibilities for the voice. Echo uses Narcissus's words to speak her desires, to create her subjectivity. She takes the object at the end of his sentence and transforms it into the subject of her own sentence. In this sense, Echo can represent the possibility of turning fragmented voice into signification, a broken and incomplete narrative into some form of expression, objectification into agency—the need for the echoing voice of trauma to survive.

[5] When survivors narrate their traumas, their testimonies often sound foreign to them.

[6] They find that this figure can represent the voice of women before the imposition of the restraints of culture. See *The War of the Words,* 249-50.

[7] In fact, this figure, like Echo, complicates gendered categories. Disembodied and eternal Echo ends up eternal and bodiless; this woman is without "age or sex." Yet Echo is a female character and this figure is a woman: Rezia calls her "poor old woman" and the narrator notes that she is a woman "for she wore a skirt" (81). The suggestion that gender may be performative, based on the act of wearing a skirt, only underscores the gap between voice and body at work in both stories. This gap can constitute a prevalent sensation for the survivor of trauma as well who often feels a rupture between the voice that tells the story and the body that lived it.

[8] Interestingly, the association of trees with survival that emerged in Clarissa's thoughts returns in this passage. This woman stands "like a wind-beaten tree for ever barren of leaves." The correlation of leaves of trees with the passing away of the dead returns when the woman seems to blot out "the passing generations—the pavement was crowded with bustling middle-class people—vanishes like leaves, to be trodden under..." (82). Here, the leaves of trees point to a parting with the dead that must accompany survival, much as Clarissa must leave thoughts of Septimus's suicide and return to her party.

Works Cited

Briggs, Marlene A. "Veterans and Civilians: The Mediation of Traumatic Knoweldge in *Mrs. Dalloway.*" In *Virginia Woolf and Communities: Selected Papers from the Eighth Annual Conference on Virginia Woolf.* Ed. Jeannette McVicker and Laura Davis. New York: Pace UP, 1999. 43-49

Caruth, Cathy. *Unclaimed Experience: Trauma, Narrative and History.* Baltimore: Johns Hopkins UP, 1996.

Freud, Sigmund. *Beyond the Pleasure Principle.* In *The Standard Edition of the Complete Psychological Works of Sigmund Freud.* Translated by James Strachey. vol 18. ch 3. London: Hogarth, 1953-74.

Gilbert, Sandra M. and Susan Gubar. *The War of the Words.* Vol. 1 of *No Man's Land: The Place of the Woman Writer in the Twentieth Century.* New Haven. Yale UP, 1988.
Hussey, Mark. *Virginia Woolf A to Z: A Comprehensive Reference for Students, Teachers and Common Readers to Her Life, Work and Critical Reception.* New York: Facts on File, 1995.
Knox-Shaw, Peter. "The Otherness of Septimus Warren Smith." *Durham University Journal* (Jan 1995): 99-110.
Miller, J. Hillis. *Fiction and Repetition: Seven English Novels.* Cambridge: Harvard UP, 1982.
Ovid. *The Metamorphoses.* Translated by Allen Mandelbaum. New York: Harcourt, Brace & Co., 1993.
Scott, Bonnie Kime, ed. *The Gender of Modernism: A Critical Anthology.* Bloomington: Indiana UP, 1990.
Showalter, Elaine. *The Female Malady: Women, Madness and English Culture: 1830-1980.* New York: Pantheon, 1985.
Woolf, Virginia. *The Diary of Virginia Woolf.* Vol. 5. Ed. Anne Oliver Bell. New York: HBJ, 1977.
——. *Mrs. Dalloway.* 1925. New York: Harcourt, 1981.
——. "Preface." *Mrs. Dalloway.* New York: Modern Library, 1928.

Suzette A. Henke
Virginia Woolf and Post-Traumatic Subjectivity

Ever since Virginia Woolf's death in 1941, her life has been treated by critics as a case history imbued with mysterious symptoms and an implicit etiology waiting to be unraveled. As late as the 1960s, readers inquired about polarized possibilities of madness or sanity, depression or mania, sociopathy or schizophrenia. As an implicit analysand, Woolf remains pinned, like a butterfly on a wall, to historical and contextual memory. Psychoanalytic critics struggle to resurrect an intact biographical subject from Woolf's letters, diaries, notebooks, novels, and polemical prose, even as they consider the author's aesthetic mutation of private experience in her fictional pathographies. Only faint traces of an amorphous authorial persona, revealed in textual production, offer the historical remnants of an analysand rife for contemporary understanding.

Thomas Caramagno has, for instance, provided in his book *The Flight of the Mind* startling, thorough, and convincing evidence that the historical Virginia Woolf might, in fact, have suffered from manic-depressive illness. And Louise DeSalvo, in *Virginia Woolf: The Impact of Childhood Sexual Abuse on Her Life and Work,* has effectively argued a case for the kind of mental stress and debilitation associated with incest trauma. In this essay, I want to propose still another diagnostic category that may prove incremental rather than alternative to earlier hypotheses. It now seems possible that Woolf's authorial subject position reflects and re-creates a number of her own traumatic experiences rehearsed, amalgamated, and reconfigured over a lifetime of literary production. Whatever our speculations about the historical author, it is essential to take into account the resonance of post-traumatic stress disorder found everywhere in Woolf's canon.

In "A Sketch of the Past," Virginia Woolf recalls the traumatic moment when her brother Gerald lifted her onto a dining room shelf and "began to explore [her] body." "I can remember," she writes, "the feel of his hand going under my clothes. . . how I stiffened and wriggled as his hand approached my private parts. . . . [W]hat is the word for so dumb and mixed a feeling?" (69). Was this the inaugural trauma of Virginia's childhood? Or did it occur the morning of May 5, 1895, when the Stephen children were allowed to view the still-warm corpse of their deceased mother Julia? "I remember very clearly," Woolf writes, "how even as I was taken to the bedside I noticed that one nurse was sobbing, and a desire to laugh came over me, and I said to myself as I have often done at moments of crisis since, 'I feel nothing whatever.' Then I stooped and kissed my mother's face. It was still warm. She [had] only died a moment before" (92). Already the young Virginia has begun to exhibit symptoms of post-traumatic stress disorder, characterized by psychic numbing and emotional anesthesia. As Cathy Caruth explains, the traumatized subject must come to terms with a "peculiar paradox: that in trauma the greatest confrontation with reality may also occur as an absolute numbing to it, that immediacy . . . may take the form of belatedness" (*Trauma* 6).

Physicians in the early twentieth century were well acquainted with the symptoms of hysteria, whose etiology seemed mysteriously allied with the influence of the womb and ovaries on woman's mental stability. Only with the eruption of similar symptoms in males fighting on the front during World War I were nerve specialists like Sigmund Freud able to diagnose the effects of combat neurosis or "shell shock" on a ravaged military population. Such post-traumatic stress, however, seemed closely allied with active combat or the fear thereof.

It is no wonder that Virginia Woolf, introduced by George Rylands to Freud's *Collected Works* in 1924, began to take an active interest in the new science of psychoanalysis. Hermione Lee tells us that once the Hogarth Press had agreed to publish Freud's papers, his theories "became one of the dominant topics of Bloomsbury. . . . In her letters to Jacques Raverat, psychoanalysis featured as something Virginia was holding at bay, though the language of her confessions to him was influenced by what she was hearing of Freud" (465). With head and conversation buzzing with an awareness of postwar trauma, Woolf sought to depict, in the character of Septimus Smith, a war veteran suffering the effects of post-traumatic stress disorder. Like Freud himself, Woolf "linked her personal history to world history, as she linked Septimus's madness to the 'cataclysms' of war" (Lee 459). According to Hermione Lee, Smith's figure amalgamates Woolf's own autobiographical trauma with her observations of the postwar malaise suffered by friends like Ralph Partridge and Gerald Brenan. "[T]ogether, these young men out of the war, with their disturbingly intense emotional lives and their uncertainty about the future, seemed to her to represent the postwar trauma of a whole generation" (Lee 459).

Freud's inaugural association of traumatic symptoms with female hysteria and male combat neurosis paved the way for later psychiatric acknowledgements of post-traumatic stress disorder as a real illness affecting countless men and women in quotidian situations. As Judith Herman observes in *Trauma and Recovery*, it was only in the 1970's, with the dawn of the women's movement, that therapists "recognized that the most common post-traumatic disorders are those not of men in war but of women in civilian life" (28). I would like to suggest that Virginia Woolf intuitively grasped a similar connection, and that she imbricated her personal experience of post-traumatic stress disorder into an astonishingly accurate portrait of the shellshocked Septimus Smith. In 1985, I published an article in *Literature and Psychology* that argued the case for an anatomy of schizophrenic symptoms at the heart of *Mrs. Dalloway*. I now want to alter this implicit diagnosis significantly, since, over the past decade, Woolf's characterization of Septimus has emerged for me from an etiological miasma as a particularly striking figure of the shellshocked soldier he was, I suspect, always meant to be.

Dr. Bessel van der Kolk, describing the symptoms of post-traumatic stress disorder, explains: "Intrusive responses are hyperactivity, explosive aggressive outbursts, startle responses, intrusive recollections in the form of nightmares and flashbacks, and reenactment of situations reminiscent of the trauma. . . . The numbing response consists of emotional constriction, social isolation, retreat from family obligations, anhedonia (lack of pleasure in physical sensation), and a sense of estrangement" (3). Victims of post-traumatic stress disorder often suffer from severe dysphoria, which might be characterized as the opposite of euphoria—a general sense of malaise and alienation.

The American Psychiatric Association, in the fourth edition of its *Diagnostic and Statistical Manual of Mental Disorders*, delineates the following symptoms characteristic of post-traumatic stress disorder: "recurrent and intrusive recollections of the [traumatic] event, . . . 'psychic numbing' or 'emotional anesthesia,'" and feelings of alienation characterized by a "markedly reduced ability to feel emotions" (424-25). Further effects associated with interpersonal stress disorders include "self-destructive and impulsive behavior; dissociative symptoms; somatic complaints; feelings of ineffectiveness, shame, despair, or hopelessness; . . . hostility; social withdrawal" (425). As Judith Herman observes, traumatic events "shatter the construction of the self that is formed and sustained in relation to others" and "cast the victim into a state of existential crisis" (51).

Most literary critics would agree that Septimus Smith's bereavement over the death of his commanding officer Evans is deeply repressed and experienced psychologically as a traumatic wound to the ego. After Evans is killed in battle, Septimus "congratulate[s] himself upon feeling very little and very reasonably" (*MD* 86). Suffering from anhedonia, he retreats into a zombie-like state of emotional paralysis interrupted by intrusive fantasies of Evans's reappearance. Invoking a lyrical ode to Time, Septimus feels convinced that "Evans answered from behind the tree" (*MD* 70). Sitting with his wife Rezia in Regents Park, he is startled by the sudden apparition of Evans's ghost, along with an entourage of dead war heroes glaring at him from "behind the railings" (*MD* 25). (These spectral apparitions are Smith's hallucinatory misprision of animals in the London zoo). Flashbacks of combat affectively evoke in Septimus violent startle responses, as well as aggressive emotional outbursts that prove frightening to his young Italian wife.

Smith clearly exhibits one of the primary symptoms of post-traumatic stress disorder—that of psychic numbing or emotional anesthesia. Tormented by a morbid but unshakable stoicism, Septimus manically confesses his inability to feel as a nameless war crime for which he masochistically demands punishment from England's bogus soul-doctor, Sir William Bradshaw. Septimus's aberrant behavior is impulsive and self-destructive, his cognitive processes dissociated and confused. Shame, despair, hopelessness, and hostility characterize the fragmented landscape of existential crisis. During periods of hyperactivity, Septimus experiences a radical swing between self-hatred and apotheosis. One moment, he feels despicable and accuses himself of unspeakable crimes. The next, he cherishes Messianic fantasies of himself as a martyred Christ figure: "Look the unseen bade him, . . . who was the greatest of mankind, Septimus, lately taken from life to death, the Lord who had come to renew society, . . . the scapegoat, the eternal sufferer" (*MD* 25).

For further insight into the fictional evolution of Septimus Smith's traumatized subject position, one might compare the completed novel with Woolf's holograph manuscript of "The Prime Minister," a draft version of the first section of *Mrs. Dalloway*. In "The Prime Minister," Septimus emerges as a deviant and idiosyncratic figure. When he stands up in a crowded restaurant and begins raving hysterically, he impresses the diners as weirdly unstable. Manifesting intrusive symptoms of post-traumatic hyperactivity, the young man fears that his heart will suddenly explode and "fly into pieces" (Henke, *Prime Minister* 134). Laughing wildly, he makes an unsuccessful effort to control this hysterical outburst and to "dam the hole in the wall . . . made by his laugh; for something warm and disquieting had trickled through the hole" in the form of post-traumatic nightmare. On the street, Septimus hears a barrel organ "playing a divine melody" that celebrates the end of the war but impels him sardonically to assess Europe's recent liberation: "Now was Europe free. Now Mrs. Lewis and Ellis Robertson could tear up their [appalling photographs of frozen bodies and] dead children" (Henke, ibid.). Tormented by relentless and uncontrollable flashbacks, Septimus is driven to extravagant fantasies of self-destruction. He is so obsessed with lugubrious recollections of battle that he imagines himself in the role of traditional scapegoat: "One might give one's body to be eaten by the starving, and then . . . be a martyr, and then, as I am going to die, I will kill the Prime Minister" (Henke, ibid.). In Woolf's inaugural portrait of this shellshocked veteran, Septimus articulates a death-wish associated with memories of the Great War and with hordes of indigent refugees left in its wake. He plans to sacrifice himself for the physical redemption of the starving masses by literally offering his body as eucharistic food for the hungry. Envisaging himself as the man-god slain to expiate the sins of a guilty community, he simultaneously becomes a self-appointed judge and an avenging angel commissioned to assassinate the British Conservative Prime Minister.

Between this early manuscript and the final version of *Mrs. Dalloway*, Woolf made some pivotal emendations. In the completed novel, Septimus's hallucinations are more sympathetically rendered through subjective, lyrical expression. Woolf wisely chose to delete earlier allusions to assassination and cannibalism. In *Mrs. Dalloway*, Septimus has been humanized and is more successfully integrated into the larger panoply of postwar society. His visions are poetic, even seductive, as he fantasizes the dissolution of his ego in a benevolent, pantheistic universe, where "leaves were alive; trees were alive. . . . Sounds made harmonies with premeditation" (*MD* 22).

Elsewhere, I have tried to compare the characteristic symptoms ascribed to schizophrenia in the fourth edition of the *Diagnostic and Statistical Manual* with those associated with post-traumatic stress syndrome; and, in turn, to examine both nosologies in light of symptoms precipitated by normal bereavement (*Shattered Subjects* 89-92). Sigmund Freud took great care in his paper on "Mourning and Melancholia" to distinguish between ordinary mourning and pathological melancholia. But where does bereavement end and madness begin? And what if the psychiatric community fails, as it did in the case of Septimus Smith (and perhaps in the case of Virginia Woolf), to distinguish among manifestations of intense mourning, post-traumatic stress disorder, and schizophrenia? As Cathy Caruth explains, one of Freud's central insights was that "history, like trauma, is never simply one's own, that history is precisely the way we are implicated in each other's traumas" (*Unclaimed Experience* 24).

Virginia Woolf, a lifelong agnostic, once confided to her friend E. M. Forster that her so-called bouts of madness had served in lieu of religious belief to provide her with creative inspiration through semi-mystical visions of transcendence. Whether Woolf's purported malady be attributed to manic-depression, schizophrenia, or post-traumatic stress disorder, it seems apparent that she herself ascribed a positive, visionary, and redemptive value to the periods of psychic dissociation that defied accurate or conclusive diagnosis during her lifetime. For her alter-ego Septimus Smith, the supplement to trauma is messianic prophecy: "The supreme secret must be told to the Cabinet; first that trees are alive; next there is no crime; next love, universal love" (*MD* 67). In Smith's mystical ravings, trees emanate a quivering consciousness, and the skin of the world palpitates with anxiety and wonder. "All taken together meant the birth of a new religion" (*MD* 23).

Writing out her own traumatic memories through elusive webs of autobiographical testimony, Woolf managed to offer the readers of *Mrs. Dalloway* a poignant figure of a shellshocked veteran suffering from post-traumatic stress disorder. In the character of Septimus Smith, she constructed a convincing simulacrum of traumatized subjectivity. The troubled young man finally succumbs, in panic, to feelings of estrangement and despair, alienation and existential crisis. But his suicidal leap from a Bloomsbury window, so obviously a defeat for the maimed historical subject, might nonetheless be interpreted as a revolutionary act of defiance and romantic heroism. He has, like Shelley's Adonais, successfully preserved his beleaguered subjectivity from the inevitable corruption of the world's slow stain. As Clarissa Dalloway reflects: "A thing there was that mattered. . . . This he had preserved. . . . There was an embrace in death" (*MD* 184).

Works Cited

American Psychiatric Association. *Diagnostic and Statistical Manual of Mental Disorders*. 4th ed., rev. Washington, D. C.: American Psychiatric Association, 1994.

Caramagno, Thomas C. *The Flight of the Mind: Virginia Woolf's Art and Manic-Depressive Illness*. Berkeley: U of California P, 1992.

Caruth, Cathy, ed. *Trauma: Explorations in Memory*. Baltimore: Johns Hopkins U P, 1995.

———. *Unclaimed Experience: Trauma, Narrative, and History*. Baltimore: Johns Hopkins U P, 1996.

DeSalvo, Louise. *Virginia Woolf: The Impact of Childhood Sexual Abuse on Her Life and Work*. Boston: Beacon Press, 1989.

Henke, Suzette A. *Shattered Subjects: Trauma and Testimony in Women's Life-Writing*. New York: St. Martin's Press, 1998.

———. "Virginia Woolf's Septimus Smith: An Analysis of 'Paraphrenia' and the Schizophrenic Use of Language." *Literature and Psychology* 31.4 (1985): 13-23.

———. "Virginia Woolf's *Prime Minister*: A Key to *Mrs. Dalloway*." In *Virginia Woolf: Centennial Essays*. Ed. Elaine Ginsberg and Laura Gottlieb. Troy, NY: Whitston, 1983. 127-41.

Herman, Judith Lewis. *Trauma and Recovery*. New York: Harper Collins, 1992.

Lee, Hermione. *Virginia Woolf*. New York: Alfred A. Knopf, 1997.

Van der Kolk, Bessel A. "The Psychological Consequences of Overwhelming Life Experiences." In *Psychological Trauma*. Ed. Bessel A. van der Kolk. Washington, D. C.: American Psychiatric Press, 1987. 1-30.

Woolf, Virginia. *Mrs. Dalloway*. 1925; New York: HBJ 1990.

———. "A Sketch of the Past." In *Moments of Being*, second edition. Ed. Jeanne Schulkind. HBJ 1985. 61-137.

Jane Lilienfeld
Accident, Incident and Meaning: Traces of Trauma in Virginia Woolf's Narrativity

My paper will argue that Virginia Woolf re-enacted the traumatic shattering of the culturally-situated subject through narrative, for such fracturing is both method and implication of modernist and postmodernist narrativity (McNaron; DeMeester). Hence in Woolf's oeuvre, the troubled issue of subjectivity for the trauma survivor offers an important vantage point from which to interrogate the conflicted discourse of modernist/postmodernist constructions of the subject position.[1] Stylistically Woolf denied the erasure of interiority even while depicting fragmented positionalities of self because her complex manipulation of free indirect discourse maintained the illusion of the intricate emotional depths of culturally-inscribed human consciousness.

Bessel van der Kolk, Judith Lewis Herman, and Janet Liebman Jacobs define trauma as an indelible biochemical brain event which shatters what they term the core self (Herman 61), and may forever alter human perception and relations. However, researchers hasten to point out that what may be one person's trauma, for another may be difficult-but-surmountable past experience (van der Kolk 155; Herman 34-6). Further, the cultural context in which trauma is conceptualized can exacerbate the severity of the experience (7-9; van der Kolk 24-25, 36-39). Additionally, in settings hostile to the concept of human suffering, the medical profession is often not exempt from the culturally imposed silencing of (gendered) traumatic experience (Herman 12-22).

The narrativity of accident is crucial to representations of trauma because causality is disrupted by traumatic experience. For many, traumatic events are at first interpreted as accidents—unforeseen and inexplicable—a random chain of circumstances which seem to make no rational sense. Violence and abuse may be perceived as accidental because these assaults shatter the human desire for security and justice—hence the survivor's inadvertent denial of the human causes of violence and abuse (Herman 178; van der Kolk 15). But accident is chemically inscribed in the very experience of trauma, which is registered as sensual and emotional overloading of preverbal segments of the brain. Traumatic experience disrupts narrative because trauma is neither remembered nor experienced as sequential; trauma fragments time as well as core self (van der Kolk 282-89).

The representation of accident is central to Woolf's narrative methods. Woolf's well-known essay "Modern Fiction" proposed the dismembering of narrative sequence: plot was not to follow the laws of probability, nor heterosexual romance, nor cultural and literary convention (Du Plessis 54-55, 60-61). Instead, Woolf substituted the seemingly random impingement of event, experience, sensation (*CR*1 149-150). In Woolf's novels, the material of narrative becomes indirect, unverifiable—sites of diverse consciousnesses focalized through multiple voices.

Returning to this passage in "Modern Fiction" in light of the work by many of those critics who have examined the representation of trauma in Woolf's work, I wondered whether Woolf has described, not what she termed "an ordinary mind on an ordinary day" (*CR*1 149), but instead, intrusive traumatic imagery? Woolf's descriptions of the so-called "ordinary mind" as it is ceaselessly assaulted by sensual and visual onslaughts voice what it feels like, not just to re-experience unsought trauma memory, but to perceive the daily details of life from the vantage point of having survived trauma (Herman 36-7; van der Kolk 513-14).

These assaultive "atoms as they fall on the mind" (*CR*1 150) become floods of tears, and then a pounding rainstorm which suggests bombardments of bullets in chapter 1 of *Jacob's Room*. In the justly famous opening of *Jacob's Room*, Mrs. Flanders's tears transform the embodied world. Perception is fragmented and so powerful that well constructed buildings sway; ships' masts become liquefied. Her tears cause accidents and accidents cause tears (*JR* 7).

Tears cascade next as rain in the final paragraph of chapter 1 (*JR* 14). The relentless rain kills the flower. The randomness of the crab's abandonment after its entrapment adds to the horror of its admirable persistence. If the rain be thought of as the imagery of unbidden traumatic memories, the forceful repetition of "trying" and "trying again" with no hope of escape, suggests a shower of unsought visualizations, a fitting metaphor for the first world war in which civilians feared attack as did entrenched soldiers. Indeed, as Allyson Booth points out, this paragraph is an excellent example of "the persistence with which the landscape of the trenches gets superimposed onto the landscape of England" (68), reflecting "the narrator's habit of attuning [the reader] to the point of view of someone sprawled flat on the ground, as a soldier or corpse might be sprawled" (68).[2]

In the passages I have just noted, Woolf voices the intertwined nature of personal and political representations of trauma. Numerous papers presented at this conference assert that this twinning provides the narrative spine of *Mrs. Dalloway*. Most readers accept by now the pairing of Septimus Warren Smith and Clarissa Dalloway, a doubling which encompasses the troubled division of gender and social class.[3] This doubling enacts the contention that what the male medical establishment of the 1920s called "combat neurosis" is an equivalent to what that same group labeled women's "hysteria" (Herman 32).

Through such doubling, Virginia Woolf confronts the reader with political choices—certainly about sexuality, but also about the trivialization of trauma, for both Septimus and Clarissa, passing as heterosexuals, are trauma survivors. Just as he saw the man he loved, Evans, blown up by a shell in front of his eyes, Clarissa saw Sylvia, her sister, killed by a falling tree, an accident Clarissa at first blamed on their father, Justin Parry ((*MD* 83-84), an analogue of Septimus's hatred and fear of patriarchal authorities. While he has severe shell shock, she has frequent and intrusive displaced memories which she experiences as premonitions of future disaster, for "it was very, very dangerous to live even one day" (*MD* 7).[4]

If Septimus imagines worlds of meaning and meaninglessness from the sky writing, Clarissa jumps with fear at the sound of a car's exhaust in the street (*MD* 13). Clarissa knows what Septimus feels because she feels it too. As numerous critics have proven, his supposedly mad maunderings are her unspoken fears and fragmented memory traces.

The traumatic material that Woolf critics have noted in *Mrs. Dalloway* occurs in the narrative's artful manipulation of memory. Medical discourses of trauma speculate that in the moment of traumatic experience, the perceptual apparatus shreds the experience as it occurs. It is not stored as a continuous, verbalized story, but as fragmented, preverbal segments of feelings, visions, and, at times, dissociated or somatic symptoms (van der Kolk 287-89). Parts of the event may be remembered while other parts may be simultaneously repressed (van der Kolk 282). Certainly this is how the narrative "stores" the moment of Sylvia's accidental death which Clarissa witnessed (*MD* 83-84). This event arises in the narrative without preparation for the reader just as the event occurred on the Parry's property, without warning. Never once is a direct image or verbal recall of Sylvia's death situated in Clarissa's free indirect discourse. Instead, the witnessed accident is remembered by Peter—who may not have seen it happen—to whom Clarissa might have spoken of the accident, as an aside in his musings on Clarissa's past.

In the narrative representation of this accidental death, Woolf subtly suggests the re-traumatizing of the trauma survivor, an experience that Septimus also undergoes. To do so, Woolf has constructed an opaque ellipsis (Genette 52, 205). Modernist novels excel at depictions of disclosed denial, as I argue at length in my book (119-124, 133-136). In *Mrs. Dalloway*, this crucial memory, subject to narrative trivialization by Peter and unvoiced in Clarissa's free indirect discourse, is disclosed to the reader while denied by the characters, for the reader can see that the memory of Sylvia's death is not available to the one character to whom it is most important. An extended though non-sequential exposition of accidental death occurs not in Clarissa's consciousness, but in that of Septimus (*MD* 70-71, 93-101), thus linking by analogy the random death of a beloved and admired sister with the combat death of a beloved and admired commander.

Peter speculates about the effect on Clarissa of this accident by implying that the late Victorian cultural insistence on the repression of emotion forced Clarissa to become a flighty do-gooder, an activity he trivializes, as he does all of Clarissa's feelings and actions (*MD* 82-84). Peter's almost jovial dismissal of this horrifying event might represent his inability to bear emotional witness to a trauma in order to escape being contaminated by it (Herman 7-9; van der Kolk 398-413), a rejection of human fellowship similar to that which is exemplified by the brutality of Septimus's doctors Bradshaw and

Holmes.[5] What Clarissa thinks about the consequences of her witnessing Sylvia's terrible death can only be discerned indirectly.

For just as clinicians say that traumatic memory may become re-enacted at a preconscious level, so the residue of Sylvia's death can be ever-present for the attuned reader. It is suggested by Clarissa's pervasive fear and constant attempts at self-soothing (*MD* 3, 9). It is suggested by her inability, as she calls it, to love (*MD* 31-32). It is suggested by her inability to tolerate the risk of choosing to live her life as a lesbian (*MD* 33-37), and perhaps as a consequence of this choice, by her rejection of Peter as a suitor and her safe choice of a man of wealth and position instead (*MD* 202-203). What Clarissa calls the iciness of her withdrawal to the narrow "bed" (*MD* 32) manifests the psychic numbing and avoidance of stress which unmourned trauma may produce in survivors (van der Kolk 538-9). Through the doubled trauma responses of Septimus and Clarissa, *Mrs. Dalloway* depicts the complicated linkage of personal and cultural trauma.

Throughout this paper I have discussed interiority as if it were unproblematized. But it is not. However, the feminist study of the consequences of trauma for human self-structure has the potential to reconfigure discussions of modernist and postmodernist narrative methods. And to that reconfiguration, a study of Woolf's narrative strategies is essential.

Virginia Woolf was one of the pioneers of the fictional representation of dissociation, disconnection, numbing, and denial (aspects of the psychological repercussions of trauma) as both personal and cultural experience, without stripping her narratives of the power of human relationship to connect reader to text, and self to other.

Through her modernist and postmodernist narrative methods, Woolf implicates the reader as an engaged witness of trauma.[6] The sudden deaths in her novels, the violations undergone by women and children, and the representation of the painful re-enactment and re-experience of the emotional aftershocks of trauma are manifested by subtle and complex narrative strategies which make these experientially comprehensible to the reader without minimization or distortion. Through non-linear temporality mapped onto multi-layered geographic space voiced through interlocking, multiple sites of free indirect discourse, Woolf's narrativity replicates a complicated and engaged representation of dismembered interiority without eliciting psychic disconnection in the reader, thus modeling a humane and sustaining way to disclose the unspeakable and unimaginable.

Notes

[1] Although one now frequently hears that the binary opposition between political, feminist identity and postmodernist constructions of the self has been resolved, Jane Flax's challenge remains unanswered: ironically, the intellectual articulation of non-unitary, divergent selves presupposes a coherent Caucasian male consciousness which can speculate about its components (Flax 209-221). The experience of being a trauma survivor, Flax argues, eliminates the safety and power of an articulated con-

sciousness and of an observing ego which can initiate and respond to human interactions (218-219). Woolf's representations—within an aesthetic which can be interpreted via postmodernist discourse—of shattered selves with whose complicated interiority readers can identify challenge the empathic shallowness of postmodern claims about the fragmented positionalities of self. Critical investigations of the methods and effectiveness of Woolf's representations model ways to interrogate postmodernist claims about subjectivity. See also Henke xiv-xix, Caughie and Waugh.

2 Froula has speculated that the multi-voiced narrative position absorbs the absent male subject by vocalizing him through a gendered, yet problematic subjectivity which meditates on being and non-being.

3 Barrett makes the important point that Doris Kilman also serves as Clarissa's double. For a discussion of the complexity of Woolf's characterization of Clarissa, see Smith.

4 Molly Hoff offers a different interpretation, reminding readers that Woolf may have read Margot Asquith's *Memoirs* (published in 1920), which cites the tragic accident in which Mrs. Asquith's sister was injured by a falling tree. Hoff analyses the narrative references to Greek stoicism and insistence on the dangers of expecting too much safety and happiness in human life (4-5).

5 I disagree with Karen DeMeester who seems to blame Clarissa Dalloway for her class-based survival strategies, while empathizing with Septimus Warren Smith's madness. DeMeester's otherwise excellent article implies an evaluation of traumatic outcomes measured along a hierarchical scale of damage, a suggestion underlined by her refusal to acknowledge the class and gender differences that separate Clarissa and Septimus.

6 For a superb discussion of Woolf's complicated yet accessible narrativity, see the critical essays on Woolf published in Kathy Mezei's *Ambiguous Discourse*.

Works Cited

Barrett, Eileen. "Unmasking Lesbian Passion: The Inverted World of *Mrs. Dalloway*." Eileen Barrett and Patricia Cramer, eds., *Virginia Woolf: Lesbian Readings*. New York: NYUP, 1997. 146-167.

Barrett, Eileen, and Patricia Cramer, eds. *Re: Reading, Re: Writing, Re: Teaching Virginia Woolf: Selected Papers from the Fourth Annual Conference on Virginia Woolf*. New York: Pace UP, 1995.

Booth, Allyson. "The Architecture of Loss: Teaching *Jacob's Room* as a War Novel." Barrett and Cramer, *Re* 65-72.

Caughie, Pamela. *Virginia Woolf and Postmodernism: Literature In Quest and Question of Itself*. Urbana: U of Illinois P, 1991.

Daugherty, Beth and Eileen Barrett, eds., *Virginia Woolf: Texts and Contexts: Selected Papers from the Fifth Annual Conference on Virginia Woolf*. New York: Pace UP, 1996.

DeMeester, Karen. "Trauma and Recovery in Virginia Woolf's *Mrs. Dalloway*." *Modern Fiction Studies* 44.3 (1998). 649-673.

DuPlessis, Rachel Blau. *Writing Beyond the Ending: Narrative Strategies of Twentieth-Century Women Writers*. Bloomington: Indiana UP, 1985.

Flax, Jane. *Thinking Fragments: Psychoanalysis, Feminism, and Postmodernity in the Contemporary West*. Berkeley: U of Chicago P, 1990.

Froula, Christine. "War, Civilization, and the Conscience of Modernity: Views from *Jacob's Room*." Daugherty and Barrett 280-295.

Gennette, Gerard. *Narrative Discourse: An Essay in Method*. Trans. Jane E. Lewin. Ithaca: Cornell UP, 1992.

Henke, Suzette. *Shattered Subjects: Trauma and Testimony in Women's Life-Writing*. New York: St. Martin's, 1998.

Herman, Judith Lewis. *Trauma and Recovery: The Aftermath of Violence, From Domestic Abuse to Political Terror.* New York: Basic Books, 1992.
Hoff, Molly. "Who is Sylvia?" *Virginia Woolf Miscellany* 40 (Spring, 1993): 4-5.
Jacobs, Janet Leibman. *Victimized Daughters: Incest and the Development of the Female Self.* New York: RKP, 1994.
Lilienfeld, Jane. *Reading Alcoholisms: Theorizing Character and Narrative in Selected Novels of Thomas Hardy, James Joyce, and Virginia Woolf.* New York: St. Martin's, 1999.
Mezei, Kathy, ed., *Ambiguous Discourse: Feminist Narratology and British Women Writers.* Chapel Hill: U of North Carolina P, 1996.
McNaron, Toni. "The Uneasy Solace of Art: The Effect of Sexual Abuse on Virginia Woolf's Aesthetic." *Women's Studies International Forum* 15.2 (1992): 251-266.
Smith, Laura A. "Who Do We Think Clarissa Dalloway is Anyway? Research into Seventy Years of Woolf Criticism." Barrett and Cramer, *Re* 215-222.
van der Kolk, Bessel A. et al. *Traumatic Stress: The Effects of Overwhelming Experience on Mind, Body and Society.* New York: Guilford, 1996.
Waugh, Patricia. *Practising Postmodernism/Reading Modernism.* New York: Arnold, 1992.
Woolf, Virginia. *Jacob's Room.* New York: HBW, 1922.
——. "Modern Fiction." *The Common Reader, First Series.* Annotated Edition. Edited and Introduced by Andrew McNeillie. c 1984. New York: HB, 1925, 1998. 146-154.
——. *Mrs. Dalloway.* San Diego: HB, 1925, 1998.

Marilyn Schwinn Smith
Narration, Memory and Identity: *Mrs. Dalloway* at the End of the Century

Clarissa Dalloway's predilection for flowers, or, as Peter Walsh would have it, for cabbages, is disproportionately mirrored in the ecstatic response to the natural world of her precariously balanced double, the war veteran Septimus Smith (Dowling 88). A remarkable quantity of imagery celebrating the beauty and fecundity of the natural world appears in the poetry of war, in response to what French poet Charles Vildrac calls tripping "between death's legs" (250). This literary connection between the experience of trauma and what, from my own dream-life, I call "fruits and vegetables" takes place at the intersection of event and memory within consciousness.

Central to the significance of *Mrs. Dalloway* as a modernist novel is its depiction of consciousness. Ironically, psychologists—the primary target against whom Woolf deploys her transcription of consciousness—are now looking at consciousness and reading it just as Woolf wrote it. After over a century of rejecting the phenomenal experience of memory as an inappropriate field of study (Larsen 163-70), psychologists doing research in the fields of eyewitness and autobiographical memory apply stylistic and grammatical

Trauma and Wellness

analyses to the memory narratives they solicit from their subjects. Before turning to the memory narrative of *Mrs. Dalloway*, I would like to put before you a few poetic texts which prompted my thinking about the significance of Clarissa's response to flowers.[1]

The French soldier in Charles Vildrac's poem "Relief" emerges from a harrowing, nighttime withdrawal from the front line into the peaceful blue of morning and exclaims: "Ah, the appletrees in blossom! I'll put blossoms into my letters" (Vildrac 250). The soldier is fully present in the springtime morning; the terror of the previous hours remains only as impetus to the intensity of feeling: "Ah, the appletree in blossom." Such moments are ubiquitous in British literary representations of the Great War and are often understood as an escape from war's horror. Escape may be a suitable interpretation of the roses in Siegfried Sassoon's "Repression of War Experience," for example, in a collection reviewed by Woolf ("Two Soldier-Poets"). A convalescing soldier, struggling to retain his sanity, achieves a momentary respite from the memory of war:

> Now light your pipe; look, what a steady hand,
> Draw a deep breath; stop thinking; count fifteen,
> And you're as right as rain . . . .
> Why won't it rain? . . .
> I wish there'd be a thunder-storm to-night,
> With bucketsful of water to sluice the dark,
> And make the roses hang their dripping heads. (Sassoon 51)

The passage contains a graphic signal—the ellipsis—to mark pauses in the soldier's train of thought. These pauses indicate the efficacy of the speaker's ritual behavior in shifting the speaker's consciousness, an effect further marked by the switch in tense.

Sometimes, natural imagery is not a response to the immediate situation, but erupts into the soldier's consciousness as memory. In Marina Tsvetaeva's epic of the Russian civil war, we watch a sentry not removed from danger (as the soldier just relieved from front-line duty or at home recovering from injury), but patrolling the final line of defense separating his besieged White army from the soon to be victorious Red army. Suddenly, with only the mediation of the three dots of ellipsis to signal a radical shift in being, the line breaks, to continue one ladder-step down with the soldier's exclamation: "Ekh, if only I remain alive, Rasp—berry ripening! Fresh cucumbers!"—an outburst which resolves into a primitive image of the sentry ingesting all of Russia (Tsvetaeva 295, my trans.).

I experience such moments not as the negative connotations of escape would suggest, as signs of weakness, but as powerful statements of the will to live. I feel in them an affinity to the quality of archaic heroism: a direct challenge to death's dominion, an equally primordial lust situated in these narratives where Homer had placed Achilles' rage and battle lust. This alternate interpretation is borne out in a poem by the Hungarian, Miklós Radnóti.[2] The death march of Jewish slave laborers, driven back to Hungary from camps in Serbia by the retreating German army is subject of a poem written shortly before his murder. Presenting himself from the rational perspective of a third person, Radnóti mocks resistance to death: "He is a fool who, already fallen on the ground   gets up and walks again" (346, trans. Hiripi). Radnóti is uncompromising in his grasp of reality, from which nature imagery or thoughts of home are said to represent an escape:

> But he is a fool   because above the houses
> for a long time   only the burnt wind is blowing,
> the wall is lying on the ground   the plum tree is broken
> and fears   inhabit the night at home. (346, trans. Hiripi)

Perhaps it is the plum tree which provokes a shift in consciousness. It begins as the speaker expresses desire for what keeps the fool walking—the world as it was before the war. It is completed as that world, in dream-like memory, assumes center stage, obliterating current reality:

> on the old cold verandah
> peaceful bees would be humming,   as the plum-jam is cooling,
> and the late summer silence would be sitting in the sun   in the sleepy gardens
> and in the foliage fruits   would be rocking nakedly,
> and Fanni [the poet's wife] would be waiting blonde   in front of the fence
> and a shadow would be cast   slowly by the slow morning[.] (346, trans. Hiripi)

This lullaby should induce submission to the reasonable lure of death. But the poet returns from the garden into the present, like Aeneas from the underworld, and speaks: "Do not go on friend, shout at me! and I will get up!" (346, trans. Hiripi).

Like *Mrs. Dalloway*, these poems offer multiple perspectives on the human experience of trauma and memory. There is the moment of trauma itself—"tripping through death's legs"—intruded upon by memory: ecstatic—"Rasp—berry ripening," or idyllic—"in the foliage fruits would be rocking nakedly." These memory images have the power to replace horrific reality, to displace death with life. There is also the afterlife of trauma, where its survival in memory has the power to replace sanity with insanity, to displace life with death. The important point is that the past, through the agency of memory, displaces and becomes the present. Somewhere, amongst the flowers, but in contiguity with trauma, stands Clarissa Dalloway. It is toward her experience, toward her ordinary life, that I will direct the following observations regarding trauma, memory, and their literary representation. Harriet Murav, discussing use of the term *trauma* in "problems of representation related to the Holocaust," notes that it "cannot be described in the conventions of realist narrative." It is, "among other things, the suspension of the victim's sense of reality, continuity, and coherence." She concludes in words clearly applicable to the challenge which the innovative narrative of *Mrs. Dalloway* poses to conceptions of reality. "[A]ny trauma, and not only those that are the result of catastrophic historical events affecting huge numbers of people, can necessitate for its representation a story that accords with no one else's sense of what is likely or probable" (Murav 244).

This necessity is answered in *Mrs. Dalloway* by Woolf's complex use of "represented speech" to unite within a single, expansive consciousness (the narrative voice of the novel) both external and internal realities. Makiko Minow-Pinkney has analyzed the fluidity of the novel's speech, indicating how descriptive narration imperceptibly metamorphoses into internal monologue and the boundaries among the narrative voices are helplessly blurred (Minow-Pinkney 55-6, 58). The modernist texture of this unique narrative voice is largely determined by the prominent role of Memory. Gregory Nagy reminds us that the Greek word *mi-mnē-skō*, as it is used in the Homeric texts, does not so much mean to "remind," as it indicates the capacity of the mind, through the agency of the muses, to be in touch with other times and places. The authority of the archaic poet resides in the capacity of his consciousness to be present in other times or place—to be present in the past (Nagy 17). This mental activity of memory, so fundamental to our literary tradition, is central to Woolf's novel. Its processes are currently the focus of psychological theories of eyewitness and autobiographical memory. Research into the experience and aftereffect of trauma has come to rely increasingly on narrative accounts based on memory.

The passage I have selected contains elements reminiscent of the poems cited earlier. In "Mulberry's the florists," just prior to that moment "when—oh! a pistol shot in the street outside!", Clarissa is actually selecting the flowers the novel's opening sentence foretold. As she moves from flower to flower, her mind becomes increasingly occupied with memories provoked by the sensual details of the flowers. They remind her of young girls on a summer evening, perhaps of herself as a young girl. The memory narrows to a particular time of day and the narrative takes a distinct grammatical turn:

> and it was the moment between six and seven when every flower—roses, carnations, irises, lilac—glows; white, violet, red, deep orange; every flower seems to burn by itself, softly, purely in the misty beds; and how she loved the grey-white moths spinning in and out, over the cherry pie, over the evening primroses! (*MD* 13)

Minow-Pinkney's analysis of the novel draws attention to just such ambiguity in use of the tense system. She says, "from a formal point, past and present are indistinguishable" (56). Melba Cuddy-Keane, commenting on the choice in the Gorris-Atkins film "to work more with time than with multiple consciousness," makes a related observation: "the characters seem not to be recollecting the past so much as living the present *through* the past" (173, 174). This mixture of times and tenses is a well researched topic in contemporary memory theory. Citing the work of Harvey and Capps, Pillemer documents the cognitive reality of the narrative switch from past to present tense for the speaker—the past has overwhelmed the present in the consciousness of the subject (*Momentous* 155-62, "Remembering" 145-62). This is the situation for sufferers of post-traumatic stress disorder. This is the phenomenon described by veterans of the Great War, in poetry of the war and in accounts of the war's continuing impact (Dowling 84-96). Current research also rates texts containing abundant and specific sensual detail highly in terms of accuracy and authenticity (Larsen 178-86). Marking a radical change in psychological theory, scholars can now cite Proust's classic text, which predicates the act of recollection on sensual stimuli, as descriptive of the actual mechanism of memory (Rubin 49-51). Woolf's text does no less.

Saturation with sensual detail connects the entire scene in Mulberry's with Proust's classic text. The phrase, "it was the moment [. . .] when," (13) explicitly connects the passage cited with the Proustian formula, "au moment où." The reference to Proust also provides a key to the relation of memory and trauma to Clarissa. Clarissa certainly does not experience the trauma of the war veteran. Hers, after all, is a representative, ordinary life. Proust's formula gives Woolf the mechanism to recover lost time. Clarissa's trauma occurred after the summer at Bourton, a summer filled with flowers and cabbages, with her entrance into the adult world and its implicit loss.

Let's look at some of the detail of Clarissa's memory. The scene in Mulberry's possesses the dream-like quality of Radnóti's garden—flowers in the place of plums, moths in the place of bees, cherry pie in the place of cooling plum jam. Both scenes are clearly the place to which the subject returns as the locus of meaning. Memory of summer at Bourton, like the memory of Radnóti's garden, enables Clarissa to continue, to get up and continue walking in the post-lapsarian reality in which she is a hostess.

Moths, which occur most frequently among the novels in *Jacob's Room* (*Concordance* 1949, 1953), remind us again of Sassoon's poem "Repression of War Experience." The connection to Sassoon is strengthened when we recall Woolf's 1917 review of Sassoon's poetry, which is clearly related to her technique in *Mrs. Dalloway* (Dowling 85). She wrote in words anticipating Proust:

> To call back any moment of emotion is to call back with it the strangest odds and ends that have become somehow part of it, and it is the weeds pulled up by mistake with the flowers that bring back the extraordinary moment as a whole. ("Mr Sassoon's" 121)

The poem begins:

> Now light the candles; one; two; there's a moth;
> What silly beggars they are to blunder in
> And scorch their wings with glory, liquid flame —
> No, no, not that, — it's bad to think of war,
> When thoughts you've gagged all day come back to scare you;

> And it's been proved that soldiers don't go mad
> Unless they lose control of ugly thoughts
> That drive them out to jabber among the trees. (51)

We have in this poem a blueprint for Septimus Smith. Trees become the motif of Septimus's insanity, as the flowers indicate Clarissa's hold on sanity. Lucrezia attempts to silence her husband's "jabber among the trees" by following the psychiatric injunction "to make her [. . .] husband take an interest in things outside himself": "'Look, look, Septimus!' she cried" (*MD* 21). Overstimulated by the visual effects of trees in Regent's Park, Septimus struggles to retain a grasp on his sanity: "But he would not go mad. He would shut his eyes; he would see no more" (22). Septimus engages in ritualized behavior comparable to that of Sassoon's soldier: "There was his hand," only to be foiled when he looks beyond himself: "there are the dead." The vision of the war had "come back to scare" him: "Evans was behind the railings!" (25). Seeing only sheep where Septimus sees the dead, Rezia responds to the crisis with five more imperatives: "Look" (25-6).

The stimulating action of the natural world's beauty on Septimus's and Clarissa's mental processes is presented throughout the novel in parallel, yet subtly distinguished, series of images. The colorful imagery intimately linking Clarissa with flowers is echoed in Septimus's past.[3] "Yet he could be happy when he chose. [. . .] All the little red and yellow flowers were out on the grass, like floating lamps he said, and talked and chattered and laughed, making up stories" (66). This is notably Rezia's memory. Or again, echoing the effect of Sally on the adolescent Clarissa, there is Miss Pole, who "lit in him such a fire as burns only once in a lifetime, without heat, flickering a red gold flame, infinitely ethereal and insubstantial [. . .] he saw her, one summer evening, walking in a green dress in a square. 'It has flowered' the gardener might have said" (85). But this is notably a narrative account, not Septimus's memory. Septimus has been severed from this past: "something happened [. . .] so prying and insidious were the fingers of the European War, [. . .] ploughed a hole in the geranium beds" (85). Between Septimus and flowers is what Gertrud Koch labels the black box of trauma, effecting a discontinuity in memory (Koch 130).

Septimus Smith is injected into the novel with the sound of the "pistol shot" while Clarissa stands musing among the flowers. The narrative links the two in adjoining sentences: "Mrs. Dalloway, coming to the window with her arms full of sweet peas, looked out with her little pink face pursed with enquiry. Every one looked at the motor car. Septimus looked" (15). As Clarissa stands with flowers, Septimus sees, on the drawn blinds of the motor car, "a curious pattern like a tree" (15). This pivotal moment joins, in mirror relationship, Septimus to Clarissa. The sound, which "made Mrs. Dalloway jump," shocks Clarissa back from her life-sustaining memory into the present (14). Finding "himself unable to pass," Septimus is sent back into the life-denying trauma of the past (14).

Notes

[1] I came to *Mrs. Dalloway* through another project, a review of literary techniques signaling that a shift in consciousness has occurred. My poetic texts were initially selected for the coincidence of natural imagery, trauma and a signaled shift in consciousness.

[2] Poetic translations of "Forced March" appear in the cited anthology (347) and in *Foamy Sky: The Major Poems of Miklós Radnóti*. Trans. Zsuzsanna Ozsváth and Frederick Turner. Princeton: Princeton UP, 1992 (116). I have used a literal translation provided by Éva Hiripi in order to convey the meaning with precision. Radnóti mimics graphically the prisoner's staggering gait by a line-central gap of several spaces on either side of a caesura. The effect is a strikingly jagged line running from top to bottom through the center of the poem. The cognitive shift occurs exactly halfway through this 20-line poem. The first clause of line 11 ends with a colon—the only colon in the poem—then the gap. The colon is the grammatical equivalent to the use of the ellipsis we have seen in other examples marking cognitive shifts.

[3] Ann Bliss, in her conference paper "The Relationship between Clothing and Sexuality in *Mrs. Dalloway*," develops an argument drawing on patterns of color in the novel. Her analysis intersects suggestively with mine, perhaps along the lines of: "Colors of Nature and Sanity in *Mrs. Dalloway*."

Works Cited

Capps, Lisa and Elinor Ochs. "Out of Place: Narrative Insights Into Agoraphobia." *Discourse Processes* 19 (1995): 415-421.

A Concordance to the Novels of Virginia Woolf. Vol. 2. Comp. James M. Haule and Philip H. Smith. New York: Garland, 1991.

Cuddy-Keane, Melba. "*Mrs. Dalloway*: Film, Time, and Trauma." In *Virginia Woolf and Her Influences: Selected Papers from the Seventh Annual Conference on Virginia Woolf*. Ed. Laura Davis and Jeanette McVicker. New York: Pace UP, 1998. 171-175.

Dowling, David. *Mrs. Dalloway: Mapping Streams of Consciousness*. Boston: Twayne, 1991.

Harvey, Alynn Day. "Evidence of a Tense Shift in Personal Experience Narrative." *Empirical Studies of the Arts* 4.2 (1986): 151-162.

Koch, Gertrud. "The Angel of Forgetfulness and the Black Box of Facticity: Trauma and Memory in Claude Lanzmann's Film *Shoah*." *History and Memory: Studies in Representation of the Past* 3.1 (1991): 119-134.

Larsen, Steen F. "What Is It Like to Remember? On Phenomenal Qualities of Memory." In Thompson, ed. 163-190.

Minow-Pinkney, Makiko. "*Mrs. Dalloway*." Chapter 3. *Virginia Woolf and The Problem of the Subject*. New Brunswick, NJ: Rutgers UP, 1987. 54-83.

Murav, Harriet. *Russia's Legal Fictions*. Ann Arbor: U of Michigan P, 1998.

Nagy, Gregory. *The Best of the Achaeans. Concepts of the Hero in Archaic Greek Poetry*. Baltimore: Johns Hopkins UP, 1979.

Pillemer, David B. *Momentous Events, Vivid Memories*. Cambridge, MA: Harvard UP, 1998.

Pillemer, David B., Amy B. Desrochers, and Caroline M. Ebanks. "Remembering the Past in the Present: Verb Tense Shifts in Autobiographical Memory Narratives." In Thompson, ed. 145-62.

Radnóti, Miklós. "Eröltetett Menet." *The Lost Rider: A Bilingual Anthology*. Ed. Péter Dávidházi. Budapest: Corvina, 1997. 346.

Rubin, David C. "Beginnings of a Theory of Autobiographical Remembering." In Thompson, ed. 47-67.

Sassoon, Siegfried. "Repression of War Experience." *Counter-Attack and Other Poems*. New York: Dutton, 1918. 51-53.
Thompson, C. P., ed. *Autobiographical Memory: Theoretical and Applied Perspectives*. Mahwah NJ: Erlbaum, 1998.
Tsvetaeva, Marina. "Perekop." *Stikhotvoreniia i poemy*. Ed. A. Sumerkin. Vol. 4. New York: Russica, 1983. 290-327. [No published translation exists.]
Vildrac, Charles. "Relief." Trans. Christopher Middleton. *The Penguin Book of First World War Poetry*. Ed. and with intro. Jon Silkin. 2nd ed. London: Penguin, 1981. 249-50.
Woolf, Virginia. "Mr Sassoon's Poems." Rev. of *The Old Huntsman and Other Poems*, by Siegfried Sassoon. *TLS* 31 May 1917: Kp C76. *The Essays of Virginia Woolf*. Ed. Andrew McNeillie. Vol 2. New York: HBJ, 1987. 119-22.
——. *Mrs. Dalloway*. 1925. New York: HBJ, 1981.
——. "Two Soldier Poets." Rev. of *Counter-Attack and Other Poems*, by Siegfried Sassoon, and *Poems*, by Geoffrey Dearmer. *TLS* 11 July 1918: Kp C115. *The Essays*. 269-72.

Life and Death Writing

Julia Briggs
In Search of New Virginias

During the summer of 1920, Virginia Woolf reread *Don Quixote*: "the sadness, the satire," she asked herself, "how far are they ours, not intended—or do these great characters have it in them to change according to the generation that looks at them?" (*D2* 55). Though she thought a great deal about this question, and asked it over and over again in different ways in her novels, she never finally decided upon an answer. As the twentieth century draws to an end, we can see that Woolf belongs simultaneously to our time and to hers: the rich harvest of narrative that she left behind in the form of diaries and letters, as well as fictions, was itself a product of a particular historical moment, a moment before the telephone took over and consigned so many conversations to oblivion. Not only Woolf herself but her family and friends left written documentation of their activities so thick that it is possible to reconstruct what she was doing, often from day to day, sometimes from hour to hour. Fascinating though this is, Woolf was the first to insist upon the difference between the outer and inner life; as she put it in *Orlando*, "Thought and life are as the poles asunder" (*O* 184). Living was only one strand in her consciousness; the still center, the thinking, reading and writing, the silence that seethed with creativity, is seldom registered in her diaries, letters, or even her reading notebooks. Now that the facts of her life have been so authoritatively established, one can turn back to the texts themselves, and find in the questions they throw up, the footprints of that other life of thought. Embarking on a new account of Woolf's life as a writer, I found myself addressing a series of unanswered and often unrelated questions and forced to recognise how much of that inner landscape still remains to be charted and mapped. In what follows, I have pursued several distinct lines of approach: I begin with a question about beginning that brings together her creative and erotic life; I then pick up an obscure allusion that invites contextualisation, go on to a brief consideration of the textual revisions she made, and finally look at the impact of an intertext, an English poet that she re-read, and who in turn provides another angle on her last novel.

One key moment in the life of a writer, any writer, is the conception of the first published work; an obvious question for one kind of biography to begin with is how and when did the seed of her first novel come to her, and what form did it take? The genesis of Woolf's later novels is often to be found in her diaries, where she wrote out for her own observation her life as a writer. *To the Lighthouse* started with a picture of her father: "I see already The Old Man," she recorded (*D*2 317); *The Years* and *Three Guineas* began as a book "about the sexual life of women" which came to her in the bath on 20 January 1931 (*D*4 6); *Night and Day*, though less well documented in its early stages, is first heard of as "poor Effie's story," the story of "The Third Generation" (*D*1 4, 19). But the originating moment of *The Voyage Out* is a vanishing point, though, by contrast, the difficulty of its bringing to birth is well attested: it was written and rewritten over five or six years, and fragments from at least four and perhaps six or eight different versions have survived. (Leonard recalled her burning a whole cupboard full of drafts.)

"How adorable the young are—like new brooms," Woolf wrote of Daphne Sanger in 1922: "At her age I was for knowing all that was to be known, & for writing a book—a book—But what book? That vision came to me more clearly at Manorbier aged 21, walking the down on the edge of the sea"(*D*2 197). The young Stephens stayed at Manorbier, on the Pembrokeshire coast, immediately after their father's death in 1904, yet no more is heard of this ambition for a further three years, until, in the summer after Thoby's death and Vanessa's marriage, Virginia confided in her friend Violet Dickinson her hopes and fears for her future as a writer: "I shall be miserable, or happy; a wordy sentimental creature, or a writer of such English as shall one day burn the pages" (*L*1 299). In October 1907, she wrote to Vanessa, who was absorbed in pregnancy, of her own conception: "why should I intrude upon your circle of bliss? Especially when I can think of nothing but my novel?" (*L*1 316).

In these years, Virginia did not keep a diary, or if she did, it has not survived; the first identifiable reference to her first novel thus occurs in someone else's diary: Clive Bell, who notoriously lacked patience and persistence, briefly kept a diary for most of the month of January 1908.[1] On January 2 he wrote "Reading Froude's Carlyle, Dante and Virginia's Sarah, first part poor, last part excellent, very penetrating and often exquisite." "Sarah" was clearly the new, the first novel, the name referring either to its heroine (later Rachel) or else the name of the boat on which the Ambroses would set sail, in another early draft called the "Sarah Jane" (*Melymbrosia* xxx, 263; ultimately it would become the "Euphrosyne"). What is certain is that by January 1908, Clive Bell, whom Virginia had passionately resented the previous year, had become her reader, admirer and first critic. As an old man Clive reminded Leonard of a sentence in which Virginia had told him that he was "the first person who ever thought I'd write well"—"which seems to me the finest feather I shall ever be able to stick in my cap" (Bell 1, 212).

By August that year, she had completed a hundred pages of the new book, and sent them to Clive: "the wonderful thing that I looked for is there unmistakably .... I believe this first novel will become a work that counts, " he replied (Bell 1, 208-9). From the outset, he had recognised her need for encouragement, and his praise for her writing veered between the poetic, as when he urged her to "reach up to the tall fruit of your imagination and feel it growing warm and ripe" (CB to VS, 4.10.08), and the prophetic, as when he predicted her future status as "V[irginia]. S[tephen]., the great contemporary novelist (1882-1972)" (CB to VS, 7.4.08). Through the years of working on *The Voyage Out*, she showed Clive the various drafts as she composed and revised them, something she would never do with anyone else. She only showed Leonard her work when she considered it finished. She came to count on Clive's support not merely as her literary advisor, but also, in some sense, as a lover, and so she referred to him, looking back many years later: "I am seeing Clive rather frequently . . . enough of my old friend, & enough of my old lover, to make the afternoons hum" (*D2* 171). Intense though it was, their relationship remained unconsummated.

In her first anguished reaction to Vanessa's marriage, she had found Clive repulsive, describing him, in a strangely phallic image, as "that funny little creature twitching his pink skin and jerking out his little spasm of laughter." Yet a letter to Ethel Smyth about heterosexual desire, written twenty-five years later, may refer to Clive: "when 2 or 3 times in all, I felt physically for a man, then he was so obtuse, gallant, foxhunting and dull that I—diverse as I am—could only wheel round and gallop away." Certainly, their early letters discuss kisses—offered, but not always taken, and whether they had "achieved the heights." Clive, the most aggressively and confidently masculine member of Thoby's Cambridge circle, on more than one occasion pleaded shyness with her, reversing their expected roles. Perhaps his proximity to her—they often saw each other every two or three days—his passionate and possessive devotion, combined with his status as her brother-in-law made him at once safe and familiar, safe because each was anxious to avoid a crisis in their intimacy, either with each other or with Vanessa.

It is difficult to do justice to Clive's contribution to *The Voyage Out*, and to separate it from their "affair" (Virginia's term), which she evidently wanted and encouraged up to a point, even though it undermined her intimacy with Vanessa seriously, and perhaps permanently. Did she, unusually for her, find him sexually attractive? Did her need to write, to write experimentally, and to find support for her work, propel her into the relationship? In after years, Clive became the parrot, the worldling, and his vanity and womanising became jokes, but between 1908 and 1910, she jealously watched how he divided his attention between her and Vanessa—it was "the swing of that pendulum [that] carried so much of my fortune with it: at any rate of my comfort" (*D1* 86). While the portrait of Terence Hewet in *The Voyage Out* owes much to Clive, as does his ironic nickname, "monk" (*VO* 117), the love scenes between Rachel and Terence, and Terence's strong feminist sympathies register the distance between the character and his initial model. Woolf's inventive powers always drew her away from her starting points, although a scene com-

Life and Death Writing

posed for *Jacob's Room* and later abandoned captures something of that note of hesitancy, of unresolved searching that characterizes their correspondence.

In the published text, Jacob and Sandra Wentworth-Williams visit the Acropolis at night, but the nature of their experience remains elusive: "They had vanished. There was the Acropolis; but had they reached it? The columns and the Temple remain; the emotion of the living breaks fresh on them year after year; and of that what remains?" (*JR* 141). The equivalent scene in the holograph draft suggests the poignancy of desire within a relationship that can never be fulfilled (it is difficult to follow because it has been so heavily corrected):

> . . .& felt [in the soft dark its strength, its fearful / rough/ excitement.]
> To kiss him—
> She might have wanted that—no, not that.
> To kiss her?—no. not that.
> What then?
> Presumably they both wished only for one thing — certainty
> That something survives, still means, yes even in the chasms of dark years the thing we felt . . .
> They wanted certainty; separate, they wanted that the thin shell dividing them should break. Once united, something in the waste of chaos survives.
> (*JR, Holograph* 266-7; I read "chasms" for "charms")

While Sandra is accorded greater subjectivity in the holograph draft than in the published text, there is also a recognition that a relationship based on artificial or transient feelings can nevertheless generate its own immortal longings—the merest doggerel longs to become great poetry.

The holograph of *Jacob's Room* at times reads like a prose poem; it is an extraordinarily free and exhilarating text. When Woolf came to revise it, she wrapped it up and brought it closer to the "real" world by adding a penultimate chapter that has no equivalent in the holograph notebooks. Significantly numbered thirteen, it describes London on the afternoon and evening of 4 August 1914, a watershed in world history, when Lord Edward Grey waited with his Cabinet for the German response to Britain's ultimatum. Woolf created a series of vignettes of London on that hot afternoon: Jacob and Bonamy seated on one side of Hyde Park; Clara, on the other, taking the dog for a walk and seeing a runaway horse; the clock at Verrey's in Regent Street; Bacon the mapseller in the Strand, Timmy Durrant in Whitehall, and finally the members of the Cabinet themselves, who "looked too red, fat, pale or lean to be dealing . . . with the course of history" (*JR* 152).

Meanwhile two processions are holding up the city's traffic—the first assembles at Trafalgar Square, "where they had been testifying to their faith, singing lustily, . . . as they marched behind the gold letters of their creed" (*JR* 150). "Another procession, without banners, was blocking Long Acre," holding up the "dowagers in amethyst and gentlemen spotted with carnations" on their way to the Opera House (*JR* 153). The first procession is a pro-war demonstration which will march beneath the windows of Whitehall, but what is the second, without banners, blocking (but only temporarily) the way? With this oblique reference, Woolf emphasises the way history, "reality," her readers' knowledge, might be something that the novelist can take for granted, that readers will bring to her text, rather as *Jacob's Room* becomes a protest against the Great War when we bring to it our knowledge of the war and of the fate of Jacob's generation.

The second procession was concerned with peace—they did not unfurl their banners to avoid provoking the pro-war demonstrators that crowded the streets that evening. It was *en route* to Kingsway Hall, where women suffragists had called a meeting to support peace and British neutrality, but its intent had already been overtaken by news of the government's ultimatum to Germany that morning. In the event, the meeting went ahead, and Millicent Fawcett, president of the National Union of Women's Suffrage Societies, spoke to an audience of 2,000 women on the wickedness of war. Two potentially contradictory resolutions were drawn up—that women should actively support the efforts of their local communities, and that the government should be urged to pursue initiatives for peace. The women's movement, already split as to whether to remain within the law in seeking the vote, now further divided over attitudes to the war. Many followed the NUWSS, when it threw its weight behind the war effort, and towards the end of the war, the women's movement was rewarded by the extension of the vote. But for those who were pacifists as well as feminists, war represented precisely the form of patriarchal oppression which they most deeply opposed. Woolf had not yet identified her position on this issue in so many words, though her continuing friendship with pacifists like Margaret Llewelyn Davies and Mary Sheepshanks, even her suspicion that Pippa Strachey was "a jingo" (*D*1 117) may be indicative—like her reference to a forgotten procession, which failed to hold up the march of history: "[O]ne must follow; one must not block the way," she warned, as ladies and gentlemen in evening dress flowed under the arch of the Opera House (*JR* 153). *Three Guineas* lay far ahead.[2] Despite the wealth of thoughts and ideas recorded in her surviving writings, a great deal more of her inner life is only registered thus incidentally or indirectly.

Moving on from the mysteries of contextuality to those of textuality, I must begin by observing that the discoveries of holograph drafts and corrected galley proofs, fascinating as they are, have quite understandably distracted attention from existing problems in the various textual states of Woolf's novels. A certain amount of work has been carried out on the significant and at times substantial differences between the British and American versions of Woolf's texts, differences so large that readers on opposite sides of the Atlantic find themselves actually reading different books—and this is particularly true of her most popular novels—*Mrs Dalloway*, *To the Lighthouse* and *Orlando*. Meanwhile, what post-publication changes she made to her British texts are commonly overlooked and have certainly never been systematically examined. A striking example occurs in the last few pages of *A Room of One's Own*,

Life and Death Writing

where Woolf launches into a series of little codas: "when a woman speaks to women she should have something very unpleasant up her sleeve. Women are hard on women. Women dislike women," she observes. Even so, "The truth is, I often like women. I like their unconventionality. I like their subtlety. I like their anonymity. I like—but I must not run on in this way" (*AROO* 100).

This was how the text appeared in the British first edition, the American first edition and all subsequent American editions. Yet sixteen days later, in the second British impression, Woolf's enthusiasm for women had changed: instead of liking their subtlety, she liked their completeness. The sequence now runs, "I like their unconventionality. I like their completeness. I like their anonymity," reading thus in all British editions thereafter until January 1992, when Woolf's published works came out of copyright in Britain, and *A Room of One's Own* was widely reprinted in texts that had been reset from the British first impression of the first edition for the sake of greater accuracy; they therefore restored "subtlety" and lost "completeness," although "completeness" must have constituted Woolf's "final intention," textually speaking. This reversion to the first impression (and to "subtlety"), must be counted a loss since, if any textual change could be considered a feminist revision, it must surely be the change from "subtlety" to the very different claim made for women by "completeness."

As a textual crux, this prompts the further question: what other post-publication changes did Woolf make that have so far gone unnoticed? It cannot confidently be answered at present, since there have been so few attempts to collate the British impressions and editions published by Woolf's own Hogarth Press during her lifetime. Indeed, there has been a widespread critical assumption that she made no significant post-publication changes, that she did not revise her texts after publication—an assumption sometimes contradicted by notes to friends or diary entries, but one that has in turn discouraged further investigation.

We do not yet know how much more there may be to learn about Woolf as reviser of her own texts. We do know from her talk on "Professions for Women" (*CE2* 287-8) that she practiced a conscious self-censorship, and we can see where those acts of self-silencing have cast their shadows across her published work—in Jacob's essay on "The Ethics of Indecency" (*JR* 65), for example, or the many digs in *Orlando* at the necessity for disguise and concealment, the towels draped around the naked body and its functions. Yet although she normally toned down her drafts in preparation for publication, her revisions were not invariably directed towards greater repression. There is the counter-example of *Three Guineas*, Woolf's most controversial polemic, a book so far ahead of its time that not even Leonard could bring himself to like it. Woolf added new material to her footnotes for the American edition, apparently recognizing that this new audience might sympathize more strongly with her position than her British readers had done. The two most striking examples of such expansion occur in footnote 41 to chapter 2 and footnote 47 to

171

chapter 3. To the first, concerned with misogyny, she adds a paragraph beginning "Presumably the need for a scapegoat is largely responsible, and the role is traditionally a woman's (See Genesis)" (*TG* 365). The second example concerns parents sharing the rearing of children, and here she adds the information that "an English Member of Parliament has resigned in order to be with his children" (*TG* 365).[3]

Turning, finally, from textuality to intertextuality, I want to consider two examples of Woolf's use of poetry. Of course, there are numerous key poetic intertexts throughout her work—the invocation to Sabrina from Milton's *Comus* in *The Voyage Out* (*VO* 309); Fidele's dirge "Fear no more the heat o' the sun" in *Mrs Dalloway* (*MD* 10); Shakespeare's sonnet no. 98 ("From you have I been absent in the Spring") in *To the Lighthouse* (*TTL* 131), as well as many other poems—familiar lines and tags echo through the whole oeuvre. The story "Monday or Tuesday," written in 1920 to provide the title for her collection of her short stories, celebrates variety and multifariousness: "Flaunted, leaf-light, drifting at corners, blown across the wheels, silver-splashed, home or not home, gathered, scattered, squandered in separate scales, swept up, down, torn, sunk, assembled—and truth?" (*CSF* 137). Its compound words and piled-up participles recall another celebrant of variety in the natural world:

> Let life, waned, ah let life wind
> Off her once skeined stained veined variety upon, all on two spools; part, pen, pack
> Now her all in two flocks, two folds— (Hopkins 98)

The poems of Gerard Manley Hopkins were published posthumously in 1918. A year later, Woolf wrote to her friend Janet Case to say how much she liked them: "instead of writing mere rhythms and sense as most poets do, he makes a very strange jumble; so that what is apparently pure nonsense is at the same time very beautiful, and not nonsense at all" (*L2* 379).

In the case of Hopkins, two letters to Janet Case show that Woolf had read and responded to his work. My final example, from the other end of Woolf's career, concerns a poet to whom she makes no other reference, although she had reviewed a prose work by him twenty years earlier. Indeed, without the first typescript of *Pointz Hall,* we should not have known that she had read his poetry at all, let alone evolved her own distinctive response to it. The opening scene here resembles that of *Between the Acts,* but the conversation that takes place is quite different. Rupert Haines, the sexy gentleman farmer, addresses old Mr Oliver:

> "Did you ever hear, Sir," (so he called the old man) "of a chap" (here he hesitated as if from awkwardness at trespassing clumsily into some higher sphere) "of a poet" (he made a correction as if he stood in the presence of a superior) "called" (he brought the name out pursing his lips) "Thomas?" . . .
> "Thomas?" he repeated. "A surname," said Haines.
> Whereupon, there was a collision between the ladies. For Mrs. Perry, .

.. said "Thomas", and Mrs. Giles very slowly raised her head, swanwise, and, as if certain weights had moved into position behind her eye, making the shallow heavy; the surface dark, said, "Old Man's Beard!"

Haines turned in his chair. And there was another collision. "Hm," he said, meaning, so you've read that. And I never thought it; so we're not such fools either of us; not such simpletons . . .

"'I Like the Cuckoo' is it? and the deaf man who hears a voice. . . ."

They quoted; remembered; forgot; stumbled.

"I wish," she said, shifting in her chair as they came to an end of what they remembered, "I'd known him—Did you, Mr. Haines?" He shook his head (*PH* 38- 9).

But old Mr. Oliver's mind is running on Byron and his legend, which "hung like a wreath of Traveller's Joy, in a dusty lane." Oliver quotes "So we'll go no more a-roving by the light of the moon," and the narrative voice wonders "How many winters and spring had changed those perfect rings, that wreath of Traveller's Joy . . . into the little bare sprig of Old Man's Beard? And why was that leaf so stringent, so pungent to him and to—[Mr. Haines] looked at Mrs. Giles, hoping that she would help him in asserting the right of the living to their own opinions" (*PH* 39).

For Rupert Haines and Isa Giles, "there was nothing but smoke" in Oliver's recitation from Byron. As poetry, it does not speak their language; it is "not for us . . . not in the way that Thomas was." Thomas's name, on the other hand, produces an electric current between them, a frisson of mutual interest that is distinctly erotic: there was "a decided prick in their own . . . the same nerve; in the thigh it was in her case, and tingling still in connection with his. She still felt it as she sat" (*PH* 40).

Byron and Thomas, both deeply romantic and in their own way, legendary poets, are implicitly compared. Thomas, it seems, has become for Isa's generation what Byron had been for her father-in-law's. But they are also linked, for Byron's love lyric, "So, we'll go no more a-roving" is itself an echo of a traditional song whose refrain –"I'll go no more a-roving with you, fair maid,"—is quoted in Thomas's second "Old Song" (Thomas 20). Thomas was exactly the right poet for this passage, and the novel to follow: killed in the Great War at the age of 39, his poetic oeuvre was entirely composed during the last three years of his life, partly at the instigation of his friend Robert Frost, who in the spring of 1914 pointed out how much of his prose was the raw material of poetry. While he would have seemed too "Edwardian" to the generation of thirties poets who felt that poetry should focus on planes, pylons and politics, Thomas's celebration of the countryside would have appealed to a romantic gentleman farmer.

This discussion of Thomas's poetry was excised from the second typescript of *Pointz Hall*, and from the published text of *Between the Acts*— only the reference to Byron remained—yet Thomas's preoccupation with the English landscape and its impact on English literature, and with the words and traditions embedded in both, has been deeply absorbed into the finished novel:

173

one of his best known poems, "Words," invokes the genius of the English language. Although Woolf cut him from the opening dialogue as too wordy, too literary, he remains, an unnamed presence within the text, evident in a series of references to scents, memories, Englishness, once the reader has been alerted to look for them. At the heart, not just of *Pointz Hall*, but of *Between the Acts* lies the question of Englishness, and what the love of England might mean if it could ever be redeemed from the nightmares of nationalism, patriotism, jingoism—for in Germany and Italy nationalism had led to the persecution, torture and death of outsiders—whether foreigners, Jews, gypsies, homosexuals or communists. The solution, if there is one, lies in the concept of a linguistic community both affectionately and mockingly celebrated by Miss La Trobe in her pageant—something that springs from the English landscape, English language and English history, something that is sufficiently immaterial to be free of class and gender, something rooted in books rather than blood.

Yet already in Woolf's first typescript, Thomas's presence is troubled and distorted by Isa's misrememberings, or even misappropriations, for she misquotes both the poems that are mentioned. Thomas did not write a poem called "Old Man's Beard" but one called "Old Man." Old Man's Beard is a name for wild clematis (also called Traveller's Joy, and so linked with Byron and "We'll go no more a-roving"). "Old Man" is a name for *artemisia abrotarium*, or Southernwood, a grey-green herb which gives off a pungent smell when its leaves are crushed. Similarly the poem on the cuckoo, which Isa remembers as "I Like the Cuckoo," is actually spoken by a deaf man and begins "That's the cuckoo, you say. I cannot hear it./When last I heard it, I cannot recall . . ."

Isa's misrememberings silently draw attention to exactly those qualities in Thomas's poetry that make him a modernist, that give him affinities with poets who seemed superficially very different from him, for Thomas, like Woolf herself, sought in his art for what is absent, what is missing, what cannot be heard or spoken. In drawing him into her text as a poet of fugitive and forgotten feelings and lost sounds, Woolf performed the task that criticism has recently begun to address, his revaluation as a modernist poet. She rewrote him, just as, in his own way, he rewrites *Between the Acts*, once his presence is recognized, as a haunting as elusive as that of the past, which became for Woolf, following Thomas, "an avenue lying behind, a long ribbon of scenes and emotions" (*MOB* 78); a haunting as elusive as the scent in the last stanza of "Old Man":

> I have mislaid the key. I sniff the spray
> And think of nothing; I see and I hear nothing;
> Yet seem, too, to be listening, lying in wait
> For what I should, yet never can, remember:
> No garden appears, no path, no hoar-green bush
> Of Lad's-love, or Old Man, no child beside,

> Neither father, nor mother, nor any playmate;
> Only an avenue, dark, nameless, without end.
>
> (Thomas 9)

Notes

[1] I am grateful to James Beechey, who is writing a biography of Clive Bell, for information on his diary, currently in the collection of Olivier Bell, and to the Society of Authors, as Literary Representative of the Estate of Clive Bell, for permission to quote from it.

[2] See also Kathryn Harvey, "Politics 'through different eyes': *Three Guineas* and Writings by Members of the Women's International League for Peace and Freedom." *Virginia Woolf: Texts and Contexts: Selected Papers from the Fifth Annual Conference on Virginia Woolf*. Eds. Beth Righel Daugherty and Eileen Barrett. New York: Pace UP, 1996. 235-40; and "Feminist History and Global Politics: Historical Notes on Woolf and the Women's International League." *Virginia Woolf and the Arts: Selected Papers from the Sixth Annual Conference on Virginia Woolf*. Eds. Diane F. Gillespie and Leslie K. Hankins. New York: Pace UP, 1997. 142-9.

[3] For a fuller account of these arguments, see my article "Between the Texts: Virginia Woolf's Acts of Revision," *TEXT* 12, 2000.

Works Cited

Bell, Clive. Unpublished correspondence in the Monk's House Papers, University of Sussex Library.

Bell, Quentin. *Virginia Woolf*. 2 vols. London: Hogarth, 1972.

Hopkins, Gerard Manley. *The Poems*. Eds. W. H. Gardner and N. H. MacKenzie. 1967. Oxford: Oxford UP, 1970.

Thomas, Edward. *The Collected Poems*. Ed. R. George Thomas. 1978. Oxford: Oxford UP, 1983.

Woolf, Virginia. *Between the Acts*. 1941. Ed. Stella McNichol; intro. Gillian Beer. Harmondsworth: Penguin, 1992.

———. *Collected Essays*. Ed. Leonard Woolf, 4 vols. London: Hogarth, 1966.

———. *The Complete Shorter Fiction*. Ed. Susan Dick. 1985. London: Hogarth, 1989.

———. *The Diary of Virginia Woolf*. Ed. Anne Olivier Bell. 5 vols. London: Hogarth, 1977- 1984.

———. *The Letters of Virginia Woolf*. Eds. Nigel Nicolson and Joanne Trautmann. 6 vols. London: Hogarth, 1975-1980.

———. *Jacob's Room*. 1922. Ed. Sue Roe. Harmondsworth: Penguin, 1992.

———. *Jacob's Room: The Holograph Draft*. Ed. Edward L. Bishop. NY: Pace U. P., 1998.

———. *Melymbrosia*. Ed. Louise A. DeSalvo. NY: NY Public Library, 1982.

———. *Moments of Being*. Ed. Jeanne Schulkind. 1976. London: Triad, 1978.

———. *Mrs. Dalloway*. 1925. Ed. Stella McNichol; intro. Elaine Showalter. Harmondsworth: Penguin, 1992.

———. *Orlando*. 1928. Ed. Brenda Lyons; intro. Sandra Gilbert. Harmondsworth: Penguin, 1993.

———. *Pointz Hall: The Earlier and Later Typescripts of "Between the Acts."* Ed. Mitchell A. Leaska. NY: University Publications, 1983.

———. *A Room of One's Own*. 1928. Ed. Michele Barrett (with *Three Guineas*). Harmondsworth: Penguin, 1993.

———. *To the Lighthouse*. 1927. Ed. Stella McNichol; intro. Hermione Lee. Harmondsworth: Penguin, 1992.

———. *Three Guineas*. 1938. Ed. Michele Barrett (with *A Room of One's Own*) Harmondsworth: Penguin, 1993.
———. *The Voyage Out*. 1915. Ed. Jane Wheare. Harmondsworth: Penguin, 1992.

June Elizabeth Dunn
"Beauty Shines on Two Dogs Doing What Two Women Must Not Do": Puppy Love, Same-Sex Desire and Homosexual Coding in *Mrs. Dalloway*

Virginia Woolf, in both her diaries and letters, playfully expresses her feelings or opinions by identifying with animals, especially dogs, and makes specific reference to dogs as coding for same-sex desire in her novels. Encoded canine images of same-sex desire in her most famous dog story, *Flush*, her 1933 biography of Elizabeth Barrett's dog, has already been explored (see Vanita; Eberly). In this paper I will scratch at and pursue dog imagery reflecting lesbian desire in Woolf's earlier novels. Specifically, I would like to suggest that the canine associations with lesbian desire in *Night and Day* between the devotee Sally Seal and the suffragist Miss Markham are further developed in the relationship between the devotee Milly Brush and the ardent Tory Millicent Bruton in *Mrs. Dalloway*. *Mrs. Dalloway* is also the first novel in which Woolf first expresses her desire for Vita Sackville-West, her lover—a theme she continues in *Orlando* and *Flush*. While Eileen Barrett and others have noticed the homoerotic friendship of Septimus Warren Smith and his commanding officer Evans, who are described as "two dogs playing on a hearth-rug" in *Mrs. Dalloway* (*MD* 93), dog imagery is additionally used in the novel as a reflection of Clarissa and Elizabeth Dalloway's lesbian desire, and a parallel to Woolf's own desire for Vita.

In *Night and Day*, Sally Seal is rescued from her "mental ambiguity" (81) and Mary Datchet from marriage by the influence Kit Markham and her dog Sailor have on both women. Sally Seal, a woman consumed with "philanthropic enthusiasm" and "always in some disorder," is only able to maintain some level of equilibrium because her "worship of Miss Markham" "kept her in her place" (81). Mary Datchet, who is "determined to be a great organizer" in the suffrage movement (79), is at first ambiguous regarding her feelings towards Ralph Denham, chastising herself for "doing now what she had often blamed others of her sex for doing . . . endowing [a man] with a kind of heavenly fire, and passing her life before it for his sanction" (164). Shortly before a suffrage meeting, Mary's thoughts of Ralph Denham and marriage obscure the importance of her work so much that she thinks about her Italian lessons and that she should perhaps "take up the study of birds" (164). The sight of Sally Seal "inducing a very large dog to drink water out of a tumbler" "awaken[s]" Mary to "reality" upon reaching the landing outside the suffrage office (164). Sally tells her that Miss Markham, the founder of their suffrage society, has arrived "and this is her dog," whom Mary pats, commenting "A very fine dog, too" (164). Sally observes: "A kind of St. Bernard, she tells me—so like Kit to have a St. Bernard. And you guard your mistress well, don't you, Sailor? You see that wicked men don't break into her larder when she's out at *her* work—helping poor souls who have lost their way" (164).

It is highly probable that Miss Markham, who is a spinster and a suffragist, is also a lesbian and that Woolf was aware of the lesbian proclivity of the suffragists. As Pat Cramer points out in her introduction to *Virginia Woolf: Lesbian Readings*, Woolf would be confirmed in this connection when suffragist and lesbian Ethel Smyth told her a "number of lesbians found each other within the suffrage movement" (119). It is Miss Markham's lesbianism embodied in her dog Sailor that protects her from men and that also allows her to help a poor soul like Mary Datchet from being distracted from her true sexual nature by men such as Ralph Denham. When Mary complains during the meeting that her friends, and in particular Ralph, "think all this kind of thing is useless," Miss Markham responds by laughing and saying, "Oh, they're that sort, are they?" and as a result, Mary's spirits are "considerably improved" (*MD* 168). Miss Markham's influence is enhanced by the devotion of Sally. It is Sally, after all, who induces Miss Markham's dog to drink out of a tumbler, and it is Sally who is glad that "Kit has a big dog" because she didn't think Kit "looked well" (170). Although the size of the dog may matter to Sally, it's how Kit's dog performs its duty which is more important, and given Sally's dogged devotion to both Kit and her pooch, Sailor is undoubtedly, in the words of Mary, "a very fine dog."

The kenneling of another sort of lesbian pedigree occurs in *Mrs. Dalloway* with Lady Bruton and Milly Brush's relationship. While Sailor in *Night and Day* may embody lesbian desire, Lady Bruton and Milly Brush in *Mrs. Dalloway* are attributed canine qualities to reflect their lesbian desire. Eileen Barrett in "Unmasking Lesbian Passion: The Inverted World of *Mrs. Dalloway*" applies Havelock Ellis' theories of "female sexual inversion" (or lesbianism) to Milly Brush's disdain for men and her deficiency of female charm; similarly Lady Bruton's "excessive dedication to her 'masculine avocations'" is evidence of both women being "on the borderland of true sexual inversion" (156). Furthermore, their lesbianism is not only implicit in the canine associations with their names, but also in the dog-like obedience Milly Brush displays towards Lady Bruton. Whereas Lady Bruton may be a "brute" in regard to her penchant for societal order no matter the cost, she still is a "woman of pedigree" (*MD* 114); and though Milly may brush people the wrong way, she is very much like the "brush" of a dog's tail, wagging herself for Lady Bruton's approval. For instance, Lady Bruton need only to "nod or turn her head a little abruptly" for Milly to take "the signal" (116), and when Lady Bruton asks Milly to "fetch the papers" Milly does so with almost show-dog precision: she "went out, came back; laid papers on the table" (118-119). The lasting impression everyone has of Lady Bruton as they leave her company is of her standing in the doorway "while her chow stretched behind her, and Miss Brush disappeared into the background with her hands full of papers" (120). Kit Markham may be the rescuer of lesbian souls, but Lady Bruton is the image of lesbian impenetrability who protects her relationships through absolute dogmatic control.

For Woolf, herself, her description of dogs often reflected her thoughts. For instance, Shot "is melancholy" when Leonard is away in London and Woolf is at Asheham recovering from her September 1913 suicide attempt (*L2* 35), and Max, in 1915, was quite sick "having voided a large worm" after hearing Leonard "read aloud a passionate poem by [D. H.] Lawrence" (73). Moreover, dogs reflected Woolf's lesbian desire. As Jane Lilienfeld notes, Woolf's "language of lesbian love" is found not only in the "encoded imagery of 'wallabies' and 'kangaroos' in her letters to Violet Dickinson" (Lilienfeld 41) but also in Violet's dog Rupert (44-45): "I think with joy of certain exquisite moments when Rupert and I lick your forehead with a red tongue and a purple tongue; and I twine your hairs round our noses" (*L1* 338). The encoded lesbian imagery which is part of Woolf and Violet's romantic relationship is "transformed" in Woolf and Vita's love affair into other animal imagery including "the muddy Grizzle of Woolf's letters to Vita" (Lilienfeld 41). It is perhaps no coincidence that Woolf's own dog Grizzle was suffering frequently from mange (a contagious skin condition which creates intolerable itching,) during the time Woolf was finishing *Mrs. Dalloway* as the Dalloways' dog Grizzle is similarly afflicted with distemper, another contagious disease in dogs. Grizzle's mange, on the one paw, mirrors Woolf's incessant irritation with people such as her bothersome assistant whom she refers to as "a poor dog" at whom she "scarcely [has] a word to throw" and Woolf compares Grizzle's mange to her assistant's fungus-covered fingers (*L3* 167). Grizzle's mange also becomes representative of Woolf's desire for Vita, which she cannot seem to satiate, a desire which she first begins to express both in her diary and letters in December 1922.

David Eberly links *Flush* to *Orlando* because "its subject [Vita] and its method" are the same and because Woolf borrowed a photograph of a dog from Vita to use as Flush's model (Eberly 21). While *Orlando* may be considered Woolf's "love letter" to Vita (*L3* xxii), Woolf's friendship with her began in 1923 and evolved into a sexual relationship in 1925 during the period she was writing *Mrs. Dalloway*. Not surprisingly, Vita preoccupied Woolf's thoughts during this time. On September 15, 1924, Woolf writes to Vita that she "felt rather spirited up" from reading Vita's story *Seducers in Ecuador,* which was dedicated to Woolf, so much that Woolf "wrote a lot" that morning "300 words"—and "God knows there are very few people I feel that way about, even the ones I admire" (*L3* 131-132). On that very same day Woolf also writes in her diary:

Life and Death Writing

Here I am, peering across Vita at Mrs. Dalloway; & can't stop, of a night, thinking of the next scene, & how I'm to wind up. Vita, to attempt a return, is like an over ripe grape in features, moustached, pouting, will be a little heavy; meanwhile, she strides on fine legs, in a well cut skirt . . . Oh yes, I like her; could tack her on to my equipage for all time; & I suppose if life allowed, this might be a friendship of a sort. The clock strikes 7, & I wonder if I hear Leonard . . . in the kitchen. Grizzle pricks an ear; lies flat again" (*D2* 313).

In this passage, Woolf not only connects her attraction to Vita to the writing of *Mrs. Dalloway*, but she also uses Grizzle as a conduit for expressing her lesbian desire. Grizzle's canine sense first picks up Woolf's attraction for Vita and then "lies flat again" as Woolf suppresses Vita when she imagines she hears Leonard. In addition to using Grizzle as the carrier of her desire, Woolf also applies archetypal canine imagery to reflect her attraction towards Vita. In a letter to Jacques Raverat in December 1924, Woolf comments upon Vita's "exquisite" legs and describes her as a "breastless cuirassier," "virginal, savage, patrician" who, if she were Woolf "should merely stride, with 11 Elk hounds, behind me, through my ancestral woods" (*L3* 150), the image of a modern day "Diana of the Hunt" who is often portrayed with her pack of hounds (Walker 58-60). The following month Woolf again writes to Raverat and asks him if he has "any views on loving one's own sex," telling him that she "want[s] to incite [her] lady to elope with [her]" (*L3* 155-156). Vita's association with dogs becomes even more discernible and connected with *Mrs. Dalloway* when she promises a puppy (Pinka, who would ultimately become the model for Flush) to Woolf in February of 1925. Woolf wonders how she "can live up to a Sackville Hound" (162) from her "aristocrat" who is "violently Sapphic" (155).[1]

As Woolf's love affair with Vita progresses, Grizzle's presence in her correspondence becomes more prevalent. Woolf teasingly pleads with Vita in her first letter to her after their love affair began not to snuff "poor Virginia . . . and Dog Grizzle (who is scratching under [her] bed)" out of her heart (224). Vanita points out that Woolf expresses two dimensions of love, "hopeless devotion and joyful eroticism," in her relationship with Vita "through an elaborately worked-out set of animal images, among which one of the prominent images is that of the dog" (Vanita 249). It is Grizzle's image which holds prominence for Woolf after *Mrs. Dalloway's* publication and it is Grizzle's mange which becomes the conveyance for expressing her unrequited desire for Vita:

But I'm in a rush—have just taken Grizzle to a vet . . . Ah, if you want my love for ever and ever you must break out into spots on your back. And you won't; for if ever a woman was a lighted candlestick, a glow, an illumination which will cross the desert and leave me—it was Vita: and thats the truth of it: and she has nothing, nor ever will have, in common with dog Grizzle who stands before me, raw, greasy, mudstained (*L3* 226).

179

During Vita's trip to Persia, Woolf again expresses her desire for her by writing about Grizzle's mange:

> Did I tell you how Grizzle is in hospital? No; I concealed it lest you should be anxious: the mange: rainbow stripes have appeared across her back. . . And I want a little spoiling. No: I don't forget you (245-246).

The urgency of Woolf's desire is reflective of Grizzle's condition—the dog is in the hospital—and in a subsequent letter, she describes herself and Grizzle as being "rather mangy" and that they "will rush down to meet [Vita]" and "lick [her] all over" when she returns (253).

In *Mrs. Dalloway*, however, Grizzle's mange is replaced by distemper, and aside from reflecting the family tension, the distemper also reflects the suppression of lesbian desire. Eileen Barrett notes that Madge Symonds Vaughan has been cited by many critics as Woolf's model for Sally Seton, and that Clarissa and Sally's friendship is "the intermingling of the intellectual and erotic, the personal and the political that [Woolf] experienced in her own feminist friendships" (Barrett 151). Woolf's relationship with Vita was very much an "intellectual and erotic" one, and like Sally who is "an extraordinary beauty of the kind [Clarissa] most admired, dark, large-eyed" and who "could say anything, do anything" (*MD* 34), Vita was similarly endowed. In *Portrait of a Marriage: V. Sackville-West & Harold Nicolson*, Nigel Nicolson comments upon his mother's "exceptional tomboyishness": although she liked to remember herself as "an unsociable and unnatural girl with long black hair and long black legs" (59), others considered her "lovely" and "a beauty" (79). Furthermore, both Sally Seton and Vita "had French blood in [their] veins" (*MD* 34), Vita's mother having been reared in France (Nicolson 10). Like Clarissa, who questions "this falling in love with women" (33) after confronting the notion that her daughter may be falling in love with Doris Kilman (10) and then recalls her first love Sally Seton (33), Woolf recalls her own love for Madge Symonds Vaughan through her burgeoning desire for Vita. Woolf refers to Vita as "a dear old rough coated sheep dog" (*L3* 224) after their affair begins, and in *Mrs. Dalloway*, Clarissa leaves the room and flings herself upon Rob, "that great shaggy dog which ran after sheep" and goes "into raptures" (*MD* 64) over the dog after learning from Sally Seton about a neighbor who had married his housemaid subsequent to her having borne his child (63). Clarissa declares that she "shall never be able to speak to [the woman] again" when Sally questions whether knowing this information would make a difference in "one's feelings" about the woman (63). Even though she loves Sally, Clarissa fears the repercussions of such a relationship and displaces her anxiety onto the woman's transgression. Later at dinner, Clarissa sits next to Richard Dalloway, her future husband. Although Clarissa expresses lesbian desire through her passion for her dog, she suppresses it by marrying Richard Dalloway and regaining heterosexual convention.

Likewise for Elizabeth Dalloway, her mother's party helps transition her from a young woman who "really cared for her dog most of all" and Miss Kilman (10), to a young woman who leaves behind Doris Kilman and her dog to attend the party and talk to Willie Ticomb (211) who thinks "she [is] like a poplar, she [is] like a river, she [is] like a hyacinth"(205). While Willie's desire for Elizabeth makes her think of "how much nicer to be in the country and do what she liked," she ignores Grizzle her poor dog, who she is certain is howling (205). Richard Dalloway notices the shift in Elizabeth because he at first does not recognize who the "lovely girl" is and then realizes "that it [is] his Elizabeth . . . [who] look[s] so lovely in her pink frock!" (211). Elizabeth is "happy" that her father is pleased with this change yet Grizzle is unattended as a result (212). For both mother and daughter, the suppression of their lesbian desire is manifest in Grizzle's behavior, whose noisy howling and misery reflect their muted anquish.

Though Woolf uses dog imagery in her diaries and letters and in her novels to express a number of emotions, same-sex desire is the most prominent sentiment contained within the imagery. Like her characters Sally Seal and Kit Markham and Lady Bruton and Milly Brush, Woolf assimilates dog imagery into the expression of her lesbian desire. As she tells her nephew Quentin, "Beauty shines on two dogs doing what two women must not do" when she relates her observation of two female dogs "becoming enmeshed" with each other (*L4* 34). While Woolf's love affair with Vita did not begin until seven months after *Mrs. Dalloway* was published, Woolf's attraction to her was very much apparent during the course of her writing the novel. Through canine imagery, especially that of her dog Grizzle, Woolf expresses her desire for Vita unabashedly as much as the Dalloway's dog Grizzle signals the suppression of Clarissa and Elizabeth's lesbian desire. Furthermore, Clarissa's remembrance of "the most exquisite moment" of her life, when she was in love with Sally Seton, was written into the novel in August 1923 (Wussow 31), months after Woolf had begun expressing her attraction to Vita in her diary and letters. If *Orlando* is considered Woolf's love letter to Vita, and *Flush* regarded as Woolf putting closure on their relationship, then *Mrs. Dalloway* could be considered their courtship novel. As Pat Cramer argues in "Notes From Underground," *Mrs. Dalloway* is a "coming out" novel. The novel's significance to Woolf and Vita's relationship is made unintentionally ironic by Leonard in his carrying out Woolf's final wishes. After Woolf's death on March 28, 1941, Leonard wrote to Vita informing her that Woolf wanted him to give one of her manuscripts to Vita. "Leonard first offered [Vita] *Flush* . . . [but] he indicated that he had originally thought of offering her *Mrs. Dalloway*" which he sent to her on June 21, 1941 (Wussow xii-xiii), the novel which signaled the beginning of Woolf and Vita's romantic and literary friendship.

Notes

[1] In a paper I presented at the Eighth Annual Virginia Woolf conference, I discussed how Woolf incorporates elements of the Sherlock Holmes stories, particularly those from *The Hound of the Baskervilles*, to mock Arnold Bennett, who believed that unlike Woolf, Sir Arthur Conan Doyle could create characters who are real and true (Bennett 87). The "brute with the blood red nostrils" that pursues Septimus Warren Smith in *Mrs. Dalloway* becomes the Baskerville Hound of heterosexual and social class convention.

Works Cited

Barrett, Eileen. "Unmasking Lesbian Passion: The Inverted World of *Mrs. Dalloway*." *Virginia Woolf: Lesbian Readings*. Ed. Eileen Barrett and Patricia Cramer. New York: New York UP, 1997. 146-164.

Bennett, Arnold. "Is the Novel Decaying?" *The Author's Craft and Other Critical Writings of Arnold Bennett*. Ed. Samuel Hynes. Lincoln: University of Nebraska Press, 1968.

Cramer, Patricia. "Introduction." Barrett and Cramer 117-127.

Eberly, David. "Housebroken: The Domesticated Relations of *Flush*." *Virginia Woolf: Texts and Contexts: Selected Papers from the Fifth Annual Conference on Virginia Woolf*. Eds. Beth Rigel Daugherty and Eileen Barrett. New York: Pace UP, 1996. 21-25.

Lilienfeld, Jane. "'The Gift of a China Inkpot': Violet Dickinson, Virginia Woolf, Elizabeth Gaskell, Charlotte Brontë, and the Love of Women in Writing." Barrett and Cramer 37-56.

Nicolson, Nigel. *Portrait of a Marriage: V. Sackville-West & Harold Nicolson*. New York: Atheneum, 1973.

Vanita, Ruth. "'Love Unspeakable': The Uses of Allusion in *Flush*." *Virginia Woolf Themes and Variations: Selected Papers from the Second Annual Conference on Virginia Woolf*. Ed. Vara Neverow-Turk and Mark Hussey. New York: Pace UP, 1993. 248-257.

Woolf, Virginia. *Night and Day*. 1919. New York: HBJ, 1973.

——. *Mrs. Dalloway*. 1925. New York: Harvest/Harcourt Brace, Co. 1997.

——. *The Diary of Virginia Woolf*. Vol. 2. Ed. Anne Oliver Bell. New York: HBJ, 1977.

——. *The Diary of Virginia Woolf*. Vol. 3. Ed. Anne Oliver Bell. New York: HBJ, 1978.

——. *The Letters of Virginia Woolf*. Vol. 3. Ed. Nigel Nicolson and Joanne Trautmann. New York: HBJ, 1977.

——. *The Letters of Virginia Woolf*. Vol. 4. Ed. Nigel Nicolson and Joanne Trautmann. New York: HBJ, 1979.

Wussow, Helen M. *Virginia Woolf "The Hours": The British Museum Manuscript of Mrs. Dalloway*. New York: Pace UP, 1997.

Val Gough
"A Responsible Person Like Her": Woolf's Suicide Culture

As Olive Anderson has pointed out, the meaning of suicidal actions can only be accurately deciphered through reconstructing their context as completely as possible, and part of that context is the "suicide culture" in which those who have died by suicide have passed their lives. What people think and feel when they find themselves caught up in a situation in which suicide could be the outcome is partly settled by the ways of thinking and feeling about suicide which they have consciously and unconsciously absorbed from childhood onwards (Anderson 4). Religious beliefs and personal philosophies, psychosexual history, and an individual's own etiquette of personal crises will have a bearing, but so will contemporary cultural representations of suicide and discourses about suicide.

Although Woolf's psychosexual history has been amply studied and related most persuasively to her final suicide, with several primary factors established—her early experiences of death and her sexual abuse; her manic depression; her final fear of recurring "madness"—there is more work to be done on Woolf's particular suicide culture and the impact it had upon her death. Our understanding of the causes of Woolf's suicide needs to be supplemented by a study of the changing history of discourses *about* suicide, as well as of the way that sociohistorical factors such as occupation, environment, geography, age, class, national identity and gender might have influenced Woolf's decision. In my thinking about Woolf's suicide culture I have been influenced by critics such as Susan Kenney, who has argued that we cannot absolve Woolf of responsibility for her own death. She says: "Leonard's stated conclusion is that she committed suicide because she was insane, and because he was not watching, which like the coroner's verdict of suicide while the balance of her mind was disturbed dissolves into a Catch-22 of circular reasoning, the assumption being that if you commit suicide you must be crazy, because if you weren't crazy you wouldn't commit suicide" (Kenney 269). Carolyn G. Heilbrun also argues that Woolf's suicide was "A free act, a choice" (Heilbrun 248) and she continues, "She must have thought with great logic about suicide" (Heilbrun 249). Thus one of the underlying premises of my analysis is that Woolf's final suicidal action was the result of her own rational interrogation of suicide over a period of many years. This thoughtful, responsible interrogation took place in a personal and intellectual climate open to the notion of suicide as a rational choice, and in a wider cultural context in which suicide functioned in popular consciousness as a heavily overdetermined literary, artistic and cultural trope.

After Woolf's death, Vanessa predictably blamed Woolf's madness but also acknowledged that there seemed to be something different about Woolf's frame of mind this time. She wrote to Vita on April 2 1941, "how strange it seems" (Marler 475) and she wrote to Jane Bussy a few weeks later that Woolf's state of mind was "still to me mysterious, for she had seemed nowhere near the state in which she had been several times before when I had dreaded this" (Marler 478). Studying aspects of Woolf's suicide culture alongside the other already well-established factors (her sexual abuse, her fear of artistic failure and recurring mental illness, and the pressures of the war and impending invasion) might move us slightly closer to understanding that mystery which is Woolf's death.

Woolf grew up during a time of particular fascination with suicide as both social phenomenon and artistic metaphor. Suicidology was a new science pioneered in Europe not Britain, but it was England which contemporary European suicidologists viewed as the centre of suicidal activity. Emile Durkheim, founding father of suicide studies, viewed the English character as fundamentally suicidal and Britain as a hotbed of romantic suicide. In scientific consciousness, then, if not in reality, England was particularly associated with suicide. Since mid-century, visual art like Henry Wallis's celebrated painting *Chatterton* (1855-6) had helped to make suicide fashionable, and there was a concomitant resurgence in "Wertherism," the vogue for romantic suicides in imitation of Goethe's *The Sorrows of Werther* (1774). Hence, among late-Victorian Londoners, suicide was far from being a taboo subject. On the contrary, the middle and working-classes relished stories of suicide, which did not necessarily arouse feelings of horror or condemnation. The amount of space given to reports of suicide in every section of the British press was then much greater than it is now (Anderson 195). And as a child, Woolf clearly shared this late Victorian relish for sensationalist stories about suicide. Writing to her mother at the age of five or six she describes the gruesome case of a man who appears to have thrown himself under a train: "Mrs. Prinsep says that she will go in a slow train cos she says all the fast trains have accidents and she told us about an old man of 70 who got his legs caute in the weels of the train and the train began to go on and the old gentleman was draged along till the train caute fire and he called out for somebody to cut off his legs but nobody came and he was burnt up. Goodbye your Loving Virginia" (qtd. Lee 107). The *Hyde Park Gate News* produced by Virginia demonstrates a similar relish for the sensational and gruesome. Satirical and ruthlessly anti-emotional, the stories were often macabre and horrific, and clearly owe something to the general thirst for sensationalism of the period.

The particular motifs which recurred in visual, literary and journalistic discourses about suicide would have deeply impressed themselves upon the young Virginia. Indeed, whilst Louise DeSalvo has shown just how deeply the idea of drowning was bound up with Woolf's psychosexual history, her sexual abuse and subsequent feelings of suffocation and inadequacy, it is also worthwhile noting that among the recurring suicide tropes of Victorian literature and the popular press, the romantic image of female suicide by drowning was one of the most potent. In fact, suicide was associated with drowning to the extent that the most frequently used phrase for suicide was "making a hole in the water." Sentimental images of self-drowned deserted or fallen women were immortalised in poems like Thomas Hood's immensely popular "The Bridge of Sighs" and in paintings like G. F. Watts's *Found Drowned* (1848-50). In numerous visual and literary images, as Barbara T. Gates points out, women seemed to drown in their own tears, or return to the waters of the womb (Gates 135). John Everett Millais's *Ophelia* appeared in 1851-2 and Elaine Showalter argues that "the figure of Ophelia eventually set the style for female insanity" (Showalter 92). It is more than likely that such a network of associations had an impact upon Woolf's own thinking about female suicide and her own overdetermined use of the metaphor in both personal and public narratives. Her own final choice of suicide method not only re-enacts the feelings of suffocation she suffered due to her sexual abuse, as Louise DeSalvo has shown, but also makes use of the defining trope for female suicide originating from the period of that abuse. Another recurrent image associated with suicidal women was that of women plunging through the air from a height, often from a bridge or tall building. Such images bear a different message to those of the Victorian Ophelias. As Gates says, "these women are not deadened or will-less, but rather their soaring is, for a moment, an act of autonomy or self-assertion" (Gates 142). Jumping from a height also recurs as a theme in Woolf's personal and literary narratives, as well, of course, as in her own actions. That other methods of suicide such as cutting, poison, hanging or shooting do not recur as tropes in Woolf's writings, both personal and fictional, with anything like the frequency of drowning and jumping, indicates that we cannot ignore the impact of contemporary discourses on Woolf's thinking about suicide.

If Woolf grew up in a context in which suicide was particularly sensationalised in the popular press and contemporary literature, it was also a time when suicide was debated seriously by intellectuals and bohemians alike. At the turn of the century, apologias for suicide abounded in advanced circles (Anderson 245). Victorian atheism, in particular, cleared a space for debates about suicide, and such debates were also carried on in novels like Mary Augusta Ward's *Helbeck of Bannisdale* (1898), which presented a religious struggle so hopeless and tragic that it could be resolved only through the overt suicide of one of its two protagonists, Laura Fountain, who drowns herself. Woolf's own family heritage of muscular agnosticism opened up the possibility of a philosophy of suicide based on religious scepticism. It was to Leslie Stephen that Ward gave a special bound copy of her novel, omitting the last chapter, for she felt that Laura's death might "depress one who had known so much sorrow" (Ward 185). Leslie had already written his own *Science of Ethics* (1882) in which he had asked:

> If we suppose that a man, knowing that life meant for him nothing but agony, and that moreover his life could not serve others, and was only giving useless pain to his attendants, and perhaps involved the sacrifice of health to his wife and children, should commit suicide, what ought we to

think of him? [He goes on to say:] May we not say that he is acting on a superior moral principle, and that because he is clearly diminishing the sum of human misery? . . . The conduct may spring either from cowardice or from a loftier motive than the ordinary, and the merit of the action is therefore not determinable; but, assuming the loftier motive, I can see no grounds for disapproving the action which flows from it. (Stephen 391-2).

Leslie was, in fact, an admirer of efficient suicides. On his way to America in 1888, he wrote to Julia: "Someone threw themselves overboard from steerage. After all, it is a cleaner way of committing suicide than most" (qtd. Lee 100).

Such openness to suicide as an ethical option was supported by contemporary eugenic theories, which also gave credence to suicide as a socially tolerable act, seeing it as a beneficial elimination of the least fit part of the race's breeding stock. Eugenicists saw irrational suicide as a manifestation of degenerative disease transmitted by inheritance, as part of the mechanism which ensured "the survival of the fittest." Suicide was even preached by some as a social duty. The most influential proponent of this view was Henry Morselli, who argued that "suicide is an effect of the struggle for existence and of human selection" (Anderson 70). Woolf appears to have been somewhat influenced by such Social Darwinism and sometimes seems to endorse the language of degeneracy and eugenics. As Hermione Lee point out, she writes in her notes for *Mrs. Dalloway* of not wanting the "insane," shell-shocked Septimus Smith to be a "degenerate" type, and she depicts him being much preoccupied with Darwinian evolution, the history of civilisation and his own "degradation" (Lee 188). Woolf's interest in euthanasia also seems to have contributed to her thinking about suicide: as her father lingered on, suffering from cancer, Woolf wished for his death, writing to Violet Dickinson "If only it could be quicker!" (*L*1 123-83). Yet she then felt tremendous guilt about that feeling, and she portrayed such ambivalence in *The Years*. When Woolf heard of George Duckworth's death in 1934 she wrote to Vanessa: "Leonard says Laura is the one we could have spared" (*L*5 300) and her infamous comment when she saw a group of retarded people—that "They should certainly be killed"—also reflects her openness to ideas of euthanasia (*D*1 13). In 1939 she wrote about her friend Margaret Llewelyn Davies, complaining that she "lives too carefully of life." "Why" Woolf asks, "drag on, always measuring & testing one's little bits of strength & setting it easy tasks so as to accumulate years?" (*D*5 214). Watching Leonard's aged mother pitifully hanging on to life she wondered whether she would be like that. Suicide, she felt would be more dignified, and she disliked the thought that "one will not perhaps go to the writing table & write that simple & profound paper upon suicide which I see myself leaving for my friends" (*D*3 231).

There is evidence that her early suicide culture encouraged Woolf to develop her own personal, rational philosophy of suicide. She had a long discussion with Vanessa on the ethics of suicide in 1903 (*PA* 211-213), and in 1905 she wrote to Eleanor Cecil praising a poem which she had seen in the

Daily Chronicle, whose subject was the death of a woman who had hanged herself. "Why do I write all about suicide and mad people?" she asked (*L*1 202-3). Suicide was often on Woolf's mind in the early years, not so much as a morbid death-wish but as an awareness of suicide as an active choice. Her 1906 story "Phyllis and Rosamond" depicts two pairs of sisters, a liberated pair and an inhibited pair. Listening to the story of the inhibited pair, one of the liberated sisters exclaims: "My God. . .What a Black Hole! I should burn, shoot, jump out of the window; at least do something!" (*CSF* 17-29). In fact, Woolf had a life-long fascination with suicide as an oppositional strategy. In her depiction of suicide as a form of resistance, Woolf was in line with Durkheim's association of suicide with insubordination to the established order, and with the unconventionality of emancipated political and intellectual elites. Suicide was one of three subversive issues which many years later Woolf named when she railed against the censorship of *The Well of Loneliness* and the policing of thought which she recognised it as a symptom of: "What of other subjects known to be more or less unpopular in Whitehall, such as birth-control, suicide and pacifism? May we mention these? We await our instructions!" (qtd. Lee 526).

If Woolf saw suicide as an act of resistance, she also recognised that the way the law treated suicide made it a form of punishment for transgression. Woolf was clearly fascinated by the way suicide and the stigma attached to it functioned as a form of social policing, and it is the figure of the criminalized female suicide, Judith Shakespeare, which Woolf uses in *A Room of One's Own* to epitomise the marginalization of women. Previous to 1823, suicides had been buried at a cross-roads, as Judith is, because these were signs of the cross; because steady traffic over the suicide's grave could help to keep the person's ghost down; and because ancient sacrificial victims had been slain at such sites. Seen as ultimate sinners, suicides had been staked to prevent their restless wanderings as lost souls, and the law after 1823 still treated suicides punitively: they had still to be buried without Christian rites and at night, and their goods and chattels were still turned over to the Crown. It was not until 1882 that the penalties imposed by common and statute law for the crime of *felonia de se* (or self-murder) were removed. Not until 1925 did Parliament downgrade the legal status of attempted suicide into a minor offence, and suicide remained illegal in Britain until 1961.

Another aspect of Woolf's suicide culture worth noting is the way that contemporary suicide mythology—the myths and conventional wisdoms surrounding suicide—may have led Woolf and those around her to believe in a personal propensity towards suicide. Suicide mythology has always associated self-murder particularly with women, although this is not borne out by statistics. But Woolf and those around her may well have internalised the belief that because of her gender, Woolf was more prone to suicidal tendencies. For the late Victorians, women were associated with suicide through two potent images: that of drowning, as I've already mentioned, and that of Indian suttee.

Barbara T. Gates has shown how British concern about suttee in the Victorian period bordered on obsession, and was fuelled by anti-Hindu feeling. It also, Gates argues, functioned as a displacement anxiety about the role of Western women and the so-called redundant woman or spinsters, whom many Victorians wanted to believe had no place to go but death. Above all, suttee reinforced the association of suicide with women, or what Gates calls the "femininization of suicide" (Gates 98). Jane Marcus has shown how in *The Waves*, Woolf associates Rhoda's suicide with suttee, through her use of Shelley's poems, specifically "the Indian girl's song" (Marcus 137). Other aspects of suicide mythology may have been internalised by Woolf, particularly the myth of the tortured artist, in which literary genius has habitually been associated with mental instability and suicide. Again, this might have been a myth which encouraged Woolf to see herself as more prone to suicide. Likewise the contemporary association of suicide with influenza. It was regarded as well-established that influenza caused melancholia: "They get all forms of insanity from influenza" a police surgeon told the jury at a suicide inquest (Anderson 169). Woolf may have also been encouraged to associate suicidal tendencies with influenza because of her brother Thoby's suicidal behaviour as a boy when he caught influenza at school. Because Woolf herself was particularly prone to bouts of influenza, did she feel herself to be more prone to suicide?

Myths about suicide will have indeed influenced Woolf—consciously and unconsciously—in complex and overdetermined ways, but so will actual socio-economic factors. Occupation, environment, geography, age, class, national identity and gender all relate in close and complex ways to suicide incidence, and although Woolf liked to see herself as an outsider, her suicide actually conforms to well-established patterns of socially determined behavior. Thus, for example, analysts of suicide statistics have always noted how commonly individuals take their lives with the special instruments of their trade, so that soldiers might use guns, butchers might use knives, or chemists use poison. And indeed, Woolf's occupation as a writer may have well influenced the method she chose for her suicide, for she appears to have chosen to die by literalizing one of her own most potent and recurring literary metaphors. Woolf used suicide as a literary trope of defiance, and it is possible to see her own suicide as a defiant *literalizing* of her own artistic metaphors. She used one of the tools of her trade as a method of self-murder.

Another factor may have been Woolf's age, for increasing age is associated with increasing suicide rates. We know Woolf associated death with loss and guilt, but as she grew older she also began to treat death as yet another peak experience to be scrutinised. She wrote in her diary that she intended to

> describe the approach of age, & the gradual coming of death. As people describe love. To note every symptom of failure; but why failure? To treat it as an experience that is different from the others; & to detect every one of the gradual stages towards death which is a tremendous experience, & not as unconscious at least in its approaches, as birth is. (*D5* 230)

Life and Death Writing

Geography is also a factor worthy of consideration when considering Woolf's suicide. Did *where* Woolf live in the last few years of her life influence her decision to commit suicide or the method she used to do so? Although popular mythology associated the City with high suicide rates, actual suicide statistics show that rates in rural areas and small market towns tended to be higher. In fact, nearby to Rodmell, the town of Lewes had a long history of suicides, having twice the national average rate, and the county of Sussex also had very high suicide rates. Although Woolf often found village life claustrophobic, she was well aware of the despair caused by the poverty and hardship endured by many rural folk. "If I were Mrs Bartholomew I should certainly do something violent" (*D3* 236). In 1938 a well-known figure in Rodmell—the old woman who lived up at "Mount Misery"—drowned herself in the Ouse. Where the Woolfs lived had particular associations with suicide, for the previous owner of Monks House, Old Jacob Verrall, had reputedly starved himself to death (Lee 423). Finally, it is probably most significant that there was a river nearby. Suicide statistics show that suicide rates are higher in areas where places of suicide opportunity, such as rivers, bridges or tall buildings, exist. Such observations merely touch upon some of the possible socio-economic factors of Woolf's suicide, and certainly indicate many areas for further research.

Other influences may have been at work too, such as the fear of scandal. Woolf's final choice of suicide method may also have been influenced by the issue of concealment, for drowning was the method most easily confused with accidental death. We can presume that the Woolfs shared the middle and upper-class distaste for publicity in cases of sudden or violent death. It is notable that suicide among the upper and professional classes was always considerably under-registered in most neighbourhoods, and even more significantly, that verdicts of insanity—rather than the much more scandalous verdict of suicide—were almost always found in middle and upper class cases. Did Woolf decide to kill herself by drowning rather than by some other method, partly to preserve her bourgeois respectability?

Finally, it is worth pausing to note how Woolf herself was an accomplished suicidologist of sorts, who strove for social accuracy in her fictional depictions of suicide. She was clearly aware of the suicide habits of Londoners, their attraction to particular suicide magnets like the Serpentine for drowning and the Monument for jumping. A description of death by drowning of a woman in the Serpentine appears in one of her early writer's notebooks, and she jokes about drowning herself in the Serpentine in a 1912 letter to Violet Dickinson "Then I shall take a dive into the Serpentine, which, I see, is 6 feet deep in malodorous mud" (*L1* 499). Much later, in *Mrs. Dalloway*, Woolf achieves notable social accuracy in the details of Septimus's suicide: in the City of London, those who took their own lives tended to be, like Septimus, middle-class people, or semi-skilled workers, master tradesmen, wholesalers, retailers or clerks and commercial travellers. If the City had its own peculiar method, it was—as Septimus does—to jump from a height, its two most infamous suicide spots being the Monument and the Iron Gallery at St. Paul's Cathedral. Moreover, soldiers were always notorious for being prone to suicide, even before shell-shock was recognised. And Septimus and Rezia's moment of trauma in Regent's Park reflects the way that the royal parks of London were well known as the accustomed haunts of the desperate. Further, Woolf's association of Septimus with a crisis of masculinity and a homosexual subtext resonate with the tendency of medical writers and "advanced" thinkers to associate suicide with a "loss of tone" and a decline in standards of "courage and manliness," thought to be due to the increasing safety of daily life. It is even possible that contemporary popular wisdom about the relationship of climate to suicidal acts may have also influenced Woolf. By 1911, heat was routinely associated with suicide, for the summer of 1911 was extremely hot and the effects of sunstroke and dehydration on the propensity to suicide were much discussed. The complex associations of the recurring lines from *Cymbeline*, "fear no more the heat o' the sun" include, I would argue, this association of a hot climate with suicidal tendencies. Repeatedly, characters in the novel remark that "the sun is hot," and this is one of the final thoughts of Septimus before he jumps from the window: "Life was good. The sun hot" (*MD* 226). Whilst, as Caroline Webb has shown, the phrase "the sun is hot" accrues associations in the novel of life affirming defiance, my reading would add a more ambivalent subtext. At any rate, it is clear that Woolf's depiction of Septimus's suicide is of considerable social accuracy, as well, of course, of personal significance and metaphoric resonance.

This paper has examined neglected aspects of the *context* of Woolf's suicide. Only by taking the full range and complexity of Woolf's suicide culture into account can we even begin to understand Woolf's enigmatic death. My ideas on the impact of suicide culture on Woolf have been offered merely as a point of departure for further research on Woolf's suicide; research which would seek to contextualize her thinking about suicide, as well as be mindful of its *own*—perhaps very different—cultural context.

Works Cited

Anderson, Olive. *Suicide in Victorian and Edwardian England*. Oxford: Clarendon Press, 1987.

DeSalvo, Louise. *Virginia Woolf: The Impact of Childhood Sexual Abuse on Her Life and Work*. London: Women's Press, 1989.

Gates, Barbara T. *Victorian Suicide: Mad Crimes and Sad Histories*. Princeton: Princeton U P, 1988.

Heilbrun, Carolyn G. "Virginia Woolf in her Fifties." *Virginia Woolf: A Feminist Slant*. Ed. Jane Marcus, Lincoln: U of Nebraska P, 1983. 236-53.

Kenney, Susan M. "Two Endings: Virginia Woolf's Suicide and *Between the Acts*." *University of Toronto Quarterly* 44.4 (1975): 265-89.

Lee, Hermione. *Virginia Woolf*. London: Chatto & Windus, 1996.

Lester, David. *Suicide in Creative Women*. New York: Nova Science, 1993.

Marler, Regina, Ed. *The Selected Letters of Vanessa Bell*. London: Bloomsbury, 1993.

Marcus, Jane. "Britannia Rules *The Waves*." *Decolonizing the Tradition: New Views of Twentieth-Century "British" Literary Canons.* Ed. Karen R. Lawrence. Urbana & Chicago: U of Illinois P, 1992, 136-64.

Showalter, Elaine. *The Female Malady: Women, Madness, and English Culture 1830-1980.* New York: Pantheon, 1985.

Stephen, Leslie. *The Science of Ethics.* London: Smith, Elder & Co., 1882.

Ward, Mrs Humphrey. *A Writer's Recollections, 2 Vols.* New York: Harper, 1918.

Webb, Caroline. "Life after Death: The Allegorical Process of *Mrs. Dalloway*." *Modern Fiction Studies* 40.2 (1994): 279-98.

Woolf, Virginia. *Mrs. Dalloway.* New York: Harcourt, 1953.

Textual Re-takes

Kathryn N. Benzel
Woolf's Early Experimentation with Consciousness: "Kew Gardens," Typescript to Publication, 1917-1919[1]

In Michael Cunningham's novel *The Hours*, he describes a park that his character Virginia Woolf envisions in a dream:

> It seems, suddenly, that she is not in her bed but in a park; a park impossibly verdant, green beyond green—a Platonic vision of a park, at once homely and the seat of mystery, implying as parks do that while the old woman in the shawl dozes on the slatted bench something alive and ancient, something neither kind nor unkind, exulting only in continuance, knits together the green world of farms and meadows, forests and parks. Virginia moves through the park without quite walking; she floats through it, a feather of perception, unbodied. ... Virginia moves through the park as if impelled by a cushion of air; she is beginning to understand that.... It is the true idea of the park, and it is nothing so simple as beautiful. (29-30)

In an uncanny way this description, 80 years later, gets to the heart of the issues I want to explore here in Woolf's short story "Kew Gardens." In her story Woolf represents Kew as if it were otherworldly, larger than its physical existence, greater and finer than the four couples who walk randomly past the struggling snail. "Kew Gardens," then, is Woolf's idea of a park found in the consciousness of the characters who mingle with the garden images. The park is represented not as a physical entity but as a collection, sometimes consistent, sometimes discordant, of characters' thoughts. But how are we to know if Woolf meant to create such an idealization of a park? Since there are no diary records and very little correspondence about "Kew Gardens," we can only speculate about its origin, creation and revision. The typescript with holograph revisions at the Harry Ransom Humanities Research Center at the University of Texas at Austin suggests that as early as August 1917 Woolf may have typed "Kew Gardens" and started revising it. A faded penciled date "Aug 7, 1917" appears at the top of the first page and next to the title appears a faded penciled "July." In publication Woolf does add "in July" to the last sentence of the first paragraph; "the men and women who walk in Kew Gardens *in July*" (*CSF* 90 my italics). Still there is no evidence in Woolf's correspondence to support these dates, and her Asheham diary, started on 3 August 1917, doesn't mention the story; however, in an August 15, 1917 letter to Lady Ottoline Morrell, Woolf recounts, "Katherine Mansfield describes your garden, the rose leaves drying in the sun, the pool, and long conversations between people wandering up and down in the moonlight" (*L2* 174). This sounds like an outline for "Kew Gardens." Also Katherine Mansfield visited Woolf at Asheham August 18-21 (or August 22—the dates are confused in Woolf's and Mansfield's correspondence) to discuss Hogarth Press's publication of her *Prelude*. During that time they read a play by Robert C. Trevelyan and sent a signed note confirming their pleasure with it; Lytton Strachey was also there. Mansfield as well sent a letter to Woolf in August suggesting that a manuscript of "Kew Gardens" did exist in August 1917, and that Mansfield read it. In the letter she says, "Yes, your Flower Bed is *very* good. There is a still, quivering changing light over it all and a sense of those couples dissolving in the bright air which fascinates me."[2] Thus there is reason to speculate that Woolf was working on her short story as early as August 1917.

In the period preceding her work on the "Kew Gardens" typescript, 1913-1917, Woolf was plagued with depression. Under Leonard Woolf's watchful eye she began to recover sporadically; in March 1915 Leonard hospitalized Virginia briefly while he moved them into Hogarth House in Richmond, near Kew Gardens. In the spring of 1917 she involved herself with the printing press which she and Leonard purchased to begin Hogarth Press. At that time she was typesetting, hand printing, and binding their Publication No. 1, *Two Stories*, including Leonard's "Three Jews" and Virginia's "The Mark on the Wall." During the summer of 1917 Leonard Woolf was administering a "rest cure" and in several letters to Vanessa Bell, Woolf complains about Leonard's nursing; she was made to remain in quiet settings, with her writing and visits limited.[3] In spite of these restrictions, she finally re-establishes her regime for writing novels and in August began again her diary. While working, I believe on "Kew Gardens," she also wrote *Times Literary Supplement* essays and began to think about her next novel, *Night and Day*. It's unclear if Woolf wrote "Kew Gardens" in a flash as she says she wrote her preceding story, "The Mark on the Wall,"[4] or whether she thought about it carefully, revising copiously. What the 1917 date on the typescript suggests, however, are the possibilities 1) that Woolf was writing more than *Times Literary Supplement* essays during the time when she was supposed to be taking her "rest cure," perhaps hiding her writing, like Jane Austen, from Leonard's watchful eye, and 2) that she communicated with Katherine Mansfield about the development of "Kew Gardens." This communication is significant in itself since Woolf rarely showed any uncompleted work to anyone.

Important to the Woolfs' move to Richmond is, of course, Kew; it became a place of respite and contemplation for her. In her diary and correspondence there is much mention of her walking in the gardens on "free" days and meeting friends and colleagues there, walking through the rhododendron and azaleas, the orchid house, the palm houses, in the rain and fog, and sitting on benches watching people. The intimacy with which she writes of Kew in her diary suggests she viewed the gardens as her own private space, her very own garden, a place for reflection. Certainly the story's lush, sensual descriptions of the flowers with their emerging throats, fleshy, heart-shaped/tongue-shaped leaves, and the trembling snail, reflect Woolf's emotional attachment to the gardens. In "Kew Gardens" the flowerbeds, butterflies, even the snail portray the inevitability and tranquillity of the natural world that Woolf found both comforting and mysterious at Kew. Interspersed among the glorious flowers and buzzing insects, the narrator describes the characters passing the flowerbed and interrupting the "atmosphere" of this garden world by the questions, unpredictability, and discord of their human world. For example, the old man's agitation and the aeroplane in the last paragraph disrupt the solitude and silence of the gardens. Through these interruptions, the reader discovers that "one's happiness, one's reality" (*CSF* 91)—that is, the human world—is not clearly defined, but rather like the transparent colors in the garden, the human world is indeterminate, transient, and undefinable, much like Woolf's own experience of the mysterious Kew.

Significantly during this early period, Woolf begins to develop an aesthetic system based on readership (Rosenberg; Benzel). In "Hours in a Library," a November 1916 *Times Literary Supplement* essay, she describes books as treasures and the reading experience as full of passion, excitement, and a spirit of curiosity—like a pirate seeking treasure. Her *TLS* reviews from this time, of Jane Austen, Charlotte Brontë, E. M. Forster, and George Gissing, focus on her replicating her own act of reading as a hunt for their treasures.[5] This excavation of texts uncovers Woolf's search for "aesthetic emotions" found underneath "others of a literary nature" (*L2* 257). I believe as Woolf works on the typescript of "Kew Gardens" at this time that her revisions suggest her attempt to create such "a case of atmosphere," a "mood" as she calls it in a letter to Vanessa Bell (*L2* 257).[6] In Woolf's "Kew Gardens, then, she attempts not only to represent the indeterminacy and mystery of life represented by the gardens and people in Kew, but also to have the reader experience this in the reading. I would like to suggest that Woolf's revisions demonstrate an experimental narrative strategy—generalizing and abstracting—which engages readers in an aesthetic experience of their own making, one which both recognizes and replicates the indeterminacy of life.

As "Kew Gardens" develops in the revised typescript, Woolf explores consciousness though the characters' memories and thought processes in order to represent this indeterminacy of life. Later in her essay "Modern Novels" she labels it "myriad impressions—trivial, fantastic, evanescent, ... an incessant shower of innumerable atoms, ... the semi-transparent envelope, or luminous halo" ("Modern Novels" *E3* 33). She sees a new narrative method where "there would be no plot, little probability, and vague general confusion"

("Modern Novels" *E*3 33). Such abstraction, "luminous halo," and generalization, "vague general confusion," encourage the reader to become a treasure hunter, digging out the story, making sense of the absences and silences, the suggestions and implications.

The revisions found in the "Kew Gardens" typescript hint at Woolf's attempts to create her "case of atmosphere." First, in general Woolf changes from present tense verbs to past tense, and this past tense reflects characters' memories and the difficulty of communicating reality in any determined linear pattern or organized logic. All of the characters depicted in the story are absorbed in recollections of the past. For instance, as the first couple walks by the garden, Simon and Eleanor each remember a moment in their youths where they were made aware of their feelings. In addition to changing the verbs to past tense in the typescript, Woolf appends to Simon's explanation, "For me ^ a square silver shoe buckle, and a dragonfly," ^"there are no words: only" (Typescript 3). His memory flashes in an instant between the physical reality recalled and its inexpressibility. Because the words are separate from the physical reality, they seem inconclusive. However, this addition in the typescript ("there are no words") does not appear in the published version, and readers see only descriptions of nature and inconsequential objects (e.g., the shoe buckle). If we analyze this typescript emendation and its subsequent deletion in the published text, two important questions arise. 1) If Woolf cannot use words, how can she represent the natural and human worlds that make up the "atmosphere" of Kew? 2) If there are no words, how can Woolf describe this memory which seems essential to Simon's sense of self? By finally erasing "there are no words," Woolf strikes a balance between her understanding of the inadequacy of language to represent and her desire to do exactly that. The conclusion is that words can, perhaps, only suggest rather than actually represent any reality. Words do not so much explain the actual scene as outline it, suggesting mood and atmosphere.

Such impressionistic interpretation is found also in Woolf's use of nature metaphors to replicate human consciousness. The raindrop expanding into colors suggests a sort of free association thinking or immediate perception. The snail's struggle to conquer the leaf suggests a kind of logical, methodical thinking. Generalizing from these metaphors of the raindrop and the snail, Woolf represents human consciousness as a combination of perception and reasoning whose connections are often ephemeral and transitory. For example as various characters' thoughts are presented they echo such metaphors. Eleanor's recollection of her first kiss is associated with "the first red water-lilies I'd ever seen" (*CSF* 91). The old man's movement through the garden is likened to an "impatient carriage horse;" the "elder man has a curiously uneven and shaky method of walking, jerking his hand forward and throwing up his head abruptly" (*CSF* 92). Finally "the wordless voices" of Kew flash "their colours into the air" like "the petals of myriads of flowers" (*CSF* 95).

Another typescript revision suggesting Woolf's concern with representation of consciousness is found again in the scene with the old man and his young companion. The old man, consumed with memories of war and widows and his imaginative renderings, cannot distinguish between reality and fantasy when he thinks that shadows are women and that flowers speak. He tries to transmit his remembered feelings to his young companion, William, but to no avail. In the typescript Woolf deletes "But we must remember William," which would suggest some spoken communication between them, and adds "Women! Widows! Women in black—" (Typescript 5), an abstract conflation of the old man's memory of widows and his immediate perception of women dressed in black. By conflating the old man's present moment of perception with his memory, Woolf captures the intangibility of life and its inability to be held in consciousness or communicated accurately in words. What appears in the typescript as dialogue between the old man and the young man (old man's command "we must remember") becomes, with its deletion, a representation of the old man's thinking. The reader has the task of creating the old man's portrait from "out of whatever odds and ends he can come by, some kind of whole—a portrait of man" (*CR* 1).

Other revisions suggest the process of thinking rather than any conclusive belief or fact. Both "believe" and "in fact" are deleted and replaced with words "he thought" (Typescript 2), "as if in deliberation" (Typescript 4), "long pauses came between the remarks" (Typescript 9), all which suggest uncertainty. This indeterminacy of thinking, memory, and reflection is also found in additions which suggest the "mystic" quality of words,[7] inarticulate speech of the heart: "there are no words" (Typescript 3) (subsequently erased in published version), "incoherent words" (Typescript 5), "words uttered in a curious tone" (Typescript 9). All this attention to words and their power or powerlessness to represent reflects Woolf's ongoing concern with reading as an act that replicates the indeterminacy of life. Again, if there are no adequate words to depict the human world, the reader is left with vagueness, generalization and abstraction, Woolf's "case of atmosphere" or "mood."

The various human scenes which interrupt the garden suggest the transience of the human world. Each scene poses some question or dilemma that is never quite articulated and remains unresolved, in a sense disintegrates or is subsumed into the vaporous colors of the garden. Three important scenes support this theme of vagueness and uncertainty. First, in the typescript the old man wants to describe or explain electric batteries or some machine to the older women in the third scene. He calls forth some scientific explanation and then mysticism: "—In the interests of Science Madam—the spirits madam—" (Typescript 6, *CSF* 92). When this passage is deleted in the published version, not only is the old man seen as unable to distinguish between the physical world of science and the ephemeral world, but also his inarticulation makes abstract the nature of reality—its physicality and his "atmosphere."

Second, a substantial passage concerning the two elderly women is deleted which describes their relationship as a "competition" in which the "smaller woman ... [is] conquered"; it's unclear exactly what the competition is about though it seems to be something about "fluency of speech"; "the ponderous one fell silent" (Typescript 7). By deleting this passage Woolf allows the relationship between the two women to become vague, and the preceding lines of dialogue seem disconnected to any reality. As a means of characterization, then, deleting this aspect of their relationship—some competition—serves to generalize the women rather than particularize them in a specific reality. In addition both of these scenes in the typescript show cancellations and additions which generalize the characters into figures of "the old man," "the ponderous woman," "the old woman."

Third, the last sentence of the typescript and published text are very different. In both the typescript and published version the snail is last seen just before the young couple, the last couple, passes by the flower bed: as the snail confronts the dead leaf, he has "inserted his head into the opening, and was taking stock of the high brown roof, ... when two other people came past" (Typescript 8, *CSF* 94). The last sentence of the typescript reads: "...like a vast nest of Chinese boxes all of wrought steel, turning ceaselessly, the city murmured; on the top of which the voices cried aloud, and the snail in the oval flower bed emerging on the other side of the dead leaf went on quietly towards his goal" (Typescript 11-12). There is something satisfying about the snail completing his journey in the typescript; even though the couples and their journeys are vague and incomplete, the snail at least makes it to some kind of conclusion. Though the sentence having to do with the snail's journey is not canceled or revised in the typescript, the published version completely deletes the snail. The published version reads: ". . . like a vast nest of Chinese boxes all of wrought steel turning ceaselessly one within another the city murmured; on the top of which the voices cried aloud and the petals of myriads of flowers flashed their colours into the air" (*CSF* 95). When Woolf eliminates the snail from the conclusion of the published version, the feeling of indeterminacy developed through the couples is re-emphasized in the natural world as gardens' colors vanish into the air. There is no definite conclusion to any of the story; readers do not know if the snail succeeds or if any of the couples' dilemmas are resolved.

In conclusion, these revisions demonstrate Woolf's concern with the emotional rhythms found in "Kew Gardens" (memories, affection, love, discord). As a means of intensifying and dramatizing the emotions, getting beneath "literary nature," Woolf uses generalization and abstraction to create impressionistic renderings of the natural and human worlds. These impressions bind together the forms, shapes, colors, and texture of the written work into an aesthetic emotion—a feeling of mystery and uncertainty. The typescript revisions of "Kew Gardens" suggest, in my analysis, that the mood of vagueness and transience becomes a significant force in creating a reading experience that replicates human consciousness. The text becomes not an object but a process of creating aesthetic meaning through the reader's recreation of emotional textures and rhythmic patterns of human consciousness. Not unlike Michael Cunningham's description of Woolf's park in *The Hours*, "Kew Gardens" "is nothing so simple as beautiful" (30).

Notes

[1] This paper is part of a larger project on "Kew Gardens," one aspect of which I presented at the 1995 Virginia Woolf Conference.

[2] Anthony Alpers's *The Life of Katherine Mansfield* (New York: Viking Penguin, 1980), 251, as quoted in Dick, (297).

[3] Several letters to Vanessa Bell indicate that Leonard would become upset with Woolf overdoing herself: she had to promise not to walk or bicycle and to keep quiet. Speaking about her weight she says, "I dont see how one can expect to keep the results of a rest cure permanently" (*L2* 170).

[4] Woolf recounts her early writing techniques and short fiction in a 1930 letter to Ethel Smyth: "I shall never forget the day I wrote The Mark on the Wall—all in a flash, as if flying, after being kept stone breaking for months" (*L4* 231).

[5] See *The Essays of Virginia Woolf*, Vol 2. (Ed. Andrew McNeillie. New York: HBJ, Publishers, 1987).

[6] In a letter to Vanessa Bell, Woolf writes, "I'm sending my story [Kew Gardens]; you will see that's its a case of atmosphere, and I dont think I've got it quite. Don't you think you might design a title page? Tell me what you think of the story. I'm going to write an account of my emotions towards one of your pictures, which gives me infinite pleasure, and has changed my views upon aesthetics; ... but all this is very complicated, and I must write a special letter about it. Its a question of half developed aesthetic emotions, constantly checked by others of a literary nature—in fact its all very interesting and intense" (*L2* 257).

[7] In her essay "On Being Ill" Woolf describes this mystic quality as "what is beyond their surface meaning, [we] gather instinctively this, that and the other—a sound a colour, here a stress, there a pause ... a state of mind which neither words can express nor the reason explain" (*CE4* 200).

Works Cited

Alpers, Anthony. *The Life of Katherine Mansfield*. New York: Viking Penguin, 1980.
Benzel, Kathryn N. "Reading Readers in Virginia Woolf's *Orlando: A Biography*." *Style* 28.2 (Summer 1994): 169-182.
Cunningham, Michael. *The Hours*. New York: Farrar Straus Giroux, 1998.
Dick, Susan, Ed. *The Complete Shorter Fiction of Virginia Woolf*. New York: HBJ, 1985.
Rosenberg, Beth. *Virginia Woolf and Samuel Johnson: Common Readers*. London; Macmillan Press, 1995.
Woolf, Virginia. *Collected Essays*. Vols 1-4. New York: HBJ, 1953.
——. *The Common Reader: First Series*. [1925] Ed. Andrew McNeillie. San Diego: HBJ, 1986.
——. "Hours in a Library." *The Essays of Virginia Woolf*. Vol. 2. Ed. Andrew McNeillie. New York: HBJ, 1987. 55-61.
——. *Letters of Virginia Woolf*. Vols. 1-5. Eds. Nigel Nicolson and Joanne Trautman. New York: HBJ, 1975-79.
——. "Kew Gardens." Typescript. By permission of Harry Ransom Humanities Research Center, the University of Texas at Austin. 1-12.

―――. "Kew Gardens." Dick, Susan, Ed. *The Complete Shorter Fiction of Virginia Woolf*. New York: HBJ, 1985. 90-95.
―――. "Modern Novels." *The Essays of Virginia Woolf*, Vol. 3. Ed. Andrew McNeillie. New York: HBJ, 1988. 33-37.
―――. "On Being Ill." *Collected Essays*. Vol. 4. New York: HBJ, 1953. 193-203.
Woolf, Virginia and Leonard Woolf. *Publication No. 1, Two Stories*. Richmond: Hogarth Press, 1917.

Peter Naccarato
Re-Defining Feminist Fiction in *The Years*

While Woolf may be recognized mostly for her contributions to modern fiction, she also serves as a critical figure for feminist scholars who look to her essays for insightful and influential commentary concerning the role of women in society. While *A Room of One's Own* has become a standard text in most women's studies classes, other essays, including *Three Guineas*, "Professions for Women," "Thoughts on Peace in an Air Raid," and many others, reflect Woolf's deep commitment to social change and her desire to contribute to it through her writing. While it may seem convenient, or even natural, to divide Woolf's work into two groups—her fiction and her essays—and to use this generic divide as the foundation for intellectual and disciplinary divisions between Woolf the "author" and Woolf the "feminist" (between the literary and the political, the creative and the critical, the artistic and the social, or what Woolf, herself, defined as the separation of "fact" from "vision"[1]) such divisions impose limitations that Woolf struggled to overcome as she wrote and revised *The Years*. If these limitations presented problems for Woolf as she attempted to merge "fact" and "vision" in the pages of this novel, they continue to do so as we work to build bridges between her fiction and her essays and use these bridges to re-define the modern period and to consider the contribution of feminist ideology to its literary productions. Such forced divisions obscure the intricate relationship between genre, disciplinarity, and gender through which they are constructed and maintained by sustaining the distinction between the "masculinized" discourse of science (including the social sciences) and the "feminized" discourse of the arts.[2]

While I cannot include a detailed exploration of the connection between disciplinarity and gender here, let me offer a few sentences aimed at contextualizing my argument that Woolf's experiment with genre in *The Years* exposes an otherwise obscured network through which the modern disciplinary hierarchy is maintained and naturalized. Feminist historians of science have emphasized the codification of gender difference into the forms and modes of knowledge production and circulation that emerged from the Scientific Revolution.[3] Because the specific historical conditions that made the Scientific

Revolution possible were intricately connected with contemporaneous social, political, and economic circumstances, the concept of knowledge that emerged from these transformations and the procedures for its production, organization, and circulation must be recognized as ideological. Scientific knowledge is gendered, in other words, as certain ideological assumptions were incorporated into the machinery of science, and the scientific theorizing that was produced through this machinery served as "a legitimization strategy for certain ideological assumptions" (Zita 199). Gender difference is incorporated into the emerging discourse of modern science as its purpose and methodology assume masculine identifications. This "masculinization" of science not only provided the criteria through which specific scientific disciplines could claim intellectual and cultural authority; it would also establish the conditions for "consigning other kinds of work and values to the sphere of the feminine" (Christie 107). Thus one of the primary ways in which disciplines would be identified and hierarchized was through their similarity to or differentiation from a highly gendered scientific method. Those disciplines that embraced its values of objectivity and rationality shared in its privilege while those that employed alternative modes and practices—including the emerging disciplinary category of Literature—were identified as feminine. By incorporating gender difference into its structure, this emerging disciplinary system both validated its hierarchical distinctions between different "kinds" of knowledge by grounding them in culturally specific gender ideology while also verifying that ideology through its claim of scientific objectivity. Thus at the time, when Virginia Woolf embarked on a project aimed at challenging generic boundaries, she found herself confronting a system of disciplines whose classifications depended on both genre and gender to maintain a hierarchy.

Woolf's interest in crossing these generic boundaries is highlighted in her own recollections concerning the origins of *The Years*, which can be located in a talk Woolf gave, on January 21, 1931, to the London branch of the National Society for Women's Service concerning professions for women. Several days after this lecture, Woolf wrote to Ethel Smyth that the speech had caused "a sudden influx of ideas, which I want to develop later, perhaps in a small book" (*L4* 280). Her diary confirms that the speech provided the impetus for her next project: "I have this moment, while having my bath, conceived an entire new book—a sequel to a Room of Ones Own—about the sexual life of women: to be called Professions for Women perhaps—Lord how exciting! This sprang out of my paper to be read on Wednesday to Pippa's society" (*D4* 6). While the next year and a half was spent completing *The Waves*, by November 1932, Woolf recorded that she had "totally remodeled" her essay:

> It is to be an Essay-Novel, called the Pargiters—& its to take in everything, sex, education, life &c; & come, with the most powerful and agile leaps, like a chamois across precipices from 1880 to here & now—Thats the notion anyhow, & I have been in such a haze & dream & intoxication, declaiming phrases, seeing scenes, as I walk up Southampton Row that I

can hardly say I have been alive at all, since the 10th Oct. Everything is running of its own accord into the stream. (*D4* 139)

In her initial outline, Woolf already articulated the broad range she wanted to cover in this new project. Rather than limiting herself to the exploration of characters in fictional situations, she wanted to connect this work with other kinds of writing in order to "take in everything." Approximately six weeks later, Woolf recorded that she had "written [herself] to the verge of total extinction" (*D4* 132). Since beginning the project on October 11, she had written over sixty-thousand words. Already anticipating the amount of revision and compression that would be required, she was, nonetheless, confident that she had "secured the outline & fixed a shape for the rest" (*D4* 132).

In her original formulation, this essay-novel would combine fictional chapters with social commentary. The issues and problems addressed in each essay would be fictionalized in alternating chapters as she told the story of the Pargiter family. Even at this early stage, she was motivated by the possibility of bridging two different kinds of writing. While the fictional chapters would be focused on specific characters, the essay portions would bridge this fiction with a more explicit interrogation of the society depicted within it. By February of 1933, however, after completing revisions of the first chapter, Woolf decided to leave out the "interchapters." Both Woolf's initial ambition to write an essay-novel and her subsequent decision to separate this text into its component parts illuminate Woolf's desire to combine two separate genres–the novel (*The Years*) and the essay (*Three Guineas*)—and, by doing so, to challenge the divide between literary or artistic expression, on the one hand, and social or political commentary, on the other. In tracing Woolf's struggle with *The Years*, we can better understand the influence of generic and disciplinary classifications upon the production and circulation of knowledge and appreciate Woolf's effort to cross these well-protected boundaries. At the same time, we can use the example of Woolf's attempt to combine "fact" and "vision" in her novel to better understand how genre functions as a classificatory system that maintains a series of divisions upon which modern disciplinarity is grounded.

The story of the Pargiter family, *The Years* is divided into eleven chapters, which are titled chronologically from "1880" to "Present Day." Through the course of these chapters, the reader follows the Pargiter clan across three generations, from Colonel Abel Pargiter, whose wife, Rose, lies dying in bed in the opening chapter to the diverse experiences of his seven children; from his son, Edward's days at Oxford to his daughter, Rose's support for Parnell and the fight for Irish independence; from these seven children living through their mother's funeral at the beginning of the novel to a reunion, some fifty years later, where their children now view them as the old generation. Interspersed throughout this particular family story are historical markers which remind the reader of the larger social backdrop against which the Pargiters' stories unfold. In addition to marking seasonal changes in the descriptive preludes which begin each chapter—the perpetually changing weather, the fluttering leaves, the vast and cloudless sky, the falling snow—these introductory paragraphs also include historical markers of the passage of time, from the stream of landaus, victorias and hansom cabs that opens the novel to the hooting horns and roaring traffic at the opening of the 1914 chapter, for example. At the same time, the particular story of the Pargiter family which is at the novel's center is intimately connected with specific historical events, whether Rose Pargiter's activist work for "the Cause" or a scene in which a dinner party is interrupted by a bombing raid during World War I; whether North Pargiter is discussing his military service in Africa or Eleanor Pargiter is remembering when she saw her first airplane. The personal story of the Pargiter family and the social context within which their lives unfold are intricately blended.

In order to understand how Woolf's specific experience with *The Years* provides a broader insight into the function of generic and disciplinary boundaries, I want to distinguish between the two different kinds of generic experimentation that she attempted. First, and most explicitly, she wanted to combine two distinct genres into one text: the essay-novel. Then, as Woolf moved from combining two different generic categories into one book towards blending different "kinds" of writing into her novel, she shifted her focus to a second mode of generic experimentation. Rather than erasing the line between separate generic categories by writing the essay-novel, Woolf's later attempt to combine in "one book" a variety of "forms" demonstrates a more subtle type of generic manipulation in which the "kinds" of writing identified as the exclusive terrain of particular genres would merge and, thus, the primary means through which separate genres are defined and maintained would be erased. Because any specific genre can only be defined by "its interrelation with and differentiation from others" (Cohen 207), Woolf's attempt to combine separate generic modes of writing threatened the balance between similarity and differentiation which serves as the basis for generic identification. In other words, the "one book" to which Woolf refers must fall within a generic category. Its ability to do so would be determined by the extent to which it embodied characteristics which were similar to other books classified within this category.

This challenge to generic categories is significant not just for its ramifications within "Literature." Because the entire disciplinary structure is grounded upon a relational model in which any one discipline is identified by its similarity to and differentiation from other disciplines, an attempt to expand the boundaries of Literature would necessarily affect the entire disciplinary hierarchy. While Woolf rejected her initial plan to pursue the essay-novel and decided, instead, to incorporate the ideas and issues from the essay portions of the text into the novel itself, she soon realized that such an incorporation was in and of itself a challenging task. In many of her diary entries, Woolf discussed this decision as an attempt to combine the masculinized discourse of facts and history with the feminized "tug of vision" (*D*5 139). Her own categories underscore the disciplinary boundaries she was attempting to cross.

Published in 1937, *The Years* was very well received, becoming a best-seller in both England and America. In addition, several critics and friends offered enthusiastic endorsements[4]; despite these positive reviews and tremendous sales records, there were several negative reviews as well. Moreover, the novel's historical place within the Woolf canon has been long debated. Those who identify *The Years* as her worst novel have sought to account for this apparent failure, many of whom attribute it to the over-ambitious scope of the project—"a summing up of all I know, feel, laugh at, despise, like, admire, hate and so on" (*D*4 198). Such criticisms rely on generic assumptions about the novel and Woolf's refusal to meet these expectations by bringing to this particular form issues, questions, ideas, and modes of writing which were understood to be outside of its scope. These critics argue that one of the primary challenges Woolf confronted in this project was the question of form. Woolf's early decision to abandon the essay-novel format and, instead, to incorporate her social commentary into the fictional text itself did not mark the end of her generic experimentation; rather, it marks the beginning of one of Woolf's most challenging experiments with form and content.

Arguing that "formal symmetry was never achieved in *The Years* because the author failed to synthesize fact and vision" (Middleton 162), critics use Woolf's own preliminary plans as the yardstick against which to measure her success in achieving these ends. According to many of these critics, Woolf's "struggle to embody ideas in imaginative fiction" is a failure (Radin xvii); her decision to take on "the ambitious task of combining fact and vision, of creating a multileveled novel that would include everything: the personal and the familial, the political and the spiritual" (Radin 147) eventually reveals her inability to accomplish this goal. Rather than read this as a personal limitation on Woolf's own artistic capabilities, however, I am suggesting that it underscores how the system of genre classification assisted in curtailing Woolf's efforts to combine "fact" and "vision," thereby securing those crucial divisions upon which the disciplinary hierarchy was grounded.

Most comparisons of the published novel with drafts, galleys, and page proofs—including Charles Hoffman's "Virginia Woolf's Manuscript Revisions of *The Years*" (1969), Mitchell Leaska's publication of *The Pargiters* (1977), in which he compiled the essay-novel portion of Woolf's initial draft, and Grace Radin's *Virginia Woolf's* The Years: *The Evolution of a Novel* (1981), which included the "two enormous chunks" Woolf excised during her final revisions—concluded that during this process of revision, Woolf muted or, in some cases, completely erased some of her most compelling ideas. For Hoffman, historical fact was sacrificed as Woolf's focus moved increasingly towards artistic vision. While he acknowledges that she was able to offer a "careful detailing of the Victorian period in the first section of the novel," he suggests that "this process was not followed for the other historical periods"

(Hoffman 89). Thus, in Hoffman's assessment, Woolf's artistic vision gradually overwhelms her historical grounding. Similarly, Leaska suggests that as Woolf attempted to compact the essay chapters into the novel itself she was forced to realize that "the truth of fact and the truth of the imagination simply would not come together" (xvii). During this process of compression, he argues, many ideas which "were originally written with the broader explicitness of prose" are revised so extensively that in the published novel "we come across splinters of memory, fragments of speech, titles of quoted passages left unnamed or forgotten, lines of poetry or remnants of nursery rhymes left dangling in mid-air, understanding between characters incomplete, and utterances missing the mark and misunderstood" (xviii). Rather than completing her "new and profoundly challenging experiment in form, calling into action both the creative and the analytical faculties almost simultaneously" (vii), Woolf finally published a novel which "communicates the *failure* of communication" (xviii).

According to Radin, "during the long period of revision and compression that precedes [the novel's] publication, Woolf's original intentions lost their force" (xvii). In comparing Woolf's early drafts with the published novel, Radin recognizes "the extent to which feminist, pacifist, and sexual themes have been deleted, obscured, or attenuated" (148). Especially when discussing the first of the "two enormous chunks" that Woolf excised just prior to the novel's publication, Radin suggests that rather than "deal[ing] incisively with the roots of war in British society," Woolf "cho[se] to soften the antiwar impact of *The Years* by deleting this episode" (84). In Radin's own account, one of the primary reasons for "the deletion of much of the ideological material" was Woolf's desire to "express her ideas through her art" (149). Despite Woolf's enormous efforts to "embody its arguments and ideas in imagery and dramatic incidents" (149), Radin concludes that we must recognize "Woolf's failure to unify *The Years*" (152); in the end, Radin is left to speculate about what kind of novel might have been written if "Woolf could have created the kind of synthesis she had been struggling to achieve" (158).

In working to achieve this synthesis, Woolf feared that her overt sociopolitical commentary would reduce her novel to propaganda; this was a fear she had seen realized when reading Aldous Huxley's *Point Counterpoint*, which she found "raw, uncooked, protesting" (*D4* 238). In searching for a more harmonious way to express her social concerns in her art, Woolf was "engaged in a struggle to transform this recalcitrant material into art without losing sight of what she meant to say" (Radin 62). The process of revision from initial manuscript drafts of *The Pargiters* to the final published version of *The Years* is one in which the forcefulness of Woolf's initial sociopolitical commentary was sacrificed as she worked to meet generic specifications. Consider, for example, Woolf's struggle with the character of Elvira (re-named Sara in the published novel). Recalling that in her essays on fiction, Woolf argues that "the foundation of good fiction," is characters who were "real, true, and convincing," we should not be surprised to realize that Woolf believed that her characters would provide the primary means through which she could pursue political and social commentary while remaining faithful to her own definition of fiction. In her early outline, Woolf planned to contrast Eleanor Pargiter with her cousin, Elvira. If Eleanor was to be "the stable, sensible, community-minded woman," Elvira would be "a portrait of an erratic, unstable, perceptive, artistic sensibility" (Radin 42). By "contrasting the factual and the visionary through the personalities of Eleanor and Elvira" (40), Woolf believed she could use the contrast between characters to produce a kind of commentary which would be generated and expressed through art. In her thorough discussion of the transformation of Elvira into Sara, Radin underscores the difficulty Woolf faced with the character of Elvira, who "seemed so alive in the author's mind, [but who] eluded translation into print" (61). What this process of transformation reveals, I suggest, is the extent to which Woolf's desire to create characters who were "real, true, and convincing" as she had defined these terms in her own theories of fiction conflicted with her attempt to use Elvira as a means of expressing her own socio-political commentary.

In early 1935, with Elvira already renamed Sara, Woolf recorded in her diary: "Sara is the real difficulty: I can't get her into the mainstream, yet she is essential" (*D4* 238). While in the manuscript draft, Elvira represents a crucial point of view if the juxtaposition between her and Eleanor is going to be effective: "as a fictional character she lacks dimension; she is more of a mouthpiece than a human being" (Radin 63). Ironically, Radin's criticism of Elvira echoes Woolf's critique of the Edwardians in her essays on fiction. Like Mr. Galsworthy, for whom Mrs. Brown provided the means of expressing views on class inequality and other social ills, Woolf created a character whose function as a "mouthpiece" for her own social and political opinions prevented her being "real, true, and convincing." During the process of revision, Woolf's need to make Sara an interesting and believable character required her to "delete some of the dialogue and soften the argumentative edge of the Elvira/Sara scenes" (Radin 62). In giving her depth and complexity, however, Woolf would create a character who remained elusive. From the Elvira who was to "convey some of the most important ideas behind the novel," Woolf moves to Sara, whose ideas "are presented so indirectly that they can be overlooked by all but the most careful readers" (Radin 63). While such complexity makes Sara a more interesting fictional character, it also dulls Woolf's representation of her own political and social beliefs in her art. In other words, Woolf could not bridge her need to explore Sara's internal complexities which would make her an interesting character with the need to make Sara the voice of her own social commentary.

While many critics have used this and other examples to argue for the failure of *The Years*, I would suggest that they offer more useful insights not into Woolf's literary abilities, but into the complex network of genre, gender and disciplinarity that her project challenged. Rather than using her experience with *The Years* to bolster the division between Woolf's literary endeavors and her political or feminist concerns, I am suggesting that this novel—from its inception to its publication—underscores the fact that while these artificially constructed boundaries change over time, they nonetheless offer strong resistance against those who attempt to transgress them.

Notes

[1] "But the Pargiters. I think this will be a terrific affair. I must be bold & adventurous. I want to give the whole of the present society—nothing less: facts, as well as the vision. And to combine them both. I mean, The Waves going on simultaneously with Night & Day. Is this possible?" (*D*4 152).

[2] The efforts of male authors (Eliot, Pound, Hulme, etc.) to masculinize modernism, in fact, underscore the extent to which literature had become increasingly feminized in relation to the more masculine discourse of science.

[3] See, for example, Evelyn Reed's *Sexism and Science* (Pathfinder P, 1978), Evelyn Fox Keller's *Reflections on Gender and Science* (Yale UP, 1985), Sandra Harding's *The Science Question in Feminism* (Cornell, 1986), and Ruth Bleier's edited collection *Feminist Approaches to Science* (Pergamon P, 1986).

[4] On 12 March 1937, both the *Times Literary Supplement* and *Time and Tide* published positive reviews. In her diary, Woolf records that at the end of April, the *Times Literary Supplement* concluded its Centenary article with a reference to "that great artist V[irginia] W[oolf] & The Years" and that both Maynard Keynes and Stephen Spender thought that *The Years* was her best book (*D*5 77-80).

Works Cited

Christie, J. R. R. "Feminism and the history of science." *Companion to the History of Modern Science*. Ed. R.C. Olby, G.N. Cantor, J. R. R. Christie, M. J. S. Hodge. London and New York: Routledge, 1990.

Cohen, Ralph. "History and Genre." *New Literary History*. Winter, 1986: 203-232.

Hoffman, Charles G. "Virginia Woolf's Manuscript Revision of *The Years*." *PMLA* 84, No. 1 (January, 1969): 79-89.

Leaska, Mitchell A. "Virginia Woolf, the Pargiter: A Reading of *The Years*." *Bulletin of the New York Public Library*, 80 (1977): 172-210.

Middleton, Victoria S. "*The Years*: A 'Deliberate Failure.'" *Bulletin of the New York Public Library*, 80 (1977): 158-171.

Radin, Grace. *Virginia Woolf's* The Years*: The Evolution of a Novel*. Knoxville: U of Tennessee P, 1981.

Woolf, Virginia. *The Common Reader: First Series*. Ed. Andrew McNeillie. New York; London: HBJ, 1950.

——. *The Diary of Virginia Woolf*. Ed. Anne Oliver Bell. 5 vols. New York: HBJ, 1977.

——. *The Letters of Virginia Woolf*. Ed. Nigel Nicolson. 6 vols. New York: HBJ, 1975-1980.

Zita, Jacquelyn N. "The Premenstrual Syndrome: 'Dis-easing' the Female Cycle." *Feminism and Science*. Ed. Nancy Tuana. Bloomington and Indianapolis: Indiana UP, 1989.

Jane de Gay
An Unfinished Story: The Freshwater Drafts of "The Searchlight"

This paper will focus on a collection of drafts relating to Woolf's short story "The Searchlight," which differ significantly from the version published by Leonard Woolf in *A Haunted House* (1943). Unlike the published version, which is set in London in the 1930s, these drafts describe a scene at Freshwater on the Isle of Wight in the 1860s amongst the circle of Woolf's great-aunt, the Victorian photographer Julia Margaret Cameron. Although the recent publication of one of the drafts in the *Virginia Woolf Bulletin* (no. 1, 1999) may herald a reappraisal, the Freshwater narrative has generally been regarded as an unsatisfactory experiment which Woolf abandoned in favor of the version which appeared in *A Haunted House*. This paper will question that view by arguing that Woolf did not dispense with the Freshwater version: on the contrary, she was developing it into a story in its own right, under the new title, "A Scene from the Past," when she died.[1] I will demonstrate that, although it is not a polished piece of work (even the final version includes a partial, handwritten attempt to rewrite the final paragraph), "A Scene from the Past" deserves more serious attention than it has been given. In particular, I will argue that Woolf's references to Julia Margaret Cameron in the Freshwater story further her examination of questions of biographical and historical truth which, as Raskin points out, preoccupy her in many versions of "The Searchlight."

"A Scene from the Past" begins with a photographic session at Cameron's studio at Freshwater, where an old man (later identified as Sir Henry Taylor, a writer and colonial official) poses to be photographed dressed as King Arthur, and a young woman plays the piano. When Cameron leaves them for a moment, the pair escape to Freshwater Down where the man describes a childhood experience, drawn from Taylor's *Autobiography,* of looking through a telescope and seeing a man kissing a woman. He describes how the experience made him aware of his own loneliness as a child who "never knew . . . a mothers love," and the young woman is moved to tears by his confession. At this point, the narrative stance shifts, and Woolf names Sir Henry Taylor and provides a synopsis of his career, drawn from Leslie Stephen's essay on him in the *Dictionary of National Biography*. She adds that, unlike the *DNB* entry, the account she has given cannot be verified because "the book in [which] this story is told, and the album in which you could see him [Taylor] draped in a shawl posed as King Arthur were destroyed only the other day by enemy action" ("Scene" 5).

The story published by Leonard Woolf is sufficiently different from the Freshwater version for the two to be considered as closely related but ultimately distinct pieces of work. Only the middle section of the Freshwater version, concerning the boy looking through a telescope, appears in the story published by Leonard Woolf. In the latter, the telescope narrative is framed by a modern scene in which a Mrs. Ivimey sees a searchlight cast into the sky by the airforce in a practice exercise, reminding her of a story about her own great-grandparents, which she proceeds to narrate to her companions. This version contains nothing about Cameron and lacks the concluding discussion of how the account might be verified.

The prevailing view of the relationship between these stories is that outlined by Graham: that Woolf abandoned the Freshwater version in favor of the Ivimey story, which represented her last word on the subject. Graham notes that after some early sketches of the telescope story in 1929-30, Woolf returned to it in January 1939 and wrote the first draft of the story about Mrs. Ivimey. This date is recorded on the first of the Ivimey drafts and also in Woolf's diary where she records writing "the old Henry Taylor telescope story thats been humming in my mind these 10 years" (*D5* 204). Graham places the Freshwater drafts next: these were written in 1941, for the earliest version includes the phrase "what we call in 1941 potatoes." He suggests that Woolf experimented with the Freshwater narrative, but abandoned it because "she found this form of the story fundamentally inadequate," and then revived the Ivimey version which she took through three further drafts, the last of which was copied out by a professional typist. Graham argues that Woolf was by this time "too thoroughly professional to bring a version to this final form unless certain that it was to be published" (385).

Graham's dating is problematic because it would mean that Woolf produced at least seven drafts of the Freshwater version and three typescripts of the Ivimey story in less than three months in 1941. Although not impossible, this is an extremely tight schedule. Furthermore, as Rebecca Mason has argued, there is evidence that Woolf completed the Ivimey version earlier than the Freshwater story, possibly as early as 1939. Vanessa Bell's biographer Frances Spalding notes that Bell read the story in May 1939 and was thinking about illustrating it, and that she wrote to Woolf on 31 May that it "seems to me lovely—only too full of suggestions for pictures almost" (309). This implies that Woolf regarded the story as sufficiently polished to show her sister, and that she was contemplating having it published with illustrations by Bell. Woolf then had the story professionally typed, but for some reason did not proceed with publication. This typescript, which is in Smith College Library, came to light after Graham's essay was written; Susan Dick took it as the final version and used it as the basis for her edition of "The Searchlight" in the revised *Complete Shorter Fiction* of 1989 (*CSF* 6, 310). As Mason points out, the Smith typescript includes a handwritten note giving Woolf's address as 37 Mecklenburgh Square, London, and, so, because she lived at that address from August 1939 to September 1940, when the building was bombed, this typescript must have been prepared during that period. (The address is in Woolf's hand, perhaps suggesting that she was planning to post it to a publisher.) There are a few small holograph corrections to the Smith typescript and its carbon copy (*CSF* 310), which suggest that Woolf continued to tinker with the Ivimey story, but it is nonetheless true to say that she did not develop it significantly after having it typed professionally no later than September 1940.

The Freshwater story, on the other hand, clearly was begun in 1941, for that date appears in the first draft. Woolf was inspired to write this story and commemorate Cameron in late January 1941 while reading the autobiography of her cousin Herbert Fisher. Woolf mentions Fisher's book in her letters and diary for the period (*L6* 461, 464; *D5* 355), and refers to it in the opening sentence of the first, manuscript draft of the Freshwater story. In this new story, Woolf revisits themes from her early sketches and the Ivimey piece: she initially entitled it "The Searchlight," but changed this to "The Telescope/A Scene from his Past" in the next draft. The title "A Scene from the Past" is used for all but one of the subsequent typescripts. Whereas Mason concludes that Woolf was revising "The Searchlight" at her death, I suggest that the Freshwater story of 1941 had its own momentum, and that with its different framing narrative and title, it was developing away from the Ivimey version and the searchlight motif. In the following discussion, I will take the Freshwater story on its own merits, and ponder why the Freshwater setting and the figure of Julia Margaret Cameron held such an appeal for Woolf. In doing so, I build on the work of Gillespie, Wussow, and others who have demonstrated Woolf's fascination with photography.

The Freshwater story began as a reaction against Herbert Fisher's autobiography. As Woolf remarked in a letter to Lady Simon, the book was both "charming" and "rather nettled me" (*L6* 464). Part of its charm was Fisher's narration of their common family history, including the romantic tale of an ancestor who had been associated with Marie Antoinette and a story about Cameron's father, who died from excessive drinking and whose body allegedly exploded out of its coffin. Woolf's commendation of the book to Ethel Smyth suggests that she was intrigued to be part of this family history: "If you want to know where I get my (ahem!) charm, read Herbert Fisher's autobiography. Marie Antoinette loved my ancestor; hence he was exiled; hence the Pattles, the barrel that burst, and finally Virginia" (*L6* 461; see Fisher 10-12). However, while Woolf was happy to associate herself with family myths, she was irritated when Fisher claimed to reveal "facts." Woolf told Lady Simon that she resented being "exposed as a novelist and told my people are my mother and father, when, being in a novel, they're not" (*L6* 464). The "people" Woolf refers to are Mr. and Mrs. Ramsay in *To the Lighthouse:* while Woolf had long admitted privately that they were based on her parents, her annoyance in this case suggests that she disliked her fiction publicly being collapsed into dry historical details. Such a prizing of fiction over "fact" prevails in "A Scene from the Past."

In the Freshwater story, Woolf sought both to claim her share in family history and to displace Fisher from it. This can be seen in the opening lines of the first manuscript draft of the Freshwater story:

de Gay

> It was not altogether a joke, sitting to ~~Mrs.~~ Julia Margaret Cameron at Freshwater in the Sixties, Herbert Fisher tells us in his <auto>biography. [—] That casual remark ~~brings back a serves to light up a scene,~~ serves [—] ~~much~~ <in> ~~the same way as that~~ <of> the searchlight, [prodding?] the night for German raiders ~~serves to bring out home a~~ to make a little island of light in the hall, to ~~recall,~~ bring back a scene. ("The Searchlight" 1) [2]

This is a reference to Fisher's recollections of visiting Freshwater and being photographed by Cameron which was "a sore trial to the patience of a child" (15), but Woolf immediately goes on to introduce the scene in Cameron's studio as though it were her own personal memory. This is an act of imaginative reclamation, because she never knew Cameron, who died in 1879, three years before Woolf was born. The image in this quotation of a scene being recalled in a flash of light also refers to Cameron's medium: it suggests the flash of a camera by which a scene is captured on film, and the power of photography to preserve a record of events and people in a form that enables them to be viewed after they have ceased to be. In other words, it is Cameron's own art that has enabled Woolf to practise her feat of time-travel by recalling Cameron as though she had known her. The reference to the flash of light does not appear in later typescripts of the Freshwater story, and, as we will see, Woolf focuses instead on the themes of Cameron's photographs, rather than the photographic process. It is here that she leaves behind the searchlight—the controlling image of the Ivimey story—and moves forward into her new project.

Woolf's attempt to engage with Cameron may be read as a feminist strategy to celebrate a female relation (whom she had already commemorated in *Freshwater*), and to circumvent the first-hand account of Fisher, a man "stamped and moulded by the patriarchal machinery" (*MOB* 132), who is not mentioned in later drafts. This is a literal example of the kind of female tradition which Virginia Blain has described metaphorically as "thinking back through our aunts." Blain argues that women writers find it helpful to negotiate their relationship with the past by adopting an aunt-figure, for an aunt is positioned outside the linear progression of the patriarchal family, and can offer subversive and alternative views of family history. Rather than constructing a lineage of "cultural matriarchy" through Cameron, as Olsen has suggested, Woolf adopts Cameron and her ideas in "A Scene from the Past," in order to re-write and lay claim to the past in a freer and more imaginative way. In looking to Cameron, Woolf denies chains of inheritance and circumvents both her parents and their problematic roles of inducting her into Victorian society. Her ironic treatment of the *DNB* not only denigrates her father's work, but also bypasses her mother's writing, for Woolf makes no mention of the entry on Cameron, which was written by Julia Stephen.

In "A Scene from the Past," Woolf claims Cameron imaginatively not simply by saturating the story with details about her life and circle—including references to Henry Taylor and the poem "Maud," by another Cameron associate, Tennyson—but also by manipulating those details. For example, Woolf's description of Taylor posing as Arthur "draped in an Indian shawl" ("Scene" 1) is not based on a real photograph. Although the description is reminiscent of a portrait of Taylor which Woolf printed in her 1926 catalog of Cameron's work, *Victorian Photographs of Famous Men and Fair Women,* Taylor does not appear as Arthur in that portrait. In fact, when Cameron compiled a set of photographic illustrations to Tennyson's *Idylls of the King,* she used a much younger model, William Warder, as King Arthur (Gernsheim 42-43), and she consistently portrayed him in the traditional medieval knight's costume of chain-mail and helmet.[3] Woolf thus plays with facts to fuse Taylor with Tennyson and the Arthuriad. The reference to the Indian shawl is another complex allusion: it relates to an anecdote from Taylor's autobiography which Woolf narrates in her introduction to the Cameron catalog. Woolf had described how Sir Henry and his wife Alice, "suffered the extreme fury" of Cameron's affection, "Indian shawls, turquoise bracelets, inlaid portfolios, ivory elephants, 'etc.' showered on their heads." When the Taylors returned an Indian shawl which Cameron had given them, she sold it and bought a sofa for Putney Hospital with an inscription that it was a gift from Lady Taylor herself. "It was better," Woolf concludes, "to bow the shoulder and submit to the shawl" (3-4). In the story, Taylor is made to submit to the Indian shawl, for the colonial official is ironically described as being wrapped in an object from the colonized culture.

Woolf's distortions of facts were true to the spirit of Cameron's work, and served to defend a feminist reading of biography and history. In one of her earliest sketches of the Taylor story ("~~Incongrous~~ Inaccurate Memories," 1930), Woolf argued that "inaccuracy" in biography is "very often a superior form of truth which the victims themselves would be the first to welcome." Such manipulation of details may be seen as a challenge to male accounts of the past, such as those presented by Fisher or the *DNB.* Woolf saw Cameron as a purveyor of truth through fantasy. In her introduction to the 1926 catalog, Woolf writes that unlike Cameron's father who was "the greatest liar in India," Cameron herself had a "gift of ardent speech and picturesque behaviour which has impressed itself upon the calm pages of Victorian biography" (1). Where men tell lies, she suggests, women like Cameron deal in colorful truths.

"A Scene from the Past" can be seen as the culmination of these earlier meditations, for in this story Woolf seeks to access and defend a larger-than-life view of truth by alluding to Cameron's work. Although the story begins with a self-consciously posed scenario in Cameron's studio, Woolf does not break the frame when the protagonists move outside, but continues to describe them in terms which evoke a Cameron photograph: "Beautiful as they were, the old man and the girl—he had snatched a bosuns cape and clapped a sombrero on his head; she was in flowing purple; one pearl pinned the cambric ruffles to her throat—nobody marked them" ("Scene" 2). This description alludes to Cameron's use of beautiful models, and her tendency to dress her sitters in elaborate costumes. Woolf insists that this outlandish picture is a truthful depiction, for she says that even though the pair were stunning, they were not out of the ordinary for Freshwater at that time. Such a maneuver captures the spirit of Cameron's photography. As Carol Armstrong has pointed out, Cameron's work displays "a kind of excess" which secures "a confirmation of the truth of fiction that exceeds the simple reality-effect of the photograph, the consequent trust that this had to be some body's actual action, and that therefore the fiction was fact" (130). In other words, she sought to make the viewer believe in legends such as the Arthuriad by showing real people acting out these scenes.

Woolf found Cameron's penchant for showing real people in fanciful situations deeply subversive. In her 1926 essay, she praises Cameron's ability to overturn the traditional order of society: "Boatmen were turned into King Arthur; village girls into Queen Guinevere. Tennyson was wrapped in rugs: Sir Henry Taylor was crowned with tinsel. The parlour-maid sat for her portrait and the guest had to answer the bell" (6). This description suggests that Cameron's subversive strengths did not lie simply in the way in which she represented historical figures—her ability to get the viewer to believe that a servant could be Arthur or Guinevere—but in her power to get the famous men of her generation to dress up and act out roles, so that Taylor and Tennyson are effectively immortalized in fancy dress. Woolf's fanciful representation of the historical figure of Taylor thus draws on Cameron's playful depiction of him in her photographs.

Woolf's story also reflects a more subtle form of subversion practised by Cameron. As Beloff has noted, Cameron's portraits reveal an "element of serious subversion of the definition of both the 'natural' masculine and feminine. For Cameron, male goodness and nobility is not thrusting. She seems to present the Janus-face of Victorian aggressive progress, its intellectual, spiritual opposite" (115). Woolf explores this inverse side of Victorian society in her treatment of Taylor, by imagining the private life of a public figure. In re-telling his story about the telescope, Woolf empathizes with an old man recalling his lonely boyhood, rather than with Sir Henry Taylor the distinguished Victorian, thus turning him into a somewhat pathetic figure. In Taylor's own account (1 44-45), the telescope incident took place when he was a young man spending three weeks alone when his father and stepmother were away on holiday, and he found "something exciting in the sense of solitude," but Woolf renders him vulnerable in her story by presenting him as a boy who was "very lonely" over a long period. However, in describing the old man as someone who had never known a "mother's love," Woolf picks up on and elaborates a hint at suffering in Taylor's account: Taylor describes the experience of watching the couple's embrace as "the only phenomenon of human emotion which I had witnessed for three years." Thus her account draws out what was only a passing comment, but suggests that this was somewhat nearer the truth, unmaking the great man by demonstrating his need of a mother.

Textual Re-takes

Woolf tells the Taylor story in a melodramatic fashion reminiscent of the staged dramas in Cameron's photographs. The characters gesticulate wildly—the old man seizes the girl's arm, and casts his eyes upon the ground; her eyes follow his and "she saw what he saw"—and the narrative concludes with the sentimental picture of the girl breaking down in tears and exclaiming, "Dear Sir Henry!" ("Scene" 4-5). By foregrounding the melodramatic, while insisting on the veracity of this heightened account, Woolf draws on Cameron to question official, patriarchal constructions of history and biography. The tension between these different interpretations emerges briefly half-way through "A Scene from the Past," when the narrator interrupts the story to note that "if her tears and his words move your scorn, turn from your path and pause where, in Whitehall, rise the august battlements of the Colonial Office. It was there he ruled; there stands his statue today" ("Scene" 3). The juxtaposition offers a choice between accepting this sentimental scene, or preferring the official historical record presented by Taylor's respectable but lifeless monument. The tension between official historical records and an imaginative recollection of the past is brought to a head in the closing paragraph of the story, when Woolf finally identifies Taylor and summarizes his biography as presented in the *DNB*: "It is left for our oblivious age to add 'Taylor, Sir Henry. (1800—1886) Author of Philip Van Artevelde. Isaac Comnenus and The Statesman . . .'" (Ibid., 5). Like his statue, Taylor's entry in the *DNB* is a cypher which stands for something which has been lost: the modern age is *oblivious* to Taylor's achievements and the *DNB* can only stand as a poor substitute.

In "A Scene from the Past" Woolf moves towards a postmodern view of truth: on the one hand, there are details which are recorded in the *DNB*, but which stand in place of a lost reality; on the other is a reconstruction of the past through fiction which cannot be proven. Woolf's refusal to corroborate facts has subversive potential. By suggesting that the book from which she took this story and the album in which Taylor can be seen dressed as King Arthur have been destroyed in an air-raid, Woolf refuses to make the story acceptable to fact-gatherers, thus preventing her fiction from being reduced to verifiable details, as Herbert Fisher had done with *To the Lighthouse*. The "enemy action" which Woolf says had destroyed the documents may be a reference to the bombing of the offices of Autotype, where Cameron's negatives were thought to have been kept (Gernsheim 187); or to the destruction of Woolf's London home, in which family heirlooms may have been lost. However, it is more likely that the book and the album never existed—as I have suggested, Henry Taylor never posed as Arthur—and so the whole story becomes a fictional recreation of a scene from the past which Woolf had never known. In this way, we can read "A Scene from the Past" as an imaginative reconstruction of history drawn from an inventive interpretation of Cameron's life and work. It does not simply celebrate a secret feminist reading of the past which is invisible to patriarchal historians, but it suggests that the past may be reinvented in a fantasy of liberation from the burden of inheritance, maternal as well as paternal.

de Gay

By using Cameron's art as a framing device, Woolf forges an imaginative access to the past by thinking back through her aunt.

Notes

1 Woolf used "A Scene from the Past" as the title for four of the last five drafts. I will take as the definitive text the last of the Freshwater drafts: Monk's House Papers MH/B10e, 1-5, hereafter "Scene" (see Hussey for facsimile). There are at least 7 drafts of the Freshwater story—a manuscript at Smith College entitled "The Searchlight" and six typescripts identified by Graham. I have taken the last of these as definitive because a close comparison reveals a clear sense of progression from one draft to the next, the later changes generally involving slight rephrasing.

2 In the transcriptions of the manuscript included here, crossed out text represents Woolf's deletions, text in angled brackets <> indicates Woolf's insertions, and square brackets [ ] denote illegible script or doubtful readings. I am grateful to the Society of Authors as the Literary Representative of the Estate of Virginia Woolf for permission to quote from the drafts.

3 Taylor describes Cameron photographing him in "multiform impersonations of King David, King Lear, and all sorts of 'Kings, Princes, Prelates, Potentates and Peers'" (197), but does not mention Arthur.

Works Cited

Armstrong, Carol. "Cupid's Pencil of Light: Julia Margaret Cameron and the Maternalization of Photography." *October* 76 (1996): 115-41.

Beloff, Halla. "Facing Julia Margaret Cameron." *History of Photography* 17: 1 (1993): 115-17.

Blain, Virginia. "Thinking Back Through Our Aunts: Harriet Martineau and Tradition in Women's Writing." *Women: A Cultural Review*, 1: 3 (1990): 223–39.

Fisher, Herbert A. L. *An Unfinished Autobiography.* Foreword by Lettice Fisher. London: Oxford UP, 1940.

Gernsheim, Helmut. *Julia Margaret Cameron: Her Life and Photographic Work.* London: Gordon Fraser, 1975.

Gillespie, Diane F. "'Her Kodak Pointed at His Head': Virginia Woolf and Photography." *Virginia Woolf: Themes and Variations.* Ed. Vara Neverow-Turk and Mark Hussey. New York: Pace UP, 1993: 33-40.

Graham, John W. "The Drafts of Virginia Woolf's 'The Searchlight'." *Twentieth Century Literature* 22.4 (1976): 379-93.

Hussey, Mark. (ed.) *Major Authors on CD-Rom: Virginia Woolf.* Woodbridge, CT: Primary Source Media, 1996.

Mason, Rebecca. "'Words Proud and Fearless: An Examination of Virginia Woolf's 'The Searchlight' and Sylvia Plath's Ariel Collection." Diss. Smith College, 1992.

Olsen, Victoria C. "Family Fictions: Virginia Woolf and Julia Margaret Cameron." *Virginia Woolf Miscellany* 49 (1997): 5.

Raiskin, Judith. "Review: Virginia Woolf Manuscripts from the Monk's House Papers, Brighton, Sussex: Harvester Press Microform Publication Ltd." *Virginia Woolf Miscellany* 27 (1987): 5.

Spalding, Frances. *Vanessa Bell.* London: Weidenfeld and Nicolson, 1983.

Taylor, Henry. *Autobiography of Henry Taylor, 1800-1875,* 2 vols. London: Longman, 1885.

Woolf, Virginia. Introduction to *Victorian Photographs of Famous Men and Fair Women* by J.M Cameron. London: Hogarth, 1926.

———. *The Diary of Virginia Woolf.* Ed. Anne Olivier Bell, asst. ed. Andrew McNeillie, 5 vols. London: Hogarth Press, 1977–84.

———. *A Haunted House and Other Short Stories.* Ed. Leonard Woolf. London: Hogarth Press, 1943.

———. *The Letters of Virginia Woolf.* Ed. Nigel Nicolson, asst. ed. Joanne Trautmann Bankes, 6 vols. London: Hogarth Press, 1975–1980.

———. *Moments of Being: Unpublished Autobiographical Writings.* Ed. and intro. Jeanne Schulkind. London: Triad/Granada, 1978.

———. *The Complete Shorter Fiction.* Ed. S. Dick. Rev. ed. London: Hogarth, 1989.

———. "A Scene from the Past." Ts. MH/B10e: 1-5. Monk's House Papers, Brighton, England.

———. "The Searchlight." Ms. Frances Hooper Collection of Virginia Woolf Books and Manuscripts, Smith College Rare Book Room, Northampton MA.

———. "Incongrous Inaccurate Memories." Ts. MH/B9k. Monk's House Papers, Brighton, England.

Wussow, Helen. "Travesties of Excellence: Julia Margaret Cameron, Lytton Strachey, Virginia Woolf and the Photographic Image." *Virginia Woolf and the Arts: Selected Papers from the Sixth Annual Conference on Virginia Woolf.* Ed. Diane F. Gillespie and Leslie K. Hankins. New York: Pace UP, 1997: 48-56.

Wayne K. Chapman
Leonard Woolf, Cambridge, and the Art of the English Essay

Who is or ought to be afraid of Leonard Woolf? Because orthodoxy always defends itself against those who challenge it, one naturally infers that, as a precociously intellectual teenager at St. Paul's School, London, and as a young man at Trinity College, Cambridge, Leonard Woolf would become someone the Establishment might be well advised to keep its eye on. The end of the English Monarchy—and we hear more about that today—was neither shocking nor unthinkable to Woolf, at 17 or 18, although he did soon after give the empire, under King Edward VII, several years of exemplary service in Ceylon. Woolf resigned to marry Virginia Stephen and became the staunch anti-imperialist, socialist, and pivotal figure Jean Moorcroft Wilson writes about in one of her booklets, *Leonard Woolf: Pivot or Outsider of Bloomsbury?* Paradoxically, it might be said that the seeds of rebellion were sown in England's finest institutions of higher learning. Partly motivated by the need to be salient in one's thesis as an essayist, Leonard emulated the great tradition of English essay-writing with early success seemingly in his pocket.

In the Leonard Woolf Papers at the University of Sussex, for example, one finds a complete draft and fair-hand copy of the essay "Monarchy," as well as two significantly shorter and possibly later spin-offs called "The Ideal King" and "A Fallacy of History."[1] The last two are abridgements of the first, associated with Cambridge for their treatment of Emerson in an essay entitled

"Mysticism," which Rosenbaum identifies as Woolf's prize-winning Trinity English essay of 1901 (*Victorian Bloomsbury* 132). Duncan Wilson, who saw that Woolf's later politics stood on rudiments set down in school days, quotes both "The Ideal King" and "Monarchy" as though they derived from Woolf's "classical and general studies" at Cambridge (16), catching an extraordinary paradox in foreshadowing the Fabian Socialist to come: as early as 1898, Woolf said that constitutional monarchy "is a sham . . . which acts as a veil, until the people's eyes can become accustomed to look upon Reality. . . . All who have the true interests of Democracy & Liberty at heart have hopes . . . that the time will come . . . when there will be no uneducated class, . . . a time when all disguises can be done away with" (*Monarchy* 4, 33). This is a very daring position for a schoolboy to take in the context of Queen Victoria's recently celebrated Diamond Jubilee. Over sixty years later, Woolf recalled the circumstances: "I had won the Eldon Essay Prize at St Paul's, £20 and a gold medal . . . for an essay on monarchy, and I know that I got considerable pleasure (and pain) from writing it" (*Sowing* 97).

Wilson's mistake in associating the essay "Monarchy" with the Cambridge essays is understandable. In fact, the intellectual climate at St. Paul's, under the mentorship of A. M. Cooke, compared with that at Cambridge in striking ways that Woolf acknowledged in 1955, in a *London Magazine* account he soon reworked in his autobiography. Cooke encouraged him "always to exercise [his] own judgment" on a "wide reading" and bestowed on him a leather-bound copy of Bacon's *Essays*, inscribed to him in 1897 as he prepared for his last year at the school and election to the debating society, attended by G. K. and Cecil Chesterton, E. C. Bentley, and R. F. Oldershaw. One distinction between his Cambridge talks and those given at St. Paul's was that at Cambridge the societies to which he belonged were literary whereas the St. Paul's club was "exclusively political." Nevertheless, his "enthusiasm for [the arts] had been encouraged by Cooke," and his contact with the Chestertons and other debaters brought "a new breath of intellectual fresh air into . . . school life"; one found "relief to find oneself," as he remembered, "on Saturday afternoons with five or six people to whom one could say what one thought and who accepted the same intellectual standards of value whatever our disagreement might be about other things" (*Sowing* 92-3).

When Leonard Woolf went up to Cambridge in 1899, he found the same, or similar relief:

> I was astonished and delighted to find that among many of my contemporaries and seniors a love of literature and a desire to write books, intensive criticism and aesthetic speculations were accepted as natural and creditable for intelligent persons. Here for the first time I entered what might be called a literary world, a provincial literary world . . . but which yet had connections with the great metropolitan literary world of London. ("Coming to London—II" 52)

Textual Re-takes

We know that Leonard's Eldon Prize essay "Monarchy" is one of the things that went along to Cambridge. In manuscript Notebook A, inscribed at both ends with his name and the date "July 17th 1894" (he attended St. Paul's School from 1894 to 1899), we encounter the first complete draft of the essay. 68 pages of this notebook were used in the first draft. Interspersed are notes, dramatic sketches, various game scores, study questions, lists of books to read, odd notes, and chess moves between "LSW" and "ST," Saxon Sydney-Turner, Leonard's roommate at Trinity College). With another 34 folio pages to the fair copy and twelve more pages to produce the two exercises in abridgement, the young writer might have felt he had written a book. And, indeed, he had rehearsed the logic of his *magnum opus* on European political developments as "communal psychology," *After the Deluge* (in two vols., 1931 and 1939) and *Principia Politica* (1953), without Freud and without coming to quite the same conclusions.

In "The Ideal King," turning to Emerson as in the later essay "Mysticism," the young Woolf demonstrates how much he will have to pivot on the question of government initiative after eventually trying to administer good government in Ceylon. "The wise know that foolish legislation is a rope of sand," Emerson had said, "which perishes in the twisting" because, Woolf added in conclusion, "the state must follow & not lead" (f. 4). Similarly, in "A Fallacy of History," the essayist challenges the belief that "a Government should be judged by what it *makes* of its citizens," using Emerson, as before, to expose the fallacious assumptions of inexperienced statesmen who think "the laws make the city." Governments reflect the "national character" and change as the character changes, for better or worse. Perhaps showing an influence of Cambridge but as yet without G. E. Moore in it, mysticism prevails over the practical concerns of statecraft, and the piece ends in admonishment:

> [W]e shall be spared the labour of tracing fictitious "laws" which regulate the effect of different Constitutions of nations. To do this were to animate the dry bones of History which would cease to be the crabbed record of laws & constitutions & would become an all-interesting story of the mysterious workings of the World-spirit, the Zeit-geist that makes or destroys all things. (qtd. *Monarchy* 8)

His efforts to make additional capital from the carefully nuanced arguments of "Monarchy" were both, in the two shorter essays, more oppositional and conservative than the parent essay, which projects glimmerings of the politics Woolf would promote in years to come and not just the erudition on classics he attained before going up to Trinity College as an undergraduate.

The Leonard Woolf Papers at the University of Sussex Library also preserve drafts and spin-offs related to his prize-winning Trinity English essay, "Mysticism," which shows that his studies in the Classics could serve his interest in literary criticism as well as interests in history and politics. These materials also render an impression of a code of ethics and of values that are, at least, markedly proto-Bloomsbury, including a Syllabus "for a work dealing

217

exhaustively with the subject of mysticism [to have been] written in collaboration" with a number of new friends who are now either associated with the Bloomsbury Group or its milieu. In the essay, Emerson was merely one of the philosophers, "initiated mystics," or "great thinkers" treated from ancient Greece through the *Symbolistes* of late nineteenth-century France. An obvious assumption in the essay, even perhaps its *sub*-thesis, is that at Cambridge the "X Society," Apostles, and other groups in which Woolf moved as an undergraduate were what he then meant by "Open Secret Societies" of which "the Society of the Mystics" was "the greatest & the highest." As he observed, the necessity of surveying and categorizing individual mystics *in practice* (or, that is, in method or precept) missed the basic sympathy of all mystics. Those "ideas" that he called, with lavish metaphor, "a system" but which he applied to distinguish one mystic from another were not to be used to infer "that there is a school of mystics in the same way as there is a school of Stoicism, or of Kant or of Hegel." Anticipating one of the paradoxes of Bloomsbury's later flirtation with mysticism in spite of its well-heeled rationalism and Woolf's own atheism, he noted that "mystics are no hide-bound pedants of reason but form a mighty Brotherhood of the Soul to which everyone is admitted who has heard his soul speak in the silence of eternity" (Woolf Papers II.A.2.b., "Mysticism," p. 5).

What makes the essay literary? First and last, it begins and ends by refuting a literary thesis. The 22-page essay challenges the egregious German critic Max Nordau on the supposed degeneracy of such Symbolist poets as Mallarmé, Nerval, Villiers de l'Isle-Adam, Rimbaud, Verlaine, and Laforgue. Nordau thought these poets to be degenerate and imbecile because they could only think in a "mystical" or, as he believed, confused way. Woolf opens his essay by invoking Plato and the parable of a wise man from "the quaint tales of the East"—one who ends his silence with an answer to all questions: "Whatever is, is." "Anyone who has thought or read even but little about what one of the few latter-day poets has called the greatest & highest of Open Secret Societies[—]'The Society of the Mystics,'" Woolf observes, "—must have felt the wisdom of that answer of the wise man," who is silent because his people can never understand the wisdom he has stored. The misunderstanding of the multitude leads them to mistake the wise man's wisdom for "confused & unintelligible dreamings."

Nordau's false premise is rhetorically introduced in the essay, and Woolf begins to do this by observing that "Plato & Plotinus, Novalis, Ruysbroeck & Emerson are obscure to us perhaps, but perhaps also their eyes have been able to pierce farther than ours into the infinite Night that surrounds Existence." "What is a mystic?" Leonard asks, shrewdly choosing to begin his argument with a definition: a mystic is one who tries to "explain the relation of mankind to the Final Cause." The definition seems Romantic in its application, for mystics seem obscure to us because they use methods "peculiar to themselves, . . . discard[ing] 'reason' when . . . seek[ing] knowledge about the

Infinite & employ[ing] only the 'soul.'" Documentation on the so-called Perennial Philosophy is patently international and therefore multilingual in the essay (mainly English, German, and French), including Plato's *Phaedrus*, Plotinus' *Enneads*, Vaughan's *Hours with the Mystics*, Swedenborg's *Heaven and Hell*, Novalis' *Hymnen an die Nacht*, and Maeterlinck's *Trésor des Humbles* (see "Mysticism," pp. 1-4). But, while resembling George Bernard Shaw's famous repudiations of Nordau,[2] Leonard's own case projects onward in time to the idea of Wordsworthian moments of insight and being that we habitually associate with Virginia Woolf. Because of Leonard's commitment to reason as a guide in politics, we overlook the fact that in his humanism was the faith that in a "flash of inspiration . . . absolute truths" are apprehended although "toilsome processes of logic fail to attain" them. "These ideas," he said in 1901, "are no mere foolish dreams; they imply a system of philosophy whose achievements are almost as glorious as its aims & resemble a mighty dome studded with the jewels of all that is most splendid in the human race" (5). It does not follow that his skepticism and atheism with respect to the "Final Cause" (as we infer from the conclusion of the essay, where mysticism is "based on Scepticism & the inability of reason to grasp Infinity" [22]) mitigate against his faith that truth could be arrested by certain people. "[G]reat minds like Hegel['s] may . . . reject mysticism finally & build a [Platonic] ladder out of intellect alone which can reach the Infinite" that mystics see "in the beauty of picture & poem" ([22]).

And it does not follow that "great minds" were strictly those of a "brotherhood," although the gendered structure and composition of the Cambridge societies to which Leonard belonged do superimpose themselves obviously and self-consciously on his thesis. A mystic brotherhood has two kinds of members: first, "initiated mystics," or philosophers who discuss consciously the "soul-power" (besides Plato and the others named, read McTaggart, Dickinson, Russell, and Moore); and, second, "lay brethren," or "poets, artists, musicians, all 'lovers' . . . who . . . without reflection recognize the mysterious workings of the absolute beauty of the Soul" (read Leonard and his undergraduate friends who studied the initiates but aspired to be poets) (6). The bulk of the essay deals with "initiated mystics" but for the purpose of defending the disputed value of supposedly degenerated French poets whose work the young men in Leonard's circle admired and emulated.

Very much the point of a brotherhood was to promote the interests and values of its members, and, just so, Woolf and several of his companions at Cambridge pressed their interests as essayists in the direction of publishing houses that were then defining the tradition of English literature in popular anthologies. Duckworth, Dent, Kegan Paul, Unwin, Macmillan—what publisher did not offer an equivalent to The Reader's Library or Everyman's series in 1900? With sights set on the "great metropolitan literary world of London" ("Coming to London—II" 52), the essay "Mysticism" was a downpayment on the general introduction that was to have been Leonard's major but not only contribution to an anthology of essays on mystics. The argument is made by the archives, which, according to a Syllabus in his papers at the University of Sussex and to an outline of topics accompanying a letter he wrote to Saxon Sydney-Turner in late December 1900,[3] show how proto-Bloomsbury might have rallied in a team effort behind Woolf, who was to have been "general editor." The contributors were his coterie, including his talented sister Bella, who was given a chapter on "Scandinavian Mysticism."[4] However, the projected plan clouded and veered from "initiated mystics" to the "lay brethren," as he defined them in his 1901 Trinity English essay, which is probably as far as the series ever got. The Syllabus ends, signed and dated "Jan 1901," with a very tentative outline to continue with essays on "Literature & Mysticism" by Woolf, "Music & Mysticism" by Sydney-Turner, and "Painting & Mysticism" (especially Blake) by Lytton Strachey.

Apart from a long, possibly unfinished (for unresolved), 44-page essay of 1902 called "Byron," nothing from Leonard Woolf's school papers accounts for so much as his two prize-winning essays "Monarchy" and "Mysticism," considering the notes, drafts, pull-sheets, and spin-offs related to them.[5] Contemplating in them the problems of existence and essence, he strove to apply his conclusions to literary theory and criticism. Such striving also gave a literary cast to an imaginary dialogue called "Myself when young did eagerly frequent," in which Boswell, Samuel Johnson, and Francis Bacon meet in the Trinity College Library to debate the merits of "useless knowledge" and a conceivably real proposal to replace the Classics Tripos at Cambridge with one in science to "bid . . . farewell to the Siren Voices of poesie & the ancient philosophers." Bacon, the proponent of the Science Tripos, is given the floor for most of the dialogue, but Johnson, the opponent, is given the last word, ironically accusing Bacon, a father of the Enlightenment, of not listening to reason. In "Socrates," a six-page essay in which Woolf looks for "a really workable 'theory of life,'" or a common viewpoint from which to regard history and literature, the eponymous philosopher seems the one character of history to come down to us (via "[h]istorian & novelist, essayist & philosopher") as one in "theory & action." His secret is that "his life & . . . his philosophy [aimed at] the discovery of the Good which he identified with truth"; and Schopenhauer, as in the essay "Mysticism," supplies the antithesis. In Woolf's view, Socrates "could never have understood the harsh judgment of the modern philosopher [that] 'Vermin is the rule everywhere upon the earth.'" In a related fragment or short address known by its first line, "Vermin, says the German philosopher, is the rule all over the world," Woolf assails "the rubbish-heaps of formulae & catch-phrases with which the ordinary man clothes his mind & thoughts," recalling Bacon's argument, in Woolf's dialogue, that literature and useless learning dwelt on "mere tricks of language" to produce a waste of learning unconvincingly represented by the Trinity College Library. But here, as in "Words, words, words," an academic theme on "fossil poetry," the writer was more intent to study his medium than profound implications.

Essays on "Lucretius," "Pastoral Poetry" and "The Agamemnon of Aeschylus" were similarly minor exercises.

Only a critique of Robert Browning entitled "A poet hidden in a cloud of thought" and a formal apologia called "Classical Education & Literature" seem to make critical ends of beginnings made in the essay "Mysticism." Unable to rescue Browning from the charge of obscurity, Woolf nevertheless defined "obscurity" just as the word "mysticism" had required definition. Critically, the fault really belonged with the "feebleness" of the uninitiated "reader's brain," not with "confusion of thought in the writer's"; Browning's thinking "was as clear as crystal but his difficulty was to make it intelligible to the ordinary mind." Perhaps not excellent, the essay would serve as an apprentice piece for Woolf's later criticism as the literary editor of *The Nation and Athenaeum* and strikes an attitude common among the Modernists. Similarly, "Classical Education & Literature" was not inspiringly written, lacking the tension of either the Bacon-Johnson dialogue or "Socrates" but taking up the defense of classical English education from Johnson against "Weltschmerz," or "world weariness." Literature, like all the arts, was defined as "a means pursued by the highest minds of fighting [the] Weltschmerz, an Excalibur which won in early life need be given up only when it has fought our last battle for us." Like Woolf's faith in the intellectual pursuit of the mystics without divinity, literature permits us to "carve out of our inner consciousness an Ideal, a human ideal to take the place of the one we have lost, the one which involved the divine." He might have accounted himself one of the condemned souls for whom Pater proclaimed art to be the successor to lost religious faith, but Woolf's stance owes more to Arnold and the historical waxing and waning tides of Hebraic and Hellenic cycles of civilization. As a modern writer and practitioner of the art of the English essay, his "word-splitting & logic-chopping" was yet "imbued with some idealistic cravings" laid down in the soil by the Greeks and Romans where the roots ran deep. There were shades of the initiated and lay brethren of the "Open Secret . . . Society . . . of the Mystics," of course, as there were for anyone who studied "accurately & minutely the flowering fields of Greek Genius," especially at Cambridge a hundred years ago.

Notes

[1] Quotations from "Monarchy" and the essays related to it are from Leonard Woolf, *Monarchy* (1999), including the editor's introduction and notes. For permission to quote from other unpublished papers, I thank the Estate of Leonard Woolf and, for her helpfulness, Elizabeth Inglis, Manuscripts Section, University of Sussex Library.

[2] Shaw's *Regeneration: A Reply to Max Nordau* (1895) and *The Sanity of Art* (1908) were direct responses to Nordau's *Degeneration*, the English translation of 1895, and "Entartung," respectively. A contentious Jewish critic known for his Zionism, Nordau's notoreity in England largely stemmed from Shaw's rather vigorous renunciations.

[3] See HM 42125, Henry E. Huntington Library, San Marino, California.

[4] Various historical parts of the work were assigned to Sydney-Turner and C. F. Angus, a fellow member of the Trinity Sunday Essay Society. The musically adept Sydney-

Turner was also to have contributed "a mystical opera" to be "brought out in the same series," so the anthology, as such, had the capacity of being issued in multiple volumes. Part I, "The Soul of Mysticism," belonged to Woolf, as did Part II, "The Origin of Mysticism"; Platonism was divided between roommates Woolf and Sydney-Turner; Neoplatonism was Woolf's; Angus was assigned "Christianity & Mysticism" with Woolf back in for "early" and "later" German Mysticism and with Sydney-Turner initially in for "German Mysticism & its relation to Platonism" but replaced by Lytton Strachey and Sydney-Turner on "English and American Mysticism" and by a surveillance of mysticism in Ireland (by Sydney-Turner), France (by Strachey), and Egypt (by Angus) with "Brahmanism" to be written by Woolf and Angus; the Editor queried the topic of "The Future of Mysticism," to be written by himself, followed by his sister's work and a piece on "Sufism" by Angus.

5 Detailed reading notes for "Mysticism," as well as the essay itself and the other compositions discussed below, are found in file II.A.2.b. in the Leonard Woolf Papers at the University of Sussex Library.

Works Cited

Nordau, Max Simon [i.e. Max S. Suedfeld]. *Degeneration*, . . . trans. from the 2nd ed. of the German work of 1894. London: Heinemann, 1895.

——. *The Malady of the Century*. London: Heinemann, 1896.

Rosenbaum, S. P. *Victorian Bloomsbury*. Volume 1 of *The Early Literary History of the Bloomsbury Group*. New York: St. Martin's Press, 1987.

Shaw, George Bernard. *Regeneration: A Reply to Max Nordau*. London: Constable, 1895.

——. *The Sanity of Art*. N.p.: n.p., 1908.

Wilson, Duncan. *Leonard Woolf: A Political Biography*. London: Hogarth Press; New York: St. Martin's, 1978.

Wilson, Jean Moorcroft. *Leonard Woolf: Pivot or Outsider of Bloomsbury?* Bloomsbury Heritage Series No. 3. London: Cecil Woolf, 1994.

Leonard Woolf. *After the Deluge: A Study of Communal Psychology*. 2 vols. London: Hogarth Press, 1931 and 1939.

——. "Coming to London—II." *The London Magazine* 2.10 (Oct. 1955): 49-54.

——. *Monarchy: an hitherto unpublished manuscript*. Ed. and intro. by Wayne K. Chapman. Bloomsbury Heritage Series No. 22. London: Cecil Woolf, 1999.

——. *Sowing: An Autobiography of the Years 1880 to 1904*. London: Hogarth Press, 1960.

——. Unpublished Manuscripts. Leonard Woolf Papers II.A.2.b. Cambridge Essays. University of Sussex Library.

Pressing the Public Sphere

Patrick Collier
Woolf, Privacy, and the Press

Like many people who become public figures, Virginia Woolf was protective of her privacy. Especially later in her life, Woolf attempted to shield herself from uncomfortable amounts of attention from fans and, to a greater extent, the press. But "privacy" meant more to Woolf than, for example, being shielded from reporters who wanted to see the interior of her home. She did see her privacy, in the most common sense of that term, as threatened by her limited celebrity. But further, and perhaps more importantly, "privacy" is an issue that is intimately connected with Woolf's sense of the proper conditions for *composition*. The privacy she defined and sought in this context was a defense against yielding too much authority to the audience and thus compromising her individual vision. This privacy was also, for Woolf, threatened by critics, literary journalism, and the literary marketplace generally—all of which threatened to upset the proper balance of power between writer and audience, not at the moment of publication or sale but rather at a more crucial and sensitive stage, the moment of composition.

"Reviewing," one of Woolf's last essays, begins with the peculiar image of garment workers mending clothes in a shop-window as pedestrians outside look in. Woolf offers this image as an analogy for the scrutiny under which novelists and poets work—the scrutiny of reviewers, who cast the unwelcome light of their observation on work that would more appropriately be performed in "the darkness of the workshop" (*CE2* 213). She figures the writer as the earnest "obscure workman" and the reviewer as a voyeur who destroys the writer's privacy—a privacy essential to the mindset required for creative work: "The review," she writes, ". . . increases self-consciousness and diminishes strength. The shop window and the looking-glass inhibit and confine" (214).

Woolf had reason to be unhappy with literary journalism in 1939, the year in which she published "Reviewing." Her critical reputation had sagged in the thirties, when a number of critics labeled her as a coterie-based novelist with a narrow audience; the decade also saw a number of strident published attacks on the Bloomsbury group as a whole.[1] Moreover, "Reviewing" is part of a more general critique of the press that Woolf developed in the thirties—a critique that found its most sustained expression in *Three Guineas*. But neither attacks on her circle nor her increasing distrust of the press fully explains the image of creative writers toiling, in public view, in the shop window—Woolf's figuration of the book review as an invasion of the novelist's *privacy*. Understanding the connection between privacy and Woolf's growing hostility to reviewers requires that we consider her idiosyncratic ideas about privacy and composition—her difficult and ever-shifting understanding of the paradoxical nature of writing as a simultaneously private and public act—and her discomfort with authorship as a visible, public position.

In the first half of the twentieth century, changes in the press and publishing had created the possibility of a greater degree of celebrity for writers than ever before. Newspapers had initiated the "personal interview" and "profile" in the last decades of the nineteenth century, and these genres created publishing opportunities for journalists with connections to well-known writers. Increases in literacy and the related explosion in publishing created the phenomena of the "best-seller" and the "blockbuster," resulting in large audiences interested in learning about their favorite authors (McAleer 48, 56). Memoirs and biographies of popular authors from the 1910s, twenties, and thirties offer accounts of writers deluged with fan mail or mobbed as they disembarked from trains and ships. Ethel M. Dell, one of the most popular British novelists of the period, was trailed by reporters on her yearly holidays in Europe and received so much fan mail, "a sack full a day" according to Penelope Dell's biography, that she had to employ a friend and her sister to type up and organize responses (41-2). Many authors, booksellers, and publishers exploited this celebrity, setting up public appearances and book-signings to maintain authors' visibility and nurture their audiences.

Though Woolf became an established and well-known writer in the late twenties, and wrote one virtual bestseller (*The Years*), she herself never achieved the degree of celebrity of a Hall Caine or an Ethel Dell. Fame on that scale fell most often to such writers of "fiction" whose work was targeted to a mass audience. As Joseph McAleer observes, the late nineteenth century had seen the rise of the distinction between "fiction" and "literature" as a means of differentiating works aimed at the lucrative mass-audience from those geared to the limited, but still profitable, traditionally upper-middle-class reading public (40-1). But this expansion of literary celebrity is relevant to Woolf for two reasons.

First, it constituted a sort of public authorial behavior Woolf disliked and chose to distance herself from. In a letter, she told Vita Sackville-West that she was horrified by the prospect of public book-signings (*L5* 348). The ambition and self-promotion of the formerly popular author Lucy Clifford showed when the two met in 1920:

> ... if I could reproduce her talk of money, royalties, editions, & reviews, I should think myself a novelist; & the picture might serve me for a warning.

> ... Brave, I suppose, with vitality & pluck, but oh the sight of the dirty quills, & the scored blotting paper & her hands and nails not very clean either, & money, reviews, proofs, helping hands, slatings—what an atmosphere of rancid cabbage & old clothes stewing in their water! (*D2* 12).

An undeniable hint of class snobbery emerges in Woolf's evocation of "rancid cabbage and old clothes stewing in their water." More importantly, though, Woolf's distaste centers on the signs of commercial ambition, reminders that writing is both a material and a commercial pursuit: review clippings, ink, page proofs, and "money" provide Woolf with a "warning" of what it means to be a novelist: it means, in short, that one must seek attention, cultivating and gathering positive reviews.

The expansion of literary celebrity is relevant to Woolf for a second reason: if Woolf and writers of her ilk were not subject to the sort of mass-celebrity which greeted such writers as Dell, Edgar Rice Burroughs, and Margaret Mitchell, they did become celebrities on a smaller scale. Memoirs of publishers and others who moved among the high-brow literati constituted a minor genre at the time, attesting to a market for accounts of such writers. In a well-known incident, Woolf herself was outraged when a *New York Times* reporter hovered outside her door with his request for entry to do a story on the homes of famous writers; and she borrowed details from her diary entry on the incident when she created Mr. Page, the comically reductive reporter in *Between the Acts* (*D5* 72-3, *BA* 97, 150, 181-2). In 1933 the *New Statesman* published an article detailing the excesses of the celebrity-chasing media. The article drew this reply from Woolf:

> If you ask these "celebrities" why they have consented to make their faces or their houses or their views public property they will reply, for the most part, that they have done so unwillingly, but that unless they consent they will be branded as prigs, curmudgeons or cranks. Often, they will add, the request is made by friends whom it is difficult to refuse, or by struggling journalists in urgent need of the few guineas that the interview or the portrait will procure them. In short, a mild form of blackmail is applied, and out of weariness or good nature they succumb (*L5* 236).

The inverted commas around "celebrities" indicate Woolf's attempt to separate herself and like-minded writers, who consent to such interviews unwillingly, from popular novelists who both had a great deal more recognition—and thus actually *were* celebrities by Woolf's definition—and who were more likely to exploit their notoriety voluntarily.

Critics have disagreed on the question of how much public notice Woolf actually desired, with Alex Zwerdling going so far as to suggest that Woolf at one point abandoned the goal of reaching a broad audience and wrote her masterpieces of the twenties with her circle of friends as the imagined audience (8-9).[2] Indeed the question of who precisely her audience was—and what her proper relationship with it should be—were vexing questions for Woolf, questions for which she never reached a settled answer. Poor reviews and minimal sales, such as those that followed *Night and Day* in 1921, could send her careening to the extreme of saying she wrote for herself alone, and that to do otherwise would compromise her artistic vision.[3] She wondered in her diary in 1921 whether it would not be best to "write for half a dozen instead of 1,500" (*D2* 107). "I have made up my mind that I'm not going to be popular, & so genuinely that I look upon disregard or abuse as part of my bargain," she wrote in February, 1922. "I'm to write what I like & they're to say what they like. My only interest as a writer lies, I begin to see, in some queer individuality" (*D2* 168). Such moments, as Hermione Lee has pointed out, alternated in the early twenties with periods marked by "a preoccupation with reputation and with fame . . . [a] feeling that she was now on the right path and in the right context for her work" (438).

More commonly, Woolf's attitude towards her audience at any given time marked a provisional compromise between the claims of the audience and the integrity of her individual voice. Woolf seems to have felt that writing for an audience always necessitates a compromise: the author's unique and idiosyncratic vision has to be tempered so it can communicate something to a reader. The phenomenon of the book review complicates this matter further, since the reviewer stands between the novelist and the audience. By looking at some of Woolf's statements about this relationship between artist, press, and public, we can begin to see how the concept of "privacy" is an important aspect of her negotiation of the writer's authority against the claims of the audience and the unwelcome mediation of the press.

Woolf addresses the pressure the literary press exerts upon the writer in the 1924 essay "The Patron and the Crocus." As the essay makes clear, Woolf felt that the particular conditions of literary journalism threatened to skew the artist's work from the first moments of composition. Woolf acknowledges that writing needs to reach an audience to matter—"[t]he crocus," she writes, "is an imperfect crocus until it has been shared" (*E4* 213). She finds that difficulties lie not in the reading habits of the audience but in its multiplicity, its fragmentation—conditions both reflected and shaped by literary journalism. The press is simultaneously a means of access and a barrier to the artist, who faces an array of confusing choices when considering audience:

> There is the daily Press, the weekly Press, the monthly Press; the English public and the American public; the best-seller public and the worst-seller public; the highbrow public and the red-blood public; all now organised self-conscious entities *capable through their various mouthpieces of making their needs known and their approval or displeasure felt.* Thus the writer who has been moved by the sight of the first crocus in Kensington Gardens has, before he sets pen to paper, to choose from a crowd of competitors the particular patron who suits him best (*E4* 213, emphasis added).

The relationship between reader and artist has here become multiply mediated. Writers can only "know" their audiences through the mediation of their "mouthpieces," who presumably express their aesthetic preferences, although

Woolf seems dubious as to how accurately they do so. Crucially, the force of this multiply-mediated relationship is felt at the moment of composition, *"before [the writer] sets pen to paper."* Woolf *could* conceive of a healthy compromise between the demands of writer and reader, one that allowed the reader to enter into the privacy of the author's writing room. But here, congress between the reader and writer is complicated by a maddeningly diverse public press. And the press here appears as an unwanted visitor in the study—a force that exerts an unwanted *a priori* influence on the writer's craft.

Woolf's displeasure with the state of literary journalism—a displeasure made more vexing by her own prolific record as a reviewer and essayist in the literary press—led her to construct a number of idylls of a more charitable, organic, and, crucially, *private* form of literary criticism. In a 1925 essay on George Moore, Woolf remarks that

> [t]he only criticism worth having at present is that which is spoken, not written—spoken over wine-glasses and coffee-cups late at night, flashed out on the spur of the moment by people passing who have not time to finish their sentences, let alone consider the dues of editors or the feelings of friends (*E4* 260).

She similarly disliked public literary criticism when it took the form of university lectures, writing in the 1934 essay "Why?" that "this lecturing about English literature . . . this passing of examinations in English literature, which led to all this writing about English literature, was bound in the end to be the death and burial of English literature" (*DM* 148). "Reviewing" similarly posits a "private" form of literary criticism: a ban on "reviewing" in its current form, to be replaced by the one-on-one consultation between the serious writer and the serious critic. The unfinished essay "Anon," which sketches a brief and highly polemical history of English literature, helps to contextualize all of these statements, as it figures the onset of publication as a fall from innocence:

> At once come into existence some of those innumerable influences that are to tug, to distort, to thwart; as also they are to stimulate and draw out. The poet is no longer a nameless wandering voice, but attached to his audience, tethered to one spot and played upon by outside influences. . . . As the book goes out into a larger, a more varied audience these influences become more and more complex. According to its wealth, its poverty, its education, its ignorance, the public demands what satisfies its own need—poetry, history, instruction, a story to make them forget their own drab lives. The thing that the writer has to say becomes increasingly cumbered ("Anon" 390).

If the onset of printing brings with it a sort of tyranny of the audience, it also creates a disabling self-consciousness, a sort of vanity, on the part of the writer, who is "no longer a wandering voice, but a man practising an art, asking for recognition, and bitterly conscious of his relation to the world, of the world's scorn" (391).

Written within two years of "Reviewing" and five years after *Three Guineas*, "Anon" helps to clarify the connection, for Woolf, between privacy and successful literary production. Privacy is a complicated and multivalent term for her. It includes freedom from what Woolf saw as slavishness to the audience, an audience represented by its "mouthpiece" the reviewer, who appears, figuratively, peeping through the shop-window at private labor. It includes freedom from the "vanity" that tempts the artist to desire public recognition; while we may not share this definition of vanity with Woolf, it was a charge she levelled at herself, repeatedly, when public response to her work upset her. Finally, and crucially, privacy does not, as the shop-window metaphor might suggest, mean solitude: on the contrary, it consists in an intimate and fruitful congress with another mind, such as that prescribed in "Reviewing" between the writer and a sympathetic critic, or between the writer and her friends, who can provide the best kind of criticism—spoken criticism. At her healthiest, and in better times, Woolf could see potential for such congress, with unknown readers, in the act of writing for publication. As Jeanne Dubino has pointed out, the concept of the "common reader" is predicated on the idea of such a relationship, on the ability of a well-read and well-intentioned readership to bring what Woolf approvingly called "the pressure of an audience" to bear upon the writer's inspiration (133).[4] At the end Woolf could no longer envision this symbiosis, and reached out for a number of desperate and fanciful solutions, among them her half-serious call for a ban on reviewing and "Anon's" nostalgic idyll of a prelapsarian, unmediated relationship with the audience.

Notes

[1] For accounts of these attacks and of Woolf's general critical fortunes in the 1930s, see the biographies by Lee (622-4) and Bell (184).

[2] More common in Woolf studies is the sense that Woolf was fighting against the modernist grain in trying to appeal to a broader audience of "common readers." Beth Rigel Daugherty, for example, argues that "at a time when the reader was scorned, attacked, ignored, and divided into classes, the barriers between 'art' and the 'masses' were getting higher and higher, and 'high modernism' was practicing detachment and disdain, Woolf chose to invoke and address common readers" (170). I am more inclined to see Woolf herself as divided—unable to settle on a fixed position as to how large and diverse her proper audience should be. For views similar to mine, see Mares 131, and Lee 438.

[3] See Lee 438-440 on Woolf's ambivalent feelings about success and fame in the years 1920-22.

[4] Dubino notes that in "The Patron and the Crocus" Woolf figures the reader and writer as sexual partners, Siamese twins, and, finally, allies, "suggesting that the writer and reader are political entities whose alliance could result in a great republic of the imagination" (133). For other thoughtful expositions of the concept of the "common reader," see Rosenberg, who reads the common reader as a "rhetorical construct" used to set up a dialogic relationship between Woolf and the reader, and Froula, who views the common reader as a means of establishing "elastic and unstable boundaries" between reader and writer, resulting in "collaborative authority" over the text (519).

Rosenberg also provides a useful summary of earlier readings of the common reader as a democratic or egalitarian concept (7 n. 2).

Works Cited

Bell, Quentin. *Virginia Woolf.* Vol. 2. London: Hogarth Press, 1972.

Daugherty, Beth Rigel. "'Readin', Writin', and Revisin': Virginia Woolf's 'How Should One Read a Book?'" Dubino and Rosenberg, 159-76.

Dell, Penelope. *Nettie and Sissie: The Biography of Ethel M. Dell and Her Sister Ella.* London: Hamish Hamilton, 1977.

Dubino, Jeanne. "Creating 'The Conditions of Life': Virginia Woolf and the Common Reader." *Re: Reading, Re: Writing, Re: Teaching Virginia Woolf: Selected Papers from the Fourth Annual Conference on Virginia Woolf.* Ed. Eileen Barrett and Patricia Cramer. New York: Pace UP, 1995. 129-36.

Dubino, Jean and Beth Carole Rosenberg. *Virginia Woolf and the Essay.* New York: St. Martin's, 1997.

Froula, Christine. "Modernism, Genetic Texts, and Literary Authority in Virginia Woolf's Portraits of the Artist as Audience." *Romantic Review* 86.3 (1995): 513-16.

Lee, Hermione. *Virginia Woolf.* London: Chatto and Windus, 1996.

Mares, Cheryl. "Woolf and Her Contemporaries." Dubino and Rosenberg 159-76.

McAleer, Joseph. *Popular Reading and Publishing in Britain 1914-50.* Oxford: Clarendon Press, 1992.

Rosenberg, Beth. "Conversation and the Common Reader." *Virginia Woolf Miscellanies. Proceedings of the First Annual Conference on Woolf.* Ed. Mark Hussey and Vara Neverow-Turk. New York: Pace UP, 1992. 1-7.

Woolf, Virginia. "Anon." Ed. Brenda Silver. *Twentieth Century Literature* 25.3 & 4 (1979): 382-98.

——. *Between the Acts.* New York: HBJ, 1941.

——. *The Diary of Virginia Woolf.* Ed. Anne Olivier Bell with Andrew McNeillie. Vols. 2 and 5. New York and London: Harcourt Brace, 1980.

——. "George Moore." *Collected Essays.* Ed. Leonard Woolf. Vol. 1. London: Hogarth Press, 1966. 181-84.

——. *Letters of Virginia Woolf.* Ed. Joanne Trautmann and Nigel Nicolson. Vol. 5. New York and London: Harcourt Brace, 1979.

——. "The Patron and the Crocus." *Essays of Virginia Woolf.* Vol. 4. Ed. Andrew McNeillie, London: Hogarth Press, 1994. 212-15.

——. "Reviewing." *Collected Essays of Virginia Woolf.* Vol. 2. Ed. Leonard Woolf. London: Hogarth Press, 1966. 204-17.

——. "Why?" *Death of the Moth and Other Essays.* London: Hogarth Press, 1942. 144-49.

Zwerdling, Alex. "The Common Reader, the Coterie, and the Audience of One." Hussey and Neverow Turk 7-9.

Melba Cuddy-Keane
"A Standard of One's Own": Virginia Woolf and the Question of Literary Value

In my previous work on Woolf's essays, I focused on provisionality and positionality, highlighting the way Woolf exposes underlying assumptions and ideologies and thus stimulates readers to read self-reflexively and dialogically (1996; 1997). I want here to turn to another facet of Woolf's "diamond shape": the Woolf who, by her own admission, is an "exacting" critic; the Woolf who, though lacking the Victorians' clear "standard of culture" to judge by, nevertheless advocates having a "standard of one's own."[1] Evaluative issues figure prominently in both her writing and her publishing career, as they do in the cultural debates of her time.

Not much is written today about evaluation. As Barbara Herrnstein Smith has noted, serious inquiry into literary value has been derailed in our century by axiological skepticism—skepticism about "the claim of certain norms, standards, and judgments to objective validity" (54)—and by feminist and postcolonial critiques of the embedded ideological biases in our value systems. Millennial consciousness has evidently rekindled the desire to reify cultural monuments but, judging by the vigorous response in the electronic lists to which I subscribe, there is nothing so likely to provoke a reader's rage than the lists of "100 Greatest Works" or "100 Greatest Thinkers" that *other* people make.

Yet, day to day, our actions express and confirm evaluative measures. Why do we buy one book rather than another? Choose particular authors for our teaching or research? Speak with passion about one writer and find ourselves thoroughly bored by another? Why are we interested in the Virginia Woolf Conference? Why are we interested in English Literature at all?

We live in a constant paradox—unable to find a justificatory discourse for our values and yet constantly making evaluative choices in our daily acts. And this same paradox can be located in Woolf's own writings about books. How strongly she unmasks, in *A Room of One's Own,* the infiltration of socially gendered values into literary judgments: "This is an important book, the critic assumes, because it deals with war. This is an insignificant book because it deals with the feelings of women in a drawing room" (74). And Woolf goes further to interrogate the competitive ethic that underlies all fixing of labels of merit, as well as the positivist, empiricist discourse that asserts such labels can be fixed: "I do not believe," she writes, "that gifts, whether of mind or character, can be weighed like sugar and butter . . . . No, delightful as the pastime of measuring may be, it is the most futile of all occupations, and to submit to the decrees of the measurer the most servile of attitudes" (105-06). Yet, in this same work, Woolf criticizes Charlotte Brontë's awkward narrative transition in *Jane Eyre* and suggests that the promising contemporary novel by the fictional Mary Carmichael still leaves considerable room for improvement. And these are not slips of practice, for Woolf makes constant theoretical claims for the importance of evaluative acts. In "How Should One Read a Book?" Woolf locates the "true complexity of reading" in the difficult but necessary transition from the first stage of receiving impressions to the second stage of passing judgment, adding that readers must judge "with great sympathy and yet with great severity" (*CR2* 270). And, as she writes in "Phases of Fiction," making judgments is not only good reading practice; it is simply unavoidable: "nobody reads simply by chance or without a definite scale of values" (*CE2* 56).

Confronted with the problematic paradox of discredited judgments bound to the inevitable process of judging, Herrnstein Smith proposes an approach through "contingencies of value." Smith begins from a critique of "the two classic axiologies of Western critical theory" (55): Hume's "Of the Standard of Taste" (1757) and Kant's *Critique of Judgment* (1790). For Hume, common, universal values can be established rationally and logically through the best practices of the best critics, proved through the validating operations of time. In contrast, in Kant's idealist philosophy, a precognitive and disinterested apprehension of beauty justifies the claim of aesthetic judgments to universal validity. But despite their radically opposite epistemologies, Smith contends that both works are "transparently circular" and "self-canceling" (72). Analyzing the numerous "buts" in Hume's argument, Smith shows how his reasoned process of admitting exceptions ends by thoroughly excavating his general universalizing principles; in Kant, the problem lies in his numerous specifications of the conditions necessary for pure and disinterested judgment—conditions that require such an elimination of "contaminating" (69) circumstances that the experiencing subject is eliminated as well.

But for Smith, the failure of axiology does not leave us stranded in the subjective. "Subjective," she argues, implies "personally whimsical," applicable to the individual alone; in contrast, a theory of contingency approaches value as "a changing function of multiple variables"—variables determined by such factors as history, culture and situation (11; 15). In Smith's model, value is understood as a measure of how well a work performs a desired or desirable function for the community of readers who may at any time be involved with it. Value does not inhere in the work itself but is produced "by the dynamics of a system" (15)—a system that includes not only the value of the work for the reader but the reader's estimate of the probable value of the work for other people. And whereas for Hume the value of a work is ascertained through its lasting appeal to common human nature, Smith suggests that the survival of a work has more to do with its adaptability: works will survive in time if they can continue to relate in different ways to different questions readers bring to them; if they can be "amenable to multiple reconfiguration" (51).

The advantage of Smith's model is that it takes us beyond confrontations of differing values to an analysis of the way value operates. Instead of disputing the selections on the lists of 100 great books, we would analyze both the institutional production of value and the "*counter*mechanisms" within the community for challenging, contradicting, and subverting normative claims (40). Regarding Woolf, such analysis would mean both situating her evaluative discourse in relation to debates about literary value in her time and analyzing the multiple functions she performed within her career: as a reader for the press; as a private reader; as a public reviewer and critic; and as a feminist cultural worker. A reading thus grounded in what Smith defines as "the fundamental character of literary value, which is its mutability and diversity" (28), would release us from imposing or expecting consistency in Woolf's practices, countering what has been a prevailing tendency to treat Woolf herself as formalist text. We would never state simply "Woolf thought" but always specify that "Woolf wrote in this context, for this community, and with this function."

At the Hogarth Press, for example, Woolf made definitive value judgments, accepting or rejecting manuscripts. She recommended publication of two novels by the working-class writer John Hampson (John Simpson) but decided his next was "so bad" she had to advise against it (*D*4 142). She approved "a good MS by a man called Graham" and the Press published his novel *The Good Merchant* the following year (*D*4 195). As a reader/editor, Woolf had standards and used them, often, as we know, recording her response privately to herself, or to select correspondents, in acerbic terms.

Yet, in the full range of her editorial activity, her absolutes frequently had soft edges. Shortly after her death, John Lehmann wrote, "For years nearly all the manuscripts that were submitted to the Hogarth Press passed through her hands, and she was always anxious to encourage even the slightest signs of talent among newcomers, and to urge publication whenever it was possible" (45). And Woolf was ready to take chances on all kinds of writing, supporting the publication, for example, of an epic-length novel written by a salesman, which Willis describes as a "good read about the fortunes of a furniture store" (266). It may be simply our limited grasp of the range of Woolf's editorial interests that makes her mentoring of the 16-year old poet Joan Easdale appear "very odd" to J. H. Willis (187) and "peculiar" to Hermione Lee (615). While the Hogarth Press was undoubtedly implicated in the institutional production of value, Woolf's evaluative practice was not limited to "high modernist" principles and she combined her definitive editorial judgments with efforts to encourage new voices, and even voices antithetical to each other, to get into print.

Given this complexity, it is not surprising that Woolf should both excel at the delivery of sharp, opinionated views and yet, as an essayist, take an approach to value judgments that is questioning, problematizing, and self-reflexive. Frequently, she subjects conventional judgments to ideological critique. Although she seems surprisingly to repeat the cliché that Jane Austen was a limited writer who knew the wisdom of "never trespass[ing] beyond her boundaries" (*CR*1 137), Woolf then turns the word "limitation" around to expose its reverse side as the exercise of choice. "For example," Woolf continues, "she could not make a girl talk enthusiastically of banners and chapels."[2] Austen's ironic eye, Woolf implies, is skeptically trained on false homage; an absence of enthusiasm here, like the lack of charm and humor in George Eliot, is a mark not of failure but of a "difference of view," a "difference of standard" (*CR*1 171).

At other times, Woolf's scrutinizing lens turns back on herself. Anatomizing Hemingway's strengths and weaknesses, she simultaneously critiques her own critical judgments. Her assumptions are revealed: "A prejudice of which the reader would do well to take account is here exposed; the critic is a modernist" (*E*4 451). Ultimately, she exposes the impurity, the perspicacity, indeed the whole ambiguity of the evaluative process: the essay ends, "So we reveal some of the prejudices, the instincts and the fallacies out of which what it pleases us to call criticism is made" (455).

Using yet another technique, Woolf contextualizes value through acts of settling and unsettling. "Modern Fiction" is known for its opening advocacy of modernism, but equally crucial to this essay is the subsequent shifting of perspective. Having upheld Joyce and Chekhov over Wells, Bennett, and Galsworthy, Woolf twists around to expose the modernists' limitations. Joyce's treatment of indecency is too didactic; the Russians lack the English "instinct to enjoy and fight rather than to suffer and understand" (*CR*1 154). The essay as a whole takes us far beyond its opening "modernist manifesto" and depicts the history of the novel as a process of endless substitution. Every lack becomes the ground for further change and innovation, and no form constitutes a final, immutable repository of value.

You may have noticed that, by adopting Herrnstein Smith's model of functionalism, I have shifted the discussion of value back to provisionality and positionality. But what if I shift outside Smith's discourse and approach Woolf from the opposite phenomenological view? For Smith stays within the discourse of logic and rationality—appropriate for analyzing Hume, who works from a reasoned ground himself, but less so for Kant, for whom the aesthetic is a precognitive apprehension, existing *a priori* to analyzable experience.[3] By her own admission, Smith subjects Kant's account of the conditions of disinterested judgment to a late twentieth-century understanding of identity, in which there is no possibility of a self existing apart from the multiply contingent contexts of language, culture, and individual history. What Smith overlooks is that, using a different cognitive model, Kant locates "pure" sensation outside the realm of knowledgeable experience and thus beyond the bounds of logical disputation.

Given Woolf's critique of the limitations of rational thought, we might expect that, like Kant, she would situate value outside logical analysis. However, there is little in her writing to suggest she upheld a transcendent, universal ideal of beauty. It is true that she defined the modernist writer as "spiritual" but she also illustrated "the flickerings of that innermost flame" (*CR*1 151) with the cemetery scene in *Ulysses*—a scene redolent with Bloom's thoughts about "corpse manure" and the "tallowy kind of cheesy" of decomposing bodies (*Ulysses* 108). Woolf's "turn" on spirituality undermines its conventional Victorian associations and links it instead with the body and the "dark places of psychology" (*CR*1 152). Her troping reflects what Northrop Frye identified as Romanticism's reversal of the traditional topos for the journey of identity: metaphors of heaven and ascent into a higher transcendent reality are rewritten as metaphors of descent into sensual unconscious life (64-66).

It is in these terms that Woolf's theory incorporates a non-rational apprehension of value, an intuitive judgment deriving not from a Kantian supersensual imagination but from a Woolfian "undermind"—a level of unconscious or preconscious activity integral to both writing and reading. For Woolf, a crucial touchstone of value is a writer's "sincerity" or "conviction," a quality hard to define but achieved when, free from all conscious impediment, a writer's perceptions and perspective are communicated whole and entire.[4] In turn, we as readers sense a writer's conviction when the text sinks into the depths of our minds, when "we seem not to read so much as to recollect what we have heard in some other life" (*E*2 115). The judgments we then make about a writer's sincerity depend upon such seemingly subjective elements as "taste" and "feeling" (*CR*2 268) but, though fallible, this process is not merely personal and provisional. The activity of the "undermind" engages our unconscious memory of everything we have read, ideally—and this connects to her urging the widest reading possible—the collective, textual unconscious of the human race. By drawing on common emotion and collective knowledge, these judgments reach toward a "universal validity" (*E*3 489) even while recognizing their basis in the emotional impact of the work on the individual reader.

In the context of the twenties and thirties, Woolf's evaluative practice offered a significant alternative to the ongoing debates about standards. While Pound and Leavis were busy constructing lists for readers to read, though clashing over whether the canon should be Classical or English,[5] Woolf tried instead to give readers the tools for making choices for themselves. The title for my talk comes from Woolf's 1924 contribution to the journal of the Worker's Educational Association, as part of a symposium on the question, "What is a Good Novel?" While most contributors tried to specify the textual features that constitute good novel writing, Woolf characteristically emphasized the reader's activity, urging her readers to engage in the ceaseless, ever-changing process of devising "a standard of one's one."

In our own time, Woolf's approach continues to offer an empowering countermechanism for challenging the burgeoning lists, perhaps answering Smith's call for "a non-canonical theory of value and evaluation" (24). Woolf avoids the axiological imperative, contextualizing value in relation to the needs of the historical moment and the ideologies of individual readers. At the same time, Woolf's model of contingency is doubled by a belief in the importance of intuitive, preconscious responses, informed by the assimilated knowledge of all our reading. Given our current interest in cognitive models, Woolf's practice thus articulates a stimulating and possibly importable paradigm for valuation theory—a tri-part process comprising (1) definitive judgments for practical action; (2) reflective speculation about our underlying assumptions; and (3) intuitive responses based on unconscious processing. I got drawn into explaining what my paper was about to my mother's stockbroker who responded, "Wow. That's great. That's exactly what I do when I evaluate stocks!" An extreme but possibly useful example of Woolf's adaptability, demonstrating Smith's point that works will survive in time if they can continue to relate in different ways to different questions readers bring to them; if they can be "amenable to multiple reconfiguration."

Notes

[1] The words and phrases in quotations marks are taken from *Mrs. Dalloway* (38), "Modern Fiction" (*CR1* 148), "The Modern Essay" (*CR1* 215) and "What is a Good Novel?" (110).

[2] Woolf refers here to the chapel scene in Chapter 9 of *Mansfield Park*—a scene that may well be an allusive intertext in Woolf's more stringent critique of imperialism and church-going in Chapter 17 of *The Voyage Out*. Woolf presumably has in mind Mary Crawford's lively puncturing of the hypocrisy of religious observances. Woolf may have misremembered Fanny's longing for the poetry of banners—or she may be crediting Austen's light touch in adumbrating Fanny's possibly naïve attachment to a romantic past.

[3] I would like to thank a former graduate student, Paul Lamarre, for prompting me to question the boundaries of Smith's discourse.

[4] Ellen Tremper similarly identifies "conviction" as an important valuative word for Woolf, associating it as well with the unimpeded activity of the unconscious in the initial stages of both creation and reception.

[5] For their different approaches to a common desire for canon formation, see Ezra Pound, *How to Read* (London 1931) and F. R. Leavis, *How to Teach Reading: A Primer for Ezra Pound* (Cambridge 1932).

Works Cited

Cuddy-Keane, Melba. "The Rhetoric of Feminist Conversation: Virginia Woolf and the Trope of the Twist." *Ambiguous Discourse: Feminist Narratology and British Women Writers*. Ed. Kathy Mezei. Chapel Hill: U of North Carolina P, 1996: 137-61.

——. "Virginia Woolf and the Varieties of Historicist Experience." *Virginia Woolf and the Essay*. Ed. Beth Carole Rosenberg and Jeanne Dubino. New York: St. Martin's, 1997: 59-77.

Frye, Northop. *Fables of Identity: Studies in Poetic Mythology*. New York: Harcourt, Brace and World, 1963.

Joyce, James. *Ulysses*. New York: Random House, 1966.

Lee, Hermione. *Virginia Woolf*. London: Chatto and Windus, 1996.

Lehmann, John. *In My Own Time: Memoirs of a Literary Life*. Boston: Little, Brown, 1969.

Smith, Barbara Herrnstein. *Contingencies of Value: Alternative Perspectives for Critical Theory*. Cambridge, Mass.: Harvard UP, 1988.

Tremper, Ellen. *"Who Lived at Alfoxton?": Virginia Woolf and Romanticism*. Lewisburg: Bucknell UP, 1998.

Willis, J. H., Jr. *Leonard and Virginia Woolf as Publishers: The Hogarth Press, 1917-41.* Charlottesville: U of Virginia P, 1992.

Woolf, Virginia. *Collected Essays.* Vol. 2. Ed. Leonard Woolf. London: Hogarth, 1967.

——. *The Common Reader: First Series.* 1925. Ed. Andrew McNeillie. New York: Harcourt, 1984.

——. *The Common Reader: Second Series.* 1932. Ed. Andrew McNeillie. New York: Harcourt, 1986.

——. *The Diary of Virginia Woolf.* Ed. Anne Olivier Bell. 5 vols. New York: Harcourt, 1977-84.

——. *The Essays of Virginia Woolf.* 4 vols. to date. Ed. Andrew McNeillie. London: Hogarth, 1986-.

——. *Mrs. Dalloway.* 1925. San Diego: Harcourt, 1981.

——. *A Room of One's Own.* 1929. San Diego: Harcourt, 1981.

——. "What is a Good Novel?" *The Highway: A Journal of Adult Education*, 16.3 (Summer 1924): 109-10.

John Young
Canonicity and Commercialization in Woolf's Uniform Edition

This paper considers Virginia Woolf the publisher alongside Virginia Woolf the author. While the Hogarth Press has long been known for making Woolf "the only woman in England free to write what I like," it also made her free to be published as she liked. Hogarth, Jane Marcus argues, "gave Woolf a way of negotiating the terms of literary publicity, and a space somewhere between the private, the côterie, and the public sphere" (144-5). I will examine one such negotiation, the Uniform Edition of Woolf's works, a series designed to capitalize on her growing recognition and marketability. Once the Woolfs had become, in Leonard's words, "more or less ordinary publishers" (Rosenbaum, 7), they began marketing their books in "more or less ordinary" ways, and these included a construction of Woolf through the Uniform Edition as both canonical and commercial, a crucial combination, I will conclude, for modernist women writers.[1]

Focusing on the publishing dynamics of Woolf's books offers a more fully historicized portrait of her career. I address the Uniform Edition through what George Bornstein calls the "textual aura" (226), a version of Walter Benjamin's aura updated to include the notions of textual materiality emphasized by Jerome McGann and Peter Shillingsburg. Reproductions which ignore a book's textual aura, Bornstein demonstrates, "tend to set the text free from its original time and place, locating it in our own principally as an aesthetic rather than historicized object" (225). There is a certain irony in applying Benjamin's original notion of aura to mechanically printed books, which can never be "authentic" objects in his sense. But while books may exemplify Benjamin's maxim that "the work of art reproduced becomes the work of art designed for reproducibility" (224), publishers still manufacture some mark of originality in first, and especially limited, editions.[2] A book that appears in "only" 100 copies, for example, creates in its consumers a sense of authenticity, if on a smaller scale than other art objects. Since all Woolf's books from *Jacob's Room* on bore the line "Published by Leonard & Virginia Woolf at the Hogarth Press," by investigating the Woolfs' publishing decisions we can also interpret her texts' material codes.

The Uniform Edition made Woolf's works more accessible than ever before, creating a textual aura that manifests itself in the books' own commodification. Hogarth historian J. H. Willis, Jr., explains:

> To put a living novelist's works into a standard edition is to make a claim for the permanence and importance of the writer's work, to establish a canon, suggest the classic. All the more interesting and revealing is such a development when the novelist is in mid-career, forty-seven years old, and a partner in the publishing firm. By their editorial decision, the Woolfs seem to have declared publicly the commercial value of Virginia's novels and their claim to artistic greatness (156).

Hogarth's Autumn 1929 catalog announced five new publications from its most prominent author: the first four Uniform Editions (*The Voyage Out*, *Jacob's Room*, *Mrs Dalloway*, and *The Common Reader*) and *A Room of One's Own*. Perhaps surprisingly (from our contemporary perspective), the catalog lists the reprint series first. The Uniform Edition appeared with this blurb (probably written by Woolf herself)[3]: "The Hogarth Press begins this autumn the publication of a cheap uniform edition, of small and convenient size, of the works of Virginia Woolf. Of the four volumes now published *Jacob's Room* and *Mrs Dalloway* have been out of print for some time." At 5s. each, the Uniform Editions were the same price as the regular first edition of *Room*, a reduction designed in response, we can assume, to that book's £2 2s. special edition, limited to 100 copies and signed by the author.

In this catalog, we see Hogarth's twin engines of literary commodification at work: the Uniform Edition, frequently advertised as "New and Cheap," capitalizes on Woolf's growing marketability and recognition to encourage the consumption and collection of all her works. At the same time, the limited edition of *Room* motivates a different consumer response, the desire to own a special literary object, signed by the author herself. By no small coincidence, 1929 was Woolf's second-most profitable year as an author, earning her nearly £3000 (or enough for six rooms of her own), and surpassed only slightly by the enormous success of *The Years* (Lee, 550). Woolf's new readers, who had discovered her in *To the Lighthouse* or in the very popular *Orlando*, could now easily and inexpensively begin retracing their steps through her career. As the catalog notes, *Jacob's Room* and *Mrs. Dalloway*, the two most desirable entries so far, were then out of print, thus making them particularly appealing to readers who had come lately to Woolf's work. By issuing the Uniform Editions as part of an expanding set—the back jacket for each publication lists both those titles already published in the series and those that were "In Preparation"—Hogarth fosters its consumers' desire to own an entire collection.

"Virginia Woolf" the brand name thus becomes legible as both canonically and commercially significant: aesthetically important enough to merit a "permanent edition" (*L4* 68) as Woolf called it, and popular enough to sell well in both limited and "cheap" editions. This authorial image stands in marked contrast to the one Woolf cultivates in *A Room of One's Own*, her other publication of 1929. There, Woolf portrays herself in an ongoing dialogue with her audience, the opposite version of textual authority from Charles Lamb's image of Milton. As Christine Froula concludes, texts like *Room* "actively invest authority in the audiences they both mirror and hail into being" (525). But the implicit claim of the Uniform Edition shifts its author back into a more Miltonic mode: Woolf represents herself here as the kind of stable authority for whom Lamb could think "changing the words in that poem seemed to him a kind of sacrilege" (*AROO* 7). Just as Woolf knows Milton's poem and Thackeray's novels in their public, stable forms, so too can her audience now engage a uniform version of her texts. Readers interested in *The Voyage Out*, for example, which had appeared in different English and American editions, now have one text stamped by the author and publisher as *the* standard edition. Whereas Milton's early versions of *Lycidas* were available only to the Oxbridge library's male visitors, the competing versions of *Voyage* were both, albeit briefly, in circulation from the Hogarth Press, with the Uniform Edition identified as the preferred, or "permanent," version. (I will return to this example below.) The Woolf of the Uniform Editions thus does *not* tell her audience "call me Mary Beton, Mary Seton, Mary Carmichael or by any name you please—it is not a matter of any importance" (*AROO* 5), because she must remain recognizable as "Virginia Woolf" the brand-name. Once *Room* appeared in the Uniform series, in 1930, its linguistic leanings toward feminist versions of authority began to intersect with its new bibliographical markings of a textual monument. Far from the anonymity dictated to female authors, Woolf canonizes herself in the Uniform *Room* as a timeless author for her readers to "think back through" (76).

The Uniform Edition of *The Voyage Out*, apparently the only one with significant linguistic differences from previous editions (Willis, 155), presents a special case for this kind of authorial refashioning because of its now well-known textual history. In the original edition of Woolf's first novel, published by Duckworth in 1915, Chapter XVI includes several scenes Woolf cut for its American publication in 1920. When Duckworth reissued *Voyage* and *Night and Day* in 1920, and again in 1927, he purchased the sheets from the American edition, thus keeping the shorter version in circulation. As Louise A. DeSalvo notes, the original edition "presents Rachel and Terence Hewet

Pressing the Public Sphere

together alone for the longest period of time in the novel. It is the one glimpse provided of the kind of life they might have shared had Rachel lived long enough to become Terence's wife" (344). Rachel and Terence agree to call each other by their first names and discuss the gendered division of societal roles, including Rachel's anxiety over prostitution. This version of Chapter XVI, as several critics have noted, is a more overtly feminist one in contrast to the more muted novel which crossed the Atlantic.

In 1929, Hogarth bought both sets of sheets from Duckworth and sold two different copies of the novel: first in its American version as a "Third Impression," and then with the cut sections restored for the Uniform Edition, set from the sheets of the original Duckworth publication and listed as a "New Edition" on the copyright page. According to Woolf bibliographer B. J. Kirkpatrick there were apparently 500 copies available of the "Third Impression" (and 100 sold), compared to 3200 copies published for the "New Edition" (6). This switch has been the source of some confusion among Woolf scholars; Willis, for example, finds it "curious" that "the text so carefully reworked by Woolf was never reprinted by the Hogarth Press" (155). In Hogarth's 1990 edition, Elizabeth Heine speculates that Woolf may have "decided that the changes she had made for the American edition . . . reflected not what she had accomplished in publishing the novel in 1915, but the rejection of everyday detail and the development of new forms with which she was experimenting five years later" (400).

By examining the textual aura of the Uniform *Voyage*, we can find other explanations for Woolf's decision in the crucial difference between publishing her first novel with her abusive half-brother in 1915 and republishing it as the best-known and best-selling author of her own firm in 1929. The back jacket, with its list of those volumes "Already Published" and "In Preparation," establishes Woolf's growing and self-made canon. As a Hogarth edition of the novel, the Uniform *Voyage* thus provides Woolf the opportunity to re-make her Duckworth books. By censoring her more daring feminist statements, Woolf produced an arguably more commercial version of her first novel. But at the same time, she reclaimed her textual authority from Duckworth's social power. "She did not want to go on being censored or controlled" by Duckworth, Hermione Lee writes of the decision to make Hogarth Woolf's sole British publisher (369). By restoring *Voyage's* original text for Hogarth's 1929 publication, Woolf casts aside the Duckworth imprint from her first novel and remakes it on her own terms, as the opening volume in Hogarth's "Collected Edition" of her works (*D3* 225). Textual cuts that may once have represented both an accession to commercial interests and an aversion to Duckworth's textual authority could now be restored under the sign of Woolf's own commercial and canonical success.

By re-producing *The Voyage Out* in the Uniform Edition, Woolf monumentalizes her textual authority in a book that marks itself as relatively stable and timeless (even if it would not seem sacrilegious to imagine Woolf changing the words). Simultaneously, she restores a text which had questioned the gender imbalances of literary and social history. "'Just consider,'" Terence tells Rachel in one of the passages deleted for the American edition, "'it's the beginning of the twentieth century and until a few years ago no woman had ever come out by herself and said things at all. There it was going on in the background, for all those thousands of years, this curious silent unrepresented life'" (200). In order to narrate this "unrepresented life," Woolf faced the perpetual feminist choice of working within the established system or of creating new structures outside the tradition. Through her publishing practices, Woolf merged both options, fashioning herself as a commercial and canonical authority.

This merger of canonicity and commercialization is, I conclude, the most significant feature of the Uniform Edition's textual aura. Critical accounts of modernism have tended to privilege self-consciously high-cultural books and their publishing histories, presenting modernism as distanced from mainstream audiences rather than in its complex interactions with popular culture and commercialism. This perspective ignores the role of publishers as a gateway into literary culture; the absence of almost any women from publishing power, especially among mainstream presses, created special problems for female modernists. For women writers, the market was often the only way into the canon, so commodification became the sole available means of establishing textual authority. In contrast to Fredric Jameson's insistence that "for modernism, the commodity form signals the vocation *not* to be a commodity, to devise an aesthetic language incapable of offering commodity satisfaction, and resistant to instrumentalization" (16), we can see in Woolf's publishing decisions the blending of commercial appeal with her aesthetic language. In April 1921, while at work on *Jacob's Room* and gloomy over the slow sales of *Monday or Tuesday*, Woolf mused, "What depresses me is the thought that I have ceased to interest people—at the very moment, when, by the help of the press, I thought I was becoming more myself. One does *not* want an established reputation, such as I think I was getting, as one of our leading female novelists" (*D2* 107). Woolf worries that, on the heels of the more conventional novel *Night and Day*, she may be lumped together with the "leading female novelists"—such as Duckworth's best-selling Elinor Glyn, for example—as a popular producer of domestic fiction. Hogarth's freedom, by contrast, produces "that queer, & very pleasant sense, of something which I want to write; my own point of view. I wonder, though, whether the feeling that I write for half a dozen instead of 1500 will pervert this?— make me eccentric,—no, I think not" (*D2* 107). As a publisher, Woolf went on to rewrite the connotations of being a "leading novelist" by constructing an authorial space from which the market need not negate the canon. As books like the Uniform Editions attest, Woolf found an audience far larger than half a dozen or even 1500, and with it, the ability to revise the patriarchal traditions associated with canonical and commercial success. While Woolf remained ambivalent about the consequences of her marketability, she also began to embrace her economic power, for what it meant both as an author and an employer. Writing in April, 1929, she reflected: "And 7 people now depend on us; & I think with pride that 7 people depend, largely, upon my hand writing on a sheet of paper. That is of great solace & pride to me. Its not scribbling; its keeping 7 people fed and housed ... they live on my words. They will be feeding well off Women & Fiction next year for which I predict some sale (*D3* 221). Woolf was correct, of course, about the sales of *Women & Fiction* under its revised title and about her existing commercial status at its publication; after earning just more than £2000 in 1929, Woolf was free to construct her own public image (*Downhill*, 64). After all, as she would conclude in *A Room of One's Own*, "Intellectual freedom depends upon material things" (108).

Notes

[1] This paper is part of a larger study, in which I argue that modernist women writers, who found the greatest freedom from publishers' reinscription of patriarchal traditions by publishing themselves, fashioned their own brand of cultural capital by directly engaging relatively popular markets. I focus primarily on Woolf and Hogarth and Gertrude Stein and the Plain Edition, published by Alice B. Toklas.

[2] Bornstein notes that, "Although Benjamin himself saw the aura as 'withering' in the age of mechanical reproduction, we may revise Benjamin by emphasizing that, for literary works, original mechanical reproductions can create their own aura and that it is the earlier auras that wither under successive reproductions of the work, particularly if the 'work' is thought of as identical merely to its words" (224). I concur that books produced in special or limited editions—or in editions that become rare regardless of publishers' intentions—aim for a diluted sense of Benjamin's aura, as they mark themselves implicitly as rarer and thus more "authentic" than versions of the same work produced in popular editions.

[3] "Given the small organization of the Hogarth Press," S. P. Rosenbaum surmises of the jacket copy for Woolf's books, "it is reasonable to conclude that these blurbs were written by the author. And who wrote the copy for the Hogarth Press's catalogue announcements of the Woolfs' books? Again these descriptions can be considered authorial—or quasi-authorial, perhaps, if Leonard wrote them with Virginia's approval" (22-3). The interaction between Woolf's "outside" and "inside" writing is a fruitful area for study. The original jacket copy for *A Room of One's Own*, for example, states simply, "The conditions that are favourable to imaginative work are discussed, including the right relation of the sexes" (*Women & Fiction*, xli), in what seems a watering down of *Room*'s internal argument for the popular audience of bookshop browsers.

[4] Quoted from the collection of the Manuscripts, Archives, and Special Collections office at the Washington State University Library.

[5] No doubt part of the financial success of these years derived from the cheaper printing costs of the Uniform Editions. As Willis explains, the "inexpensive trade edition meant to the press greater ease of production, lower reprinting costs, and certain marketing advantages in the attractive, uniform volumes" (155-6). Edward L. Bishop notes that the Uniform jackets' hand-drawn designs "preserve the link with the avant-garde, [while] the jade-green cloth boards with the gold lettering on the spine assert Woolf's entry into the literary establishment" (58).

[6] As Leonard Woolf notes, *Orlando* was "the turning-point in Virginia's career as a successful novelist" (143). In all, she earned slightly more than £3700 on her books between 1928 and 1929.

[7] On the author as a brand name, see Andrew Wernick, "Authorship and the supplement of promotion," in *What Is An Author?*, eds. Maurice Biriotti and Nicola Miller (Manchester: Manchester University Press, 1993).

[8] In discussion following the conference panel, Julia Briggs said Woolf made other revisions in Uniform texts as well. I hope soon to collate the Uniform and later editions, but at present I am certainly willing to take Briggs at her word. Assuming such revisions to be present, the Uniform Edition would represent another instance of Woolf's post-publication revising habits, similar to the changes made between English and American editions, but now more in line with Henry James's famous revisions for the New York Edition of his works. See *Henry James's New York Edition: The Construction of Authorship*, ed. David McWhirter (Stanford: Stanford University Press, 1995).

[9] Hogarth's standard practice was to list each Uniform Edition as a "New Edition." While not technically true from a bibliographer's point of view, the new cover does create a new version. As Hans Zeller argues, "Since a text, as text, does not in fact consist of elements but of the relationships between them, variation at one point has an effect on invariant sections of the text. ... A new version implies a new intention" (241).

[10] In their introduction to the Shakespeare Head Press edition, C. Ruth and Lawrence Miller conclude that the switch was purely a financial decision by Leonard Woolf, made after Richard Kennedy had ordered the wrong size paper for the Uniform Edition (xxx). As the Millers note, references in Woolf's diaries and letters to the Uniform Edition are scarce, but it still seems likely that she was more than "indifferent" (xxx) about which version of her novel would launch the series.

[11] On this topic, see especially Shari Benstock, *Women of the Left Bank: Paris, 1900-1940* (Austin: University of Texas Press, 1986), and *The Gender of Modernism: A Critical Anthology*, ed. Bonnie Kime Scott (Bloomington: Indiana University Press, 1990).

[12] Rosenbaum describes Glyn's books as "forgettable but immensely popular romantic novels of passion on tiger-skin rugs" (13). After the initial strong sales for *The Waves* began to fade, Woolf worried again that she was "in danger, indeed, of becoming our leading novelist, and not with the highbrows only" (*D4* 49). Woolf's concern that she will become a "leading novelist," like her anxiety about that phrase following the reception of *Night and Day*, addresses the anxiety of her joint commercial and intellectual public presences.

Works Cited

Benjamin, Walter. "The Work of Art in the Age of Mechanical Reproduction." In *Illuminations*. Ed. Hannah Arendt. New York: Schocken Books, 1968.

Bishop, Edward L. "From Typography to *Time*: Producing Virginia Woolf." In *Virginia Woolf: Texts and Contexts*. Eds. Beth Rigel Daugherty and Eileen Barrett. NY: Pace University Press, 1996. 50-63.

Bornstein, George. "Yeats and Textual Reincarnation: 'When You Are Old' and 'September 1913.'" In *The Iconic Page in Manuscript, Print, and Digital Culture*. Eds. Bornstein and Theresa Tinkle. Ann Arbor: University of Michigan Press, 1998. 223-248.

DeSalvo, Louise A. "Woolf's Revisions for the 1920 American and English Editions of *The Voyage Out*." *Bulletin of Research in the Humanities* 82 (1979): 338-366.

Froula, Christine. "Modernism, Genetic Texts and Literary Authority in Virginia Woolf's Portraits of the Artist as the Audience." *The Romanic Review* 86 (1995): 513-526.
Heine, Elizabeth. "Virginia Woolf's Revisions to *The Voyage Out*." In *The Voyage Out: The Definitive Collected Edition.* Ed. Heine. London: Hogarth Press, 1990.
Jameson, Fredric. *Postmodernism, or, The Cultural Logic of Late Capitalism.* Durham: Duke University Press, 1991.
Kirkpatrick, B. J. *A Bibliography of Virginia Woolf.* Third ed. Oxford: Clarendon Press, 1980.
Lee, Hermione. *Virginia Woolf.* New York: Alfred A. Knopf, 1997.
Marcus, Jane. "Virginia Woolf and the Hogarth Press." In *Modernist Writers and the Marketplace.* Eds. Ian Willison, Warwick Gould, and Warren Chernaik. New York: St. Martin's Press, 1996. 124-150.
McGann, Jerome. *The Textual Condition.* Princeton: Princeton University Press, 1991.
Rosenbaum, S. P. "Leonard and Virginia Woolf at the Hogarth Press." University of Texas Faculty Seminar on British Studies. Austin: Harry Ransom Humanities Research Center, 1995.
Shillingsburg, Peter L. *Resisting Texts: Authority and Submission in Constructions of Meaning.* Ann Arbor: University of Michigan Press, 1997.
Willis, J. H., Jr. *Leonard and Virginia Woolf as Publishers: The Hogarth Press, 1917-41.* Charlottesville: University Press of Virginia, 1992.
Woolf, Leonard. *Downhill All the Way: An Autobiography of the Years 1919-1939.* London: The Hogarth Press, 1967.
Woolf, Virginia. *The Diary of Virginia Woolf.* Ed. Anne Olivier Bell. Vols. 2-4. New York: HBJ, 1978, 1980, 1982.
——. *The Letters of Virginia Woolf.* Vol. 4. Eds. Nigel Nicolson and Joanne Trautmann. New York: HBJ, 1979.
——. *A Room of One's Own.* 1929. New York: HBJ, 1981.
——. *The Voyage Out.* 1915. London: Penguin Books, 1992.
——. *Women & Fiction: The Manuscript Versions of* A Room of One's Own. Ed. S. P. Rosenbaum. Oxford: Shakespeare Head Press, 1992.
Zeller, Hans. "A New Approach to the Critical Constitution of Literary Texts." *Studies in Bibliography* 28 (1975): 231-264.

Moving Images

Suzanne Bellamy
"Painting The Words": A Version of Lily Briscoe's Paintings from *To The Lighthouse*

Words and images, writing and visual art, writers and artists. The space between is as anarchic and vulnerable as the table in Lily's mind when she thinks of Mr. Ramsay: "It lodged now in the fork of a pear tree, its four legs in the air" (*TTL* 27). This complex geography, the domain of dual creativity, preoccupies me as an artist, writer, and Woolf researcher. Lily Briscoe's oeuvre and existence in Woolf is the diamond mine to which I return often, looking for the treasure, the place where the words and the painting meet. Woolf's great experiment with Lily Briscoe, creating the painter, the paintings, the process, the resolution of forms, continues to open to new exploration. It was probably only a matter of time before transference happened, and I crossed the anarchic line.

The idea to paint Lily's painting came to me on a walk down a dusty Australian country road early one morning. I have read *To The Lighthouse* many times, and felt growing in my brain the images enmeshed in the text. Now I wanted to see if there was really a more formal approach to this embedded visual text in the novel. Had anyone else painted the paintings? I knew only of the old video of *TTL* in a 1980s BBC production, with a misjudged impressionistic image of Lily's painting. I knew that wasn't right. What did it look like? There's the question. And of course I knew that Woolf had the ultimate freedom in this, because she could have several paintings floating at once, and had no restriction on producing the thing itself, the solid artifact. I felt, however, that she was serious about the painting in the novel, that it carried the form beyond the words, was the parallel text, or multiple text. The non-verbal gave deep structure to the work, and yet what can this mean in a book of words?

How complex this is. On the one hand there seems to be an acknowledgement, shared with Proust, that there is a territory where words cannot go, where something else must become the vehicle. At the same time, Woolf moves into the world I am calling the visual surreal, the place where visual form is forged out of a use of words that touches all the senses and bridges to a plane of multiple fusions. Cheryl Mares, in "Reading Proust: Woolf and the Painter's Perspective," explores this rich territory of the two writers' relationship to painting. Was this a literary game for Woolf, or could the paintings be made to work parallel to the words, in a parallel universe? The parallel universe can also work both ways, and the words themselves and their structures are changed by their dance with the visual.

Lily's paintings in the novel exist in several forms, in two versions ten years apart, and textually can also be seen as incorporating all her visual and thought impressions as she plays the part of the eyes of the novel. As an example, her vision of Mr. Ramsay's work as a scrubbed kitchen table, upsidedown in a pear tree, is pure surrealism and can be painted as such. Lily's paintings are her formal canvas, and her continuous process of seeing/feeling/ thinking/ transforming become her canvas-in-action, that place as she experiences her life, where everything changes, where alchemy happens. "It was when she took her brush in hand that the whole thing changed" (*TTL* 21).

It became a creative game between us, Lily and I, her elusive painting and my attempts to follow the signs and proceed to manifestation. There was an element of play from the beginning, hide and seek, synchronicity, the one in the other, all surrealist techniques (Chadwick). The surrealist form became the theme of the whole project. I did not want to illustrate the novel, I wanted to take Lily's journey in paint, and for this I wanted a companion.

Rules of the Game

I had met artist Isota Tucker Epes at the Woolf conference in St. Louis the previous year, and I immediately wrote to her to join me in the project. Each of us had produced art series on Woolf, and were equally very much intellectual in our approach as well. Two versions of this project, independently produced, would be a good base for this experiment. There would always be another way to see, to paint Lily's work, and Woolf's vision. Two was a good starting point. Our agreed brief was to paint Lily's painting, and in the process we would hope to shed some new light on the novel, perhaps to find another or parallel reading. Little did I know at that time that Isota and I would go on a complex journey, produce several paintings, destroy some, and even at the end know we hadn't really finished. This has been a rich mine indeed. The game involved Isota, me, and Virginia. Our agreement was to work completely uninfluenced by each other, an ocean apart for the whole time, and only finally to see each other's work when we opened our session at the conference. We kept to this deal, and only after the session, with J. J.Wilson, at a pub in Newark, could we unburden ourselves of the unexpected creative stresses of the journey. So intense were these that we are now embarking on *The Waves*, for 2000.

My Paintings... Method

The influence of my long and accumulated reading around the questions of Lily's painting had to be faced head on at this point. I had to move into the studio and away from the books and ideas, to let the form happen as Lily let it, in the mix of witness, thought, and process, down with the salt cellars and the tablecloth (*TTL* 100). From the start, in my mind I saw three paintings. No matter what I did, there they sat in my brain. I tried to blend them into one, in an early rejected version, which was useful and gave me the idea of the floating triangles/sails, but couldn't hold the power of the eclipse, which would not be denied.

I thought about Panthea Reid's description of the novel as tripartite (Reid 285), which had lodged in my mind like the table in the tree, but I disagreed with Reid's emphasis on Roger Fry as the dominant influence on Woolf/Briscoe. Lily was not in Fry territory any more. Something new was being discovered about the creative process and the new conflicting territories of modernism. I felt Woolf taking from many sources, deliberately and in a prefiguring way, with echoes not only of Cézanne but Matisse, Picasso, Kandinsky perhaps, and some early form of female surrealism, later flowering in Fini, Kahlo, Leonora Carrington (Chadwick).

I wasn't painting the novel though—I was adamant—but it sat there, in three, with one dominant starting point. And the dominant image was always the central panel, which in the beginning was black, a black panel. Clearly I was seeing the structure of the novel as a whole, and like an oriental triptych it could be read left to right, right to left, or focussed on the present middle with wings of past memory and future vision. Here the central panel was the deepest vision, contemporaneous presents. Here was the choice. Was this Lily's painting or Woolf's, and were they one? Lily became Woolf became Lily, and I became a voyager.

I wasn't painting the novel, I repeated, and all the more emphatically, as it became clearer in rereadings that several other embedded paintings floated within the text. In fact the whole novel bursts with individual creative projects. While Lily has the brushes and the easel, others paint in their minds, principally Mrs. Ramsay herself, who sees through the frame of the window at night and on the stairs, in the reverse to Lily (*TTL* 129-132).

The Panels

A lot of surrealist synchronicity followed. As I reread the novel, I was struck by the multiplicity of references to light and shadow, by the sun eclipsed, by the whole idea of the eclipse, after which shadows disappear, and a new light is born (e.g. *TTL* 88, 133, 143-147, 234-235). I knew Woolf had taken the 1927 journey to see the eclipse in Yorkshire, with Vita. The central panel, in my painting and in the novel, the thing which held it all together, was an eclipse, absence, the death of Mrs. Ramsay, the war, the loss of light and the loss of Vita?... an absent presence. Then my reading and seeing brought a different source of light to the foreground. It was not all black, it was not absence, it was not dark. My painting began to glow like a dark jewel, triangulations of deep purple and red light, an eclipsed solar light making it possible to SEE the inner forms of generated light in the earth, in life, inner life . . . it became exciting. I was seeing a densely alive void between states of ordinary perception. Was this the time before the solar god of patriarchy, a glimpse of the oldest earth energies, or the renewal or birthing of a new light source?

But then the oddest things began to happen. I had been reading Peter Conrad's *Modern Times, Modern Places* and imagining conversations between Stein, Einstein, Woolf, Proust, Marinetti on acceleration of time and the birth of new light and new colorfields. Diane Gillespie kindly answered email requests for comment. She told me about the new Jane Goldman book on Woolf (*Feminist Aesthetics*), and I immediately got it. Sun and Fish, Eclipse, Prismatics, Colour Theory. I was thrilled. Then I realised that the 1927 eclipse journey happened after *TTL* came out, a few months after in fact. Was it then the 1919 eclipse to which she was referring? Was she somehow prefiguring the 1927 eclipse? All through *TTL* there is a palpable experience of eclipse, of being there.

And then, one day on the radio, I heard that there was to be another eclipse in the UK, this year, the first full one on the mainland since 1927. . . August 11th 1999, and right over Talland House too. Was this a sign? Enough for me!

The other sections of the triptych then fell into place. The first became Lily's original attempt, her unfinished painting, and it was here I felt I allowed Lily to paint her thoughts, and to be the true surrealist painter I now came to see her to be. In an unfinished and perhaps unsuccessful attempt, Lily loads the painting with all the elements of the scene, house, window, chair, bay, black rock, lighthouse, the white wall and the jacmanna, the purple shadow on the steps, the light source from within (deliberate or a writer's folly?), and the tree with the upended table. Whether Woolf had at this time seen surrealist art or read surrealist material is still uncertain. Manuela Palacios has raised these general questions about Woolf and surrealism in recent conversations on the email Woolf list, deciding Woolf had not seen Dali's work before 1931, and suggesting surrealism may have been pollinating different artists in different countries in the same period of time(Woolf listserv, 29 Sept. 1999).

I was aware from reading Reid, Gillespie, and Hussey, that there was much speculation as to the possible source of the painting. Debates about the Madonna form of Mrs. Ramsay and James abound—and are uncontested by me —as do the extant photos of Woolf, her mother and brother on the steps of Talland House. I have incorporated a sketchy James and the wicker chair in the window. For me though, and for Lily, they are unfinished, unresolved, and in the final panel they disappear entirely, for all of us. There are other interesting new ideas about who Lily might be modeled upon, including the ideas of Jocelynne Harris from New Zealand who raises issues about the New Zealand painter Frances Hodgkins, at the 1999 Conference. There was also an Australian painter, Clarice Beckett, whose style and sensibility seemed to make her an ideal Lily model for me until I found that there was no clear evidence she had travelled abroad. Another Australian painter, Stella Bowen, visited Bloomsbury in the 20s, knew Mansfield and may have met Woolf. Her painting style certainly resonates with what we know about Lily (Modjeska). These are questions for future work, and I mention them here to make the point that older certainties are not settled on these issues. I take Diane Gillespie's argument that the influence of Fry on Woolf's ideas was declining by this time in the 20s, and she was drawing on many possible diverse sources and models. The creation of Lily Briscoe seems now to have been a truly multitudinous form.

Influenced by so many theories, rejecting old ways of seeing (including Mr Paunceforte), Lily nonetheless was not an abstract painter, not quite Vanessa Bell or Roger Fry. She was grasping for a new form. (Diane Gillespie remarked to me via email that she often thought of Lily's painting as like Vanessa Bell's painting *Studland Beach*, the rounded forms and color of that work.) I let Lily's way of seeing in the novel determine how she painted. She says that it's the jump between what one sees and what one can get down on the canvas where the failure happens. I let her try to fuse the two. She sees with a surrealist gaze, for me at least, but I don't want to overstate this to the exclusion of her formal commitment to modernist colorfields, energy patterns, and the decentred human. While the final painting is clearly fueled by memory, she also invokes her inner vision of the original scene to move towards a form of abstraction that has a mystical/transcendent aspect. It is a form of abstraction imbued with loving.

Mrs. Ramsay is the subject of her heart, her loving passion, clearly, and the core of the work, but the paintings bear witness also to the explosive dissolving of Mrs. Ramsay from the scene, from the composition. Or do they? Interestingly Isota and I both reached the dilemma of this central image, in the scene with Mrs. Ramsay to one side. Both of us took a predominantly surrealist approach (table in the tree and floating /buried triangle) and both of us grappled with the mystery about the shadow, the inner sources of light, both from within the window and from within the earth's surface. Never will I forget, in the session, Isota calmly telling us, "I finally found I had to murder Mrs. Ramsay." Tough love.

I would wake up each morning and see the panels in my mind. From the start, as well as the central black one, I also saw them standing vertically not horizontally. This also defied the convention of the horizontal/horizon, long inner views rather than wide scapes, a method used mainly by Oriental painters or those influenced by them. Only then did I see the matter of Lily's Chinese eyes, in three references (*TTL* 19,121). This somehow gave me the clue to how I was seeing the construction of the landscape itself, for there was a landscape . . . a view to the lighthouse. It was not a Western horizon at all;

Moving Images

the paintings became oriental in their depiction of the scene, travelling up and out to sea, like a Chinese road painting. Like Lily, I was freed from perspective altogether. This positioning held also for the eclipse view.

In each panel the solar light, afternoon, dark night, then morning, held the top right. Perspective shifted, but the formal elements of the story remained. Not abstraction, not impressionism, not strictly post impressionist formalism either. A fusion perhaps, but with, for me, a form closest to surrealism. This is clearest in the central panel, where the floating window holds the foreground, emitting a golden inner light but which is also just a shell. The earth is shrouded in the patterns of the overlayed lace tablecloth (Mrs. Ramsay, a whole way of life, the table), lit by the interior diamond clusters, crystalline forms of purple. The line of the coast, similar in each of the panels, draws in the energy of the outer earth, is shaped by it, and holds it like a crucible. Triangles unite all three panels, as do windows and the fugitive sun.

The third painting in the triptych held the key to the fate of Lily and the emotional form of the novel's resolution. I personally then realized in my reading I had moved from the elegiac, the loss of Lily's object of love, to her release and freedom, the birth of her free creative self in passing through the eclipse and to a new seeing, her own, on the white wall, a clean white canvas, white and uncompromising (*TTL* 181). Here again, after the work was done, I saw the role of the white wall in a new light. In the first painting, the wall is counterpoint to Mrs. Ramsay's triangular shadow in the window. The wall is white, bright, but also showcase to the brilliant jacmanna (*clematis jacmannii*, a very showy purple clematis popular in pre-war gardens.) [1] In my third panel, in Lily's new vision, the wall is empty, is open. It is her new canvas. Just as the purple triangle has been released from the window, so too the wall is no longer carrying anything but its own potency, its white emptiness, ready for new work.

The triangulations, which move from the shadow of Mrs. Ramsay in my first panel, through the deep glowing triangulations of the eclipse world, now burst from the window into the air, across the ocean, become the sails of the sea and fly up past the sun itself. Lily as artist and as independent woman is born in the process of seeing, painting, letting go and returning to her new vision, post eclipse. It is surrealist transformation.

Conclusion

As an experiment in transgression, this project has been very fruitful. In the end, no explanations here can encompass what is happening in the artwork. Things happened in the paintings which were not arbitrary, but which are not open to easy interpretation. Triangulations abounded, in the novel, in the paintings, in the collaboration with Isota and Virginia, in the biographical dimensions between Lily, Virginia, and Vanessa. So much of this project has also had the sense of homage. Mine to Woolf, Woolf's to Vanessa, Lily's to Mrs. Ramsay. What better form of loving than to enter the journey of creative process? Part of Woolf's achievement in *To The Lighthouse* surely is this one, to try to describe the path to creation through the field of the heart.

Something had happened to me in the process of the painting itself. Before I began, I had read Lily as still enmeshed in her loss and love for Mrs. Ramsay, and the words took me there. Now, through the paint, I had come to see Lily the artist as not enclosed in grieving at all, but as someone who had painted her way to a separate rebellious independent place, with a new and open white canvas. Is this an indication of a creative tension in the novel, a contradiction, or the true center of Woolf's vision for Lily? The latter I think, and certainly the conclusion of my own journey.

Note

[1] *Clematis jacmannii*, the jacmanna prominent in the first section of the novel, and in my panel by the white wall, acting as counterpoint to the purple shadow of Mrs. Ramsay, created a lively discussion in the session. I had thought it was Nelly Moser but several people, principally Jean Moorcroft-Wilson, emphatically asserted otherwise. It seemed somehow significant that Woolf scholars also knew a lot about clematis, more perhaps than Woolf herself. The clematis mystery game deepened for me when I was on my last flight, across America, before the Conference, seated next to a woman reading a French manuscript. At baggage claim in Baltimore, she picked up a huge box. "What's in there?" I asked. "Clematis," she said. Mmmmm.

Works Cited

Chadwick, Whitney. *Women Artists and the Surrealist Movement*. London: Thames and Hudson, 1985.

Conrad, Peter. *Modern Times, Modern Places. Life and Art in the 20th Century*. Hong Kong: Thames and Hudson, 1998.

Gillespie, Diane F., Ed. *The Multiple Muses of Virginia Woolf*. Columbia and London. University of Missouri Press, 1993.

——. *The Sisters' Arts. The Writing and Painting of Virginia Woolf and Vanessa Bell*. New York: Syracuse University Press, 1988.

——.(ed.) *Roger Fry*. Oxford: Shakespeare Head Press. Blackwell,1995.

Goldman, Jane. *The Feminist Aesthetics of Virginia Woolf. Modernism, Post-Impressionism and the Politics of the Visual*. Cambridge: Cambridge University Press, 1998.

Hussey, Mark. *Virginia Woolf A to Z*. New York: Oxford UP, 1995.

Mares, Cheryl. "Reading Proust : Woolf and the Painter's Perspective." *The Multiple Muses of Virginia Woolf*. Ed. Diane Gillespie. Columbia and London: University of Missouri Press, 1993. 58-89.

Modjeska, Drusilla. *Stravinsky's Lunch*. Pan Macmillan Australia, 1999.

Reid, Panthea. *Art and Affection. A Life of Virginia Woolf*. New York: Oxford UP, 1996.

Woolf, Virginia. *To The Lighthouse*. London: Dent. Everymans Library, 1938. Australia, 1999.

Moving Images

The Lighthouse

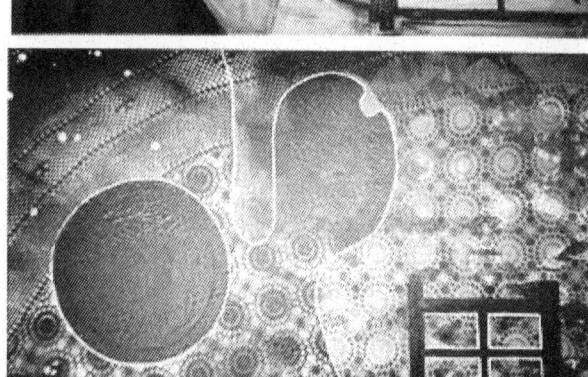

Time Passes

The Window
Triptych, acrylic on canvas

Isota Tucker Epes
The Liberation of Lily Briscoe

When my fellow artist Suzanne Bellamy telephoned me from Australia in January 1999 to suggest that we each paint a version of Lily Briscoe's canvas and write a paper on the process of completing the picture, I thought it was a marvelous idea. Little did I suspect what lay ahead!

I have always loved *To the Lighthouse* since I first read it in 1933 at age 15; moreover, I have read and reread it at various stages of my long life and have assigned it many times to my English classes, teaching it each time from a slightly different perspective, but always finding it, from my own personal standpoint, an example of literature at its best. Yet never in all those years did I think it contained one of Woolf's strong political statements. Now, converted by my own painting of Lily's canvas, I have completely changed my mind, and the purpose of this paper is to explain how that came about.

When I set out on this project in February, I began by reviewing my series of paintings entitled "An Essay: Virginia Woolf," which I exhibited at the Third Woolf Conference in 1993. Each of these pictures contained an image of Woolf at a certain stage in her career and each tried to depict one or another of the concepts she was exploring at the time in her writing. It was interesting to look at the slides of those canvases, gone to new owners for almost a decade, and to remember the excitement of working on them day after day. Curiously, though, the images themselves were of no help to me at all in envisioning Lily's painting.

At this point I was completely baffled as to why, having done the earlier series, this Briscoe project was giving me so much trouble. The reason, I have decided now, is this. Normally, when a visual artist's goal is to communicate an abstract idea, she selects an image or a variety of images treated in a specific way and placed in a certain relationship to each other; this arrangement, she believes, speaks for her.

In *To the Lighthouse*, Woolf gives us a few of the specific images employed by Lily in her painting—the window, the steps, the purple shadow, the central tree—but never tells us, except for suggesting the placement of the tree, how these images relate to one another nor, indeed, what concept they were intended to communicate. Therefore, in recreating Lily's canvas, one must reverse the usual process of composition and discover the overall concept by experimenting with the relationships of the specific images. All the while, one must remember that one is working, not with one's own ideas, but with Lily's, insofar as one can discern them in certain passages of the novel. "Oh well," I suddenly decided, "why not stop this futile analyzing and start playing with the paint?" Which is what I did with considerable relief.

Early in February, I began by making a loose, experimental design on a half sheet of Arches paper, letting my hand work quite freely. Mrs. Ramsay

Moving Images

The Third Attempt

The Final Painting

became a huge, blue window on the right, so prominent it crowded against a little central tree and contorted the natural shape of its branches. Perched in the upper left corner was a tiny white table, all that was visible of Mr. Ramsay.

When I looked at the hopelessly distorted composition I was shocked to see that I, like the enamoured Lily, had tumbled into the trap of Mrs. Ramsay's manipulative charm with which she endeavored to dominate her small domestic world. And, like Lily at the dinner table sliding the saltcellar (alias, the tree) to the center of her imagined painting, I already found myself chafing against my entrapment. It was easy to discard this initial trial balloon.

Unsure where to go next, I took refuge, as so many artists do, in starting a large, aimless oil painting on which I wasted the next two months. And what a dreary travesty it was, crowded to the gills, a project that cast Lily as some sort of documentor of the Ramsay summer household! At least Mr. Ramsay had assumed a more interesting role in this version: he was depicted as a tall figure striding into a high wind, and above his head a lighthouse had landed on the now more sizable white table of intellectual inquiry.

Again Mrs. Ramsay was represented by a blue window, not so large, but still dominating the scene, and this time Mrs. Ramsay's silhouette with James was visible on its dark surface. To the far right, six Ramsay children scooted off on a path to mysterious destinations of their own, each carefully identified. (I was particularly pleased with Jasper in Norfolk jacket, and knee britches, shouldering his shotgun.) Mr. Carmichael dozed, book on belly, in his reclining chair, while Mr. Tansley and Mr. Bankes paid discreet homage to Mr. Ramsay just above him. Finally one day even Prue and Andrew made a brief appearance, Prue seated upon a tombstone dressed in white and Andrew lying in a crumpled corpse in military garb upon the ground. Shocked at my own tasteless "kitsch," I slabbed white gesso over the entire canvas, then sanded the dried surface to wipe out its memory. "Symbols *only* from now on," I vowed. "No cheap illustration."

So it was that I moved on to a second oil painting, dealing in this one, as in the original discarded sketch, only with the simplest symbolic images. At once I felt I was back on track and that I was truly Lily's ally in a project that was making progress. In fact, when I finished this third effort, I was so sure I had completed the job that I had slides made of the painting. (See illustration 1, a black and white print taken from one of the slides, entitled "The Third Attempt.")

In this version, Mr. Ramsay had assumed his rightful half of the canvas, or most of it, and his white table is quite prominent. Moreover, it is firmly lodged on the branches of a much more substantial tree that stands squarely in the center of the picture. Beneath the table's legs, Cam and James steer their sailboat into the 20th century and (I like to tell myself) Mr. Ramsay's little lighthouse is at least able to aid them with cerebral navigation for the journey, even though Mr. Ramsay himself seems mired in Victorian mores forever.

Moving Images

Meanwhile, Mrs. Ramsay still remains too much the focal point of the composition. Quite unconsciously I designed the stairs beneath the blue window so that they appear to follow the viewer as he shifts his position, skewering his attention on the purple shadow. Also I was unhappy with the way Mrs. R.'s geranium pots, her hedge, and her red hot pokers seem to fill up an undue amount of space as though she were consciously trying to block the view of the sea and the sky, just as she tried to block Lily's artistic dreams by her insistence on a conformist marriage. In an effort to correct these flaws, I began to paint out large areas of the composition, but at this point, I developed a severe eye allergy to the oil paints and had to put them away, throwing away a whole month's work at the same time.

Time was a-wasting. It was now May 31 and the Woolf Conference in Newark, DE was just 10 days away. Switching to acrylic paint because of its faster drying time, I began my final canvas, the one I exhibited at the University of Delaware in June. (See illustration 2, "The Final Painting".) It is a stark image, but instinct told me from the very first to keep it as simple as possible. Moreover I began by using the same symbolic images I had used in "The Third Attempt," so what, I wondered as I began, would make this piece any more satisfactory than its predecessor? At that moment, I had what seemed to me a vision of my own. Filling one large brush with tinted white and another with ocean green, I simply struck out the dark window, leaving in the right foreground only the steps, quite simple ones now, with the purple shadow lying quietly on their muted surfaces.

Now, I realized, the focus of the entire painting centers on the right horizon, carrying the viewer's eye far, far off where the pale sky meets the variegated sea. *Now* Lily can stare with her pinched little Chinese eyes to the furthest shores of imagination and create whatever art she chooses!

The project is finished now, but at a price. For, to accomplish our end, Lily and I have had to murder our beloved Mrs. Ramsay and to brush her influence from our lives. No alternative was possible, if Lily was to go free and the picture to get its final stroke of painting. Yet even as we took this action, we knew that Mrs. R. was as much a victim of a patriarchal society as Lily herself would have been, had she not rebelled against the older woman's domination. A strong person, this matriarch, like such women in male-dominated societies through time, seized the only power permitted her: she became the tyrant ruler of her small, domestic kingdom, insisting that every female within its borders subscribe to a pattern of strict conformity and marry according to its rules in order that each, with time, would inherit a similar kingdom of her own. What could we do but mourn this lady even as we rejected her influence?

Curiously, it was not critical analysis, but the process of painting that led me too this new understanding of what I now see as the central (and *very* political) theme of *To the Lighthouse*. Nor am I surprised to make this discovery so late in my life because I learned long ago that reading and rereading Mrs. Woolf's writing is like handling a living organism that grows and transforms itself over and over, reflecting with each transformation a new, more subtle light. But who knows this better than you, the scholars who have for years shaped and reshaped the understanding of her readers everywhere?

Anna Snaith
Photographs by Dominic Rowland

"At Gordon Sq. and nowhere else": The Spatial and Social Politics of Bloomsbury

Writing of Gordon Square, Bloomsbury, Woolf describes "the sense of space" of "deep large pattern one gets there," a "sense of thoughts all liberated" (*D*1 86). Her comments point to the connections between material, spatial freedom and intellectual, political emancipation which this area of London offered her. Her move from Kensington to Bloomsbury in 1904 has been well documented: the literal distance covered in that move from southwest to northeast London can be read as a symbolic shift from the Victorian to the Edwardian. The turn of the century can be seen as encapsulated for Woolf in that move. As she describes in her essay "Old Bloomsbury" Vanessa's decision regarding the location of the siblings' new home had everything to do with its situation on the opposite side of London from Kensington (*MOB* 200).

Woolf's sense of liberation was in part a result of the embryonic Bloomsbury Group, but as early as 1910 Lytton Strachey used the single word Bloomsbury synonymously with the Bloomsbury Group (Lee 801). I want to undo this elision and think instead about what the geographical area of Bloomsbury, London, meant to Woolf in the first decade of this century. Woolf was constantly attuned to spatial politics, as she was to the history of London itself; in particular, she was well aware of the implications of urban architecture and geography for women. Whether it be St. Paul's for Elizabeth Dalloway or the Law Courts for Eleanor Pargiter, these are the markers of patriarchy which dominate the public arena both literally and metaphorically. Space for Woolf is anything but neutral. She would surely have agreed with the theorist of space Henri Lefebvre that, "any space implies, contains and dissimulates social relationships" (82). Yet again, Woolf is ahead of her time—yet again she turns the centuries, the decades, before they turn themselves. The feminist geographer Nancy Duncan has called recently for "a feminist deconstruction of the controversial distinction between metaphorical or discursive and so-called 'real' space" (Duncan 3). The room of one's own, a space at the center of Woolf's feminism, enacts just such a deconstruction, making inseparable material and symbolic space.

Moving Images

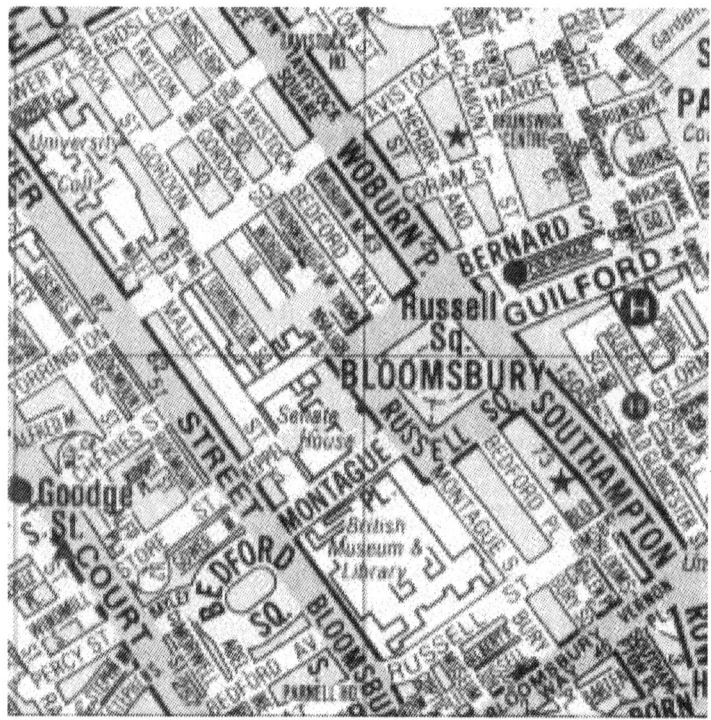

The significance of Bloomsbury for Woolf goes further than personal association, however. Her reaction to Bloomsbury provides evidence of her involvement in and knowledge of women's history, politics and activism. Not only did many women reformers of the period live in Bloomsbury, but many suffrage groups met in its upstairs rooms. It was also an area of London in which single, independent women could rent rooms or flats. The socio-cultural history of Bloomsbury is crucial to a discussion of the area's symbolic value for Woolf.

Bloomsbury is bounded by Tottenham Court Road on the east, Gray's Inn Road on the west, Euston Road on the north and Holborn on the south. The area takes its name from William Blemund, lord of the manor, Blemundsbury, in the 13th century (Clinch 127). By the 17th century, the manor had passed into the hands of the Bedford family but not until the 18th and 19th centuries were the houses that now form Bloomsbury being built (Morris 172). The building of Gordon Square, for instance, began in the 1820s, but was not completed until the 1860s (Woodford 12). These squares were initially intended for upmarket professionals, but by the 1880s and 1890s fashion began to move west and Bloomsbury became a rather less desirable address. As Thomas Burke writes of Bloomsbury at the turn of the century: "its streets whose houses had been homes became nests of lodging houses for hard-up clerks or nests of the sorrier sort of bordel" (Burke 12). Bloomsbury was characterized as an area of "shabby-genteel poverty" (Burke 12) as suggested in Woolf's comment while searching for housing in 1904: "Jack [Hills]... showed us the neighbourhood which he thinks bad and says we should never get anybody to come and see us, or to dine" (*L*1 120). In C. F. Keary's novel *Bloomsbury* (1905) the protagonists are described as living in "the back of beyond. Right over in Bloomsbury" (5).

The market value of Bloomsbury properties and the area's bohemian reputation around the turn of the century was crucial to its role as a site of women's politics and history. In contrast to the sign which Eleanor sees in a window in the West End in the 1891 section of *The Years* which reads "rooms let to single gentlemen only" (*TY* 111), Bloomsbury was an area in which single, independent women could find accommodation in flats, rooms or bedsits. With the rise in "surplus" women came a shortage of suitable accommodation. Women's journals of the late 19th century debated the question of women's independent living at length. Subsidized boarding houses sprang up in Bloomsbury, often run by philanthropic organizations, where women could live communally with a private bedsitting room but shared dining and living areas (Vicinus 295-6). While Virginia and Vanessa lived with two male siblings at 46 Gordon Square, we know, for example, that in 1903 a Miss Lidgett lived alone at No. 40 in the Square (Spencer). The *Holborn and Finsbury Guardian*, a local weekly newspaper covering the Bloomsbury area, carried ads in 1905 for rooms and flats available for rent by single working women.

Woolf's move to Bloomsbury instigated her own entry into the world of professional work. The private room of one's own, a phrase she herself uses in a letter to Madge Vaughan at this time (*L*1 162), occasions her entry into the

Moving Images

public world of journalism with her first reviews for *The Guardian* in December 1904 and 1905. Across Gordon Square from No. 46 was Dr. Williams' historical and theological Library. When Woolf applied for a ticket in 1905, she described herself as a "'journalist who wants to read history'" (*L*1 190), and she wrote to Violet Dickinson: "I do feel a professional lady" (*L*1 190). Her public self-definition as a working woman situates her in the larger community of working women living in Bloomsbury.

Dickinson's first present to Woolf at Gordon Square was an inkpot with, in Woolf's words, "a well for ink deep enough to write a dozen articles for the Guardian" (*L*1 153). The house is a place of writing, it is to be christened with "good black ink" (*L*1 153). Her illness during 1904 had meant Dr. Savage preventing her from returning to London and from writing. Her enforced exile from Bloomsbury intensifies her constant anticipation during 1904 of the room waiting for her: "Gordon Square is full of books and pictures...[it] is the *only* place where I can be quiet" (*L*1 152). Gordon Square let her write, let her plunge deep into the inkpot uncensored. This involved writing Bloomsbury itself as a site of liberation and feminism—something she did in her diaries, short stories, letters and novels.

This fight against the patriarchal medical profession which preceded her arrival in Bloomsbury heightened her awareness of the politics of the area. Septimus Smith, also a victim of the medical profession, kills himself on the

railings of a "large Bloomsbury lodging house" (*MD* 195). Her fictional representations of Bloomsbury focus, however, on the area as a site of suffrage politics. In *The Years*, Rose, an active suffragette, takes Sara to a suffrage meeting in Bloomsbury (134). In the Third Essay of "The Pargiters" Nora Graham invites Delia to "join a queer little society that met in the Gray's Inn Road" (57).

Snaith

Woolf inscribes history into her texts, the political activists who did indeed inhabit the rooms of Bloomsbury. Ray Strachey describes "the meetings which multiplied in halls and drawing-rooms, in schools and chapels, at street corners" (20). A Bloomsbury guide book of the time describes the many societies which "made the district the headquarters of their activities"(*The Bloomsbury Book* 5). The International Franchise Club met at 66 Russell Square, the Men's League for Women's Suffrage at 40 Museum Street (Morris, 1974 34) and the Women's Freedom League in Barter Street off Southampton Row (Sturtevant 33). In October of 1906 the headquarters of the WSPU moved from Manchester to 4 Clement's Inn just below the south boundary of Bloomsbury (Pankhurst 62). The Pankhursts themselves lived at 8 Russell Square between 1888 and 1893 (Pankhurst 24, 30), and Millicent Garrett Fawcett, who became president of the National Union of Women's Suffrage Societies when it broke from the WSPU, lived at 2 Gower Street, a stone's throw from Gordon Square, from 1884 to 1929 after the death of her husband, Henry Fawcett (Rubinstein 72). Even closer to home, at 51 Gordon Square lived Lady Jane Strachey, who sat on the committee of the NUWSS and worked for the Women's Local Government Society (Sturtevant 18). Jane Strachey's daughters Philippa and Marjorie were active in the suffrage campaign: Philippa organised the famous Mud March suffrage rally in February 1907 (Lee 233), and her daughter in law, Ray Strachey, author of *The Cause*, visited the Square during this period, attending her first Bloomsbury Group party in 1909 (Lee 233). While it was not until 1910 that Woolf worked for an

Moving Images

NUWSS society and attended rallies, during the years leading up to that she was mixing and discussing with women who were.

Suffragettes would have been an important public presence on London streets protesting and selling papers. "One might argue" states Barbara Green, "that Virginia Woolf was emboldened to streetwalk, because the suffragette marched first" (Green 38). Woolf's move to Bloomsbury coincided with "the flowering time of the Women's Movement" (Strachey 20), and while Woolf did not find herself able to participate in militant activism, she was certainly aware of the feminist inhabitants of Bloomsbury, the women's history being made there and the connections between her own writing and that activism.

In *Night and Day*, a text which explores public versus private fulfilment, Mary Datchet's place in the public world of work emanates from a "suffrage office...at the top of one of the large Russell Square houses, which had once been lived in by a great city merchant and his family, and was now let out in slices to a number of societies" (*ND* 71). Although the text, and Mary herself, are ambivalent about the Suffrage cause and the efficacy of the Society and its workers, the value of Mary's independence is not in question. This independence is specifically linked to Bloomsbury. On her journey home Mary's mood changes with the geographical area; while her politics, her activism and her independence are "in some way connected with Bloomsbury" (158), the male world of Lincoln's Inn Fields (the law courts) makes her "cold and depressed" (159). On Mary's way to work, Woolf reverses the conventional Modernist image of automaton commuters: Mary likes "to think herself one of the workers" (70). She enjoys the shared public space and relishes her indistinguishability, proof of her part in the communal world of work. She "ranged herself entirely on the side of the shopkeepers and the bank clerks" (70). Her enjoyment of London, she recognizes, is "entirely due to the fact that she had her work" and that work is situated in and integrally linked to Bloomsbury (*ND* 69).

Bloomsbury was also a focal point for women's educational reform and the founding of new schools and colleges for women. Across Gordon Square is University College London which opened its doors to women in 1878 (Vicinus 127). This drew women students to the area both to live and study. The building at the corner of Gordon Square became a College Hall and Home for Ladies in 1848 (in the same building as Dr. Williams' Library) (Twinn 18). No. 47 Bedford Square was opened as a Ladies' College in 1849 (Vicinus 123). In 1880 it became a school of the University of London and in 1909 Bedford College for Women (Woodford 71). This meant that female lecturers were seeking accommodation as were female students. In her autobiography, M. Vivian Hughes, a lecturer at Bedford College, describes her move, with a fellow teacher, into a new building, "Ladies' Residential Chambers" with private bedrooms but a communal dining room where they meet "a variety of interesting women, all of them at work of some kind—artists, authors, political workers" (Hughes 37).

It was, of course, in 1905 that Woolf herself started work in education, teaching history and literature courses at Morley College for working men and women. Woolf notes that she is "rising in philanthropic circles" (*L*1 193) and although the college was not in Bloomsbury she would have been aware of similar institutions close to home, such as the Working Women's College at 29

Queen's Square founded by Elizabeth Malleson and Barbara Bodichon in 1864 (Sturtevant 13). In early 1905 Mrs. Humphry Ward wrote to Vanessa and Virginia asking them to work at the settlement for working class people which she had founded in 1890 in Gordon Square (*PA* 220). Woolf's philanthropy did not extend as far as to support the anti-suffragist Mrs Humphry Ward. The settlement moved in 1897 to Tavistock Square (Sutherland 223) and is still in existence at 42 Queen's Square, Bloomsbury.

Literary space, for Woolf, goes hand in hand with the spaces of independent living and political activism occupied by women in Bloomsbury. In Woolf's first short story, "Phyllis and Rosamond", written in 1906, two young girls escape their home in Belgravia to attend a party at the Miss Tristrams in Bloomsbury, which is reminiscent of the Thursday evening gatherings at the Stephens' in Gordon Square. As Phyllis travels by cab to the Tristrams, the immense, sprawling trees in Bloomsbury symbolize the "room, and freedom" of the place. The "roar and splendour of the Strand" and the "talk and life" of the Tristrams represent the unconstrained movement, both physical and metaphorical, of the inhabitants (24). Bloomsbury represents motion and excess; the talk from the party spills out into the street, not contained by the limits of the home. "But if one lived here in Bloomsbury, she began to theorize [...] one might grow up as one liked" (24).

The move, like Woolf's own, from Kensington to Bloomsbury, is one of expansion. "What was even more exhilarating" she writes in "Old Bloomsbury", "was the extraordinary increase of space" (*MOB* 201). The sense of experimentation, the psychological and intellectual space are found in the literal spaciousness, the "light and air" of the Bloomsbury squares compared to the "muffled silence" of Hyde Park Gate (*MOB* 201). In Mrs Oliphant's novel *A House in Bloomsbury*, the narrator describes the houses in Bloomsbury as "aired and opened up by many spacious breathing places" (21). The protagonist, Dora, who lives with her father in a flat below a single woman, is described as having "floating hair and large movements, [which] seemed to take up a great deal more space than her father": signifiers of her independence (30).

We can see that as well as an awareness of Bloomsbury's cultural and political history, Woolf was tapping into a tradition of writing about Bloomsbury in terms of emancipation. In Olive Birrell's *Love in a Mist* (1900), Hilda Forester takes a flat in Bloomsbury with two other women: the flat is an "escape from her present mode of life" (228). In Radclyffe Hall's *The Unlit Lamp* (1924), Elizabeth Rodney gives her friend Joan Ogden the lease of a Bloomsbury flat for her birthday. Here, the chance of their own flat represents sexual emancipation as the two women can develop the lesbian relationship which is the "unlit lamp." Jehane Bruce, in Violet Hunt's *A Workaday Woman* (1906), "lives alone in a flat, and pays its rent and supports herself on regular journalism and occasional fiction" (3). The narrator, Caroline, feels a "sensation of unaccustomed liberty" as she sets out to visit Jehane at Hardicanute Mansions, Bloomsbury (13).

In C. F. Keary's novel *Bloomsbury* (1905) Mya Nepean and Joyce Freeling share a room in Nasmyth House in Mecklenburgh Square (where Woolf lived prior to World War II). The locale is associated with socialist politics and bohemianism. The women attend art classes and art lectures at a working people's college in Queen's Square (37). On the way home they hear voices from an upper Bloomsbury room and conclude that it must be a "revolutionary meeting" (40). The women they come into contact with in Bloomsbury include Sydney Grove, who has a lectureship at Bedford College and lectures on history at various girls' schools.

The centrality of Bloomsbury, particularly Gordon Square, for Woolf, testifies to the importance she placed on issues of space and geography. To the questions which postmodern geographers are asking today—"can concrete geographical . . . circumstances . . . be understood as expressions of abstract social relations" (Pile 1)—Woolf answers yes. Her use of spatial metaphors shows her conception of space as being concerned with networks which create and define space. The networks of women's politics and reform underpin her own private liberation. Gordon Square embodies privacy: "I long for a large room to myself, with books and nothing else, where I can shut myself up, and see no one, and read myself into peace. This would be possible, at Gordon Sq.: and nowhere else" (*L*1 147). It is from that room, however, that she can become public, literally and metaphorically. Gaston Bachelard reads the house as cradle, bosom, an enclosed space, but for Woolf the public spaces of Bloomsbury were just as important (Bachelard 6-7). The streets and squares connected her to other women, other streetwalkers. As Barbara Green argues: "the physical spaces that house the fragments of history . . .connect the world of militant and constitutionalist suffragists with the world of Woolf's Bloomsbury. Both the private archive and the feminist library hold a central position in suffrage activism and in Woolf's imaginings" (Green 164). Literal sites of resistance—those upstairs rooms of Bloomsbury—and the spaces in which history is recorded become textual spaces for Woolf.

Bloomsbury and its politics of space, then, was crucial to Woolf's life and writing at the turn of the last century. As we approach the turn of this century how is Woolf marked in the spaces of contemporary Bloomsbury? She has had a "mews" named after her in 1994, in truth a back alley, symbolic perhaps of the hidden spaces she occupies in contemporary British culture, and the hidden spaces women activists occupy in histories of Bloomsbury. She gives her name to a Burger Bar in the Hotel Russell in Russell Square, also symbolic of the harnessing of her iconography for the purposes of tourism. Perhaps in the 21st century she will occupy the spaces of cultural prominence that her place in women's history merits.

Notes

[1] For a discussion of Dr. Williams' Library see Morris pp. 10-11 and Rev. Kenneth Twinn, "An Ivory Tower in Gordon Square," *Camden History Review*, No. 1, Camden History Society, 1973: 17-18.

[2] Pankhurst writes that "The Inn was at once a rallying-ground for women of all grades and classes" (62).

[3] Pankhurst writes of the house: "the two great inter-communicating drawing-rooms were soon a centre of meetings and conferences for advanced causes. Radicals, Socialists, Fabians and Agnostics gathered there, free-thinkers and libertarians of every school and country" (24). In 1893 the house was pulled down to make way for the Hotel Russell which stands on the site today.

[4] The Women's Sunday Procession, for example, on June 21, 1908, consisted of 30,000 women protesters and ¼ million spectators (Green 74).

[5] See Squier for a discussion of Mary's identification with London more generally (129).

[6] See, for example, Woodford. The only women reformers mentioned are the Pankhursts and erroneously at that (55).

Works Cited

Bachelard, Gaston. *The Poetics of Space*. Trans. Maria Jolas. Boston: Beacon Press, 1969.

Birrell, Olive. *Love in a Mist*. London: Smith Elder & Co., 1900.

The Bloomsbury Book. Arts and Crafts Quarterly, 1926.

Burke, Thomas. *Living in Bloomsbury*. London: George Allen and Unwin, 1939.

Clinch, George. *Bloomsbury and St. Giles*. London: Truslove & Shirley, 1890.

Duncan, Nancy (Ed.). *Body Space*. London: Routledge, 1996.

Green, Barbara. *Spectacular Confessions: Autobiography, Performative Activism and the Sites of Suffrage 1905-1938*. London: Macmillan, 1997.

Hall, Radclyffe. *The Unlit Lamp*. London: Cassell & Co. Ltd., 1924.

Hughes, M. Vivian. *A London Home in the Nineties*. London: OUP, 1937.

Hunt, Violet. *The Workaday Woman*. London: T. Werner Laurie, 1906.

Keary, C. F. *Bloomsbury*. London: David Nutt, 1905.

Keith, Michael and Pile, Steve (Eds.). *Place and the Politics of Identity*. London: Routledge, 1993.

Lee, Hermione. *Virginia Woolf*. London: Chatto and Windus, 1996.

Lefebvre, Henri. *The Production of Space*. Trans. Donald Nicholson-Smith. Oxford: Blackwell, 1991.

Lodge, Mrs. *The Mystery of Bloomsbury Crescent*. London: Digby, Long & Co.,1896.

Morris, Joan. "Shoulder to Shoulder: The Suffragettes' Local Connections." *Camden History Review*. No. 2. Camden History Society, 1974: 34.

Morris, W. G. *The Squares of Bloomsbury*. London: The Homeland Assoc. Ltd.

Oliphant, Mrs. *A House in Bloomsbury*. London: Hutchinson & Co., 1894.

Pankhurst, E. Sylvia. *The Life of Emmeline Pankhurst*. London: T. Werner Laurie Ltd., 1935.

Rubinstein, David. *A Different World for Women: The Life of Millicent Garrett Fawcett*. London: Harvester, 1991.

Spencer, Joan A. *39-47 Gordon Square*. Unpublished booklet held in the Camden

Public Library, Local History Archives.
Squier, Susan Merrill. "The Classic City Novel and *Night and Day*." *Women Writers and the City*. Knoxville: U of Tennessee P, 1984: 114 – 133.
Strachey, Ray. *The Cause*. London: G. Bell & Sons Ltd., 1928.
Sturtevant, Katherine. *Our Sisters' London: 19 Feminist Walks*. The Women's Press, 1991.
Sutherland, John. *Mrs. Humphry Ward: Eminent Victorian, Pre-Eminent Edwardian*. Oxford UP, 1991.
Twinn, Rev. Kenneth. "An Ivory Tower in Gordon Square." *Camden History Review*. No. 1. Camden History Society, 1973: 17-18.
Vicinus, Martha. *Independent Women: Work and Community for Single Women 1850-1920*. London: Virago, 1985.
Woodford, F. Peter (ed.). *Streets of Bloomsbury & Fitzrovia*. Camden History Society, 1997.
Woolf, Virginia. *The Complete Shorter Fiction*. Ed. Susan Dick. Triad Grafton, 1991.
——. *Diary*. Vol. 1. Ed. Anne Olivier Bell. London: Hogarth Press, 1978.
——. *Letters*. Vol. 1. Ed. Nigel Nicolson and Joanne Trautmann. London: Hogarth Press, 1975.
——. *Mrs Dalloway*. Ed. Claire Tomalin. Oxford: Oxford UP, 1992.
——. *Night and Day*. London: Penguin, 1969.
——. "Old Bloomsbury". *Moments of Being*. Ed. Jeanne Schulkind. London: Grafton, 1989.
——. *The Pargiters*. Ed. Mitchell Leaska. London: Hogarth Press, 1978.
——. *A Passionate Apprentice*. Ed. Mitchell Leaska. Toronto: Lester & Orpen Dennys, 1990.
——. *The Years*. Ed. Hermione Lee. Oxford: Oxford UP, 1992.

Leslie Kathleen Hankins
Tracking Shots through Film History: Virginia Woolf, Film Archives and Future Technologies

> The scene, if I may ask you to follow me, was now changed. The leaves were still falling, but in London now, not Oxbridge; and I must ask you to imagine a room, like many thousands, with a window looking across people's hats and vans and motor-cars to other windows, and on the table inside the room a blank sheet on which was written in large letters WOMEN AND FICTION, but no more. The inevitable sequel to lunching and dining at Oxbridge seemed, unfortunately, to be a visit to the British Museum. (*AROO* 25)

Moving Images

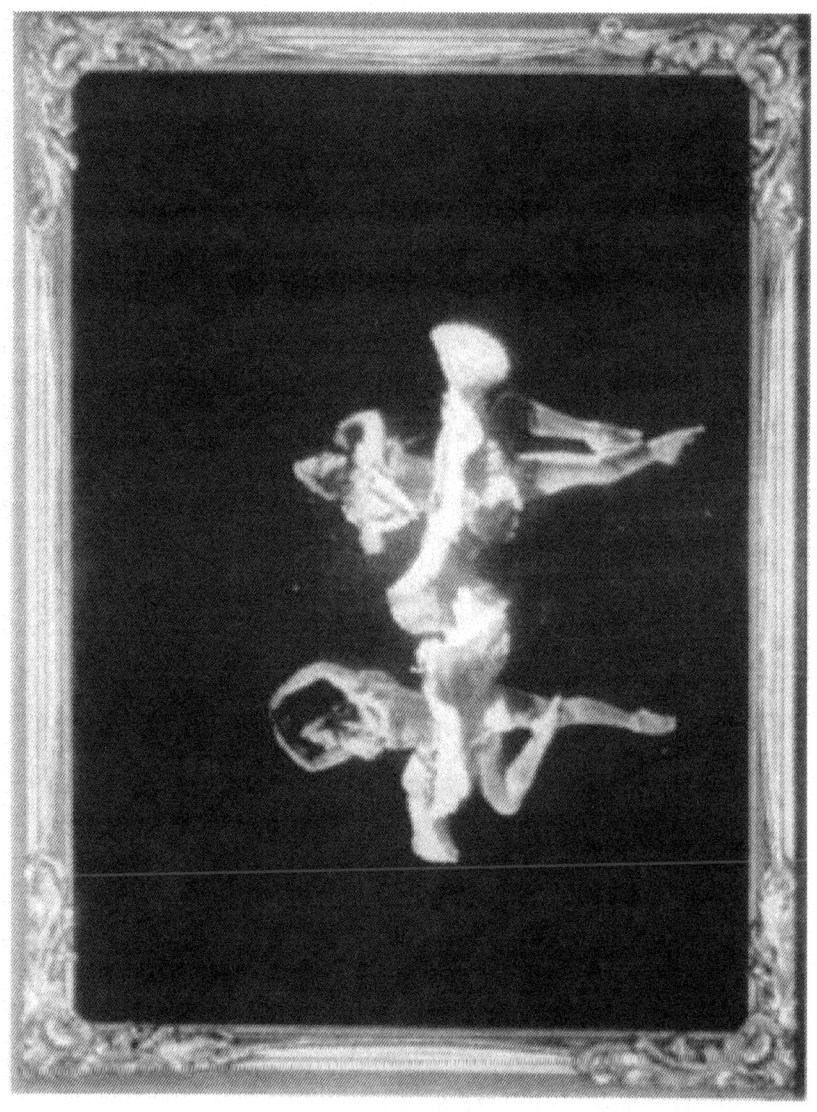

Hankins

Not the British Museum, but a screening room of the British Film Institute and a blank sheet emblazoned WOOLF AND CINEMA become the "inevitable sequel" for a scholar tracking Woolf's connections to film. Fleeting references to movies in Woolf's diaries, letters and essays release a swarm of questions. Thinking idly of Chaplin, D. W. Griffith, Germaine Dulac and Alice Guy-Blaché, I wondered what films Virginia Woolf encountered in British picture palaces or on marquees and in advertisements in her strolls about London in the 1920s. What was popular film culture like? What was on the average film program? shorts? feature films? film adaptations? documentaries? avant-garde films? What connections might we find between Woolf's art and British films? Time to plot a research trip to explore the British Film Institute, I resolved. Desperately seeking news of a few films of interest, I sent off for the catalogue: *The British Cinema Source Book: British Film Institute Archive Viewing Copies and Library Materials* and, upon its arrival "opened a volume of the catalogue, and ..... the five dots here indicate five separate minutes of stupefaction, wonder and bewilderment" (*AROO* 26). The catalogue was crammed with the titles of thousands of films, most of which, it is fair to say, were obscure, as a segment selected at random testifies:

> *Unveiling of War Memorial by Admiral of the Fleet Earl Jelicoe of SCAPA GCB, OM, GCVO, on Sunday June 13* (1926)
> *Vanity Fair* (Tense Moments with Great Authors series) (1922) d. Walter Courtenay Rowden.
> *Vapourer Moth, the* (Secrets of Nature series) (1924)
> *Visit of HRH Princess Mary and Viscount Lascelles To Halifax* 13.3.25 (1925)
> *Wandering Jew, the* (1923) d. Maurice Elvey
> *War Neuroses*: Netley 1917, Seale Hayne Military Hospital (1919)
> *What's Wrong with the Cinema?* (1925)
> *Where Their Caravan was Wrested* (1915)
> *Where There's Life There's 'Ope* (1927) d. D. M. Connan
> *Whirl of Charleston, the* (On with the Dance series) (1927) d. Harry B. Parkinson
> *Winners of "The Capitol" Challenge Cup* (1928)
> *With a Skirmishing Party in Flanders* (1915)
> *With Britain's Monster Guns in Action* (1916)
> *With the British Forces in France* (1915)
> *Woman He Scorned, the* (1928) d. Paul Czinner
> *Woman Redeemed, a* (1927) d. Sinclair Hill
> *Women's Work on Munitions of War* (1918)
> *Wonderful London* first series

"How shall I ever find the grains of truth embedded in all this mass of paper, I asked myself, and in despair began running my eye up and down the long list of titles" (*AROO* 27). I first noted peculiar or compelling titles, anything suggestive for Woolf's fiction. Winnowing that list, "making a perfectly arbitrary choice of a dozen [. . .] or so, I sent my slips of paper" (*AROO* 27) listing a

Moving Images

variety of films, including newsreels, mainstream comedies, public affairs films, serials, avant-garde films and experimental films:

> *'Old Bill' Through the Ages* (1924) d. Thomas Bentley
> *Kino the Girl of Colour* (1920) d. William Friese-Greene, Claude Friese-Greene.
> *Dancing Grace—Studies of Madame Lopokova* (*Eve's Film Review* series) (1922)
> *Some Classical Dancing by the Pupils of Margaret Morris (1922)* from *Around the Town* series
> *Visit of HRH Princess Mary and Viscount Lascelles to Halifax (1921)*
> *Cut it Out: A Day In the Life of a Censor* (1925) d. Adrian Brunel
> *Running a Cinema* (*Memoirs of Miffy* series) (1921)
> SECRETS OF NATURE series
> *The Battle of the Plants* (1926),
> *The Swallow-Tail Butterfly* (1926)
> *Plant Movements* (1920)
> *LGOC Scenes of London* (1924)
> *Cosmopolitan London* (1924) (*Wonderful London* first series) d. Frank Miller, Harry B. Parkinson.
> *Snapshots of London* (1924) (*Wonderful London* second series) d. Harry B. Parkinson, Frank Miller.
> *Some War-Time Types: The WLA Girl* (1918)
> *Shooting Stars* (1927) d. Antony Asquith
> *Bluebottles* (1928) d. Ivor Montagu

The selections promised connections—however tenuous—with Woolf's essay "The Cinema" or with her cinematic novels. The hope was to replicate the multi-faceted cinematic milieu of England in the 1920s and to unearth some treasures that would complicate and illuminate the relationship between Woolf and the cinema. Ushered into the small, vault-like basement screening room of the British Film Institute, I was daunted by the leaning tower of slightly rusty film reel canisters of all shapes and sizes, most of which seemed to have been in storage for decades. Thus began the test of stamina and eyesight, screening reel after reel of the films of the obscure. Woolf's comments about confronting the mass of literature written by her contemporaries seemed to echo through the vault: "But can we go to posterity with a sheaf of loose pages, or ask the readers of those days, with the whole of literature before them, to sift our enormous rubbish heaps for our tiny pearls?" (*E4* 236). Pearls? or rubbish? Both. But the whole gave a broader and more nuanced picture of the film milieu and the cultural moment of the 1920s. "Snapshots of London" and the *Wonderful London* series captured the vital London backdrop of Woolf's *Mrs. Dalloway*. The "Cosmopolitan London" film celebrated London in ways reminiscent of Woolf's "Street-Haunting: A London Adventure," as one of the film's title cards attests: "To the Londoner all things are possible. If he wearies of the sameness of his surroundings, he need but walk around the corner or invest in a 2 penny bus ride—and at once he is among strange faces and scenes reminiscent of foreign climes." Unfortunately, the film, conjuring up Hugh

Hankins

Whitbread rather than Virginia Woolf, alternated the multi-cultural cosmopolitan scenes with title cards bearing ethnocentric, anti-Semitic and racist commentary.[1] It was a chilling reminder of an often overlooked aspect of the 1920s. The *Secrets of Nature* series captured visuals Woolf often incorporated into her fiction, such as images of transforming moths and butterflies; films in the series using fast and slow motion cinematography to make plants dance are suggestive for Woolf's time lapse drama of vegetation in the "Time Passes" section of *To the Lighthouse*. Woolf screened and reviewed some of Friese-Greene's early experiments with color film; his "Kino the Girl of Colour" gave an example of such demonstration films. Because the Archduke Harry in *Orlando* was patterned somewhat on Lord Lascelles, screening the "Visit of HRH Princess Mary and Viscount Lascelles to Halifax" offered information and amusement. Film culture in England was portrayed in two comic films; "Running a Cinema" spoofed the film market of the time and "Cut it Out: A Day in the Life of a Censor" by Adrian Brunel, a comic scathing portrayal of censorship, dovetails with Woolf's indictment of censors in *Orlando*. All in all, this eclectic assortment of films offered the rare opportunity to situate Woolf in the British cinematic milieu of the 1920s, not only next to the masterpieces of the period, but also along with the worthy candidates for oblivion. It is easier to understand Woolf's mixed feelings about the movies when faced with this mélange of the mediocre and the mesmerizing. And, as critics attempting to obtain peripheral visions of the culture surrounding Woolf, we may learn from such ephemeral films what common cultural attitudes were—about modernity, entertainment, travel, film, science, history, class, gender, race, and war.

Several compelling films: "Some Classical Dancing by the Pupils of Margaret Morris" (1922), "'Old Bill' Through the Ages," (1924) and "Dancing Grace—Studies of Madame Lopokova," (1922)—invited further analysis. On April 5, 1924, at the Holborn Empire Woolf saw a set of films demonstrating a new color film process and wrote a paragraph for the "From Alpha to Omega" column in the *Nation and Athenaeum* (*E3* 404-4). One of the films was "The Dance of the Moods" featuring "a number of dancers from the Margaret Morris School of Dancing" (editor's footnote, *E3* 403). The film in the British Film Institute archives, "Some Classical Dancing by the Pupils of Margaret Morris—Nymphs of the Water-Garden" (1922) from the *Around the Town* series, though black and white and not the identical film, is surely representative. Purportedly "classical" dancers move in highly stylized posed grace through the setting of an ornate swimming pool with statuary, and their dancing is reflected in the pool. The dancers sport tunics, bare feet and short hair in pseudo-Grecian headbands. The tone is serious (one might say pretentious) and the dancers are synchronized figures resembling moving statues. The tableaux suggest Woolf's tongue-in-cheek tableaux of the Ladies of Chastity, Purity, and Modesty in *Orlando*.

Moving Images

Another film was quite a find. For years I've been haunted by a reference found while searching in the New York Public Library archives: in *Today's Cinema News and Property Gazette* of March 6, 1924 a full page yellow poster (13) advertising "'Old Bill' Through the Ages," directed by Thomas Bentley, followed by an interview with the director about the upcoming release which promised "History Without Tears" (21) as the director claimed the film as " not a comedy, but a burlesque .... It is a travesty of the highpoints of history"(21). The subject and tone of the film anticipate Woolf's *Orlando* (though Woolf's aristocratic protagonist is a switch from Bentley's working class hero); Bentley remarks, "The treatment of historical episodes is thoroughly up to date and adult, and it is just this mixture of the modern and the antique that has given me such wonderful possibilities" (21). Efforts to locate this intriguing film proved fruitless until the vaults of the British Film Institute produced, to my delight, a viewing copy. A pertinent popular culture film, it introduces the "Old Bill" figure, a working class Brit Everyman, against the backdrop of Big Ben, St. Pauls and other landmarks:

> There is an heroic figure symbolic of the plain Briton; Symbolic of the average everyday man who catches his train and does his job, loves his wife and spanks his children; Symbolic too, with his modest heroisms and good humoured patience, of the real stuff, both warp and weft of which the gorgeous tapestry of our History has been woven through the centuries.

In the opening scene in the trenches of World War I, an officer gives Old Bill a can of tinned lobster and Old Bill purloins from the Captain's bookshelf a text which turns out to be *The History of England from Norman Times*. While digesting the tinned lobster and this tome, Old Bill falls into a fitful sleep punctuated by his dreams of a romp through history. A very common Common Reader, "Old Bill" is incarnated downwardly mobile through British history, beginning as "Bill the Conqueror," then as "a courtier of Good Queen Bess Queen of an England great in literature no less than Arms," and even changing sex when "Old Bill starred as Aunt Sally for 11 years" to evade the Puritans after they pass the "Total Abolition of Pleasure" Act in 1624. At the end, Old Bill, as demobbed ex-Private Busby, is toasted by his officer after the war as "Bill the spirit of our Empire." This popular culture burlesque might have commanded Woolf's attention as she wrote her 1928 novel of Orlando, an aristocrat, who is likewise placed against a burlesque backdrop of centuries of history—as well as when she penned Miss LaTrobe's pageant of English history in *Between the Acts*.

Another promising film was "Dancing Grace—Studies of Madame Lopokova," a two minute film from *Eve's Film Review* series (1922), which captures in dance the Bloomsbury figure Madame Lopokova, one of Woolf's intimate social circle. Biographical links aside, the film proved an impressive meditation on cinema as art, and on the relationship between cinema and the acknowledged high arts of ballet and painting. An ornate picture frame surrounds the whole moving image, reminding us in a rather heavy-handed way that film should be seen as high art. The film shows Lopokova dancing a simple ballet number, after which a title card announces, "The 'slow' camera adds new motion to Madame's movements—" and the film shows the dance repeated, in slow motion. Then, another title card appears: "A further stage was reached when our special camera took things in hand and 'framed up' a few surprise moments of its own—!" whereupon the film doubles the dancing Lopokova, creating a fantasy *pas de deux* in which she dances with herself. The film is a fascinating self-conscious investigation of the promise and potential cinema brings to the arts, as the film plays with cinematic experimentation, doubling and speed, techniques Woolf plays with in her fictions and discusses in her essay on the cinema.

The holdings of the film archives—old blockbusters, travel shorts, oddball local interest films, science trick films, dance films and cinematic postcards of London—offer invaluable insights about the multifaceted British film culture of the 1920s; such compelling archives beg to be made more widely accessible to the common scholar and students. Yet, one cannot spend much time in archives without being reminded that historically they have been closer to the Oxbridge library with the patriarchal guardian angel at the door than to the cheap college Woolf proposes in *Three Guineas* or the "towerless and classless" society she envisions in "The Leaning Tower." Today's technologies, including scanning, CD-ROMs, DVDs and websites, would seem to offer scholars magnificent and easy opportunities to share archival treasures in public forums, and to move beyond the inevitable elitism of archives (which require travel funding, letters of introduction and fees). Though archives provide vital services preserving and storing rare old films, difficulties viewing, copying and sharing the films remain challenging. For example, unlike the fairly reasonable copy and permissions fees for reproducing photographs and written texts, fees for copying film clips and obtaining copyright permission to include them in scholarly work are exorbitant. To obtain a copy of the two minute long Lydia Lopokova film, for example, would cost over $1,500 for permissions. Working on a CD-ROM companion for a book on Woolf and the Cinema involves prohibitive fees, searches for copyright information for old obscure films, some territorial archives, and other archives which, though willing to help, lack equipment and staff to make copies. As we move more and more into the "Information Age," it bodes ill that the common scholar is likely to be economically disenfranchised from participating. Though these frustrations need not dampen enthusiasm for combining Woolf's texts and current technologies, they must give one pause.

Given these drawbacks, yet drawn on by the lure of new technologies, we might wonder if it would be wiser to generate multi-media or hypermedia adaptation projects than to hassle with archival materials. Certainly, current technologies hold out hope for adapting Woolf's creative visions in innovative ways. If—as I've suggested before[2]—one productive approach to adapting Woolf's novels would be to move backwards in time, exploiting the technologies and aesthetics of avant-garde filmmakers of her day, another experimental approach is to leap into the future, using emerging technologies to create hypermedia experiments incorporating Woolf's texts into new contexts. Woolf urges writers to "reveal the flickerings of that innermost flame which flashes its messages through the brain" ("Modern Fiction" *E4* 151) and projects ways film might be able to express such a vision if "left to its own devices" ("The Cinema" *E4* 593). But she also suggests that both words and film are—as long as they are kept separate at least—inadequate. In "The Cinema" Woolf alternates between condemning words and condemning film in a rhetorical ricochet which dizzies the reader. But must we choose between words and visuals? Woolf's wrenching rhetoric, akin to the "violent changes" and "fantastic contrasts" she suggests for future film, in fact may catapult us free to combine words and visuals in innovative ways using new hypermedia.[3] Explorations of the theories and aesthetics of film adaptation, coupled with CD-ROM and Web technologies, encourage us to find fresh ways to bridge the divide between film and literature. Stimulated by Woolf's assertions (rhetorical or genuine) that words were inadequate to capture her visions and by her less ambivalent judgment that cinema failed to successfully adapt literature—and spurred on by critical evaluations of the films of Woolf's texts by today's filmmakers—it is tempting to consider alternative possibilities for multi-media adaptation. Theorizing the relationship between hypermedia and Woolf, and composing adaptations which *combine* Woolf's texts with visuals—rather than attempt to *translate* the texts into visuals—may prove to be the logical extension of the investigation of Woolf and the cinema, transforming the study into one of Woolf and the screen.

From here it is but a short segue to a vignette from Suzanne Bellamy's essay, "The Pattern Behind the Words," in the collection *Virginia Woolf: Lesbian Readings* edited by Patricia Cramer and Eileen Barrett. Bellamy describes her vision:

> When I first saw the Woolf persona, she stood absorbed at a huge easel-like circuit board, tipped at an angle like an architect's bench. On both sides of her were hundreds of tiny objects in containers and trays, exotic materials unknown to me, like jewels and unknown metals, tiny shapes. She had an array of tweezers and tools that she used to pick up these objects, and obviously amazing eyesight, I thought, helped by the abundant prismatic light in her studio.
> The board she worked on seemed to be moving as she built shapes in intricate detail. I asked her whether she could tell me what her current work involved. "The pattern behind the words," she said. Speaking very much in character, with comfortable references to her earlier opus, she said she was now absorbed at a deeper level, creating forms in the shape of brain patterns themselves, synaptic constructions with patient experimentation. Now when I recall my first sighting of Woolf's work in progress, it was like a computer-generated circuit board. (Bellamy 34)

Just as Woolf's daring invention of Judith Shakespeare plays with the facts to jolt the reader into new ways of looking at the past, Suzanne Bellamy's inventive vignette stimulates the reader to look at the future relationship of technology and Woolf in innovative ways. We might, of course, temper this utopian moment with a few readings of Mark Hussey's "How Should One Read a Screen?" given at the conference and published in Pamela Caughie's collection, *Virginia Woolf in the Age of Mechanical Reproduction*. Somewhere between Bellamy's inspired vision of Woolf's computing afterlife and Hussey's cautionary tale of terminal anxiety, we wait in anxious anticipation for future technologies which work for the common screener. Scholars may look forward to towerless and classless "cheap" archives made accessible to Anon, a future for intellectual property toward which Woolf gestures in *Three Guineas*:

> Indeed, the actual world is much more difficult to deal with than the dream world. Still, Madame, the private printing press is an actual fact, and not beyond the reach of a moderate income. Typewriters and duplicators are actual facts and even cheaper. By using these cheap and so far unforbidden instruments you can at once rid yourself of the pressures of boards, policies, and editors. They will speak your own mind, in your own words, at your own time, at your own length, at your own bidding. And that, we are agreed upon, is our definition of "intellectual liberty." "But," she may say, "the public"? How can that be reached without putting my own mind through the mincing machine and turning it into sausage?" "The public, Madame," we may assure her, "is very like ourselves; it lives in rooms; it walks in streets, and it is said moreover to be tired of sausage. Fling leaflets down basements; expose them on stalls; trundle them along on barrows to be sold for a penny or given away. Find out new ways of approaching "the public" . . . (*TG* 97-98).

And, artists and audiences alike may anticipate tempting technologies for screening Woolf's words and other media into innovative adaptations for the future:

> How all this is to be attempted, much less achieved, no one at the moment can tell us. We get intimations only in the chaos of the streets, perhaps, when some momentary assembly of colour, sound, movement suggests that here is a scene waiting a new art to be transfixed. ("The Cinema" 595).

Notes

[1] The documentary tours Piccadilly Circus with its French and Italian restaurants and Tottenham Court and café bars, and warns viewers: "But we do not advise you to linger long in the unsavoury Whitcomb Street district, where there is a certain notorious cafe bar (Grand Cafe) famous for its negro clientele. 'White Trash' are not encouraged here." The film describes "the swamping hive of Jewish humanity off the Whitechapel Road" and "The Chink" and, after portraying a racially mixed woman and child, notes "Yes there are nicer places in London than Limehouse—and one is glad to get back to the center of things and see . . . [a scene of the changing of the Guard] . . . something which reminds us that there is still something British in Wonderful London!"

[2] See Hankins, "Kindle" and "Colour."
[3] At this conference I was delighted to encounter the prototype projects of Michael Groden on *Ulysses* and Clifford Wulfman on *The Waves*, projects which offer stimulating glimpses of such innovation.

Works Cited

Barrett, Eileen and Patricia Cramer, eds. *Virginia Woolf: Lesbian Readings*. New York: NYU Press, 1997.

Bellamy, Suzanne. "The Pattern Behind the Words." *Virginia Woolf: Lesbian Readings*. Eds., Eileen Barrett and Patricia Cramer. New York: NYU Press, 1997. 21-36.

Burrows, Elaine with Janet Moat, David Sharp and Linda Wood. *The British Cinema Source Book: BFI Archive Viewing Copies and Library Materials*. London: BFI Publishing. 1995.

Hankins, Leslie Kathleen. "'Colour burning on a framework of steel': Virginia Woolf, Marleen Gorris, Eileen Atkins and *Mrs. Dalloway*(s)." *Women's Studies: An Interdisciplinary Journal*. Special Issue, "Virginia Woolf in Performance. 28. 4. Ed. Sally Greene, (Summer 1999): 367-77.

——. "'To Kindle and Illuminate': Woolf's Hot Flashes Against Ageism—Challenges for the Cinematic Lens." *Virginia Woolf and Her Influences: Selected Papers from the Seventh Annual Conference on Virginia Woolf*. Eds. Laura Davis and Jeanette McVicker. New York: Pace University Press, 1998. 26-35.

Hussey, Mark. "How Should One Read a Screen?" *Virginia Woolf in the Age of Mechanical Reproduction*. Ed. Pamela Caughie. New York: Garland Press, 2000. 249-265.

To-Day's Cinema News and Property Gazette. March 6, 1924: 13, 21.

Woolf, Virginia. *A Room of One's Own*. 1929. New York: Harcourt, 1981.

——. "The Cinema," *The Nation & Athenaeum*, July 3, 1926: 381-3. Reprinted as Appendix II "The Cinema/The Movies and Reality." *The Essays of Virginia Woolf*. Vol. 3. Ed. Andrew McNeillie. London: The Hogarth Press, 1994. 591-595.

——. *The Essays of Virginia Woolf*. Vol. 3. Ed. Andrew McNeillie. San Diego: HBJ, Publishers, 1988.

——. *The Essays of Virginia Woolf*. Vol. 4. Ed. Andrew McNeillie. London: The Hogarth Press, 1994.

——. "How It Strikes a Contemporary" 1923. *The Essays of Virginia Woolf*. Vol. 3. Ed. Andrew McNeillie. San Diego: HBJ, Publishers, 1988. 353-360.

——. "The Leaning Tower" 1940. *The Moment and Other Essays*. New York: Harcourt, 1948. 128-154.

——. "Modern Fiction." 1925. *The Essays of Virginia Woolf*. Vol. 4. Ed. Andrew McNeillie. London: The Hogarth Press, 1994. 157-165.

——. *Three Guineas*. 1938. San Diego: HBJ, Publishers, 1966.

Filmography

"Nymphs of the Water Garden." *Some Classical Dancing by the Pupils of Margaret Morris*. *Around the Town* series. 1922.

Bentley, Thomas, dir. *'Old Bill' Through the Ages*. Ideal Studies. British Film Service. 1924.

Dancing Grace—Studies of Madame Lopokova. *Eve's Film Review* series. Pathé. 1922

Lesley Higgins and Marie-Christine Leps
From Contingency to Essence: Fictions of Identity in Novels and Films

> "The problem's not the hero, but the struggle. Can you make a film about a struggle without going through the traditional process of creating heroes? It's a new form of an old problem." – Michel Foucault, "Film and Popular Memory"

Virginia Woolf knew that powerful biographies never tell the story of a personal journey, but rather analyze the discursive practices which shape subjectivities and delimit their itineraries. She also knew that the plots we read and the plots we live by are inextricably linked; that the same cultural, political, and economic pressures apply to both kinds of fiction. *Mrs. Dalloway* (1925), for example, rewrites the day-in-the-life narrative so that Clarissa Dalloway's preparations for a lavish party are made to make sense both as the predictable telos of a privileged upper-class life and as the figure of patriarchal, imperial England after the First World War. The text thus exposes the public determinations of the private sphere: any individual moment of civilized pleasure is governed by the same power-knowledge relations which drive a veteran to suicide and compel his eminent physician to prescribe "order" and "proportion" for shell-shock. *Orlando: A Biography* (1928) inverts this strategy by allowing the eponymous character to experience being him- and her-self from the 1580s to the 1920s; as the undying subject of modernity changes and crosses sexes, the rarefaction produced by vectors of gender, class, and race comes to light.

Not surprisingly, both novels became films in the 1990s, when the nature and representation of identities saturated contemporary culture and warfare. The first segment of our argument examines the problematics of identity and subjectivity in Woolf's biographical experiments. The second considers Marlene Gorris's *Mrs. Dalloway* (1998) and Sally Potter's *Orlando* (1993) in order to explore the different interpretive possibilities afforded by the directors' present and by the cinematic medium. These analyses allow us, finally, to suggest how Woolf's past work continues to impinge upon contemporary modes of knowing and being.

I. A day in the life of modernity

Woolf's innovative texts counter any notions that life is individual, substantial, and knowable in its past and present. *Mrs. Dalloway* and *Orlando* insist that subjectivity is social, relational, and constructed; that identity is but an alibi that masks, with the semblance of coherence and closure, various and at times contradictory cultural investments. Contingency, not essence, obtains. Furthermore, Woolf's revolutionary forms contrarily demonstrate that meaning is not the integral, causal, and developmental figure promoted by conventional texts (whether social-scientific, political, or literary); traditional biographies and realist novels are co-conspirators in the subjectivization of individuals commonly identified as men and women, nobles and servants, soldiers and politicians. *Mrs. Dalloway* deftly registers the extent to which regulatory mechanisms govern the one and the many. Characters' ostensibly random, independent meanderings along the streets of London are shown to follow prefigured political, economic, gender, ethnic, and class lines. Clarissa Dalloway, seemingly undamaged by the recent war, is continually juxtaposed with the demobilized Septimus Warren Smith, who can only reaffirm that "life is good" by ending it. Physicians have been prescribing liberal doses of the English way-of-life for his anguish (porridge, soccer, outings), insisting that he keep his sense of "proportion, divine proportion" as they prepare his isolation and confinement. But Warren Smith recognizes his current enemies only too well: "human nature, in short, was on him—the repulsive brute, with the blood-red nostrils" (*MD* 92)—and this is what finally kills him. War, for Woolf, is not a temporary aberration, but the *reductio ad absurdum* of her culture's way of life.

Tied to this life-death tandem is a series of characters whose lives and positions instantiate the major institutional forces of governance: the judiciary, the army, the Empire, the industrial middle class, the church, health care services, and academia. By moving from one strand of thought to another, from the present to the past, from quotidian observations to daydreams and hallucinations, the narrative demonstrates the extent to which "the utmost happiness to be enjoyed in this life" (qtd. in Foucault 1980 2:251) serves only to strengthen the state.

The text carefully traces the ever-narrowing paths followed by all the characters: "the wild, the daring, the romantic" Sally Seton becomes Lady Rosseter, wife of the cotton manufacturer, with the big house in Manchester and the "five enormous boys" (*MD* 72, 171); Peter Walsh, the minor Anglo-Indian bureaucrat, is so effectively subjectivized that the predictable string of failures which constitutes his life (as student, socialist, husband, civil servant, lover) does not prevent him from maintaining his admiration for "the triumphs of civilisation," the "splendid achievement [of] . . . London; the season; civilisation" (*MD* 151, 55); and so on. Plot development relentlessly demonstrates how people's lives are diminished until they become normal, ordinary, perfectly understandable for everyone, and yet strange and incomprehensible to themselves: "But often now this body she wore. . . , this body, with all its capacities, seemed nothing—nothing at all. She had the oddest sense of being herself invisible; unseen; unknown; . . . this being Mrs. Dalloway; not even Clarissa any more, this being Mrs. Richard Dalloway" (*MD* 10-11).

The temporal compression of *Mrs. Dalloway* is answered by the expansiveness of *Orlando*, which traces the various ways in which the possibilities of life have been governed and circumscribed throughout modernity. Gender's enforcing hand is dramatized by placing Orlando in a perpetual, playful state of becoming: a young English aristocrat (a favorite of Elizabeth I) becomes an official of Queen Anne's government in Constantinople who becomes a woman who, returning to George II's London, needs to cross-dress to remain mobile yet becomes a wife who becomes a Victorian mother who ends up a celebrated writer, at "the twelfth stroke of midnight, Thursday, the eleventh of October, Nineteen hundred and Twenty Eight" (*O* 329), on a wild goose chase. . . literally. In the final segment, Orlando the woman feels "haunted": "[F]or though one may say, as Orlando said. . . Orlando? still the Orlando she needs may not come; these selves of which we are built up, one on top of another, as plates are piled high on a waiter's hand, have attachments elsewhere, sympathies, little constitutions and rights of their own . . . for everybody can multiply from his own experience the different terms which his different selves have made with him" (*O* 308). Subjectivity (displayed and displaced in this passage's pronominal shifts) is enacted as a series of contingent selves in a text which questions the meaning and limits of gender in the spaces of social and narrative representation. Yet the number of selves allowed to come out always depends upon historical circumstances.

Never, in either book, is the reader presented with an unobstructed view of the characters or their situations; a narrative presence mediates the reader's apprehension and calls attention to the constructedness of life forms—biological, social, and biographical. In *Mrs. Dalloway*, the narrator functions as a conductor, orchestrating the reader's perception of disparate streams of consciousness, all the while subtly keeping time ("Big Ben was beginning to strike, first the warning, musical; then the hour, irrevocable" [*MD* 117]). This narrative procedure of knowledge production (mapping the relational character of identity) is thematized in the novel when Peter Walsh remembers Clarissa Dalloway's theory "to explain the feeling they had of dissatisfaction; not knowing people; not being known. For how could they know each other? . . . [T]o know her, or anyone, one must seek out the people who completed them; even the places . . . . [T]he unseen part of us, which spreads wide, the unseen might survive, be recovered somehow attached to this person or that, or even haunting certain places, after death. Perhaps–perhaps" (*MD* 152-53). *Completion* is the novel's project, shared by narrator and reader: a specific disposition of presences that makes possible new meanings by differently articulating intersections of the epistemological and ontological.

In *Orlando*, the narrator's identifying presence functions more like that of an overbearing, loud-speaking, self-obsessed tour guide repeatedly bemoaning the difficulties of his task. This playful, ironic device not only parodies Woolf's other writings, but life-writing in general. While purportedly tracing the becoming of Orlando, the narrator stubbornly remains at the surface, constantly insisting that nothing of interest ever takes place, evacuating meaning until the only recourse is to "leave a great blank here," on page 253. Discontinuous historical tableaux stage social conventions of being and doing: gender roles and political offices are rendered through a flurry of fashion statements, tea parties, banquets of state, wax seals, and legal parchments. Yet, the serious work of the fictional parody is to reiterate inescapable forces of governance which limit the possibilities of life through gender, class, race, and sexual orientation. Orlando can only survive through submission to monarchical whims, Augustan misogyny, Victorian crinolines, property entailments, marital estate, and bodily "twangings and tinglings" (*O* 245).

II. Moving pictures

But how to translate such experimental fictions into film? In her 1926 essay "The Cinema," Woolf hypothesizes that "there must be some residue of visual emotion not seized by artist or painter-poet which may await the cinema.... Something abstract, something moving, something calling only for the very slightest help from words or from music to make itself intelligible—of such movements, of such abstractions, the films may in time to come be composed" (*E4* 351).[1] Marlene Gorris's *Mrs. Dalloway* and Sally Potter's *Orlando* realize this potential in several ways. Both films emphatically stage the pastness of the past: Gorris uses different film stocks (Kodak for richly colored memories; Fuji for a bloodless post-war present) (Lacey C3); Potter chromatically coordinates and keys each historical set design, allowing the colors and the lighting to "brin[g] it all to life" (Glaessner 14). Lavish costuming in both films is accentuated by camera work that focuses on embroidery, jewels, hat design, a frayed cuff, the sound and smoke of a locomotive, thus foregrounding the metonymic ruse which allows small details to signify entire social modes of production.

Soundtracks intensify differently. Gorris uses the sounds of combat in the midst of a pastoral park scene or Bond Street to manifest the war's continuing, invasive presence in Warren Smith's afflicted life—a physical connection also imposed upon the listening audience. The plangent notes of strings, piano, and exploding mortars connect his daily hallucinations with the moment of pause preceding his suicide, thereby concretizing the functional equivalence between the way of life promulgated by his physicians and the way of death necessitated by economic and political imperatives. Intermixing the sounds of combat with those of classical music, using opera as the aural correlative of mortal anguish, forcefully signifies the inextricable relation between civilization and war. Potter's carefully-crafted soundtrack (she co-wrote the score with David Motion) includes the enhanced presence of heartbeats, bird song, scratching skate blades, wind and rain, thereby registering the sounds (and synaesthetically, the feeling) of everyday life as the audience knows them in the midst of the "irreality"[2] of her cinematic narrative.

Complementary visual and auditory textures thus bring the past to life with a keen immediacy of sensation. These cinematic pleasures come at a cost, however: the price of substantiation. In both films, the past *is* the past (singular, shared, linear, inalterable), and it leads to the present. In the film *Mrs. Dalloway*, the consistent and progressive character of the flashbacks—so different from the temporally unsettling and tunnel-like intrusions of Woolf's novel—concretize the past as a *real* set of events with an essential, commonly available meaning. The film concludes nostalgically with a freeze-frame of Clarissa, Sally, and Peter enjoying the leisure and luxury of youth, before marriage. Such an ending confirms Gorris's film as the story of lost opportunities, missed love affairs, and wasted potential. Even the rich and powerful, we are told, have their unhappy moments. Woolf's *Mrs. Dalloway* conveys the infinite multiplicity of the past, known only partially, and always refracted through the voluntary and involuntary memories of troubled consciousnesses. Scenes from the past impinge on the present, impede perception, and limit the future. Nonetheless, the novel ends, stubbornly, with the recognition and reaffirmation of Clarissa's presence ("For there she was" [*MD* 194]) as "gift" and potential for transformation through understanding. Only Clarissa instinctively accepts Septimus's suicide and recognizes the soul-forcing, "obscurely evil" strength of social order and proportion; only Clarissa is inflamed with an all-consuming anger; only she knows her parties as a tribute to life and an offering to others. The film, on the other hand, tends to hystericize Clarissa (especially during the party) and elevate Peter into a dashing, tanned, romantic hero untouched by political complications.[3]

However parodically, Woolf's *Orlando* tightens the correlation between gendered identities and social order. The opening sentences interlace the governmental strands of patriarchy, property, and empire: "He—for there could be no doubt of his sex, though the fashion of the time did something to disguise it—was in the act of slicing at the head of a Moor which swung from the rafters. . . . Orlando's father, or perhaps his grandfather, had struck it from the shoulders of a vast Pagan . . . and now it swung, gently, perpetually, in the . . . attic rooms of the gigantic house of the lord who had slain him" (*O* 13). Potter's *Orlando* begins, as it ends, as a story of personal development and ultimate freedom. Orlando is introduced as a sensitive young man, at home in a pastoral setting, who simply craves the affections of another. The introductory, female voice-over description is interrupted by the character himself at the moment of pronominal identification: "But when he—'that is, I' [Swinton's Orlando interjects, looking straight at the camera]—came into the world [the voice-over continues], he was looking for something else. Though heir to a name that meant power, land, and property, surely when Orlando was born, it wasn't privilege he sought, but company." From the outset, subjective camera techniques inscribe the viewer as complicitous company with a shared horizon of understanding: comments addressed to the camera, simple understatements such as "very interesting person" (Queen Elizabeth I), "terrific play" (*Othello*), or "it would never have worked; a man must follow his heart," do not explain an unfamiliar scene so much as suggest that the protagonist is already our contemporary, as distant from the past as we are. Eventually, so complicitous has the audience become that words are superfluous—Orlando's knowing gaze in the audience's direction suffices to punctuate key moments of the diegesis with shared irony.

Thus Orlando's desires and future are always assured in Potter's film, and indeed will come to include literary success, a beautiful daughter, and a singing angel who proclaims, "At last, I am free. At last, at last, to be free of the past. And of a future that beckons me. I am coming, I am coming. Neither a woman nor a man. We are joined, we are one, with a human face." Granted, the angel (impersonated by Jimmy Somerville, who sings throughout the film) is a send-up of the *deus ex machina* trope. Granted, this figure parodies the movie's teleological drive as signaled by the constant motivation for change: this Orlando never ages because Queen Elizabeth stipulates perpetual youth as the condition for granting him property; this Orlando becomes a woman because he will not take up arms and kill another; this Orlando eschews marriage; and so on. According to Potter, these alterations were necessary "to strengthen some of the narrative muscle for cinematic purposes—to supply little bits of motivation for the story's premise, to make it psychologically convincing on film" (qtd. Indiana 90). Just so: to paraphrase Foucault, Potter's film is about the hero's personal journey, not about social, political, and economic struggles as they shape individuals. Orlando is always essentially Orlando, whatever the mirror may reveal. "Same person. No difference at all," says Orlando as she admires her new female body; then, turning to address the camera, she adds, "Just a different sex." Woolf's novel would have it otherwise. Change is unmotivated and unexplained in her biography. The narrator's initial stipulation of sameness at the moment of biological transformation is soon contradicted; gender colonizes the body, inflects its desires, and directs its actions elsewhere. "Thus," the narrator reluctantly acknowledges, "there is much to support the view that it is clothes that wear us and not we them; we may make them take the mould of arm or breast, but they mould our hearts, our brains, our tongues to their liking" (*O* 188).

Both films, but especially Potter's, ultimately reiterate the liberal humanist dream of personal freedom and expression. Potter's Orlando is finally liberated from the fetters of gender, property, and privilege, and accompanied by a video camera-wielding daughter. Completing the narrative framing device, the voice-over asserts, "But she is changed. She is no longer trapped by destiny. And, ever since she let go of the past, she found her life was beginning." Woolf's Orlando knows no such easy answers. Social pressures are maintained rather than denied: only her son's birth entitles her position at the family estate; her compulsory husband, "now grown a fine sea captain," returns home in an airplane. But this "classic" happy ending is immediately subverted by the final figure of the wild goose "[springing] up over his head" (*O* 329), which confirms the fictional satire.

III. Final credits

Why would Potter do such a thing—affirm an essential identity for all human beings? Perhaps because of her present: an era of multiplying genocides euphemistically known as ethnic cleansings, when the recognition of difference, in terms of race, religion, or sexual orientation, justifies war on the European and African continents, the fire-bomb deaths of three boys in Northern Ireland, or the lethal beating (yet another) of a gay man in a U.S. college town. Declaring sameness could be more strategic, politically.

Yet there is a moment in Woolf's novel, judiciously translated to the screen by Potter, which inscribes the reader/viewer in the implied author's attempt to alter the balance of power relations, dislodge acceptable truths, and thus foreshadow the possibility of amending conditions of existence. Orlando's biographer pauses briefly to mention the following curiosity: "Near London Bridge, where the river had frozen to a depth of some twenty fathoms, a wrecked wherry boat was plainly visible, lying on the bed of the river. . . . The old bumboat woman, who was carrying her fruit to market on the Surrey side, sat there in her plaids and farthingales . . . for all the world as if she were about to serve a customer, though a certain blueness about the lips hinted the truth" (*O* 36). Having noted the presence of the frozen corpse, however, the narrator quickly moves on to describe enthusiastically the "brilliancy" of the Great Frost, when aristocrats could dine and dance on the frozen Thames. Yet this act of narrative enfolding makes manifest the ethical responsiveness of the writing subject—marks its outrage, and summons the reader. With vivid directness, Potter's modified point-of-view shot forces the viewer into the woman's place under the ice's snowy surface. The scene begins with the sovereign's laughing face staring directly down, into the camera; on either side, two male courtiers replicate his gaze and gaiety, while a third witness looks sideways towards them, embodying a critical yet silent objection. Next, positioned behind the observers, the camera reveals the object of mirth: the peasant woman's frozen body. Then immediately, a larger shot features the king's attendants clumsily maneuvering a cloth to prevent his feet from ever touching the ice. The royal progress is subsequently framed by subjects either laboring to survive or enjoying their leisurely ice-skating. Rather than dismissing or obviating the constraints of gender, class privilege, and governance, this particular episode compellingly transmits their deadly effects.

Ultimately, however, both films work through identification: the viewer is made to sympathize with characters, to pity workers, and to consider war as an inhuman aberration. Woolf's reader is always led to understand that personal empathy must be tempered by social critique; war is revealed as the necessary cost of a masculinist, militaristic society. Instead of aspiring to an essential sameness, the reader is urged by Woolf's austere pragmatism to acknowledge, analyze, and negotiate with contingency and difference.

Notes

1 For further discussion of "The Cinema" see Hotchkiss and Shaughnessy.
2 For a discussion of the film's "irreality" and satire, see Pidduck.
3 During the party, Clarissa is rescued from near-collapse by her husband, who shepherds her away from the Bradshaws's discussion of shell-shock and suicide (her overreaction is signaled by point-of-view close-ups of their mouths). The scene revealing

her psychic connection to Warren Smith is demeaned by displacing it to the window: unwittingly or not, the effect is to reiterate a cliché of the classic Hollywood "woman's film," in which images of hysterical or paranoid women "looking through windows or waiting at windows abound" (Doane 72-73). Unlike the whey-faced Richard Dalloway or Hugh Whitbread, the fit and younger-looking Peter maintains his ability to attract female interest and desire—not only from Clarissa, but from Daisy, the "girl in India," and a beautiful stranger in Regent's Park.

Works Cited

Doane, Mary Ann. "The 'Woman's Film': Possession and Address." In *Revision: Essays in Feminist Film Criticism.* American Film Institute Monograph Series. Eds. Mary Ann Doane, Patricia Mellencamp, and Linda Williams. Frederick, MD: U Publications of America, 1984. 67-82.

Foucault, Michel. *Omnes et Singulatim: Towards a Criticism of "Political Reason."* The Tanner Lectures on Human Value. Ed. S. M. McMurrin. 2 vols. Cambridge: Cambridge UP, 1980-1981.

——. "Film and Popular Memory." *Foucault Live: Collected Interviews, 1961-1984.* Ed. Sylvère Lotringer. Trans. Lysa Hochroth and John Johnston. New York: Semiotext[e], 1989. 122-32.

Glaessner, Verlina. "Fire and Ice." *Sight and Sound* n.s. 2 (August 1992): 12-15.

Hotchkiss, Lia M. "Writing the Jump Cut: *Mrs. Dalloway* in the Context of Cinema." In *Virginia Woolf: Texts and Contexts, Selected Papers from the Fifth Annual Conference.* Eds. Beth Daugherty and Eileen Barrett. New York: Pace UP, 1996. 134-39.

Indiana, Gary. "Spirits Either Sex Assume: Gary Indiana Talks with Sally Potter." *Artforum* 31 (Summer 1993): 88-91.

Lacey, Liam. "To the festival, Mrs. Dalloway." Rev. of *Mrs. Dalloway* by Marlene Gorris. Toronto *Globe and Mail* 11 September 1997: C3.

Pidduck, Julianne. "Travels with Sally Potter's *Orlando*: Gender, Narrative, Movement," *Screen* 38. 2 (1997): 172-89.

Shaughnessy, Nicola. "Is s/he or isn't s/he?: Screening *Orlando*." In *Pulping Fictions: Consuming Culture Across the Literature/Media Divide.* Eds. Deborah Cartmell et al. London: Pluto P, 1996. 43- 55.

Woolf, Virginia. *Mrs. Dalloway.* New York: HBJ, 1990.

——. *Orlando: A Biography.* New York: HBJ, 1973.

Michelle N. Mimlitsch
Envisioning/Revisioning Woolf in Film at the End of the Twentieth Century

The recent film adaptation of *Mrs. Dalloway* begins not in London, 1923, but in Italy, 1918, where we watch Septimus Warren Smith witness the death of his friend and officer, Evans. Of course, we all know that is *not* how *Mrs. Dalloway* begins . . . at least not as Woolf wrote it. Wondering why Marleen Gorris chose this beginning, however, offers an almost-too-perfect entré for this presentation.

This paper began with two distinct, but I believe complementary, ideas. The first has to do with "envisioning"—my label for the film industry's ongoing project of making books into movies, visual cultural productions that can be seen and therefore appreciated in the dominant mode of our time. The second is concerned with what I have called "revisioning" in my title—the process by which a film adaptation (like any other new creation based on an earlier work) *revises* its original in ways that reflect its creator's interpretation of the source text.

Motion pictures have always borrowed from prose fiction. The obvious affiliation between the two forms as they have evolved is rooted in their shared predilection for narrative. As Morris Beja writes in his textbook on the subject of *Film and Literature* (1979), "written stories . . . and filmed stories . . . are really two forms of a single art—the art of narrative literature" (xiv). Prose fiction has long supplied something of which the film industry was in continual need: good stories. When filmmakers attempt to bring a "literary" novel to the screen, however, there must be more at work than a simple need for a good plot—especially if that novel emphasizes what Woolf called "the inside of [the] mind" (*CDB* 182) in her critique of film adaptations in "The Cinema." In just the last decade we have seen film adaptations of many extremely abstract or "textual" books: Henry James's psychologically nuanced *The Portrait of a Lady* (1881), Vladimir Nabokov's verbally and thematically illusory *Lolita* (1955), E. M. Forster's *Howards End* (1910) with its lengthy meditations voiced by the extradiegetic narrator, and, of course, both *Orlando* (1928) and *Mrs. Dalloway* (1925).[1] These are not lively adventure stories begging for an action-filled film version, nor are they recent bestsellers likely to lure audiences through clever co-marketing. Rather, they are works that the filmmakers who choose them find relevant today and therefore worth revisioning. A little bit like the readers who memorize classics in *Fahrenheit 451* (1953), these filmmakers bring texts they value to film, the form that according to Brian McFarlane "might be claimed . . . [to have] displaced the novel as the twentieth century's most popular narrative form" (vii). In so doing, they simultaneously make the narrative available to audiences who might never read the book and imprint it with their own understanding of the source's intentions, meanings, and relevance.

It is this very act of interpretation that so often disgruntles readers—like Woolf—who have appreciated the text in its own right (or rather, if we are to be accurate, have appreciated their own understanding and interpretation of the text). There are doubtless many reasons why we tend to privilege a literary source over a film adaptation thereof—perhaps we encountered it first, or simply prefer to read, or have absorbed the message of cultural value conveyed by the fact that we study literature in high school, but not film. Whatever the cause, as scholars of literature we seem always tempted to use the standard of faithfulness in judging an adaptation, despite often-repeated arguments in adaptation theory such as McFarlane's that although "the adducing of fidelity to the original novel as a major criterion for judging the film is pervasive[, n]o critical line is in greater need of re-examination and devaluation" (8). McFarlane's *Novel to Film* (1996) gathers comments from many critics to the effect that insistence upon fidelity simply isn't useful, and can obscure more productive approaches to comparing an adaptation and its source. For example, as film writer Christopher Orr has suggested, film adaptations "[constitute] a privileged site for a comparative investigation of the discursive practices of film and literature" (73) as well as for assessing the ideological perspectives of the adapters: "a film adaptation is a product of the culture that created it and thus an expression of the ideological forces operative in that culture at a specific historical moment" (73).

In addition to offering a lens through which to observe the ideologies of the filmmakers, movies that achieve any level of mainstream distribution should also be considered a barometer of wider cultural trends and concerns. While many tiny independent films are made every year from radical and challenging perspectives, their screenings are generally limited to film festivals or other arts venues with highly targeted audiences. Films like *Orlando* and *Mrs. Dalloway* (1997), on the other hand, achieve wider distribution because their producers have convinced the marketing executives at distribution companies that enough people will pay to see the film to make it worth their while. As Leslie K. Hankins has noted of *Orlando*, this may explain some adaptive choices, like the "Lesbian Erasure" she finds in the film. As we notice such marketing maneuvers, then, we might ask ourselves, what does Woolf *mean* to a non-scholarly audience, now, today, this moment of June 1999? What in her works has resonated with our cultural moment in this last decade of the twentieth century?

Viewing Gorris' *Mrs. Dalloway*, we find in just the first minutes of the film the concepts that dominate its narrative. Although the film is more attentive than many adaptations to fidelity to its source, its opening scenes indicate the ways in which it will diverge therefrom—reorganizations of the novel that reflect our current assessments of the natures of both history and feminism in the 1990s. From the scene at the Italian front, the film shifts to Clarissa Dalloway at her mirror in June, 1923. She thinks, in a voiceover, "Those ruffians, the gods, shan't have it all their own way. Those gods who never lose a chance of hurting, thwarting, and spoiling human lives are seriously put out if all the same you behave like a lady. Of course now I think there are no gods there's no one to blame. It's so very dangerous to live just one day." As she proceeds to go out for her flowers, we see a one-legged veteran on the street just before she encounters Hugh Whitbread, who explains that his wife is "a good deal out of sorts. The war may be over but there's still the echo of it. The Bexborough boy was killed, you know, and she is very close to Lady Bexborough... and Evelyn takes things badly." Opening the film in the trenches, of course, privileges the novel's "war book" aspects, framing whatever follows in the context of the horrors of the Great War. This is reinforced visually by the maimed veteran in the background and in dialogue through an interesting reworking of Clarissa's conversation with Hugh. While cleverly mentioning Lady Bexborough and her dead son in an almost offhand fashion just as the novel does, it also recasts the war as the cause for Evelyn Whitbread's illness rather than the "internal ailment" (6) that the novel specifies. Gorris' decision to foreground the war in this fashion undoubtedly has multiple motivations, but it seems particularly striking when we remember the attention the European wars of this century have received in various media as the 1900s wind to a close. Pat Barker's *Regeneration* trilogy, including Booker Prize winner *The Ghost Road* (1995), has revitalized the Great War as a topic for literary discussion in the past decade; in 1996 PBS broadcast an eight-episode series titled "The Great War and the Shaping of the Twentieth Century"; and anyone who watches the History Channel on cable will quickly conclude that little else aside from war (Great or otherwise) took place in "Our Century." By privileging the war-related elements of Woolf's *Mrs. Dalloway*, Gorris participates in our process of reevaluating the history of this bloodiest of human centuries, reminding us of Woolf's pacifism while reflecting our end-of-the-century need to better understand the violent conflict that has in too many ways shaped our culture.

Interestingly, Sally Potter's *Orlando* participates in our dialogue on war as well, through her addition of a motive behind Orlando's sex change—a modification that particularly vexed some viewers. Woolf's *Orlando* begins with the youth "in the act of slicing at the head of a Moor which swung from the rafters" (13). Potter omits this scene, opening instead with Orlando under the Oak Tree, attempting to compose poetry. This change takes on importance within the context of the war-related motivation Potter gives to Orlando's eighteenth-century sex change. As the Kahn's enemies invade, Orlando agrees to aid in the defense. When the Archduke Harry shoots a man, however, Orlando is so troubled by Harry's callous statement that "He's not a man, he's the enemy" that he walks away from the fighting, looking dazed amidst the noises of battle and, tellingly, a baby crying. His second long sleep and the transformation into a woman immediately follow. The film version of Orlando's conversation with Shelmerdine about gender confirms the connection between the battle and the change of sex. Orlando asks if Shelmerdine has fought in battles, "like a man," and then speculates: "If I were a man . . . I might choose not to risk my life for an uncertain cause. I might think that freedom won by death is not worth having. In fact . . ." But here Shelmerdine interrupts her, saying, "You might choose not to be a real man at all. Say if I was a woman . . . I might choose not to sacrifice my life caring for my children, or my children's children, nor to drown anonymously in the milk of female kindness. But instead, say, to go abroad. Would I then be . . ." In her turn Orlando interrupts, finishing his question, "A real woman?". While Orlando's unwillingness to risk her life may be interpreted as a kind of cowardice—a failure to be a "real man," the scene's implicit critique of the gender roles of real women suggests another reading, one that undermines the assumption that real men fight in battles.

Furthermore, just as the crying baby in the Turkish battle scene injects the suffering of children in war into the movie, the passage from the Victorian period to the present through a composite tableau of the two World Wars reminds us of the impact that modern war has had on women—a theme reminiscent of many of Woolf's writings. As the Victorian episode ends we hear a small airplane flying overhead. As much a harbinger of the future as the train in the 1850 sequence, it drops a bomb into the Victorian mist; with its impact the colors change and the scene becomes one of First World War trenches—mud, barbed wire, and broken-down wagon wheels. Simultaneously, the pregnant Orlando's costuming in a 1940s dress and the number of explosions suggest World War II and the blitz, and particularly the suffering of women and children in total war. Despite the fact that Woolf places the Great War in parentheses in her 1928 text, Potter has commented that to bring the narrative to a conclusion in our present "It seemed clear that I had to refer to the First and Second World Wars and the effect they had on consciousness" (Donohue, 12). Like Gorris' foregrounding of the Great War in *Mrs. Dalloway*, Potter's revision of *Orlando* reflects our contemporary compulsion to understand and respond to the conflicts that have shaped our times. Simultaneously, by bringing Woolf's pacifism into the narrative, Potter reminds us of the degree to which our understanding of an author's complete oeuvre often influences our interpretation of a single work.

Along these lines, Madeline Moore's paper in the panel on Potter's *Orlando* at the 1994 Woolf conference argues for such framing of several of the changes Potter made to the elements and themes of Woolf's novel. Connecting the change of sex to a crisis in battle, she posits, "must be understood . . . within contemporary ethical concerns" (196). Similarly, she reminds us that Potter's revision of the novel's conclusion—changing Orlando's child to a girl and "freeing" her from her property—makes sense to modern female viewers: "Potter's film glorifies the bravery of a character who relinquishes money and the possibility of being part of a couple, and extols the relationship to her daughter. This is a feminism American and English women of the '90s certainly recognize" (196).

Returning to Gorris' *Mrs. Dalloway* with this thought in mind, we can observe a similar, if subtler, interpretation of Woolf's text influenced by contemporary feminist perspectives. Clarissa's first thoughts in the film are of "those ruffians" who hurt and spoil human lives. In the novel, this language appears nearly half-way through, in Peter's thoughts about Clarissa (77). By shifting it forward and into Clarissa's consciousness immediately following the scene in the trenches, Gorris recasts Clarissa's resistance to a random, brutal fate as an intentional refutation of the powers that lead to war. Her next thought, "It's so very dangerous to live just one day," bridges these thoughts of violent ruffians and the announcement that she will buy the flowers herself (the moment we know the novel begins). In Woolf's text, the declaration that "she always had the feeling that it was very, very dangerous to live even one day" does not appear until after the conversation with Hugh. So, here again, Gorris has privileged an aspect of the novel by moving it forward in the film's narrative and allowing it to set the tone for what follows. As the movie progresses, it becomes clear that for Clarissa the danger of everyday life is not so much "those ruffians" but her own timidity. In a series of scenes crucial to the film's exposition of the romantic triangle constituted by Peter Walsh, Clarissa, and Richard Dalloway, it becomes apparent that Gorris interprets Clarissa's weak heart as a faint one too, an emotional condition that explains—in a way Woolf's text does not—why Clarissa would choose to marry Richard. Like the novel, Gorris' film depicts the conflict between Peter's overwhelming desire and Clarissa's need for solitude even in marriage. The film goes on, however, to add an element of fear to Clarissa's motivation in choosing Richard. In the quarrel at Bourton in which Peter demands that Clarissa tell him the truth about her relationship with Dalloway, the novel's Clarissa refuses to reply. In Gorris' adaptation, however, she exclaims, "He makes me feel safe! . . . You want so much of me Peter; I just can't do it—throw everything away and go across the world with you. I'm not brave in that way." Later at the party, in an exchange not present in the novel, Peter asks Sally why Clarissa wouldn't marry him. Her reply reiterates Clarissa's: "She was afraid," a statement that does not distinguish between the fear of being overwhelmed and the need to feel safe, allowing both factors to remain in play.

While audiences today can certainly relate to Clarissa's fear of being smothered, we may find it difficult to understand why she would choose stuffy, inarticulate Richard Dalloway instead; why not go off on her own, or with Sally, or wait for a better man who asked less of her? Why, within the framework of the film, does her need to feel safe justify choosing Richard? In yet another recontextualizing of language from the novel, Gorris offers an explanation for this, too. Woolf's parenthetical comment, "(they spoke of marriage always as a catastrophe)" (34) becomes a thwarted feminist conversation between Clarissa and Sally. Clarissa expresses her sense that marriage is far better for men than for women, to which Sally replies "Marriage is a catastrophe for women!" Clarissa goes on to add, however, that it seems inevitable—expressing a sense of constraint thoroughly in keeping with her upbringing and era, but generally incompatible with ours. Combined with her need to feel safe, this comment provides a *reason* for marrying Richard: he is the better choice when marriage remains inescapable.

Significantly, while Peter and Sally talk at the party, the film moves back and forth between them and Clarissa at her window, pondering Septimus' suicide. Strikingly, she concludes, "That young man killed himself, but I don't pity him. I'm somehow glad he could do it, throw it away. It's made me feel the beauty, somehow feel, very like him . . . less afraid." With these thoughts she goes back down to the party, where another small but significant revision to the novel takes place: Clarissa declares to Peter, "Here I am at last" suggesting a change within her that is completely absent from the novel's third-person "For there she was" (194). The film fades on couples dancing at the party, most recently joined by Clarissa, partnered with Peter. By reinterpreting the meaning of Septimus' suicide for Clarissa and "revisioning" the closure of the narrative, Gorris offers an interpretation of the novel likely to appeal to an audience that may well wish Clarissa had chosen Peter. Moreover, by suggesting that she has outgrown at least some of her fear, Gorris recuperates Clarissa as the feminist heroine many readers seek but struggle to find in the novel. Thus, just as Potter's *Orlando* reflects a broader reading of Woolf's pacifism, so too Gorris' interpretation of *Mrs. Dalloway* draws in Woolf's feminism while also reminding us of the much more limiting cultural restraints upon women of Woolf's time in contrast to our own.

Both of these directors, then, have made adaptations that emphasize two of the "causes" we most closely associate with Woolf: feminism and pacifism. Their modifications to the sources foreground these issues and reflect the contexts in which they are discussed today. This adaptive process reveals not only that active concern with pacifism and feminism cannot yet be relegated to the "historic recreation" aspect of costume drama, but also the filmmakers' conviction that Woolf's fiction still contributes to our understanding of these issues. Their exercise of "adaptive license" suggests a dialogue with Woolf, in which they advise her of what has happened since she wrote, while continuing to listen to what her works offer to a culture trying to make sense of a century of war and to women still seeking personal strength and independence despite significant changes in their social roles. Woolf might be disappointed to find us still talking about war and the roles of women as we turn toward the twenty-first century, but she would surely be glad to be a part of the conversation.

Note

[1] James Ivory's *Howards End* was released in 1992, Jane Campion's *Portrait of a Lady* in 1996, and Adrian Lyne's *Lolita* in 1998.

Works Cited

Beja, Morris. *Film and Literature: An Introduction.* New York: Longman, 1979.
Donohue, Walter. "Immortal Longing." [An interview with Sally Potter.] *Sight and Sound* 3/1 (1993): 10-12.
Hankins, Leslie K. "Redirections: Challenging the Class Axe and Lesbian Erasure in Potter's *Orlando*." In *Re: Reading, Re: Writing, Re: Teaching Virginia Woolf.* Ed. Eileen Barret and Patricia Cramer. New York: Pace UP, 1995: 168-84.
McFarlane, Brian. *Novel to Film: An Introduction to the Theory of Adaptation.* Oxford: Clarendon Press, 1996.
Moore, Madeline. "Virginia Woolf and Sally Potter: The Play of Opposites and the Modern Mind in *Orlando*." In *Re: Reading, Re: Writing, Re: Teaching Virginia Woolf.* Ed. Eileen Barret and Patricia Cramer. New York: Pace UP, 1995: 184-97.
Mrs. Dalloway. Dir. Marleen Gorris. First Look Pictures and BMG Independents, 1997.

Mimlitsch

Orlando. Dir. Sally Potter. Sony Pictures Classics, 1993.
Orr, Christopher. "The Discourse on Adaptation." *Wide Angle* 6/2 (1984): 72-76.
Woolf, Virginia. "The Cinema." 1926. In *The Captain's Death Bed and Other Essays.* NY: Harcourt, 1950: 180-86.
——. *Orlando; A Biography.* 1928; San Diego, Harvest/HBJ, n.d.
——. *Mrs. Dalloway.* 1925; San Diego, Harvest/HBJ, 1990.

Disciplinary Traversals

Shiela Pardee
Assuming Psyche's Task: Virginia Woolf Responds to James Frazer

In Virginia Woolf's first novel, *The Voyage Out* (1915), there is already evidence of an engagement with ethnographic study and primitive mythology which has been more often noted in her later work.[1] In her first novel she responds especially to the tendency of British anthropology during the Victorian era to classify the practices of other cultures based on their assumptions about what constituted "good" and "evil" for Britons. Using the evolutionary model of Darwinism and assuming a history and future of human progress, Victorian anthropologists and ethnographers rated human groups according to scales of development in body types, social and political institutions, arts, technology, and religious expression. However, as increasingly detailed hierarchies produced exceptions in every category, a counter-emphasis developed.[2] In general, Victorian description of other peoples and cultures had emphasized differences between the British and the "others"; Modernist descriptions began increasingly to emphasize similarities. In *The Voyage Out*, Woolf draws on ethnographic description to emphasize the ritual elements in British social practices and their basic similarity to the practices Victorians cataloged and read as the curiously "primitive" practices of "savage" people.

In this new generation's turn toward recognition of "the savage within," the relationship between classical studies and anthropology is crucial. Familiarity with classical history engendered acknowledgment of equivalence between the relationship of the Roman Empire to the "savage" Britons and the relationship of the British empire to the "savage" Africans. Victorian emphasis on the inevitability of progress was gradually replaced by a modernist emphasis on historical cycles of progress and regression. The popularity of Gibbon's *History of the Decline and Fall of the Roman Empire*, a book St. John Hirst urges upon Rachel in *The Voyage Out*, is an expression of this emphasis. The study of Greek prehistory, aided by archaeological discoveries, brought together contradictory images of Greece as the epitome of civilization and of the early Greeks as illiterate savages. The literary scholar in *The Voyage Out*, Miss Allen, expresses confusion about such contradictory images during a discussion of "discoveries in Crete." When she thinks of Greece, she says, she thinks of "naked black men," which she is sure is "quite wrong" (114). In 1890, following Victorian ethnographer E. B. Tylor, who theorized that the superstitious beliefs of European peasants were "survivals" of earlier "primitive" customs, classical scholar James G. Frazer wrote *The Golden Bough*, an explication of a passage in Virgil with reference to an Italian folk custom and similar practices worldwide. Woolf's friend, classical scholar Jane Harrison, was influenced by Frazer, but she discarded his idea that primitive societies developed rituals to conform with pre-scientific ideas about nature, asserting instead that the rituals themselves were primary and served practical purposes which may no longer be apparent, and that mythical and artistic elaborations of the rituals came later.

In 1909, Frazer read a paper at the Royal Institution in London, which evolved into the volume *Psyche's Task*, dedicated to "all who are engaged in Psyche's task of sorting out the seeds of good from the seeds of evil." Frazer wrote that even if the "great institutions which form the framework of modern society . . . have sometimes been built on" the "rotten foundations" of superstition, "it would be rash to conclude that they must all come down" because "in spite . . . of his absurdities man moves steadily upwards" (vii). Virginia Stephen and her friends, many of them educated at Cambridge where Frazer was a Fellow, were less optimistic.

Frazer's optimism, however, is also qualified. From his famous "armchair" position of academic and domestic security, Frazer is sure that savagery and superstition do not reside in himself. He believes that superstitions "linger" because of "the natural, universal, and ineradicable inequality of men" (166). Better ideas form "in the upper stratum" of people, he says, and slowly filter down to those at "the bottom" (168). The "intellectual progress" of humanity as a whole is slow. "The surface of society, like that of the sea, is in perpetual motion; its depths, like those of the ocean, remain almost unmoved" (171).

Frazer was a Cambridge man of the 1870s, like Woolf's characters Ridley Ambrose and William Pepper in *The Voyage Out* (20). Pepper is an expert naturalist who lectures to fellow travelers "upon the unplumbed depths of ocean." He describes in detail "the white, hairless, blind monsters lying curled on the ridges of sand at the bottom of the sea, which would explode if you brought them to the surface" (23). Helen and Rachel are not impressed; Helen calls Pepper "a bore" (23). Glancing back at Pepper laughing and gossiping with Ambrose about Cambridge acquaintances, "they saw [him] as though he had suddenly loosened his clothes, and had become a vivacious and malicious old ape" (17). Later, Rachel compares Pepper to a fossilized fish (19). Virginia Woolf distrusted the blind, institutionally-nurtured confidence of the older generations of Cambridge men which included her father, Leslie Stephen. Although she was skeptical about scholarly discourse in general, she seems very much in control when she uses anthropological discourse in *The Voyage Out* to critique the patriarchal form and political assumptions of empire.

That confidence is registered strongly, for example, in the mocking remarks of Helen and Rachel regarding the deficiencies of Pepper and Ambrose, and in their excursions into the night streets of an unfamiliar South American town "looking for life" (98). But Helen and Rachel also have deep fears and episodes of shaken confidence. Helen has "presentiments of disaster" in the native village. She "became acutely conscious of the little limbs, the thin veins, the delicate flesh of men and women, which breaks so easily and lets the life escape." She thinks of the "falling branch," the "foot that slips" and the possibilities of crushing and drowning (286). Rachel also has moments of sympathetic anxiety about others which are placed in contrast to the confident optimism of men. When Richard Dalloway talks of unity and progress, Rachel thinks of "a lean black widow . . . longing for someone to talk to" (66). When Terence talks of the income and freedom they will have in London, Rachel thinks of the less fortunate, about women who "die with bugs crawling across their faces." She kept and occasionally looked at the novel[3] which had given her these unsettling ideas, "as some medieval monk kept a skull, or a crucifix to remind him of the frailty of the body" (301). In a similar way, Woolf keeps ethnographic discourse in the background as a reminder of the common vulnerability of all people to the forces of nature; the common use of ritual to control behavior; and the wasted potential of less-powerful individuals, usually women, restricted by community expectations of ritual practice.

She makes a surprising application of this ethnographic discourse in *The Voyage Out* by recording the rituals of social and courtship behavior of the English tourists rather than the native population. The tourists vary in their understanding and enjoyment of rituals such as church and social engagements, but their ritual participation is little influenced by this. St. John Hirst goes to church, even though he reads Sappho during the service. Rachel finds the visits and letters expected after her engagement a taxing bore, but she participates to please Terence. In addition, Woolf demonstrates that the British community practices subtle, generalized forms of ritual equivalent to some of those found in Frazer's descriptions.

One of Frazer's preoccupations was the confinement of adolescent girls after puberty. In his examples, the girls are kept alone in the dark, tended by older female relations (often aunts), and forbidden to walk or sit on the ground. These taboos were observed, according to Frazer, for reasons of sympathetic magic (100), because menstruating women were thought to be uncommonly powerful, and controlling them was necessary to prevent catastrophe and insure fertility. The theoretical approach of Jane Harrison, which insists on the primacy of ritual, might suggest that the caging ritual was developed for the practical purpose of controlling women's sexuality until marriage, and that the elaborate explanations came later. Woolf demonstrates that British adolescent women like Rachel were also kept confined to control their sexuality and protect them from predatory men.

Woolf seems preoccupied with images of confinement in *Melymbrosia,* an early draft of *The Voyage Out.* She describes the confining city of London "dropped down from the skies as a cruel gin or cage over myriads of ant like creatures" by "some malicious arm" (DeSalvo, xxxi). Woolf continues the theme of confinement with her description of a plant attempting to grow after "whole months or winters close packed" and "squeezed" with "no airy crevice." It would, "if it still adventured upwards . . . though now maimed and blunted, knock its head against a flat sheet of some foreign substance." Eventually, "the sap would dry in the veins for no rain or sun would visit it, and it would lie there passive against the stone, white and soon shriveled" (xxxi). Louise DeSalvo considers it "obvious" that "Woolf meant this as a metaphor for the fate of human beings as well as that of plants" (xxxi). Woolf was already very familiar with images of women in British patriarchal society as stunted plants and caged birds from reading late Victorian and contemporary feminist writers, and she evokes those images here.

In addition, these dismal images of confinement evoke Frazer's descriptions of the confinement of adolescent girls. In one example, "girls are shut up in a little room or cell . . . in almost total darkness." After years of confinement, "bodily growth is stunted by the long want of exercise"; when she is released, "her complexion is pale and wax-like." Like upper-class British women kept "protected" at home, these girls occupy themselves with "handiwork" (*Golden Bough* 229). In another example, girls were placed at puberty "in small huts in which they had to remain on their hands and knees for six months; then the hut was enlarged enough to let them kneel upright, and they had to remain in this posture for six months more" (230).

In most of Frazer's examples, the women must avoid contact with the ground. In *The Voyage Out,* Woolf also attaches this ritual avoidance to British sexual ritual. When Terence and Rachel recall the walk in the woods during which they declared their love for each other, the experience seems unreal and neither can remember what had been said. The one thing that "seemed to unite them" and the one thing that they both recall is that they "sat upon the ground" (282). The sexual implications of being on the ground alone together automatically invoked their culture's prohibition against premarital sex. This prohibition is powerful enough to cause both Hewett and Hirst to assume, after seeing Arthur and Susan in a similar position, that the couple is engaged. The decision to marry is not a rational one for either couple: it is the result of a conditioned assumption designed to control their behavior.

When Rachel becomes engaged, new social demands threaten to take control of her life. She becomes more aware of Helen's role in guiding her toward marriage, and she realizes that her close relationship with Helen is

Disciplinary Traversals

threatened. The impressionistic passage from *The Voyage Out* in which Helen catches up to the young couple, knocks Rachel down, and rolls her around on the ground, marks their changed relationship. The dominant elements in the description are Rachel's position of powerlessness and the sinister, ubiquitous grasses that surround her.

> The grasses and breezes sounding and murmuring all round them, they never noticed that the swishing of the grasses grew louder and louder, and did not cease with the lapse of the breeze. A hand dropped abrupt as iron on Rachel's shoulder; it might have been a bolt from heaven. She fell beneath it, and the grass whipped across her eyes and filled her mouth and ears. Through the waving stems she saw a figure, large and shapeless against the sky. Helen was upon her. Rolled this way and that, now seeing only forests of green, and now the high blue heaven, she was speechless and almost without sense. At last she lay still, all the grasses shaken round her and before her by her panting (283).

Helen's roughhousing play with Rachel is both friendly and charged with eroticism.[4] It would be a mistake, however, to ignore Helen's use of matriarchal power to wrestle her engaged niece down and force her to submit to her new role. Helen must reclaim Rachel for the community the young woman would prefer to ignore, and she must ensure continuity of the community's control of her sexuality. As Marianne DeKoven puts it, Helen "simultaneously represents and is alienated by" the "moribund, pernicious regimes of class and gender" which control the behavior of the group (91). In terms of the ethnographic examples available to Woolf from Frazer and from Charles Domville-Fife, the South American correspondent of the *Times*, she submits Rachel to the equivalent of a ritual pre-nuptial beating.[5]

According to Domville-Fife, after being shut up at puberty in a hut, the girl is promised to the young man "offering the best present." Then, in the presence of the whole tribe, the girl is "flogged with whips of grass cord"[6] and the "evil spirit" is commanded "to leave the girl." It is considered "a good sign" if "the girl falls forward in a faint" because this allows time for "the new spirit of docility" to "enter its life-long home" in the bride-to-be (176). For Rachel, as for the South American women, the period of relative freedom after her adolescent confinement is brief, and the goal of allowing her to emerge at all is to attract a suitable husband. Once that goal is attained, community control returns as forcefully and as unexpectedly as "a bolt from heaven."

In the community described by Domville-Fife, both women and men participate in the ceremony of expelling evil spirits from the bride-to-be. In *The Voyage Out*, Helen and Terence seem to conclude the pact of marriage together as Rachel lies stunned by their combined physical strength, economic power, and erotic attractiveness. She sees them "looming over her," laughing and kissing, and "fragments of speech came down to her on the ground. She thought she heard them speak of love and then of marriage" and "sitting up, she too realised Helen's soft body, the strong and hospitable arms, and happiness

295

swelling and breaking in one vast wave"(283). It is only after the business of the marriage contract has been concluded and the young woman has submitted, that she can be received once again into the embrace representing the acceptance and support of the female community. The conclusion of this ritual restores the young couple's self-consciousness about their sexuality and the necessity of demonstrating control over it. "Falling into line behind Mr. Flushing, they were careful to leave at least three yards distance between the toe of his boot and the rim of her skirt" (284).

Throughout the novel, Woolf reveals a painfully heightened awareness of the extremes of manipulation women undergo as a result of cultural constraints designed to isolate them from sexual experience and power. She demonstrates the ritual constraints practiced among her own people, so that young women "can't walk alone" (82) but must remain shut up and isolated, guarded, as in other cultures, by older women. During her conversation with Helen after being kissed by Richard Dalloway, Rachel suddenly understands the restrictions she has had to endure. "[S]he saw her life for the first time a creeping hedged-in thing, driven cautiously between high walls, here turned aside, there plunged in darkness, made dull and crippled for ever—her life that was the only chance she had—the short season between two silences." She felt that she hated men, even though she liked Dalloway and liked being kissed (82). After her engagement, Rachel feels vaguely dissatisfied and complains that she hates "these divisions . . . why should one be shut up and by oneself in a room? . . . . she wanted many more things than the love of one human being" (302).

Woolf responds quite directly to the ideas of James Frazer, who writes in *Psyche's Task* that "a mass, if not the majority, of people in every civilized country is still living in a state of intellectual savagery . . . in fact, the smooth surface of cultured society is sapped and mined by superstition. Only those whose studies have led them to investigate the subject are aware of the depth to which the ground beneath our feet is thus, as it were, honeycombed by unseen forces" (170). Woolf represents these unseen forces with an oozing cave in Rachel's dreams where an atavistic male figure drools and gibbers. For Frazer, the superstitions of the masses are the treacherous, hidden, irrational, maternal gaps which swallow knowledge and reason. For Woolf, they are spaces of confinement and limitation made odious by being occupied by "reasonable," "civilized" men, "the maternal deformed by patriarchy" (DeKoven 37).

Woolf ventured bravely into a masculine world of anthropological discourse to make an example of British patriarchal rituals. Frazer's thesis in the series of lectures published as *Psyche's Task* was that superstitious observances such as the confinement of women had a positive aspect in that they strengthened respect for institutions such as marriage and private property! Woolf's work reverses this position, implying that the subjugation of woman to patriarchal institutions is the bad seed that should be discarded.

Disciplinary Traversals

Notes

[1] The studies of Moore and Froula on matriarchal mythologies and female initiation rites, respectively, in *The Voyage Out* are especially relevant as demonstrations of this engagement. See also Patricia Maika and Sandra Shattuck for their assessments of Jane Harrison's influence on *Between the Acts* and Jane Marcus for the importance of Harrison's ethnographic texts to Woolf's work in general (2-3). Haller and Molly Hoff have also demonstrated Woolf's use of myth and ritual.

[2] See Stocking and Kuklick for historical analysis of British anthropology.

[3] Ann Ardis suggests that this could be an allusion to Zola's *Nana*, "specifically to the famous scene at the end in which he graphically describes her putrescent body, then figures her metaphorically as the dung heap upon which all the flies of Paris feast."

[4] Tvordi, DeSalvo, and Zimmerman demonstrate the erotic nature of the relationship between Helen and Rachel.

[5] Domville-Fife does not provide sources or information on previous publication in his compilation, but Frazer explores the significance of ritual beating in general in *GB* (213-217) and gives a briefer description of a similar pre-marital ritual beating ceremony of the Uaupes of Brazil. Frazer's source is Wallace (496).

[6] Frazer gives another instance of using grass for a symbolic "beating" in *Psyche's Task* (51).

Works Cited

Ardis, Ann. E-mail to the author. 9 Nov. 1999.

DeKoven, Marianne. *Rich and Strange: Gender, History, Modernism*. Princeton: Princeton UP, 1991.

DeSalvo, Louise. Introduction. *Melymbrosia by Virginia Woolf: An Early Version of The Voyage Out*. New York: New York Public Library; Astor, Lenox and Tilden Foundations, 1982.

——. *Virginia Woolf's First Voyage: A Novel in the Making*. Totowa, New Jersey: Rowman and Littlefield, 1980.

Domville-Fife, Charles. *The Real South America*. London: George Routledge & Sons, 1922.

Frazer, James G. *The Golden Bough: A Study in Comparative Religion*. 1890. *The Golden Bough: The Roots of Religion and Folklore*. Avenel, New Jersey: Gramercy Books, 1981.

——. "Psyche's Task." *The Devil's Advocate and the Scope of Social Anthropology*. London: Macmillan, 1927.

Froula, Christine. "Out of the Chrysalis: Female Initiation and Female Authority in Virginia Woolf's *The Voyage Out*." *Tulsa Studies in Women's Literature* 5, (Spring 1986): 63-90.

Hoff, Molly. "Coming of Age in *Mrs. Dalloway*." *Woolf Studies Annual* 3. New York: Pace UP, 1997. 95-121.

Kuklick, Henrika. *The Savage Within: The Social History of British Anthropology, 1885 - 1945*. Cambridge: Cambridge UP, 1991.

Maika, Patricia. *Virginia Woolf's* Between the Acts *and Jane Harrison's Con/spiracy*. Studies in Modern Literature 78. Ann Arbor, Michigan: UMI Research Press.

Marcus, Jane. "Introduction: Virginia Woolf Aslant." *Virginia Woolf: A Feminist Slant*. Lincoln: U of Nebraska P, 1983.

Moore, Madeline. "Some Female Versions of Pastoral: *The Voyage Out* and Matriarchal Mythologies." *New Feminist Essays on Virginia Woolf*. Ed. Jane Marcus. Lincoln: U of Nebraska P, 1981.

Shattuck, Sandra D. "The Stage of Scholarship: Crossing the Bridge from Harrison to Woolf." *Virginia Woolf and Bloomsbury: A Centenary Celebration.* Ed. Jane Marcus. Basingstoke : Macmillan, 1987.
Stocking, George W., Jr. *After Tylor: British Social Anthropology 1888-1951.* Madison, Wisconsin: U of Wisconsin P, 1995.
Tvordi, Jessica. "*The Voyage Out:* Virginia Woolf's First Lesbian Novel." *Virginia Woolf: Themes and Variations. Selected Papers from the Second Annual Conference on Virginia Woolf.* New York: Pace UP, 1993.
Wallace, Alfred Russel. *A Narrative of Travels on the Amazon and Rio Negro with an account of the Native Tribes and Observations on the Climate, Geology, and Natural History of the Amazon Valley.* 1895. New York: Greenwood Press, 1969.
Woolf, Virginia. *The Voyage Out.* 1915. San Diego; New York; London: HBJ, 1968.
Zimmerman, Bonnie. "Exiting from Patriarchy: The Lesbian Novel of Development." In *The Voyage In: Fictions of Female Development.* Ed. Elizabeth Abel. Hanover: The U of New Hampshire P, 1983.

Elyse Myers
Virginia Woolf and the "Voyage Out" from Victorian Science

By means of enthusiastically received public lectures, newly constructed museums and an explosion in the publication of popular scientific periodicals, classical science reasoned its way to a central position in 19th-century British life. Advanced by Sir Isaac Newton in the 17th-century, the classical paradigm of scientific epistemology operates according to a logic of rigid cause-and-effect determinism and posits a clear separation between the scientist and "his" object of study. Such faith in the objectivity of the material world and the certainty of its cause-effect progression inspired the English mechanical philosopher Robert Boyle, in the 1660s, to describe the natural world as "a great piece of clockwork" (qtd. in Shapin 34). This paradigm underwrote Francis Bacon's 17th-century development of a scientific method centered on controlled observation, classification, and inductive reasoning. Given sufficient time and material, science, according to this model, will finally acquire total and conclusive knowledge about the mysteries of the universe. As Steven Shapin contends, the scientific method established by Bacon was designed to discipline the production of knowledge so as to eliminate individualist thinking which might undermine the authority of the 17th-century British government. By standardizing the scientific project as an exercise in controlled observation and collection of facts, intellectual authorities ensured that even children could contribute to the collective labor of producing a socially unified world view. Likewise, popular 19th-century science periodicals and, even more authoritatively, Victorian leaders such as the Prince Consort, fostered the consolidation of state power in an era of rapid industrialization and potential social

Disciplinary Traversals

unrest by avidly promoting Bacon's scientific protocols. Speaking before the British Association for the Advancement of Science as its President in 1859, Prince Albert declared that the knowledge secured by science delivers a fully factual account of the universe: "Facts are objective and belong to everybody—they remain the same facts at all times and under all circumstances. . . . It is with facts only that the Association deals" (qtd. in Benson 299). Thus, to many Victorians, science promised the revelation of objective truth about the natural world and represented the essence of progress. To others, however, the increasingly pivotal role played by science in society posed a threat. Its imperialist aim to scrutinize, classify and control targeted not only the mysteries of the external world, but also those of the human body. The female body, in particular, became an object of study and rationalization in the 19th-century. Indeed, Virginia Woolf's 1915 novel, *The Voyage Out,* arguably works to subvert the sovereignty of this entrenched system of monolithic "truth" production. Of notable interest with respect to this line of study is the character of Rachel, whose experiences most forcefully challenge the laws and legends of classical science. Whereas others might momentarily doubt the certainty that 2 p.m. follows 1 p.m., or that England exists independently of one's view of it, for Rachel, these exceptions increasingly assume the status of rule. For her, only "a moment's respite was allowed, a moment's make-believe, and then again the profound and reasonless law asserted itself . . ." (*VO* 263).

Such a moment of "make-believe" occurs early in the narrative, standing behind Rachel's seemingly innocent observation in the following passage: "She looked at the ground; it pleased her to scrutinise this inch of the soil of South America so minutely that she . . . made it into a world where *she was endowed with the supreme power.* She bent a blade of grass, and set an insect on the utmost tassel of it, and wondered if the insect realised his strange adventure . . ." (emphasis added, 141). As an English woman in the process of being "educated as the majority of well-to-do girls in the last part of the nineteenth century were educated" (33), it is her culturally constituted faith in the value of observation, domination, knowledge, and power which underpins this "imperializing" gesture on Rachel's part. The epistemological foundations of Newtonian science allow her to conceive of herself as a subject entirely detached from the object she observes, to control the position of this object by relying upon empirically-based predictions (if she first bends the blade of grass, then the insect will remain on this perch), and to presume to know the full experience of the viewed object by enlisting the logic of cause-and-effect relations (moving the insect should cause it to experience a "strange adventure"). Yet a later passage in the novel overturns the scientifically-ordered structure of this scene and, simultaneously, divests Rachel of her sense of power. In a seeming inversion of the earlier episode, Rachel now assumes the perspective of the *object* she formerly observed. Thus, subject and object blend; Rachel becomes like a bug in the grass: "A hand dropped abrupt as iron on Rachel's shoulder; it might have been a bolt from heaven. She fell beneath

299

it, and the grass whipped across her eyes and filled her mouth and ears. Through the waving stems she saw a figure, large and shapeless against the sky. . . . Over her loomed two great heads, the heads of a man and a woman" (283). Indeed, while the perspective has altered, the details of this scene are strangely similar to those of the earlier incident. What accounts for the difference between the earlier and later episodes is the absence from the latter of the predictability, the cause-and-effect certainty, and hence the very intelligibility which organizes the former. Unlike other characters in the novel, then, Rachel herself experiences the suspension of the classically assigned places of up and down, before and after, subject and object—of Newtonian physics itself.

Before discussing Rachel's ultimate defection from Newton's "clockwork" world, I think it's profitable to consider why Rachel resists, deliberately or not, the scientific paradigm so avidly sanctioned by Victorian culture. We might take a cue from narrative developments immediately preceding Rachel's perspectival shift from subject to object in the above-cited passage. Moments before her "fall," Hewet obliquely proposes marriage to Rachel for the first time. Why might this proposal compel Rachel to retreat from ordered reality? An unexpected link between the scientific method celebrated in 19th-century England and the institution of matrimony offers a possible answer. In his writings, Bacon genders Nature as female and urges, "let us establish a chaste and lawful marriage between Mind and Nature . . . [for] Nature betrays her secrets more fully when in the grip . . . of art than when in enjoyment of her natural liberty" (qtd. in Lloyd 47). The Baconian model of science which survived the centuries to flourish in 19th-century England was arguably no less threatening to women's freedom, and indeed, it may be due to this very disciplinary muscle that it was so readily conscripted into Victorian culture. Just as Shapin notes the power with which Bacon's scientific method furnished the 17th-century British monarchy, so too have feminist historians of science speculated on the role Victorian science performed in installing women securely in the domestic sphere. Indeed, while the original language of Bacon's empirical epistemology had inscribed within it notions of sexual hierarchy, this hierarchy was increasingly actualized in the performance itself of scientific inquiry so that, by the 19th century, the material female body became the object par excellence of taxonomic study. As Marina Benjamin argues, the Victorian "science of woman shared with natural history an emphasis on specular knowledge. . . . Through the science of woman, women were subject to the scrutiny of the scientific eye and transformed from companions of mankind into beings that presented yet another species for the male gaze to rest upon" (12).

Indeed, *The Voyage Out* does not fail to record this gendered polarization between observers and observees. Remarkable are the instances in which Hewet turns his own taxonomizing lens on Rachel. Directly following his musings on how to truly know people, Hewet commands Rachel to "'sit on the floor and let me look at you'. . . . He examined her curiously. 'You're not beautiful,' he began, 'but I like your face. I like the way your hair grows down

Disciplinary Traversals

in a point, and your eyes too'" (*VO* 297). During a similar examination earlier in the narrative, when Rachel asks Hewet why he's interested in studying her, he replies, "'Partly because you're a woman'. . . . When he said this, Rachel, who . . . had reverted to a childlike state of interest and pleasure, lost her freedom and became self-conscious. She felt herself at once singular and under observation" (215). Then, in a rhetorical move well-calculated to chime with Rachel's own sentiments, Hewet concludes that "'one never knows what any one feels. We're all in the dark'. . . . [But] what he said was against his belief; all the things that were important about her he knew" (218). Hewet, it is clear, subscribes fully to the Baconian epistemological axiom that observation of an object's exterior is the avenue to full knowledge and understanding of it.

Sally Shuttleworth contends that it is this very conflation of women's identities with their bodies that Victorian economic ideology sought to establish. As industrialization of the nation's production sector and the growth of a capitalist economy accelerated in tandem throughout the century, so too arose the need for the creation of a leisured consumer class. Moreover, the capitalist demand for an expanding labor force raised the premium on the biological role of reproduction. The relegation of women to the domestic sphere would answer to both of these historically-specific, economic imperatives. According to Shuttleworth, "Victorian scientists and social theorists increasingly sought out and extolled biological evidence of the sexual division of functions in all forms of life" (53). A new fascination with the taxonomy of gender emerged which focused on slotting women into the functional identities of wives and mothers. Accordingly, in its scrutiny of women's bodies, science singled out for special—indeed, obsessional—attention the reproductive organs and especially their attendant process, menstruation. As an external operation of the body which could be observed, charted and predicted, the menstrual cycle was construed in the discourse of Victorian science as homologous with the (unobservable) female psyche. Knowledge of the former guaranteed knowledge of the latter. Appropriately enough, it is Mr. Dalloway—the model capitalist—who teaches Rachel the social worth and weight of her body by employing, for her edification, exactly the same analogy between women and sewer systems that many popular scientific texts of the time used in order to describe the female reproductive system. Mr. Dalloway images the proper place for women as the subterranean recesses of the city, "concealed from the public eye" (*VO* 66), but nevertheless performing there the critical task of safeguarding the smooth flow of the social circulatory system. By construing women as properly confined to the under-workings of a city, Richard simultaneously references a popular trope for the female body. Thus, inscribed within his own metaphorical representation of the separate, gendered social spheres is a coded affirmation that women are the captives of their own bodies. This image so effectively forces Rachel to feel the barriers erected by her own body that soon after this encounter she dreams of entrapment in a sewer and/or uterine-like space: "She dreamt that she was walking down a long tunnel, which grew so narrow by degrees that she could touch the damp bricks on either side. At length the tunnel opened and became a vault; she found herself trapped in it, bricks meeting her wherever she turned . . ." (77).

Enter Terence Hewet, who, as already noted, turns his taxonomizing attention towards Rachel. She, having lately been tutored into her naturalized gender role by the likes of Richard Dalloway, submits to Hewet's marriage proposal. She nevertheless cannot escape the notion that "this body of his was unreal; the whole world was unreal" (282), which surfaces immediately after Hewet speaks of marriage. In defiance of Newtonian physics, Baconian empiricism, and Victorian ideology, Rachel rejects the totalization of her identity as a "block of matter" (292) and fancies instead "that we're nothing but patches of light" (292-3). For his part, Hewet feels "immensely solid" (293). Like a well-schooled Victorian Englishman, he believes in the rationality of the material world, wherein objectivity *is* possible, effects *do* proceed predictably from given causes. Indeed, "according to him, too, there was an order, a pattern which made life reasonable . . ." (299). As matter is intelligible for Hewet, so are women, for as his country's science says, women are essentially matter. Thus, even while he magnifies the value of her various body parts, Hewet diminishes her mind on grounds of her gender, charging, "'You've no respect for facts, Rachel; you're essentially feminine'" (295). But Rachel does perceive the critical fact that the scientifically and socially naturalized institutions of marriage and maternity participate in a vast ideological program of control. In a futile gesture of defiance against such mindless disciplining, she asserts, "'I won't have eleven children . . . I won't have the eyes of an old woman'" (294).

In the end, Rachel does refuse to continue seeing with the eyes of a society so enamored of visual empiricism—and she does so, in large measure, by transgressing the ordered coordinates of the Newtonian universe, by departing from the block of matter that so essentializes her: her body. When she ultimately retreats to her bed, Rachel removes herself from the world in which the clock, and all it signifies, reigns. Time no longer respects the boundaries of man-made minutes, and "Rachel woke to find herself in the midst of one of those interminable nights which do not end at twelve, but go into the double figures . . ." (330). In the absence of time-frames that obediently depict the before-and-after relationships of continuity, the sacred union of cause-and-effect dissolves. For Rachel, "the outer world was so far away that the different sounds . . . could only be ascribed to their cause by a great effort of memory" (329-330). As it frees her from the Newtonian mechanics that build a reality out of obedient blocks of matter, Rachel's final collapsed condition permits her to discount her body as much as possible. Thus, "for long spaces of time she would merely lie conscious of her body floating on the top of the bed and her mind driven to some remote corner of her body, or escaped and gone flitting round the room" (347).

Disciplinary Traversals

But is Rachel's final escape from her body merely an act of resistance that fails to offer a more promising alternative to the form of knowledge production installed by the popular scientific discourse of the 19th-century? Arguably, even as it questions the presiding place Baconian science allots to vision in the quest for knowledge, Woolf's novel offers, in its stead, the possibility of discovering truth value in sound—and in seemingly disorganized sound, at that. When Hewet reads aloud from notes of congratulation on their engagement, Rachel fumes against the emptiness of the words that, eunuch-like, are employed expressly because their lack of potency serves to reify rather than rupture social order and propriety: "'They're sheer nonsense!' Rachel exclaimed. 'Think of words compared with sounds!'" (292). This is not the only instance in which Rachel privileges less organized over more organized sound. The patchwork piano tunes she plays at the dance initially perplex, but finally liberate her dancing audience, for their lack of convention requires the dancers to "'invent the steps" (166). Knowing through listening, as opposed to knowing through seeing, better accommodates the chaotic, ever-changing flux of being that flows beneath the visible surface of both subjects and objects. While Newton's paradigm foregrounds visual empiricism, Evelyn Fox Keller and Christine Grontkowski warn us that the faculty of sight is alone in its ability to seemingly operate independently of time. Because sight can support the illusion of a stationary world, it promotes faith in the concept of eternal truths. By contrast, knowledge derived by means of the ear dispels the fictive atemporality of the object under study, intimating instead that "the real" is always in process.

During their expedition at the top of Monte Rosa, Hewet asks Rachel, "'What are you looking at?'.... She was a little startled, but answered directly, 'Human beings.'" (135). We cannot *not* watch and visually order the world around us in our ongoing endeavors to communicate with and understand it. Yet, as *The Voyage Out* suggests, to privilege the orderly processes of communication over the chaotic (or noisy) processes of creation actually serves to limit the range and integrity of our knowledge. As William Paulson notes, attending to the noise that is everywhere around us "keeps us from being so fully integrated into a silently functioning system that we would cease to be aware of it as system" (181) and regard it instead as natural truth. That Woolf's 1915 novel would question the optical even as it elevates the aural as the epistemological basis of subject-object relations strikes me as a remarkably prescient anticipation of the de-throning of vision in the late 20th-century paradigm of science. Indeed, according to Keller, at a time when a new discourse of chaos has helped unsettle the Newtonian myth that rigid laws order the universe, when we know that the apparent objectivity and truth-value of vision are not "features of reality, but only of our relatively coarse daily observations, it seems appropriate to reassess our commitment to the ideals which these features imply" (200). *The Voyage Out* does indeed call into question the ideals of objectivity and certainty upon which the classical paradigm of science is founded. And by reading Woolf's novel through and beside contemporaneous discourses of science, we can develop a greater awareness of how we are positioned by *our own* cultural assumptions about what counts as knowledge. This effort, in turn, assists us in embarking on our own voyages out into new ways of understanding.

Works Cited

Benjamin, Marina. "A Question of Identity." In *A Question of Identity: Women, Science and Literature*. Ed. Marina Benjamin. New Brunswick, NJ: Rutgers UP, 1993. 1-21.

Benson, Donald R. "Facts and Constructs: Victorian Humanists and Scientific Theorists on Scientific Knowledge." In *Victorian Science and Victorian Values: Literary Perspectives*. Ed. James Paradis and Thomas Postlewait. New Brunswick, NJ: Rutgers UP, 1985. 299-318.

Keller, Evelyn Fox and Christine R. Grontkowski. "The Mind's Eye." In *Feminism and Science*. Ed. Evelyn Fox Keller and Helen E. Longino. Oxford: Oxford UP, 1996. 187-202.

Lloyd, Genevieve. "Reason, Science and the Domination of Matter." In *Feminism and Science*. Ed. Evelyn Fox Keller and Helen E. Longino. Oxford: Oxford UP, 1996. 41-53.

Paulson, William R. *The Noise of Culture: Literary Texts in a World of Information*. Ithaca: Cornell UP, 1988.

Shapin, Steven. *The Scientific Revolution*. Chicago: U of Chicago P, 1996.

Shuttleworth, Sally. "Female Circulation: Medical Discourse and Popular Advertising in the Mid-Victorian Era." In *Body/Politics: Women and the Discourses of Science*. Ed. Mary Jacobus, et al. New York: Routledge, 1990. 47-68.

Woolf, Virginia. *The Voyage Out*. New York: HB, 1948.

Michael Whitworth
"The Lighted Strip of History": Virginia Woolf and Einsteinian Simultaneity

The umbrella metaphor for this conference, "Turning the Centuries," pictures time as a book; time as something we can stand outside and manipulate, something through which we can move backwards and forwards at will; time, moreover, as something marked with fixed points at which we have to turn the page or commence a new volume. There are, however, other images of time: time as a substance within which we are trapped, like flies in amber, or like a body in a peat bog (*TTL* 26). Time could be a ticker tape or a scroll, lacking distinct markers, with human beings as its characters. Time too can be thought of as a ray of light moving through space: this image was central to Einstein's special theory of relativity, and is the central image of this paper. Considerations of the "philosophical" precedents for Woolf's treatment of time have been dominated by Bergson, from Delattre (131-37) to Stevenson (104, 134-35; see also Majumdar and McLaurin 24, 35). The "ray of light" leads instead to astronomy and to Einstein, whose contribution has been often overlooked or assimilated to a Bergsonian model (Stevenson 107-09). If the "limber, shifty, contingent" modes of representation that Woolf adopted (Beer 116) owed something to the ideas of representation employed by the new physicists, it is possible that her conception of simultaneity owed something to them as well.

Ironically, I need to start by setting down some markers of my own. Introductions to modernism and its intellectual context usually cite 1905 and 1916 as the dates at which Einstein published his theories of special and general relativity. From these unquestionable facts it is usually allowed to follow that any literary works subsequent to 1905 and 1916 were open to the influence of Einstein's theories. This simplifies a more complex situation in a number of respects. Firstly, though we speak of "Einstein's" theory, the ownership of relativity theories was by no means clear in these early days: in the early scientific literature, Einstein's name was often hyphenated with others (Staley 263-65). Secondly, though we speak of each theory as a separate thing, each was composed of component ideas which had been in circulation for some considerable time. Einstein's ability to synthesize these ideas led to him being perceived as their owner, and led to their becoming more widely known. However, literary relations with science usually involve partial appropriations, assimilations of scientific discourse into a mixture of other discourses; such processes tend to analyze theory into its components, though the analysis involved is often intuitive, not scientific. Thirdly, although the dates 1905 and 1916 dominate literary summaries of intellectual history, the crucial year for British literary writers was 1919. In May 1919, the Astronomer Royal, Arthur Eddington, carried out an experimental test of Einstein's general theory. This attracted some publicity at the time, but it was only after 6 November 1919, when Eddington announced that he had proved the theory, that relativity was widely written about and widely discussed. In the years following, there was a significant boom in popular science writing.

In this popular writing, the image of starlight travelling through space took on immense importance. It had been known since 1675 that light takes time to travel (Flammarion, *Popular Astronomy* 317), but Einstein's Special Theory was the first physical theory in which this became significant. Because light has a finite velocity, our perceptions of events always reach us slightly after the fact. While this may not matter to someone looking across a room or out of the window, it makes a great deal of practical difference to the astronomer and the philosopher. In looking at a distant star, we are always already looking at history. In the absence of a universal time frame, the whole vocabulary of time is compromised: the terms "now" and "then" become relative; we need to distinguish between absolute and apparent simultaneity. If the sun were to go out, "now," like a lightbulb being switched off, it would take eight minutes for us to realize it.

This last example is vivid, but the 1920s popularisations as frequently popularised the idea by asking the reader to imagine an observer watching the earth from a distant planet; for such an observer, one of our historical events would appear to be happening in their present moment. The idea apparently originated in Camille Flammarion's *Lumen*, published in French in 1872 and in English in 1897 (89-92). Flammarion used the example of the Battle of Waterloo. This illustration and its descendents were used in several of the 1920s popularisations: Edwin Slosson used it in 1920, while Charles Nordmann substituted the Battle of the Marne; in 1928 Maurice Maeterlinck used the marriage of Napoleon III in a similar way (Slosson 42-45, Nordmann 76, Maeterlinck 153). In the period immediately after the First World War these ideas are full of complex emotional and intellectual connotations. In 1920 H. H. Turner, the Professor of Astronomy at Oxford, wrote that because of the finite speed of light, "our universe is not co-existent: the past close around us belongs to the peaceful present, but the nearest star is still in the midst of the late War . . ." (xi).

We do not know if Woolf read any of these books, but I would emphasize that all were published in Britain, and many were reviewed in journals like the *Times Literary Supplement*, *The Athenaeum* and the *New Statesman*, at a time when Woolf was contributing to or was associated with them (for example, the reviews by Sanger and Sullivan). The subculture of popular science writing was not, bibliographically speaking, entirely separate from the world of Woolf's writing. In any case, a detailed consideration of the publishing context for these ideas must not be allowed to obscure the importance of conversation. Flammarion's image of the Battle of Waterloo is vivid, compact and compelling, and could fall very easily into conversation, just as, at the end of *Between the Acts*, swift allusion can be made to new ideas of matter: "nothing's solid" (*BTA* 118). The publishing context is valuable precisely because it gives us an idea of possible conversations; the contents of a generalist journal like *The Athenaeum* or *New Statesman* suggest all sorts of interdisciplinary possibilities. Woolf did not need to meet the most eminent physicists personally in order to absorb these ideas. I know of no compelling evidence that she met Jeans or Eddington, and generally speaking, too much emphasis is put on the presence of the great oracles. At the same time, the now forgotten popularisers and intellectual all-rounders are treated too dismissively; Judith Killen, for example, refers to them as "nameless hacks," as if their anonymity detracted from their accuracy (78).

The Battle of Waterloo was particularly resonant within a British context. The date 1815 was not only a date known to every schoolchild, it had become the type of a piece of factual information known to everyone. It assumed immense historiographical significance, being not so much a new page in history, as a new chapter or indeed a new volume; this was literally the case, with many volumes of history taking 1815 as their final or opening chapter. Woolf was perfectly aware of this, and of the sense that the Battle inaugurated the Victorian era (*E*1 317, *E*1 331).

In her earliest allusion to the finite speed of starlight, Woolf does not use the Battle of Waterloo as a historical marker. In *Night and Day*, Katharine Hilbery prefers the "star-like impersonality" (*ND* 34) of mathematics to the confusion of prose; in chapter 16 she turns her attention to the impersonality of the stars themselves. She resorts to them, we are told, much as a literary person would resort to books, "absent-mindedly" moving from volume to volume (*ND* 161). The stars, it is implied, are a form of library in which every moment of human history exists simultaneously, like the British Library of *Jacob's Room* in which Plato and Aristotle sit "cheek by jowl" with Shakespeare and Marlowe (*JR* 93). But in a subsequent passage the stars offer an insight deeper into history, and then into prehistory:

> Somehow it seemed to her that they were even now beholding the procession of kings and wise men upon some distant part of the earth. And yet, after gazing for another second, the stars did their usual work upon the mind, froze to cinders the whole of our short human history, and reduced the human body to an ape-like, furry form, crouching amid the brushwood of a barbarous clod of mud. (*ND* 164)

The time scales of evolutionary history are juxtaposed with those of Christian history. In a loose sense, this is a relativistic view of time: Katharine is imagining time as if it were simply another dimension of space in which one can move back and forth at will. The idea that the past and the present were simultaneously present was encouraged by the thought experiments of relativity, although they have no basis in the theory more strictly defined: no body can move faster than light, so one can neither overtake the present moment nor move back in time past it. Whether Woolf's sources for this idea are pre-Einsteinian or Einsteinian is difficult to determine. The draft of chapter 16, originally titled "Chapter Seventeen" and dated "Jan 5th 1917," contains the scene of Katharine star-gazing, but does not allude to the finite velocity of light. Exactly when Woolf added the detail is not known, nor would knowing necessarily resolve the question of her sources. As she does not use the Battle of Waterloo as a specific example, it is possible that her source was not Flammarion's *Lumen*, but his *Popular Astronomy*. This work expounds and explores the implications of light's finite velocity almost to the point of tedium, but does not use the events of 1815 as a reference point (317-19, 617-18):

> As the aspect of worlds changes from year to year, from one season to another, and almost from one day to the next, we can represent this aspect as escaping into space and advancing in Infinitude to reveal itself to the eyes of distant beholders. (617)

Although in isolation the verbal detail is a slender piece of evidence, one cannot altogether ignore the translator's choice of "beholders," the slightly elevated register of which anticipates Woolf's (or Katharine's) use of "beholding."

If in *Night and Day* the idea of starlight provides a connection with the past, then in *To the Lighthouse* it provides an image of posterity. Lily, looking at the distant view of the sandhills, feels it outlasts the gazer by a million years, and communes already "with a sky which beholds an earth entirely at rest" (*TTL* 25); again, "beholding" is the phrase of choice. Mr. Ramsay invokes the same stellar perspective: he considers his achievement as if he were looking from a mountain top down at the "long wastes of the ages," from which vantage point he can see "the perishing of stars" (*TTL* 41). He asks what would survive of him: "His own little light would shine, not very brightly, for a year or two, and would then be merged in some bigger light, and that in a bigger still. (He looked into the darkness, into the intricacy of the twigs)" (*TTL* 41). As in *Night and Day*, there is nothing left in the universe save "stars and the light of stars" (*ND* 164). Mr. Ramsay's problem is that he is not a "star" of the philosophical firmament.

In *The Waves* Bernard refers quite explicitly to the light of stars falling on his hand "after travelling for millions upon millions of years" (*TW* 206): this informs his earlier description, during the Hampton Court scene, of our English past as being "one inch of light" (*TW* 174), and Louis's reference to "the lighted strip of history" (*TW* 173). In this whole scene, the presence of the past is particularly vivid. The Battle of Waterloo is not mentioned, but for Bernard, "all depends upon the Battle of Blenheim" (*TW* 175). Teasingly, too, at the end of the episode, Bernard is clutching a return ticket to Waterloo (*TW* 180): this is realistically accurate, in that Waterloo would be the usual London station for Hampton Court; but it is also symbolic of the new conception of time and history created by the new physics. When Bernard speaks of the past as "one inch of light" he goes on to describe how his sense of history has changed:

> I try to recover, as we walk, the sense of time, but with that streaming darkness in my eyes I have lost my grip. This Palace seems light as a cloud set for a moment on the sky. It is a trick of the mind—to put Kings on their thrones, one following another, with crowns on their heads. (*TW* 174)

Bernard repeatedly ridicules the crown as being "a golden teapot," and with it ridicules the Royalist version of history as the lives of Kings and Queens. But the trick of the mind is the treatment of historical events as sequential, the idea of the Kings following one another. Bernard more usually associates this dull sequentiality with the lives of small shopkeepers—Tuesday following Monday—but here it is attributed to the monarchy, or at least to a popular idea of the monarchy as something embodying linear order.

Flammarion's account of light in *Popular Astronomy* introduces a new resonance to the title of *The Waves* with regard to sequentiality. As each changing aspect of the world escapes into space (in the passage quoted above), it "is followed by another, and so on successively; and it is as if a series of waves bearing from afar the past of worlds should become present to observers ranged along its passage!" (617). While this image of waves as bearers of past

Disciplinary Traversals

time is ultimately less profoundly significant for this novel than the idea of waves as Platonic forms, Flammarion's association of it with linear succession suggests that it may have been in Woolf's mind in writing this passage.

The mathematically minded will notice that Bernard diminishes the scope of English history by many orders of magnitude. If light travels at 186,000 miles a second, then an inch of light would accommodate no more than a fraction of a second of English history. There is not, however, much to be gained from studying science and literature if one reduces it to a process of correcting factual errors, although this can be revealing in particular cases (Deery 73-74). Whether or not Woolf was conscious of the error, this miscalculation allows the phrase "one inch of light" to refer back to the conclusion of *Orlando*, where the truth is described as "an inch of silver." To give the full context: Orlando is driving out of London, thinking of the wild goose, and pressing hard on her accelerator:

> Always it flies fast out to sea and always I fling after it words like nets . . . which shrivel as I've seen nets shrivel on deck with only sea-weed in them; and sometimes there's an inch of silver—six words—in the bottom of the net. But never the great fish who lives in the coral groves. (*O* 216)

If one may allow this equivalence between the inch of light and the inch of silver, then the passage in *Orlando* deepens the significance of the passage in *The Waves*. The new physics suggests that language will never catch the ultimate referent of history, the great fish or the wild goose. However, the ray of light, the inch of silver, presents the simulacrum of historical events, making them seem present, though they continually evade capture.

There is one last teasing example. In "How Should One Read a Book?" (1926), Woolf had used the examples "Paris is the capital of France" and "King John signed the Magna Charta" (*E4* 389) as examples of facts upon which everyone can agree. In the 1932 revision for the second *Common Reader*, she stated "The battle of Waterloo was fought on a certain day; but is *Hamlet* a better play than *Lear*? Nobody can say" (*CE2* 1). Woolf appears to be inscribing a subtle irony into her example: while no one would disagree about the date of the battle, the new physics had made it clear that the time frame within which it was located was relative to the observer.

Whether or not we label it "Einsteinian," this way of thinking about time has a larger significance for Woolf's work. Even in the novels where she does not invoke the image of starlight, she is interested in juxtaposing different moments within her characters' lives, and different moments within British history. Though Flammarion imagines the Battle of Waterloo as "still" raging and "still" visible, Septimus Warren Smith imagines an unnamed battle of the First World War. The new physics made this idea of history something more than a trick of memory and mind: it appeared to be a fundamental feature of the physical world.

Notes

[1] The facsimile of the manuscript in Hussey, ed. *Virginia Woolf*, gives this section the page numbers 76-84.
[2] I am grateful to Holly Henry, whose paper "Nebulous Networks" offers other pointers to the importance of the *Popular Astronomy*.
[3] I am grateful to Kathryn Sowden for drawing this passage to my attention.

Works Cited

Beer, Gillian. *Virginia Woolf: The Common Ground*. Edinburgh: Edinburgh UP, 1996.

Deery, June. "Cultural Trespass?: Aldous Huxley's Forays into Modern Physics." *University of Dayton Review* 21.3 (1992): 73-84.

Delattre, Floris. *Le roman psychologique de Virginia Woolf*. Paris: J. Vrin, 1932.

Flammarion, Camille. *Lumen*. Trans. A. A. M. and R. M. London: William Heinemann, 1897.

———. *Popular Astronomy: A General Description of the Heavens*. Trans. J. Ellard Gore. London: Chatto and Windus, 1894.

Hussey, Mark, ed. *Virginia Woolf*. Major Authors on CD-ROM series. Woodbridge, CT: Primary Source Media, 1997.

Killen, Judith. "Virginia Woolf in the Light of Modern Physics." Diss. U of Louisville, Kentucky, 1984.

Maeterlinck, Maurice. *The Life of Space*. Trans. Bernard Miall. London: Allen and Unwin, 1928.

Majumdar, Robin, and Allen McLaurin, eds. *Virginia Woolf: The Critical Heritage*. London: Routledge and Kegan Paul, 1975.

Nordmann, Charles. *Einstein and the Universe*. Trans. Joseph McCabe. London: T. Fisher Unwin, 1922.

Sanger, C. P. "Easy Books on Einstein." *New Statesman* 18 (1922): 596. Unsigned review, authorship identified by reference to signed copies at the *New Statesman* offices, London.

Slosson, Edwin. *Easy Lessons in Einstein*. London: George Routledge and Sons, 1920.

Staley, Richard. "On the Histories of Relativity: The Propagation and Elaboration of Relativity Theory in Participant Histories in Germany, 1905-1911." *Isis* 89 (1998): 263-99.

Stevenson, Randall. *Modernist Fiction: An Introduction*. Hemel Hempstead: Harvester Wheatsheaf, 1992.

Sullivan, J. W. N. "Einstein's Problem." *The Athenaeum* no. 4698 (1920): 641-42.

Turner, H. H. Introduction. *The Foundations of Einstein's Theory of Gravitation*. By Erwin Freundlich. Cambridge: Cambridge UP, 1920. ix-xii.

Woolf, Virginia. *Jacob's Room*. Ed. Sue Roe. London: Penguin, 1992.

———. *Night and Day*. Ed. Julia Briggs. London: Penguin, 1992.

———. *Orlando*. Ed. Brenda Lyons. London: Penguin, 1992.

———. *To the Lighthouse*. Ed. Stella McNichol. London: Penguin, 1992.

———. *The Waves*. Ed. Kate Flint. London: Penguin, 1992.

Edward Barnaby
Visualizing the Spectacle: Woolf's Metahistory Lesson in *Between the Acts*

The *spectacle* and *metahistory* are two concepts that emerge from Marxist criticism during the latter half of this century, and two ideological dynamics that converge in Virginia Woolf's novel *Between the Acts*. Writing in the late 1960s in France, Guy Debord describes the product of modern capitalism as the "Society of the Spectacle." Such a society is essentially a totalitarian state in which everything from religion to philosophy to history has been transformed into images for visual consumption by a populace that has, in turn, been transformed into a politically passive audience. Metahistory, on the other hand, is Hayden White's more recent term for the attempt to theorize historical discourse with the hope of preventing it from being absorbed into the spectacle. Metahistory forces one to remain conscious of the literary and aesthetic structures through which history is told, and to develop an awareness of how these structures allow ideology to enter a particular reconstruction of the past. While the historical pageant that takes place in *Between the Acts* reveals the existence of a politically passive society of spectators in England prior to the Second World War, Woolf's literary gesture of taking this pageant as the subject of her novel simultaneously participates in a metahistorical inquiry into the nature and consequences of a society's relationship to its past. While Miss LaTrobe, the director of the pageant, apparently fails to stir the political consciousness of her fictional audience by the end of the performance, Woolf's portrayal of this failure within the novel makes the metahistorical perspective visible by illustrating the dynamics of an aesthetic representation's ideological power over the spectator.

This speaks to the larger issue of the social function of the novel as a genre. *Between the Acts* lies at the intersection of two schools of ideological criticism concerning the modern novel. Literary critics such as Georg Lukács, Phillip Rahv, Italo Calvino, and Milan Kundera regard the novel's fundamental concern as the mediating function of language, a self-consciousness of form that exposes the subjective nature of any totalitarian worldview that passes beneath its lens regardless of the guise of objectivity in which such ideology is couched. While nineteenth-century novelists directed this capacity of the genre primarily at the established Churches of Europe and the emerging cult of science, many twentieth-century novelists have focused this power on the rise of fascist government in Central and Eastern Europe. In his book *A Theory of Literary Production*, Pierre Macherey gives this argument a particularly visual turn when he writes that "Art, or at least literature, because it naturally scorns the credulous view of the world, establishes myth and illusion as visible objects" (Macherey 132). The assumption here is that once fascist mystification is made visible, it loses its power over the mind of the spectator. On the other hand, other Marxist critics such as Debord and Althusser suspect aesthetic and literary culture of contributing to the mystification of the interests of the dominant class instead of exposing them. What the novelist makes visible merely serves as more fodder to sate the voracious spectator and is not a source of political awareness. Frederic Jameson argues in his book *The Political Unconscious* that the aesthetic of realism in modern art and literature functions as a political "strategy of containment" in which the distinction between the spectacle and daily life collapses and the political capacity of the individual becomes, in effect, delimited by the representations that surround him (Jameson 52).

Does Woolf's attempt in *Between the Acts* to make visible the process of producing history thus raise her readers to the level of metahistorical awareness or plunge them deeper into the contemplation of spectacle? Perhaps it is first necessary to examine how history is visualized in the novel. The discussion that opens the novel concerning something as mundane as the location of a new cesspool leads Mr. Oliver to construct a genealogy of the landscape. As the narrator explains,

> the site they had chosen for the cesspool was, if he had heard aright, on the Roman road. From an aeroplane, he said, you could still see, plainly marked, the scars made by the Britons; by the Romans; by the Elizabethan manor house; and by the plough, when they ploughed the hill to grow wheat in the Napoleanic wars. (*BTA* 4)

One could add to this litany of geo-historical artifacts the dozens of landing strips dug into the landscape during the World Wars that remain visible to this day from aloft. The construction of history is also made visible in the portraits and artifacts assembled in Pointz Hall to assert a viable family lineage. The house itself is the visual icon around which local legend and folklore is preserved in the collective memory of the town. Even the barn is transformed into a visual historical gesture, which, being described as a steeple-less church that more closely resembles a temple, interjects a classical and pagan presence within a horizon otherwise framed by the architecture of Christianity.

From these subtle visual manifestations of the process of constructing history that open the novel, Woolf shifts to the more overt visual motif of the mirror. Ironically, the mirrors she sets forth make visible the inherent incompleteness of any self-image that one constructs, including the fabricated image of the past known as history. Woolf exemplifies Macherey's argument that the true insight of realism is not the clarity of its reflection of the world, but the inherent incompleteness of its reflection, which exposes the bad faith of any mode of representation, including history, that positions itself as an objective totality. Whether it be the construction of one's identity or the reconstruction of one's past, reality cannot be synthesized into a single image. The trifold mirror in Isa's bedroom not only fragments her self-image into "three separate versions of her . . . face," but also fails to envelope her eye within the totality of its representation (*BTA* 13-4). In its incompleteness, the mirror permits her gaze to wander "outside the glass" to "a slip of terrace, lawn and tree tops" where "the perambulator; two nurses; and her little boy George" compete with the inner identity Isa creates based on the image of her face in the mirror (*BTA* 14).

Grasping at the romantic notion that books are indeed mirrors of the soul, Isa turns to the mirror of art in order to construct an identity for herself and her historical era. However, by virtue of the three-hour trainride from town to the country home, the library at Pointz Hall has become cluttered with shilling-shockers purchased to ease the boredom of travel and promptly discarded as so many carcasses of consumed spectacle upon the guest's arrival at the house. Traditional literature proves to be an equally unsatisfactory mirror for Isa's soul because its aristocratic preoccupations produce an incomplete representation of ages past. As the narrator succinctly states, "Nobody could pretend . . . that the looking-glass always reflected the anguish of a Queen or the heroism of King Harry" (*BTA* 16). While such a statement is reminiscent of Thackeray's attempt in *Vanity Fair* to position the realist novel as the most objective and inclusive means of representing society to itself, Woolf takes the argument in the opposite direction by relativizing realism as merely one among many aesthetic constructs through which images of the self and the past are formulated in literature. Isa browses without satisfaction through a spectrum of literary works bounded by poetry on one extreme and science on the other, with both private and public histories falling in between:

> Keats and Shelley; Yeats and Donne. Or perhaps not a poem; a life. The life of Garibaldi. The life of Lord Palmerston. Or perhaps not a person's life; a county's. *The Antiquities of Durham*; *The Proceedings of the Archaeological Society of Nottingham*. Or not a life at all, but science—Eddington, Darwin, or Jeans. (*BTA* 19-20)

There are two ways of reading this progression. The nineteenth-century understanding of the relationship between the arts and sciences would dictate that the list ranges from the subjectivity of poetry to the objectivity of science. Woolf, however, would have us read the list from a metahistorical perspective through which each of these genres are revealed as ideas mediated by a certain use of language that can lay no greater claim to objectivity or subjectivity than the others. Biography is the poem of a life, history the poem of a county, and science the poem of the universe. Like the trifold mirror in Isa's bedroom, no single perspective achieves a totality of representation. Instead, each one makes visible its particular representations of the real.

While Thackeray would argue that literary realism in the novel incorporates the entire spectrum of verbal representation from poetry to history to science and, thus, produces objectivity out of its radical subjectivity, Woolf demonstrates that even the apparent realist objectivity of direct reportage in a newspaper article deconstructs into fictional components of fantasy and romance. The narrator comments as Isa reads a story in the *Times*:

> "A horse with a green tail . . ." which was fantastic. Next, "The guard at Whitehall . . ." which was romantic and then, building word upon word, she read: "The troopers told her the horse had a green tail; but she found it was just an ordinary horse. And they dragged her up to the barrack room where she was thrown upon a bed. Then one of the troopers removed part of her clothing, and she screamed and hit him about the face. . . ." (*BTA* 20)

The realistic style of the article in no way makes the situation described more real to Isa than a fantasy or romance. She regards the story from the standpoint of spectacle, appreciating the visual composition of the scene as she would a painting or a tableau on the stage. The narrator notes that the description is "so real that on the mahogany door panels she saw the Arch in Whitehall; through the Arch the barrack room; in the barrack room the bed," yet any overt indication that Isa sees the political injustice of the reported events is suppressed (*BTA* 20).

Just as the newspaper transforms the interactions of society into aesthetic objects for disinterested contemplation, Miss La Trobe's historical pageant subverts her own agenda by advancing a call for political action within a theatrical medium that subdues its audience into complacency. The few characters in the novel to whom the ideology of visual representation has become transparent resist the passive role of the spectator that is foisted upon them as members of the audience. Giles Oliver broods over the general atmosphere of passivity in which he is mired:

> Books open; no conclusion come to; and he sitting in the audience. "We remain seated" "We are the audience." Words this afternoon ceased to lie flat in the sentence. They rose, became menacing and shook their fists at you. This afternoon he wasn't Giles Oliver come to see the villagers act their annual pageant; manacled to a rock he was, and forced passively to behold indescribable horror. (*BTA* 59-60)

Although for the most part the fictional audience of the pageant never reaches this level of awareness, the readers of Woolf's novel become a sort of meta-audience of the pageant with full access to Woolf's metahistorical perspective. Woolf's narration makes visible to this meta-audience the literary and aesthetic structures, indeed the words-as-objects, with which Miss La Trobe constructs her account of British history.

Two such structures that operate conspicuously within the pageant are emplotment and focalization. In his book *Metahistory*, Hayden White discusses the politics of emplotment, namely the poetic arrangement of historical narrative to create a story with dramatic interest, usually one that follows either a tragic or comic progression. There is a certain conservatism linked to the sense of inevitability and necessity with which the events are described as taking place, as any good story will make certain to its readers that it could not be told in any other way. La Trobe portrays British history as a bildungsroman in which a young nation develops to maturity and attains reason, as evidenced by the child whom she casts for the opening scene to symbolize the innocent

Disciplinary Traversals

England of the Middle Ages. She is also quite concerned throughout the pageant that nothing disrupt the emotional momentum of the historical plot she has constructed out of scenes from plays and music from various epochs.

Focalization, on the other hand, refers to the extent of the narrator's presence in a given text. While works of fiction often indulge in a high level of focalization, scientific texts strive for what Pierre Carrard describes as "zero focalization" in his book *The Poetics of the New History* (Carrard 105). Whereas the novel exploits the presence of the narrator to foreground its aesthetic structures, historical and scientific texts achieve an effect of objectivity by concealing the selections and omissions made by their narrators. Woolf engages in radical focalization techniques in *Between the Acts* by emphasizing not only Miss La Trobe's liberal splicing and editing of primary sources, but also the fictional nature of the so-called primary sources themselves through which the audience is intended to derive a general spirit of the age. A generic scene from a Renaissance drama serves to resurrect the Elizabethan era, while a scene from an eighteenth-century farce serves as a window upon the Age of Reason. The historical basis of the pageant is revealed to be a collection of narratives retold by the meta-narrator La Trobe.

Whether one prefers to call it dramatic distance or a willful suspension of disbelief, the narrator notes that there is something about the dynamics of theater that prompts the audience to accept whatever is placed before it: ". . . the audience sat gazing; and beheld gently and approvingly without interrogation, for it seemed inevitable, a box tree in a green tub take the place of the ladies' dressing room" (*BTA* 134-5). Along with this acceptance of the somewhat abstract visual representation, however, comes a failure on the part of the audience to scrutinize the political implications of the events depicted. Far from enjoying any critical separation from the representation, the audience longs to be absorbed into complete empathy with the spectacle itself. Mrs. Swithin congratulates Miss La Trobe for achieving this emotional bridge between actor and spectator, which would have been considered a theatrical victory by the standards of the nineteenth-century melodrama. "What a small part I've had to play!" Swithin acknowledges, "But you've made me feel I could have played . . . Cleopatra!" (*BTA* 153). La Trobe, however, was evidently hoping for less of a catharsis and more of a Brechtian alienation effect, as her aim was not to enable the audience to share vicariously in the glory of the past, but to inspire them to take an active role in shaping their future. Philip Rahv makes a similar argument in an essay titled "The Literary Class War" in which he calls for a proletarian form of catharsis that instead of purging the audience of its emotions rallies it to positive action outside the theater. Unable to face her failure in this respect, La Trobe willfully misinterprets Swithin's praise as saying "You've stirred in me my unacted part" (*BTA* 153).

Other than Isa, Giles, and William Dodge, whom the narrator describes as "caught and caged; prisoners; watching a spectacle," the remainder of the audience is, in effect, transformed into a collection of lotus-eaters by the end of the pageant (*BTA* 176). Not even La Trobe's experimental dose of pure reality can release them from the totality of the spectacle. Allowing the audience to gaze out at the landscape beyond the momentarily empty stage for too long causes them to perceive the experiment not as a concentrated dose of realism, but as a gap in representation that leaves them distracted, restless and craving spectacle more than ever in order to fill the void. The distance between realism and reality is made visible and illustrates that, in spite of its pretensions to objectivity, historical realism is merely one among many modes of aesthetic representation. Fearing that her experiment might ruin the dramatic momentum of the pageant, La Trobe quickly proceeds to the final scene, titled simply "Ourselves" in the program. She is forced to portray the historical present without recourse to the economy of representation afforded by scenes from old plays, period costumes and other kitschy visual cues that immediately evoke a given era. In response to this challenge, La Trobe resorts to a symbolic tableau in which men and women of all races are portrayed in the act of building a wall. Once again Woolf underscores focalization by simultaneously viewing the historical image through the eyes of both a newspaper reporter and a clergyman. While the reporter interprets the scene as an allegory of the League of Nations in the modern spirit of global activism, the reverend's remarks after the pageant absorb the message of the play within the providential rubric of accepting one's station in life.

The narrator notes that as soon as the reverend ascends the stage, the audience "folded their hands in the traditional manner as if they were seated in church" (*BTA* 191). However, while the fictional audience is permitted to consume the pageant as spectacle, aided by the conveniently distilled synopses of the play offered by the clergyman and the reporter, the meta-audience reading Woolf's novel is liberated from the spectacle by watching this process take place. Thus we return to the initial question of whether the novel is able to make visible the concealed dynamics of the visual spectacle itself. Althusser would see in this scene evidence of various state apparati, in this case organized religion, the mass media and the performing arts, having conspired to conceal the social awareness of people like La Trobe, Isa and Giles within the outlook of the dominant class. However, Macherey would see Woolf's literary treatment of this process as making it irreversibly transparent and exposing it to the readers of her novel.

Just as the spectators become self-congratulatory while contemplating the cathartic restoration of order embodied by the rebuilt wall on stage, the entire cast picks up mirrors and other reflecting objects and holds them up to the audience while shouting fragments of their lines from throughout the pageant. Out of this historical collage emerges a single voice that attempts to break the spell of the spectacle and force the audience to participate actively in the task of reconstructing its past and constructing its future. However, instead of pointing to the incompleteness of all forms of aesthetic representation, this breaking down of the fourth wall, so to speak, is largely dismissed by the audience as inappropriate theatrical form on La Trobe's part. Instead of exposing the spectacle's lack of totality, the several unplanned interruptions during the pageant, such as the brief afternoon cloudburst and military planes flying overhead, are chalked up to the inconveniences of an outdoor venue.

As the audience disperses after the pageant, Woolf assembles a pastiche of fragments overheard from their conversations. Even those who were impressed enough by the implications of the pageant to prolong the discussion of it afterwards do so with the rational detachment required to dissect the aesthetic object, but not the critical sensibility to analyze its social implications as an aesthetic product. As one anonymous spectator remarks, "And if we're left asking questions, isn't it a failure, as a play? I must say I like to feel sure if I go to the theatre, that I've grasped the meaning . . . Or was that, perhaps, what she meant?" (*BTA* 200). This futile quest for an objective representation of the self and of the past is precisely what Woolf attempts to dismiss as worthless, indeed self-destructive, by making visible the gaps, the omissions, the selectivity and the role of accidentals in the mounting of this historical pageant. It is the metahistorical insight that cannot be dramatized and which narrative cannot relate, the moments Between the Acts, to which the audience should look.

Works Cited

Carrard, Pierre. *Poetics of the New History: French Historical Discourse from Braudel to Chartier.* Baltimore: Johns Hopkins UP, 1992.
Debord, Guy. *The Society of the Spectacle.* 1967. Trans. Donald Nicholson-Smith. New York: Zone, 1995.
Jameson, Frederic. *The Political Unconscious: Narrative as a Socially Symbolic Act.* Ithaca: Cornell UP, 1981.
Macherey, Pierre. *A Theory of Literary Production.* Trans. Geoffrey Wall. London: Routledge, 1978.
Rahv, Phillip. "The Literary Class War." In *Essays on Literature and Politics, 1932-1972.* Eds. Arabel J. Porter and Andrew J. Dvosin. Boston: Houghton Mifflin, 1978. 271-3.
White, Hayden. *Metahistory: the Historical Imagination in Nineteenth-Century Europe.* Baltimore: Johns Hopkins UP, 1973.
Woolf, Virginia. *Between the Acts.* San Diego: Harcourt Brace & Company, 1970.

Ann Murphy and Jeanne McNett
Women's Learning, Women's Work

Our delivery of this paper at the Ninth Annual Virginia Woolf Conference at the University of Delaware, June 13, 1999, was an experiment. We shared our basic ideas in a dialogue, and we welcomed our listeners to participate when they had something to add. This effort to open up the process of paper presentation, to make it a more inclusive, active forum for sharing and testing our ideas, operates on assumptions that community is critical to the building of understanding. As Thomas Kuhn has helped us to understand, our ideas themselves are not ours; they belong to a vast community of thinkers (7). This paper is an abbreviated summary of that presentation.

Woolf's radical 1938 essay, *Three Guineas*, examines the root causes of war and asks how women can help end war without first achieving economic independence and a voice in public discourse. Her essay brilliantly identifies the contradictions at the heart of feminism, pacifism and social change: to oppose war effectively, women must first gain an income and a public identity, becoming part of precisely those educational and professional structures that foster the competition and violence that create war. Yet in joining this procession around the mulberry tree in order to challenge it, women risk being co-opted by precisely the social forces we want to subvert and challenge.

Woolf, of course, offers no neat solution to this dilemma, and the tensions she identifies remain intractable. However, she offers the possibility that, rather than accepting the values and assumptions in patriarchal education and the professions, middle class women can consciously affirm and maintain their outsider status as a way to re-examine the very nature of that education and those professions. Membership in Woolf's Society of Outsiders can thus be a critical advantage rather than a liability, allowing us a perspective from which to recognize and oppose the procession of educated men.

As we close our century, we look back on the enormous changes women have experienced in education and work and examine the extent to which Woolf's hopes for the radicalizing potential of women's presence have been fulfilled, as well as the extent to which women have fallen into those traps Woolf foresaw, and others she did not explicitly anticipate.

Women In The Academy

In describing the nineteenth-century struggle to open higher education to women, Woolf poses three central issues: (1) What we teach ("What sort of education will teach the young to hate war?" [Woolf 22]); (2) How we negotiate the compromises between radical feminist education and practical professional needs ("...[S]tudents must be taught to earn their livings...the college for the daughters of educated men must induce bequests and donations from rich men...encourage competition...accumulate great wealth" [Woolf 35]); and (3) How we teach ("...we can examine...the aim of...teaching, and refuse to teach any art or science that encourages war..." [Woolf 36-37]).

What we teach
• A profound revolution has occurred in the United States in terms of who is teaching and who is attending college. In significant ways the procession has truly been transformed. In the process, feminists, people of color and others in the Society of Outsiders have challenged what we teach, both by redefining the canon and by developing radical new ways of reading. Yet institutional resistance to these changes is formidable. Feminist scholars have more often been

Disciplinary Traversals

transformed *by* the academy than succeeded in transforming it; the very success of feminist scholarship has created an often divisive star system which undercuts our community as Outsiders; and radical new ways of reading have been diffused and depoliticized into a dry, marginalized jargon, alienating both our students and the public.

• In an irony which even Woolf did not fully anticipate, while we have failed to transform the academy, we have become the focus of a pervasive and systematic media attack on our perceived left-wing radicalism, our incomprehensible ways of reading, and our "easy" working conditions. Thus many public debates about higher education in America assume

> that traditional core subjects, especially in the humanities, have been displaced by radical new curricula that undermine the students' regard for the accomplishments of Western civilization and that call into question all standards and values (Kolodny 45).

Accommodation vs. Challenge in the Academy

• The revolutionary fervor of 1970s feminism in the academy has failed to restructure the institutions in which we teach. We have not overthrown the tenure process. Nor, for example, have we ensured access to affordable day care for faculty, support staff, and students in the academy.

• Many women entering higher education, especially those in the humanities, have maintained their Outsider status—albeit inadvertently—in the ways they define their work. The values women often bring to higher education, reflecting and reinforcing prevailing gender stereotypes, have not transformed the academy; rather they have often marginalized women whose professional contributions do not meet previously established male criteria for tenure and promotion:

> . . .Women, as a group, carry heavier teaching loads, bear greater responsibility for undergraduate education, and have more service commitments. . . have less access to graduate teaching assistants, travel funds, research monies, laboratory equipment,[and]. . .inside the university, as outside it. . . assume primary responsibility for nurturing the young and serving men, but receive little credit for doing so (Park 55).

• Woolf urges women to challenge the values and assumptions of the academic procession by deliberately foregoing the "honors" of the procession. More often, however, we seem merely to be reinforcing essentialist gender roles, positioning ourselves as Outsiders without creating an alternative community to sustain us. The often inadvertent reinforcement of gender stereotypes is surely not what Woolf means by affirming freedom from unreal loyalties.

> Since 1970 the number of full-time faculty members in the United States has risen by approximately half, while the number of part-time faculty members has tripled. . . .the proportion of faculty members who were full-time dropped from nearly 80% to under 60%. . .Women. . .[are more heav-

ily represented] among non-tenure line and part-time faculty members than among tenure-line appointments (Holt & Anderson 135).

- The exploitation of part-time/adjunct faculty is a serious feminist and economic issue. Both the disgraceful working conditions of these teachers and the comparative silence about this issue within academic discourse suggest that we are not simply failing to build "an experimental college, an adventurous college" (Woolf 33), but are complicit in the creation of a corporate model of higher education, based on an underclass of academic migrant workers.
- Evidence of the corporatization of values in the academy abounds: the dramatic shift in focus from humanities to business; the transformation of our vision of education from older, elitist notions of "culture" and "tradition" to explicitly materialist notions of "excellence," and "leadership training"; and the growing tendency to regard students as "consumers."

> Twenty-five years ago. . . colleges and universities were classified in terms of academic mission: research universities, comprehensive universities, liberal arts colleges, community colleges. . . An updated taxonomy. . . sorts institutions by market niche: brand-name. . . mass-providers. . . and convenience institutions. . . [and finally, consider] the for-profit University of Phoenix, which, with 50,000 students, is. . . the largest private university in the nation. . . Every student in a given program takes the same courses in the same sequence. . . Faculty do not prepare their own courses; uniform syllabi are issued every three years. (Baker 21, 22)

Revisiting these familiar trends in higher education in the light of Woolf's essay asks us to revitalize our vision of ourselves as *conscious* outsiders, as members of a *Society* of Outsiders with its own values and community. It also reminds what is at stake in the corporate values now dominating the academy:

> What this society *wants* of those who graduate from its schools and colleges with degrees in the humanities . . . are, at worst, docility and grammatical competence, at best, reliability and a high level of textual skills. What this society does *not* want from our educational institutions is a group of people imbued with critical skills and values that are frankly antagonistic to those that prevail in our marketplaces, courts, and legislative bodies (Scholes 19).

How should we teach?

- Those of us fortunate enough to have achieved tenure must change not just *what* we teach but *how*; we must "pour scorn upon . . . degrees, and upon the value of examinations . . . refuse to bolster up the vain and vicious system of lecturing . . . And, of course, if we are offered honours and degrees for ourselves we can refuse them" (Woolf 36-37).
- We can define ourselves as Outsiders in the classroom by deconstructing faculty-student power relations, by employing radicalizing pedagogies, by encouraging students to think critically and analytically about the values of their society, and by taking multiculturalism seriously in our teaching.

Disciplinary Traversals

• We can define ourselves as part of a Society of Outsiders among our colleagues and work to create an alternative community which sustains and nurtures one another.

Women In The Professions

Participation in the professions may help us gain control of our economic lives and build our participation in the public discourse; yet in so doing we may succumb to the very forces for which we have tried to build alternatives, ending up neither ethical nor free. Woolf understood at a complex level how organizational culture operates within a bureaucracy to ensure its continuation. In *Three Guineas* she warns against three specific dangers of the professions whose relevance continues: an organization's traditions and rituals (the procession), extreme wealth, and nationalism.

Dangers of the Procession

• Even the briefest analysis of metaphorical structures used in business to describe major activities indicates the prevalence of war metaphors as critical to their traditional approaches. Business strategies, price wars, and marketing campaigns all lead to an implicit acceptance of war as a way of thinking, and appropriate referent. Certainly there are alternative metaphors which may be used to give shape to the chaos of the market which we have not sufficiently explored. Woolf suggests that if we understand how organizations work, in and of themselves, separated from their metaphorical connections, we might avoid their ". . . undeniable effect[s] . . .[to] make people who practice them possessive, jealous of any infringement of their rights, and highly combative if anyone dares dispute them" (Woolf 66).

• Woolf's metaphorical observations of how organizational cultures operate to control their participant's values are supported by the work of organizational theorists such as Mary Jo Hatch, who has analyzed how socialization actually occurs within the organization, how corporate symbols, traditions and rituals operate. Her work suggests that in the professions we may have missed opportunities to encourage the valuation of difference. Perhaps in our efforts to be a part of our organizations, we have not avoided their dangerous aspects and, seduced by their symbolic vehicles, we have missed opportunities to create alternatives.

> [Researchers find] key symbols [of organizational culture] that are widely recognized by organizational members, but which are associated with a multitude of meanings and interpretations. The puzzle [of organizational culture] is solved when you examine the concept of sharing closely. There you will discover that sharing has two contrary meanings. The meaning most of us immediately think of has to do with common experience; when we share we are directly involved with others in a way which recognizes our similarity. . . . But sharing also means that we divide something into individual pieces (shares) and distribute them among ourselves, as in share cropping. This second meaning emphasizes our separateness (204).

- As organizational forms evolve, honest connections among members become critical. This change leads to a new level of openness and may increase opportunities to influence the organization.

> Organizations are no longer built on force but on trust. The existence of trust between people does not necessarily mean that they like one another. It means they understand one another. Taking responsibility for relationships is therefore an absolute necessity. It is a duty. Whether one is a member of the organization, a consultant to it, a supplier to it, or a distributor, one owes that responsibility to all one's coworkers: those whose work one depends on as well as those who depend on one's own work (Drucker 72).

- There is no one, right way to understand, think about and thereby reify business structures. Because business adds value, it has the largely unexplored potential to offer constructive approaches with depth and meaning for participants as well as consumers This argument, made convincingly by Michael Novak, may not readily occur to people unfamiliar with the daily operations of business, yet it might interest those who seek change within the corporate world. Outsiders are essential to any effort to change how business operates. Judy Rosener, in her *America's Competitive Secret: Women Managers*, argues that women, precisely *because we are outsider*s, are better equipped to institute change, unencumbered as she understands us to be by yesterday's paradigms.

Dangers of Extreme Wealth

- Top earning women corporate officers in the US make $.63 cents on every $1.00 in salary and bonus made by men (Catalyst 1998 Survey). A June, 1999 *Financial Times* survey outlines similar salary gaps in Europe, which average 27% (parallel to that of the US) and are as high as 36% (Taylor 9). The dangers of extreme wealth seems to be an area in which most women have yet a need to explore the desirable mean.
- The prevalence of women in the management of nonprofit organizations may indicate that for many women, salary, beyond a satisfactory level, may not be as effective a motivator as it appears to be for men. Woolf recognizes this difference in her reference to Octavia Hill's letter: "You and I know that it matters little if we have to be the out-of-sight piers driven deep into the marsh. . . . The bridge is what we care for and not our place in it . . ." (Woolf 165). Do we fully understand why the majority of nonprofit organizations are funded at reduced levels and managed by women? Is this an example of under-valuation or less egoistic motivators? If the latter, how can such efforts be protected from the less altruistic forces in the marketplace?

Dangers of Nationalism

The danger of nationalism is directly connected to bureaucracy's ability to absolve the individual of moral responsibility at a personal level for actions taken in the name of the organization—a process Max Weber captured in the differences between formal and substantive rationality. While formal rationality may lead to an "iron cage, . . . a cog in an ever moving mechanism," substantive rationality involves a logic which examines the desired and unintended *ends* of an action (Hatch 33). The Society of Outsiders has opportunity to move the discussion to considerations of the ends achieved by particular actions, an approach Woolf suggests we follow: "Let us never cease from thinking—what is this 'civilization' in which we find ourselves? What are these ceremonies. . . ? What are these professions and why should we make money out of them? Where in short is it leading us, the procession of educated men?" (63).

• Much of the international economy is shifting from one based on natural resources and physical labor to one based on goods and services. National borders are no longer barriers; nationality is increasingly less important. In addition, the process of globalization may advantage women in less developed nations as well as in developed ones, as corporations reduce their borders, integrate internal systems with suppliers and buyers, and build a global workforce. Because women think more contextually, take a broader perspective and are more flexible than are men, we have the advantage of our gender in our globalizing economy (Fisher 4).

• This world view is built on assumptions about which the reader may have serious doubts; unfortunately, its exploration is beyond the scope of this presentation. The tension of women's participation in the corporate world is one which merits further exploration from all viewpoints. The process of globalization does go beyond nationalism, and it is fair to say that there is no constructive place for nationalism in a globalized marketplace, although national culture would still play an important role. Globalism may increase the dangers associated with stronger corporate cultures as corporations render national governments relics of a simpler time. Unchallenged, such developments would constitute an increased rather than reduced danger because they would avoid the control which national governments may now exercise on corporate activities which may be seen to counter-balance irresponsible corporate citizenship.

Conclusion

In *Three Guineas* Woolf identifies the contradiction at the heart of both academic and professional worlds: access to learning and work, which are essential to our role in public discourse, may also enmesh us in precisely the world we could be challenging. She warns us that in both education and the professions there are corruptive forces. That is a warning we need to hear—now more than ever. Yet she also offers ways that women can escape the patriarchal dangers of capitalism and build an alternative system. We need not join the procession of the sons of educated men. Those processions are not ours, Woolf suggests; we do not need to share in their tacit collusion. Instead, we can take our share and continue to rebuild.

What has happened for women in the academy and in the professions in the sixty years since *Three Guineas* was published illustrates the depth and relevance to today's world of Woolf's perceptions. The Society of Outsiders still offers perspectives of value to educators and business people as we enter the twenty-first century in a global marketplace, collaborating across borders and cooperating with our competitors. This is a world in which the patriarchal procession is becoming increasingly dysfunctional. As we move into the new century, building on women's achievements during the Twentieth Century, we would do well to draw on both Woolf's insightful observations and our own experiences to rethink the role of our participation in The Society of Outsiders.

Works Cited

Baker, Lynne Rudder. "Should the Humanities Be Saved?" *Umass Alumni Magazine.* 3.2 (Winter 1999): 18-23.

Bauer, Dale, and Susan Jarratt. "Feminist Sophistics: Teaching with an Attitude." *Changing Classroom Practices.* Ed. David Downing. (U of Illinois Press, forthcoming).

Catalyst Census of Women Corporate Officers and Top Earners. The Catalyst Homepage. 9 Nov. 1999. <www.catalystwomen.org>.

Drucker, Peter. "Managing Oneself." *Harvard Business Review* 77.2 (1999): 64.

Fisher, Helen. *The First Sex: The Natural Talents of Women and How They Are Changing the World.* New York: Random House, 1999.

Hatch, Mary-Jo. *Organizational Theory: Modern Symbolic and Postmodern Perspectives.* New York: Oxford University Press, 1997.

Holt, Mara and Leon Anderson. "The Way We Work Now." *Profession 1998.* Modern Language Association of America.

Kolodny, Annette. *Failing the Future: A Dean Looks at Higher Education in the Twenty-first Century.* Durham: Duke University Press. 1998.

Kuhn, Thomas. *The Structure of Scientific Revolutions.* 2nd ed. Chicago: U Chicago P, 1970.

Novak, Michael. *Business as a Calling: Work and the Examined Life.* New York: The Free Press, 1996.

Park, Shelley M. "Research, Teaching, and Service: Why Shouldn't Women's Work Count?" *Journal of Higher Education.* 67 (Jan.-Feb. 1996): 46-84.

Rosener, Judy B. *America's Competitive Secret: Women Managers.* New York: Oxford University Press, 1995.

Scholes, Robert. *The Rise and Fall of English.* New Haven: Yale University Press, 1998.

Stewart, T. *Intellectual Capital.* New York: Doubleday, 1997.

Taylor, Robert. "Pay gap between the sexes widest in Western Europe." *Financial Times* 29 June 1999: 9.

Woolf, Virginia. *Three Guineas.* 1938; New York: HBJ, 1966.

Laurie Quinn
A Woolf with Political Teeth: Classing Virginia Woolf Now and in the Twenty-First Century

Poised within a few short months of the millennial turn, the Ninth Annual Virginia Woolf Conference takes the long view of time, as measured in centuries, as marked by transitions that lead from one expanse to the next. Mindful of the significance of those briefer moments of being, which stretch to become the hours, the years, and the centuries, I will shape this discussion around two texts that may reveal what wider historical vistas tend to obscure. Each reveals the workings of class, not as an abstracted concept or a statistical category, but as lived and represented experience.[1] In reading them together, I deliberately blur the classed boundaries between the two, so that a little-read, "poor relation" of a text, probably best known to feminist socialist academics, comes to illuminate a now-famous work emblematic of Woolf's literary genius. The first is the "Introductory Letter" Woolf wrote for the Co-operative working women's autobiographical collection *Life As We Have Known It*, published by Hogarth Press in 1931.[2] The second is that well-known novel, published in 1925 and traversing through one post-War London day in mid-June, *Mrs. Dalloway*. In their concern with the particular, the daily, the brief-but-intense, both texts inscribe class into the historical moments from which they emerge in ways that are invaluable to our own classed practice of reading and criticism now and in the coming century.

Edited by Margaret Llewelyn Davies, who asked Woolf to contribute a preface, *Life As We Have Known It* records what Woolf described as "voices [that] are beginning only now to emerge from silence into half articulate speech" ("Introductory Letter" xxxix). The first-person narratives powerfully detail how, as mothers, wives, and workers, these women's lives were influenced by the Co-operative Movement. My consideration of a piece of Woolf's writing which appears within the same covers as those voices so different from hers is thus intrinsically a cross-class project, though the "Introductory Letter" itself is addressed to Davies, not to the working women writers. Well aware of the class implications of this genteel genre, Woolf crafts a form which can display the very tensions she wants to reveal between her own writerly position and the Co-operative women's. Instead of representing what she did not experience, namely, an easy solidarity across classes, Woolf chooses to show that women of distinct classes might use writing differently toward the same progressive political ends.

In its feminist integrity, the letter pays attention to the details of difference, and does not claim that gender can always trump class. Indeed, Woolf at first describes the barrier between herself and the working-class women as "impassable" (xxviii). But the "Introductory Letter"—which emerges from a remarkable mix of actual political events, social connections and disconnections, reading and writing processes, and the shifts in consciousness that are part of all these experiences—represents Woolf's learning how to make a more legitimate connection to these writers and to take a more nuanced look at their lives, rather than merely making left-leaning excuses.

Written in May 1930, the "Introductory Letter" begins with the anecdotal tone familiar to readers of the author's nonfiction, and centers around Woolf's description of her memories of the Working Women's Congress she herself attended as an observer seventeen years before, in 1913. Woolf is candid about her discomfort with her own privilege at the meeting. While she was a socialist who lived in economic comfort under the systems of capitalism and empire, the women she saw and heard at the Congress, those worn down daily by those systems, were those for whom socialism was both a political philosophy *and* an urgent practical need.

In the early passages which capture her observations of real-live workers, Woolf does seem inclined to underestimate differences among flesh-and-blood women of the working classes, to overestimate their noble hardiness. Her narrative of the conference up to a certain point keeps circling back to her own inability to imagine the content of the lives revealed in the speeches of the women, whose names are sometimes listed in sequence, but who are mostly referred to without distinction as "they." In Woolf's eyes, "their" faces and clothing sometimes blend into an undifferentiated mass. But this is not a "real" letter; it is an even more self-consciously designed rhetorical performance which takes letter form, as in *Three Guineas*. At first revealing her perception of the impossibility of genuine connection between herself and the women attending the Congress, Woolf sets her early impressions and initial alienation up for a fall within the narrative of the letter. She works toward an anecdote which shows us a Virginia Woolf who is capable of being shaken out of her class-based biases.

Later on that summer, Woolf goes to Davies's office in Hampstead to discuss her impressions of the Congress, and begins to tell her friend about the impassable divide she had been pondering when she was an observer. Davies, the activist seeking to influence the political consciousness of her literary-minded friend, unlocks a desk drawer to reveal to Woolf a pile of writings by the working women from whom Woolf feels alienated. Davies explains that if Woolf read those writings, "the women would cease to be symbols and would become instead individuals" (xxix). Though Woolf is eager, in her retelling, to see the writings, Davies feels uncertain of whether showing them to a writer like Woolf constitutes a betrayal of the women who wrote them, and between this reluctance and the many interruptions of personal and wider history, it takes seventeen years for Davies to collect the papers and for Woolf to write the introduction. In Woolf's own depiction, it is only over a long span of time and through the mediating realm of language, through reading and writing, that she discovers how to draw appropriately qualified connections between her life and the lives of some working-class women.

Disciplinary Traversals

In crafting the piece, Woolf uses the rhetorical "turn" of the opening drawer to show how, after Davies challenges her assumptions, the writings can begin to affect her—and to affect the content of her "Introductory Letter." Woolf moves on to include specific details of the women's lives, and her discussion of their work and their intellectual-political struggles attests to her increasing engagement with the women as individuals and as writers. Resisting any oversimplification of this process of change, Woolf notes that although the combination of reading the women's stories and having memories of their faces and voices produced a shift in her *own* consciousness, such a response might not be typical.

Conjuring a literary critic, Woolf speculates on *his* reception of the writings she is introducing, but her attention to his hypothetical dismissals soon gives way to extensive quoting of the working women's writings. Interjecting with such phrases as "Could she have said that better if Oxford had made her a Doctor of Letters?" and "It has something of the accuracy and clarity of a description by Defoe" (xxxviii), Woolf proceeds rhetorically to remove herself from the "debate" she has imagined: "Whether that is literature or not literature I do not presume to say, but that it explains much and reveals much is certain" (xxxix). This diffident tone and apparent self-erasure, followed by an insistence on the validity of at least part of her own answers to those rhetorical questions, are recurring characteristics in Woolf's nonfiction, and suggest a central tension. Gendered enactments of self-doubt coexist here with her ability to see through the tropes of power. Emerging from the tension, the voice of the educated man's daughter can be heard moving consciously toward her Outsider's viewpoint, speaking from a liminal space somewhere between working-class women and the cultural elite. Woolf's feminist understanding of the biases of the male establishment allows her to destabilize, through her rhetorical shifts, the whole notion of aesthetic judgment. Though she appears to leave open the question of whether or not the writings are "literature," she seems to begin to forge her own standard here, hinting that whatever "explains much and reveals much" is literary. Those who could "presume to say" what the literary worth of this collection might be would judge from a gender and class-based confidence, from a certain sense of entitlement in the realms of taste. Woolf, barred from that presumption as a woman though half-permitted by virtue of her class to try her hand at judging, may be articulating in this passage that a less stable, but far richer way of seeing the literary and the political is available to us. In any case, the letter's incorporation of her own initial obtuseness, and the literary critic's imagined dissenting voice, deliberately sets class authorities up for failure. We are left with the momentum of Woolf's growing understanding and with the undeniable details of the women's narratives, and thus with a sense of what remains to be done among women.

I think that Woolf's legacy to us in this instance is not so much her "letter of introduction" given on the working women's behalf but her willingness to record, though in a complex style faithful to her understanding of artful prose, her own imperfect involvement in the process of trying to connect across classes. Woolf engages with the difficulties that arise when working-class struggle and feminist struggle try to merge. If we read Woolf for those very interstices, rather than reducing the tensions to lapses in, or triumphs of, her political integrity, we may find ourselves more willing to make our own attempts—still, no doubt, imperfect—to grapple with class, race, and other differences honestly and consistently. Mary Childers, in an important reading of the "Introductory Letter," writes of feminist Woolf criticism: "A willingness to hear the voice of the relatively privileged woman crack under the pressure of class position is essential to a feminism that acknowledges differences among and within women" (62). Though this is indeed vital to feminist criticism in general, I do not see Virginia Woolf's novels and essays as examples of such "cracking" so much as they are chronicles of her growing resistance to the expectations of class privilege. Woolf searches, often though not always successfully, for forms that can serve her increasingly difference-conscious feminism, and I read the complex text of the letter as one of her successes.

It is certainly worth remembering, especially at the *Ninth* Annual Virginia Woolf Conference, that even Woolf's extant body of writing was itself almost eclipsed amid the historical-material processes of publication and canonization. Thanks to feminist literary critics, Woolf has been constructed instead as the foremost foremother of literary feminism, as the rescued/reconstructed, deserving genius. But, as Woolf herself would have been quick to recognize, the genius we now claim for her could probably not have found voice in a woman who did not share at least some of Virginia Woolf's many privileges. Given that Woolf self-consciously exposed the limits and the potential of point of view, both as an aesthetic category and as a political identity position, I find that Woolf's portrayals of the worlds she herself knew well—the worlds of privilege—are her most vital and potentially revealing legacy for feminist criticism now.

Here, then, a glance at a scene from *Mrs. Dalloway* in which Woolf's writing strikingly illuminates power relations. Among its many riches, *Mrs. Dalloway* serves as an especially revealing case study on issues of class as they operate in and around Virginia Woolf's writing. Woolf wrote in her diary that she conceived of *Mrs. Dalloway* as a way to "criticize the social system and to show it at work, at its most intense," and self-reflexively added "but here I may be posing" (*D2* 248); this moment suggests Woolf's ongoing sensitivity to the problem of critiquing the very system in which one enjoys privilege. Woolf's development of the interconnected and shifting perspectives of the novel and its characters points to the fact that she lived during times in which life narratives became newly unpredictable. But the enduring powers of the systems of class and gender are not lost on Woolf, as the novel consistently reveals.

In the scene I want to note, Richard Dalloway, securely ensconced in the English male world of privileged civic-mindedness, is walking to give Clarissa the flowers he has bought to express his unspoken love for her and gratitude for their marriage. As he walks, contemplating the "miracle" (174) of his life with Clarissa, Richard is characterized as one who has "championed the down-trodden and followed his instincts in the House of Commons" (175); on his walk he notices people who might be in need of his benevolent protection—prostitutes, costermongers, children trying to cross the street unhelped by police officers. Thinking that "it is a thousand pities never to say what one feels" (175), Richard sees the poor in the same detached but vaguely sympathetic way as Clarissa tends to do during her walk; he has more *power* than she to shape the worlds of those on whom his gaze falls, but also more power to harm them with his Conversionary missions. His gaze falls on a "female vagrant . . . stretched on her elbow (as if she had flung herself on the earth, rid of all ties, to observe curiously, to speculate boldly, to consider the whys and the wherefores, impudent, loose-lipped, humorous)" (176). Approaching this woman, who recalls the figure of the singer at the underground entrance in her elemental connectedness to the earth, Richard carries the flowers for Clarissa—those natural emblems made into cultural, conventional gestures of feeling—"like a weapon" (176) and "smile[s] goodhumouredly" in response to the woman's laugh, while *"considering the problem of* the female vagrant" (176, my emphasis). Richard's inability to acknowledge the woman's individual humanity, even as he senses it briefly in the "spark between them" (176); his pseudo-reformer's point of view, indeed, his inability to have the kind of shift in consciousness that Woolf herself records in the "Introductory Letter," is underscored by what he sees next—Buckingham Palace. As he gets closer to his home, with Big Ben sounding in the air, Richard contemplates the impressive dignity of Crown and Empire. Woolf's writing is rich with such class- and gender-conscious criticism of power systems, and this aspect of her literary politics remains integral to the process of "classing Virginia Woolf."

    In the title of this paper, I call for a twenty-first century Virginia Woolf with political teeth. Mindful of the residual benefits of Freudian terrors about the devouring female body, I use the phrase to spark our re-recognition of the ways in which Woolf can turn this century as a properly dangerous political animal. The unmasking of class privilege is one incomplete imperative of her legacy to feminists, because like it or not, Virginia Woolf has been Nortonized, with all the attendant political defanging. Woolf, whose best writing destabilizes the categories of power, sometimes from *within* those categories of power, has become the token woman modernist. *A Room of One's Own*, widely anthologized now, will hardly seem radical to our students unless *we* point out that the colleges in which they read their Virginia Woolf are nearly as inaccessible to working-class students now as Oxbridge was to women. Instead of collaborating in locking Woolf into her famous room, financially secure but quite alone, we can offer a classed construction of Woolf which will help us to continue asking the hard questions of feminist scholarship.

    Though she was gifted in helping us to imagine the silenced lives of women from the working classes, those lives which, as we turn the century, largely remain "half hidden in profound obscurity," it is not enough to read Woolf's accounts of her working-class sisters' absences. We must continue her search for the women writers we have lost and are still losing, making sure their writing survives. And we must write, read and teach in ways that break the silences that still surround the lives and writings of those for whom the metaphorical, rhetorically politicized dilemma of where to send three improbable guineas remains the fancy of a privileged imagination.

Notes

1. Significant amid her own lived experiences, Woolf's teaching at Morley College from 1905 to 1907 gave her an early opportunity to traverse contemporary English class hierarchies. Such work afforded Woolf different understandings of class than she might have gleaned from her domestic interactions with servants, for instance.
2. As Jane Marcus has pointed out, the version of this text chosen by Leonard Woolf for publication in Woolf's *Collected Essays* as "Memories of a Working Women's Guild" is an earlier, quite different version first published in the *Yale Review*. My discussion here refers to the "Introductory Letter," the text which was published with *Life As We Have Known It*.
3. In an insightful reading of the "Introductory Letter," Leila Brosnan explores Woolf's crafting of this form as a complex way of including the working women in a "discursive network, which, while it is aware of class divisions, achieves a power of speech through gender and genre solidarity" (126). Though Brosnan's insightful reading is faithful to the complexity of Woolf's choices, my reading differs from hers in that I would not claim that Woolf uses generic innovations as a way of transcending her privileges in order to achieve solidarity; rather, I think Woolf is deliberately using the form to show how difficult such solidarity is in practice.
4. Here I want to acknowledge a few of the many feminist scholars whose work on Virginia Woolf has shaped and indeed made possible my own thinking about her legacy. Foremost, Jane Marcus; also particularly helpful to this discussion, Leila Brosnan, Mary Childers, Juliet Dusinberre, Kathy Phillips, and Rachel Blau DuPlessis.

Works Cited

Brosnan, Leila. *Reading Virginia Woolf's Essays and Journalism: Breaking the Surface of Silence*. Edinburgh, Scotland: Edinburgh UP, 1997.
Childers, Mary. "Virginia Woolf on the Outside Looking Down: Reflections on the Class of Women." *Modern Fiction Studies* 38 (1992): 61-79.
Marcus, Jane. *Art and Anger: Reading Like A Woman*. Columbus: Ohio State UP, 1988.
Woolf, Virginia. *The Diary of Virginia Woolf*. Ed. Anne Olivier Bell. 5 vols. New York: Harcourt Brace, 1984.
——. "Introductory Letter." *Life As We Have Known It*. By Co-operative Working Women.
Ed. Margaret Llewelyn Davies. 1931; New York: Norton, 1975.
——. *Mrs. Dalloway*. Orlando: Harcourt Brace, 1997.

Notes on Contributors

ANN ARDIS (1) is Director of the University Honors Program and Associate Professor of English at the University of Delaware. She is the author of *New Women, New Novels: Feminism and Early Modernism* (1990), and is now editing a collection, *Women's Experience of Modernity, 1875-1945*.

MONICA AYUSO (86) was born in Argentina is currently Assistant Professor in the English Department at California State University, Bakersfield. She completed a Doctorate from the University of Florida with a dissertation entitled, "Thinking Back Through Our Mothers: Virginia Woolf in the Spanish American Imagination." She specializes in ethnic, racial, and gender studies.

EDWARD BARNABY (311) is a Henry Mitchell MacCracken Fellow in the Department of English at New York University.

EILEEN BARRETT (111) is Professor of English at California State University, Hayward. With Patricia Cramer, she co-edited *Virginia Woolf: Lesbian Readings*.

SUZANNE BELLAMY (244) is an Australian studio artist and writer working on the visual and textual meeting places in the work and life of Virginia Woolf. She has exhibited work at the last three Woolf conferences, and last year collaborated with American artist Isota Tucker Epes on painting the canvases of Lily Briscoe. This collaboration continues this year, with *The Waves* as the focus. She is also preparing a large essay and print study on Gertrude Stein and Virginia Woolf, in conversation on language and geography. This will also be exhibited at the Baltimore conference.

KATHRYN N. BENZEL (192), Professor of English at University of Nebraska-Kearney, has published and presented on Virginia Woolf, Dorothy Richardson, Laura (Riding) Jackson, and Interdisciplinary studies. She recently published *Charleston, A Voice in the House* (London: Cecil Woolf Publishers, 1998) and is currently writing *Virginia Woolf's Aesthetics of Reading* and co-editing with Ruth Hoberman a collection of criticism on Virginia Woolf's short stories.

CHARLES BOEBEL (40) taught for many years at Manchester College before retiring to become a full-time writer. He lives in North Manchester, Indiana, and writes mainly about the American Midwest, with occasional excursions into academic and literary topics.

ALISON BOOTH (24) is Associate Professor at the University of Virginia. Her publications include *Greatness Engendered: George Eliot and Virginia Woolf* (1992), and the collection *Famous Last Words: Changes in Gender and Narrative Closure* (1993). *How to Make It as a Woman*, on collective role-model biographies, should appear early in the new millennium.

Virginia Woolf: Turning the Centuries

JULIA BRIGGS (166) is Professor of English and Women's Studies at De Montfort University, Leicester, England; General Editor for Penguin's edition of Virginia Woolf's works in the Modern Classics series. She is at work on an intellectual biography of Woolf.

PAMELA L. CAUGHIE (34) is Professor of English and Director of Women's Studies at Loyola University Chicago. She is author of *Virginia Woolf and Postmodernism* (1991) and *Passing and Pedagogy*, (1999), as well as articles and book chapters on Woolf, modernism, feminism, and pedagogy.

WAYNE K. CHAPMAN (215) is Professor of English at Clemson University and was Director of the Sixth Annual Virginia Woolf Conference; editor of Virginia Woolf International: *The South Carolina Review* (1996), Ireland in the Arts and Humanities 1899-1999: *The South Carolina Review* (1999), editor of *The Countess Cathleen: Manuscript Materials* (1999), and co-editor of *Women in the Milieu of Leonard and Virginia Woolf* (1998).

PATRICK COLLIER (223), a teacher and freelance writer, will receive his Ph.D. in English from the University of Delaware this spring. His book project, *Newspapers at Modernism's Great Divide*, is a study of relationships between journalism and modernist literature in Britain.

PATRICIA CRAMER (116) is Associate Professor of English and Director of the Women's Studies program at the University of Connecticut at Stamford. She has published articles on feminist teaching, Blake, Chaucer, and Virginia Woolf and is currently working on a book entitled *Virginia Woolf: The Lesbian Years*.

MELBA CUDDY-KEANE (230) is Associate Professor of English and a Northrop Frye Scholar at the University of Toronto. She is a former President of the International Virginia Woolf Society and has published on Virginia Woolf, Joyce Cary, narrative theory, and historical and cultural studies.

GABRIELLE DANE (16), currently a doctoral candidate in English at the University of Minnesota, Twin Cities, has published essays on Shakespeare; feminist and psychoanalytic theory; and women writers, including Toni Morrison, Kathy Acker, and Hélène Cixous. She is focusing her dissertation on Virginia Woolf and the notion of history.

JANE DE GAY (207) is Lecturer in English at Trinity and All Saints University of Leeds. She has published articles on Woolf in *Woolf Studies Annual*, *English Review* and *Critical Survey*, and is currently writing a book on Woolf's responses to her literary influences.

JUNE ELIZABETH DUNN (176), in addition to completing her Master of Arts degree in English at Southern Connecticut State University as a Graduate Research Fellow, is the university's Events Coordinator for the Women's Studies Program. She plans to pursue a Ph.D. in late Victorian/early twentieth century British Literature.

DAVID EBERLY (134) is a poet, critic, and gay activist, whose work has appeared in numerous anthologies and journals over the last three decades. His collection of poetry, *What Has Been Lost,* was published in 1982.

ISOTA TUCKER EPES (252), a longtime Virginia Woolf reader, has worked most of her life as an editor, writer, or teacher of English Literature. At 67, she retired from the

Notes on Contributors

classroom to study studio art. Now, fourteen years later, she still paints with pleasure and regularly enters her work in juried solo and group exhibits.

DIANE F. GILLESPIE (127), Professor of English at Washington State University, is author of *The Sisters' Arts: The Writing and Painting of Virginia Woolf and Vanessa Bell*, co-editor of *Julia Duckworth Stephen: Stories for Children, Essays for Adults* and of *Virginia Woolf and the Arts: Selected Papers from the Sixth Annual Conference on Virginia Woolf*, and editor of *The Multiple Muses of Virginia Woolf* and of *Roger Fry: A Biography* for the Shakespeare Head Press Edition of Woolf's works.

TROY GORDON (102) is a graduate student completing a dissertation at the University of Michigan, where he also teaches English, Women's Studies, and Lesbian/Gay Studies. Before graduate school he worked in Seattle cabaret theaters as an actor, pianist, singer and writer.

VAL GOUGH (183) is Lecturer in English at the University of Liverpool, U.K. She is editor of *A Very Different Story: Studies on the Fiction of Charlotte Perkins Gilman* (1998) and *Charlotte Perkins Gilman: Optimist Reformer* (2000). She has published widely on Virginia Woolf and other modernist women writers, as well as on her other literary passion, science fiction. She is currently working on a book on British women's science fiction of the inter-war period.

JUDITH GREENBERG (140) is completing a book on the role of Echo for representing trauma in Woolf, Duras, and Joyce. She has written on trauma for *American Imago* and *Woolf Studies Annual*. Currently an independent scholar, she has taught in the French Departments at Dartmouth and Williams Colleges.

SALLY GREENE (11) is an independent scholar in Chapel Hill, North Carolina. Part of her time is spent practicing law in nearby Raleigh. She is editor of *Virginia Woolf: Reading the Renaissance* (1999) and has edited a special edition of *Women's Studies: An Interdisciplinary Journal* titled "Virginia Woolf in Performance" (1999).

LESLIE KATHLEEN HANKINS (266), Associate Professor of English at Cornell College in Iowa, is writing a book on Virginia Woolf and the Screen. She has published in Gillespie's *The Multiple Muses of Virginia Woolf*, Barrett and Cramer's *Virginia Woolf: Lesbian Readings*, Greene's special issue of *Women's Studies* and Caughie's *Virginia Woolf in the Age of Mechanical Reproduction* and in previous volumes of the Selected Papers. With Diane Gillespie, she co-edited *Virginia Woolf and the Arts: Selected Papers from the Sixth Annual Conference on Virginia Woolf*.

SUZETTE HENKE (147) is Thruston B. Morton, Sr. Professor of Literary Studies at the University of Louisville. She is author of *Joyce's Moraculous Sindbook: A Study of "Ulysses"* (1978), *James Joyce and the Politics of Desire* (1990), and *Shattered Subjects: Trauma and Testimony in Women's Life-Writing (1998)*. She has published essays on Virginia Woolf, Dorothy Richardson, Anaïs Nin, Doris Lessing, Janet Frame, Keri Hulme, Maya Angelou, Sally Morgan, Samuel Beckett, and W. B. Yeats.

LESLEY HIGGINS (276), associate professor of English at York, has published extensively on modernist literary culture, Walter Pater, and Gerard Manley Hopkins. Her work on Woolf, Foucault, and mobility rights with Marie-Christine Leps frames a new study of governmentality and twentieth-century fiction.

Virginia Woolf: Turning the Centuries

MARIE-CHRISTINE LEPS (276), associate professor of English and Social and Political Thought at York University, is the author of "Apprehending the Criminal: The Production of Deviance in Nineteenth-Century Discourse" and essays on the information age.

JANE LILIENFELD (153) an Associate Professor of English at Lincoln University, an historically Black college, has published essays on Woolf, feminist theory, and 19th and 20th century women writers. She is the author of *Reading Alcoholisms: Theorizing Character and Narrative in Selected Novels of Hardy, Joyce, and Woolf*, and the co-editor of *The Languages of Addiction*.

MICHELLE N. MIMLITSCH (283) is a doctoral candidate in English at UCLA. She is completing her dissertation on the influence of early feminism on women's home front fiction of the Great War, which includes a discussion of *Mrs. Dalloway*. Her interest in film adaptations derives from a broader interest in cross-pollination among the arts.

ANN MURPHY (317) is an Associate Professor of English at Assumption College. Her research interests include women in higher education and pedagogy. Her recent work has been on Emily Davies.

ELYSE MYERS (298) is a graduate student in English at the University of Iowa. She's currently working on her dissertation, which concerns modernist literary texts, Relativity Theory and reconceptualizations of the body.

JEANNE MCNETT (317) is an Assistant Professor of Management at Assumption College. Her research interests include the role of culture in international business, pedagogy, and the role of the humanities in the practice of business.

PETER NACCARATO (199) is Assistant Professor of English at Marymount Manhattan College. His essay on Virginia Woolf will be included in Greenwood Publishing Group's forthcoming *Twentieth Century British Women Writers*. He is also co-editor of *The Years* for The Shakespeare Head Press Edition of Virginia Woolf, from Basil Blackwell.

SHIELA PARDEE (291) is a doctoral candidate at the University of Delaware. She is completing her dissertation on representations of Latin America in novels by Woolf, Conrad, and Lawrence.

GYLLIAN PHILLIPS (56) teaches at Nipissing University in North Bay, Ontario. Her work is generally focused on modernism, and specifically on music/text collaboration. She has published on Virginia Woolf and Gertrude Stein.

LAURIE QUINN (325) is completing her doctoral dissertation, *Reading for Class: Virginia Woolf, Rebecca West, and Sylvia Townsend Warner*, at the University of New Hampshire. This paper is derived from that project, and from her ongoing intellectual and political investment in the myriad intersections of class issues and feminism.

STEPHEN RAMSAY (6) is a Senior Programmer at the Institute for Advanced Technology in the Humanities and a graduate student in English at the University of Virginia. He is currently writing a dissertation on computational methods and literary analysis.

JUDITH ROOF (93) is the author of *Reproductions of Reproduction: Imaging Symbolic Change, Come As You Are: Sexuality and Narrative,* and *A Lure of Knowledge: Lesbian Sexuality and Theory.* She is Professor of English at Michigan State University.

Notes on Contributors

CATHERINE SANDBACH-DAHLSTRÖM (78) is Associate Professor of English at Stockholm University, author of *Be Good Sweet Maid: Charlotte Yonge's Domestic Fiction*, and numerous articles on Feminist Theory and Virginia Woolf. Her book on Virginia Woolf, *Conversing About Collusion,* is forthcoming. She is the senior editor of the Swedish journal of Women's Studies.

BONNIE KIME SCOTT (1) is Professor and Director of Graduate Studies in English at the University of Delaware. Her books include *Joyce and Feminism, James Joyce* (feminist readings), *The Gender of Modernism, Refiguring Modernism* (2 vols.), and *Selected Letters of Rebecca West,* as well as several edited conference collections.

TRACEY SHERARD (62) received her Ph.D. in 1998 from Washington State University, where she currently teaches courses in composition and literature. She has published articles on the work of Virginia Woolf, Thomas Pynchon, James Baldwin, and Toni Morrison in journals such as *African American Review* and *GENDERS.*

MARILYN SCHWINN SMITH's (158) interest in Woolf grew from her work on the Russian poet Marina Tsvetaeva, a contemporary of Woolf's. The magnificent scene in *Orlando* on the frozen Thames will serve as introduction to a lecture Dr. Smith is currently preparing on the English perception of Russia during the Renaissance.

ANNA SNAITH (256) is a Lecturer in English at Anglia Polytechnic University in Cambridge, England. She is the author of *Virginia Woolf: Public and Private Negotiations* (2000) and the editor of 'The Three Guineas Letters' (*Woolf Studies Annual* 2000). She is currently working on a book on postcolonial women writers living in London in the period 1890-1930.

LISA GOLMITZ WEIHMAN (69) has recently completed her doctoral work in the English Department of New York University. Her research centers on questions of gender and nationalism in the literature of twentieth-century England and Ireland, and she is currently revising her dissertation, *Deconstructing the Nation: Women's Literary Politics 1880-1941* for publication.

MICHAEL WHITWORTH (304) teaches at the University of Wales, Bangor. He has published articles on Woolf, Eliot, and Conrad, and on various aspects of science and literature. He is currently completing a book on modernism and the new physics, and is compiling a bibliography of Sir Herbert Read.

JOHN YOUNG (236) is a lecturer at the University of Michigan. He received his Ph.D. from Northwestern University in 1998, and is currently at work on a book manuscript that combines editorial and feminist theory to investigate relationships between modernist women writers and publishers.

Virginia Woolf Turning the Centuries

Ninth Annual Virginia Woolf Conference
University of Delaware, June 10-13, 1999

THURSDAY, JUNE 10 (All sessions held in Perkins Student Center)
9:30 a.m.   Registration opens at Perkins Student Center, lobby
10-1 p.m. Optional tour of Winterthur. Bus leaves at 10 from Perkins Student Center.
11 a.m.   Campus tour available, leaving from Perkins Student Center lobby.
1-2:30 p.m.   **Concurrent Session 1**
Period Studies 1—Revisiting the Long 18th Century   Collins Room
Donald Mell, University of Delaware (chair)
    Gabrielle Dane, University of Minnesota – Twin Cities, "Thinking Back Through Her Fathers: Virginia Woolf and Edward Gibbon"
    Michele Hilton, University of Toronto, "Woolf's Criticism of Jane Austen and the Reception of *Night and Day*"
    Jody R. Rosen, CUNY Graduate Center, "Writing Herself a Companion, Writing Herself Chaste: Women Traveling Alone in the Eighteenth Century"
Disciplinary Traversals 1—Science and Technology   Kirkwood Room
Elaine Safer, University of Delaware (chair)
    Emily Blair, University of California – Davis, "Virginia Woolf's Motor Car: Repetition and Identity"
    Susan M. Rochette-Crawley, University of Northern Iowa, "Science and Sentience: Imagination, Space, Time, and Optics in Virginia Woolf's Short Fiction"
    Elyse Myers, University of Iowa, "Virginia Woolf and the 'Voyage Out' from Victorian Science"
    Barbara E. Weaver, Clemson University, "Teaching Woolf's *A Room of One's Own* to First-year Engineering and Science Students with Laptop Computers"
Accompanying Mrs. Dalloway   Alumni Room
Jessica Berman, University of Maryland—Baltimore County (chair)
    Ann Bliss, California State University – Hayward, "The Relationship between Clothing and Sexuality in *Mrs. Dalloway*"
    Linda Raphael, George Washington University, "Other Minds and Marital Quarrels: Mrs. Dalloway and Mrs. Ramsay"
    Marilyn Smith Schwinn, Five-College Associate, "Narration, Memory, and Identity: *Mrs. Dalloway* at the End of Century"
2:30-4 p.m.   **Concurrent Session 2**
Cultures of War 1   Alumni Room
Karen Levenback, George Washington University (chair)
    Karla Alwes, SUNY Cortland, "'Ancestral voices prophesying war': Woolf's 'masculine fiction' in *Three Guineas*" [paper to be read]
    Catherine Hollis, University of California – Berkeley, "Moments of Shock: Life Writing in 1939-1940"
    Lisa Golmitz Weihman, NYU, "The Problem of National Culture: Virginia Woolf's *Between the Acts* and Elizabeth Bowen's *The Last September*"
Remote Inscriptions 1   Collins Room
Theodore Braun, University of Delaware (chair)

Peter G. Christensen, University of Wisconsin-Milwaukee, "Marguerite Yourcenar: Translator of Virginia Woolf"

Emily Dalgarno, Boston University, "Dostoyevsky and Woolf's Modernism"

Susanna Rich, Kean University, "Is it Lucretius?—*De Undarum Natura*"

Ted Taylor, Rutgers University, "Self-Portraits for the Self"

Subjectivity 1—Changing the Subject: Virginia Woolf and Poststructuralist Theories of Subjectivity   **Kirkwood Room**

Moira P. Baker, Radford University, (chair) "'Writing Against the Current': The Politics of Subjectivity in *Three Guineas*"

Mary Trianosky, Hollins College, "A Day Revealed: Woolf's Challenge to Traditional Discourses of Sexuality"

Jennifer Kurtz, Radford University, "'These long waves, these endless paths': Social Institutions and Identity Formation in *The Waves*"

Woolf as Biographer/ Biography   **Gallery**

Windy Counsell, University of Delaware (chair)

Elisabeth H. Ellington, Brandeis University, "Writing Virginia Woolf's Lives: Biographical Potential in the 21st Century"

Gyllian Phillips, Nipissing University, " 'She was no scholar': Placing Mrs. Browning"

Anna Snaith, Anglia Polytechnic University, "'At Gordon Sq. and nowhere else': The Spatial and Social Politics of Bloomsbury"

Simone Waddell, University of Delaware, "Reinventing Biography: Virginia Woolf's Departures from Leslie Stephen's Essays in Biography"

4-4:30 p.m.   **Snack**

4:30-6 p.m.   **Plenary Panel: Virginia Woolf: Scanning the**
                          Centuries   **Collins Room**

Barbara Green, Notre Dame University (chair)

Sally Greene, Independent Scholar, "Virginia Woolf: Renaissance Woman"

Alison Booth, University of Virginia, "Those Well Lit Corridors of History: The Victorians"

Pamela Caughie, Loyola University, "Virginia Woolf in the Age of Mechanical Reproduction"

6-7:30 p.m.   **Buffet Reception**   **Gallery**
                          Welcome: George Miller, English Department Chair;
                          Bonnie Kime Scott and Ann Ardis, Conference Co-Directors
                          Woolf Society Players

7:30-9 p.m.   **Concurrent Session 3**

Feminist Studies 1—Feminist Resistance   **Collins Room**

Mary Pinkerton, University of Wisconsin—Whitewater (chair)

Craig Hamilton, University of Maryland, "The Exit Metaphor and Woolf's *The Voyage Out*"

Petra Ragnerstam, Lund University, "Cultured Resistance in Virginia Woolf's *To the Lighthouse*"

Peter Naccarto, Adelphi University, "Re-Defining Feminist Fiction in *The Years*"

Conference Program

Same-Sex Desire and Homosexual Coding   **Alumni Room**
Lynnette Beers (chair)

    June Elizabeth Dunn, Southern Connecticut State University, "'Beauty shines on two dogs doing what two women must not do': Puppy Love, Same-Sex Desire, and Homosexual Coding in Woolf"

    Henry Krusiewicz, Midland Lutheran College, "To Lie Down with Dogs: Trained Beasts in Woolf's *Flush* and Barnes' *Nightwood*"

    Colleen Lamos, Rice University, "Queer Woolf?"

    Tracey Sherard, Washington State University, "'Parsifal in the Forest of Gender': Wagner, Homosexuality, and *The Waves*"

Investing in Futures: Woolf and Literary Value   **Kirkwood Room**
Patrick Collier, University of Delaware (chair)

    Melba Cuddy-Keane, University of Toronto - Scarborough, "'A Standard of One's Own': Virginia Woolf and the Question of Literary Value"

    William H. Harrison, SUNY-Geneseo, "From Carrots to Canon": Leonard and Virginia Woolf on Middlebrows, Modern Fiction, and Literature"

Morton P. Levitt, Temple University, "Woolf in Time"

    Alisha Rohde, Ohio State University, "Investing in Futures: Early Developments in Woolf's Literary Value"

Narrative Ploys   **Gallery**
Elisabeth Ellington, Brandeis University (chair)

    Sarah E. Davis, University of Delaware, "Piercing the Veil: Revealing the Veiled Feminine Voices of Virginia Woolf and Jane Austen"

    Mary C. Madden, University of South Florida, "A Porcupine in the Parlor: Virginia Woolf's Quills Hit Their Mark: An Analysis of Satire in the Work of Virginia Woolf"

    Flora P.H. Ni, Providence University, "Fighting a Masculine War with a Feminine Writing: Paradox in Virginia Woolf's Style"

    Elizabeth Primamore, CUNY Graduate Center, "Woolf and the Sexual Life of Women: *The Pargiters*, A Revisionist's Text and Personal History of Sexuality"

FRIDAY, JUNE 11 (All sessions in Perkins Student Center)

8-9 a.m.   **Continental breakfast**
                Campus tour available.

9-4 p.m.   Woolf Film viewing, Library Media Center.
                See Special events section of program for schedule.

9-10:30 a.m.   **Concurrent Session 4**

Period Studies 2—Woolf and the Victorians   **Collins Room**
Barbara T. Gates, University of Delaware (chair)

    Julia S. Gray, University of Rochester, "The Development of Free Indirect Discourse: An Investigation of Narrative Form and Function in George Eliot and Woolf"

    Ann K. Hoff, CUNY Graduate Center, "Modern Autobiographical Representations of a Victorian Childhood"

    Jennifer L. Kellog, Clemson University, "Virginia Woolf and Lytton Strachey in the Shadow of the Victorians"

Shiela Pardee, University of Delaware, "Assuming Psyche's Task: Virginia Woolf Responds to James Frazer"

Cultures of War 2—*Between the Acts* **Alumni Room**
Katharine Kerrane, University of Delaware (chair)
    Nancy Knowles, University of Connecticut – Storrs, "Virginia Woolf's *Between the Acts* as Pacifist Art"
    Tonya Krouse, Brandeis University, "Fascism Begins at Home: Performing Gender and Sexuality *Between the Acts*"

Woolf and Women's Studies in the 21st Century:
A Roundtable Discussion **Bacchus Theatre**
Jeanette McVicker (chair), SUNY – Fredonia
Vara Neverow, Southern Connecticut State University
Diana Swanson, Northern Illinois University
    Andrea Herrera, SUNY – Fredonia
    Mark Hussey, Pace University

Subjectivity 2—Seeing the Self **Kirkwood Room**
Allison Carpenter, University of Delaware (chair)
    Thomas March, NYU, "Woolf's Clarissa Dalloway: The Voyage in from *The Voyage Out*"
    Christina Seluzicki, Bryn Mawr College, "Sea-ing the Self: Virginia Woolf and Katherine Mansfield's Struggle for Wholeness"
    Nadia Wagner, Kean University, "Fathoming the Mind: A Jungian Reading of Woolf's *Jacob's Room*"
    Yuan-Jung Cheng, National Sun Yat-sen University, "'The Unheard Melodies': A Poetics of Madness in *Mrs. Dalloway*"

10:30-11 a.m. **Coffee**

11-1 p.m. **(Long) Concurrent Session 5**

Forms of History 1: Reformulations **Kirkwood Room**
Anne M. Boylan, University of Delaware (chair)
    Ann Browning, UNC – Chapel Hill, "Woolf, A.S. Byatt, and Four Queen Elizabeths"
    Audrey Johnson, Washington State University, "Orlando and the Spirit of the Age: Virginia Woolf's Re-Vision of Victorian Historiography"
    Jason B. Jones, Emory University, "Virginia Woolf's *The Years*: Towards a Non-Reparative History"
    Edward Barnaby, NYU, "Visualizing the Spectacle: Woolf's Meta-history Lesson in *Between the Acts*"
    Manuela Palacios, University of Santiago de Compostela, "Sketches of the Past: Virginia Woolf as Art Historian"

Feminist Studies 2—Conversations at the Turn of the Century **Collins Room**
Ann Ardis, University of Delaware (chair)
    Susan Torrey Barstow, University of Virginia, "*Freshwater* and the Recovery of Feminist History"
    Deirdre Flynn, University of California – Berkeley, "Wearing Her Mother's Victorian Dress: Woolf's Image of the Modern Woman"

Conference Program

    Evelyn Haller, Doane College, "Virginia Woolf and Willa Cather Dancing with Leon Bakst"

    Anne MacMaster, Millsaps College, "Contrast as Continuity: Woolf's *The Years* and Wharton's *The Age of Innocence* on the Turn into the Twentieth Century"

    Catherine Sandbach-Dahlstrvm, Stockholm University, "Feminist Conversation: Woolf, De Beauvoir and the Dialogic"

First Encounters: Reading Woolf and Joyce . . . Together in High School Alumni Room
Kathy Hill-Miller, Long Island University—C.W. Post Campus (moderator)
    Peter Greer, Department of English, Phillips Exeter Academy (chair)
    Lauren Brumsted, '99, Phillips Exeter Academy
    Nita Pettigrew, Department of English, Phillips Exeter Academy
    Jonathan Chow, '99, Phillips Exeter Academy
    Sarah Ream, Department of English, Phillips Exeter Academy
    Brian Lowe, '99, Phillips Exeter Academy

Period Studies 3—Modernism and Modernity   Bacchus Theatre
Patrick Collier, University of Delaware (chair)
    Ruth Hoberman, Eastern Illinois University, "*The Years*, Kitsch, and Modernism"
    Robert Hurd, University of Maryland, "The Aesthetic of Everyday Life in Virginia Woolf's *To the Lighthouse*"
    Garry Leonard, University of Toronto – Scarborough, "Modernism as a Symptom of Modernity in *Mrs Dalloway*"

1-2:30 p.m.   **Lunch** on one's own
2:30-4 p.m.   **Featured Panels**

Sexuality and Subjectivity in Woolf's Life and Work Bacchus Theatre
    Madeline Moore (chair), University of California-Santa Cruz, "Virginia Woolf's Sexuality and the Problematics of Subjectivity"
    Suzette Henke, University of Louisville, "Virginia Woolf : Trauma and Subjectivity"

"Painting the Words": Two Versions of Lily Briscoe's Canvas in *To the Lighthouse* Collins Room
J.J. Wilson, Sonoma State University (chair)
    Isota Tucker Epes, Artist, Falls Church, VA
    Suzanne Bellamy, Artist, Braidwood, Australia

4-4:30 p.m.   **Snack**
4:30-6 p.m.   **Concurrent Session 6**

Remote Inscriptions 2—Woolf in Diaspora   Collins Room
Ellen Pifer, University of Delaware (chair)
    Monica Ayuso, California State University - Bakersfield, "Remote Inscriptions: *To The Lighthouse* and *The Waves* in Julieta Campos' Caribbean"
    Arianne Burford, Washington State University, "Making Waves: 'Discovering' Virginia Woolf's and Jamaica Kincaid's Disruption of Empire in *The Waves*, *Between the Acts*, and *At the Bottom of the River*"

Conference Program

Donna Camoesas, Dickinson State University, "At the Crest of the Stream: Woolf, Lispector, and *Aqua viva*"

Anju Kapur, College of New Jersey, "Modernism as Philosophical Enterprise: Virginia Woolf and Arundhatti Roy"

Disciplinary Traversals 2—Religion and Philosophy   **Kirkwood Room**

Kathryn Miles, University of Delaware (chair)

Michael Lackey, University of St. Thomas, "Post-God Intimacy in Woolf's *To the Lighthouse*"

Catherine Mintler, Kenwood Academy High School, University of Illinois – Chicago, "The Novel as Hegelian Work of Art: Sublation of the Particular Arts and the Origin of the Woolfian Moment *in To the Lighthouse*"

Katherine Bennett, Mills College, "*To the Lighthouse* Over an Ocean of Wisdom: A British Conception of Buddhist Philosophy Counters the Western Rationalist Tradition

Trauma and Wellness   **Bacchus Theatre**

Terri Brint Joseph, Chapman University (chair)

Diane F. Gillespie, Washington State University, "Metaphors of Illness and Wellness: John Donne, Virginia Woolf, and Susan Sontag"

Judith Greenberg, Williams College, "Woolf's Ancient Song: Traces of the Dead Echoing into the Future"

Annalisa Weaver-Zox, Claremont Graduate University, "Madness Enters 'The Sacred Circle': Gender, Psychiatry and 'an inner meaning expressed' in *Mrs. Dalloway*"

Androgyny   **Alumni Room**

Anne Thalheimer, University of Delaware (chair),

Yael S. Feldman, NYU, "Who is Afraid of Androgyny? Recuperating Woolf's Androgyny for General Consumption"

Sarah Johnson, Midland Lutheran College, "The Other for the Other: Binaries and Bisexuality in *The Waves*"

Ayako Mizuo, Loughborough University, "The Place of Imagination and Autobiography: Virginia Woolf's Aesthetics of Sexual Difference"

Scott Warnock, Temple University, "The Elision of Gender and the Limits of Language in *Orlando* and *The Heavenly Twins*"

6-7 p.m.   **Play Reading** *Orlando 2000: A Dramatic Speculation*
       by Charles Boebel   **Bacchus Theatre**

7-8:30 p.m.   Dinner on one's own

8:30 p.m.   **Keynote**: **Julia Briggs, DeMontfort University,**
       "Finding New Virginias"
       Lois Potter, University of Delaware (chair)

SATURDAY, JUNE 12   (All sessions held in Gore Hall on the mall)

8-9 a.m.   **Continental breakfast**   **Gore 204**
       Meeting: The future? of *The Virginia Woolf Miscellany* **Gore 204**
       J.J. Wilson presiding

9-10:30 a.m.   **Concurrent Session 7**

Speaking of Greeks   **Gore 219**

Pierre-Eric Villeneuve, Brock University (chair)

Conference Program

        Pascale Dubé, University of Quebec – Montreal, "Woolf and *The Voyage Out* or Woolf's First Antigone"

        Theodore Koulouris, University of Sussex, "The Greeks, the Academics, and the 'Other': Virginia Woolf and Helenism"

        Susan Omundsen, University of Sydney, "Decoding Woolf's Feminist Mythology in *To the Lighthouse*" [paper to be read]

        Stephen Ramsay, University of Virginia, "'On Not Knowing Greek': Virginia Woolf and the New Ancient Greece"

Disciplinary Traversals 3—Physics   Gore 316

Julian Yates, University of Delaware (chair)

        Holly Henry, Pennsylvania State University, "Standing on the 'globe of glass': Virginia Woolf and the Solar Eclipse"

        Greg Grewell, Washington State University, "Woolf's Chaos: The Dynamicism of *The Waves*"

        Michael Whitworth, University of Wales, "'The Lighted Strip of History': New Physics Moving the Markers"

Pressing the Public Sphere   Gore 204

Christopher Keirstead, University of Delaware (chair)

        Patrick Collier, University of Delaware, "Woolf, Privacy, and the Press"

        Anne Fernald, Purdue University, "A Feminist Public Sphere?: Woolf's Revisions of the 18th Century"

Alice Staveley, Oxford University, *"Three Guineas* Goes to Market"

        John Young, University of Michigan, "Canonicity and Commercialization in the Uniform Edition"

10:30-11 a.m.   **Coffee**

11-1 p.m. **(Long) Featured Panels**

New Applications of Queer Theory   Gore 204

Gregory Weight, University of Delaware (chair),

 Judith Roof, Indiana University, "Revisiting Gay and Lesbian Readings of Woolf"

        Troy Gordon, University of Michigan "The Place of Cross-Sex Friendship in Woolf Studies,"

Respondents:

Pat Cramer, University of Connecticut – Stamford

Eileen Barrett, California State University - Hayward

Electronic Archives   Gore 223

Laura Davis, Kent State University (chair)

        Patricia Clements, University of Alberta, Susan Brown, Guelph University, and Kathryn Harvey, "The Orlando Project"

        Michael Groden, University of Western Ontario, *"Ulysses*: The Challenge of Presenting the Modernist Novel in an Electronic Environment"

        Mark Hussey, Pace University, "How Should One Read a Screen?"

        Clifford E. Wulfman, Yale University, "Breaking on the Electronic Shore: Hypertext and *The Waves*"

1-2:30 p.m. **Lunch** on one's own. Meeting of the International Woolf Society **223 Gore**

Conference Program

2:30-4 p.m.   Concurrent Session 8
Media-ted Metamorphoses: Subjectivity, Temporality, Textuality   Gore 223
Peter Feng , University of Delaware (chair)

Lesley Higgins and Marie-Christine Leps, York University, "The Subject of Time in *Mrs. Dalloway* and *Orlando* (novels and films)"

Michelle N. Mimlitsch, UCLA, "Envisioning/Revisioning Woolf in Film as We Approach the 21st Century"

Alyssa J. O'Brien, University of Rochester, "'Not being Clarissa any more': The Metamorphosis of *Mrs Dalloway*"

Steven Putzel, Pennsylvania State University, "Woolf Adapts Woolf for the Stage: Three 'Caricatures'"

Feminist Studies 3—Turning the Century with Feminist Criticism   Gore 219
June Elizabeth Dunn, Southern Connecticut State University (chair)

Ann Gibaldi Campbell, UNC – Chapel Hill, "Turning the Century: From the House of Man to the 'Our' of Women"

Laurie Quinn, University of New Hampshire, "A Woolf with Political Teeth: Classing Virginia Woolf for and in the 21st Century"

Diana Royer, Miami University, "Dead White Feminist Females: Millennial Housecleaning and the Fate of Virginia Woolf"

Karin E. Westman, College of Charleston, "With 'money and a room of her own': The Legacy of Woolf's Advice for the Woman Artist at Century's End"

Woolf and the Other   Gore 204
Lil Crisler, University of Delaware (chair)

Joseph Flanagan, University of Delaware, 'What's History without the Empire?': The Colonial Death Drive in *The Waves*"

Karen Gaffney, University of Delaware, "'This Was the Skeleton Beneath': *The Voyage Out* and Construction of Others"

Maren Linett, University of Michigan, "'The Jew in the Bath'*: The Years* and its Draft Versions"

Who's NOT Afraid of Leonard Woolf   Gore 316
Wayne Chapman, Clemson University (chair), "Leonard Woolf, Cambridge, and the Art of English Essay"

Jean Wilson Moorcroft, University of London, "Leonard Woolf and the Hogarth Press"

Karen Schiff, Clemson University, "Vanessa Dell and the Big Bad Woolfs: 'Kew Gardens' and Negotiations about Hogarth Aesthetics"

4-4:30 p.m.   Snack
4:30-6 p.m.   Concurrent Session 9
Subjectivity 3   Gore 219
Allison Carpenter, University of Delaware (chair)

Lisa L. Hill, Southeastern Oklahoma State University, "Poetics as Rhetorics: Rereading 'the Subject' Through Virginia Woolf"

Deborah Jacobs, Independent Scholar, "The Souls of Womenfolk, — or What Virginia Knew"

Conference Program

Roberta Schreyer, State University of New York at Potsdam, "A Postmodern Theory of Intersubjectivity in Woolf's Work"

Remote Inscriptions 3—Continuing Influences   Gore 223

Kathryn Miles, University of Delaware (chair)

Jennifer Guarino, University of Delaware, "The Two Floating Rhodas: A Contemporary Re-Writing of *The Waves*"

Georgia Johnston, Saint Louis University, "Historical Intertexts: Cunningham's *The Hours* and Woolf's *Mrs. Dalloway*"

Justyna Kostkowska, Middle Tennessee State University, "Written on the Body: Jeannette Winterson's Palimpsest of Virginia Woolf, or the Full Circle"

Stephanie Harzewski, Independent Scholar, "'What the Light Looks Like': Carole Maso, Virginia Woolf, and the Process of Illumination"

Woolf's Short Stories   Gore 316

Susan Suchy, Chapman University (chair)

Kathryn N. Benzel, Univ. of Nebraska - Kearney, "Woolf's Early Experimentation with Consciousness: 'Kew Gardens,' Typescript to Publication"

Jane de Gay, The Open University, "An Unwritten Story: The Victorian Version of Virginia Woolf's 'The Searchlight'"

Laura Lojo-Rodríguez, University of Santiago de Compostela, "From One Age of Literature to Another: Virginia Woolf's 'The Mark on the Wall'"

Jorge Romero-Sacido, University of Santiago de Compostela, "The Search for Truth as the Shaping Force of Discourse: Virginia Woolf's 'Monday or Tuesday'"

Woolf and Traumatic Narrative: Fictional Strategies and Cultural Responses   Gore 204

Jane Lilienfeld, Lincoln University (chair), "Accident, Incident, and Meaning: Traces of Trauma in Virginia Woolf's Narrativity"

David Eberly, John F. Kennedy School of Government, "Safety Pins and Semicolons"

Patricia Cramer, University of Connecticut – Stamford, "'Plain as a Pike's Staff': A Response to Recent Biographers"

6:30-8 p.m.   **Orlando Costume Ball and Banquet**   Gore Rotunda

Costumes are entirely optional. Various stores on Main St. offer resources.

8-9 p.m.   **After Dinner Features**

Creative interpretations 1:   Gore 204

Rosemary Monaco, S. Illinois. Univ.-Edwardsville (chair)

Allison Funk, "Letters to Virginia Woolf" (poetry), and

Robin Lippincott, excerpts from *Mr. Dalloway* (novel)

Creative interpretations 2:   Gore 223

John Fuegi and Jo Francis out-takes from *Virginia Woolf: The War Within*

Turning the Patterns: Gore 219

Open discussion of current patterns in Woolf studies, anticipating tomorrow's panels and next year's conference, and looking back through "Virginia Woolf Turning the Centuries," so far. Bonnie Kime Scott and Ann Ardis (chairs)

SUNDAY, JUNE 13 (Sessions held in Gore and Smith Halls—Smith is across S. College Avenue via pedestrian bridge)

8-9 a.m.   **Continental breakfast**   Gore 204

Conference Program

Meeting to plan next year's Conference, Jessica Berman (chair)
9-10:30 a.m.   **Concurrent Session 10**

The Ethics of Suicide   Gore 316
Pierre-Eric Villeneuve, Brock University (chair), "Words for a Century: Woolf's Last Letters"
    Val Gough, University of Liverpool, "'A responsible person like her': Woolf's Suicide Culture"

Education Engendered   Smith 120
Carole M. Kley, Rutgers University (chair)
    Beth Rigel Daugherty, Otterbein College, "Virginia Woolf's Educational Inheritance: The Stephen Household and Nineteenth Century Debates about Education for Girls"
    Paula Makris, Case Western Reserve, "Homosocial Education and Patriarchal Gender Roles: The Classics in *Jacob's Room*"
    Jeanne McNett and Ann Murphy, Assumption College, "Women's Learning, Women's Work: Virginia Woolf for the Twenty-first Century"

The Cultures of War 3—Breaking Time: Woolf and the Wars   Gore 219
Ellen Tremper, Brooklyn College (chair), "A Shift on the Scale"
    Georgette Fleischer, Columbia University, "From 'Time Passes' to 'A Sketch of the Past': Virginia Woolf's Parenthetical Responses to World War I and World War II"
    Suzanne Laizik, Columbia University, "'The future shadowed their present': *Between the Acts* and World War II"

Remote Inscriptions 4   Gore 223
Shelley Puhak, University of Delaware (chair)
    Madelyn Detloff, University of California – Irvine, "Dead Women at the Bottom of the Sea: The Cultural Symbolics of Woolf's Suicide at the Century's End"
    Robert Foote, Mills College, "Dalloway, Derrida, and the Gift: Life After Deconstruction"
    Lisa K. Stein, University of Kentucky, "Beyond Benjamim: The Evolution of the Flaneur from Dickens to Woolf"
    Judy Suh, University of Pittsburgh, "Re-membering Trauma: Mrs. Dalloway's Critique of Nostalgia"

10:30-12 p.m.   **Concurrent Session 11**

The Illustrated Woolf   Smith 120
Brenda Lyons, Greenfield Community College (chair), "Orlando and Flush: The Case of Disappearing Photographs"
    Krystyna Colburn, University of Massachusetts – Boston, and Vara Neverow, Southern Connecticut State University, "Paterfamilias, Pater Ecclesias, Pater Patrias: Photographic Portraits of the Domestic Father and the Public Father Taken from a Monks' House Album"
    Leslie Kathleen Hankins, Cornell College, "Tracking Shots through Film History: Woolf and Film Archives"

Forms of History 2: Keeping Time   Gore 223
Robert E. Foote, Mills College (chair)
    Alice T. Gasque, University of South Dakota, "Time in *Between the Acts*: The Pageant and Its Frame"
    Anneli Kallero, Lund University, "Being and Time in Virginia Woolf's *The Waves*"

Conference Program

        Brian Richardson, University of Maryland, "Beyond Feminist Aesthetics?"

        Thomas W. Sheehan, University of California – Berkeley, "Transitional Moments: Time In *Between the Acts*"

Disciplinary Traversals 4: Art   **Gore 316**

Elisa Kay Sparks, Clemson University (chair), "'The beauty, which is almost entirely colour': Colors and Being and Meaning in the Early Work of Woolf and O'Keefe"

        Jocelyn Harris, University of Otago, "The Case of the Woman Artist: Virginia Woolf and Frances Hodgkins"

12-1 p.m.   **Endnote performance: Ntozake Shange**   **120 Smith**
               "**Many Trails of a Poet**"
               J.J. Wilson, Sonoma State University (chair)

1-2 p.m.   **Closing reception**   **Gore Rotunda**

Farewell from Jerry Beasley, incoming English Department Chair, University of Delaware

Special conference features

Library exhibit: Visit the first floor exhibition area of the University of Delaware library for a display that demonstrates the extent of Woolf's influence and the diversity of materials which have been published in response to the lively and continuing interest in her life and work. Selections range from Vanessa Bell's sketches to Woolfian offerings on the web. Examples from the extensive collection of the Hogarth Press imprints in the Library's Special Collections department are generously represented. Thursday and Friday, additional Hogarth imprints are located in a case outside Special Collectionsj, which is open Monday through Friday, 9-5.

Library film viewing: Downstairs in the library's Media Room on Friday June 11, there will be continuous showings of Woolfian films.

9 AM   *A Room of One's Own*
11   *Mrs. Dalloway*
1 PM   *Orlando*
3   *Virginia Woolf: The War Within*

t-shirt and poster sales: limited edition t-shirts designed by Suzanne Bellamy are on sale at the registration desk for $19. Posters with graphic design by Cynthia Clabough, featuring the same Bellamy design, are available for $10. UD Bookstore has cylinders for safe carrying. Sales benefit the travel scholarship fund.

Silent Auction: A tradition at Woolf Conferences, the brainchild of Krystyna Colburn, who gives her time, energy and material to the effort. Proceeds go to the travel scholarship fund. Visit the display case in the lobby of Memorial Hall (the building in the center of the mall, between the library and the Georgian part of the mall that includes Gore Hall). Items up for auction include books, memorabilia and collectables. To place a bid, write your name and address, the item number, and the amount you bid on the paper provided, then put it into the box located near the case.

The new memorial hall:

Once you have visited the silent auction, you are cordially invited to enjoy the quiet spaces of our newly refurbished English Department building. A particularly nice spot to relax or to hold quiet conversations is the third floor lounge. Notice that Virginia Woolf is one of 24 authors commemorated in writing around the Memorial Hall Dome, adjacent to the lounge. Notice that hers is the first name visible as you come up the stairs to the third floor!

Conference Program

bookstores:
Two local bookstores—Rainbow Books, located at 58 E. Main Street, and the University of Delaware Bookstore, located in the Perkins Student Center on Academy Street—are participating in the conference. They have both stocked many titles relating to Woolf, as well as recent works by Ntozake Shange and Michael Cunningham. The University Bookstore will be open from 8 a.m. to 5 p.m. Thursday and Friday. Rainbow Books, which will also be selling a small number of conference t-shirts and posters, is open from 10 a.m. to 7 p.m. Thursday, 10 a.m. to 9 p.m. Thursday-Saturday and 10 a.m. to 6 p.m. Sunday. Rainbow Books also features a small restaurant and coffee bar.

travel scholarship fund:
Every year the Conference endeavors to raise money to help meet the travel expenses of conferees with limited funds. These are distributed after the conference, when all revenues are in. We thank those of you who checked off the box on the registration form and made a donation in that manner. Additional contributions will be gratefully received at the registration desk or by either of the conference directors. Krystyna Colburn has generously designated proceeds from the silent auction to the fund. Profits from t-shirt and poster sales also go to this fund, and we thank Suzanne Bellamy and Cynthia Clabough for contributing their artistic efforts to this cause. At the time we went to press the following individuals had contributed: Eileen Barrett, Jessica Berman, Krystyna Colburn, Beth Daugherty, Laura Davis, Isota Epes, Anne Fernald, Diane Gillespie, Julia Gray, Lynne Gray, Anne Howard, Mark Hussey, Georgia Johnston, Anneli Kallero, Jeanette McVicker, Flora Pi-hua Ni, Steven Putzel, Susanna Rich, Diana Royer, Sara Ruddick, Lise Schlosser, Bonnie Kime Scott, Elisa Sparks, Ellen Tremper, J.J. Wilson. See your folder for an updated list.

And announcing for next year:
10th Annual Virginia Woolf Conference, June 8-11, 2000
"VIRGINIA WOOLF OUT OF BOUNDS"
The University of Maryland, Baltimore County (UMBC)
The conference will highlight work on Woolf that crosses regional, temporal, and disciplinary boundaries of all kinds. As the inaugural conference of the millennium, it will continue to address the future of Woolf studies, especially as an opportunity for new intellectual exchanges and mixtures. Proposals are also invited on such topics as:
Woolf in post-colonial contexts, Woolf and contemporary theory, Woolf and the East, Woolf and science, Woolf and history, Inter-textual Woolf/ "sightings" of Woolf, Woolf in translation. The conference particularly invites proposals on pedagogical issues such as: Woolf in the Women's Studies Curriculum, in the ESL classroom, in the AP English/High School Curriculum, and in composition study.
Inquiries to: Jessica Berman, Woolf Conference Director
English Department, UMBC, 1000 Hilltop Circle, Baltimore, MD 21250
Phone: (410) 455-2384   fax: (410) 455-1030   e-mail: jberman@umbc.edu
Or Dori Concannon, UMBC — Continuing Education, 4th floor, Technology Center
1450 South Rolling Rd., Baltimore, MD 21231
Phone: (410) 455-1322   Fax: (410) 455-2336

Index

Abraham, Julie 107, 110n, 138
Adams, William Henry Davenport 27
adjunct faculty 320
Aeschylus 7
After the Deluge 217
agnosticism 17, 151
Ajax 7
Albert, Prince Consort 299
Algren, Nelson 84n
Allan, Tuzyline 95
Allen, Miss (*VO*) 292
Allen, Paula Gunn 117, 124n
Allen, Walter 134
Althusser, Louis 312, 316
Ambrose, Helen (*VO*) 103, 114, 292, 294-96
Ambrose, Ridley (*VO*) 292
Amfortas 64-65
Anderson, Olive 183
androgyny 21, 22, 102, 108
anhedonia 149
"Anon." 145, 228
anthropology 291f.
Antigone 6
Anzaldua, Gloria 117
Apostles 218
Ardis, Ann 297n
Aristotle 307
Armstrong, Carol 212
Arnold, Matthew 7, 8, 221
Arnold, Thomas 9
Artaud, Antonin 8
Arthur, King 207f.
Asheham 178, 193
Asquith, Margot 157n
Astell, Mary 28
Athenaeum, The 306
Auden, W. H. 41
"Aurora Leigh" (Woolf) 56f.
Aurora Leigh 56f., 81
Austen, Jane 25, 28, 31n, 80, 81-2, 194, 232-33

Bachelard, Gaston 264
Bacon, Francis 298, 300
Baillie, Joanna 25
Bair, Deirdre 84n
Bakhtin, Mikhail 80
Ballard, George 27
Bankes, William (*TTL*) 103, 107, 114
Barber, Stephen 103, 105, 108, 110n, 114
Barker, Pat 286

Barrett, Eileen 3, 95, 100n, 177, 180, 273
Barry, Iris 35
Barthes, Roland 12, 15n
Bast, Mrs. (*TTL*) 29
BBC 35, 39
Beatles, The 42, 47
Beckett, Clarice 248
Beechey, James 175
Beer, Gillian 35
Behn, Aphra 26, 31n
Beja, Morris 284
Bell, Clive 167-68
Bell, Vanessa 119, 136, 167, 168, 193, 194, 198n, 248
Bellamy, Suzanne 1, 112, 252, 273-74
Benjamin, Marina 300
Benjamin, Walter 34f., 236, 241n
Bennett, Arnold 37, 182, 233
Bennett, Paula 111
Benstock, Shari 95, 96, 242n
Bergoffen, Debra 83, 84
Bergonzi, Bernard 35
Berman, Jessica 3
Bernard (*TW*) 65-66
Betham, Matilda 29, 31n
Betham-Edwards, Matilda 29
Between the Acts 15, 69f., 311f.; compared with Bowen's *Last September* 72-77; cross-sex friendship in, 103-07; film influence on, 271; nationalism in, 69f.; physics and 306; sexuality and war in, 119-20
Beyond the Pleasure Principle 140
Bible 131
Big Ben 329
biography: 24-32,; *Three Guineas* and, 27-28; Woolf's experiments with, 56f., 276f.; of Woolf, 147, 166-67
Biographical Dictionary of the Celebrated Women of Every Age and Country, The 31n
Biographies of Good Women 30n
Birrell, Francis 26
Birrell, Olive 263
Bishop, Edward L. 10n, 241n
Blackmer, Corinne 95
Blain, Virginia 210
Bliss, Ann 164
Bloomsbury 258, 264
Bloomsbury group: attacks on, 223; synonymous with London neighborhood 256f.
Bodichon, Barbara 263
Boebel, Charles 1
Boone, Joseph 100n
Bond, Cynthia D. 32n
Bonheur, Rosa 27
Book of Sibyls, A 26

348

Index

Booker, M. K. 68n
Booth, Alison 80
Booth, Allyson 154
border crossing 38
Borges, Jorge Luis 90
Bornstein, George 236, 241n
Bowen, Elizabeth 71f.
Bowen, Stella 248
Bowlby, Rachel 83, 109
Boyle, Robert 298
Bradshaw, Dr. (*MD*) 121, 150, 154
Braidotti, Rosi 80
Brecht, Bertolt 8, 315
Bredbeck, Gregory W. 118, 124n
Brenan, Gerald 148
Briscoe, Lily 1, 103, 107, 108, 114, 244f., 252f.
Briggs, Julia 3, 242n
British Film Institute 268
Brontë, Charlotte 194, 230
Brontë, Emily 28
Brontë sisters 25, 81-2
Brosnan, Leila 330n
Brown, Antonio 109n
Brown, Mrs. 29
Brown, Susan 2
Browning, Elizabeth Barrett 25, 56f., 138
Browning, Robert 73, 221
Brunel, Adrian 270
Brunelleschi, Filippo 13
Brush, Milly (*MD*) 181
Bruton, Lady Millicent (*MD*) 177-78, 181
Buckingham Palace 329
Burckhardt, Jacob 11, 12, 14
Burke, Thomas 257
Burroughs, Edgard Rice 225
Bussy, Janie 184
Butler, Josephine 30n
Butler, Judith 96-97, 100n, 103, 117, 118
Byron, George Gordon 173

Caballero, Fernan 29
Calvino, Italo 311
Cambridge University 215f., 292
camera 34f., 88-89
Cameron, Julia Margaret 207f.
Campos, Julieta 86f.
Caputi, Jane 121
Caramagno, Thomas 147
Carlyle, Jane 25, 27
Carlyle, Thomas 26
Carmichael, Mary (*AROO*) 231, 238
Carpenter, Mary 30n
Carrard, Pierre 315

Carrington, Dora 121
Carrington, Leonora 246
Carter, Eliza 27
Carter, Elizabeth 29, 30n
Caruth, Cathy 140, 148, 151
Case, Janet 172
Case, Sue-Ellen 100n
Cassandra 8
Castelvetro 8
Castle, Terry 97, 100n, 102, 112, 113
Catalyst 322
Catherine of Siena 27
Caughie, Pamela 1, 2, 59, 61n
Cause, The 27, 30n, 260
Cecil, Eleanor (Nelly) 186
Celebrated Englishwomen of the Victorian Era 27
Cerasano, S. P. 15n
Ceylon 217
Cézanne, Paul 246
Chaplin, Charlie 268
Chaucer 7
Chekhov, Anton 233
Childers, Mary 327, 330n
Christianity: Gibbon on, 17, 20; discourses of heterosexuality of, 63, 64, 68n, 121
"Cinema, The" 38, 269, 273, 274, 279
Civilization of the Renaissance in Italy 11
Cixous, Hélène 41
Clark, Cheryl 118
class: in *BTA* 70; and *Life As We Have Known It* 325f.; in *Mrs. Dalloway*, 328-29; and suicide, 189-90
clematis jacmanii 249, 250
Clements, Patricia 2
Cliff, Michelle 114
Clifford, Lucy 224
Clough, Anne 28, 30n
Cochran, Jo Whitehorse 32n
Code, Rev. Joseph B. 27
Coleridge, Sara 27
common reader 6, 113, 271
Conrad, Peter 247
Cook, Blanche Wiesen 94, 112
Corday, Charlotte 27
Cornhill Magazine, The 26
Cox, Ka 136
Craig, Edith 27
Cramer, Patricia 3, 115, 177, 181, 273
Cuddy-Keane, Melba 1, 2, 10n, 34-35, 36, 161
Cumberland, Debra 58
Cunningham, Michael 192, 198
Curie, Mme. 27
Cvetkovich, Ann 120
Cymbeline 142, 172, 190

349

Index

Dali, Salvador 247
Dalloway, Clarissa (*MD*): and cross-sex friendship 103, 114; on death, 141f.; in film version, 285, 288; and lesbian desire, 97-99, 111-12, 113-14, 121, 138, 156; and Septimus, 154, 158, 277
Dalloway, Clarissa (*VO*) 301-02
Dalloway, Elizabeth (*MD*) 181, 256
Dalloway, Richard (*MD*) 328-29
Dalloway, Richard (*VO*) 296
Datchet, Mary (*ND*) 176, 261
Daugherty, Beth Rigel 77n, 228n
Davies, Emily 30n
Davies, Margaret Llewellyn 4, 27, 170, 186, 325f.
da Vinci, Leonardo 13
Davis, Laura 2
Davis, Natalie Zemon 25
de Beauvoir, Simone 78f.
Debord, Guy 311, 312
Decline and Fall 17, 19-20, 21,
Deconstruct This: Radical Feminism Fights Back Against Postmodernism 123n
Defoe, Daniel 327
DeKoven, Marianne 295, 296
de Lauretis, Teresa 96, 100n, 111, 117
Dell, Ethel M. 224
DeMeester, Karen 157n
Denham, Ralph (*ND*) 14-15, 176
DeSalvo, Louise 3, 84n, 147, 184, 238, 294
Diagnostic and Statistical Manual of Mental Disorders 149, 151
Dick, Susan 208
Dickinson, Violet 112, 167, 178, 186, 189, 259
Dictionary of National Biography 27, 207, 211
DiGaetani, John 62, 68n
Dobkin, Alix 117, 123n,
Dodge, William (*BTV*) 103, 104-05, 106-07, 109, 114, 315
Domville-Fife, Charles 295
Donne, John 127f.
Don Quixote 166
Dowling, Linda 10n
Drucker, Peter 322
Dryden, John 6
Dubino, Jeanne 132n, 133n, 228, 228n
Duchess of Newcastle 25
Duckworth, George 186
Duckworth, Gerald 137, 148
Duckworth publishers 26, 31n, 238-39
Dulac, Germaine 268
Duncan, Nancy 256
Dunn, June 3
DuPlessis, Rachel Blau 68n, 109, 330n
Durkheim, Emil 184

Dusinberre, Juliet 330n
Dworkin, Andrea 120

Easdale, Joan 232
Eberly, David 61n, 95, 178
Echo & Narcissus 143-45, 146n
eclipse 246-47
Edgeworth, Maria 25
Einstein, Albert 247, 305-06
Eisenstein, Sergei 36
Electra 7
Elements of Style 134
Eliot, George 25, 27, 80, 81-2,
Eliot, T. S. 14, 39, 41, 132
Elvedon 64
Eminent Victorians 26
Epes, Isota Tucker 2, 245, 248
Epstein, William H. 24
erotic, Woolf's use of 120
ethnography 291f.
Evans, Mary 82
Ezell, Margaret 25

Faderman, Lillian 119
Fahrenheit 451 284
Farwell, Marilyn 94, 96, 100n, 112
Famous Blue-Stockings 27
Far from the Madding Crowd 91
Fawcett, Millicent Garrett 27, 31n, 170, 260
Feminine Mystique, The 41
feminism: meetings, 41; and queer scholarship, 116f.; and space, 256; Woolf as icon of, 78, 199; and scholarship, 25, 28
Fernald, Anne E. 15n
Fetterley, Judith 96
Fini, Leonor 246
Fisher, Herbert 209, 213
Flammarion, Camille 305-06, 308, 309
Flax, Jane 156n
Flush 24, 56f., 176, 178
Fogel, Daniel 128
Forster, E. M. 151, 194, 284
Foster, Jeanette 93, 94
Foucault, Michel 68n, 99, 117
Four Margarets 31n
Four Quartets 41
Fowler, R. 10n
Fraenkel, Eduard 10n
Frazer, James 291f., 312
Freshwater 207f.
Freud, Sigmund; Freudianism 100n, 121, 140, 148, 149, 151, 217, 329
Freyd, Jennifer 135

350

Index

Frith, Simon 36
Froula, Christine 157n, 228n, 238, 297n
Fry, Elizabeth 27, 30n
Fry, Roger 79, 246
Frye, Northrop 234
Fulbrook, Kate 83
Fuss, Diana 96, 100n, 117

Gage, Carolyn 117
Galileo 13
Galsworthy, John 233
Garrity, Jane 39
Gates, Barbara T. 188
Gay, Peter 17
gay studies (*See* also lesbian studies; queer theory) 3, 102f., 116f.
Gibbon, Edward 16-24, 291
Gillespie, Diane 247
Gissing, George 194
Gladstone, William 9
globalism 323
Glyn, Elinor 240
Goethe 183
Goldberg, Carl 122
Goldman, Emma 27
Goldman, Jane 247
Goldsmith, Margaret 27
Gordon Square 264
Gordon, Lyndall 82
Gordon, Troy 3, 114-15, 116f.
Gorris, Marlene 283, 286, 289
Graham, J. W. 208, 214n
Grahn, Judy 117
Gray, Bennison 134-35
Great American Foundresses 27
Greek Anthology, The 6
Greek: history, 292; language 6-10
Green, Barbara 261, 264
Greene, Nick (*O*) 132n
Grey, Lord Edward 169
Griffith, D. W. 268
Groden, Michael 2, 275n
Grontkowski, Christine 303
Grossman, Lionel 21
Grosz, Elizabeth 100n
Guardian, The 259
Guy-Blaché, Alice 268

Haines, Rupert (*BTA*)
Halberstam, Judith 120
Hall, Radclyffe 263
Hamilton, Cicely 27, 31n
Hampson, John 232

Hankins, Leslie K. 4, 114, 285
Hare, Augustus 131
Harris, Jocelyn 247
Harrison, Jane 84n, 292, 293-94
Harry Ransom Humanities Research Center 192
Hart, Lynda 120
Harvey, Kathryn 2, 175
Hatch, Mary Jo 321
Haunted House, A 207
Hazlitt, William 26
Hegel, G. F. W. 79, 83, 85n, 218
Heilbrun, Carolyn 84n, 102, 108, 183
Heine, Elizabeth 239
Hellenism 9
Hemingway, Ernest 233
Hendrix, Jimi 42
Hennessy, Rosemary 31n, 103
Henry, Holly 310
Herman, Judith 149, 153
Herrman, Anne 109
Herschel, Caroline 29, 31n
Hewet, Terence (*VO*) 168, 238-39, 294, 296, 300-02
Heywood, Elizabeth 80
Hilbery, Katharine 14-15, 307
H[ilda]. D[olittle]. 41
Hill, Octavia 30n, 322
Hills, Jack 257
Hirst, St. John (*VO*) 19, 103, 114, 291
history: omissions in Woolf's version of, 24f.; simplification in gender studies of, 78; and new physics, 304f.; Woolf's thinking about, 16-24, 25
Hitler, Adolf 35
Hodgkins, Frances 248
Hoff, Molly 157n
Hoffman, Charles 203-04
Hogarth Press 26, 133n, 148, 171, 232, 236f.
Holmes, Dr. (*MD*) 121, 156
Holmes, Sherlock 182
homosexuality: 104f., 176f.; Neville's (*TW*), 63-67; Foucault on, 68n
Hood, Thomas 185
Hoogland, Renée 97, 100n
hooks, bell 108
Hopkins, Gerard Manley 172
Hopi 9
"Hours in a Library" 194
"How Should One Read a Book?" 231, 309
"How Should One Read a Screen?" 274
Hume, David 8, 231, 233
Humm, Maggie 83, 85n
Hussey, Mark 2, 34, 146n, 247, 274
Huxley, Aldous 204

351

Index

Hyde Park Gate News 184
Hypatia 27

incest *See* sexual abuse
International Franchise Club 260

Jacobs, Janet Liebman 153
Jacobs, Peter 62
Jacob's Room: allusions in, 169-70; influence of camera on 36-37; draft of, 169; moths in, 162; tears in, 154
Jagose, Annamarie 100n, 119
James, Henry 242n, 284
Jameson, Fredric 240
Jeffreys, Sheila 118
Jex-Blake, Sophia 31n
Jinny (*TW*) 64
Joan of Arc 27, 29, 30n, 31n
Johnston, Georgia 27
Johnson, Maisie 1
Johnson, Samuel 21, 26, 28
Johnston, Judith 78n
Joplin, Janis 41, 51
Joyce, James 80, 233

Kahlo, Frida 246
Kandinsky, Wassily 246
Kant, Immanuel 9, 231, 233
Keller, Evelyn Fox 303, 304
Kennard, Jean 112
Kenney, Susan 183
Keynes, John Maynard 206n
Killen, Judith 306-07
Kilman, Doris (*MD*) 113-14, 138, 157n, 181
Kineke, Sheila 59
King Lear 7, 309
Kingsley, Mary 25, 28
Klepfisz, Irene 118
Knapp, James 68n
Kolk, Bessel van der 149, 153
Kregloe, Carmen 121
Kuhn, Thomas 318
Kundera, Milan 311

Lacan, Jacques 13
Last September, The 72f.
Laurence, Patricia 77n
Lamarr, Paul 235n
Lawrence, D. H. 38, 178
La Trobe, Miss 70-71, 106, 108, 114, 174, 311, 314, 315, 316

"Leaning Tower, The" 81
Leaska, Mitchell 203-04
Leavis, F. R. 234, 235n
Le Doeuff, Michèle 83, 84
Lee, Hermione 82, 132n, 148, 186, 232
Lefebvre, Henri 256
Lehmann, John 232
lesbian-feminism 111, 116f.
lesbian studies (*See* also gay studies; queer theory) 3, 93f, 102f., 111f., 116f., 176f.
Levine, Howard 135
Lewis, Thomas 61n
Life As We Have Known It 4, 27, 325f.
Lilienfeld, Jane 95, 112, 178
Locke, Alain 39
Locke, John 8
Lopokova, Lydia 271-72
Lorde, Audre 117, 120
Louis (*TW*) 63, 103
Lukács, Georg 311
Luftig, Victor 104, 110n
Lundgren-Gothlin, Eva 83
Lycidas 238

Macherey, Pierre 311, 312, 316
Machiavelli 12
MacKail, J. W. 6
MacKinnon, Catherine 120
Maeterlinck, Maurice 306
Malleson, Elizabeth 263
Manresa, Mrs. 1, 106, 120
Mansfield, Katherine 193
Marcus, Jane 82, 94, 95, 109, 188, 236, 330n
Mares, Cheryl 245
Marinetti, Filippo 247
Markham, Kit (*ND*) 176-77, 181
"Mark on the Wall, The" 193
Marsh, George 37
Marshall, Paule 30
Martin, Biddy 100n, 103
Martin, Mrs. 29
Martineau, Harriet 30n
Marx, Karl 79
Mason, Rebecca 208
Matisse, Henri 246
McAleer, Joseph 224
McFarlane, Brian 284-85
McGann, Jerome 236
McNaron, Toni 95, 112
McNett, Jeanne 2
McWhirter, David 15
Mecklenburgh Square 69, 208, 264
Meese, Elizabeth 96, 100n, 112, 117
Meisel, Perry 12, 85n

Index

Meiselman, Karin 135
Melymbrosia 294
Memoirs of Several Ladies of Great Britain 27
Men's League for Women's Suffrage 260
Merleau-Ponty, Maurice 79, 83, 85n
Mezei, Kathy 157n
Michelangelo 12
Michelet, Jules 12, 13-14, 15
millennium 1, 39, 325
Miller, C. Ruth & Lawrence 242n
Miller, J. Hillis 142, 144, 146n
Miller, Nancy 79
Milton, John 238
Mimlitsch, Michelle 4
Minow-Pinkney, Makiko 35, 161
Miriam, Kathy 121
Mitchell, Margaret 225
Mitford, Mary Russell 25, 27, 28
"Modern Fiction" 153-54, 233, 273
"Modern Novels" 194
Moi, Toril 79, 82
Moments of Being 119
"Monday or Tuesday" 172
Monk's House 69-70
Moore, George 79, 227
Moore, G. E. 217, 219
Moore, Madeline 287, 297n
Moraga, Cherríe 108, 117
More, Hannah 30n, 31n
Morley College 262, 330n
Morselli, Henry 186
Morton, Donald 120
Mrs. Dalloway 4, 88, 276; 1920s films as backdrop, 269; and modernism, 99-100; narrator in, 278; and survival, 144; in relation to *Life As We Have Known It* 325f.; lesbian desire in, 137-38, 177-78
Mrs. Dalloway (film) 276, 279-80, 283-86, 287-89
multiculturalism 320
Munt, Sally 100n
Murav, Harriet 160
Murphy, Anne 2
mythology 291f

Nabokov, Vladimir 284
Nagy, Gregory 161
narrative: in *JR* 36-37; in Campos and Woolf, 87f.; and trauma, 153f., 160f.; in *MD* 158f.
nation *See* nationalism
Nation & Athenaeum 221
nationalism: Gibbon and Woolf's versions of, 20-21; as theme, 70f.; and racism in film, 274; and professions, 321, 322-23

Negro in Literature and Art, The 30
Neville (*TW*) 63, 64-67
New Negro, The 39
New Statesman 225, 306
Newton, Isaac 298
New York Times 225
Nicolson, Harold 26
Nicolson, Nigel 180
Nietzsche, Friedrich 8
Night and Day 14, 167; poor sales of, 225-26; same-sex desire in, 176f., 193; and suffrage, 261
Nightingale, Florence 25, 27, 28
non-profit organizations 322
Nordau, Max 218
Nordmann, Charles 306
Novak, Michael 322

Odyssey, The 9
Olano, Pamela 95, 96
"Old Bloomsbury" 256
Oldfield, Sybil 25
Oliphant, Margaret 26, 31n, 263
Oliver, Bart 312
Oliver, Giles (*BTA*) 120, 314
Oliver, Isa (*BTA*) 73, 74, 103, 313-14
"On Being Ill" 127, 198n
"On Not Knowing Greek" 6-10,
Orlando: A Biography 34, 40, 166; and biography, 24, 276, 277-78; and censors, 270; play with history, 95, 271, 309; index in, 58-59; and metaphor, 127-28; narrator in, 278-79; as popular text, 1, 4; and Vita Sackville-West, 178; as satire, 12; Tillyard's criticism of, 15n;
Orlando (film): 276, 279-82, 285, 286-87
Orlando 1-2, 21, 40-42, 108; as divided subject, 59; and technology, 34, 38;
"Orlando Project, The" 2
Ormerod, Miss 84n
Orr, Christopher 285
Ovid 143

Page, Mr. (*BTA*) 225
Pageant of Great Women, A 27
Palacios, Manuela 247
Pankhursts 260, 265n
Pape-Carpentier, Marie 29
Pargiters, The 204f.
Pargiter, Eleanor (*TY*) 103, 121
Pargiter family (*TY*) 201
Pargiter, Sara (*TY*) 205
Parker, Pat 117
Parkes, Bessie Rayner 26

353

Index

Parnell, Charles Stewart 201
Parry, Sylvia (*MD*) 154-56
Parsifal 62f.
Partridge, Ralph 121, 148
Pater, Walter 7, 12, 15, 26
"Patron and the Crocus, The" 226
Paulson, William 303
Penelope, Julia 122
Pepper, William (*VO*) 292
Percival (*TW*) 62f., 121
Père-Lachaise 13-14
Peter, John 64
"Phases of Fiction" 231
Phillips, Kathy 330n
photography, technology of 34f
"Phyllis & Rosamond" 187, 263
Picasso, Pablo 246
Pilkington, Laetitia 25
Plato 9, 219, 307
Pointz Hall 70, 75, 109, 312
Pointz Hall 172, 174
Pomjalovsky, Nicholas (*TY*) 103, 122
Poole, Roger 84n
Poresky, Louise 63, 68n
Porter, Roy 20
Potter, Sally 281, 286-87, 289
Pound, Ezra 234, 235n
Pridmore-Brown, Michelle 35
"Prime Minister, The" 150-51
Principia Politica 217
Procne and Philomel 82
"Professions for Women" 171, 199
Proust, Marcel 162, 244, 247
punctuation 134f.

queer theory 3, 93f., 102f., 111f., 116f.

racism 274n
Radin, Grace 203-04
Radnóti, Miklós 160
Rahv, Philip 311, 315
Raitt, Suzanne 110n
Ramsay, Mr. (*TTL*) 114, 209, 254f.
Ramsay, Mrs. (*TTL*) 114, 209, 248, 252, 254f.
Raspa, Anthony 132n
Raverat, Jacques 148
Reagon, Bernice 117
"Reflections at Sheffield Place" 22
Reid, Panthea 246, 247
Renaissance studies 11-16
Reti, Irene 118
"Reviewing" 223-24
Rhoda (*TW*) 65, 103, 121

Rich, Adrienne 94, 104, 118, 122
Richter, Harvena 62-63
Risolo, Donna 95
Ritchie, Anne Thackeray 26
Rivera, Diego 36
Rodmell 189
Roe, Sue 82
Roger Fry: A Biography 24
Rogers, J. A. 39
Rollin, Roger B. 132n
Roof, Judith 3, 68n, 111f., 116f.
Room of One's Own, A: 78, 106, 199, 241, 268; irony in, 129; literary judgment in, 230; partial history in, 24f.; textual apparatus in, 59; textual changes in, 171
Rosenbaum, S. P. 216, 234, 241n, 242n
Rosenberg, Beth C. 228n
Rosener, Judy 322
Rossetti, Christina 28, 31n
Ruotolo, Lucio 138
Ruskin, John 12, 15n
Rylands, George 148

Sabina 87-91
Sackville-West, Eddy 71
Sackville-West, Vita: 112; *Joan of Arc*, 26; on Aphra Behn, 31n; compared to Elizabeth Bowen, 71; Woolf's love for, 95, 122, 176, 178-79; on Woolf's sexual dysfunction, 136; letter to, 224
Sand, George 25
Sanger, Daphne 167
Sappho 25, 27, 73
Sartre, Jean-Paul 79, 82, 83, 85n
Sasha (*O*) 1, 41, 41
Sassoon, Siegfried 159, 162-63
"Scene from the Past, A" 207, 211, 213
Schlack, Beverly 132n
Schlegel, Friedrich von 7
science 199-200
Science of Ethics 185-86
Scott, Bonnie K. 13, 38, 109n
"Scribbling Dame, A" 80
Seal, Sally (*ND*) 176-77, 181
"Searchlight, The" 4
Second Sex, The 78, 81-82,
Sedgwick, Dwight Henry 127
Sedgwick, Eve 68n, 104
Seducers in Ecuador 178
Seton, Sally (*MD*) 138, 180, 277, 288
Seven Women Against the World 27
Sévigné, Madame de 25
sexual abuse 134f., 147, 183
Shakespeare, Judith 15n, 29, 81, 187, 274

Index

Shakespeare, William 131, 142, 172
Shange, Ntozake 2
Shapin, Steven 299, 300
Sheepshanks, Mary 170
shell-shock 142, 149, 155, 190, 282n
Shelley, Percy Bysshe 152
Shelmerdine, Marmaduke Bonthrop 41, 286
Sherard, Tracey 3
Shillingsburg, Peter 236
Showalter, Elaine 146
Shuttleworth, Sally 301
Simmel, Georg 37
Simon, Shena 119, 209
Six Brilliant Englishwomen 26
Six Life Studies of Famous Women 29
Six Maries, The: Devotional Readings 31n
Sinister Wisdom 123n
"Sketch of the Past, A" 148
"'Slater's Pins Have No Points'" 136-37, 138
Slosson, Edwin 306
Smith, Barbara Herrnstein 230, 231-32, 233
Smith, Patricia Juliana 96
Smith, Lucrezia (*MD*) 145
Smith, Septimus (*MD*) 103, 114, 121, 141-42, 148f., 154, 163, 189, 277
Smith College Library 208, 214n
Smyth, Ethel 31n, 168, 177, 198n, 209
Society of Outsiders 318, 320, 323
Some Eminent Women of Our Time 27
Some People 26
Somerville, Jimmy 281
Sontag, Susan 127f.
Sophocles 7, 8
Spalding, Frances 208
Spender, Stephen 119, 206n
Stalter, Sunny 39
starlight 305, 310; in *ND* 307-08; in *TTL* 308; in *TW* 308-09
Stephen, Leslie 16, 17, 26, 31n, 83, 132n, 185, 293
Stephen, Thoby 167
Stanhope, Lady Hester 25
Stein, Gertrude 241n, 247
Stimpson, Catherine 94, 112
Stockhausen, Karlheinz 42
Strachey, Lady Jane 260
Strachey, Lytton: 26, 83, 108, 256
Strachey, Philippa 170, 260
Strachey, Ray 27, 260
Strauss, Richard 144
"Street Haunting: A London Adventure" 269
Studland Beach 248
subjectivity 276f.
suffragettes 1, 261
suicide 3, 152, 183f., 282n, 288

surrealism 247
Susan (*TW*) 64, 66-67
Swanson, Dina 96, 112
Swithin, Lucy (*BTA*) 104-05, 106-07, 109, 114, 315
Symonds, J. A. 7, 8
Sydney-Turner, Saxon 217, 220, 222n

Talland House 247
Tarzan and His Mate 37
Tasso, Torquato 140, 141, 145
Taussig, Michael 35, 37-38
Tavistock Square 263
Taylor, Sir Henry 207, 212, 214n
teaching (*See also* universities) 318-19, 330
technology 34f., 272, 273
Tennyson, Alfred 211, 212
Terry, Ellen 25
textual differences 170-72
Thackeray, William 313
Thomas, Edward 172-75
"Thoughts on Peace in an Air Raid" 199
Thrale, Hester 25
Three Guineas 20, 78, 80, 115, 199, 224, 272; and professions, 321-22; on contradictions of feminism, 318f.; as life narrative, 27; genesis of, 167, 170; on intellectual property, 274; textual changes to, 171-72; examines root causes of war, 318
Thucydides 9
Tillyard, E. M. W. 12
Time & Tide 206n
"Time Passes" 269
Times (London) 9, 295
Times Literary Supplement 193, 194, 206n, 306
Tinné, Alexandrine 29
Toklas, Alice B. 241n
To the Lighthouse: influence on Campos of, 90-91; genesis of, 167; past in, 308
Tremper, Ellen 235n
Trevelyan, R. C. 193
Tristan, Flora 27
Tsvetaeva, Marina 159
Turner, H. H. 306
Tvordi, Jessica 95, 96
Tylor, E. B. 292
Two Stories 193

Ulysses 2, 88, 234, 275n
universities 318-21

355

Index

Vanita, Ruth 61n, 96, 110n, 114
Vaughan, Madge 180, 258
Verrall, Jacob 189
Vicinus, Martha 25
Victoria 27, 31n, 108
Victorian culture: 212; repression of emotion in, 155; science of 291f., 298f.
Vildrac, Charles 158, 159
Villeneuve, Pierre-Eric 15n
Vinrace, Rachel (*VO*) 19, 168, 238-39, 291, 292, 294-96, 299-304
Virgil 292
Virginia Woolf Bulletin 207
Virginia Woolf in the Age of Mechanical Reproduction 2, 34, 38, 274
"Virginia Woolf Out of Bounds" 3
Virginia Woolf: Reading the Renaissance 11
Vogue 39
Voyage Out, The 4, 19, 167, 238-39; ethnography and ritual in, 291f.; genesis of, 167f.; and Victorian science, 299f.

Wagner, Richard 42, 62f.
Walker, Alice 32n
Walsh, Peter 1, 138, 144, 155, 158, 277, 283n
Walters, Suzanna Danuta 119
war 76, 119, 121, 138; as literary topic, 286; metaphors of, 127f., 321; trauma and, 141f., 148, 150f., 154; in *JR*, 169-70; in *MD*, 277; and women's roles, 289
Ward, Mary Augusta (Mrs. Humphry) 185, 263
Washington State University 132n, 241n
Wasteland, The 9, 41
Waterloo, Battle of 306-07
Watt, G. F. 185
Waves, The 8, 275n; Percival in, 62f.; influence on Campos of, 90
Weber, Max 323
Wells, H. G. 233
Well of Loneliness, The 187
Wentworth-Williams, Sandra 169
Wernick, Andrew 242n
Wharton, Edith 136
Wheeler, Ethel Rolt 27
Whitbread, Hugh (*MD*) 269-70, 283n, 286
White, Hayden 12, 79, 311, 314
Whorf, Benjamin 9
Who's Who in Colored America 30
Wilde, Oscar 10n
Willis, J. H. 26, 232, 237, 241n
Wilson, Duncan 216
Wilson, J. J. 245
Wilson, Jean Moorcroft 215
Winchilsea, Lady 31n

Winckelmann 7
Winston, Janet 95, 136-37
Winterson, Jeanette 134
Wittig, Monique 96
Wollstonecraft, Mary 31n, 81
"Women and Fiction" 81
Women's Freedom League 260
Women's Local Government Society 260
Woolf, Leonard: as editor, 207, 330n; as essayist, 215f.; as publisher, 236-41; care of Woolf, 198n; on Wagner, 62; Woolf's need of, 79, 84n; on *VO*, 167; and Vita Sackville-West, 181-82;
Woolf studies 4, 34, 39, 104, 108-09, 230, 328
Wordsworth, Dorothy 25, 30n
Wordsworth, William 219
Worker's Educational Association 234
Working Women's College 262
Working Women's Congress 326
Writer's Diary, A 88
WSPU 260
Wulfman, Clifford 2, 275n
Wynne-Davis, Marion 15n

Years, The: Bloomsbury in, 259; lesbian desire in, 121, 122; genesis of, 167, 200; reception of, 203, 224
Yellin, Jean Fagin 32n
Yonge, Charlotte 30n

Zeller, Hans 242n
Zimmerman, Bonnie 94, 96, 100n, 112, 117, 118, 123
Zita, Jacqueline 103
Zwerdling, Alex 225

www.ingramcontent.com/pod-product-compliance
Lightning Source LLC
Chambersburg PA
CBHW021817300426
44114CB00009BA/206